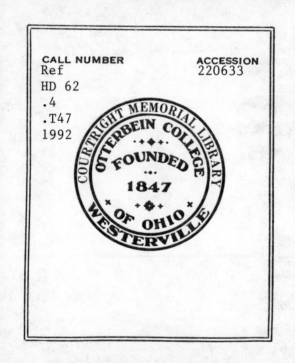

INTERNATIONAL MANAGEMENT HANDBOOK

INTERNATIONAL MANAGEMENT HANDBOOK

JOHN V. TERRY

WITH A FOREWORD BY DON TYSON

THE UNIVERSITY OF ARKANSAS PRESS ▪ FAYETTEVILLE ▪ 1992

This book was designed by Chiquita Babb using the Garamond and Futura typefaces.

The paper used in this publication meets the minimum requirements of the American National Standard for Permanence of Paper for Printed Library Materials z39.48-1984. ⊚

Library of Congress Cataloging-in-Publication Data

Terry, John V., 1920–
    International management handbook / John V. Terry.
        p.   cm.
    ISBN 1-55728-248-x (cloth : alk. paper). — ISBN 1-55728-249-8
    (pbk. : alk. paper)
        1. International business enterprises—Management.   I. Title.
    HD62.4.T47 1992
    658'.049—dc20   91-41679
                                                        CIP

To four extraordinary friends.

To Kevin Kreeger, my computer "right hand"; to his father, Walter Kreeger, whose personal interest in my books has inspired me and has helped the University of Arkansas Press sell my books; to Darrell Robison, who is probably the best pragmatic manager I have known; and to Dick Trammel, who has made northwest Arkansas a better place in which to live and work.

Acknowledgments

No person compiles a volume like this one without owing much to the professors he has studied under, to the books he has read, to the students he has taught, and to the many people in business and industry with whom he has consulted over the years.

These people are too numerous to be mentioned by name. However, the bibliography at the end of the book will give some idea as to the scope of my studies and debts.

I will specifically mention the Federal Reserve and the International Monetary Fund for assisting me with publications produced by them.

The following periodicals come in for approval for their unending coverage of world affairs vital to the writing of this book: *American Heritage, Europe, Forbes, Fortune, Harvard Business Review, Newsweek, Time, U.S. News & World Report,* among others.

Scot Danforth has been the faithful and patient editor. To him I owe much.

It is to be hoped that this book will help in some measure to the increased peace and productivity of our world.

I would like to thank the following for permission to reprint materials in this work:

Excerpt from the dust jacket from *Freedom in the Modern World* by Herbert J. Muller. Copyright 1966 by Herbert J. Muller. Reprinted by permission of HarperCollins Publishers.

Dr. Laurence J. Peter and Raymond Hull, *The Peter Principle.* Copyright 1969. Reprinted by permission of William J. Morrow and Co., Inc.

Encyclopedia of Associations, 1991, 25th edition, Volume 1, edited by Deborah M. Burek. Copyright (c) 1990 by Gale Research Inc. Reproduced by permission of the publisher.

J.V.T.

Contents

Foreword

Good management is the key to success in business and industry. Whatever else a company may have going for it, it is ultimately doomed to failure unless efficient management is its hallmark.

There was a time when a manager could know his own region or his own country and achieve a modicum of success. This time is now consigned to the past. The modern manager must know the world and know it well.

No nation can any longer afford to deny its markets to any other nation. And no industry should ignore any part of the world as a potential market. The reason is simple. We are now, like it or not, operating in a global economy, and this is not likely to ever change.

The company, and its management, that ignores this new world order will sooner or later succumb to the competitive forces that now abound.

This book attempts to bridge the gap between nations in the management process. It seeks to show why we must all make the effort to cooperate if our world is to be as peaceful and productive as it can be. And, while the book may not tell us everything we would like to know about management in a global economy, it does build a foundation that any educational institution or any business can use as a springboard for further understanding.

I welcome this book, and I hope that it will find its place in the literature of world business.

Don Tyson
Chairman
Tyson Foods, Inc.
January, 1992

Preface

The word apocalypse has long denoted the last times or the end. Theologically, the term has been used to indicate the purpose for the Apostle John's writing of the Revelation, the last book in the Bible. The Greek words in apocalypse are *apo* and *kaluptein* literally meaning to "uncover." In recent years, apocalyptic writings have not been confined to theologians. Futurists, philosophers, and others have looked at the world scene and wondered how long the world could stand under the weight of its problems.

As a student of world religions, I find that many of them adhere to the belief that there will be a cataclysmic ending of time and a life after death for the "chosen." As a pragmatist and a futurist, however, I know that none of us has this kind of knowledge. The Bible and other religious writings warn against setting dates or predicting times that are beyond our knowledge. Such writings usually admonish people to be watchful of the times and to be ready for whatever comes.

I am amazed on a daily basis at the rapidity of change that is coming upon the world and wonder if this change presages further events of an apocalyptic nature.

Quite frankly, I do not know. Therefore, in the absence of hard knowledge, we must continue to meet the problems of the day and plan for what we think will be the problems of tomorrow.

Not in all of human history have so many vital matters forced themselves upon us in such a short space of time. The very magnitude of the world's population makes humanity's problems seem insurmountable. Again, in the absence of hard knowledge, we must forge ahead.

In the decades since World War II, human beings have acquired knowledge of this universe at an undreamed-of rate. Geographic boundaries, which once seemed so formidable, have now evolved into space boundaries. We have no idea where our technological advances may lead us, but we will cope with the changes technology will bring; we always have.

The greatest and most frightening frontier facing man seems so slight and so simple that it defies serious study. And, yet, after millennia, the inability of human beings to live peacefully and productively with their fellow human beings remains the virtually untouched frontier. It is in this arena that humanity will fight its greatest battles in the years ahead, in the event those years are given to us.

This all-pervasive frontier of human beings' misunderstanding of themselves is as near to all of us as child abuse, domestic failures, and world wars. This frontier is the cause of business failures and the primary problem of underdeveloped countries. It is, by all accounts, the single most vital problem a person will ever face, save his relationship with God.

This volume is unabashedly written for all the world. Specifically, it is written for all the managers of the world, whether they are managers of small, nonprofit organizations or of giant multinational businesses. It is for all those who are chosen to achieve goals, and find that they must use other people to achieve those goals. Our changing world will not make it easier to manage people. We are now faced not only with the problems of our own domestic society, but also with a worldwide society in which we will have to become an integral part.

More Americans will migrate to other countries. Many more people from other countries will look to the United States for the home they need. We will not all speak the same language, and we will not look alike. But, despite all these differences, we will still have to manage, and we will have to do it as peacefully and productively as possible. Moreover, all of this integration of the many peoples of the world will have to take place in a period of rising nationalism, which, strangely enough, is also a period of forming international partnerships, such as the European Community.

Lest we mount the proverbial horse and ride off in all directions, let me say that this volume must serve first of all the business community of the world.

Good business management is based on the ability to create an atmosphere among people in the work situation that, if not perfect, will allow workers to be reasonably productive and happy.

Many studies in the past have accented the differences between human beings, but, in order to promote good business management, we must now be more aware of the sameness of people, wherever they are found in the world. If people within a nation, or among nations, were inherently different from each other, no philosophy of management could ever be developed, and there would be no basis upon which to build a productive work situation. However, if people are basically alike no matter where they are found, as Maslow and others have argued, then there is a basis for building a philosophy of management that transcends national boundaries, color, sex, native tongue, and creedal preferences.

If such boundaries are to be transcended, we must all know some common words and concepts that apply to the world of work. We must be somewhat aware of the different philosophies of management that are propounded in the world. Perhaps above all, we must know what is going on around us in the world. If we are to be irrevocably linked to each other, at least economically, then each will have to have insight into what the other is feeling and doing at any given point in time.

If the economies of the nations of the world are to be productive enough to feed, clothe, and house the billions of people in the world, then we are going to have to let go of our insular, xenophobic sentiments and all the other inhibiting factors that prevent success. We are going to have to replace prejudices with the passion to succeed.

As we move more and more swiftly toward a global economy, our universal ability to manage people, wherever we live and work, will be vital to the economic development and ultimate productivity of the people of the world.

This is an extraordinary age in which to live, and I would not have missed it for anything. Most of the time, however, I find my feelings much akin to those expressed by Herbert J. Muller, who wrote these words some thirty years ago: "I write in a sober, even somber mood, as one who does not despair of our future, but is not optimistic about it either. Nevertheless, I have written this volume in the pious conviction that modern history may still have a tragic dignity. Or, let me simply say that I am pleased to have lived in this era."*

In a spirit of international goodwill, this volume is designed for all people everywhere who are concerned with building a better understanding between peoples and a more productive economic world in which to live.

J. V. T.

---

*Herbert J. Muller, *Freedom in the Modern World* (New York: Harper & Row, 1966).

Introduction

The success or failure of business and industry around the world in the 1990s will depend upon the ability to manage properly. Management always relates directly to people. Anyone can be taught to manage technology, regardless of the rapidity of change. Not all people can manage other people well, and this ability is the secret to business success.

Managing people in an era of rapid change in technology demands the greatest of skills. In Alvin Toffler's majestic book, *Future Shock,* is this statement:

> Change is the process by which the future invades our lives, and it is important to look at it closely, not merely from the grand perspectives of history, but also from the vantage point of the living, breathing individuals who experience it. The acceleration of change in our time is, itself, an elemental force. This accelerative thrust has personal and psychological, as well as sociological, consequences. In the pages ahead, these effects of acceleration are, for the first time, sympathetically explored. This book argues forcefully, I hope, that, unless man quickly learns to control the rate of change in his personal affairs as well as in society at large, we are doomed to a massive adaptational breakdown.*

Two decades ago, as we tried to look squarely at the implications of the new age of technology, of information, or of communications—any one of which is an apt title for the period in which we live—we breathed a collective sigh of relief. With machines doing the jobs people once did, management would seem to be a breeze. Thus, management, after more

*Alvin Toffler, *Future Shock* (New York: Random House, 1970).

xix

than five decades of earnest searching for the secrets of motivation and productivity, decided that such knowledge would no longer be needed.

Few managers looked at the historical fact that new technology, rather than eliminating jobs, usually creates more. Technology does not, to be sure, create jobs in the same places, nor does it merely create new jobs to replace the old ones. But technology does create new jobs nonetheless, with living, breathing human beings doing those tasks.

I attribute the breakdown in management to our Age of Affluence (my designation), which existed from about 1955 to 1975. During the period, people in the United States and in many other developed nations in the world acquired more wealth and produced more wealth than in any other similar period in the world's history. Because unprecedented wealth was being produced, management was reduced to saying "yes" to every demand of labor. The increased costs, it seemed, could always be passed along to the consumer.

In addition, this affluence made it seem that every department needed more people. There was, after all, plenty of money to pay them. Industries got rich, fat, and lazy, and the vitally important aspects of the management of human beings in the workplace were generally forgotten. Workers themselves lost perspective as to what they were supposed to be doing, namely, producing new wealth in enough abundance to pay themselves, to pay for the factors of production, and to yield a profit to the entrepreneurs. Thus productivity (the wealth a worker can produce in an hour's work), began to decrease, and this decrease in productivity continued until about 1986.

It should be noted that there was not an absolute decrease in productivity in every year but that "productivity was increasing at a decreasing rate." In 1979 and 1980, we were at no increase; in short, productivity was just holding its own. In 1985, productivity began climbing slowly back, but generally at a rate lower than that of other industrially developed countries.

Unquestionably, the productivity problem was worsened in the United States by two other factors. One, financial people made their way quickly to top executive positions from 1960 to 1980. Generally, they knew little about industry, and they sought success in making the "bottom line" look good during a given quarter or year, with little regard for the future. Long-range planning was neglected as was any other major expenditure of money that did not immediately reflect well in the current financial statement. Two, the service sector was growing rapidly as the manufacturing sector was declining. It is often said that productivity in the service sector is impossible to gauge. That is not true. However, it has been more difficult to measure productivity in the service sector, and we are just now beginning to get a handle on the problem.

It took the energy crunch of 1974–75 to remind the United States of two vital economic facts: 1) resources are scarce and we cannot all have everything we want; 2) the more we wish to consume, the more we must expect to produce.

During this period productivity declined markedly in the United States; in England, France, and Italy the new-found wealth in the hands of consumers was reaching out to demand more goods and services. This demand-pull against existing supply resulted in double-digit inflation in many of the developed nations of the world.

In the United States, long considered the fountain of management knowledge, the economic problems of affluence were tragic. In book after major book, the sins of industry are cataloged. The "layers of fat" in industry were beyond belief. Organized labor has, during the golden years, pushed for everything it could get. Management was undisturbed by labor initiative, since it was getting more than its share, and it was not difficult to pass along price increases to consumers. In the face of declining productivity, this attitude was patently foolish, but it continued.

The decline in productivity, however, was not the only sign of poor management; quality was also declining, particularly in some of the most expensive items consumers buy, such as automobiles.

The United States had to face the problem squarely when its exports also declined and imports increased. With a rapidly growing deficit in the balance-of-trade account, The United States could no longer deny its weaknesses. In a very short time, the nation became the world's largest debtor.

It is now generally conceded that the quality of management is at its lowest ebb in more than fifty years. We live in a world that does not so much pit manager against manager on the domestic scene, but instead often pits the management of the companies of one nation against another in what is recognized as a global economy. Any nation opting for nationalism or isolationism will soon find itself in serious economic trouble. Yet both sentiments are rife in the world. Nongovernmental management will have to curb governments in preventing this error.

What, then, caused the decline of management in the United States? It is simple: carelessness, greed, and the idea that in affluent times profits could be made regardless of consequences. We now know better, presumably, but we face the difficult prospect of rebuilding the management structure of American industry, a rebuilding that will probably begin in the business departments of colleges and universities.

Although the management problem is acute in the United States, we are by no means the only nation in trouble. Great Britain, primarily because of her long experiment with democratic socialism, has a major problem. France has long been in economic trouble, but is seeing signs of improvement. Italy's problems resemble those of France, and in both cases many problems arise from the way labor unions relate to the governments in those countries.

Japan, now looked upon as the citadel of astute management, is facing problems of her own. Japan's ability to manage should be studied, but one conclusion at which one must arrive after study is that her success has been as much related to her culture as to her management expertise. And, as the affluence of the average Japanese family grows, so will the demands grow for different working conditions and more consumer goods. Unfortunately for Japan, she certainly cannot offer these workers "2,800-square-foot homes on two acres of ground"—one version of the American dream—because the lack of land makes it impossible. Management's problem in Japan may turn out to be the question of how Japan can keep workers happy when it cannot give workers what they want. The answer will not be easy to find.

With respect to Japan, it should also be noted that the relationship existing between government, the banking industry, labor unions, and industry is unique. It seems unlikely that the same industrial atmosphere will ever exist again in any other country. Every manager should understand, however, how this system works. Indeed, United States management can benefit greatly from learning what systems exist in all nations. It seems likely, despite Japan's uniqueness, that many countries will attempt to emulate the Japanese approach to management.

Current events in the former Soviet Union and the Eastern bloc countries pose another monumental problem for business management. It is the expressed desire of these countries to break with communism and to be free to conduct business in a more democratic atmosphere. It must be kept in mind, however, that most of the people in these nations know almost nothing about democracy, much less about proven management techniques and about what it takes to build a competitive industrial complex in an already complicated world.

For more than two generations, the people of Eastern Europe have lived in a controlled economic atmosphere in which their schooling, their work, and even their homes were the results of the decisions of others. Economic decisions were made by "central committees," and management tended to take the form of presiding over chaos. Management was safe as long as it could satisfy the central committee (often there was a nepotistic relationship existing between management and party members), and workers were given little consideration at all. Absenteeism from work was common, as were alcoholism and planned subversion of work schedules. Quality was abysmal. How are such countries now supposed to pull themselves up by the bootstraps and become industrially competitive in a world economy, particularly in the face of the obsolete infrastructures these countries are forced to work with?.

Two vital truths will have to be introduced into these countries. One truth is that economic scarcity will continue to inhibit their economies. They must learn what they can and cannot do with the resources they have. The second truth is that people will only accomplish in the industrial world that which they are motivated to accomplish. Motivation by force has been the order of the day for two generations. Now, management in these countries must understand people, and management must understand what it takes to move them to become the best with what they have.

There is no question but that both technology and management expertise will have to be exported to the Eastern bloc countries. These people are accustomed to hard work; a work ethic, per se, is not the problem. Enlightened guidance of a work ethic will be needed. Germany can be of inestimable help, but the United States should not hesitate to offer whatever kind of help is necessary.

Management, at its base, is simplistic. It is the achievement of goals through the use of people and other resources. Alas, how to motivate those people to achieve the goals is the rough road managers must learn to traverse before their management can be called successful.

It should be noted that people are allocated the priority position in this brief definition. Regardless of the sophistication of technology, failure will ensue unless people are understood and motivated. Since all true motivation is self-motivation, the study of human relations in management will take on an importance in many nations where such study has been ignored in the past.

The history of a systematic, scientific approach to management is really quite brief, less than one hundred years old. Since 1900, the tide of sound management practices has risen and fallen repeatedly, but the trend line moved upward until about 1965. From that point, at least in the United States, there has been a regression in the practice of good management, especially on the part of management in basic industries.

What should a prospective manager know in order to become a good manager? I believe it is imperative that this person look upon human beings as unique in all of creation. In Section IX of this book will be found brief descriptions of the thinking of twenty of the better-known specialists in the field of management. These descriptions are meant to convey a view of human beings and how to deal with them in groups and in the workplace, which, if followed, will help the perspective manager become a good manager. Abraham Maslow, especially, should be studied by every student of management, whether the student is still in school or already in the workplace.

Management is an art and a science. The discipline has no body of knowledge that will allow it to stand alone. One should be somewhat acquainted with anthropology, sociology, physiology, psychology, economics, history, and philosophy, whether formally or informally. If this seems impossible for the average manager, or would-be manager, it need not be. There is a plethora of good literature available, literature that is understandable at an eighth-grade reading level. For people still in school, all the courses are in place for perusal by sincere students.

Practically, the manager or would-be manager should know the language of management and economics. That is part of the reason for this volume. It is not sufficient to be able to mouth the language: it is necessary to know what the language means. Managers should know what experts have written and taught over the years. The most important aspects of this body of shared expertise will be found in Section IX. Moreover, the manager should continue his education by subscribing to periodicals in his field of expertise and being aware of the latest developments in technology and personnel skills.

Historically, authoritarian rule has been the norm in business and industry as it has been in all other areas of life. This kind of manager still exists in larger numbers than is good for industry. Sometimes authoritarianism can work for the short run; in fact, it often works very well in the short run. Never yet has it been successful in the long term, and one need only examine the current unrest in the former Soviet Union, China, and the Eastern bloc countries to see that this is so.

Without fail in studying management, one will come into contact with the study of human relations. Human relations is not a discipline in itself. Rather it is a general study of communications, motivation, leadership, group dynamics, etc. So when one pursues the study of business management very far, that person will also pursue human relations. The end of this study is to know how better to relate to people and to assist them in relating better to each other. This goal, simple as it may sound, stands in marked contrast to the goals management has pursued even in the recent past.

The obvious failure in the United States in the past two decades is well documented in the inability of the United States to compete on an international level, in the deterioration of quality produced, and in the growing dissatisfaction of workers with their jobs and with management. Two other phenomena, though certainly not confined to the 1980s, were well observed in that decade. One has to do with the blatant dishonesty of executives who were caught and punished for their acts. While workers may never rise as high as management, they rarely rise any higher than the leadership they have. The dishonesty of an industrial leader opens the door for dishonesty among the people he attempts to lead. The second relates to the acceleration of mergers and takeovers in the decade and the problems that emerged with them. One of the harmful effects of mergers and takeovers is the "golden parachute" that many managers arranged for themselves prior to any takeover or merger; it was a plan in which executives would be rewarded handsomely even if the firm ever merged or was taken over.

The manager's preparation for his own financial safety was not wrong in itself. But such arrangements were usually done, however, with complete disregard for what would happen to the employees of the firm. Managers tended not to protect the interests of the workers in the same way as they would protect their own: the prospect of losing one's job with no safety net at all because of a merger or takeover was a prime reason for lower morale among nonmanagerial personnel during the 1980s (Just recently, a few companies have arranged what they call a "tin parachute" for all employees in the event of a dramatic change in the business, but it comes as something of an afterthought. However, it has been introduced, and should gain universal approval.)

The decade of the 1980s was marked by greed in the industrial world. If industry is to improve its position in the 1990s, greed will have to be replaced with the desire on the part of management to share proportionately the fruits of the production process. Likewise, the decade of the 1980s was marked by selfishness on the part of management at all levels, beginning at the top. In the 1990s, a concern expressed in tangible ways for all people in the firm must replace that selfishness.

The decade of the 1980s was also marked by two more disastrous trends. One was the growing spirit of nationalism, and the other was the concept of protectionism. If the world economy is to enjoy even modest success, free trade will have to be a reality.

Three other international phenomena will play a strong role in future management and in the economic activities of the 1990s.

One is the coming into full fruition, in 1992, of the European Economic Community, which began with the Treaty of Rome in 1957. A "United States of Europe" could pose either monumental problems to the rest of the world, or, with the cessation of European hostilities, it could usher in a period of greater economic and cultural cooperation, not only in Europe, but in all the world.

The second event will be the takeover of Hong Kong by China in 1997. The temper of China in 1997 with respect to human rights could assist in opening all of Asia to greater economic activity, or it might prove to be another impediment to opening the world.

The third phenomenon is the marvelous growth of the Pacific Rim nations. This growth will be discussed in Section V in some detail, and it will unquestionably be a factor in management strategies in the future.

All of the renewed international economic activity of the 1990s will ride on the shoulders of management. If this management is good, the economic climate can be very good. If the management is bad, continued inflation and growing debt could result.

All good management is based on the simple axiom that is found in one form or another in every major religion: "Do unto others as you would have them do unto you." A simple principle, but one that is desperately difficult to practice. And, as the world economy expands and nations become more interdependent, it is incumbent that managers in all nations learn to speak a somewhat common language and that managers become aware of those concepts that are proven to produce better human relations and better productive results.

This volume is dedicated to the advance of management knowledge and to a one-world concept of management expertise. But nothing less than an understanding of human needs in the workplace and a sincere desire to fulfill these needs will cause management to succeed.

INTERNATIONAL MANAGEMENT HANDBOOK

 # Major International Organizations with Headquarters in Washington, D.C., or New York City

NOTE: While addresses rarely change, telephone numbers change periodically. New telephone numbers are usually provided by a taped message when a number that has been changed is reached.

Inter-American Development Bank
1300 New York Avenue
Washington, DC 20577
Telephone number: (202) 623-1000

International Bank for Reconstruction and Development
(World Bank)
1818 H Street
Washington, DC 20433
Telephone number: (202) 477-1234

International Boundary Commission, United States and Canada
United States Section
425 I Street, Suite 150
Washington, DC 20001-2599
Telephone number: (202) 632-8058

NOTE: the International Boundary and Water Commission, United States and Mexico, United States Section, is located in Texas at the following address:

4171 North Mesa, Suite C-310
El Paso, TX 79902
Telephone number: (915) 534-6700

International Cotton Advisory Committee Headquarters
1225 19th Street, Suite 320
Washington, DC 20036
Telephone number: (202) 463-6660

International Finance Corporation
1818 H Street
Washington, DC 20433
Telephone number: (202) 477-1234

International Joint Commission, United States & Canada
United States Section
2001 S Street, Second Floor
Washington, DC 20440
Telephone number: (202) 673-6222

International Labor Organization
Washington Branch Office
1750 New York Avenue
Washington, DC 20006
Telephone number: (202) 376-2315

International Monetary Fund
700 19th Street
Washington, DC 20431
Telephone number: (202) 623-7000

Organization of American States
Organization of American States Building
17th Street & Constitution Avenue
Washington, DC 20006
Telephone number: (202) 789-3000

Pan American Health Organization
525 23rd Street
Washington, DC 20037
Telephone number: (202) 861-3200

United Nations, General Assembly
Secretariat
New York, N.Y. 10017
Telephone number: (212) 754-1234

United Nations Information Centre
1889 F Street
Washington, DC 20006
Telephone number: (202) 289-8670

Embassies of Foreign Countries in Washington, D.C., or New York City

NOTE: While addresses rarely change, telephone numbers change periodically. New telephone numbers are usually provided by a taped message when a number that has been changed is reached.

Afghanistan
2341 Wyoming Avenue
Washington, DC 20008
Telephone number: (202) 234-3770

Algeria
2118 Kalorama Road
Washington, DC 20008
Telephone number: (202) 328-5300

Antigua and Barbuda
3400 International Drive
Suite 2H
Washington, DC 20008
Telephone number: (202) 362-5211

Argentina
1600 New Hampshire Avenue
Washington, DC 20009
Telephone number: (202) 939-6400

Australia
1501 Massachusetts Avenue
Washington, DC 20036
Telephone number: (202) 797-2000

Austria
2343 Massachusetts Avenue
Washington, DC 20008
Telephone number: (202) 483-4474

Bahamas, The Commonwealth of
Suite 865m
600 New Hampshire Avenue
Washington, DC 20037
Telephone number: (202) 944-3390

Bahrain, State of
3502 International Drive
Washington, DC 20008
Telephone number: (202) 342-0741

Bangladesh, People's Republic of
2201 Wisconsin Avenue
Washington, DC 20007
Telephone number: (202) 342-8372

Barbados
2144 Wyoming Avenue
Washington, DC 20008
Telephone number: (202) 939-9200

Belgium
3330 Garfield Street
Washington, DC 20008
Telephone number: (202) 333-6900

Belize
1575 I Street, Suite 695
Washington, DC 20005
Telephone number: (202) 289-1416

Benin, People's Republic of
2737 Cathedral Avenue
Washington, DC 20008
Telephone number: (202) 232-6656

Bolivia
3014 Massachusetts Avenue
Washington, DC 20008
Telephone number: (202) 483-4410

Botswana, Republic of
4301 Connecticut Avenue, Suite 404
Washington, DC 20008
Telephone number: (202) 244-4990

Brazil
3006 Massachusetts Avenue
Washington, DC 20008
Telephone number: (202) 745-2700

Brunei, State of
Watergate, Suite 300
2600 Virginia Avenue
Washington, DC 20037
Telephone number: (202) 342-0159

Bulgaria, People's Republic of
1621 22nd Street
Washington, DC 20008
Telephone number: (202) 387-7969

Burkina Faso
2340 Massachusetts Avenue
Washington, DC 20008
Telephone number: (202) 332-5577

Burma
2300 S Street
Washington, DC 20008
Telephone number: (202) 332-9044

Burundi
2233 Wisconsin Avenue
Washington, DC 20007
Telephone number: (202) 342-2574

Cameroon, The Republic of
2349 Massachusetts Avenue
Washington, DC 20008
Telephone number: (202) 265-8790

Canada
1743 Massachusetts Avenue
Washington, DC 20036
Telephone number: (202) 785-1400

Cape Verde
3415 Massachusetts Avenue
Washington, DC 20007
Telephone number: (202) 965-6820

Central African Republic
1618 22nd Street
Washington, DC 20008
Telephone number: (202) 483-7800

Chad
2002 R Street
Washington, DC 20009
Telephone number: (202) 462-4009

Chile
1732 Massachusetts Avenue
Washington, DC 20036
Telephone number: (202) 785-1746

China, The People's Republic of
2300 Connecticut Avenue
Washington, DC 20008
Telephone number: (202) 328-2500

Colombia
2118 Leroy Place
Washington, DC 20008
Telephone number: (202) 387-8338

Congo, The People's Republic of
4891 Colorado Avenue
Washington, DC 20011
Telephone number: (202) 726-5500

Costa Rica
1825 Connecticut Avenue
Washington, DC 20009
Telephone number: (202) 234-2945

Cyprus, Republic of
2211 R Street
Washington, DC 20008
Telephone number: (202) 462-5772

Czechoslovakia
3900 Linnean Avenue
Washington, DC 20008
Telephone number: (202) 363-6315

Denmark
3200 Whitehaven Street
Washington, DC 20008
Telephone number: (202) 234-4300

Djibouti, Republic of
866 United Nations Plaza
Suite 4011
New York, NY 10017
Telephone number: (212) 753-3163

Dominican Republic
1715 22nd Street
Washington, DC 20008
Telephone number: (202) 332-6280

Ecuador
2535 15th Street
Washington, DC 20009
Telephone number: (202) 234-7200

Egypt, Arab Republic of
2310 Decatur Place
Washington, DC 20008
Telephone number: (202) 232-5400

El Salvador
2308 California Street
Washington, DC 20008
Telephone number: (202) 265-3480

Equatorial Guinea
801 Second Avenue
Suite 1403
New York, NY 10017
Telephone number: (212) 599-1523

Estonia
Office of the Consulate General
9 Rockefeller Plaza
New York, NY 10020
Telephone number: (212) 247-1450

Ethiopia
2134 Kalorama Road
Washington, DC 20008
Telephone number: (202) 234-2281

Fiji
2233 Wisconsin Avenue
Washington, DC 20007
Telephone number: (202) 337-8320

Finland
3216 New Mexico Avenue
Washington, DC 20016
Telephone number: (202) 363-2430

France
4101 Reservoir Road
Washington, DC 20007
Telephone number: (202) 944-6000

Gabon
2034 20th Street
Washington, DC 20009
Telephone number: (202) 797-1000

Gambia, The
19 East 47th Street
New York, NY 10017
Telephone number: (212) 752-6213

Germany, Federal Republic of
4645 Reservoir Road
Washington, DC 20007
Telephone number: (202) 298-4000

Ghana
2460 16th Street
Washington, DC 20009
Telephone number: (202) 462-0761

Great Britain
3100 Massachusetts Avenue
Washington, DC 20008
Telephone number: (202) 462-1340

Greece
2221 Massachusetts Avenue
Washington, DC 20008
Telephone number: (202) 667-3168

Grenada
1701 New Hampshire Avenue
Washington, DC 20009
Telephone number: (202) 265-2561

Guatemala
2220 R Street
Washington, DC 20008
Telephone number: (202) 745-4592

Guinea
2112 Leroy Place
Washington, DC 20008
Telephone number: (202) 483-9420

Guyana
2490 Tracy Place
Washington, DC 20008
Telephone number: (202) 265-6900

Haiti
2311 Massachusetts Avenue
Washington, DC 20008
Telephone number: (202) 332-4090

Honduras
4301 Connecticut Avenue, Suite 100
Washington, DC 20008
Telephone number: (202) 966-7700

Hungary
3910 Shoemaker Street
Washington, DC 20008
Telephone number: (202) 362-6730

Iceland
2022 Connecticut Avenue
Washington, DC 20008
Telephone number: (202) 265-6653

India
2107 Massachusetts Avenue
Washington, DC 20008
Telephone number: (202) 939-7000

Indonesia
2020 Massachusetts Avenue
Washington, DC 20036
Telephone number: (202) 293-1745

Iraq
1801 P Street
Washington, DC 20036
Telephone number: (202) 483-7500

Ireland
2334 Massachusetts Avenue
Washington, DC 20008
Telephone number: (202) 462-3939

Israel
3514 International Drive
Washington, DC 20008
Telephone number: (202) 364-5500

Italy
1601 Fuller Street
Washington, DC 20009
Telephone number: (202) 328-5500

Ivory Coast
2424 Massachusetts Avenue
Washington, DC 20008
Telephone number: (202) 483-2400

Jamaica
1850 K Street, Suite 355
Washington, DC 20006
Telephone number: (202) 452-0660

Japan
2520 Massachusetts Avenue
Washington, DC 20008
Telephone number: (202) 234-2266

Jordan
3504 International Drive
Washington, DC 20008
Telephone number: (202) 966-2664

Kenya
2249 R Street
Washington, DC 20008
Telephone number: (202) 387-6101

Korea
2320 Massachusetts Avenue
Washington, DC 20008
Telephone number: (202) 483-7383

Kuwait
2940 Tilden Street
Washington, DC 20008
Telephone number: (202) 966-0702

Laos
2222 S Street
Washington, DC 20008
Telephone number: (202) 332-6416

Latvia
4325 17th Street
Washington, DC 20011
Telephone number: (202) 726-8213

Lebanon
2560 28th Street
Washington, DC 20008
Telephone number: (202) 939-6300

Lesotho
1430 K Street
Washington, DC 20005
Telephone number: (202) 628-4833

Liberia
5201 16th Street
Washington, DC 20011
Telephone number: (202) 723-0437

Lithuania
2622 16th Street
Washington, DC 20009
Telephone number: (202) 234-5860

Luxembourg
2200 Massachusetts Avenue
Washington, DC 20008
Telephone number: (202) 265-4171

Madagascar, Democratic Republic of
2374 Massachusetts Avenue
Washington, DC 20008
Telephone number: (202) 265-5525

Malawi
1400 20th Street
Washington, DC 20036
Telephone number: (202) 223-4814

Malaysia
2401 Massachusetts Avenue
Washington, DC 20008
Telephone number: (202) 328-2700

Mali
2130 R Street
Washington, DC 20008
Telephone number: (202) 332-2249

Malta
2017 Connecticut Avenue
Washington, DC 20008
Telephone number: (202) 462-3611

Mauritania
2129 Leroy Place
Washington, DC 20008
Telephone number: (202) 232-5700

Mauritius
4301 Connecticut Avenue
Washington, DC 20008
Telephone number: (202) 244-1491

Mexico
2819 16th Street
Washington, DC 20009
Telephone number: (202) 234-6000

Morocco
1601 21st Street
Washington, DC 20009
Telephone number: (202) 462-7979

Mozambique
1990 M Street
Washington, DC 20009
Telephone number: (202) 293-7146

Nepal
2131 Leroy Place
Washington, DC 20008
Telephone number: (202) 667-4550

Netherlands
4200 Linnean Avenue
Washington, DC 20008
Telephone number: (202) 244-5300

New Zealand
37 Observatory Circle
Washington, DC 20008
Telephone number: (202) 328-4800

Nicaragua
1627 New Hampshire Avenue
Washington, DC 20009
Telephone number: (202) 387-4371

Niger
2204 R Street
Washington, DC 20008
Telephone number: (202) 483-4224

Nigeria
2201 M Street
Washington, DC 20037
Telephone number: (202) 822-1500

Norway
2720 34th Street
Washington, DC 20008
Telephone number: (202) 333-6000

Oman
2342 Massachusetts Avenue
Washington, DC 20008
Telephone number: (202) 939-6200

Pakistan
2315 Massachusetts Avenue
Washington, DC 20008
Telephone number: (202) 939-6200

Panama
2862 McGill Terrace
Washington, DC 20008
Telephone number: (202) 483-1407

Papua New Guinea
1330 Connecticut Avenue
Suite 350
Washington, DC 20036
Telephone number: (202) 659-0856

Paraguay
2400 Massachusetts Avenue
Washington, DC 20008
Telephone number: (202) 483-6960

Peru
1700 Massachusetts Avenue
Washington, DC 20036
Telephone number: (202) 833-9860 to 9869

Philippines
1617 Massachusetts Avenue
Washington, DC 20006
Telephone number: (202) 483-1414

Poland
2640 16th Street
Washington, DC 20009
Telephone number: (202) 234-3800

Portugal
2125 Kalorama Road
Washington, DC 20008
Telephone number: (202) 328-8610

Qatar
600 New Hampshire Avenue
Suite 1180
Washington, DC 20037
Telephone number: (202) 338-0111

Romania
1607 23rd Street
Washington, DC 20008
Telephone number: (202) 262-4747

Rwanda
1714 New Hampshire Avenue
Washington, DC 20009
Telephone number: (202) 232-2882

Saint Christopher and Nevis
2501 M Street
Suite 309
Washington, DC 20037
Telephone number: (202) 833-2550

Saint Lucia
2100 M Street, Suite 309
Washington, DC 20037
Telephone number: (202) 463-7378

Sao Tome and Principe
801 2nd Avenue, Suite 1504
New York, NY 10017
Telephone number: (212) 697-4211

Saudi Arabia
601 New Hampshire Avenue
Washington, DC 20037
Telephone number: (202) 342-3800

Senegal
2112 Wyoming Avenue
Washington, DC 20008
Telephone number: (202) 234-0540

Seychelles
820 Second Avenue
Suite 203
New York, NY 10017
Telephone number: (212) 687-9766

Sierra Leone
1701 19th Street
Washington, DC 20009
Telephone number: (202) 939-9261

Singapore
1824 R Street
Washington, DC 20009
Telephone number: (202) 667-7555

Solomon Islands
820 Second Avenue
Suite 808A
New York, NY 10017
Telephone number: (212) 599-6193

Somali Democratic Republic
600 New Hampshire Avenue, Suite 710
Washington, DC 20037
Telephone number: (202) 342-1575

South Africa
3051 Massachusetts Avenue
Washington, DC 20008
Telephone number: (202) 232-4400

Spain
2700 15th Street
Washington, DC 20009
Telephone number: (202) 265-0190

Sri Lanka
2148 Connecticut Avenue
Washington, DC 20008
Telephone number: (202) 483-4025

Sudan
2210 Massachusetts Avenue
Washington, DC 20008
Telephone number: (202) 338-8565

Suriname
2600 Virginia Avenue
Washington, DC 20037
Telephone number: (202) 338-6980

Swaziland
4301 Connecticut Avenue
(Van Ness Center) Suite 441
Washington, DC 20008
Telephone number: (202) 362-6683

Sweden
600 New Hampshire Avenue
Suite 1200
Washington, DC 20037
Telephone number: (202) 944-5600

Switzerland
2900 Cathedral Avenue
Washington, DC 20008
Telephone number: (202) 745-7900

Syria
2215 Wyoming Avenue
Washington, DC 20008
Telephone number: (202) 232-6313

Tanzania
2139 R Street
Washington, DC 20008
Telephone number: (202) 939-6125

Thailand
2300 Kalorama Road
Washington, DC 20008
Telephone number: (202) 483-7200

Togo
2208 Massachusetts Avenue
Washington, DC 20008
Telephone number: (202) 234-4212

Trinidad and Tobago
1708 Massachusetts Avenue
Washington, DC 20036
Telephone number: (202) 467-6490

Tunisia
1515 Massachusetts Avenue
Washington, DC 20005
Telephone number: (202) 862-1850

Turkey
1606 23rd Street
Washington, DC 20008
Telephone number: (202) 387-3200

Uganda
5909 16th Street
Washington, DC 20011
Telephone number: (202) 726-7100

United Arab Emirates
600 New Hampshire Avenue
Washington, DC 20037
Telephone number: (202) 338-6500

Uruguay
1918 F Street
Washington, DC 20006
Telephone number: (202) 331-1313

Venezuela
2445 Massachusetts Avenue
Washington, DC 20008
Telephone number: (202) 797-3800

Western Samoa
820 Second Avenue
New York, NY 10017
Telephone number: (212) 599-6196

Yemen
600 New Hampshire Avenue, Suite 860
Washington, DC 20037
Telephone number: (202) 965-4760
Yugoslavia
2410 California Street
Washington, DC 20008
Telephone number: (202) 462-6566

Zaire
1800 New Hampshire Avenue
Washington, DC 20009
Telephone number: (202) 234-7690

Zambia
2419 Massachusetts Avenue
Washington, DC 20008

Zimbabwe
3852 McGill Terrace
Washington, DC 20008
Telephone number : (202) 332-7100

Source of Information: Congressional Directory, 100th Congress.

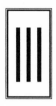

U.S. Federal Departments and Agencies Important to Management

NOTE: Addresses for Federal Departments and Agencies rarely change, but telephone numbers often do. The latest numbers are listed. When the number changes, there will normally be a taped message for the caller giving the new number of the office.

Executive Branch

Executive Office of the President
The White House
1600 Pennsylvania Avenue
Washington, DC 20500
Telephone number: (202) 456-1414

U.S. citizens and citizens of other countries do write or call the White House and will usually get an answer. Communications with the White House are usually for the purpose of expressing an opinion. Direct communications are reserved for heads of state and other dignitaries.

Office of Management and Budget
Executive Office Building
Washington, DC 20503
Telephone number: (202) 395-3000

This office prepares the annual budget for the president and does research related to the budget. Normally, neither U.S. citizens nor foreign citizens would have reason for contacting the office.

Council of Economic Advisors
Executive Office Building
Washington, DC 20506
Telephone number: (202) 395-5084

This is a group of three economists, chosen by the president, with one serving as chairman. On behalf of the president and his staff, this group does economic research and makes periodic reports. People outside government should not contact the Economic Advisory Council for information. Those interested in annual economic reports should subscribe either to the annual Economic Report of the President or the Statistical Abstract of the United States. Orders can be sent to the Superintendent of Documents, U.S. Government Printing Office, Washington, DC 20402, (202) 783-3238.

Central Intelligence Agency

The CIA is an international intelligence-gathering agency, working primarily on behalf of the Office of the President. No inquiries should be directed to this agency.

National Security Council

Members include the president, vice president, secretary of State, secretary of Defense, director of Central Intelligence, chairman of the Joint Chiefs of Staff, and the assistant to the president for National Security Affairs. No communications should be directed to this group.

Office of Administration

The "office management" division of the executive branch. Since this agency does not deal with the public directly, communicating with it would be futile.

Office of Science and Technology Policy
Executive Office Building
Washington, DC 20506
Telephone number: (202) 395-4692

Individuals and firms directly concerned with this type of government policy, whether foreign or domestic, can communicate with this office.

Office of the U.S. Trade Representative
600 17th Street
Washington, DC 20506
Telephone number: (202) 395-3204

This office welcomes any type inquiry related to international trade. The office serves as a liaison between the Office of the President and foreign countries on all matters concerning international trade. All communications, foreign or domestic, are welcome

Department of State
2201 C Street
Washington, DC 20520
Telephone number: (202) 647-4000

It is unlikely that the Department of State would respond ⌐ any unofficial communication from an individual or a comp ⌐y. The Department of Commerce or the Office of the l.ɔ. Trade Representative would advise on international commerce problems. Also, note reference below.

Department of State
Assistant Secretary for Bureau of Economic and Business Affairs
2201 C Street, Room 6820
Washington, DC 20520
Telephone number: (202) 647-7971

This division of the Department of State could be of assistance in many areas, domestic or foreign, but other departments already mentioned might serve specific needs better.

Department of State
Assistant Secretary for Bureau of Public Affairs
2201 C Street, Room 6800
Washington, DC 20520
Telephone number: (202) 647-9606

Communications having to do with activities of the Department of State could be directed to this division.

Department of the Treasury
15th Street & Pennsylvania Avenue
Washington, DC 20220
Telephone number: (202) 566-2000

Information desired from the Department of the Treasury should come from the division listed below.

Department of the Treasury
Office of the Assistant Secretary of the Treasury for Public Affairs
  and Public Liaison
15th Street & Pennsylvania Avenue
Washington, DC 20220
Telephone number: (202) 566-2000

Department of the Treasury
Office of the Comptroller of the Currency
490 L'Enfant Plaza East SW
Washington, DC 20219
Telephone number: (202) 447-1810

Communications to this department should probably be limited to persons directly involved in banking or other arms of the financial industry.

Department of the Treasury
Internal Revenue Service
Internal Revenue Building
1111 Constitution Avenue
Washington, DC 20224
Telephone number: (202) 566-5000

Anyone can communicate with this division on any matter concerning the Internal Revenue Service. Foreign nations or business firms would find this a helpful source.

Bureau of the Public Debt
999 E Street, Room 553

Washington, DC 20239-0001
Telephone number: (202) 376-4300

Information regarding the federal debt can be obtained from this division.

Department of Defense
The Pentagon

The Department of Defense, in most cases, should be communicated with through the Public Affairs Office, listed below.

Department of Defense
Public Affairs
The Pentagon, Room 2E800
Washington, DC 20301-1400
Telephone number: (202) 697-9312

Virtually any matter concerning the Department of Defense can be directed to this office.

Department of the Army
The Pentagon

Any communications for this department should be addressed to the Office of Public Affairs, listed below.

Department of the Army
Office of Public Affairs
The Pentagon
Washington, DC 20310-1501
Telephone number: (202) 695-5135

This office can answer almost any question related to the army from veterans, veterans' groups, and other citizens.

Department of the Navy
The Pentagon

Communications to the Department of the Navy should be addressed to the Office of Information.

Department of the Navy
Office of Information
The Pentagon
Room 2E340
Washington, DC 20350
Telephone number: (202) 697-7392

This office can provide information on the navy much as the army's Office of Public Information provides information on the army.

Department of the Air Force
The Pentagon

Communications with the air force should be directed to the Office of Public Information listed below.

Department of the Air Force
Office of Public Information
The Pentagon
Room 4D927
Washington, DC 20330-1000
Telephone number: (202) 697-8675

Handles virtually all communications of a public nature for the U.S. Air Force.

Department of Justice

Communications should be sent to the Public Affairs Office listed below.

Department of Justice
Office of Public Affairs
Constitution Ave. between 9th & 10th Sts.
Room 1213 Main
Washington, DC 20530
Telephone number: (202) 633-2015

Virtually any type of public information on the law and the court system can be obtained here. Foreign nations or business firms would find this division a valuable resource.

Department of Justice
Executive Office for U.S. Attorneys
Constitution Ave. between 9th & 10th Streets
Room 1619 Main
Washington, DC 20530
Telephone number: (202) 633-2121

A more specialized division of the Department of Justice that would probably be more attuned to the needs of attorneys, judges, and other legal personnel.

Department of Justice
Antitrust Division
Constitution Ave. between 9th & 10th Streets
Room 3107 Main
Washington, DC 20530
Telephone number: (202) 633-2401

Any domestic company, individual, foreign nation, or business can receive information on the antitrust laws now on the books in the United States from this division.

Federal Bureau of Investigation
J. Edgar Hoover Building
Washington, DC 20535
Telephone number: (202) 324-3000

Citizens or companies having special information related to the FBI can find answers here.

Department of the Interior
Interior Building
C Street between 18th & 19th Streets
Washington, DC 20240
Telephone number: (202) 343-1100

Department of the Interior
Office of Public Affairs
Interior Building
C Street between 18th & 19th Streets

Washington, DC 20240
Telephone number: (202) 343-6416

All matters related to the Department of the Interior, which deals with government lands, water courses, etc., can be directed to this division.

Department of the Interior
Bureau of Land Management
Interior Building
C Street between 18th & 19th Streets
Washington, DC 20240
Telephone number: (202) 343-1100

Any question having to do with federally owned lands can be directed to this division.

Department of Agriculture
Independence Avenue between 12th & 14th Streets SW
Washington, DC 20250
Telephone number: (202) 655-4000

This department has a gold mine of information available for any individual, business, or government that wants it, and the information is not confined to the United States, but the the world. Often the information is without cost.

Department of Agriculture
Commodity Credit Corporation
12th Street & Independence Avenue, SW
Washington, DC 20250
Telephone number: (202) 447-8165

This is a specialized division that should probably be communicated with only by those in the financial industry or by agricultural organizations or agencies.

Department of Agriculture
Food and Consumer Services
12th & 14th Streets, SW

Washington, DC 20250
Telephone number: (202) 447-7711

This division of the Agricultural Department has a wealth of information on food standards, consumer interests in the food industry, and is open to communications from both foreign and domestic inquiries.

Department of Agriculture
Marketing and Inspection Services
12th & 14th Streets & Independence Avenue, SW
Washington, DC 20250
Telephone number: (202) 447-4256

As the name implies, this division deals with meat and other inspection services and marketing standards. Any individual or company, domestic or foreign, can obtain information here.

Department of Agriculture
Office of Governmental and Public Affairs
Administration Building
14th Street & Independence Avenue, SW
Washington, DC 20250
Telephone number: (202) 447-7977

This division of the Department of Agriculture deals with intergovernmental problems and the public affairs of the department.

Department of Agriculture
Economics
Administration Building, Room 227-2
14th Street & Independence Avenue, SW
Washington, DC 20250
Telephone number: (202) 447-4164

No division of this department plays a more important role in supplying vital information than does this one. Agricultural statistics, not on the United States alone but on all the nations of the world, are available to anyone, domestic or foreign. Economists and many organizations have relied on these figures for years. As with all other departments, not all information is free, but some of it will be. All of it is valuable.

Department of Commerce
Herbert C. Hoover Building
14th Street & Constitution Avenue
Washington, DC 20230
Telephone number: (202) 377-2000

See Office of Public Affairs listed below.

Department of Commerce
Office of Public Affairs
Herbert C. Hoover Building
14th Street & Constitution Avenue
Washington, DC 20230
Telephone number: (202) 377-2067

Direct all communications concerning commerce to this division. In my career in education, in business, and in industry, now spanning more than forty years, the Department of Commerce has been of untold assistance. Thirty years ago I began to encourage smaller firms in the area of international trade and was quite successful. For foreign and domestic trade, this department has valuable information in the form of periodicals and myriads of other types of literature. Also, the department has regional offices, the locations and directors of which can be obtained on request.

Particularly when starting an international division in a company, I recommend communicating with the Department of Commerce first. The department is also an unending source of vital statistics for business, education, and other institutions.

Department of Commerce
Bureau of Economic Analysis
1401 K Street
Washington, DC 20230
Telephone number: (202) 523-0693

Another division of the department that can supply statistics concerning many fields.

Department of Commerce
Bureau of the Census

Suitland, MD 20233
Telephone number: (202) 763-5190

This bureau is vital to any person or company dealing with populations and the many facets of such populations. I am a consistent user of their literature. Some information is free of cost, but the most valuable materials usually have modest fees. Any educator, business person, or organization should be aware of what this bureau can do for them. (In the 1930s, W. Edwards Deming went to this bureau as a statistician. His work there, so experts believe, has made it one of the most efficient in government.)

Department of Labor
Frances Perkins Building
Third Street & Constitution Avenue
Washington, DC 20210
Telephone number: (202) 523-8271

See Department of Labor, Office of Public and Governmental Affairs, below.

Department of Labor
Bureau of Labor Statistics
General Accounting Office Building
441 G Street, Room 2106
Washington, DC 20212
Telephone number: (202) 523-1092

This office is probably the most complete repository for statistical information to be found in the world; it is certainly the best known in the United States. Every business organization, educator, or researcher, domestic or foreign, will find this a bonanza.

Department of Labor
Office of Public and Governmental Affairs
Room s-2018
200 Constitution Avenue
Washington, DC 20210
Telephone number: (202) 523-9711

All communications not directly related to the statistical work of the Department of Labor should be addresses to this division. And literally every working person or employer in the nation, or from other nations, can find advice and help here for all problems related to labor.

Department of Health and Human Services
200 Independence Avenue SW
Washington, DC 20201
Telephone number: (202) 475-0257

See divisions below which operate within the jurisdiction of this largest of federal government departments. (Formerly the H.E.W., or the Department of Health, Education and Welfare.)

Department of Health and Human Services
Office of Public Affairs
200 Independence Avenue SW
Washington, DC 20201
Telephone number: (202) 245-1850

This office that can serve as an initial contact to help find specific information among the different offices and divisions of the Department of Health and Human Services.

Department of Health and Human Services
Offices of Human Development Services
200 Independence Avenue, SW
Washington, DC 20201
Telephone number: (202) 245-7246

This division deals with some educational problems, especially of the disabled, native Americans, the very young, the aged, etc.

Department of Health and Human Services
Office of Assistant Secretary for Health
Hubert H. Humphrey Building
200 Independence Avenue, SW
Washington, DC 20201
Telephone number: (202) 245-7694

This office serves the entire health field under the secretary of Health and Human Services.

Department of Health and Human Services
Food and Drug Administration
Office of the Commissioner
Room 14-71 PKLN
McLean, VA 22101
Telephone number: (202) 443-2410

This office deals with licensing new drugs and overseeing the safety of the food products produced and/or marketed in the United States.

Department of Health and Human Services
National Institutes of Health
9000 Rockville Pike
Bethesda, MD 20205
Telephone number: (202) 496-4000

The NIH conducts disease research in virtually every known field. It also funds seminars, research projects, etc., and it serves as the strong right arm to the health services of this large department.

Social Security Administration
6401 Security Boulevard
Baltimore, MD 21235
Telephone number: (301) 965-6433

The Social Security Administration oversees all aspects of the Social Security program, including retirement benefits, survivor benefits, etc. Moreover, The Social Security Administration handles the Medicare program and all of its facets.

Department of Housing and Urban Development
HUD Building, 451 Seventy Street SW
Washington, DC 20410
Telephone number: (202) 755-6417

HUD is in charge of all aspects of public housing, including urban development, equal opportunity housing, community planning, etc.

Department of Housing and Urban Development
Office of Public Affairs
HUD Building, Room 10132
Washington, DC 20410
Telephone number: (202) 755-6980

Most communications to this department should be sent to this office.

Department of Transportation
400 Seventh Street SW
Washington, DC 20590
Telephone number: (202) 366-4000

The Department of Transportation conducts all aspects of transportation policy in the nation, and any interested person, business, or organization, whether domestic or foreign, can communicate with it.

Department of Energy
James Forrestal Building
1000 Independence Avenue, SW
Washington, DC 20585
Telephone number: (202) 586-5000

The Department of Energy undertakes all facets of energy problems in the United States, and it maintains statistics on energy the world over.

Department of Energy
Congressional, Intergovernmental and Public Affairs
James Forrestal Building
1000 Independence Avenue, SW
Washington, DC 20850
Telephone number: (202) 586-5450

The division of the Department of Energy to which most communications should be directed.

Department of Education
400 Maryland Avenue, SW
Washington, DC 20202
Telephone number: (202) 245-3192

The Department of Education oversees all aspects of public education, and it can be freely communicated with by individuals, businesses, organizations, whether domestic or foreign.

Department of Veterans' Affairs
810 Vermont Avenue
Washington, DC 20420
Telephone number: (202) 233-3523

The newest department of the federal government. It handles virtually all matters related to veterans.

Independent Agencies

Most of these agencies reveal in their titles the type work they do. Any individual, organization, foreign government, or foreign organization is free to communicate with any of them, and these agencies provide valuable information on specific problem areas.

Advisory Commission on Intergovernmental Relations
1111 20th Street, Suite 2000
Washington, DC 20575
Telephone number: (202) 653-5540

Advisory Council on Historical Preservation
1100 Pennsylvania Avenue, Suite 809
Washington, DC 20004
Telephone number: (202) 786-0503

African Development Foundation
1625 Massachusetts Avenue, Suite 600
Washington, DC 20036
Telephone number: (202) 673-3916

Agency for International Development
New State Department Building
320 21st Street, Room 2895
Washington, DC 20523
Telephone number: (202) 647-8440

American Red Cross
National Headquarters
430 17th Street
Washington, DC 20006
Telephone number: (202) 737-8300

Appalachian Regional Commission
1666 Pennsylvania Avenue
Washington, DC 20235
Telephone number: (202) 673-7856

Board Of Governors of the Federal Reserve System
Constitution Avenue & 20th Street
Washington, DC 20551
Telephone number: (202) 452-3000

This is another valuable arm of our federal government. It is usually call a quasi-governmental agency because it is neither owned nor totally controlled by government. I have worked closely with the Federal Reserve and many of its branch banks for many years. I have found them cooperative, helpful in meeting my needs, and always courteous. Briefly, and in the main, it serves as the central bank of the United States.

Commission of Fine Arts
708 Jackson Place
Washington, DC 20006
Telephone number: (202) 566-1066

Commodity Futures Trading Commission
2033 K Street, Suite 819
Washington, DC 20581
Telephone number: (202) 254-6387

This is a most sensitive agency of government that oversees what the name implies, futures trading in commodities, and that is vital to agriculture and to all firms that deal with agricultural products in any form.

Consumer Product Safety Commission
5401 Westbard Avenue
Bethesda, MD 20207
Telephone number: (301)) 492-6660

Copyright Royalty Tribunal
1111 20th Street, Suite 450
Washington, DC 20036
Telephone number: (202) 653-5175

Environmental Protection Agency
401 M Street, SW
Washington, DC 20460
Telephone number: (202) 382-4700

Equal Employment Opportunity Commission
2401 E Street
Washington, DC 20507
Telephone number: (202) 634-6930

Export-Import Bank of the United States
811 Vermont Avenue
Washington, DC 20571
Telephone number: (202) 566-2117

This agency conducts research and deals with international commerce in the making of loans.

Farm Credit Administration
1501 Farm Credit Drive
McLean, VA 22102-5090
Telephone number: (703) 883-4000

The Farm Credit Administration conducts all aspects of farm credit, which is now a multi-billion dollar business and highly complicated. Probably only people deeply involved in farm credit would find communications with this office helpful.

Federal Communications Commission
1919 M Street
Washington, DC 20554
Telephone number: (202) 655-4000

The FCC oversees aspects of public communications, including radio, television, short-wave radio, etc.

Federal Council on the Aging
330 Independence Avenue, SW Room 4545
Washington, DC 20201
Telephone number: (202) 245-2451

A relatively new agency of government founded for the purpose of doing research on aging and making recommendations for programs for the aged.

Federal Deposit Insurance Corporation
550 17th Street
Washington, DC 20429
Telephone number: (202) 393-8400

The agency that accepts deposit insurance premiums for bank deposits and makes payment on claims when banks default.

Federal Election Commission
999 E Street
Washington, DC 20463
Telephone number: (202) 376-5140

Federal Emergency Management Agency
500 C Street, SW
Washington, DC 20472
Telephone number: (202) 646-2400

Federal Home Loan Bank Board
1700 G Street
Washington, DC 20552
Telephone number: (202) 377-6000

Federal Home Loan Mortgage Corporation
1776 F Street
Washington, DC 20013
Telephone number: (202) 789-4700

Federal Labor Relations Authority
500 C Street SW
Washington, DC 20424
Telephone number: (202) 382-0700

Federal Maritime Commission
1100 L Street
Washington, DC 20573
Telephone number: (202) 523-5707

Federal Mediation and Conciliation Service
2100 K Street
Washington, DC 20427
Telephone number: (202) 653-5290

Federal Mine Safety and Health Review Commission
Sixth Floor
1730 K Street
Washington, DC 20006
Telephone number: (202) 653-5633

Federal Trade Commission
Pennsylvania Ave. and 6th St. NW
Washington, DC 20580
Telephone number: (202) 326-2000

The Federal Trade Commission is charged with keeping business competition free and fair. It enforces antitrust legislation, prevents false advertising, and regulates the labeling and packaging of commodities.

General Services Administration
General Services Building
18th & F Streets
Washington, DC 20405
Telephone number: (202) 535-0800

The General Services Administration supervises buildings and equipment for the entire federal government complex.

Inter-American Foundation
1515 Wilson Boulevard
Arlington, VA 22209
Telephone number: (703) 841-3800

An agency to study and make recommendations on relationships between American nations.

Interstate Commerce Commission
Interstate Commerce Commission Building
12th Street & Constitution Avenue
Washington, DC 20423
Telephone number: (202) 275-7252

The Interstate Commerce Commission deals with virtually all matters related to interstate transportation and commerce.

National Aeronautics and Space Administration
400 Maryland Avenue, SW
Washington, DC 20546
Telephone number: (202) 453-1000

National Archives and Records Administration
Seventh Street & Pennsylvania Avenue
Washington, DC 20408
Telephone number: (202) 523-3220

National Commission on Libraries and Information Science
GSA Building, Suite 3122
Seventh & D Streets, SW
Washington, DC 20024
Telephone number: (202) 382-0840

National Council on the Handicapped
Suite 814, 800 Independence Avenue, SW
Washington, DC 20591
Telephone number: (202) 267-3234

National Credit Union Administration
1776 G Street
Washington, DC 20456
Telephone number: (202) 357-1000

An agency charged with the regulation of credit unions, which usually are formed in companies among professional groups. Such unions usually accept deposits from members, make loans to members, etc.

National Endowment for the Arts
1100 Pennsylvania Avenue
Washington, DC 20506
Telephone number: (202) 682-5414

National Endowment for the Humanities
1100 Pennsylvania Avenue
Washington, DC 20506
Telephone number: (202) 786-0438

National Labor Relations Board
1717 Pennsylvania Avenue
Washington, DC 20570
Telephone number: (202) 632-4950

National Mediation Board
Suite 910, 1425 K Street
Washington, DC 20572
Telephone number: (202) 523-5920

National Research Council
National Academy of Sciences
National Academy of Engineering
Institute of Medicine
2101 Constitution Avenue
Washington, DC 20418
Telephone number: (202) 334-2000

National Science Foundation
1800 G Street

Washington, DC 20550
Telephone number: (202) 357-9859

National Transportation Safety Board
800 Independence Avenue, SW
Washington, DC 20594
Telephone number: (202) 382-6600

Office of Personnel Management
1900 E Street
Washington, DC 20415
Telephone number: (202) 655-4000

Peace Corps
806 Connecticut Avenue
Washington, DC 20526
Toll free telephone number: 1-800-424-8580

A quasi-governmental organization formed under President Kennedy's administration to send people of various callings to aid developing nations.

Pension Benefit Guaranty Corporation
2020 K Street
Washington, DC 20006-1806
Telephone number: (202) 778-8840

An organization concerned with guaranteeing the payment of pensions to employees by companies or other organizations. Supposed to work much like the FDIC.

Securities and Exchange Commission
450 Fifth Street
Washington, DC 20549
Telephone number: (202) 272-2617

The organization charged with regulating the stock exchanges of the United States. It is a source of much valuable information available to both domestic and foreign enquirers.

Small Business Administration
1441 L Street
Washington, DC 20416
Telephone number: (202) 653-6545

An agency charged with assisting small businesses with direct or guaranteed loans, holding small business seminars, and providing management assistance to them.

Smithsonian Institution
1000 Jefferson Drive, SW
Washington, DC 20560
Telephone number: (202) 357-1300

An agency devoted to preserving historic artifacts, natural history items, etc., of national concern. The Smithsonian Institution exhibits these objects in Washington, D.C. The Smithsonian Institution publishes many types of literature as well.

U.S. Commission on Civil Rights
1121 Vermont Avenue
Washington, DC 20425
Telephone number: (202) 523-5571

The Commission on Civil Rights has the responsibility of promoting the keeping of civil rights legislation and recommending prosecution of violations.

International Trade Commission
701 E Street
Washington, DC 20436
Telephone number: (202) 523-0161

U.S. Nuclear Regulatory Commission
1717 H Street
Washington, DC 20555
Telephone number: (202) 492-7000

U.S. Postal Service
475 L'Enfant Plaza, SW
Washington, DC 20260-0010
Telephone number: (202) 268-2000

U.S. Railroad Retirement Board
844 North Rush Street
Chicago, IL 60611
Telephone number: (312) 751-4500

Source of Information: Congressional Directory, 100th Congress.

The World Management Outlook from Western Europe to the Middle East

The European Community, 1992

The European Community, which is to come into full fruition in December 1992, is a phenomenon without precedent in history.

The European Community has been formed in the face of national enmities that have existed for hundreds of years. Never, in peace time, has a federation of independent states been established with the goals the EC has. The magnitude of the undertaking almost defies imagination, and if it meets only one-third of its goals it will remain the most ambitious plan to retard war and promote economic growth and development.

History of the European Community

After World War II, Europe, having been decimated by world wars just a generation apart, was encouraged to seek peaceful and productive means for helping widely diverse nations come together.

The idea could not have come too soon. Since the time of the Caesars the territory represented now by these twelve countries of Europe had seen little else but war. What peace it had known was the peace of the conquered, when the conqueror was too powerful to struggle against.

The tribes and nationalities represented in the territory are almost innumerable. In spite of this, however, in modern history there have always been strong nationalistic feelings among the various nations.

At the beginning of World War II, there were approximately 165 million people in this territory. Approximately 7.7 million lost their lives during the war; more than half of the number were between the ages of sixteen and forty. This was a terrible loss of human resources. Moreover, the war caused a loss of trillions of dollars of destroyed infrastructure and productive facilities, all of which produced a catastrophe almost beyond human imagination.

In addition to these seemingly insurmountable problems were the enmities that built up as a result of the human atrocities committed by the Germans, in the main, but also by other nations to a lesser degree.

So, while union to avoid future wars seemed a reasonable thing to do, the barriers to be overcome were enormous. The United States, with General George C. Marshall as secretary of State, possibly prevented postwar suffering beyond description, though the suffering was severe enough in any event. In June 1947, Secretary Marshall proposed what became known as the Marshall Plan. It was an aid plan for Europe, administered by the Economic Cooperation Administration (ECA), which spent about 12 billion dollars from 1948 to 1951 to help the ravaged countries get back on their feet.

The Marshall Plan was a humanitarian act, to be sure, but it was not purely that. During the last year of the war the United States saw the toughness of the Soviet Union. The United States did not want a weak Europe between herself and the Soviet Union, and certainly the United States did not want an acquisitive Soviet Union preying on a weak Europe. Europe had been our most prolific trading partner, and we needed her trade. Europe, however, could only become a strong trading partner again if she became economically strong again.

As Europe rebuilt her economic strength with the assistance of the United States, she built with the latest technology, which the United States did not have in many cases. By the middle of the 1950s, Europe was on her feet and beginning to compete strongly with the United States. After the war, the notion of cooperation became a driving force throughout Europe.

In 1953 the European Coal and Steel Community, or the Schuman Plan, was established, wherein six nations pooled their coal and steel resources to create unified products and labor markets. These six countries were France, West Germany, Italy, Belgium, the Netherlands, and Luxembourg.

On January 1, 1958, the Treaty of Rome brought into existence the European Economic Community (widely known as the Common Market). This treaty, signed by the same six countries, launched an ambitious plan of creating a free-trade area among themselves and of integrating their entire economies.

In 1958 the European Atomic Energy Community (Euratom) became the third cooperating European community. Its members are pledged to the common development of Europe's nuclear energy resources through coordination of their nuclear research and development.

These organizations became the European Community in 1967, and that is the name now used to refer to all of them, although in everyday conversation, the European Community is often referred to as the Common Market.

From the beginning of the EC, derisive remarks from other parts of the world have been commonplace. Usually such remarks emerge from an inward fear that the EC's plans might indeed succeed. The facts are that the mobility of labor has been much increased, many tariff barriers are down, and there has been no threat of war. On the other hand, the EC's "red tape" continues to proliferate, and very serious problems exist, including obtaining an effective Common Market currency and addressing differing tax structures of individual countries.

Without question, however, this is the most ambitious program ever devised by an international community, and it must be given the most serious attention by those who are traditional friends and trading partners of western Europe. In the economic world it will unquestionably be the "hot topic" of 1992.

The original six members, Belgium, France, Italy, Luxembourg, the Netherlands, and West Germany were joined in 1973 by Denmark, Ireland, and Great Britain. Greece joined in 1981, and Spain and Portugal joined in 1986.

In 1978 the European Community created the European Monetary

System with an agreement to coordinate the foreign exchange rates of the member nations' currencies. Britain, at first, was reluctant to endorse the European Monetary System, but joined the agreement in 1989. The primary purpose of the European Monetary System is to minimize fluctuations in a particular currency compared to another member country's currency. This lowers the risk of doing business across borders and encourages trade within the Common Market. A European currency has also been created. It is called the "ecu," and it is worth about $1.10. It is seldom used, however.

In 1985, Jacques Delors, a former finance minister in the Socialist government of France's Francois Mitterand, became president of the EC's Commission, its executive arm. He was recently appointed to another four-year term. As soon as Delors was elected president, he, along with Lord Cockfield, an EC minister from Britain, had drafted the White Paper that laid out the 1992 program. By the end of the year they had won the endorsement of the twelve leaders of the EC nations for what they called the Single European Act. It committed the twelve nations to the 1992 program and introduced a vital reform in the governing institutions the EC had created since the original treaty in 1957.

The four key institutions in the EC are:

1. The Council of Ministers. It is the supreme body of the EC and is composed of the 12 leaders of the member nations, or their representatives, with final power to approve or disapprove EC actions.

2. The Commission. Delors is president, and the Commission is the EC's Executive Branch. It is composed of 17 commissioners (the equivalent of cabinet secretaries) appointed by the Council of Ministers. They, along with 12,000 lesser lights, called Eurocrats, are headquartered in the Berlaymont Building in Brussels.

3. The Court of Justice. It is based in Luxembourg, has 13 members, and is the EC's "supreme court." It deals mainly with trade and business disputes involving both governments and individuals.

4. The Parliament. This is a body of 518 members, elected by popular vote by the 12 EC member nations. It is the only democratic body in the EC, and has practically no official function. It controls about 30 percent of the EC's 50-billion-dollar budget, but it has few other powers. The Parliament meets in Strasbourg, France.

The EC is heavily socialistic, as one might assume, since most of the nations involved have had heavily subsidized economies in place for a long time. Agriculture, particularly, is highly subsidized under the Common Agricultural Policy. Although subsidies are common in virtually every major country in the world, some believe that the EC's subsidies will turn the EC to protectionism in the area of agriculture, which would be a blow to the United States. and other nations.

One common industry has already been started under the EC banner, with the cooperation of England, France, and West Germany. It is the Airbus Industrie, an aircraft company designed to compete with Boeing and McDonnell Douglas. This consortium was formed in 1966, and the company had planes in the skies by 1972. Today the company accounts for about 25 percent of the aircraft sales in the world. Since the beginning of Airbus Industrie, three more countries have joined the consortium: Spain, the Netherlands, and Belgium. The industry is highly subsidized; more than 15 billion dollars in subsidies have been provided for it to date.

If the European Community is to come to full fruition, there is a mountain of work yet to be done. The EC thinks its goals are achievable.

The World's Fear of the European Community

The world could not be happier to see the western European countries on a course which seems to hold a peaceful future. The two World Wars were devastating, and were at the root of the U.S. federal debt. (In 1910 the federal debt was $1.1 billion. In 1920, as a result of World War I, it had grown to $24.2 billion. In 1940, even after paying Depression welfare expenses, the federal debt was only $43 billion. At the end of World War II, in 1945, the debt stood at $258.7 billion.)

With regard to economics, however, the EC is not regarded as cheerfully by other nations. The ruling fear is that a united Europe will become isolationist and protectionist and that this vast market of more than 300 million people will be lost to the rest of the world. Moreover, there is widespread fear that a reunified Germany, possibly the most powerful international competitor in the world, will be a formidable member of the EC.

Japan has sought publicly to ignore the fear of the EC, but she may be the most apprehensive of all about the EC's protectionist tendencies. The low countries, the Netherlands, Belgium, and Luxembourg, for instance, want Japanese cars badly. However, that desire is not in tune with the plans of the EC. Japan, loaded with money, wants to make extensive investments in the EC if they are allowed.

The United States has long had extensive operations in the EC, as the EC nations have had in the U.S. The U.S. is possibly most afraid of the agricultural protectionism which already prevails, and it may become worse.

There are at least three **good reasons** why the EC surely cannot be protectionist very long. The **first is** that western Europe, along with Japan, is highly dependent upon oil from the Middle East. But many nations, the most prominent being the United States, have extensive influence in the Middle East. Oil may well become the economic tool which is used to keep the EC away from protectionist policies.

The second reason is that in spite of the vast resources of the EC, their products and industries are not, in many cases, superior to those of the rest of the world. So the EC, though perhaps able to subsidize such important industries as the Airbus Industrie, cannot subsidize all industries very long. Ultimately a profit must be made, and it must be made in a competitive market. Subsidies may be fine for a time, but ultimately a healthy economy must be built upon industries that not only pay their own way, but also make enough to keep social programs going.

The third reason is that Great Britain and Germany, both still powerful in their own ways, will not sit still for a protectionism that endangers their own roles in the international economy. Further, the fact is that protectionism has never worked in the long term; one has to feel that protectionism will not work for the EC, and indeed it may not prove to be the problem some believe it will become. If the world is to develop economically, giving each citizen in every country a higher standard of living, then free trade to the greatest degree possible will be the order of the day. And the EC is unlikely to be able to stand against this trend.

This is not to say that the EC, even with its protectionist tendencies, cannot succeed to a degree; it likely will succeed, and we had all better hope that it will. But perhaps it can act as the fifty United States act—

with healthy interstate state and competitive export trade—rather than as a body united against the rest of the world.

As noted earlier, the EC plans to be socialistic in the same manner that western Europe has been socialistic for many years. Already vast sums are being expended in Spain, Portugal, and Greece, especially in the building or rebuilding of infrastructures. This kind of expense puts a strain on any economy and, despite its size, the EC will be no different from any country in the facing of blunt economic facts. Even when socialism is democratic, which the EC will be, it is an expensive form of government and the economy tends to become overburdened by taxes. However, as I shall discuss in more detail in the conclusion, democratic socialism seems destined to be the government of the future, literally around the world, which should put the world on a fairly even economic basis.

Even with a reunified Germany and its productive capabilities in the EC, the EC will still need vast infusions of outside capital to be successful, and Japan will be the primary source of this capital. The EC cannot afford to play fast and loose with the rest of the world, pretending, economically, that it does not exist. Should the rest of the world, even in small part, put economic pressure on the EC, success would be impossible.

It is my opinion that the EC's protectionism, if indeed it is ever begun in earnest, will not stand the test of time. Too many outside nations, with too much money and representing too many markets for EC products, will be too tempting to resist.

Members of the European Community

The primary reasons for nations joining the European Community are two: (1) The possibility of preventing future wars in the area; (2) The strength which can be drawn from the other member nations, with the lesser-developed countries drawing on the combined strengths of the developed countries.

No nation ever likes to give up even a part of its sovereignty, but this is necessary in a federation such as the EC. Great Britain has balked at giving up power probably more than any other member nation. If there is to be a fully developed Economic Community, then many more national sacrifices will have to be made. Whether all of EC's goals can be accomplished is still a moot question. However, as I have stated previously, all of the ambitions of the leaders of the EC do not have to be achieved to have a successful federation.

The reunification of Germany brings a whole new look to the EC and its future. Because of the importance of reunification, and the gigantic role Germany will play in the future of the EC, I will deal with Germany before presenting the other eleven members. Let me explain to the readers that just a mention of the member nations is insufficient. As briefly as possible, effective managers need to know the strengths and weaknesses of each nation. Germany will be first.

Germany and the EC

Before examining the economic conditions that existed in the two Germanies prior to reunification, which took place on October 3, 1990, an analysis of the history of the region is in order.

Historically, probably no nation has been more feared than Germany, certainly not in modern history. The reuniting thus has had a twofold effect. There is general happiness that the German people were able to get together again; there is also fear that, once united, Germany would become the fearsome nation of old.

History continues to speak loudly. Germany, as a modern state, was formed after the defeat of Napoleon. The great European powers met at the Congress of Vienna (1815) and established the German Confederation, which formerly had been 39 independent states. These people, once divided into nearly 1,800 dominions, were fractious and quite accustomed to fighting.

In 1871, after winning the Franco-Prussian War, Otto von Bismarck established the German empire under Kaiser Wilhelm I and started a period of national expansion.

In 1914, Archduke Francis Ferdinand of Austria-Hungary was murdered in Sarajevo, upsetting a European balance of power that had existed only tenuously since the turn of the century. Germany started World War I by invading Belgium, a small and neutral nation.

After Germany's defeat in 1918, the Treaty of Versailles "settled" WW I in 1919. Germany was forced to pay 33 billion dollars in reparations, and the seeds were sown for World War II.

In 1933, Adolph Hitler came to power as Germany's Chancellor, with plans well laid for extending the nation's power and of subjugating all of Europe if possible. The sentiments in Germany were still strong against those who had placed the burden on them after WW I.

All of the exploits of this madman need not be reviewed. World War II was started with the invasion by Germany of Poland in 1939. By the end of the war in 1945, Germany had indeed overcome virtually all of Europe. Had not the United States and Russia intervened in the war there was no way for Europe to win, even though Britain remained stalwart throughout. Also, the Allied winners were more lenient this time about postwar retribution, thus avoiding the deep-seated enmities of WW I.

The dividing of Germany into East and West was the result of placating the Soviet Union after the war by giving up the east, along with half of the city of Berlin. In 1961, with tensions rising in both East and West Germany, the Communists built the Berlin Wall. Without question this had to be one of the most ridiculous acts of man's history, and it certainly gave the world a look at the "vision" of communism.

In 1989 there was a relaxing of travel between the East and the West, and with the failure of communism, the two were reunited in October 1990.

East Germany was, and is, in a pitiable condition, as are the former Eastern bloc countries and the former Soviet Union. West Germany is literally buying East Germany back from years of Communist authoritarian rule. The infrastructure of East Germany is virtually in ruins, as are the industrial plants and other businesses. Even West Germany still does not know what the cost will be to bring the East back to a semblance of normalcy.

If the rest of Europe and other nations of the world are somewhat concerned about a reunited Germany, they are not alone. Having seen, from the inside, some of the things that have happened in Germany, some of her own people are also concerned.

Officially, the Germans do not want a Europe controlled by Germany but a Europe of which Germany is a part. Time will tell. But a well-founded opinion is that Germany will not hastily give up the position she has, much of which goes back to the generous Marshall plan and the lack of punishment she was afforded after World War II.

Differences between the East and the West, as well as the failure of communism to live up to its promises, can be seen in the statistics below.

People. Population (1991 est.): 78,700,000. Density: 571 per sq. mi.

Geography. Area: 137,838 sq. mi. Capital: Berlin, population: 3,410,000. Major cities: Hamburg, population 1,597,500; Munich, population 1,206,400; Cologne, population 934,400.

Government. Type: Now a reunited Federal Republic. Head of state: president. Head of government: chancellor. Local governmental divisions: 10 laender states and 14 districts.

Economy. Industries: steel, ships, vehicles, machinery, coal, chemicals, electrical products, textiles. Chief crops: grains, potatoes, sugar beets. Minerals: coal, iron, potash, lignite, uranium. Arable land: 30 percent (West Germany); 47 percent (East Germany). Labor force: 5 percent agriculture, 40 percent industry and commerce, 54 percent services (West Germany); 10 percent agriculture, 42 percent industry and construction (East Germany).

Finance. Currency: Mark (July 1990): $1.67 = $1 U.S. GNP (1988): $1,208 billion (West Germany); $207.2 billion (East Germany). Per capita income: $19,750 (West Germany); $10,000 (East Germany). Imports: $250 billion (West Germany); $31 billion (East Germany). Exports: $323 billion (West Germany); $30 billion (East Germany). Trading partners: EC and other European countries.

Education. Literacy rate: 99 percent. Years of compulsory education: 10.

The differences in GNP and per capita income provide vivid proof of the failure of the East's Communistic system. The figures also reveal the need of the West for the East's agriculture.

In less than a decade, and perhaps in five years, the production of the East should be equal, on a size comparison basis, to the West. Germany will then be one reasonably restored country with a GNP of probably 2.5 trillion dollars or more.

Although the financial and productive strength of Germany will rival that of all the rest of the EC, I do not foresee Germany becoming a "bully" within the EC, but it could become the strong partner that will encourage all the other nations to cooperate.

Belgium

People. Population (1990 est.): 9,895,000. Density: 840 per sq. mi. Percent urban population (1980): 73 percent.

Geography. Area: 11,799 sq. mi., slightly larger than Maryland. Capital: Brussels, population 970,000. Major cities: Antwerp, population 479,000; Ghent, population 233,000; Charleroi, population 209,000; Liege, population 200,000.

Government. Type: parliamentary democracy under a constitutional monarch. Head of state: king. Head of government: premier. Local governmental divisions: 9 provinces, 3 regions, and 3 cultural communities. Amount spent on defense (1988): 3.1 percent of GNP.

Economy. Industries: steel, glassware, diamond cutting, textiles, chemicals. Chief crops: wheat, sugar beets. Minerals: coal. Other resources: forests. Arable land: 26.5 percent. Fish catch (1988): 23.3 metric tons. Labor force: 2 percent agriculture; 26 percent industry and commerce; 37 percent services and transportation; 23 percent public services.

Finance. Currency: franc (June 1990 34.81 = $1 U.S.) GNP (1988): $153 billion. Per capita income (1987): $10,340. Imports (1988): $95 billion. Exports (1988): $104 billion. Trading partners: Germany, Netherlands, France, United Kingdom, and United States.

Education. Literacy rate: 98 percent. School compulsory to age eighteen.

Belgium lives by foreign trade. About 50 percent of its total production is sold abroad.

Denmark
Kingdom of Denmark
Kongeriget Danmark

People. Population (1990 est.): 5,134,000 (the population is aging). Density: 305 per sq. mi. Percent urban population (1986): 84 percent.

Geography. Area: 16,633 sq. mi., size of Massachusetts. Capital: Copenhagen, population 619,000. Major cities: Aarhus, population 252,071; Odense, population 171,468.

Government. Type: Constitutional monarchy. Head of state: queen (or king). Head of government: prime minister.

Economy. Industries: machinery, textiles, furniture, electronics. Chief crops: dairy products. Arable land: 62 percent.

Finance. Currency: krone (June 1990 6.44 = $1 U.S.). GNP (1987): $101.3 billion. Per Capita income (1988): $19,750. Imports (1989): $26.6 billion. Exports (1988): $28.1 billion. Major trading partners: Germany, Sweden, EC, and United States.

Education. Literacy rate (1986): 99 percent. Years of compulsory education: 9. Attendance rate: 100 percent.

France
French Republic
Republique Francaise

People. Population (1990 est.): 56,184,000. Density: 252 per sq. mi. Percent urban population: 77.2 percent.

Geography. Area: 220,668 sq. mi., four-fifths the size of Texas. Capital: Paris, population (1982), 2,188,918. Major cities: Marseille, population 878,689; Lyon, population 418,476; Toulouse, population 354,289; Nice, population 338,486.

Government. Type: republic. Head of state: president. Head of government: prime minister. Local governmental divisions: 22 administrative regions, containing 95 departments. Amount spent on defense: 4 percent of GNP (1987).

Economy. Industries: steel, chemicals, autos, textiles, wine, perfume, aircraft, electronics. Chief crops: Grain, corn, rice, fruits, vegetables. (France is the largest food producer and exporter in the EC.) Minerals: bauxite, iron, coal. Other resources: forests. Arable land: 32 percent. Livestock (1988): cattle, 21.1 million; pigs, 12.5 million; sheep, 10.3 million. Fish catch (1988): 843,000 metric tons.

Finance. Currency: franc (June 1990 5.57 = $1 U.S.) Gross National Product (1988): $943 billion. Per capita income (1986): $13,046. Imports (1989): $193 billion. Exports (1989): $179 billion. Major trading partners: EC and United States. National Budget (1988): $208 billion. Consumer price change in 1989: 3.5 percent.

Education: Literacy rate: 99 percent. Years of compulsory education: 10.

France is the most viable competitor of the United States in farm products in the EC. This appears to be the first obstacle to overcome in trade between the US and the EC.

Greece
Hellenic Republic
Elliniki Dimokratia

People. Population (1990 est.): 10,066,000. Density: 196 per sq. mi. Percent urban population: 58 percent.

Geography. Area: 51,146 sq.mi., about the size of Alabama. 75 percent of the land is mountainous and nonarable. There are about 2,000 islands, only about 169 of which are inhabited. Capital: Athens, population 3,027,000. Major cities: Salonika, population 720,000; Patras, population 150,000.

Government. Type: presidential parliamentary republic. Head of state:

president. Head of government: prime minister. Local governmental divisions: 51 prefectures.

Economy. Industries: textiles, chemicals, metals, wine, food processing, cement. Chief crops: grains, corn, rice, cotton, tobacco, olives, citrus fruits, raisins, figs. Minerals: bauxite, lignite, oil, manganese. Livestock (1987): 11.0 million sheep; 5.6 million goats. Fish catch: 135,000 metric tons. Labor force: 28 percent agriculture; 29 percent industry; 40 percent services.

Finance. Currency: drachma (June 1990, 161.0 = $1 U.S.). GNP (1987): $43.5 billion. Per capita GNP: $4,350. Imports (1988): $12.3 billion. Exports: $5.4 billion. National budget (1987): $20.2 billion. Consumer price change (1988): 13.7 percent.

Education. Literacy rate (1989): 96 percent, men; 89 percent, women. Years of compulsory education: 9.

Ireland
Republic of Ireland

People. Population (1990 est.): 3,557.000. Density: 137 per sq. mi.

Geography. Area: 27,137 sq. mi., slightly larger than West Virginia. Capital: Dublin, population 502,000 (1988 est.). Major cities: Cork, population 140,000; Limerick, population 60,000.

Government. Type: parliamentary republic. Head of state: president. Head of government: prime minister. Local governmental divisions: 26 counties. Amount spent on defense (1988): 1.3 percent of GNP.

Economy. Industries: food processing, metals, textiles, chemicals, brewing, electrical and non-electrical equipment, machines, tourism. Chief crops: potatoes, grain, sugar beets, fruits, vegetables. Minerals: zinc, lead, silver, gas. Arable land: 14 percent. Livestock (1987): cattle, 6.7 million; pigs, 994,000; sheep, 2.7 million. Fish catch: 247,000 metric tons.

Finance. Currency: pound (June 1990 0.60 = $1 U.S.) GNP (1988):

$28.6 billion. Per capita income: $6,200. Imports (1989): $17.4 billion. Exports: $20.6 billion. Prominent trading partners: UK, United States, France, W. Germany.

Education. Literacy rate: 99 percent. Years of compulsory education: 9. Attendance rate: 91 percent.

Italy
Italian Republic
Repubblica Italiana

People. Population (1990 est.): 57,657,000. Density: 493 per sq. mi. Percent urban population (1988): 67 percent.

Geography. Area: 116,303 sq. mi., about the size of Florida and Georgia combined. Capital city: Rome (1988 est.), population 2,800,000. Major cities: Milan, population 1.4 million; Naples, population 1.2 million; Turin, population 1.0 million.

Government. Type: republic. Head of state: president. Head of government: prime minister. Local governmental divisions: 20 regions with some autonomy; 94 provinces. Amount spent on defense (1988): 2.1 percent of GNP.

Economy. Industries: steel, machinery, autos, textiles, shoes, machine tools, chemicals. Chief crops: grapes, olives, citrus fruits, vegetables, wheat, wine. Minerals: mercury, potash, sulphur. Arable land: 32 percent. Livestock (1987): cattle, 8.9 million; pigs, 9.1 million. Fish catch: 554,000 metric tons.

Finance. Currency: lira (June 1990 1,214 = $1 U.S. GNP (1988): $825 billion. Per capita income: $14,333. Imports (1989): $153 billion. Exports: $140 billion. Major trading partners: Germany, France, UK, and United States. National Budget (1987): $311 billion. Percent change in consumer prices (1989): 6.2 percent.

Education. Years of compulsory education: 8.

Luxembourg
Grand Duchy of Luxembourg
Grand-Duche de Luxembourg

People. Population (1990 est.): 369,000. Density: 369 per sq. mi. Percent urban population (1985): 81 percent.

Geography. Area: 998 sq. mi., smaller than Rhode Island. Capital: Luxembourg, population 86,000.

Government. Type: constitutional monarchy. Head of state: grand duke. Head of government: prime minister. Local governmental divisions: 3 districts. Amount spent on defense: 0.8 percent of GNP.

Economy. Industries: steel, chemicals, beer, tires, tobacco, metal products, cement. Chief crops: corn, wine. Minerals: iron. Arable land: 25 percent.

Finance. Currency: franc (March 1990 35.06 = $1 U.S.). GNP (1988): $4.9 billion. Per capita GNP (1988): $13,380.

Education. Literacy rate (1989): 100 percent. Years of compulsory education: 9. Attendance rate: 100 percent.

Netherlands
Kingdom of the Netherlands
Konindrijk der Nederlanden

People. Population (1990 est.): 14,864,000. Density: 931 sq. mi.

Geography. Area: 15,770 sq. mi., the size of Massachusetts, Connecticut, and Rhode Island combined. Averages 35 feet above sea level. Capital: Amsterdam, population 691,000. Major cities: Rotterdam, population 574,100; Hague, population 443,500.

Government. Type: parliamentary democracy under a constitutional monarch. Head of state: Queen (or King). Head of government: prime minister. Seat of government: The Hague. Amount spent on defense (1987): 3.2 percent of GNP. Local governmental divisions: 12 provinces.

Economy. Industries: metals, machinery, chemicals, oil refinery, diamond cutting, electronics, tourism. Chief crops: grain, potatoes, sugar beets, vegetables, fruits, flowers. Minerals: natural gas, oil (petroleum reserves: 195 million barrels). Livestock (1988): Cattle, 4.7 million; pigs, 13.4 million. Fish catch (1987): 435,000 metric tons. Labor force: 1 percent agriculture; 47 percent industry and commerce; 44 percent services; 15 percent government.

Finance. Currency: guilder (June 1990 1.66 = $1 U.S.). GNP (1988): $223 billion. Per capita income (1987): $13,065. Imports (1989): $104.2 billion. Exports: $107.8 billion. Major trading partners: Germany, Belgium, France, UK. National budget: (1988): $91 billion.

Education. Literacy rate (1989): 99 percent. Years of compulsory education: 10. Attendance rate: 100 percent.

Portugal
Republic of Portugal
Republica Portuguesa

People. Population (1990 est.): 10,528,000. Density: 261 per sq. mi. Percent urban population (1983): 30 percent.

Geography. Area: 36,390 sq. mi., slightly smaller than Indiana. Capital: Lisbon, population 2,000,000. Major city: Oporto, population 1.5 million.

Government. Type: parliamentary democracy. Head of state: president. Head of government: prime minister. Local governmental divisions: 18 districts. 2 autonomous regions. 1 dependency. Amount spent on defense (1987): 3.2 percent of GNP.

Economy. Industries: textiles, footwear, cork, chemicals, fish, canning, wine, paper. Chief crops: grains, potatoes, rice, grapes, olives, fruits. Minerals: tungsten, uranium, copper, iron. Other resources: forests (Portugal is the world's leader in cork production). Arable land: 32 percent. Livestock (1987): sheep, 2.4 million; pigs, 1.2 million; cattle, 1 million. Fish catch: 395,000 metric tons. Labor force: agriculture 21 percent; industry and commercial 34 percent; services and government 44 percent.

Finance. Currency: escudo (June 1990 145.40 = $1 US). GNP (1987): $33.5 billion. Per capita income (1986): $2,970. Imports (1989): $18.7 billion. Exports: $12.5 billion. Major trading partners: UK, Germany, France. Consumer price change in 1989: 12.6 percent.

Education. Literacy rate (1989): 83%. Years of compulsory education: 6. Attendance rate: 60 percent.

Spain
España

People. Population (1990 est.): 39,623,000. Density: 204 per sq. mi. Percent urban population: 75 percent.

Geography. Area: 194,886 sq. mi, size of Arizona and Utah combined. Capital: Madrid, population 3,500,000 (1987). Other major cities: Barcelona, population 2,000,000; Valencia, population 700,000; Seville, population 580,000.

Government. Type: constitutional monarchy. Head of state: king (or queen). Head of government: prime minister. Local governmental divisions: 50 provinces, 2 territories, 3 islands. Amount spent on defense (1987): 2.4 percent of GNP.

Economy. Industries: machinery, steel, textiles, shoes, autos, processed foods. Chief crops: grains, olives, grapes, citrus fruits, vegetables. Minerals: lignite, uranium, lead, iron, copper, zinc, coal. Other resources: forests (cork). Arable land: 31 percent. Livestock (1987): cattle, 4.9 million; pigs, 16.9 million; sheep, 17.3 million. Fish catch

(1987): 1.0 million tons. Labor force: agriculture 16 percent; industry and commercial 24 percent; service 52 percent.

Finance. Currency: Peseta (May 1990 101.55 = $1 U.S.) GNP (1989): $288 billion. Per capita income (1989): $4,490. Imports (1989): $71.4 billion. Exports: $44.4 billion. Major trading partners: EC, United States. National budget (1987): $66.7 billion. Consumer price change (1989): 6.8 percent.

Education. Literacy rate (1989): 97 percent. Compulsory education to age 14.

United Kingdom of Great Britain and Northern Ireland

People. Population (1990 est.): 57,121,000. Density: 601 per sq. mi.

Geography. Area: 94,226 sq. mi., slightly smaller than Oregon. Capital: London, population 6,700,000 (1987). Other major cities: Birmingham, population 1,008,000; Glasgow, population 715,000; Leeds, population 710,000; Sheffield, population 532,000; Liverpool, population, 476,000; Manchester, population 451,000; Edinburgh, population 440,000; Bradford, population 463,000; Bristol, population 384,000.

Government. Type: constitutional monarchy: Head of state: queen (or king). Head of government: prime minister. Local governmental divisions: England and Wales, 47 nonmetro counties; 6 metro counties; Greater London; Scotland. 9 regions, 3 islands areas, N. Ireland, 26 districts. Amount spent on defense (1987): 4.7 percent of GNP.

Economy. Industries: steel, metals, vehicles, ship building, banking, textiles, chemicals, electronics, aircraft, machinery, distilling. Chief crops: grains, sugar beets, fruits, vegetables. Minerals: Coal, tin, oil, gas, limestone, iron, alt, clay, chalk, gypsum, lead, silica. Arable land: 30 percent. Crude oil reserves: 5.8 billion barrels. Livestock (1987): cattle, 12.6 million; pigs, 7.9 million; sheep, 38.7 million; Fish catch (1987): 716,000 metric tons. Labor force: agriculture 1.7 percent; manufacturing and engineering 24 percent; services 52 percent.

Finance. Currency: pound (June 1990 .56 = $1 U.S.) GNP (1988): $758 billion. Per capita GNP: $13,329. Imports (1989): $197 billion. Exports: $152 billion. Major trading partners: Germany, United States, France, and the Netherlands. National budget (1988): $320 billion.

Education. Literacy rate (1989): 99 percent. Years of compulsory education: 12. Attendance rate: 99 percent.

Conclusion to the European Community

Although I obtained statistics from the most reliable sources at my command, differences in the years the surveys were made and how they were made will be reflected in the final figures. Usually these differences are not enough to be concerned about. Readers would be well advised, however, to review statistics at least annually and update their records.

Some other ways of dealing with statistics will also be confusing. For example: Per capita income is not the same as per capita GNP, or GDP. (Gross National Product and Gross Domestic Product are the same.) Per capita income is the national income (all the payments made to the factors of production, which are land, labor, capital, and entrepreneurship) divided by the population. GNP or GDP is the sum total of all the final goods and services produced in an economy in a year, stated in terms of dollars. Thus, if you divide either the GNP or the GDP by the population, a much higher figure than the figure for per capita income is obtained.

Other statistics that are important to study when reviewing the records of a nation include:

1. Population density. This figure often dictates the type of industries the nation can have.

2. Type of government structure. A government's structure often reveals how quickly the government can be changed or overthrown.

3. The nation's industries. Analyzing a nation's industries helps determine whether they support generally low-paying jobs or high-paying jobs.

4. The natural resources. Studying natural resources allows predictions to be made about the development of a nation's economy over time.

Comparing the U.S. and the EC

	Population (Millions)	GDP Per Capita ($)	Gov't Expend. (As % of GDP)	Unemp. Rate, 1988	Percentage of Land in Agriculture	Population Per Sq. Mile	TV's Per 1,000 Pop.	Trade With U.S., 1988 ($ Billions)	U.S. Trade Surplus/ (Deficit) ($ Billions)
Belgium	⎰10	11,802	52	10.2	47	319	301	⎰11.9	⎰2.9
Luxembourg	⎱	14,705	44	1.7	49	133	253	⎱	⎱
Denmark	5	13,241	58	5.6	66	119	386	2.6	(.7)
France	56	12,803	52	10.3	58	102	402	22.3	(2.1)
West Germany	61	13,323	47	6.2	48	245	379	20.8	(12.2)
Greece	10	6,363	43	7.4	70	76	174	1.2	.1
Ireland	4	7,541	55	17.6	81	51	260	3.6	.8
Italy	57	12,254	50	11.9	58	190	255	18.4	(4.8)
Netherlands	15	12,252	60	9.5	54	356	467	19.7	5.5
Portugal	10	6,297	44	7.0	48	111	157	1.4	.06
Spain	39	8,681	42	20.1	62	77	322	7.4	1.0
United Kingdom	57	12,340	44	8.3	77	233	534	36.4	.4
United States	244	18,338	37	5.4	46	26	813	..	..

Sources: World Development Report 1989; U.S. Department of Commerce; Organization for Economic Cooperation and Development; Statistical Offices of the European Community; Statistical Abstract of the United States 1989.

71

5. Amount of arable land. The amount of arable land is a good indicator of whether the nation can be self-supporting in agricultural products.

6. Division of the labor force. Too many people still engaged in agriculture reveals a nation that is underdeveloped. Also, the number of people engaged in government services can indicate a socialistic form of government, though it may not be so named.

7. Differences between imports and exports. A nation with consistently more imports than exports reveals that a nation is building a foreign debt, as the United States has over the past ten years.

8. Note the rate of inflation for the country for the last year reported.

9. Note section on education. The literacy rate of many countries is frequently exaggerated. More years of compulsory education, if enforced, add credence to the rate of literacy reported.

10. Check to see if the nation reporting is superior in any one economic category, the presence of which might mean quicker economic development.

A matter which shall be discussed in length later is also important for the reader. Statistics from the former communist countries, when forthcoming, are frequently not reliable. So, while I shall use statistics from communist countries, they are not completely dependable.

When a manager is seeking a foreign market, he need not be concerned whether or not his product is already produced in that market. He does need to be concerned about comparative costs, about shipping charges, about tariffs, etc. If his product is of quality and produced at the lowest cost he may well be competitive if the tariffs do not negate that advantage.

But more important than all of the statistics is the need for all managers all over the world and students of management all over the world to realize the actuality of the one-world economy. They must learn that the one-world economy is the setting in which they will have to manage. And it makes little difference whether one is in the top position in management, where the big decisions are made, or working in a lower echelon, where the manager is closer to the product. All alike must realize that the success of their companies and their own personal wealth hinges on how well they understand the world and what the world wants from them.

The European Community will succeed, though probably not to the degree it aspires to. It will become a formidable competitor not only for the United States but for the world. It is hoped that the EC will welcome investment capital from outside and will learn to trade on the basis of comparative advantage. Should the EC turn protectionist for any period of time, it will negate all possibility of success. The EC, in full bloom, would be large and formidable, but not an alliance which could stand against the rest of the world.

By December 31, 1992, that full fruition is to come. It is a historic movement and will be watched closely. Even modest success will make it the most prodigious peaceful union the world has ever known.

Several times in this volume, and particularly in this section, I have alluded to the fact that the future of governments, their politics, and economies, will be built around democratic socialism. While there might be the tendency to disparage this statement, I want to look at the facts concerning what has happened since 1930, what the tendency is now, and how this tendency will progress in the decade of the 1990s.

Those nations, particularly industrialized nations, of the world that have avoided communism have embraced democratic socialism, though they might wish to call it by some other name. We can use the United States as an example of how socialism grows, even when a nation refuses to call it by its name. In 1929, when the Great Depression began, there was virtually no program to assure a reasonable standard of living for the average family, nor had such a plan been expected, either from industry or government. Moreover, there was no type of a retirement program, no compensation for periods of unemployment, and no federal minimum wage. There were some welfare programs, though they were meager and were shunned by the average family as being a disgraceful dependence upon someone else. It is difficult to describe to people today how strongly people felt in those days about "charity."

To one who did not live during those years it is almost impossible to describe the despair most people felt at the beginning of the Great Depression. Unemployment at the trough of the Depression reached 25 percent of the labor force and another 25 percent were underemployed. Few people in those days had a chance to save money. Most families lived from paycheck to paycheck and there was little or no savings for emergencies. Coming as abruptly as it did after the "roaring twenties," the Great Depression not only scared the whole nation but left the nation vulnerable to almost any solution the government might propose.

The following statistics will give an idea of the the income of the times:

YEAR	PER CAPITA GNP		PER CAPITA GNP FOR YEARS AFTER 1945
1931:	$ 615.00	1945:	$ 1,526.00
1932:	$ 468.00	1950:	$ 1,876.00
1933:	$ 446.00	1965:	$ 3,366.00
1934:	$ 514.00	1970:	$ 4,951.00
1935:	$ 569.00	1980:	$ 11,995.00
1936:	$ 645.00	1990:	$ 19,169.00
1937:	$ 704.00		
1938:	$ 656.00		
1939:	$ 695.00		
1940:	$ 761.00		

At 475 percent inflation since 1933, our lowest per capita GNP during the Great Depression, namely 1933, would be worth $2,120 currently. This statistic gives some idea of the standard of living people had then. While coping better than one might believe, people looked for some hope that the same thing would not happen again.

In my years of teaching economics, I often tried to make students aware of the conditions in the 1930s and failed completely. They could not imagine such a time and put my descriptions down as one of those "I used to walk to school, three miles each way, through rain and snow" tales. It would be difficult, however, to exaggerate the stark realities of those times. Most people did not have bank accounts that amounted to much and the average family did not own a home. In short, when the emergency came, they had little or nothing to fall back on. Many who had been doing well in business, but were somewhat in debt, lost all they had.

By the 1930s the people of the United States were acquainted with both communism and socialism. There was, in fact, a spirit of revolution in the air. This was exacerbated by the conditions of the 1920s, which flaunted wealth and drove a wedge between the "haves" and "have nots." Change of some kind had to come.

Though Franklin Delano Roosevelt was a man of the privileged class, he sought to present himself as a champion of the people. His message provided a good image for his election, as did his marriage to organized labor. The common people hailed his election. My grandfather, using the reverent tones usually reserved for saying grace at the table, declared him to be "a God-sent man". Others were not so sure.

From 1932 until well into World War II, more and more social programs were enacted in an attempt to ward off another depression. Minimum wages laws, farm support programs, revamping of the Federal Reserve System, the introduction of favorable union laws, workman's unemployment compensation, new banking and security laws, higher taxes on the rich, Social Security, giant public programs such as TVA all marked the dawn of a new era in government intervention in what had always been seen as personal and private affairs.

The war years contributed to this government interventionism with the personal restrictions that government usually enacts during a period of great national stress, including wage and price controls, rationing, etc. After the war many benefits for veterans were passed by a grateful Congress, including extensive educational programs, housing loans, etc.

While Roosevelt is often regarded as the president who brought the United States out of the Great Depression, this is not true. From 1932 until the United States' military goods sales picked up in 1940, the United States had several mini-booms and mini-busts, but it never overcame the Depression completely. In late 1940, 15 percent of the labor force was still unemployed, and only the onset of World War II changed the economic picture.

And while John Maynard Keynes' economic theories had persuaded Roosevelt to spend on public works to aid the economy, the national debt actually increased from $19 billion in 1930 to $47 billion in 1940, hardly enough to lift an economy as large as that of the United States. The major impact of government during the Great Depression was not its expenditures, per se, but the idea implanted in the minds of the American people that the federal government was the nation's savior in times of great need. While not many people recognized it then, 1932 ended the private enterprise, or market, system in the United States as we had known it and depended upon it. From that time on, the United States has slowly but surely made her way toward democratic socialism, though we still do not call it that, and toward an economy over which the government has increasing control.

Three major wars and countless social programs have increased the United States' national debt from $17 billion in 1930 to $3.2 trillion in 1990. If we have bought "security," it was purchased at a tremendous price.

All nations of the world, even the most prominent ones, will adopt more social programs, programs in housing, health care, education, etc. This will means somewhat lessened standards of living, but less distance, also, between the rich and the poor.

Managers will not deal with other companies alone, either domestically or internationally, but with companies that are, to some degree, partners with government. So prices will not be market prices but administered prices, to some extent. There will be interminable miles of red tape. This does not mean that business cannot be done anywhere in the world. It will mean that the world will need to have a new generation of managers who know how to deal in a world market, which is by no means free.

This new association of businesses with governments will also mean that in many instances, both inside one's own country and outside it, a manager will be dealing directly with governments, since governments will be spending a much larger share of the GNP. The table on the EC and the United States, at the end of this section, addresses the amount of various GNPs that are spent by government. The EC nations, in particular, are already deeply involved in socialism, and they will become more so. But extensive social programs take a lot of money, and they do not promote the most efficient forms of government. These are the kinds of government which will prevail in the world over the foreseeable future, however. Students of management and in-service managers will wish to avail themselves of all information possible on both the history and current practice of socialism.

Appendix: Branch Offices of the European Economic Community

Commission of the European Communities
Rue de la Loi 200, B-1049 Bruxelles

Office in Belgium

Bureau in Belgie
Rue Archimede 73
1040 Bruxelles
Archimedesstraat 73
1040 Brussel
Telephone number: 235 38 44
Telex number: 26 657 COMINF B
Telecopy number: 235 01 66

Office in Denmark

Hojbrohus
Ostergade 61
Postbox 144
1004 Kobenhavn K
Telephone number: 33 14 41 40
Telex number: 16 402 COMEUR DK
Telefax number: 33 11 12 03/33 14 12 44

Offices in Germany

Zitelmannstrasse 22
5300 Bonn
Telephone number: 53 00 90
Telex number: 886 648 EUROP D
Telefax number: 5 30 09 50

Kurfürstendamm 102
1000 Berlin 31
Telephone number: 8 92 40 28
Telex number: 184 015 EUROPE D
Telefax number: 8 92 20 59

Erhardstrasse 27
8000 München 2
Telephone number: 2 02 10 11
Telex number: 184 015 EUROP D
Telefax number: 2 02 10 15

Office in Spain

Calle de Serrano 41, 5a.
28001 Madrid
Telephone number: 435-17 00 / 435 15 28
Telex number: 46 818 OIPE
Telefax number: 276 03 87

Offices in France

Bureau á Paris
61, rue des Belles-Feuilles
75782 Paris Cedex 16
Telephone number: 45 01 58 85
Telex number: Paris 611 019 COMEUR
Telefax number: 47 27 26 07

CMCI
2, rue Henri-Barbusse
13241 Marseille Cedex 01
Telephone number: 91 91 46 00
Telex number: 402 538 EURMA
Telefax number: 91 90 98 07

Office in Ireland

39 Molesworth Street
Dublin 2
Telephone number: 71 22 44
Telex number: 93 827 EUCO EL
Telefax number: 71 26 57

Offices in Italy

Via Poli, 29
00187 Roma
Telephone number: 678 97 22
Telex number: 610 184 EUROMA 1
Telefax number: 679 16 58

Corso Magenta, 59
20123 Milano
Telephone number: 80 15 05
Telex number: 316 200 EURMIL 1
Telefax number: 418 85 43

Office in Luxembourg

Batiment Jean Monnet B/O
2920 Luxembourg
Telephone number: 430 11
Telex number: 3423/3446 COMEUR LU
Telefax number: 43 01 44 33

Office in the Netherlands

Korte Vijverberg 5
2513 AB Den Haag
Telephone number: 46 93 26
Telex number: 31 094 EURCO NL
Telefax number: 64 66 19

Office in Portugal

Centro Europeu Jean Monnet
Largo Jean Monnet, 1-100
1200 Lisboa
Telephone number: 54 11 44
Telex number: 18 810 COMEUR P
Telefax number: 55 43 97

Office in the United Kingdom

Jean Monnet Street
8, Storey's Gate
London SWIP 3AT
Telephone number: 222 8122
Telex number: 23 208 EURUK G
Telefax number: 222 09 00 / 222 81 20

Office in Northern Ireland

Windsor House
9/15 Bedford Street
Belfast BT2 7EG
Telephone number: 240 708
Telex number: 74 117 CECBEL G
Telefax number: 284 241

Office in Wales

4 Cathedral Road
PO Box 15
Cardiff CFI 9SG
Telephone number: 37 16 31
Telex number: 497 727 EUROPA G
Telefax number: 226 41 05

Office in Scotland

7 Alva Street
Edinburgh EH2 4PH
Telephone number: 225 20 58
Telex number: 727 420 EUEDIN G
Telefax number: 226 41 05

Offices in the United States of America

Washington
2100 M Street NW
(Suite 707)
Washington, DC, 20037
Telephone number: (202) 862-9500

Telex number: 64 215 EURCOM NW
Telefax number: 429 17 66

New York
Suboffice to the Washington Office
3, Dag Hammarskjold Plaza
305 East 47th Street
New York, NY 10017
Telephone number: (212) 371-3804
Telex number: 012 396 EURCOM NY
Telefax number: 758 27 18

Office in Japan

Tokyo
Europa House
9-15 Sanbancho
Chiyoda-Ku
Tokyo 102
Telephone number: 239 04 41
Telex number: 28 567 COMEUTOK J
Telefax number: 261 51 94

Offices in Switzerland

Geneve
Case postale 195
37-39, rue de Vermont
1211 Geneve 20
Telephone: 34 97 50
Telex number: 282 61/2 ECOM CH
Telefax number: 34 23 31

Office in Venezuela

Caracas
Avenida Orinoco
Las Mercedes
Apartado 67 076
Las Americas 1061 A

Caracas
Telephone number: 91 51 33
Telex number: 27-298 COMEU VC
Telefax number: 91 88 76

The Former USSR and the Former Eastern Bloc Countries

Possibly never in human history have so many dynamic events taken place among the nations of the world as we have seen in the past few years. The renewed interest in the Economic Community, the rapid rise of the Pacific Rim nations, the intolerable problems in the Middle East, and the rapid push of the United States, Mexico, and Canada to unite in a Common American Market all alert us that change in the modern world does not require a lot of time.

No person I know and no author I have read saw any possibility of the breakdown of the USSR, nor of the releasing of the Eastern bloc nations from the control of the former Soviet Union. Before casting a somewhat apprehensive look into the future, it would be useful to make some comparisons between the United States, the European Community, and the former Warsaw Pact countries, which once included the USSR, Albania, Bulgaria, Czechoslovakia, East Germany, Poland, and Romania. The Warsaw Pact was dissolved on April 1, 1991.

The following figures are revealing:

NATION OR FEDERATIONS	POPULATION	GNP	PER CAPITA GNP
United States	250,372,000	$4.8 tril	$19,200
European Community	324,000,000	$4.61 tril	$14,230
Former Warsaw Pact	395,090,000	$3.62 tril	$ 8,511

It should be noted that the United States, with 25 percent less population than the EC, has a per capita GNP 26 percent higher. And, with a population of 36 percent less than the former Warsaw Pact nations, the United States has a 64 percent greater per capita GNP.

These figures do not tell all the story. Per capita GNP is simply the

GNP (or GDP, which is the same) divided by the population. Before a standard of living can be established, one has to know how much of the GNP actually went to the people in the form of a per capita income. We find, for example, that in 1989 France spent 52 percent of its GNP on government; the United States spent 37 percent; East Germany spent 59.3 percent; West Germany spent 47 percent; Romania spent 94 percent.

Thus the socialist, or communist, countries were government oriented, taking a major portion of the GNP and keeping the people, in the main, on some sort of government support, including free education, subsidized housing, guaranteed care in old age, free national health care, etc.

The Former USSR

We have witnessed in the Soviet Union movements which are as earth-shaking as any we had seen in the world since World War II. While communism has not died, it has been clearly identified as a failure.

Following is a list of the republics that made up the Soviet Union.

REPUBLIC	SQ. MI. AREA	POPULATION
Russia	6,592,800	146,000,000
Ukraine	233,100	51,377,000
Uzbekistan	172,700	19,569,000
Kazakhstan	1,049,200	16,470,000
Byelorussia	80,200	10,141,000
Azerbaijan	33,400	6,921,000
Georgia	26,911	5,297,000
Tadzhikistan	54,019	4,969,000
Moldavia	13,012	4,224,000
Kirgizia	76,642	4,238,000
Lithuania	26,173	3,682,000
Armenia	11,306	3,459,000
Turkmenistan	188,417	3,455,000
Latvia	24,695	2,673,000
Estonia	17,413	1,571,000

Some understandable confusion about the makeup of the former Soviet Union stemmed from the fact that within these fifteen republics were twenty autonomous republics. So one might have read that there were fifteen republics or twenty.

The Commonwealth of Independent States

Both economically and politically, the republics need one another. The following lists some of the economic strengths of each:

NAME	NATURAL RESOURCES AND INDUSTRIES
Russia	Steel, oil, gas, electric energy
Ukraine	Arable black soil, wheat, sugar beets, potatoes, livestock
Belorussia	Machinery, tools, appliances, steel, cement textiles
Azerbaijan	Oil, iron ore, cobalt, winter wheat, fruit
Georgia	Largest manganese mines in the world, timber, coal, food, textiles, grain, tea, tobacco
Armenia	Copper, zinc, aluminum, molybdenum, marble
Uzbekistan	Cotton, iron and steel, cars, tractors, coal, sulphur, copper, oil
Turkmenistan	Cotton, maize, carpets, chemicals
Tadzhikistan	Farming, cattle breeding, cotton, grain, rice, fruits, rich mineral deposits, coal, hydroelectric power
Kazakhstan	Deposits of coal, oil, tin, copper, lead, zinc, fish canning
Kirgizia	Cattle and horse breeding, tobacco, cotton, rice, sugar beets
Moldova	Black earth plain, grain, fruits, vegetables, tobacco, textiles, wine

It is apparent that while a commonwealth with all these resources and industrial capabilities would be a formidable power, not one republic, except possibly Russia, is prepared to be self-sufficient. Further, it should be remembered that three generations of communism failed to exploit these resources properly, even to the extent of keeping people properly clothed, fed, and housed.

One major problem, of special relevance to the present work, is the question of where the managers are going to come from in this new commonwealth. These nations possess the natural resources and existing industries to make production efficient and profitable, but they face formidable obstacles. Since 1917 the Communist state control has not produced efficient managers, but sycophantic followers of state demands. While there is already evidence in the former USSR, and in Poland and Hungary, that there are managers for small firms, the managerial expertise for large industries is not evident. Other nations, the United States, Germany, and Japan among them, should assist with the development of good managers. There will undoubtedly be coventures in the new commonwealth, and nations with the most management expertise can make the most of such arrangements, both for themselves and for the commonwealth nations. Further, the colleges and universities of the former Soviet Union can now be turned loose to train managers in free market techniques, with a heavy emphasis on human relations, an art and science much frowned upon in an authoritarian state.

If the commonwealth has the fortitude to suffer through a transition period when even food is scarce, as Poland has over the past few years, the probability is that within a few years not only can a semblance of peace reign but economic progress can be made. Trillions of dollars were lavished by the USSR upon the space program, on military hardware, and upon the export of communism. But, while this was going on, the consumer was forgotten, and the free market was nonexistent. The energy that once went into the creation of this mighty machine must now be directed toward capital goods, consumer needs, and the exploitation of the vast farmlands of the region. If the nations of the commonwealth let the people follow their own capacities in the labor market, the commonwealth might soon become the power her resources show she can be.

The Former Eastern Bloc Nations

The Eastern bloc nations, long under the thumb of the Soviet Union but now free from it since the dissolving of the Warsaw Treaty Pact on April 1, 1991, offer opportunities for trade and foreign investment on a magnitude unparalleled in the world. These nations are Poland,

Czechoslovakia, Hungary, Yugoslavia, Romania, and Bulgaria, since East Germany is already reunited with West Germany.

The history of these nations, which is so steeped in tradition, the arts, architecture, etc., has been dominated by more than fifty years of stringent living under communism. As the communist regimes fell, it was quickly learned that these nations would be faced with more years of stringent living if they were to get back to the type of life they would like and the attendant freedoms it would bring.

For these nations to pull themselves up to a reasonable standard of living, two things must happen: 1) they must support a government structure stable enough to attract venture capital from the outside; 2) they must be willing to live stringently for a few more years until the new governments and new private enterprises have a chance to build the economy. It is my opinion that the former Eastern bloc countries will do both.

With regard to government structure, the return of communism is not a problem. Settling the problems of factionalism within the countries is, but these problems are not insurmountable. Throughout the area, we will see forms of democratic socialism, which, in fact, will be a world-wide phenomenon before the end of this decade. Most individual freedoms, however, will not be affected, and competition will be sufficient to propel the engine of industry. These new governments will be free enough in their control of industry to build a reasonable standard of living for the people. The economic recovery of these nations will be supported by the growth of tourism, which within just a few years should boom.

In terms of foreign investment, especially investments in already established companies, these nations should be a bonanza in the next decade and beyond. Germany will be anxious to help the eastern European countries, while the nations of the former Soviet Union will be too involved with their own problems to help. Other countries will find this area a good place to do business as the one-world economy develops.

There is a question now as to whether or not, given time, these countries will want to become a part of the European Community. This is a very real possibility. Certainly they will not want alliances with the countries of the former Soviet Union. And, since their economies are more likely to develop along the lines of western European countries, particularly Germany and France, an ultimate union with the EC is not improbable.

Conclusion to the Former Eastern Bloc Nations

Few if any nations in the world have suffered so much since the 1930s as have these. Overrun first by the Germans and then, in part, by the Soviet Union, their populations as well as their resources have been depleted. After the USSR brought these nations into the Warsaw Treaty Organization in 1955 as an answer to the North Atlantic Treaty Organization, they remained virtually the vassals of Moscow until 1990. Between 1955 and 1990, the power of Moscow was used to put down democratic uprisings, including the uprising in Czechoslovakia in 1968. After this debacle, Albania withdrew from the pact.

These nations, with much that is noble in their pasts, deserve a better future. Managers all over the world should make a special study of the history of each of these nations and of the things the Eastern bloc nations need most now to become developed nations. The eastern European nations could make a splendid market for United States goods, and they could also become partners in the United States' overseas installations.

East Germany was quickly reunited with West Germany. Although the price of this reunification will be great, due to the enormous resources that will be required to lift the East German economy to the level of the West German economy, most Germans seem to believe that one Germany is better than two, regardless of the price. They are unquestionably correct. Germany will become the heart of the European Community, as well as its financial power. If this new Germany can keep her priorities straight she may well do much good in Europe in the foreseeable future.

The futures of the other former Eastern bloc countries are less sure. Poland seems destined to lead the way in economic recovery. Yugoslavia seems destined to remain divided, in spirit if not in essence. Hungary may possibly rank directly behind Poland in terms of the possibility for economic growth as she seeks stability of government and economic progress. She is an independent country that once defied Stalinist communism, which nearly brought on her death. There is evidence of a strong national resolve in Hungary, and it can be properly put to use in the economic sphere. Czechoslovakia, with a long background in the arts, is trying to gain equal success in forming a democratic government and in promoting her economy. Her leaders are now dedicated people, mostly with nonpolitical backgrounds. This just might be the nation to draw the most attention from prospective investors among all the old Eastern bloc group.

Romania and Bulgaria will continue to muddle along in their own ways. Strife still exists in both countries, fostered often by conflicting religions and old-fashioned ethnic distrust. Nor is the communism yet dead. Bulgaria was once Moscow's best friend among the Eastern bloc nations and solidly communist. She is also solidly agrarian, though industrialism has been getting a toehold there. Neither country will find democracy easy to assimilate.

The Middle East and Developing Countries

Unless one understands something of the history of the Middle East, which includes its origin and its religion, he will never understand the events that are now taking place there. The "Desert Storm" war of February 1991, for instance, was little more than a continuation of the many wars that have gone on there for centuries. At this point, one can see little else in the future.

According to both Biblical and secular sources, the Arabs and the Jews are descendents of the same father, Abraham, the patriarch, who first appeared about 2,000 B.C. in Ur of the Chaldees. The Arabs, in the main, are seen as the descendants of Araham through the concubine of Abraham, Hagar, and her son, Ishmael. Both Jews and Arabs lay claim to the land that God promised Abraham.

The Jews and Arabs have always been enemies, but the later adherence of the Arabs to Allah and his prophet Mohammed forever alienated the two peoples. There now exist three great monotheistic religions, Islam, Judaism, and Christianity. There are about five hundred million adherents to Islam in the world. Since the state of Israel was formed in 1948, there have been constant conflicts, and conflicts will continue.

It would be helpful to examine some statistics on the Middle Eastern nations:

NATION	POPULATION	GNP (1986,87,88)	OIL*	PER CAPITA INCOME OR GNP	
Cyprus	708,000	$ 3.5 bil.	0	$ 5,210	GNP
Turkey	56,549,000	62.0 bil.	139MB	1,160	Income
Syria	12,471,000	17.0 bil.	1.4BB	1,147	Income
Iraq	18,782,000	34.0 bil.	40BB	1,950	GNP
Iran	55,647,000	93.0 bil.	36.5BB	1,667	Income
Lebanon	3,340,000	1.8 bil.	0	690	GNP
Israel	4,371,000	36.0 bil.	700,000	5,995	Income
Jordan	3,065,000	4.3 bil.	0	1,403	GNP
Saudi Arabia	16,758,000	70.0 bil.	169BB	4,177	Income
Yemen	11,000,000	4.5 bil.	600MB	410	GNP
Kuwait	2,080,000	19.1 bil.	94BB	10,410	Income
Bahrain	512,000	4.6 bil.	173MB	9,994	Income
Qatar	498,000	5.4 bil.	3.3MB	27,000	Income
United Arab Emirates	2,250,000	22.0 bil.	33BB	11,900	Income
Oman	1,305,000	7.5 bil.	4.5BB	5,747	Income

*MB indicates millions of barrels, and BB indicates billions of barrels. This area accounts for 298,012,000,000 barrels of oil.

With the exception of Cyprus, and Israel, these nations are Moslem.

The data above reveal several areas of interest for managers, whether they are importing, exporting, or simply interested in what the competition situation is like around the world.

Oil, of course, is what the Middle East nations have to offer. Areas such as western Europe and Japan remain tied to the area because of the oil. Indeed, oil is the reason these small nations are wooed by the entire world. It seems unlikely at this point that anything but oil will ever attract much interest in the Middle East, but everything is subject to change. In the economic world it has often been presumed that the nation controlling the Middle East, even in part, can control the energy sources of the world—an assumption, I think, that has been somewhat overblown.

It will be noted in the data above that the Middle East runs from the very poor to the very rich, according to oil ownership, population, and the type of government that prevails. This will continue. The Middle East does remain a strong market for trade of many types, one of which is foodstuffs, particularly canned foods. More than thirty years ago, as I was introducing a food company to foreign trade, I made my first sale in Kuwait.

It might be possible for some of the nations to free themselves a bit from the monopoly of oil income, but there must be industries in other countries willing to invest, and they will not invest until a greater degree of stability is assured in the region. Communism, also, is still a force in the Middle East. The Middle East will remain an international tinder-box. Fighting will continue between the nations of the region as long as time continues. It is a most interesting and paradoxical part of the world.

Developing Countries

A discussion of the developing countries of the world would require a book or perhaps a library. The scope of this volume will not allow for more than brief definitions and references.

Developing countries are divided into two groups: 1) Low-income economies, with 1985 GNP per person of $400 or less and 2) Middle-income economies, with 1985 GNP per person of $401 to $1,000.

Low-Income Economies (0 to 400 Dollars)

NATION	POPULATION	GNP/GDP 1988		PER CAPITA GNP/GDP OR INCOME	
Afghanistan	15,592,000	$ 3.1	bil.	$ 220	GNP
Bangladesh	117,976,000	18.1	bil.	113	pcIncome
Benin	4,840,000	1.4	bil.	374	pcIncome
Bhutan	1,566,000	252.0	mil.	150	PCGNP

NATION	POPULATION	GNP/GDP 1988		PER CAPITA GNP/GDP OR INCOME	
Burkina Faso	8,941,000	1.4	bil.	170	PCGNP
Burma	5,647,000	1.2	bil.	238	PCIncome
Central African Republic	2,879,000	1.1	bil.	376	PCIncome
Chad	5,064,000	805.0	mil.	158	PCGNP
China	1,130,065,000	350.0	bil.	258	PCIncome
Ethiopia	51,375,000	5.7	bil.	121	PCIncome
Ghana	15,310,000	5.3	bil.	390	PCGNP
Guinea	7,269,000	2.4	bil.	305	PCGNP
Haiti	6,409,000	2.2	bil.	360	PCGNP
India	850,067,000	246.0	bil.	300	PCGNP
Kenya	25,393,000	8.1	bil.	322	PCIncome
Madagascar	11,802,000	2.1	bil	255	PCIncome
Mali	9,182,000	1.6	bil.	200	PCIncome
Mozambique	14,718,000	4.7	bil.	319	PCIncome
Myanmar (formerly Burma)	41,279,000	9.3	bil	210	PCIncome
Nepal	19,158,000	3.1	bil.	160	PCIncome
Niger	7,691,000	2.2	bil.	310	PCGNP
Pakistan	113,163,000	39.0	bil.	360	PCIncome
Senegal	7,740,000	2.0	bil.	380	PCIncome
Sierra Leone	4,168,000	.965	mil.	320	PCIncome
Somalia	8,415,000	1.5	bil.	290	PCGNP
Sri Lanka	17,135,000	7.2	bil.	400	PCGNP
Sudan	25,164,000	8.5	bil.	330	PCGNP
Tanzania	26,070,000	$ 4.9	bil.	$ 256	PCGNP
Togo	3,566,000	1.3	bil.	240	PCIncome
Uganda	17,593,000	3.6	bil.	220	PCGNP
Vietnam	68,488,000	12.6	bil.	180	PCIncome
Zambia	8,119,000	2.1	bil.	304	PCIncome
Zimbabwe	10,205,000	5.5	bil.	275	PCIncome

TOTALS:

33 nations   2,662,067,000 $759,220,000,000

AVERAGE GNP/GDP OR INCOMES: $275.65 for those nations reporting Per Capita GNP. $263.42 for those nations reporting Per Capita income.

There is a shocking reality in these statistics. Thirty-three nations, having a little more than half of the world's population, live on per capita incomes of little more than $250 per year, a vanishingly small figure compared to the $16,444 per capita income in the United States. It should be recalled that those nations reporting per capita GNP are giving a figure of the GNP divided by the population. Since not all of the GNP goes to the people, actual income could be figured at 10-20 percent less.

Add to this the fact that neither the income nor the wealth of these nations are divided equally, and the result is that nearly 2.7 billion people live continually on the ragged edge of starvation. In addition, more than half of these people live under communism, which means that they have little chance to see better days until communism is abandoned.

The statistics on middle-income economies are equally revealing:

Middle-Income Economies ($401 to $1,000)

NATION	POPULATION	GNP		PER CAPITA GNP OR PC INCOME	
Albania	3,268,000	$ 2.6	bil.	$ 960	PCGNP
Bolivia	6,730,000	4.6	bil.	570	PCGNP
Cambodia	6,993,000	10.4	bil.	960	PCGNP
Cote d'Ivoire (Ivory Coast)	12,070,000	$ 10.3	bil.	$ 921	PCIncome
Dominican Republic	7,253,000	5.5	bil.	800	PCGNP
Egypt	54,139,000	25.6	bil.	490	PCGNP
El Salvador	5,221,000	4.1	bil.	700	PCIncome
Guatemala	9,340,000	9.6	bil.	810	PCGNP
Indonesia	191,266,000	75.0	bil.	435	PCIncome
Laos	4,024,000	.500	bil.	500	PCIncome
Lebanon	3,340,000	1.8	bil.	690	PCGNP
Liberia	2,644,000	.973	bil.	410	PCGNP
Mauritania	2,038,000	.843	bil.	450	PCIncome
Morocco	26,249,000	18.7	bil.	630	PCIncome
Nicaragua	3,606,000	2.1	bil.	610	PCGNP
Nigeria	118,865,000	78.0	bil.	790	PCIncome

NATION	POPULATION	GNP	PER CAPITA GNP OR PC INCOME
Peru	21,904,000	19.6 bil.	940 PCIncome
Philippines	66,674,000	38.2 bil.	667 PCIncome
Thailand	54,890,000	52.2 bil.	771 PCIncome

TOTALS:

19 Nations   336,644,154 $ 360.616,000,000

AVERAGE PC INCOME: $ 680.40. AVERAGE PC GNP: $ 700.00

The total of the low-income and the middle-income population = 2,998,711,154. The total GNP= $1,119,836,000. Average PCGNP = $373.44. Percentage of world population in this category = 57.7%.

These statistics are staggering when they are related to the possibility of world development. Some of the small, very poor countries could become charity cases, always to be cared for by others. The larger nations, such as China and India, which have narrowly avoided developing-nation status, have several obstacles to hinder their progress. India certainly is progressing in her use of technology, but the chances that the success produced by technology will trickle down to the masses are slim. If technology were to improve India's standard of living for all of her citizens, it would happen generations into the future. India is not only faced with poverty; as with other poor regions, certain religious beliefs hinder her progress. Moreover, the poorer masses are generally uneducated. The literacy rate is 36 percent and, while the government has mandated fourteen years of compulsory education, it is obvious that few actually are so educated. Development that moves until it encompasses the masses seems almost impossible.

The situation in China is also dim. Until communism is abandoned and the doors of China opened, little more in the way of development can reach the people. Should China throw out the communist system, there is a chance for it to develop in the next two generations. I think it is even possible that such development could reach the masses in that period of time. Reuniting with Hong Kong could hasten widespread development. The Chinese are an ingenious people. Their history is to be envied, and their future could be enviable as well.

Conclusion to the Middle East and Developing Countries

While the world economy continues to expand, that expansion is by no means uniform. Speaking generally, developing countries are worse off than they were a decade ago. They are deeply in debt and need vast infusions of cash.

But nations such as the United States, which might otherwise be the source of that money, are also deeply in debt. In addition, the United States and some of her institutions stand to lose billions when those developing countries default. However, should the Americas come together into a Common Market, the nations in that area could develop well in a generation or two.

Africa and its development problems are a frightening spectacle. Tribal conditions and other local problems have contributed to impeding development. Communists in South Africa have been waiting for many years to get the hold they feel will be theirs when the barriers between blacks and whites are largely torn down.

Here are some of the countries that may develop over the next twenty-five years, and others whose development does not seem so promising.

Mexico, Central America, and South America can develop with the help of Canada and the United States, and they probably will. Africa will likely not develop. The signs of civil war are everywhere to be seen in South Africa, and the myriads of smaller countries likely will continue to be kept down by despotic regimes.

India, as much as I hope for the best, will likely not develop much either, at least in the next twenty-five years. Education of the masses must become a reality for development to happen, and, unfortunately, development must happen for education to be assured. the hopes are dim. However, markets for trade in India will be open, and no country should be unaware of the trade possibilities there. China can develop by denouncing communism. We can hope that she will do so. Indonesia and many of the smaller countries of Southeast Asia can develop. Again, for some of these countries the renunciation of communism is a condition for development. Once that is done, given the prime position of the Pacific Rim, I would not doubt that any of these countries could engage in development. There are other countries, however, such as Bangladesh, where development, if not impossible, is not probable. I cannot see where the outside resources would come from to assist in Bangladesh's development.

Regardless of how bad the economic prospects look in many parts of the world, it is absolutely essential that managers and would-be managers be familiar with all parts of the world. Twenty years ago I challenged my college students in economics, who did not see why they should be interested in world trade, to go to any local supermarket, clothing store, or discount store, and check the shelves carefully. Even then, more and more spaces on the shelves were being filled up with foreign goods. This is much more true today. An aspiring manager must not disavow history or foreign languages. A middle or lower echelon manager must not be divorced from developments in the world economy. The raw materials any manager may use, at least in part, will come from a country other than his own. Few goods or services any manager produces will stay in his country. The effective manager, at whatever stage, must understand the world economy and become a knowledgeable part of it. Managers must learn and propagate the concepts of "free trade" and "comparative advantage". Every country, in fact, that hopes to develop, or to become a working part of the one-world economy, will have to eschew protectionism and open its doors to the goods and the knowledge of developed nations.

Source of Information: The measure of nations' degree of development and information concerning the progress of the past ten years was taken from the International Bank for Reconstruction and Development's publication, *The World Development Report,* 1987, and is used by permission.

The World Management Outlook in the Far East

The Pacific Rim countries for this volume include Hong Kong, China, Australia, Japan, Malaysia, Indonesia, South Korea, North Korea, Vietnam, Taiwan, Philippines, and Thailand.

These countries, in varying degrees, will usher the Pacific into the twenty-first century as they develop economically and become full partners in the one-world economy. A complete bibliography can be found at the end of this volume.

China and the 1997 Takeover of Hong Kong

Introduction

One of the major world movements in the last decade of the twentieth century will be the takeover of Hong Kong by The People's Republic of China (mainland China) in 1997. The implications of this act reach beyond the current decade, and the takeover may do more to change the face of the global economy than will the European Community.

In 1898, Hong Kong and the surrounding islands were leased to Great Britain by China for a period of ninety-nine years. Hong Kong quickly became the most important of the British Colonies, in terms of trade and finance. Now China is poised to rule Hong Kong once again. The importance of Hong Kong to the world has been immeasurable, and the pertinent question at this time is, how much will Hong Kong change after 1997?

Along with Hong Kong and China, I will also review the so-called Pac Rim, or Pacific Rim, nations and the impact they may have on the global economy in the future. Although it has usually been the custom of Western countries to keep their eyes on the West, that will no longer be possible. With the emergence of economic strength in Japan, followed by South Korea and others, the Far East is alive to stay, and it will compete strongly in the global economy. Section V will present statistics and other material on all of the Pac Rim countries.

One current view of the 1997 takeover of Hong Kong by China assumes that China will bring into Hong Kong the hard-line communism it has embraced since 1945. I take an opposite view which I shall present in the Hong Kong section shortly. In the meantime, some background information on China would be useful.

The People's Republic of China (Mainland China)

Some authorities claim that the land has been inhabited for more than 500,000 years; however, this great and noble nation has advanced slowly. In the centuries of written history, it has generally be ruled by "dynasties," families or groups that held power for many years. The dynasties of more recent times are outlined in the following paragraphs.

Chou 1027–256 b.c. This is known as the "classical age" or the age of Confucius. There was much political disorder, but written laws came into existence, along with a money economy, iron implements, etc. Feudalism dominated.

Ch'in 221–207 b.c. China was unified under the harsh rule of Shih Huang-ti. Feudalism was generally replaced by a pyramidal bureaucratic government. A written language was standardized. Roads, canals, and much of the Great Wall of China were built.

Han 202 b.c.–a.d.220. China was further unified, but under less harshness, and Confucianism was made the basis for a bureaucratic state. Buddhism was introduced. An encyclopedic dictionary and history were compiled. Porcelain was first produced.

Three Kingdoms 220–265. China was divided into three sections, Wei, Shu, and Wu, with Wei gradually gaining domination. Confucianism was declining, and Taoism and Buddhism were increasing in influence. During this period many scientific advances brought in from India were adopted.

Tsin or Chin 265–420. This was a dynasty founded by a Wei general, with a gradual expansion to the southeast. Several barbarian dynasties ruled in North China. The growth of Buddhism continued.

Sui 581–618. China was reunified and a central government established. Confucianism still declined as Taoism and Buddhism were favored. A new system of canals was built and the Great Wall of China was reworked.

T'ang 618–906. China expanded her territory during this period. Buddhism was temporarily suppressed, and Confucianism was partly restored. Civil Service examinations were established, based on the teachings of Confucius. Much progress was made in poetry, sculpture, and painting.

Five Dynasties and Ten Kingdoms 907–960. This was a period of political unrest in China, with periodic provincial wars, political corruption, and general hardship among the people. Printing increased greatly, and paper money was first printed.

Sung 960–1279. This was a period of great progress, with the cultivation of tea and cotton becoming widespread. Neo-Confucianism gained favor over Taoism and Buddhism. A central government was reestablished. Gunpowder was used for the first time by the military.

Yuan 1260–1368. The Mongol Dynasty was founded by Kublai Khan. Relationships with the West increased. Confucian ideals were strongly discouraged. This period is considered the great age of Chinese playwriting. Revolutions in southern China and Mongolia brought the dynasty to an end.

Ming 1368–1644. Mongols were expelled from the country. Both the teachings of Confucius and the Civil Service examinations based on Confucianism were reinstated. There was considerable contact with European traders and with missionaries. The production of porcelain, fine architecture, the novel, and drama flourished.

Ch'ing or Manchu 1644–1912. A dynasty established by the Manchus (from Manchuria in northeast China). During this era there was much territorial expansion but a weakening of Chinese power, accompanied by a decline of central authority. Trade with Europe increased. In the end, foreign powers divided China into different spheres of influence. During this era the Opium War was fought, Hong Kong was ceded to Britain and the Boxer Uprising (1898–1900) was fought to curb foreign influence.

From 1912 to 1949. Although this is not designed to be a history of China, a few pages of explanation are necessary to make the reader aware of why China is in her current position and what might change relative to that position in the years form 1949 to 1997.

In succession, we have the following events beginning in 1911:

1911. Anti-Manchu revolution.

1912–1916. A Chinese Republic founded after the overthrow of the Manchus.

1916–1926. Era of the war-lords.

1927. Chiang Kai-shek started the long civil war. He was able to oust the Communists who had assisted in overthrowing the war lords.

1934–35. The Communist "Long March," which ended with the party's base established in Shaanxi.

1937. In 1931 the Japanese had captured Manchuria, and in 1937 the Japanese launched a vicious attack on China. The Japanese were opposed by Nationalists and Communists alike.

1945. The Japanese were finally defeated, and civil war again broke out between the Communists and the Nationalists.

1949. Chiang Kai-shek resigned as president in 1949 and led his Nationalists to Taiwan where the Nationalist Republic of China was set up.

1949. Mao Tse-tung was declared premier of China, and the Communists held full power.

After the takeover by the communists, industries and the land were nationalized.

Some progress began almost immediately, as an authoritarian government can often make more progress in the short term than a democratic government.

In the years 1949–90, despite the economy's general improvement in China, the new wealth touched few Chinese. Periodic objections to the rigors of communism continued throughout this period, as did periodic reversions to the more stringent brand of communism similar to that Stalin made infamous in the Soviet Union.

China must industrialize to increase the living standards of the people. I predict that well before the 1997 takeover of Hong Kong, China will renounce revolutionary communism and embrace a semi-democratic socialism. This is becoming the political and economic system for most of the nations in the world, including the United States, which will lean much more heavily toward socialism during the decade of the nineties.

Current Statistics on the People's Republic of China

China has a land area of about 3,705,390 square miles, virtually the same as the land area of the conterminous United States.

Yet the population of China is approximately 1.1 billion, or more than four times that of the United States. The population density of China is 288 per square mile as contrasted with 68 in the United States. Subsequent statistics will reveal why this is of so much concern to China.

Only 11 percent of China's land is arable, and with the current modified-communal system China is not able to feed her vast population. China has no choice but to industrialize and become a major trading nation.

The government is, of course, communist, with the head of state the premier. China is divided into twenty-one provinces, five autonomous regions, and has three main cities, Beijing, Shanghai, and Tientsin.

The industrial economy consists of iron and steel, textiles, agricultural implements, and trucks. Crops consist mainly of grain, rice, cotton, and tea. The primary minerals include tungsten, antimony, coal, iron, lead, manganese, mercury, uranium, and tin. Crude oil reserves are about 18.5 billion barrels.

The monetary unit is the Yuan, with a value of about 4.72 per U.S. dollar (March 1990). The GNP in 1988 was $350 billion, with a per capita income of $258. Real GNP growth over a five-year period has been 11.2 percent, average annual, and an inflation rate of about 10.1 percent average annual over a five-year period.

Education amounts to about 9 years of compulsory education, and the literacy rate is about 70 percent. About 190 out of 100,000 attend a university.

Sixty-eight percent of the labor force is still employed in agriculture, and only 18 percent is employed in commerce and industry. China must evolve as quickly as possible until these percentages are turned around, and even then the number of people employed in agriculture will be high. China must come into the twentieth century, and quickly.

China is not "backward" in the sense that it has never developed at all. The arts have developed since before the Middle Ages in Europe. The lack of development is economic, and at the root of that problem is the lack of education and the poor literacy rate.

If China were to renounce the revolutionary aspects of communism, promote education, and begin to open the doors to relatively free trade, she could develop quickly. Hong Kong could be the trade and finance springboard from which all of this could take place. I believe that China will begin to take economic initiative before 1997.

Though there are thousands of books on China, I will mention only three. These are: Jonathan D. Spence, *The Search for Modern China*, W. W. Norton & Company, 1990; Bette Bao Lord, *Legacies, a Chinese Mosaic*, New York: Alfred A. Knopf, 1990; Arthur Waldron, *The Great Wall of China*, New York: Cambridge University Press, 1990.

Hong Kong

To most Westerners, Hong Kong is a name that conjures up the most exotic images of the Far East. It is the most exotic place in the Far East in many ways, as it is rich and ever changing.

Until October 1997 Hong Kong is a Crown Colony of Great Britain and has proven to be the jewel of the United Kingdom. The area was leased by Britain from China in 1898 for a period of ninety-nine years. There is currently an overriding fear that China will bring into the area of Hong Kong the same militant communism now reigning in Mainland China. I do not believe that this will happen.

In December, 1990, the Hong Kong and Shanghai Banking

Corporation set up a holding company in England as a precautionary measure against the coming of Communist China. Many major industries are looking at exit routes, if they are needed, and many people have already made their way to the United States, Canada, England, and other western countries. In order to prevent migration from Hong Kong and to mollify the suspicions of other nations, China needs to take steps as soon as possible to assure the people in Hong Kong, and the rest of the world, that Hong Kong will not change as much as is feared.

One step to help alleviate these fears was taken on April 4, 1990. The Seventh National People's Congress of the People's Republic of China, at its Third session, adopted the Basic Law of the Hong Kong Special Administrative Region of the People's Republic of China. This set of laws is supposed to be the governing set of laws of Hong Kong for fifty years after the takeover in 1997. (A copy of these laws may be obtained from The Hong Kong and Shanghai Banking Corporation, Ltd., 1 Queen's Road Central, Hong Kong, or from the Hong Kong General Chamber of Commerce, 22/F United Center, 95 Queensway, Central, Hong Kong. It is a booklet of about seventy pages, and every manager at all interested in Hong Kong or the Far East should obtain one.)

China must do more than this. It is likely that only changes in the People's Republic of China itself would encourage people to believe that Hong Kong will indeed be able to operate as she has for the past ninety-three years. Additionally, Hong Kong could become the doorway of mainland China to the rest of the world. China's history is replete with advantages lost, and Hong Kong must not be added to this list. Few cities in the world are as diverse in every sense as Hong Kong is, and few are so well positioned to remain a world economic and financial center. The Far East needs Hong Kong.

Now that revolutionary communism has been discredited, even in its own cradle, this is the time for China to begin a reform, which, under the best of circumstances, would take a generation. But the first positive steps would likely convince the world not only that will Hong Kong remain the great center she is, but that all of China would follow in a spirit of internationalism and a more democratic domestic society. But if she ever is to reach her potential as an international influence, if she ever is to take here place as a leading nation of the world, both economically and culturally, China must begin by letting Hong Kong remain Hong Kong.

No nation in the world can now live within itself or for itself.

Current Statistics On Hong Kong

Population: 5.8 million, with 90 percent being urban, and 97 percent Chinese.

Land area : 403 square miles or 1,045 square kilometers.

Population growth: 2.7 percent annually.

Literacy rate: 90 percent.

Real Gross Domestic Product: $45.7 billion (HK$490.6 mil.).

Per capita GDP: $10,939.

Inflation: five-year annual average, 5.5 percent (10.4 percent, Oct. 1990).

Real GDP growth: 2.3 percent, 1989, 2.3 percent predicted for 1990.

Language: Cantonese and English. Mandarin is being learned by many. The basic law stipulates that in addition to Chinese, English may also be used as an official language by the executive, legislative, and judicial authorities of the Hong Kong SAR after 1997.

Monetary unit: Hong Kong dollar. Since 1983 has been fixed at HK$7.80 to U.S.$1. (It is allowed to fluctuate within a narrow range, that range in 1989 was HK$7.774–7,815 to U.S.$1.)

The industry of Hong Kong is widely diversified. There are about 48,000 factories producing everything from low-cost textiles to sophisticated electronic equipment. The city is the trade center and the financial center of the Far East.

Throughout the Far East, cities, states, and nations are positioning themselves to assume trade and financial leadership if China does not change by 1997. Singapore is a major bidder for such a position and virtually every Pac Rim country is assessing the situation by the day. Even Hawaii is bidding to become the trade and financial center for the Pacific.

But few, if any, cities in the world hold positions like that of Hong

Kong. It is my conviction that after 1997 Hong Kong will still be Hong Kong, and that the rigidity of Chinese communism will be modified and will not make its way into that port.

Other Pacific Rim Countries

Australia

Introduction

It is tempting in this section to write about Australasia; i.e., Australia, New Zealand, and the islands of the South Pacific, together with New Guinea. However, Australia is a continent itself, and, for the scope of this volume, Australia is the focal point of interest. What happens in Australia will have a decided effect on the rest of Australasia.

Australia had an inauspicious beginning, as did the United States and other nations which have forged into the forefront of major nations of the world. Peoples from Asia were undoubtedly the first settlers of Australia, but Europeans began to explore the South Pacific in the seventeenth century, and in 1770 Capt. James Cook explored the east coast of the continent. Inhabitants at that time were of several tribes, but they were all referred to as aborigines (people who inhabited the land from earliest times, before colonization).

In 1787, the twenty-eighth year of the reign of King George III, the British government sent a fleet to colonize Australia.

Never had a colony been founded so far from its parent state, or in such ignorance of the land it occupied. There had been no reconnaissance. In 1770 Captain James Cook had made landfall on the unexplored east coast of this utterly enigmatic continent, stopped for a short while at a place named Botany Bay and gone north again. Since then, no ship had called: not a word, not an observation, for seventeen years, each one of which was exactly like the thousands that had preceded it, locked in its historical immensity of blue heat, dust, sandstone and the measured booming of glassy Pacific rollers.

Now this coast was to witness a new colonial experiment, never tried before, not repeated since. An unexplored continent would become a jail. The space around it, the very air and sea, the whole transparent labyrinth of the South Pacific, would become a wall 14,000 miles thick.*

And so the beginning of Australia; a beginning which would dog the continent for a hundred years. For those sent to colonize the continent were convicts, soldiers of fortune, British regular soldiers, and an admixture of adventurers.

By 1830, the entire continent had been claimed by Great Britain, and settlers of a different stripe hurried to this great land, still largely unknown. The Commonwealth was proclaimed in 1901.

Current Statistics on Australia

People. Population (1990 est.): 16.6 million. Density: 5.4 per sq. mi. (Much of Australia is considered uninhabitable, but some of the land could be reclaimed for people in the next several decades.) Percent urban population (1984): 85 percent. Ethnic groups: European 95 percent; Asian, 4 percent; aborigines, 1.5 percent. Languages: English, aboriginal. Religions: Anglican, 26 percent; other Protestant, 25 percent; Roman Catholic, 25 percent.

Geography. Area: 2,966,200 sq. mi., almost the size of the continental United States. Capital: Canberra, population 297,300. Major cities (1987 est.): Sydney, population 3,500,000; Melbourne, population 3,000,000; Brisbane, population 1,200,000; Perth, population 1,100,000; Adelaide, population 993,000.

Government. Type: democratic, federal state system. Head of state: Queen Elizabeth of England, represented by a governor general. Head of government: prime minister. Local divisions: 6 states, 2 territories. Amount spent on defense (1988): 2.7 percent of GNP.

Economy. Industries: iron, steel, textiles, electrical equipment, chemicals, autos, aircraft, ships, machinery. Chief crops: wheat (a leading export, and competitive with any nation in the world), barley, oats, corn, hay,

*Robert Hughes, *The Fatal Shore: The Epic of Australia's Founding* (New York: Alfred A. Knopf, 1987), p.1.

sugar, wine, fruit, vegetables. Arable land: 9 percent. Minerals: coal, copper, iron, lead, tin, uranium, zinc. Crude oil reserves (1987): 1.6 billion barrels. Fish catch: 156, 000 metric tons. Livestock: cattle, 22 million; sheep, 162 million; pigs, 2.5 million. Other resources: Wool, 30 percent of the world's output. Labor force: 6 percent agriculture; 33 percent finance and services; 36 percent trade and manufacturing.

Finance. Currency: dollar (June 1990): 1.30 = $1 U.S. GNP (1988): $220 billion. Per capita income (1988): $14,458. Imports (1989): $44.6 billion. Exports (1989): $33.0 billion. Major partners in both exports and imports are the Japanese and the United States. National budget (1989): $65 billion. Consumer price change in 1989: 7.6 percent.

Education. Literacy rate: 99 percent. School compulsory to age fifteen. Attendance rate: 94 percent.

Australia has a number of external territories, consisting mostly of small islands, but some of them produce citrus fruits, bananas, coffee, and other crops needed on the mainland. The latest territory acquired (in 1933) was the Australian Antarctic Territory, which has 2,360,000 square miles.

Conclusion

Australia should prosper abundantly as the Pac Rim countries increase both their production and their influence on the world economy. Several Australian cities are already financial capitals, and they will become stronger as the Pac Rim expands its sphere of influence.

Robert Hughes, *The Fatal Shore: The Epic of Australia's Founding* (New York: Alfred A. Knopf, 1987), is recommended reading on Australia, and it contains a bibliography with references to virtually all the best books on Australia.

If one is inclined toward fiction, I would recommend Evan Green, *Adam's Empire: A Sweeping Novel of the Australian Outback* (New York: St. Martin's Press, 1986).

Japan
Nippon or Nihon

Introduction

Of all the countries in the world, Japan is the most respected, in some ways the most feared, certainly the most envied, and surely the most misunderstood.

Japan will always be remembered as the nation that led Asia into the twentieth century and caused all other nations to re-evaluate their national priorities. Actually, there is little that is strange about what Japan has accomplished since World War II and will probably continue to accomplish. In order to understand these accomplishments, however, one must look at the background of Japan, those things most important to the Japanese people, and those cultural mores that are difficult for any non-Asian to understand.

"Japan bashing" is an exercise in futility that has nonetheless occupied the time of U.S. citizens from those on the street to CEOs of giant multinational corporations. The question is why. For many CEOs, it is far easier to criticize a competitor than to admit managerial sins. Many people do not want us to forget World War II, though they do not seem as worried about Germany, Italy, or even the Soviet Union as they are about Japan.

With respect to Japan and her current superiority in certain industries, it must be recognized that the United States, after reaching an unofficial zenith about 1970, decided that the things that once had made us superior were no longer important. While we were enjoying our riches, others, primarily Japan, sped past us. The catching up will not be easy.

A number of experts avow that Japan has made great national progress by denying consumers many of the material things a rapidly developing nation might expect to have. I concur in this. This can be verified by the highly inflated prices the Japanese consumer pays for food and other products because of excessive tariffs. The consumers' inability to buy many products is also revealed in the savings rate, which often runs as high as 16 to 20 percent annually. What Japan has done, however, in holding down consumer spending, is to amass huge pools of capital (see Appendix A), which it is then able to invest both at home and prolifically abroad. The infrastructure of Japan is generally better than that of other industrialized nations (especially in terms of railroad travel and communications, though some parts of the country are still deprived due to lack of political clout.)

Just how long Japan will be able to keep such a tight rein on consumers is not known. If Japanese history follows that of other industrialized nations, it will probably not be long until consumers demand more of the GNP pie. Why it will be impossible for consumers to have some of the fruits of their labor found in other countries will be discussed in the conclusion to this section.

After World War II the United States did much to assist Japan in getting back on her economic feet. General Douglas MacArthur remained in Japan to oversee the first faltering steps of a demolished nation. The rearming of Japan was forbidden, so the nation was able to concentrate on its infrastructure, and upon rebuilding business, industry, and trade. Billions of dollars spent during the cold war period by other industrialized nations were put to constructive use in Japan.

Another strength in Japan is the close relationship between government, banking, industry, and unions, when this close cooperation is a necessity. There exists in Japan an informal organization called *zaibatsu* made up of industries, banks, etc., who are able to thrust themselves quickly into any situation that endangers the economic growth of the nation, such as the 1973–75 energy crunch. Although this kind of cooperative economic arrangement was outlawed by the Allied Forces after WW II, it was never dead and revived quickly upon the departure of General MacArthur.

Probably the best contribution the United States ever made for postwar Japan—and it was made with no knowledge of what the results would be—was to send W. Edwards Deming to Japan in 1950. Deming was internationally recognized for his statistical work, and one area of his expertise was statistics as they apply to industry, specifically production, and to the quality of that production. Japan took his ideas to heart immediately, while he was most often ignored by industry in the United States, and he is revered in Japan today as the mentor who put industry on the right track, both with respect to productivity and to quality.

A Brief Look at Japan's History

Japan is an island country off the coast of Asia and consists of four major islands and thousands of minor ones. The islands are volcanic in nature, and there is the almost constant threat of earthquakes and volcanic eruptions.

Experts believe that people were living in Japan at least 6,500 years ago, and perhaps earlier. They are known as the *Jomon* (cord pattern) people because of the manner in which they decorated their pottery.

Present-day Japanese came to the islands about 2,200 years ago, probably from Korea. Legends tell us that the first emperor of Japan was Jimmu Tenno, who ruled from 660 B.C., and the country has been ruled by emperors almost ever since. From the third century A.D., powerful noble families controlled the government and, from about 1192 to 1867, the country was under the rule of a series of shoguns, or military governors. National rule was recovered by Emperor Meiji about 1868.

While Japan was generally isolated from the rest of the world, some trade was carried on with the Dutch and the Portuguese in the sixteenth and seventeenth centuries.

Commodore Matthew C. Perry opened Japan to the world in 1854, when a trade treaty was signed between Japan and the United States.

Since the time of the shoguns the Japanese had been a warlike nation. After a war with Russia in 1904–5, Russia ceded the south half of Sakhalin and gave up some of her possessions in China. Japan had also fought China in 1894-95 and gained Taiwan. Japan annexed Korea in 1910. In World War I, Japan ousted Germany from Shantung and took over the German Pacific islands.

Japan took Manchuria in 1931 and began a war with China in 1932, launched World War II in the Pacific when she attacked Pearl Harbor on December 7, 1941, was disastrously defeated and officially surrendered on August 14, 1945.

Beginning with the new constitution adopted in 1947, Japan

renounced the right to wage war, the emperor renounced his claim to divinity, and the parliament, or diet, became the sole law-making authority.

Current Statistics on Japan

People. Population (1990 est.): 123,778,000. Density: 844 per sq. mi., contrasted with 68 per square mile in the United States. Percent urban population (1985): 76.7 percent. Language: Japanese (English used widely in business with foreigners). Ethnic groups: Japanese, 99.4 percent; Korean, 0.5 percent. Religions: Buddhism and Shintoism shared by the majority. Other religions, including Christianity, are also present in much smaller numbers.

Geography. Area: 145,856 sq. mi., slightly smaller than California. Capital: Tokyo, population 8.3 million. Major cities (1987): Osaka, population 2.6 million; Yokohama, population 3.1 million; Nagoya, population 2.1 million; Kyoto, population 1.4 million; Kobe, population 1.4 million; Sapporo, population 1.6 million; Kitakyushu, population 1.0 million; Kawasaki, population 1.1 million; Fukuoka, population 1.2 million.

Government. Type: parliamentary democracy. Head of state: Emperor Akahito; Head of government: prime minister. Local governmental divisions: 47 prefectures. Amount spent on defense: Less than 1 percent of GNP annually.

Economy. Industries: electrical and electronic equipment; autos, machinery, chemicals. Chief crops: rice, grains, vegetables, fruits. Minerals: negligible. Crude oil reserves (1985): 26 million barrels. Arable land: 13 percent. Livestock (1986): cattle, 4.6 million; pigs, 11.7 million. Fish catch (1987): 12.4 million metric tons. Labor force: 8 percent agriculture; 34 percent manufacturing and mining; 53 percent services and trade.

Finance. Currency: Yen (June 1990: 151 = $1 U.S.) GNP (1989): $1.8 trillion. Per capita GNP (1989): $15,030. Imports (1989): $209 billion. Exports (1989): $273 billion. Major trading partners: United States, Middle East, EC, Southeast Asia. National budget (1989): $470 billion. Consumer price change (1989): 2.3 percent.

Education. Literacy rate: 99 percent. Most students attend school for 12 years.

Conclusion

What makes Japan tick? How has this tiny nation been able to run rings around older industrial nations in just forty-five years? I doubt if anyone knows the whole answer. I can suggest some reasons:

1. The United States helped rebuild Japanese productive facilities at the end of World War II.

2. The understandings that exist between government, industry, financial institutions, and labor unions.

3. The quality consciousness instilled in the Japanese by W. Edwards Deming.

4. Participation in management, primarily through quality control circles.

5. Ability to spend "defense" money on the nation's industrial growth.

6. Controlled consumer spending and dramatic individual savings patterns.

7. A stubborn work ethic.

8. An ancient desire to succeed to maintain the family's good name.

9. Well-trained work force.

10. High tariffs on imports, which will not work much longer.

Japan's success will face new challenges in the world to come. In order to be an accepted partner in the world economy, Japan will have to begin playing the game by protecting herself less and by increasing the size and number of trading partners. Since she cannot give consumers all the things they want (such as a ranch-style house on two acres of land), many Japanese will move with companies to all parts of the world. Since lack of land area is a hindrance to meeting consumer demands Japan will have to compensate for this by letting her citizens substitute travel, migration, and in-country leisure-time centers.

My belief is that Japan will make long strides toward free trade during the 1990s. Also, foreign investments will continue to increase, and this investment is vital to the rest of the world.

I recommend the following books with different degrees of enthusiasm, but all are worthwhile: Mitchell F. Deutsch, *Doing Business with the Japanese* (New York: The New American Library, Inc., 1983). Mitsuyuki

Masatsugu, *The Modern Samurai Society* (New York: American Management Associations, 1982). David Halberstam, *The Reckoning* (New York: William Morrow and Company, Inc., 1986.) Rafael Aguayo *Dr. Deming: The American Who Taught the Japanese about Quality* (New York: A Lyle Stuart Book, published by the Carol Publishing Company, 1990).

There are literally thousands of articles in periodicals on Japan and will be many more; managers should take advantage of these. Some past articles I would recommend: "Behind the Miracle: Everyday Life in Japan." *The Wilson Quarterly,* (Autumn 1990), pp. 19–52. Special Issue: Asia in the 1990s, *Fortune* (Fall 1989). Special Issue: Asia: Megamarkets of the 1990s. *Fortune* (Fall 1990). "Should U.S. Companies Fight Like the Japanese," (March 7, 1989, International Issue), pp. 36-38. (See also appendices immediately following.)

Sources of Information: I am indebted to James W. Hollingshad, consulate-general of Japan, New Orleans, LA, 70113-3146 for the listing of Japanese banks in the following appendix and for permission to use it.

Appendix: Ten Largest Japanese Banks by Deposits (December 31, 1989)

BANK	THOUSANDS OF U.S. DOLLARS
The Dai-ichi Kangyo Bank, Ltd. (K.K. Dai-ichi Kangyo Ginko) 1-5, Uchisaiwai-cho 1-chome, Cgiyoda-Ku, Tokyo 100 JAPAN Telephone number: 03 (596) 1111 Fax number: 03 (596) 2539	$ 314,780,128
The Sumitomo Bank, Ltd. (K.K. Sumitomo Ginko) 22, Kita 5-chome, Higashi-ku Osaka 541 JAPAN Telephone number: 06 (227) 2111	288,242,189

BANK	THOUSANDS OF U.S. DOLLARS

The Mitsubishi Bank. Ltd.   278,806,753
(K.K. Mitsubishi Ginko)
7-1, Marunouchi 2-chome,
   Chiyoda-ku, Tokyo 100
JAPAN
Telephone number: 03 (240) IIII
Fax number : 03 (240) 2567

The Fuji Bank, Ltd.   278,642,535
(K.K. Fuji Ginko)
5-5, Ote-machi 1-chome,
   Chiyoda-ku, Tokyo 100
JAPAN
Telephone number: 03 (216) 2211
Telex number: J24311 FUJIBANK

The Sanwa Bank, Ltd. $ 275,972,496
(K.K. Sanwa Ginko)
10, Fushimi-machi 4-chome,
   Higashi-ku, Osaka
JAPAN
Telephone number: 06 (202) 2281
Fax number : 06 (231) 4246

The Industrial Bank of Japan   213,287,599
(K.K. Nippon Kogyo Ginko)
3-3, Marunouchi 1-chome,
   Chiyoda-ku, Tokyo 100
JAPAN
Telephone number: 03 (214) IIII

The Mitsubishi Trust & Banking Corp.   192,294,268
(Mitsubishi Shintaku Ginko K.K.)
4-5, Marunouchi 1-chome,
   Chiyoda-ku, Tokyo 100
JAPAN
Telephone number: 03 (212) 1211
Fax number : 03 (211) 1267

BANK	THOUSANDS OF U.S. DOLLARS

The Tokai Bank, Ltd. 179,030,994
(K.K. Tokai Ginko)
21-24, Nishiki 3-chome,
  Naka-ku, Nagoya 460
JAPAN
Telephone number: 052 (211) 1111

The Sumitomo Trust & Banking Co Ltd. 171,664,091
(Sumitomo Shintaku Ginko K.K.)
5-33, Kitahama 4-chome,
  Chuo-ku, Tokyo 103
JAPAN
Telephone number: 06 (220) 2121

The Mitsui Trust & Banking Co., Ltd. $ 159,219,084
(Mitsui Shintaku Ginko K.K.)
1-1 Nihonbashi Muro-machi 2-chome,
  Chuo-ku, Tokyo 103
JAPAN
Telephone number: 03 (270) 9511
Fax number : 03 (243) 1900

Total deposits of Japan's top ten banks, as of December 31, 1989, equaled
$ 2,351,939,437,000

Malaysia

Introduction

This beautiful and rich jewel of the South Pacific, which occupies part of the Malay peninsula and part of an island (Borneo) in the East Indies, should have a bright future. Blessed with a more stable government than many small countries and rich in natural resources, Malaysia should fare well in the rise of the Pacific Rim nations and in all of Asia.

The Malays came from southern China about 4,500 years ago. Successively, the area was ruled by the Portuguese, the Dutch, and the British, who formed the Straits Settlements colony in 1826.

Malaya became independent in 1957 and in 1963 joined with the British colonies of Sarawak, Sabah (British North Borneo) and Singapore to form Malaysia. Singapore left the federation in 1965 to become an independent city-state. There had been considerable tension between Singapore, the people of which are primarily Chinese, and the rest of Malaysia, where the Malays dominate. It is not likely that either would have prospered as well united as they have separately.

Current Statistics on Malaysia

People. Population (1990 est.): 17,053,000. Density: 132 per sq. mi. Ethnic groups: Malays, 59 percent; Chinese, 32 percent; Indians, 9 percent. Languages: Malay (official), English, Chinese, and Indian languages. Religions: Moslem, Hindu, Buddhist, Confucian, Taoist, and local religions.

Geography. Area: 127,316 sq. mi., slightly larger than New Mexico. Topography: mostly covered by tropical jungle, including the central mountain range. Capital: Kuala Lampur (1986 est.), population 1,000,000.

Government. Type: federal parliamentary democracy with a constitutional monarch. This supreme head of state is elected every five years from among the rulers of the nine Malay state rulers. Head of government: prime minister. Local governmental divisions: 13 states and the capital. Amount spent on defense: 4.2 percent of GNP in 1987.

Economy. Industries: rubber goods, steel, electronics (Malaysia is the third largest producer of semiconductors after the United States and Japan). Chief crops: palm oil, copra, rice, pepper. Minerals: tin (35 percent of the world's output), iron. Crude oil reserves (1987): 3.2 billion barrels. Other resources: Rubber (35 percent of the world's output). Arable land: 13 percent. Livestock (1987): 2.2 million pigs. Fish catch (1986): 571,000 metric tons. Labor force: 21 percent agriculture, 22 percent manufacturing, 11 percent tourism and trade.

Finance. Currency: Ringgit (March 1990), 2.72 = $1 U.S. GNP (1988): $34.3 billion. Per capita GNP: $2,018. Imports (1987): $12.1 billion.

Exports (1987): $18.0 billion. Major trading partners: Japan, United States, Singapore. National budget (1988): $10.8 billion.

Education. Literacy rate (1989): 80 percent. 96 percent attend primary school, and 48 percent attend secondary school. Education is being pushed harder in Malaysia, and this development will be a future help to the economy. Increasing industrialization, which should come with their natural resources, will demand higher education, but will also assure growth.

Conclusion

In comparison with most small Asian countries, Malaysia is already considered prosperous. This image will assist the country in running somewhat ahead of the average small country during the rise of the Age of the Pacific.

The relationship with Singapore, and the fact that the city-state is virtually in the middle of Malaysia, will lend financial stability and increasing trade possibilities to the country.

Indonesia
Republic of Indonesia

Introduction

Indonesia is composed of about 13,500 islands in the Asian East Indies. There is relative poverty in many of the islands, partly because of the falling prices of oil that prevailed before the Mideast Crisis of 1990–91 and partly because of the large population among the islands. It is the fifth most populous nation in the world.

Hindu and Buddhist civilization reached the tribal people of Indonesia nearly 2,000 years ago, taking root especially in Java. Islam spread along the maritime trade routes in the fifteenth century and became predominant in the sixteenth century.

In the seventeenth century, the Dutch replaced the Portuguese as the most important trade power in the area, achieving territorial control over Java by 1750. The smaller outer islands were not subdued until the early twentieth century. For the first time, all of what is now Indonesia was under the control of one country.

Following the Japanese occupation, 1942–45, nationalists led by Sukarno and Hatta proclaimed a republic. After four years of fighting, the Dutch ceded sovereignty in December 1949. West Irian, on New Guinea, remained under Dutch control. Indonesia seized Dutch property and, after much diplomatic mediation, the area was turned over to Indonesia in 1963.

General Sukarno became the first president in 1949. In 1959 he assumed dictatorial powers, and in 1963 he proclaimed himself president for life. He allied himself with communist China, and in 1965 a communist coup was quashed under the leadership of General Suharto, who stripped Sukarno of power in 1966. Sukarno was put under house arrest where he remained until his death.

General Suharto, head of the army, was named president in 1968, and he was renamed in 1973, 1978, and 1988. Both communist and Moslem opposition groups remain strong, and the army continues to have a dominant political role.

A more stable government and oil exports keep the economy of Indonesia fairly stable, but one cannot discount the influence of the Moslems, and perhaps the communists, in the future. Currently Indonesia is not highly recommended for foreign investment, but that may well change in this decade. Should China reject revolutionary communism, it would undoubtedly aid the future of Indonesia, since communism in Indonesia is Maoist in nature.

Current Statistics on Indonesia

People. Population (1990 est.): 191,266,000. Density: 255 per sq. mi., as compared to 68 per square mile in the United States. Topography: Indonesia comprises 13,500 islands, including Java, one of the most densely populated areas in the world with 1,500 people per square mile. Main islands besides Java are Sumatra, Kalimantan (most of Borneo), Sulawesi, and West Irian. The mountainous and plateau areas have moderate climates and the lowlands a normal tropical climate. Capital: Jakarta, population 8,800,000. Major cities (1988 est.): Surabaja, population 2,500,000; Bandung, population 1,400,000; Medan, population 1,700,000.

Government. Type: independent republic. Head of state: president. Local governmental divisions: 27 provinces, 246 districts, and 55 municipalities. Amount spent on defense (1985): 2.5 percent of GNP.

Economy. Industries: food processing, textiles, light industry. Chief crops: rice, coffee, sugar. Minerals: nickel, tin, oil, bauxite, copper, natural gas. Crude oil reserves (1987): 8.4 billion barrels. Other resources: rubber. Arable land: 8 percent. Livestock (1987): cattle, 6.4 million; sheep, 5.1 million. Fish catch (1987): 1.9 million metric tons. Labor force: 56 percent agriculture; 23 percent industry and commerce; 16 percent services.

Finance. Currency: rupiah (June 1990) 1,823 = $1 U.S. GNP (1988): $75 billion. Per capita income (1988): $435. Imports (1988): $13.2 billion. Exports: $19.2 billion. Major trading partners: Japan, United States, and Singapore. National Budget (1990): $21.1 billion. Inflation: five-year average of 7.6 percent annually.

Education. Literacy rate (1988): 85 percent. 84 percent attend primary school.

Conclusion

If the problem of communism can be settled, and if the Moslems become no more militant than they are now, Indonesia can become an important partner in world trade. Negative factors are the immense population, and the problem of whether or not government can remain stable. There seems to be little opportunity for Indonesia to grow at the same rate as other Pac Rim countries, but she will undoubtedly grow, with light industries, probably related to oil, leading the way. It should also be noted that 56 percent of the labor force is in agriculture. No country to date has developed greatly while being dominated by agriculture. Better methods of agriculture, using less of the labor force, and more emphasis on education are needed.

South Korea
Republic of Korea

Introduction

South Korea is one of the marvels of the entire Asian scene. As with many other Asian countries, the country has been beset over time with problems that would seem to preclude any major economic growth at all, and most certainly in our time. But the growth and development of South Korea, far from being stagnant, has already happened, and economic growth should accelerate into the twenty-first century.

Korea has a recorded history which reaches back into the first century, B.C. It was united as a kingdom under the Silla Dynasty, in A.D. 668. At times Korea was associated with the Chinese empire. The treaty that ended the Sino-Japanese War of 1894–95 declared Korea's complete independence. In 1910, however, Japan forcibly annexed Korea as Chosun.

At the Potsdam Treaty Conference (in former East Germany) in July 1945, the 38th parallel was designated as the line dividing the Soviet and the American occupations of Korea. The Soviets entered Korea above the 38th parallel in August 1945, and United States troops entered the area south of the 38th parallel in September of the same year. The Soviets organized the communists and socialists to prevent the reunification of Korea. Thus, South Korea was born.

The South formed the Republic of Korea in 1948, with Dr. Syngman Rhee chosen as president. He was forced out of office as a result of a student uprising in April 1960.

The test for both North and South Korea came when the North attempted an invasion of the South in June 1950. Ultimately, North Korea was assisted by the Chinese, and the United Nations authorized a force to assist South Korea, under the leadership of General Douglas MacArthur. The war ended, after great loss of life and property, on July 27, 1953, at Panmunjom. The fighting took place generally around the 38th parallel, and little was achieved by either side, other than the fact that the Chinese communists were held at bay and apparently gave up any further ambitions in the direction of South Korea.

In the succeeding years, South Korea, with many ups and downs in its government and otherwise, has made remarkable progress. The differences between the South and the North can be seen in the statistical comparisons between the two nations.

In spite of the calamities which have plagued the South Korean government since 1950, sufficient stability has been established and preserved to assure the growth and development of the country and to encourage foreign investment there. The volatility of the political situation has served to discourage rapid foreign investment, with student groups and unions causing the greatest problems. At this point, however, South Korea seems to have incurred the kinds of troubles a new democracy must expect, and before this decade is over the major problems should be solved.

Current Statistics on South Korea

(Compare to the statistics of North Korea on pp. 123–24.)

People. Population (1990 est.): 43,919,000. Density: 1,189 per sq. mi. Percent urban population (1988): 68 percent. Ethnic groups: Koreans. Religions: Buddhism, Confucianism, and Christianity.

Geography. Area: 38,025 sq. mi., or slightly larger than Indiana. Location: northern east Asia. Topography: the country is mountainous, with a rugged east coast. The western and southern coasts are deeply indented with many islands and good harbors. Capital: Seoul, population 10,500,000. Major cities (1989): Pusan, population 3.7 million; Taegu, population 2.2 million; Inchon, population 1.6 million; Kwangju, population 1.1 million; Taejon, population 1.0 million.

Government. Type: republic with power centralized in a strong executive. Head of state: president. Head of government: prime minister. Local governmental divisions: 9 provinces and Seoul, Pusan, Inchon, and Taegu. Amount spent on defense: 5.8 percent of GNP in 1987.

Economy. Industries: electronics, ships, textiles, clothing, motor vehicles.

Chief crops: rice, barley, vegetables, wheat. Minerals: tungsten, coal, graphite. Arable land: 22 percent. Livestock (1987): cattle, 2.8 million; pigs, 3.3 million. Fish catch (1988): 3.2 million metric tons. Crude steel production (1987): 16.7 million metric tons. Labor force: 21 percent agriculture; 27 percent manufacturing and mining; 52 percent services.

Finance. Currency: Won (March 1990): 703 = $1 U.S. GNP (1988): $171 billion. Per capita income (1986): $2,180. Imports (1989): $63 billion. Exports (1989): $62 billion. Major trading partners: United States and Japan. National budget (1988): $22.0 billion. Inflation: five-year annual average, 3.5 percent. Real GDP growth, five-year annual average, 11.4 percent.

Education. Literacy rate: 92 percent. Attendance rate, high school: 90 percent; college: 14 percent; university students per 100,000 population: 3,671. Elementary education is partly free, and there are 224 institutions of higher education, including universities.

Conclusion

The extraordinary story of South Korea can only be enhanced by the unification of the two Koreas. Talks are already being held, and I predict that reunification will be a reality before the year 2000. Surely it will be encouraged as China's leaders begin to break down the barriers of militant communism. The United States will remain a close friend of South Korea, as will Japan. These relationships, too, would be enhanced by reunification. Look for Japan, once the South and North are reunited, to make lavish investments in Korea.

However, foreign investments in Korea will be monitored closely by the Koreans. The Koreans' history gives them little reason to trust foreigners, Japan in particular. So, while Japan will try to invest heavily, so will the United States and other countries, both East and West. A reunified Korea could become a major power in the world in a matter of twenty-five years.

North Korea
Democratic People's Republic of Korea

Introduction

Ethnically and spiritually, North and South Korea are the same. After a history of being ruled either by China or Japan, at the end of World War II, the Koreas were divided with the North being taken over by Communist USSR, and the South being taken first by the United States, and then being allowed to become a republic.

The Korean War resulted because the Soviets wanted to reunite the country by force, with it all becoming communist. The United Nations thwarted this attempt. And, even with some governmental problems, the South has gone ahead to become a viable partner in the one world economy, while the Communist North remains generally underdeveloped.

After I have discussed the Pac Rim countries, the European Community, and Russia and the Eastern Bloc, I will discuss the fall of communism, and the economic and sociological weaknesses of the system which resulted in its death. Strangely enough, they parallel quite closely the very forces which make managers succeed or fail.

North Korea will wither, and eventually die as a nation unless there is reunification. It is my opinion that there will be reunification, and that it will take place during the decade of the 1990s. Those who might think this is too soon should remember the experience in the Soviet Union and in the Eastern Bloc countries.

Reunification will have to come through direct talks between South and North Korea. I do not think any outside force can cause it to happen, not the United States, the United Nations, or anyone else.

Current Statistics on North Korea

People. Population (1990 est.): 23,059,000. Density: 471 per sq. mi. Percent urban population (1985): 62 percent. Ethnic groups: Korean. Languages: Korean. Religions: activities almost nonexistent, but normally would be Buddhism, Confucianism, Chondokyo.

Geography. Area: 46,540 sq. mi., or slightly smaller than Mississippi. Location: northeastern Asia. Neighbors: former USSR and China to the North and South Korea to the south. Topography: mountainous country, with rugged coastlines. Capital: Pyongyang, population 1,283,000.

Government. Type: communist. Head of state: president. Head of government: premier. Head of Communist party is a powerful force. Local governmental divisions: 9 provinces, 3 special cities. Amount spent on defense: 24 percent GNP.

Economy. Industries: textiles, petrochemicals, food processing. Chief crops: corn, potatoes, vegetables, fruits, and rice. Minerals: coal, lead tungsten, graphite, magnesite, iron, copper, gold, phosphate, salt, fluorspar. Arable land: 19 percent. Livestock (1987): cattle, 1.1 million; pigs, 3.0 million. Fish catch (1987): 1.8 million metric tons. Crude steel production (1987): 6.1 metric tons. Labor force: 48 percent agriculture.

Finance. Currency: Won (March 1990) 0.97 = $1 U.S. GNP (1988): $20 billion. Imports (1988): $3.1 billion. Exports (1988): $2.4 billion. Major trading partners, China, Japan. Per Capita GNP: approx. $890

Education. Literacy rate (1989): 99 percent. Years compulsory education: 11.

Conclusion

In the years 1910–45 Japan occupied Korea, and industry began to thrive, due to abundant natural resources. Under communism, industries were nationalized, and farming became primarily communal. And, with nearly half the population still working in agriculture, as compared to 22 percent in the South, economic development in the North cannot be rapid. The difference in defense spending is also notable. In 1988, the North spent 24 percent of the GNP and the South spent 5.8 percent of the GNP.

We should also understand that statistics from communist countries are not always reliable, but I think that the statistics here are reasonable, though some are older than one might desire.

Perhaps in no other comparison in the world, except between West and East Germany, can the sad results of communist rule be so clearly recognized. But the reunification of the North and South, when it comes, will make Korea an industrial giant, and one large enough to make a good trading partner for China, Japan, the United States, and any other country wishing to play a role in the Age of the Pacific.

Singapore
The Republic of Singapore

Introduction

Many people in the world of business and finance believe that the emergence of Singapore as a separate nation in 1965 is directly linked to the takeover of Hong Kong by The People's Republic of China (Mainland China) in 1997. If the officials of Singapore did not have that in mind in 1965, they must have it mind now. No major trade and finance center in the Far East can afford to ignore the takeover and its implications.

However, with or without Hong Kong as she is now, Singapore is a major world trade center and will continue to grow well into the next century. She will be constrained only by her lack of territory. But since many aspects of world trade—such as finance, insurance, freight forwarding, etc.—do not depend on space, there are no pragmatic limits on the possibility of growth for Singapore.

Singapore was founded in 1819 by Sir Thomas Stamford Raffles. It was a British colony until it became autonomous in 1959. On September 16, 1963, it joined with Malay, Sarawak, and Sabah to form the Federation of Malaysia. Tensions quickly arose between the Malaysians, who were dominant in the Federation, and the ethnic Chinese, dominant in Singapore.

An agreement was made for Singapore to become a separate nation on August 9, 1965. Since that time, as statistics will reveal, Singapore has made herculean strides in economic development.

Current Statistics on Singapore

Since becoming independent in 1965, the economy of Singapore has grown at an average annual rate of 9 percent. In real terms, the Gross Domestic Product (GDP) is seven time larger than in 1965. Per capita income has increased ten-fold to S$16,000 in 1988, with "S$" signifying Singapore dollars, a figure that would amount to $8,511 in U.S. dollars. Unemployment fell from about 11 percent in 1965 to about 3 percent in 1988.

Inflation remains low and has averaged about 1 percent annually over the past five years. Except for 1965, the balance of payments has been in surplus every year. External debt is less than 1 percent of official foreign reserves, which had reached about $33.3 billion by the end of 1988. Singapore was an entrepôt economy in the 1960s, and commerce was the dominant sector.

Singapore officials see the city-nation in the light of the following quotation from the report, "The Singapore Economy: New Directions Report of the Economic Committee": "Singapore must catch up with the industrialized countries in maturity and level of development of our economy. By the 1990s, we must aim to become a developed nation. We must aspire to be as good as any developed nation in terms of education and skill level, range and sophistication of our economic activities, capital invested per worker, and productivity per worker.

"Singapore's position in the global economy, therefore, is to be economically as developed as the West, and yet more competitive."

Singapore is one of the world's largest ports. Standards in health, education, and housing are high, International banking has grown greatly.

People. Population (1990 est.): 2,703,000. The population is relatively young with 68 percent being between the years of fifteen and fifty-nine. Density: 409 per sq. mi. Ethnic groups: Chinese, 77 percent; Malays, 15 percent; Indians, 6 percent. Languages: Chinese, Malay, Tamil, and English, all of which are official. Religions: Buddhism, 29 percent; Taoism 13 percent; Moslem, 16 percent; Christian, 19 percent.

Geography. Area: 224 sq. mi., a little smaller than New York City. The nation includes 40 nearby islets. Capital: Singapore, population 2,600,000.

Government. Type: republic within the commonwealth. Head of state: president. Head of government: prime minister. Amount spent on defense (1987): 6 percent of GNP.

Economy. Industries: shipbuilding, oil refining, electronics, banking, textiles, food, rubber, lumber processing, tourism. Arable land: 11 percent. Livestock (1986): pigs, 700,000. Fish catch (1987): 15,000 metric tons. Crude steel production (1985): 300,000 metric tons. Labor force: 1 percent agriculture; 58 percent industry and commerce; 35 percent services.

Finance. Currency: Singapore dollar (S$) (May 1990) 1.88 = $1 U.S. GNP (1988): $23.7 billion. Per capita income (1985): $6,200. Imports (1989): $49.6 billion. Exports (1989): $44.6 billion.

Education. Literacy rate: 85 percent. Years education compulsory: none. Attendance rate: 85 percent.

Conclusion

Most statistics for this review were obtained from a report from the Economic Development Board, 250 North Bridge Road, #24-00 Raffles City Tower, Singapore 0617. Other worldwide development offices are listed in the following appendix.

If Singapore is to improve her position to that aspired to in the above report, two items must be approached immediately. First, education standards must be improved. Second, steps must be taken to assure that changes in governmental leadership do not change the course of this city-nation. Singapore is an economic marvel, but economic marvels are dotting the Asia-Pacific region prolifically.

Source of Information: I am indebted to the Singapore Economic Development Board for permission to adapt the Asia-Pacific map and to use the listing of worldwide offices of the Economic Development Board.

Vietnam
Socialist Republic of Vietnam

Introduction

Few names of nations stir so much emotion as Vietnam. The wars that have raged in this area for many years, and specifically the war in which the United States was involved (1961–73), have left scars that may never be completely erased. But international managers need to deal with Vietnam just as they deal with the other Pac Rim countries.

The Vietnamese people began filtering into the area about 2,500 years ago, primarily from China. From 111 B.C. to A.D. 939 Vietnam was held by China and was later a vassal state.

Conquest by France began in 1858 and ended in 1884 with the formation of the protectorates of Tonkin and Annam in the north and the colony of Cochin-China in the south. Vietnam was ruled by France as a part of the combined interests of French Indochina.

In 1940 Vietnam was taken over by the Japanese, but by this time nationalistic forces were rising against the intrusions from outside. A number of groups united to form the Vietnam (Independence) League, headed by Ho Chi Minh, a communist guerilla leader.

After WW II, when the hold of Japan was broken, France attempted to regain control. She fought nationalist and communist forces from 1946 to 1954, but finally lost in the battle of Dienbienphu, May 8, 1954.

A cease-fire accord, signed in Geneva in July, 1954, divided Vietnam along the Ben Hai River. It provided for a buffer zone, the withdrawal of the French from the North, and elections to determine the nation's future.

Under this agreement the Communists gained control of the territory north of the 17th parallel, 22 provinces with an area of 62,000 square miles and a population of 13,000,000. The capital was Hanoi, and Ho Chi Minh was named president.

South Vietnam was composed of the 39 southern provinces with a land area of 65,000 square miles and a population of 12,000,000. Nearly a million North Vietnamese fled to the South to avoid communism. On

October 25, 1955, Ngo Dinh Diem, premier of the interim government of South Vietnam, proclaimed the Republic of Vietnam and became its first president.

The Democratic Republic of Vietnam (North Vietnam) adopted a constitution on December 1, 1959, that was based on communist principles and called for reunification.

The United States entered the war in 1964 by beginning air strikes on North Vietnam. By 1973 it was evident that the United States could not win the war and needed to get out. By 1974 aid to South Vietnam was curbed, and the South was left to fight the North alone. The South lost, and Vietnam was reunited under communist North Vietnam in 1975.

Current Statistics on Vietnam

People. Population (1990 est.): 69,488,000. Density: 519 per sq. mi. Percent urban population (1988): 19 percent. Ethnic groups: Vietnamese, 84 percent; Chinese, 2 percent; remainder, Muong, Thai, Khmer, Man, Cham. Languages: Vietnamese (official), French, English. Religions: Buddhism, Confucianism, and Taoism are the most widespread. Roman Catholicism, animism, Islam, and Protestantism are present.

Geography. Area: 128,401 sq. mi., about the size of New Mexico. Location: east coast of the Indochina Peninsula. Neighbors: China on north, Laos and Cambodia on the west. Topography: 24 percent of the land is arable, including the Red river valley in the north and the Mekong in the south, plus the coastal plains. The remainder consists of semi-arid plateaus and barren mountains, with some tropical rain forests. Capital: Hanoi, population 3.1 million. Major city: Ho Chi Minh City (Saigon), population 3.9 million.

Government. Type: Communist. Head of state: president. Head of government: prime minister. Head of Communist Party is a powerful influence. Local governmental divisions: 39 provinces. Amount spent on defense: 19.4 percent of GNP in 1986.

Economy. Industries: food processing, textiles, cement, chemical fertilizers, steel. Chief crops: rice, rubber, fruits, vegetables, corn, manioc, sugar cane. Minerals: phosphates, coal, iron, manganese, bauxite, apatite, chromate. Other resources: forests. Arable land: 23 percent. Livestock (1987): cattle, 2.7 million; pigs, 11.7 million. Fish catch (1988): 871,000 metric tons. Labor force: 70 percent agriculture, 8 percent industry and commerce.

Finance. Currency: Dong (Jan. 1990): 4,500 = $1 U.S. GNP (1987): $12.6 billion. Per capita income (1987): $180. Exports (1987): $1.4 billion. Imports (1987): $3.1 billion. Major trading partners: Hong Kong, Japan. National budget (1987): $4.3 billion.

Education. Literacy rate: 78 percent.

Conclusion

As the statistics reveal, it will be virtually impossible for Vietnam to pull itself up by its bootstraps. Vast infusions of capital will be necessary, and even then the process of development will be slow, particularly with respect to raising the standard of living of the average person.

When communism is abandoned, as it will be well before the end of this decade, it is possible that Ho Chi Minh City or Saigon could become a small replica of Singapore and thus become a trade and finance city. There will be no infusion of capital, though, until moves are made toward a free-market economy and until Vietnam is willing to let foreign developers in on terms that are reasonable.

Taiwan
Republic of China

Introduction

This small island in the South China Sea began to be populated by large numbers of Chinese in the seventeenth century. The Dutch ruled the island from about 1620 to 1662, when it again came under the rule of China. The island in earlier days was called Formosa. After the Japanese war with China (1894–95), the island was ruled by Japan until 1945. In 1949, General Chiang Kai-shek led about two million Chinese

Nationalists to Taiwan after the communist take-over of mainland China and established a new Nationalist government and a free-market economy.

The United States gave much aid to Taiwan, and new industries soon began to blossom. Chiang Kai-shek promised that he would recapture mainland China, and mainland China has periodically declared that she will take over Taiwan.

Taiwan had the China seat in the United Nations until 1971, when the seat was awarded to The People's Republic of China. There was considerable tension at the time between Taiwan and the United States, but most experts conceded that mainland China had to be given the UN chair. Recognizing Taiwan, with its 17 million people as the real China, while ignoring mainland China with a population then of about 900,000,000, was incongruous.

The United States severed diplomatic relations with Taiwan in 1978, at the same time as relations were reestablished with the People's Republic of China.

Ties were then reestablished between the United States and Taiwan by the United States' forming of the American Institute in Taiwan. Taiwan, for its part, started the Coordination Council for North American Affairs in Washington. Its address is 4201 Wisconsin Ave., Washington, DC. The telephone number at present is (202) 895-1800.

Taiwan, under semidemocratic private enterprise standards, has built a highly effective economy on the island.

Current Statistics on Taiwan

People. Population (1990 est.): 20,454,000. Density: 1,460 per sq. mi. Percent urban population: 72 percent. Ethnic groups: Taiwanese, 85 percent; Chinese, 14 percent. Languages: Mandarin Chinese (official), Taiwan, and Hakka dialects. English is the business language.

Geography. Area: 13,885 sq. mi., about the size of New Hampshire and Connecticut combined. The western part of the island is flat and fertile, and it is cultivated intensively. Capital: Taipei, population 2,637,000. Major cities (1989): Kaohsiung, population 1,342,000; Taichung, population 715,000; Tainan, population 656,000.

Government. Type: democratic, with the president and vice president elected for five-year terms by a popularly elected National Assembly. Head of state: Nationalist party chairman. Head of government: prime minister. Local divisions of government: 16 counties, 5 cities. Amount spent on defense: 4.6 percent of GNP in 1987.

Economy. Industries: textiles, clothing, electronics, processed foods, chemicals, plastics. Chief crops: rice, bananas, pineapples, sugar cane, sweet potatoes, peanuts. Minerals: coal, limestone, marble. Arable land: 25 percent. Labor force: 17 percent agriculture; 41 percent industry and commerce; 42 percent services.

Finance. Currency: New Taiwan dollar (June 1990) 27.02 = $1 U.S. GNP (1988): $119.1 billion. Per capita GNP (1988): $6,200. Imports (1989): $52.6 billion. Exports (1989): $66.1 billion. Major trading partners: United States, Japan, and Hong Kong. National budget (1988): $15.6 billion.

Education. Literacy rate (1988): 90 percent. Years of compulsory education: 9. Attendance rate: 99 percent.

Conclusion

After thirty-eight years, martial law was lifted in 1987. In spite of martial law, a marked degree of freedom was present, along with democratic policies and private enterprise industries. This development, along with education and United States aid, has pushed Taiwan forward economically.

Contrary to vows by post–World War II Taiwanese leaders and leaders of mainland China, neither nation has attacked the other. Nor will they in the future, so far as it is possible to foresee. When The People's Republic of China relaxes its communist policies, it is possible that Taiwan might rejoin mainland China as a separate republic. Already talks have been conducted, but with little or no fanfare. Trade is also carried on between the two nations (more than $2 billion last year), but this is conducted through third parties in Hong Kong. When China abandons her hard-line stance, in advance of the takeover of Hong Kong in 1997, it is possible to see Hong Kong, Taiwan, and Shanghai serving as the advance guard for mainland China in foreign trade and finance.

Philippines
Republic of the Philippines

Introduction

This nation, made up of nearly seven thousand islands, has unlimited potential for development. At least two things must happen before this development can begin in earnest. One, the communist threat (of the Maoist variety) must be settled. Two, corrupt government must be changed. At this moment, enough money has been pumped into the Philippines to make her far more developed than she is. American colonialism first, and then corrupt government—particularly under Ferdinand Marcos—has bled the country dry. In addition to the threat of the Communists, Moslems in the islands are militant, and they may be as much a danger as the Communists. A stable government could probably bring this situation under control, and there is hope for the future.

The multiplicity of islands would not be a major problem, since the two main islands, Luzon to the north and Mindanao to the south, can pretty much control the others. A stable government could weld them together with little trouble.

The people of the Philippines are primarily Malays whose ancestors probably migrated from Southeastern Asia and were still generally in a gathering-type economy when first visited by the Europeans. The islands were visited by Magellan in 1521, and Manila was founded by the Spanish in 1571. The islands were named for King Philip II of Spain.

In 1898, after the Spanish-American War, the islands were ceded to the United States for $20,000,000. This annexation was followed by a vicious war that lasted six years (1899-1905), pitting United States troops against the Filipino guerrillas.

Japan attacked the islands on December 8, 1941, mid-eastern time, and continued to occupy the islands until the end of World War II. On July 4, 1946, independence was proclaimed, in line with an act passed by Congress in 1934. The islands became a republic.

Much modern history must be bypassed as beyond the scope of this

133

book. Suffice it to say that the communists have kept their guerrilla attacks alive. There continues to be political corruption beginning at all levels of government. The plantation system, a product of the colonial system, continues to keep workers poverty-stricken.

Military bases belonging to the United States in the Philippines have offered substantial employment to the people and have added much to the economy. However, the fervent nationalists among the Filipinos as well as the communists have wanted the Americans out, and our bases are being closed.

Natural resources in the islands belong to the government, and they are exploited as the government wants them to be. By law, natural resources can be developed only by citizens, or by citizens working in tandem with foreign interests so long as 60 percent of the firm engaged in development belongs to Philippine citizens.

Current Statistics on the Philippines

People. Population (1990 est.): 66,647,000. Density: 535 per sq. mi. Percent urban population (1987): 41 percent. Ethnic groups: Malays (large majority), Chinese, Americans, a few Spanish. Languages: Filipino (based on Tagalog), English (both official). Numerous other regional dialects. Religions: Roman Catholic, 83 percent; Protestants, 9 percent; Moslems, 5 percent.

Geography. Area: 115,831 sq. mi., slightly larger than Nevada. Neighbors: Malaysia and Indonesia on south; Taiwan on the north. Capital: Quezon City, with Manila being the de facto capital. Cities (1985 est.): Manila, population 1.7 million; Quezon City, population 1.3 million; Cebu, population 552,000.

Government. Type: republic. Head of state: president. Local governmental divisions: 12 regions, 73 provinces, 61 cities. Amount spent on defense (1987): 1.3 percent of GNP.

Economy. Industries: food processing, textiles, clothing, drugs, wood products. Chief crops: sugar, rice, corn, pineapple, coconut. Minerals: cobalt, copper, gold, silver, iron, petroleum. Crude oil reserves (1987): 19 million barrels. Other resources: forests, 42 percent of land area. Arable land: 26 percent. Livestock (1987): cattle, 1.7 million; pigs, 7.0

million. Fish catch (1984): 1.8 million metric tons. Labor force: 47 percent agriculture; 20 percent industry and commerce; 13 percent services.

Finance. Currency: Peso (May 1990) 22.89 = $1 U.S. GNP (1988): $38.2 billion. Per capita income (1988): $667. Imports (1988): $8.1 billion. Exports (1988): $7.0 billion. Major trading partners: United States and Japan. National budget (1989): $10.7 billion.

Education. Literacy rate: 88 percent. Attendance rate: 97 percent attendance in elementary schools, and 55 percent in secondary schools. English is taught nationwide.

Conclusion

Currently the Philippines is rated low with respect to foreign investment, due to unstable government, communist influence, and nationalism. However, there may be only two other areas of the Pac Rim nations that have more potential than the Philippines, and those two are the Koreas, if they are reunited, and Australia.

Quite beyond what happens to our military bases in the Philippines, the United States needs to remain very close to this country. The people are hard working, intelligent, hungry to learn new things, and innovative. When they are able to shake off the residue of colonial influence and put together a stable government they will be in a position to make great strides. As with many underdeveloped countries, this will not happen overnight. But it can happen, and I believe that it will in the next two decades.

Thailand
Kingdom of Thailand

Introduction

Thailand, traditionally the fabled and romantic Kingdom of Siam, is a nation most have heard of since childhood yet know little about. It is the only southeast Asian country never to have been taken over by some

European power. Thus, the problems left over from colonialism are not to be found. What is found is a vast difference between the "haves" and the "have-nots."

As is true with many of the southeast Asian countries, the early migrants to the area came from South China, so virtually all of the Southeast Asian countries have China as a mother country, if one wishes to go back far enough.

King Mongkut and his son King Chulalongkom, who ruled from 1851 to 1910, modernized the country and made trade treaties with Britain and France. In 1932 a bloodless revolution limited the power of the monarch. Japan occupied the country during World War II, and Thailand was seen as an ally of Japan. After the war, however, the nation followed a pro-West policy.

There was a bloody military coup in 1976. The causes were rising crime, inflation, rising oil prices, and labor union unrest. Troops from Vietnam crossed the border and were repulsed by the Thai forces in 1980.

Currently, Thailand is burdened with thousands of refugees from Laos and Cambodia. There is little at present to encourage one to think that Thailand can develop as a full partner with other Pac Rim countries, but this may be a misapprehension, as we shall see in the conclusion.

Current Statistics on Thailand

People. Population (1990 est.): 54,890,000. Density: 277 per sq. mi. Percent urban population (1985): 20 percent. Ethnic groups: Thais, 75 percent; Chinese, 14 percent; others, 11 percent. Languages: Thai and regional dialects. English is the primary business language. Religions: Buddhism 95 percent, Moslem, 4 percent.

Geography. Area: 198,456 sq. mi., or about the size of Texas. Topography: A plateau dominates the northeast one-third of Thailand, which drops to a fertile alluvial valley of the Chao Phraya River. Mountains with heavy forests are in the north, and the southern peninsula is covered with rain forests. Capital: Bangkok, population 4.7 million.

Government. Type: constitutional monarchy. Head of state: king. Head of government: prime minister. Local governmental divisions: 73 provinces. Amount spent on defense (1987): 3.7 percent of GNP.

Economy. Industries: textiles, mining, wood products. Chief crops: rice (a major export), corn, tapioca, sugar cane. Minerals: antimony, tin (among the world's largest producers), tungsten, iron, gas. Other resources: forests (teak is exported.) Arable land: 34 percent. Livestock (1987): cattle, 4.9 million; pigs, 4.2 million. Fish catch (1988): 2.1 million metric tons. Labor force: 59 percent agriculture; 26 percent industry and commerce; 10 percent services; 8 percent government.

Finance. Currency: Baht (March 1990), 25.98 = $1 U.S. GNP (1988): $52.2 billion. Per capita income (1986): $771. Imports (1988): $19.7 billion. Exports (1988): $11.6 billion. Major trading partners: United States, Japan, Singapore. Consumer price changes (1989): 5.4 percent. GNP growth five-year annual average: 7.2 percent.

Education. Literacy rate: 89 percent. Years compulsory education: 6. Attendance rate: 96 percent.

Conclusion

To encourage development, Thailand needs to increase requirements for education, take up more modern farming methods, and encourage outside investment for industries.

It is quite possible that Bangkok could become another Singapore on a smaller scale with regard to certain industries, such as electronics, and with regard to trade and the services.

Conclusion to the Pac Rim

When I was inducted into the U.S. Army in 1942 and reported to Fort Custer, Michigan, we were issued equipment and were put almost immediately on a troop train. Before that troop train arrived at Camp Stoneman, California, we were informed that we would be shipping out in a few days. We were not told where we were headed; in fact, we were not told anything but that we would get some training before going into combat.

When we arrived some time later in Honolulu and were shipped to Schofield Barracks for training, we felt we had reached the end of the world. Until December 7, 1941, I had never heard of Pearl Harbor. In those days it was possible, and even often the case, that one would never travel outside one's own state in a lifetime.

In my own lifetime, we have gone from the Model T Ford as the apex of engineering ingenuity to space travel.

It should not be surprising, therefore, that many people still alive and working in the world are dumbfounded by the concept of a one-world economy, but that is what we now have. And events in the world that fifty years ago we might never have heard of at all, we now know about in a matter of minutes, due to miraculous advances in communications.

Managers can no longer think in terms of their own products or in terms of domestic markets alone. They must think in terms of the world market. In order to do this, they must have some knowledge of the world in which they live. In line with this, the office of every manager should have a world globe, along with the latest world atlas and an encyclopedia of world geography.

The Possible Scope of Concern with the Pac Rim

For small businesses, particularly, hiring a consultant in international trade, for a short period of time, is usually worthwhile. Also, the Department of Commerce and its regional offices have a great deal of information for any size business wanting to engage in international trade. Much of this information could prove to be invaluable.

Managers must also be aware that they are not dealing with immature traders when they go to the Pac Rim. Most of these countries were engaged in international trading hundreds or thousands of years before the United States became a nation.

For many U.S. companies dedicated to building a good trade with Asia, this next decade will be the best opportunity yet.

Pac Rim People

People in Southeast Asia were once known for producing fireworks and cheap products. Many consumers in the West got the idea that Southeast Asian producers could make nothing better. Surely we know better by now. It is true that some of the lower-paying trades, such as the manufacture of cheap clothing, are still prominent in Southeast Asia, due mainly to a large, oppressed female labor force and lower pay. But

Southeast Asia is also the home of the latest technologies. They can do anything anyone else in the world can do, and often better. Never under-rate them.

In more than half of the Pac Rim countries discussed in this volume, better and more widespread education is needed. It would appear, at least, that the education now available to many is superior at lower grades to that we have in the United States. When higher education, par-ticularly in the less developed regions, is brought up to higher standards, their chances for development will increase.

Another generality we have attached to the Southern Pacific is that it is a heavily overpopulated and poverty-stricken region. This is true in some places, with Vietnam being the best known. The total population of the Pac Rim is approximately 1.75 billion, 1.1 billion in China alone. Some of the countries have birth rates that will not suffice for the future. Japan, for example, has a natural increase of 0.5 percent annually. This is not sufficient population growth to supply a labor force for the future. The nations that will need workers the most in the future are the ones least likely to have them.

On the other hand, the relative ages of the population tell a slightly different story. The Pac Rim population is young, with only 5.9 percent over sixty. Economically, a young population is an advantage. Only Japan, with 16.9 percent above the age of sixty, and Australia, with 15.4 percent above the age of sixty, are much different from the norm. (These two countries were excluded in calculating the 5.9 percent average.) It is not clear how many people in China are over sixty, but the figure might be as high as 18 percent. In all, the population situation would appear to be favorable in three out of four of the Pac Rim countries.

Pac Rim Monetary Problems

Japan, Hong Kong, and Singapore are all well positioned to make Pac Rim investments, if and when communism is abandoned. Western capi-tal would be welcome, but it would not be absolutely necessary for the development of the Pac Rim.

In 1988, the total Gross National Product of the Pac Rim nations was approximately $3.77 trillion, compared with a $4.8 trillion GNP in the United States alone. For most nations economic development will depend upon massive foreign trade. Another factor might help their trading position. In the opinion of some experts, worldwide inflation will be less of a problem over the next two decades than it has been in the past two. If this proves to be true, the prospects for economic development will be enhanced.

The View of the West from the Pac Rim

It goes almost without saying that the view of the West by the Pac Rim countries leaves something to be desired.

All of the Pac Rim countries were at one time or another controlled or greatly influenced by the West, except Thailand. The memories of Western exploitation, and wars that often accompanied it, still linger. There is a sense in which the East had to convince the West that it could produce anything and with quality. It would seem that the East may have to be convinced by the West that we consider them equals and are willing to abandon our air of superiority that seems to follow us wherever in the world we go.

Since 1958, when Eugene Burdick and William J. Lederer's *The Ugly American* was written, the West has been made somewhat aware of its restricted vision of other countries and other cultures. The West has a few years, but not many, to change its image if it wants to play a major role in Southeast Asia. If we are not prepared to change, we are not prepared to do much business in the Pac Rim.

The Asia–Pacific

VI | Glossary from The Peter Principle

Introduction

I had little more than started on the *International Management Handbook* when I decided that the glossary from *The Peter Principle* had to be a part of it, if I could get permission from the publisher. This marvelous little volume, though written in a whimsical style, is a mirror of present-day management, not only in the United States but around the world. And in a book of the nature of the *International Management Handbook,* which can often be weighty and sometimes unexciting, some degree of truth, written with tongue in cheek, should lighten the load.

At the end of this section I will list Peter's three books, the years in which they were published, and the publisher. I believe that all three are still available, and every manager should have them in his library.

The chapter references are to specific chapters in *The Peter Principle* within which the terms are discussed.

Alger Complex—a moralistic delusion concerning the effect of Push on promotion. Chap. 5.

Alternation, compulsive—a technique for frustrating subordinates. Chap. 12.

Aptitude tests—a popular means of hastening final placement. Chap. 9.

Arrived—achieved final placement. Chap. 3.

Auld Lang Syne Complex—sentimental belittlement of things present and glorification of things past: a sign of final placement. Chap. 12.

Buckpass, Downward, Upward and Outward—techniques for avoiding responsibility. Chap. 12.

Cachinatory Inertia—telling jokes instead of working. Chap. 12.

Caesarian Transference—irrational prejudices against some physical charactistic. Chap. 12.

Codophilia, Initial and Digital—speaking in letters and numbers rather than words. Chap. 12.

Comparative Hierarchiology—an incomplete study. Chap. 7.

Competence—the employee's ability, as measured by his superiors, to fill his place in the hierarchy. Chap. 3.

Compulsive Incompetence—a condition exhibited by Summit Competents. (See "Summit Incompetence.")

Computerized Incompetence—incompetent application of computer techniques or the inherent incompetence of a computer. Chap. 15.

Convergent Specialization—a Substitution technique. Chap. 13.

Cooks—makers of broth, some incompetent. Chap. 8.

Co-ordinator—an employee charged with the task of extracting competence from incompetents. Chap. 9.

Copelessness—a condition occasionally understood by employees, more often by management. Chap. 9.

Creative Incompetence—feigned incompetence which averts the offer of unwanted promotion. Chap. 14.

Deadwood—an accumulation at any level in a hierarchy of employees who have reached their level of incompetence.

Distraction Therapy—a treatment for the relief of the Final Placement Syndrome. Chap. 11.

Edifice Complex—a complex about buildings. Chap. 12.

Einstein, Albert—mathematician and trend setter in men's fashions. Chap. 9.

Eligible—any employee who competently carries out his duties is eligible for promotion.

Emotion-Laden Terms—not used in hierarchiology. Chap. 9.

Ephemeral Administrology—a Substitution technique. Chap. 9.

Equalitarianism—a social system which ensures the freest and fastest operation of the Peter Principle.

Exceptions—There are no exceptions to the Peter Principle.

Failure (as applied to school pupils)—see "Success."

Fileophilia—a mania for classification of papers. Chap. 12.

Final Placement Syndrome—pathology associated with placement at the level of incompetence. Chap. 11.

First things first—a Substitution technique. Chap. 13.

First Commandment—"The hierarchy must be preserved." Chap. 3.

Free-Floating Apex—a supervisor with no subordinates. Chap. 3.

Funds—Needed by Professor Peter. Chap. 7.

Gargantuan Monumentalis—giant burial park, big mausoleum and huge tombstone syndrome. Chap. 12.

General Purpose Conversation—stock, meaningless phrases. Chap. 12.

Good follower—supposedly a good leader: a fallacy. Chap. 6.

Heep Syndrome—a group of symptoms indicating the patient's belief in his own worthlessness. Observed by D. Copperfield, reported by C. Dickens. Chap. 9.

Hierarchal Exfoliation—the sloughing-off of super-competent and super-incompetent employees. Chap. 3.

Hierarchal Regression—result of promoting the incompetent along with the competent. Chap. 15.

Hierarchiology—a social science, the study of hierarchies, their structure and functioning, the foundation for all social science.

Hierarchy—an organization whose members or employees are arranged in order of rank, grade or class.

Hierarchy, Cheopsian or feudal—a pyramidal structure with many low-ranking and few high-ranking employees. Chapter 8.

Hull's Theorem—"The combined Pull of several Patrons is the sum of the separate Pulls divided by the number of Patrons." Chap. 4.

Hypercaninophobia Complex—fear caused in superiors when an inferior demonstrates strong leadership potential. Chap. 6.

Image Replaces Performance—a Substitution technique. Chap. 13.

Incompetence—a null quantity: incompetence plus incompetence equals incompetence. Chap. 10.

Input—activities which support the rules, rituals and forms of a hierarchy. Chap. 3.

John Q. Diversion—undue reliance on public opinion. Chap. 12.

Lateral Arabesque—a pseudo-promotion consisting of a new title and a new work place. Chap. 3.

Leadership competence—disqualification for promotion. Chap. 6.

Level of Competence—a position in a hierarchy at which an employee more or less does what is expected of him.

Level of Incompetence Syndrome—a position in a hierarchy at which an employee is unable to do what is expected of him.

Life-Incompetency Syndrome—a cause of frustration. Chap. 8.

Maturity Quotient—a measure of the inefficiency of a hierarchy. Chap. 7.

Medical Profession—a group showing apathy and hostility toward Hierarchiology. Chap. 11.

Meekness—a technique of Creative Incompetence. Chap. 15.

Obtain Expert Advice—A Substitution technique. Chap. 13.

Order—"Heav'n's first law.": the basis of hierarchal instinct. Chap. 8.

Output—the performance of useful work. Chap. 3.

Papyromania—compulsive accumulation of papers. Chap. 12.

Papyrophobia—abnormal desire for a "clean desk." Chap. 12.

Party—a hierarchal organization for selecting candidates for political office. Chap. 7.

Patron—one who speeds the promotion of employees lower in the hierarchy. Chap. 4.

Percussive Sublimation—being kicked upstairs: a pseudo-promotion. Chap. 3.

Peter Principle—in a hierarchy, every employee tends to rise to his level of incompetence.

Peter's Bridge—an important test: can you motivate your patron? Chap. 4.

Peter's Circumambulation—a circumlocution or detour around a superincumbent. Chap. 4.

Peter's Circumbendibus—a veiled or secret circumambulation (see above).

Peter's Corollary—in time, every post in a hierarchy tends to be occupied by an employee who is incompetent to carry out his duties.

Peter's Inversion—internal consistency valued more highly than efficiency. Chap. 3.

Peter's Invert—one for whom means have become ends in themselves. Chap. 3.

Peter's Nuance—the difference between Pseudo-Achievement and Final Placement Syndromes. Chap. 5.

Peter's Palliatives—provide relief for incompetence symptoms. Chap. 15.

Peter's Paradox—employees in a hierarchy do not really object to incompetence in their colleagues. Chap. 4.

Peter's Parry—the refusal of an offered promotion. (Not recommended.) Chap. 14.

Peter's Placebo—an ounce of image is worth a pound of performance. Chap. 13.

Peter's Plateau—the level of incompetence.

Peter's Prescriptions—CURES for individual or world ills. Chap. 25.

Peter's Pretty Pass—the situation of having one's road to promotion blocked by a super-incumbent. Chap. 4.

Peter's Prognosis—spend sufficient time in confirming the need, and the need will disappear. Chap. 13.

Peter's Prophylactics—an ounce of prevention. Chap. 15.

Peter's Remedies—means of preventing total-life-incompetence. Chap. 15.

Peter's Spiral—the non-progressive course followed by organizations suffering from high-level incompetence. Chap. 10.

Peterian Interpretation—the application of hierarchiological science to the facts and fictions of history. Chap. 15.

Phonophilia—an abnormal desire for possession and use of voice transmission and recording equipment. Chap. 12.

Professional Automatism—an obsessive concern with rituals and a disregard of results. Chap. 3.

Promotion—an upward movement from a level of competence.

Promotion Quotient—numerical expressions of promotion prospects. Chap. 13.

Protégé—see "Pullee".

Proto-hierarchiologists—authors who might have contributed to hierarchiological thought. Chap. 8.

Proverbs—as repositories of hierarchiological fallacies. Chap. 8.

Pseudo-Achievement Syndrome—a complex of physical ailments resulting from excessive Push. Chap. 5.

Pull—an employee's relationship—by blood, marriage or acquaintance—with a person above him. Chap. 4.

Pullee—an employee who has Pull. Chap. 4.

Random Placement—a cause of delay in reaching the level of incompetence. Chap. 9.

Rigor Cartis—abnormal interest in charts, with dwindling concern for realities that the chart represents. Chap. 12.

Saints—good men but incompetent controversialists. Chap. 8.

Secrecy—the soul of Push. Chap. 5.

Seniority Factor—downward pressure which opposes the upward movement of competent employees. Chap. 5.

Side-Issue Specialization—a substitution technique. Chap. 13.

Socrates Complex—a form of Creative Incompetence. Chap. 14.

Staticmanship—the timely renunciation of One-upmanship. Chap. 8.

Study Alternate Methods—a Substitution technique. Chap. 13.

Substitution—a lifesaving technique for employees on Peter's Plateau. Chap. 13.

Success—final placement at the level of incompetence. Chap. 8.

Summit Competence—a rare condition. Chap. 9.

Super-competence—doing one's work too well: a dangerous characteristic. Chap. 3.

Super-incompetence—complete lack of output and input; grounds for dismissal. Chap. 3.

Super-incumbent—a person above you who, having reached his level of incompetence, blocks your path to promotion. Chap. 4.

Tabulatory gigantism—obsession with large-size desks. Chap. 12.

Tabulology, abnormal—the study of unusual arrangements of desks, workbenches, etc. Chap. 12.

Tabulophobia Privata—inability to tolerate the presence of desks. Chap. 12.

Teeter-Totter Syndrome—inability to make decisions. Chap. 12.

Temporary relief—results of medical treatment for Final Placement Syndrome. Chap. 11.

Universal hierarchiology—an untapped field of study. Chap. 7.

Utter Irrelevance—a Substitution technique common at upper levels of commerce. Chap. 13.

The Peter Principle was authored by Dr. Laurence Peter and Raymond Hull (New York: William Morrow & Co., 1969). Two more books by the same author and publisher, *The Peter Pyramid,* 1975, and *The Peter Plan,* 1986, are highly recommended

VII International Banking and Finance

Central Banks of the Nations of the World

Afghanistan

Da Afghanistan Bank
Ibni Sina Watt
Kabul, AFGHANISTAN

Albania

Banque de l'Etat Albanais
Sheshi Skenderbej 1
Tirana, ALBANIA

Argentina

Banco Central de la Republica Argentina
Reconquista 266
1003 Buenos Aires, ARGENTINA

Aruba

Centrale Bank van Aruba
Havenstraat 2
Oranjestad, ARUBA

Australia

Reserve Bank of Australia
65 Martin Place
GPO Box 3947
Sydney (NSW) 2001, AUSTRALIA

Austria

Oesterreichische Nationalbank
Otto-Wagner-Platz 3
Postfach 61
A-1011 Wien, AUSTRIA

Bahamas

The Central Bank of the Bahamas
P.O. Box N 4868
Nassau N.P., BAHAMAS

Bahrain

Bahrain Monetary Agency
P.O. Box 27
Manama, BAHRAIN

Bangladesh

Bangladesh Bank
Motijheel Commercial Area
P.O. Box 325
Dhaka 1000, BANGLADESH

Barbados, West Indies

Central Bank of Barbados
P.O. Box 1016
Bridgetown, BARBADOS, W.I.

Belgium

Banque Nationale de Belgique, S.A.
Boulevard de Berlaimont 5
B-1000 Bruxelles, BELGIUM

Belize

Central Bank of Belize
P.O. Box 852
Belize City, BELIZE

Bermuda

The Bermuda Monetary Authority
48 Church Street
Sofia Building
Hamilton HM 12, BERMUDA

Bolivia

Banco Central Bolivia
Ayacucho esq. Mercado
Cajon Postal No 3118
La Paz, BOLIVIA

Botswana

Bank of Botswana
Khama Crescent
P.O. Box 712
Gaborone, BOTSWANA

Brazil

Banco Central do Brasil
Caixa Postal (P.O.B.): 04.0170
70074 Brasilia DF, BRAZIL

Bulgaria

National Bank of Bulgaria
2, Sofiiska Komuna Strm.
1000 Sofia, BULGARIA

Burma

Union of Burma Bank
24-26 Sule Pagoda Road
Rangoon, BURMA

Burundi

Banque de la Republique du Burundi
B.P. 705
Bujumbura, BURUNDI

Cambodia

National Bank of Cambodia
22-24 Moha Vithei 9 TOLA
Phnom-Penh, CAMBODIA

Canada

Bank of Canada
234 Wellington Street
Ottawa KIA 0G9, CANADA

Central Africa

Banque des Etats de l'Afrique Centrale
Republique du Cameroun
Boite Postale 1917
Yaounde, CENTRAL AFRICA

Chile

Banco Central de Chile
Casilla 967
Agustinas 1180
Santiago de Chile, CHILE

China

The People's Bank of China
San li He
Beijing, CHINA

Colombia

Colombia National Bank (Banco de la Republica)
Carrera 6a No 14-85

P.O. Box 3531
Bogota, COLOMBIA

Costa Rica

Banco Central de Costa Rica
Calle 4a., Avenidas Fernandez Guell y la.
1000 San Jose, COSTA RICA

Cuba

Banco Nacional de Cuba
402 Cuba Street
P.O.B. 736
La Habana 1, CUBA

Cyprus

Central Bank of Cyprus
36 Metichiou Street
P.O. Box 5529
Nicosia, CYPRUS

Czech and Slovak Federal Republic

Statni Banka Ceskoslovenska
Na prikope 28
CS-110 03 Praha 1
CZECH AND SLOVAK FEDERAL REPUBLIC

Denmark

Danmarks Nationalbank
Havnegade 5
DK-1093 Copenhagen K, DENMARK

Dominican Republic

Banco Central de la Republica Dominicana
Ave. Dr. Pedro Henriquez Urena
Apartado Postal 1347
Santo Domingo, R.D., DOMINICAN REPUBLIC

Ecuador

Banco Central del Ecuador
Plaza Bolivar (La Alameda, Av. 10 de Agosto y)
Briceno, Casilla 339
Quito, ECUADOR

Egypt

Central Bank of Egypt
Kasr el Nil Street 31
Cairo, EGYPT

El Salvador

Banco Central de Reserva de El Salvador
1a. Calle Poniente y
7a. Avenida Norte
San Salvador, EL SALVADOR

England

Bank of England
Threadneedle Street
London EC2 8AH. ENGLAND

Ethiopia

National Bank of Ethiopia
P.O. Box 5550
Addis Ababa, ETHIOPIA

Fiji

Reserve Bank of Fiji
G.P.O. Box 1220
Suva, FIJI

Finland

Suomen Pankki—Finlands Bank
P.O. Box 160 (Snellmaninaukio)
SF-00101 Helsinki, FINLAND

France

Banque de France
39, rue Croix-des-Petits-Champs
Boite Postale 140-01
F 75049 Paris Cedex 01, FRANCE

Gambia

Central Bank of the Gambia
1-1 Buckle Street (WEST AFRICA)
Banjul, GAMBIA

Germany

Deutsche Bundesbank
Wilhelm-Epstein-Strasse 14
Postfach 10 06 02
D-6000 Frankfurt 1, GERMANY

Ghana

Bank of Ghana
P.O. Box 2674
Accra, GHANA

Greece

Bank of Greece
21, E. Venizelos Avenue
P.O. Box 3105
GR-102 50 Athens, GREECE

Guyana

Bank of Guyana
P.O. Box 1003
Georgetown, GUYANA

Haiti

Banque de la Republique d'Haiti
Angle Rue du Magasin de l'Etat
B.P. 1570
Port-au-Prince, HAITI

Honduras

Banco Central de Honduras
Avenida Juan Ramon Molina 5. Calle
Tegucigalpa D.C., HONDURAS

Hungary

Magyar Nemzeti Bank (National Bank of Hungary)
Szabadsag ter 8/11
H-1850 Budapest, HUNGARY

Iceland

Central Bank of Iceland (Sedlabanki Islands)
Kalkofnsvegur 1
P.O. Box 160
150 Reykjavik, ICELAND

India

Reserve Bank of India
Shahid Bhagat Singh Road
Post Box 10007
Bombay 400 023, INDIA

Indonesia

Bank Indonesia
Jalan M.H. Thamrin No.2
P.O. Box 1035
Jakarta 10010, INDONESIA

Iran

The Central Bank of the Islamic Republic of Iran
Ferdowsi Avenue
P.O. Box 11365/8551
Tehran, IRAN

Iraq

Central Bank of Iraq
Rashid Street

P.O. Box No. 64
Baghdad, IRAQ

Ireland

Central Bank of Ireland
Dame Street
P.O. Box No. 559
Dublin 2, IRELAND

Israel

Bank of Israel
P.O.B. 780, Kiryat Ben Gurion
Jerusalem 91007, ISRAEL

Italy

Banca d'Italia
Via Nazionale 91 (Casella Postale 2484, 00100
ROMA CENTRO CORRISPONDENZE)
I-00184 Roma, ITALY

Jamaica

Bank of Jamaica
Nethersole Place
P.O. Box 621
Kingston, JAMAICA

Japan

The Bank of Japan
No. 1-1, 2-Chome, Hongoku-cho, Nihonbashi, Chuo-ku
C.P.O. Box 203
Tokyo 100-91, JAPAN

Jordan

Central Bank of Jordan
P.O. Box 37
Amman, JORDAN

Kenya

Central Bank of Kenya
Haile Selassie Ave.
Nairobi, KENYA

Korea

The Bank of Korea
110, 3-ka, Namdaemoon-ro, Chung-gu
C.P.O. 100-794, KOREA

Kuwait

Central Bank of Kuwait
13006—Safat
P.O. Box 526
KUWAIT

Laos

Banque d'Etat du Laos
Rue Yonnet
Boite Postale No 19
Vientiane, LAOS

Lebanon

Banque de Liban
rue Masraf Loubane
Boite Postale 11-5544
Beirut, LEBANON

Lesotho

Central Bank of Lesotho
P.O. Box 1184
Maseru, LESOTHO

Liberia

National Bank of Liberia
Broad Street

P.O. Box 2048
Monrovia, LIBERIA

Libya

Central Bank of Libya
P.O. Box 1103
Tripoli, LIBYA

Madagascar

Banque Centrale de Madagascar
Boite Postale 550
Antananarivo (101), MADAGASCAR

Malawi

Reserve Bank of Malawi
P.O. Box 30063
Lilongwe 3, MALAWI

Malaysia

Bank Negara Malaysia
Jalan Dato' Onn
50480 Kuala Lumpur, MALAYSIA

Malta

Central Bank of Malta
Valletta, MALTA

Mauritius

Bank of Mauritius
Sir William Newton Street
P.O. Box No.29
Port Louis, MAURITIUS

Mexico

Banco de Mexico
Avenida 5 de Mayo No.2
Apartado Postal 98 bis
06059 Mexico D.F., MEXICO

Morocco

Bank Al-Maghrib
277, avenue Mohammed V
Boite Postale 445
Rabat, MOROCCO

Netherlands

De Nederlandsche Bank N.V.
Westeinde 1
1017 ZN Amsterdam
NETHERLANDS

Netherlands Antilles

Bank van de Nederlandse Antillen
Breedestraat 1 (P)
Willemstad, Curacao
NETHERLANDS ANTILLES

New Zealand

Reserve Bank of New Zealand
2 The Terrace
G.P.O. Box 2498
Wellington C.1
NEW ZEALAND

Nicaragua

Banco Central de Nicaragua
Pista de la Resistencia
Managua D.N., NICARAGUA

Nigeria

Central Bank of Nigeria
Tinubu Square
Privare Mail Bag 12194
Lagos, NIGERIA

Norway

Bank of Norway (Norges Bank)
Bankplassen 2
Postboks 1179 Sentrum
0107 Oslo 1, NORWAY

Oman

Central Bank of Oman
Muttrah Business District
P.O. Box 4161
Ruwi, OMAN

Pakistan

State Bank of Pakistan
I.I. Chundrigar Road
Post Box No.4456
Karachi, PAKISTAN

Papua New Guinea

Bank of Papua New Guinea
P.O. Box 121
Port Moresby
PAPUA NEW GUINEA

Paraguay

Banco Central del Paraguay
Av. Pable VI y Sgto. Mareco, Co. Santo Domingo
Asuncion, PARAGUAY

Peru

Banco Central de Reserva del Peru
Jr. Antonio Miro Quesada 441-445
Apartado 1958—Correo Central
Lima 100, PERU

Philippines

Central Bank of the Philippines
Manila, PHILIPPINES

Poland

Narodowy Bank Polski
rue Swietokzyska 11/21
Boite Postale 1011
PL 00-950 Varsovie
POLAND

Portugal

Banco de Portugal
148, Rua do Comercio
1101 Lisboa Codex
PORTUGAL

Romania

Banca Nationala A Romaniei
Strada Lipscani 25
Bucuresti, ROMANIA

Rwanda

Banque Nationale du Rwanda
Boite Postale No 531
Kigali, RWANDA

Saudi Arabia

Saudi Arabian Monetary Agency
P.O. Box 2992
Riyadh, SAUDI ARABIA

Seychelles

Central Bank of Seychelles
P.O. Box 701
Victoria, Mahe
SEYCHELLES

Sierra Leone

Bank of Sierra Leone
Siaka Stevens Street
P.O. Box 30
Freetown, SIERRA LEONE

Singapore

The Monetary Authority of Singapore
MAS Building
P.O. Box 52
Singapore 9001
SINGAPORE

Solomon Islands

Central Bank of Solomon Islands
P.O. Box 634
Honiara
SOLOMON ISLANDS

Somalia

Central Bank of Somalia
Corso Somali 55
P.O. Box 11
Mogadishu—S.D.R.
SOMALIA

South Africa

South African Reserve Bank
P.O. Box 427
Pretoria 0001
SOUTH AFRICA

Spain

Banco de España
Apartado de Correos 15
28080 Madrid, SPAIN

Sri Lanka

Central Bank of Sri Lanka
34-36 Janadhipathi Mawatha
P.O. Box 590
Colombo 1, SRI LANKA

Sudan

Bank of Sudan
P.O. Box 313
Khartoum, SUDAN

Surinam

Centrale Bank van Suriname
P.O.B. 1801
Paramaribo, SURINAM

Swaziland

Central Bank of Swaziland
P.O. Box 546
Mbabane, SWAZILAND

Sweden

Sveriges Riksbank
11 Brunkebergstorg
s-103 37 Stockholm, SWEDEN

Switzerland

Schweizerische Nationalbank
Postfach
CH-8022 Zurich
SWITZERLAND

Syria

Banque Centrale de Syrie
29 Aya Street
Damas, SYRIA

Taiwan

Central Bank of China
No.2, Roosevelt Road, Sect. 1
Taipei, 10757, TAIWAN

Tanzania

Bank of Tanzania
10 Mirambo St., P.O. Box 2939
Dar es Salaam, TANZANIA

Thailand

Bank of Thailand
273 Samsen Road
P.O. Box 154 BNC
Bangkok 10000
THAILAND

Tonga

National Reserve Bank of Tonga
Private Bag No. 25, P.O.
Nukualofa, TONGA

Trinidad, West Indies

Central Bank of Trinidad and Tobago
P.O. Box 1250
Port of Spain
TRINIDAD, WEST INDIES

Tunisia

Banque Centrale de Tunisie
Rue de la Monnaie
B.P. 369
Tunis, 1001, TUNISIA

Turkey

Turkiye Cumhuriyet Merkez Bankasi
Istikal Caddesi No. 10
06100 Ulus/Ankara
TURKEY

United Arab Emirates

Central Bank of the United Arab Emirates
P.O. Box 854
Abu Dhabi, UAE

Uganda

Bank of Uganda
37/343, Kampala Road
P.O. Box 7120
Kampala, UGANDA

Uruguay

Banco Central del Uruguay
Casilla de Correo 1467, Correo Central
(Calle Paysandu y Florida)
Montevideo
URUGUAY

Venezuela

Banco Central de Venezuela
Esquina de Las Carmelitas
Apartado Postal 2017
Caracas 1010
VENEZUELA

Vietnam

State Bank of the Socialist Republic of Vietnam
Hanoi, VIETNAM

West African Monetary Union

West African Monetary Union
Avenue Abdoulaye Fadiga (B.P. 3108)
Republique de Senegal
Dakar
WEST AFRICAN MONETARY UNION

West Indies

Eastern Caribbean Central Bank
P.O. Box 89
Basseterre, St. Kitts
WEST INDIES

Yugoslavia

Narodna Banka Jugoslavije
P.O. Box 1010
UY-11001 Beograd
YUGOSLAVIA

Zaire

Banque du Zaire
Boulevard Colonel Tshiashi
B.P. 2697
Kinshasa-Gombe
ZAIRE

Zambia

Bank of Zambia
Bank Square, Cairo Road
P.O. Box 30080
Lusaka, ZAMBIA

Zimbabwe

Reserve Bank of Zimbabwe
76, Samora Machel Avenue
P.O. Box 1283
Harare, ZIMBABWE

This listing of the central banks of the world was provided by the Division of Banking Regulation and Supervision, Board of Governors of the Federal Reserve System, Washington, DC 20551

Prominent International Banks

Deposit figures are in thousands of dollars.

BANK, COUNTRY:	DEPOSITS (IN DOLLARS, 1990)
Dai-ixhi Kangyo Bank, Ltd., Tokyo, Japan:	314,780,128
Sunitomo Bank Ltd.,Osaka, Japan:	288,242,189
Mitsubishi Bank, Ltd., Tokyo, Japan:	278,806,753
Fuji Bank, Ltd., Tokyo, Japan:	278,642,535
Sanwa Bank, Ltd., Osaka, Japan:	275,972,496
Industrial Bank of Japan, Ltd., Tokyo, Japan:	213,287,599
Banque Nationale de Paris, France:	192,525,992
Mitsubishi Trust & Banking Corp., Tokyo, Japan:	192,294,268
Deutsche Bank, Frankfurt, Germany:	184,378,643
Tokai Bank Ltd., Nagoya, Japan:	179,030,994
Norinchukin Bank, Tokyo, Japan:	176,329,604
Credit Lyonnais, Paris, France:	176,099,988
Sumitomo Trust & Banking Co., Ltd., Osaka, Japan:	171,664,091
Credit Agricole Mutuel, Paris, France:	169,711,546
Barclay's Bank Plc, London, UK:	167,127,661
National Westminster Bank Plc, London, UK:	163,014,110
Mitsui Trust & Banking Co., Ltd., Tokyo, Japan:	159,219,084
Mitsui Bank, Ltd., Tokyo, Japan:	157,894,949
Bank of Tokyo, Ltd., Japan:	152,933,845
Long-Term Credit Bank of Japan Ltd., Tokyo, Japan:	148,398,357
Société Generale, Paris, France:	141,977,467
Taiyo Kobe Bank, Ltd., Kobe, Japan:	136,538,177
Dresdener Bank, Frankfurt, Germany:	135,670,068
Yasuda Trust & Banking Co., Ltd., Tokyo, Japan:	135,105,776
Daiwa Bank, Ltd., Osaka, Japan:	131,680,308
Hong Kong & Shanghai Banking Corp., Hong Kong:	118,504,960
Commerzbank, Frankfurt, Germany:	106,668,460
Swiss Bank Corp., Basel, Switzerland:	100,865,736

BANK, COUNTRY:	DEPOSITS (IN DOLLARS)
Toyo Trust & Banking Co.,Ltd., Tokyo, Japan:	100,172,771
Union Bank of Switzerland, Zurich:	96,997,909
Westdeutsche Landesbank Giorzentrale, Duesseldorf, Germany:	96,532,850
Bayerische Vereinsbank, Munich, Germany:	95,993,000
Nippon Credit Bank, Ltd., Tokyo, Japan:	88,179,792
Midland Bank Plc, London, UK:	88,034,800
Banca Nazionale del Lavoro, Rome, Italy:	84,811,188
Lloyds Bank Plc, London, UK:	84,335,950
Bayerische Hypotheken-und. Wechsel-Bank, Munich, Germany:	83,191,003
Istituto Bancario San Paolo de Torino, Turin, Italy:	79,614,718
Kyowa Bank, Ltd., Tokyo, Japan:	78,919,007
Banka Commerciale Italiana, Milan, Italy:	77,865,384

Twenty Largest U.S. Commercial Banks

NAME AND ADDRESS	ASSETS (IN THOUSANDS, 1990)
Citibank 399 Park Avenue New York, NY 10043 Telephone number: (212) 559-1000	$ 104,996,000
Bank of America NT and SA 555 California St. San Francisco, CA 94104 Telephone number: (415) 622-3456	69,640,000
The Chase Manhattan Bank, NA One Chase Manhattan Plaza New York, NY 10081 Telephone number: (212) 552-2222	$ 58,241,477

NAME AND ADDRESS	ASSETS (IN THOUSANDS)
Morgan Guaranty Trust Company 23 Wall Street New York, NY 10015 Telephone number: (212) 483-2323	45,471,746
Manufacturers Hanover Trust Co. 270 Park Avenue New York, NY 10017 Telephone number: (212) 286-6000	42,876,000
Security Pacific Bank 333 South Hope St. Los Angeles, CA 90017 Telephone number: (213) 613-6211	36,095,333
Wells Fargo Bank, NA 420 Montgomery St. San Francisco, CA 94104 Telephone number: (415) 396-0123	35,109,059
Chemical Bank 277 Park Avenue New York, NY 10017 Telephone number: (212) 310-6161	33,298,000
Bankers Trust Company 280 Park Avenue New York, NY 10017 Telephone number: (212) 775-2500	33,261,373
First National Bank of Chicago One First Plaza Chicago, IL 60670 Telephone number: (312) 732-4000	27,372,437
NCNB Texas National Bank 1401 Elm Street Dallas. TX 75283 Telephone number: (214) 744-9600	$ 20,474,765

NAME AND ADDRESS	ASSETS (IN THOUSANDS)
Continental Illinois National & Trust Co., of Chicago 231 South LaSalle St. Chicago, IL 60697 Telephone number: (312) 828-2345	17,763,339
First National Bank of Boston 100 Federal Street Boston, MA 02110 Telephone number: (617) 434-2200	17,687,897
Bank of New York 48 Wall Street New York, NY 10015 Telephone number: (212) 530-1784	16,665,898
Marine Midland Bank, NA 140 Broadway New York, NY 10015 Telephone number: (212) 440-1000	16,659,085
First Interstate Bank of California 707 Wilshire Blvd. Los Angeles, CA 90017 Telephone number: (213) 614-4111	16,613,623
Mellon Bank, NA One Mellon Bank Center Pittsburgh, PA 15258 Telephone number: (412) 234-5000	15,603,197
Boston State Deposit & Trust 1 Boston Place Boston, MA 02106 Telephone number: (617) 956-9700	15,464,313
Irving Trust Company One Wall Street New York, NY 10005 Telephone number: (212) 635-1111	$ 14,154,585

NAME AND ADDRESS   ASSETS (IN THOUSANDS)

Republic National Bank of New York
452 Fifth Avenue
New York, NY 10018
Telephone number: (212) 930-6000   13,897,318

NOTE: The rapid economic changes in the United States have caused banks to merge, names to change, and assets to shift rapidly. The figures contained here are the latest available. In some cases, only addresses may remain the same by the time this book is published. Such is our changing world.

A Review of the Federal Reserve System

The scope of this book demands a review of the Federal Reserve System, which acts as the central bank of the United States. To this end, it would be helpful to analyze the financial conditions and present a brief summary of the banking institutions that existed in the United States prior to the Fed's emergence in 1913.

The Constitution of the United States made no provision for a banking system in the new nation, though it did make the federal government responsible for some sort of monetary system. The problems which the new federal government had in founding a monetary system were compounded by the fact that there was a great deal of disagreement about what sort of central government the new nation ought to have. Alexander Hamilton's argument for a strong central government and Thomas Jefferson's stand in favor of leaving most of the power to the various states represented the two poles of the debate.

In 1791 Alexander Hamilton was secretary of the Treasury, while Thomas Jefferson was secretary of State and George Washington was president. Hamilton wanted a central bank of the United States to preside over the monetary affairs of the fledgling government. Jefferson declared that the Constitution gave the government no authority to set up a central bank, which was technically correct. But Hamilton argued that the Constitution did give the federal government the power over many monetary and fiscal matters, and that a bank was necessary to carry out such matters.

Hamilton won the debate, and the First Bank of the United States was formed in 1791, with a capital stock of $10 million dollars. Two million of this was subscribed by the federal government, with the remainder paid by private individuals. Five of the First Bank directors were chosen by the government and twenty were chosen by private investors. The main bank was in Philadelphia with branches in other major cities. The First Bank performed all of the basic banking functions. It was the largest bank, and the largest corporation, in the United States.

While the First Bank of the United States did a commendable job, its size and the fact that it appeared to favor eastern businessmen over western farmers brought it to an end in 1811, when Congress failed by one vote to renew its charter.

Without a central bank, the country found itself in a monetary crisis. Then the War of 1812 aggravated the problem. (A war requires a central bank to increase the money supply quickly and sufficiently to pay the war bills as they come due. Trying to do this by public subscription, as was tried in 1812, was virtually impossible then, and it would be totally impossible today.) In 1816, the final year of James Madison's presidency, a bill to charter a Second Bank of the United States was introduced by Henry Clay, speaker of the House, who had opposed rechartering the First Bank.

By a narrow margin, the Second Bank was chartered for twenty years. It was capitalized for $35 million, one-fifth of which was subscribed by the federal government, with the balance paid by private individuals. One-fifth of the directors were appointed by the president, and the rest by stockholders.

If anything, the Second Bank was too successful, and it soon began to be feared by some business people and politicians alike. Andrew Jackson, a man well-liked by the common people of the new republic, became president in 1829, when the bank charter still had seven years to run. At the end of the seven years Henry Clay was able to push a bill through Congress to recharter the Bank, but it was vetoed by President Jackson and it became the last of the central banks of the United States.

While the Second Bank was chartered, numerous state-chartered banks were formed, and they had been jealous of the Second Bank and the power it was building both for government and for some business people. The state-chartered banks, for the most part, were undercapitalized, poorly managed, awash in bad loans, and generally unable to carry the monetary responsibility of the nation. Nonetheless, in lieu of a central bank monetary policy was left up to the various state banks for the next twenty-five years.

Monetary policy had to come into focus during the Civil War. In 1863, Congress passed the National Banking Act; legislation at last began to bring some semblance of order to the financial world of the United States. The National Banking Act provided for the creation of nationally chartered banks, all of which were required to have "national" in their names, or "N.A.," which stands for "National Association". The same requirement still stands today for federally chartered banks.

While state-chartered banks had issued currency almost indiscriminately, the federally chartered banks were required to back their currency with U.S. government securities. Limits were set on certain kinds of loans, and periodic examinations of each bank were to be made by the comptroller of the currency.

In spite of the emergence of the national banks, many state banks remained in business. They no longer issued currency, but the days of such currency was passing anyway, and the demand for deposits in banks formed the backdrop for making loans.

In spite of the National Banking Act of 1863, the banking situation improved but little. There was still no central bank to which the government could turn, and the existing banks worked without central check-clearing services or any of the activities a central bank would have carried on.

Because of the lack of central control of monetary policy, the financial gyrations in the economy led the nation from booms to busts with alarming regularity. The reserves held by banks were generally immobile.

The financial panic and economic depression of 1893 were so pervasive that economic uncertainty became the order of the day in the nation. Another panic in 1907, though it did not trigger a depression, made it clear that something had to be done about the U.S. monetary situation.

The Federal Reserve System

While there was a nationwide concern over monetary policy after the 1907 panic, the country was divided over how the problem could be solved. A conflict existed between the giant "city" banks, and the small "country" banks, a conflict that remains, to some extent, to this day. The "common people," generally represented by the country banks, have always felt that monetary policy was controlled by the rich city banks and by the large industrialists.

Woodrow Wilson signed the Federal Reserve Bill on the evening of December 23, 1913. The framework of the Federal Reserve System as it now exists is outlined below. I should mention that the Fed, as it got under way in 1914, was weak and its actions did not have pervasive consequences in the market as they do today. Still, the formation of the Federal Reserve System was a long step in the right direction. The nation now had a central bank. The System is composed of a seven-member Board of Governors. It has its headquarters in Washington, D.C., with a nationwide network of twelve Federal Reserve Banks and twenty-five branches.

The Board of Governors
of the Federal Reserve System

Members of this board are appointed by the president and confirmed by the Senate to serve fourteen-year terms. This length of service and staggered terms are intended to insulate the members from ongoing political pressures.

The staggering is such that one term expires every two years. Should a member resign or die, the president appoints another to fill the unexpired term. Any member who has served only a partial term may be reappointed for a full term, but a member who has fulfilled his term cannot be reappointed. The president designates one member of the Board as chairman and another as vice chairman for terms of four years. As of this writing, Alan Greenspan, an economist, is chairman.

Not more than one member can be appointed from any one of the twelve Federal Reserve Districts. The president is urged to consider appointments from all sectors of the economy, including financial, agricultural, industrial, etc.

The Board of Governors is primarily responsible for the nation's monetary policy. The Federal Open Market Committee (FOMC) makes the primary decisions affecting the cost and availability of money and credit. FOMC is composed of the seven members of the board and five Reserve Bank presidents, one of whom is the president of the Federal Reserve Bank of New York.

The Board of Governors also sets reserve requirements; i.e., the percentage of total deposits that member banks must maintain with the Fed in the form of vault cash, or deposits in the Fed. The discount rate, or the rate of interest the Fed charges member banks for borrowing, is set by the Board in concert with the member banks. Changes in this rate are recommended by the boards of directors of the Reserve Banks and are subject to the approval of the Board of Governors.

The Board sets margin requirements on credit extended by broker-dealers, banks, and others to purchase or carry stock. It maintains contact with the central banks of the world and with organizations concerned with the international monetary system. Its supervisory duties extend to operations of domestic corporations involved in international banking or finance and certain other operations of foreign banks and banking organizations in the United States. The Board is also charged with the oversight of the Federal Reserve Banks.

The Board also has the responsibility for implementing the major federal consumer credit laws, such as Truth in Lending and Equal Credit Opportunity.

Meetings of the Board occur several times each week, and they are conducted in compliance with the government's Sunshine Act, which allows for some of the meetings to be public. All meetings regarding consumerism are open to the public. Meetings concerning matters of financial information are usually closed.

A report to Congress twice each year accounts for actions of the Board on economic matters and monetary policy. The chairman of the Board appears often before committees of Congress to report on many aspects of the economy. A full annual report is also made to Congress.

Many statistical reports are made by the Board for the benefit of banks, businesses, researchers, students, etc. Many of these reports can be found in the monthly publication, the *Federal Reserve Bulletin.*

The Federal Open Market Committee (FOMC)

This is the most important monetary policy-making body in the Federal Reserve System. It is charged with making policy designed to promote economic growth, full employment, stable prices, and a sustainable pattern of international trade and payments. The Committee makes decisions governing open-market operations (the buying and selling of government and Federal Agencies' securities), thereby directly influencing the availability of money in the nation and its cost.

The FOMC is composed of the Board of Governors and five Federal Reserve Bank presidents. The president of the New York Fed serves on a continuous basis. The other four members serve on a rotating basis for a period of one year. Rotation is conducted so that each year one member is elected to the Committee by the Board of Directors from each of the following bank groups: (a) Boston, Philadelphia, and Richmond; (b) Cleveland and Chicago; (c) Atlanta, St. Louis, and Dallas; (d) Minneapolis, Kansas City, and San Francisco.

By law, the Committee determines its own organization, which looks something like this:

A. Chairman
B. Vice Chairman
C. Staff Officers, including:
    1. Secretary, who keeps notes on all matters of policy;
    2. Economists to prepare and present to the Committee information

regarding business and credit conditions, plus domestic and international economic and financial developments;

3. a General Counsel to furnish legal advice;

4. two managers of the System Open Market Account, one for domestic and one for foreign operations, to execute and to report to the Committee on open market transactions.

The law requires that the FOMC meet at least four times each year in Washington, D.C. Meetings can be called by the Board of Governors or by three Committee members. Usually the meetings are from five to eight weeks apart, on a schedule set at the beginning of the year. The meetings are not open to the public.

Policy decisions become part of the annual report made by the Board of Governors to the Congress. Policies made and followed have much to do with the levels of reserves in member banks and the ease or difficulty for customers desiring to get loans. The total amount of credit available in the economy is the result of these policies.

Federal Reserve Banks

There are twelve regional Federal Reserve Banks and twenty-five branch banks, which are located to serve the economic and monetary needs of each region of the country. All are under the direction of the Board of Governors.

The Federal Reserve Banks are located in New York, Boston, Philadelphia, Cleveland, Richmond, Atlanta, Chicago, St. Louis, Minneapolis, Kansas City, Dallas, and San Francisco.

Federal Reserve Branches are located in Buffalo, Cincinnati, Pittsburgh, Baltimore, Charlotte, Birmingham, Jacksonville, Miami, Nashville, New Orleans, Detroit, Little Rock, Louisville, Memphis, Helena, Denver, Oklahoma City, Omaha, El Paso, Houston, San Antonio, Los Angeles, Portland, Salt Lake City, and Seattle.

In addition to the President and staff, each Federal Reserve Bank has a nine member Board of Directors which oversees its operations under the general supervision of the Board of Governors.

The board consists of three Class A directors representing member banks; three Class B directors representing the public; three Class C directors, also representing the public, but appointed by the Board Of Governors. Two of the directors are designated as chair and deputy chair for one-year terms.

Federal Reserve Banks generate their own incomes, though theoretically they are nonprofit-making. In 1988, they turned $17.3 billion over to the Treasury Department after paying all of their own expenses.

In conjunction with the Board of Governors, Federal Reserve Banks have broad supervisory authority over member banks and bank-holding companies. They conduct field examinations of member banks and holding companies, and they have the authority to approve certain types of bank and bank-holding company applications.

The following government services are performed by Federal Reserve Banks. They handle operating accounts of the U.S. Treasury, hold in their vaults collateral for government agencies to secure public funds on deposit with private depository institutions, and receive for deposit to the Treasury accounts items such as federal unemployment taxes, individual income taxes withheld by payroll deduction, corporate income taxes, and certain federal excise taxes.

Since the adoption of the Monetary Control Act of 1980, Fed services are available to all depository institutions whether such institutions are members of the Fed or not. Some service charges are usually made. The following services are performed by the Federal Reserve Banks for depository institutions. They distribute coin or currency to depository institutions according to need at specific times of the year, store cash for depository institutions when demands are light, destroy bad coin and currency (replacement coin and currency is obtained from the Treasury's Bureau of Engraving and Printing and the Bureau of the Mint), process checks through a central check-clearing system handling about 8 billion checks per year, maintain a network through which depository institutions can transfer funds and securities nationwide in a matter of minutes, and operate automated clearing houses (ACHs) for the electronic exchange of payments among participating depository institutions. The ACH is used primarily to carry out recurring transactions, such as direct deposits of payrolls and mortgage payments.

Federal Reserve Bank Board of Directors

The nine member Board of Directors at each regional Federal Reserve Bank is charged with being well versed in the economies and the prevailing credit conditions of its region. Each branch bank also has a Board of Directors, with either five or seven members.

Branch bank directors are not elected. The majority are appointed by the Reserve Bank, and the rest are appointed by the Board of Governors. The branch Board chairman is named from among the directors appointed by the Board of Governors. Branch directors serve one-, two-, or three-year terms, depending on the size of the branch, and are usually limited to two successive terms.

Advisory Committees of the Fed

The Consumer Advisory Council. This organization consists of thirty members representing a wide range of consumer interests.

Federal Advisory Council. This group meets in Washington four times each year and consists of one member from each Federal Reserve Region. The member is usually a banker. This council, because it does represent all of the Fed regions, is asked to make recommendations on monetary policy in the nation, but it has no policy-making power.

Thrift Institution Advisory Council. Its purpose is to offer information and views on the special needs of thrifts. Group is composed of representatives from S & L's, savings banks, and credit unions.

Academic Consultants. This organization provides a forum for the exchange of views between the Board and members of the academic community in economics and banking. Meetings are held in Washington three to four times a year.

Member Banks of the Federal Reserve System

NUMBER AND QUALIFICATIONS FOR MEMBER BANKS

There are 5,245 member banks in the Federal Reserve System, of which 4,198 are National Banks and 1,047 are State Banks. In 1989 there were 13,100 banks in the United States.

Federally chartered banks (National Banks) must be members of the Federal Reserve, and state-chartered banks may choose to be members if they qualify.

HOW MEMBER BANKS CAPITALIZE FEDERAL RESERVE BANKS

Member banks of each Federal Reserve region capitalize the Fed Bank by pledging up to 6 percent of their capital to buy stock in that bank. (Only about 3 percent has been required to date.) Member banks receive 6 percent interest on the stock.

Reserves of member banks are kept with the regional Fed Bank or in the vaults of the member banks. The reserves must meet legal standards daily. Twelve percent reserves is the most-used figure now, meaning that reserves must equal 12 percent of the demand deposits of the banks. Savings deposits require smaller reserves, usually 3 percent. No interest is paid on reserves. Although member banks of a regional Federal Reserve Bank technically own it, they do not control it, and they have only advisory powers with respect to policy. Ultimate control of the regional Federal Reserve Banks rests with the Board of Governors.

The federal government does not own the Federal Reserve Banks, nor can it control them. While the president usually likes for the Federal Reserve chairman to agree with his monetary policy, it is not compulsory. Moral suasion is often used by the president and by Congress to get the Federal Reserve chairman to support a particular monetary policy, but Fed independence remains.

Although member banks of the Fed comprise only about two-fifths of the commercial banks in the United States, the Fed exerts indirectly as much influence over nonmembers as it exerts directly over members.

Conclusion to the Federal Reserve System

Monetary policy in the United States has been more stable since the Federal Reserve Banking System was organized. However, the Fed is not loved by all politicians or bankers. Although the Fed is a creation of Congress, it is not owned or controlled by Congress, nor by any Administration. Since both would like to control it, this often causes problems.

It is my opinion that dissatisfaction with the Fed will grow in the next decade as the federal government becomes more powerful and programs more socialistic. Therefore, I predict that by the year 2005 will have a third Bank of the United States. As with the other two, it will be funded partly by the federal government and partly by private capital. The federal government will have more control over the bank, and this will create a central bank for the country structured more like the other central banks of the world.

Important Addresses

The addresses below will open to all managers or other interested people anywhere in the world a gold mine of information on the Federal Reserve Banking System of the United States. Much of the information is without cost, but there is a small charge for some publications.

Board of Governors of the Federal Reserve System
Publications Services
MS-138
Washington, DC 20551
Telephone number: (202) 452-3244

Federal Reserve Bank of Boston
Public Services Dept.
P.O. Box 2076
Boston, MA 02106-2076
Telephone number: (617) 973-3459

Federal Reserve Bank of Cleveland
Public Affairs Dept.
P.O. Box 6387
Cleveland, OH 44101-1387
Telephone number: (216) 579-3079

Federal Reserve Bank of Atlanta
Public Information Dept.
104 Marietta Street, N.W.
Atlanta, GA 30303-2713
Telephone number: (404) 521-8788

Federal Reserve Bank of Chicago
Public Information Center
230 South LaSalle Street
P.O. Box 834
Chicago, IL 60690
Telephone number: (312) 322-5111

Federal Reserve Bank of Dallas
Public Affairs Department
Station K
Dallas, TX 75222
Telephone number: (214) 651-6289, or 6266

Federal Reserve Bank of Kansas City
Public Affairs Dept.
925 Grand Avenue
Kansas City, MO 64198
Telephone number: (816) 881-2402

Federal Reserve Bank of New York
Public Information Dept.
33 Liberty Street
New York, New York 10045
Telephone number: (212) 720-6134

Federal Reserve Bank of Richmond
Public Services Dept.
P.O. Box 27622
Richmond, VA 23261
Telephone number: (804) 697-8109

Federal Reserve Bank of San Francisco
Public Information Dept.
P.O. Box 7702
San Francisco, CA 94120
Telephone number: (415) 974-2163

Federal Reserve Bank of Minneapolis
Public Affairs
250 Marquette Avenue
Minneapolis, MN 55480
Telephone number: (612) 340-2446

Federal Reserve Bank of Philadelphia
Public Information Dept.
P.O. Box 66
Philadelphia, PA 19105
Telephone number: (215) 574-6115

Federal Reserve Bank of St. Louis
Public Information Office
P.O. Box 442
St. Louis, MO 63166
Telephone number: (314) 444-8444, Ex. 545

Sources of Information: The Board of Governors of the Federal Reserve System and the twelve regional Federal Reserve Banks. Three publications have been particularly helpful: "Federal Reserve System: Public Information Materials," Issue 10, 1990-1991; "Historical Beginnings . . . The Federal Reserve," published by the Federal Reserve Bank of Boston.

Appendix to the Federal Reserve Banking System

After the Depression "bank holiday" in late 1932 and 1933, when all the commercial banks in the country were closed for over nine months, Congress decided that the banking system needed to be shored up against such events in the future.

Congress therefore passed the Banking Act of June 16, 1933, which established the Federal Deposit Insurance Corporation. The FDIC's major task was to insure commercial bank depositors against loss in the event of economic problems that might cause runs on the banks. The first insurance covered $2,500, and this gradually rose until currently it covers $100,000 per account. The FDIC is also empowered to examine banks, to counsel weak banks, to encourage the merger or sale of weak banks, to close banks that are essentially insolvent, and to pay off the claims against such banks.

With the failure of more than 700 banks in the last decade, the Federal Deposit Insurance Corporation has been busy settling claims. The current problem with savings and loan institutions and the FSLIC (the savings and loan equivalent of the FDIC) and mounting problems for the FDIC has brought renewed scrutiny to the size of such insurance. It is probable that the $100,000 insurance limit per account will be changed. Some suggest that accounts should be insured up to a given amount, with the client permitted to buy insurance on the deposits over that figure.

The FDIC collects premiums from all participating banks. (All banks that are members of the Fed must belong to FDIC, and most other banks choose to.) The FDIC invests these funds and holds them for use when they are needed. The government does not contribute to the fund, but the fund is allowed by law to borrow up to $3 billion from the Department of the Treasury in times of emergency.

Boundaries of Federal Reserve Districts and Their Branch Territories

1–12 Federal Reserve Districts
--- Boundaries of Federal Reserve Branch Territories
★ Board of Governors/Washington, D.C.
■ Federal Reserve Bank Cities
● Federal Reserve Branch Cities
▲ *Regional Check Processing Offices*
✕ *Culpeper Communications and Records Center*

Source: Board of Governors of the Federal Reserve System.

The Federal Reserve System

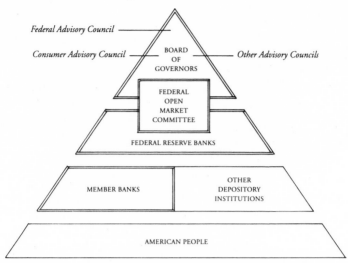

The System's formal organization is outlined with a double line.

World Securities and Stock Exchanges

Argentina

Bolsa de Commercio de Buenos Aries
Sarmiento 299
Buenos Aires 1353

Australia

Stock Exchange of Adelaide
55 Exchange Place
Adelaide, 5001 S.A.

Brisbane Stock Exchange
Network House
344 Queen Street
Brisbane, 4001, Queensland

Stock Exchange of Melbourne
351 Collins Street
Melbourne, 3301 Victoria

Stock Exchange of Perth
68 St. George's Terrace
Perth, 6001 W.A.

Sydney Futures Exchange
13-15 O'Connell Street
Sydney, N.S.W. 2000

Sydney Stock Exchange
Australia Square
Sydney, N.S.W. 2000

Austria

Wiener Boersekammer
Wipplingerstrasse 34
A-1011 Wien, 1

Belgium

Fondsen-En Wisselbeurs Van Antwerpen
Korte Klarenstraat 1
2000 Antwerpen

Bourse de Bruxelles
Palais de la Bourse
1000 Bruxelles

Fondsen-Ed Wisselbeurs Van Gent
Kouter, 29
9000 Gent

Bourse de Fonds Publics de Liege
Boulevard D'Avroy, 3/022
4000 Liege

Brazil

Bolsa de Valores do Rio de Janiero
Praca xv de Novembro 20
Rio de Janiero RJ
Bolsa de Valores de Sao Paulo
Rua Alvares Penteado No. 151-60 Andar
01012 Sao Paolo, SP

Canada

Alberta Stock Exchange
300 5th Avenue, S.W.
Calgary, Alberta T2P 3C4
(403) 262-7791

Montreal Exchange
Tour de la Bourse
800 Victoria Square
Montreal, Quebec H4Z 1A9
(514) 871-2424

Toronto Futures Exchange
Toronto Stock Exchange
The Exchange Tower
2 First Canadian Place
Toronto, Ontario M5X 1J2
(416) 947-4700

Vancouver Stock Exchange
Stock Exchange Tower
609 Granville Street
Vancouver, British Columbia V7Y 1H1
(604) 689-3334

Winnipeg Commodity Exchange
500 Commodity Exchange Tower
360 Main Street
Winnipeg, Manitoba R3B 0V3
(204) 942-8431

Winnipeg Stock Exchange
167 Lombard Avenue
Winnipeg, Manitoba R3B 0V3
(204) 942-8431

Chile

Bolsa de Commercio de Santiago
Casilla 123-D
Santiago

China, Republic of (Taiwan)

Taiwan Stock Exchange
8-10th Floor, City Building
85 Yen-Ping South Road
Taipei

Colombia

Bolsa de Bogota
Carrera 8, 13-82 Piso 8
Bogota

Denmark

Kobenhavns Fondsbors
6 Nikolaj Plads
DK-1007 Copenhagen

Ecuador

Bolsa de Valores de Quito
Avenue Rio Amazonas 540 y Jeronimo
Carrion, Piso 8
Apartado Postal 3772
Quito

Egypt

Cairo Stock Exchange
4-A Cherifein Street
Cairo

Finland

Helsingin Arvopaperiporssi
Fabianinkatu 14
001000 Helsinki 10

France

Bourse de Bordeaux
Palais de la Bourse
13-Bordeaux

Bourse de Lille
68 Palais Bourse
Place du Theatre
59-Lille

Bourse de Lyon
Palais du Commerce
Place de la Bourse
Marseille

Bourse de Nancy
40 rue Henri Poincare
54000 Nancy

Bourse de Nantes
Palaise de la Bourse
Place du Commerce
44-Nantes

Bourse de Paris
4, Place de la Bourse
75080 Paris

Paris Commodity Exchange
Bourse de Commerce
2, rue de Viarmes B.P. 53/01
75040 Paris

Great Britain

Belfast Stock Exchange
Northern Bank House
10 High Street
Belfast BRI 2BP

London Commodity Exchange
Cereal House, 58 Mark Lane
London EC3R 7NE

London International Financial Futures
Exchange (LIFFE)
Royal Exchange
London EC3

London Stock Exchange
Old Broad Street
London EC2N IHP

Midlands & Western Stock Exchange
Margaret Street
Birmingham B3 3JI

Northern Stock Exchange
2/6 Norfolk Street
Manchester M2 IDS

Provincial Stock Exchange
Room 402, 4th Floor
London EC2N IHP

Scottish Stock Exchange
Stock Exchange House
69 St. George's Place
Glasgow G2 IBU & 12 Dublin Street
Edinburgh EHI 3PP

Greece

Athens Stock Exchange
10 Sophocleous Street
Athens 121

Hong Kong

Hong Kong Futures Exchange
Hong Kong Stock Exchange
Exchange Square
GPO Box 8888

India

Bombay Stock Exchange
Dalal Street
Fort, Bombay 400001

Calcutta Stock Exchange Association
7, Lyons Range
Calcutta 700001

Delhi Stock Exchange Association
3 & 4/4B Asaf Ali Road
New Delhi 110002

Madras Stock Exchange
Stock Exchange Building
11 Second Line Beach
Madras 600001

Indonesia

Stock Exchange of Indonesia
Perserikatan Perdagangan
Uang dan Efek-Efek
P.O. Box 1224/Dak
Jakarta-Kota

Ireland

Irish Stock Exchange
28 Anglesea Street
Dublin 2

Israel

Tel Aviv Stock Exchange
113 Allenby Road

Tel-Aviv 65127

Italy

Borsa Valori di Bologna
Piazza della Costituzione, 8
Palazzo degli Affair
40100 Bologna

Borsa Valori de Firenze
Piazza Mentana, 2
50122 Firenze

Borsa Valori di Genova
Via G. Boccardo, 1
16121 Genova

Borsa Valori di Milano
Piazza delgi Affari, 6
20123 Milano

Borsa Valori di Napoli
Via S. Aspreno, 2
80133 Napoli

Borsa Valori di Palermo
Via E. Amari, 11
90139 Palermo

Borsa Valori di Roma
Via de'Burro, 147
00186 Roma

Borsa Valori di Torino
Via S. Francesco de Paola, 28
10123 Torino

Borsa Valori de Trieste
Via Cassa di Risparmio, 2
34100 Trieste

Borsa Valori di Venezia
Via XXII Marzo, 2034
30124 Venezia

Jamaica

Jamaica Stock Exchange
Bank of Jamaica Tower
P.O. Box 621
Nethersole Place, Kingston

Japan

Fukuoka Stock Exchange
2-14-2 Tenjin, Chuohku
Fukuokashi

Hiroshima Stock Exchange
14-18 Ginzancho
Hiroshimashi

Kyoto Stock Exchange
66 Tateuri Nishimachi
Tohdohin Higashihairu
Shijohdohri, Shimokyoku
Kyoto

Nagoya Stock Exchange
3-3-17 Sakae, Naka-ku
Nagoyashi

Niigata Securities Exchange
1245 Hachibancho
Kamiohkawamaedohri
Niigatashi

Osaka Securities Exchange
Kitahama 2-chome
Higashi-Ku
Osaka 541

Sapporo Stock Exchange
5-141 Nishi
Minami Ichijoh, Choku
Sappororshi

Tokyo Stock Exchange
2-1-1 Nihombashi-Kayaba-cho
Chuo-ku, Tokyo, 103

Kenya

Nairobi Stock Exchange
Stanbank House
Moi Avenue
P.O. Box 43633
Nairobi

Luxembourg

Societe de la Bourse de Luxembourg
11, avenue de la Porte-Neuve
2227 Luxembourg

Malaysia

Kuala Lumpur Stock Exchange
4th Floor Bock C, Damansara Centre
Damansara Heights
Kuala Lumpur 23-04

Mexico

Bolsa Mexicana de Valores
Uraguay #68
Mexico I.D.F.

Bolsa de Valores de Monterrey
Escobedo Sur #733
Monterrey, N.L.

Morocco

Bourse des Valeurs de Casablanca
Chamber of Commerce Building
98 Boulevard Mohamed V
Casablanca

Netherlands

Amsterdam Stock Exchange
Beursplein 5, P.O. Box 19163
1000 GD Amsterdam

European Options Exchange
DAM 21
1012 JS Amsterdam

New Zealand

Auckland Stock Exchange
C.M.L. Centre
Queen Street
Auckland 1.

Christchurch Invercargill Stock Exchange
128 Oxford Terrace
P.O. Box 639
Christchurch

Dunedin Stock Exchange
Queens Building
109 Princess Street
P.O. Box 483
Dunedin c.1

Wellington Stock Exchange
Government Life Insurance Building
Brandon Street
P.O. Box 767
Wellington c.1

Nigeria

Nigerian Stock Exchange
NIBD House, 15th Floor
63/71, Broad Street
P.O. Box 2457
Lagos

Norway

Aalesunds Bors
Roysegate 14
6001 Aalesund

Bergens Bors
Olav Kyrresgate 11
Postboks 832
5000 Bergen

Fredrikstad Bors
Nygaardsgaten 5
Fredrikstad

Oslo Bors
Tollubugaten 2
Oslo 1

Trondheim Bors
Dronningensgt
Trondheim

Pakistan

Karachi Stock Exchange
Stock Exchange Road
Karachi 2

Lahore Stock Exchange
17 Bank Square
Lahore

Peru

Bolsa de Valores de Lima
Jiron Antonio Miro Quesada 265
Apartado 1538
Lima 100

Philippines

Makati Stock Exchange
Makati Stock Exchange Building
Ayala Avenue
Makati, Metro Manila

Manila Stock Exchange
Manila Stock Exchange Building
Prensa Street, Cor.Muelle de la Industria
Binondo, Manila

Metropolitan Stock Exchange
Padilla Arcade, 2nd floor
Greenhills Commercial Center
San Juan, Metro Manila

Portugal

Bolsa de Valores de Losboa
Praca do Commercio
Torreao Oriental
Lisboa

Singapore

Stock Exchange of Singapore
702/1403, Hong Leong Building
Raffles Quay
Singapore 0104

Singapore International Monetary Exchange
24 Raffles Place
29-04 Clifford Centre
Singapore 0104

South Africa

Johannesburg Stock Exchange
P.O. Box 1174
Diagonal Street
Johannesburg, 2000

South Korea

Korea Stock Exchange
1-116 Yoido-Dong
Youngdeungpo-Ku
Seoul

Spain

Bolsa de Barcelona
Paseo Isabel 11, Consulado 2
Barcelona 3

Bolsa de Bilbao
Jose Maria Olabarri 1
Bilbao 1

Bolsa de Commercio de Madrid
Plaza de la Lealtad 1
Madrid 14

Bolsa Oficial de Commercio de Balencia
Calle Pascual y Genis, 19
Valencia

Sri Lanka

Colombo Brokers' Association
P.O. Box 101
59 Janadipathi Mawatha
Colombo 1

Sweden

Stockholms Fondbors
Box 1256
S-111 82 Stockholm

Switzerland

Borsenkammer des Kantons Basel-Stadt
Freie Strasse 3
CH-4001 Basel

Berner Borsenverein
Aabergergasse 30
CH-3011 Bern

Chambre de la Bourse De Geneve
10, rue Peitot
Case Postale 228
1211 Geneve

Bourse de Lousanne
Societe de Banque Suisse
16, Place St-Francois

Bourse de Neuchatel
Coq d'Inde 24
2000 Neuchatel

Effktenborsenverein Zurich
Bleicherweg 5
Postfach
8021 Zurich

Thailand

Securities Exchange of Thailand
Siam Center, 4th Floor
965 Rama 1 Road
Bangkok, Metropolis 5

United States

American Stock Exchange
AMEX Commodities Corporation
86 Trinity Place
New York, NY 10006
(212) 306-1000

Boston Stock Exchange
One Boston Place
Boston, MA 02108
(617) 723-9500

Chicago Board of Trade
LaSalle at Jackson
Chicago, IL 60604
(312) 435-3500

Chicago Board Options Exchange
LaSalle at Van Buren
Chicago, IL 60605
(312) 786-5600

Chicago Mercantile Exchange
International Monetary Market
30 South Wacker Drive
Chicago, IL 60606
(312) 930-1000, (800) 843-6372

Chicago Rice and Cotton Exchange
444 West Jackson Boulevard
Chicago, IL 60606
(312) 341-3078

Cincinnati Stock Exchange
205 Dixie Terminal Building
Cincinnati, OH 45202
(513) 621-1410

Coffee, Sugar and Cocoa Exchange
4 World Trade Center
New York, NY 10048
(212) 938-2800

Commodity Exchange, Inc. (COMEX)
4 World Trade Center
New York, NY 10048

Intermountain Stock Exchange
373 South Main Street
Salt Lake City, UT 84111
(801) 363-2531

Kansas City Board of Trade
4800 Main Street
Kansas City, MO 64112
(816) 753-7500

Midamerica Commodity Exchange
444 West Jackson Boulevard
Chicago, IL 60606
(312) 341-3000

Midwest Stock Exchange
440 South LaSalle Street
Chicago, IL 60605
(312) 663-2222

Minneapolis Grain Exchange
150 Grain Exchange Building
Minneapolis, MN 55415
(612) 338-6212

New York Cotton Exchange
4 World Trade Center
New York, NY 10048
(212) 938-2702

New York Futures Exchange
20 Broad Street
New York, NY 10005
(212) 656-4949, (800) 221-7722

New York Mercantile Exchange
4 World Trade Center
New York, NY 10005
(212) 938-2222

New York Stock Exchange
11 Wall Street
New York, NY 10005
(212) 656-3000

Pacific Stock Exchange
301 Pine Street
San Francisco, CA 94104
(415) 393-4000

Philadelphia Stock Exchange
Philadelphia Board of Trade
1900 Market Street
Philadelphia, PA 19103
(215) 496-5000

Spokane Stock Exchange
225 Peyton Building
Spokane, WA 99201
(509) 624-4632

Germany

Berliner Wertpapierbörse
1000 Berlin 12
Hardenbergstrasse 16-18

Rheinisch-Westfalische Börse zu Dusseldorf
4000 Dusseldorf
Ernst-Schnieder-Platz 1

Frankfurter Wertpapierbörse
Börsenplatz 6
6000 Frankfurt am Main 1

Hanseatische Wertpapierbörse Hamburg
2000 Hamburg 11
Adolphsplatz, Börse, Zimmer 151

Bayerische Börse in München
8000 Munchen 2
Llenbackplatz 2a

VIII Short Listing of Typical Trade Associations

Trade associations are established to promote a certain product or products or a certain service or services. Usually, such an association will be composed of several companies in the same industry with mutual interests. Some, but not all, associations do their promotional work on a worldwide basis.

This listing was adapted from the enormous wealth of information in the *Encyclopedia of Associations,* 1991, 25th Edition, Volume 1, edited by Deborah Burek. Copyright (c) 1990 by Gale Research, Inc. Reproduced by permission of the publisher. Gale Research, Inc., is located at 835 Penobscot Building, 645 Griswold Street, Detroit, MI 48226. This organization can provide more information on foreign and domestic trade associations.

American Apparel Manufacturers Association (AAMA)
2500 Wilson Blvd., Suite 301
Arlington, VA 22201
Telephone number: (703) 524-1864

Founded in 1962, this organization is the result of the uniting of several apparel organizations. It is a resource depository for virtually any type of information on the apparel business as a whole. Equally accessible to foreign and domestic inquiries. It publishes the *AAMA Newsletter,* which appears monthly, and other publications.

American Cloak and Suit Manufacturers Association (ACSMA)
450 Seventh Avenue
New York, NY 10123
Telephone number: (212) 244-7300

The American Cloak and Suit Manufacturers Association was founded in 1919 for contractors producing women's coats and suits for wholesalers and other manufacturers.

American Fur Industry (AFI)
363 7th Avenue, 7th Floor
New York, NY 10001
Telephone number: (212) 564-5133

The American Fur Industry was founded 1958 for fur manufacturers and others involved in the fur industry. Its aim is to promote the fur industry and to foster higher standards. It publishes *American Fur Industry* a quarterly newsletter.

American Fur Merchants' Association (AFMA)
363 7TH Avenue
New York, NY 10001
Telephone number: (212) 736-9200

The American Fur Merchants' Association was founded in 1900. It serves dealers, brokers, silk and supply houses, banks, factories, auction companies, wholesalers, importers and exporters of furs. It also publishes a periodic bulletin.

Association of Rain Apparel Contractors (ARAC)
225 W. 39th St.
New York, NY 10018
Telephone number: (212) 819-1011

The Association of Rain Apparel was founded in 1948. It represents manufacturers of ladies' outwear and rainwear.

American Association of Exporters and Importers (Foreign Trade) (AAEI)
11 W. 42nd Street

New York, NY 10036
Telephone number: (212) 944-2230

The American Association of Exporters and Importers was founded in 1921. It engages in all aspects of international trade and serves the people who are related to it, domestic and foreign. In addition, it holds seminars and serves as a general clearinghouse for information for all concerned with international trade. The AAEI's publications include the AAEI Membership Directory and periodic bulletins, as well as a broad range of import-export–related documents.

American League for Exports and Security Assistance
(Foreign Trade) (ALESA)
122 C Street, N.W., Suite 740
Washington, DC 20001
Telephone number: (202) 783-0051

The American League for Exports and Security Assistance was founded in 1976. It supports and encourages the sale of American defense products abroad, in agreement with foreign policy, security, and the economic goals of the nation. It also works for the development and implementation of a national export policy and tries to insure favorable treatment for exports in all pertinent legislation and national priorities.

American Association of International Executives (Foreign Trade) (ASIE)
c/o Anthony M. Swartz
Dublin Hall, Suite 419
1777 Walton Road
Blue Bell, PA 19422
Telephone number: (215) 643-3040

The American Association of International Executives was founded in 1964. It represents persons holding positions in international trade who have qualified for membership through ASIE examinations as Certified Documentary Specialists (CDS), Certified International Executive (EIE-EM), or Experienced International Executive (EIE-EM); other classes of membership do not require examination. The ASIE sponsors seminars on key foreign trade subjects and other topics. Its publications include:

American Society of International Executives—Roster, which appears annually, and the *ASIE Bulletin,* which appears bimonthly. The ASIE also publishes a column in *Import/Export Management* magazine.

American Traders Group (ATG)
P.O. Box 167
Annandale, VA 22003
Telephone number: (703) 256-2386

The American Traders Group was founded in 1983. It supports exporters of U.S. goods and good trade relations between nations. The ATG specializes in the supply and operation of supermarket operations and ventures. Its publications include *Validated Export Price Lists,* which appears quarterly.

American West Overseas Association (AWOA)
W. R. Diekroeger, Exec. Dir.
19451 195th Place
Hudson, CO 80642
Telephone number: (303) 536-4206

American West Overseas Association represents manufacturers, wholesalers, and sales representatives engaged in the export of American Western wear, riding equipment, and other related products. It conducts publicity and public-relations programs aimed at foreign consumer and trade publications. It also acts as a liaison with commercial officers in U.S. embassies and the U.S. Department of Commerce. It publishes an export letter for its membership.

American Pulpwood Association (Forest Industries) (APA)
1025 Vermont Avenue, N.W., Suite 1020
Washington, DC 20005
Telephone number: (202) 347-2900

The American Pulpwood Association is concerned with all matters pertaining to forestry and the pulpwood industry, both domestic and foreign. Its concerns include new tree-growing methods and machinery in growing, protecting, harvesting, and utilizing pulpwood. It also monitors labor training and safety. The APA is a depository of a gold mine of information in its field. It is also accessible to individuals or firms, either domestic or foreign. It produces many publications on the subject of forestry and specifically on the pulpwood industry.

Association of American Wood Pulp Importers (AAWPI)
c/o Barry Miller
Central National Gottesman, Inc.
100 Park Avenue
New York, NY 10017
Telephone number: (212) 532-7300

The Association of American Wood Pulp Importers was founded in 1911. It represents companies importing pulpwood. It seeks to establish trade customs and rules for wood pulp import and sales.

American Association of Small Research Companies (AASRC)
c/o Lawrence Levy, President
222 Third Street, Suite 3150
Cambridge, MA 02142
Telephone number: (617) 491-7906

The American Association of Small Research Companies was founded in 1972. Members are small research and development companies. The AASRC seeks to further the welfare of high technology and small research and development companies. It publishes a periodic newsletter and brochures.

American Business Association (ABA)
292 Madison Avenue
New York, NY 10017
Telephone number: (212) 949-5900

The American Business Association was founded in 1972. It represents owners of businesses and individuals in executive, managerial, and sales capacities. It provides financial services to business professionals. Its services include group travel packages, insurance, loans, and discount car rentals. It publishes the *ABA Business Brief,* which appears quarterly.

American Business Women's Association (ABWA)
9100 Ward Parkway
P.O. Box 8728
Kansas City, MO 64114
Telephone number: (816) 361-6621

The American Business Women's Association was founded in 1949 and has one hundred thousand members. The association is composed of women business owners, and also business women in all areas of the national economy. It has a strong educational bent, helping to prepare women for leadership positions in business. The ABWA publishes *Connect,* which appears quarterly and a newsletter.

American Society of Professional and Executive Women (ASPEW)
1429 Walnut Street
Philadelphia, PA 19102
Telephone number: (215) 563-4415

The American Society of Professional and Executive Women was founded in 1979 and has 25,200 members. Its purpose is to promote, through practical information and benefits, a positive attitudinal environment for career women involved in all areas of American enterprise. It also conducts seminars and provides discount library services and executive recruitment. The ASPEW publishes *Successful Women,* which appears bimonthly.

Coalition to Promote America's Trade (CPTA)
1101 15th St., N.W., Suite 205
Washington, DC 20005
Telephone number: (202) 785-3060

The Coalition to Promote America's Trade was founded in 1984. It is primarily a lobbying group united to lobby against legislation that would broaden the definition of domestic subsidies to include final products containing imported natural resources. If legislation were to be changed to encompass such products, those products would become subject to U.S. trade duty laws, from which they are currently exempt. The CPTA publishes lobbying materials.

Committee on Fair Trade with China (CFTC)
c/o Edward Furia
P.O. Box 288
Medina, WA 98039
Telephone number: (206) 455-5650

An organization that lobbies the U.S. Congress to have China classified as having a "planned market economy" in the U.S. in order to provide a "pragmatic nonideological reason" for China to continue economic reform.

Committee for Production Sharing (CPS)
1629 K St., N.W.
Washington, DC 20007
Telephone number: (202) 296-3232

The Committee for Production Sharing was founded in 1986. Its goal is to enhance U.S. competitiveness through combining technology and content in partnership with developing country labor and factor cost.

Committee for Small Business Exports (COSBE)
P.O. Box 6
Aspen, CO 81612
Telephone number: (303) 925-7567

The Committee for Small Business Exports was founded in 1979, and it has one hundred members. It represents owners and officers of small manufacturing, trading, and consulting companies involved in exports and lobbies in order to improve incentives and reduce financial and legal impediments surrounding small companies involved in exports. It publishes a periodic newsletter.

Council for Export Trading Companies (CETC)
1225 Connecticut Ave., N.W., Suite 415
Washington, DC, 20036
Telephone number: (202) 861-4705

The Council for Export Trading Companies was founded in 1982. It works primarily with small- to medium-sized companies and their exports through the formation of export trading companies. (Export trading companies, or ETC's, are antitrust-exempt entities permitted by law to sell American goods and services abroad. The CETC lobbies Congress and various departments of the federal government. It publishes a periodic newsletter and periodic research reports.

Czechoslovak-U.S. Economic Council (CUSEC)
c/o U.S. Chamber of Commerce
1615 H Street, N.W.
Washington, DC, 20062
Telephone number: (202) 463-5482
Fax number: (202) 463-3114
Telex number: 248302

The Czechoslovak-U.S. Economic Council was founded in 1975 and has sixty members. It consists of executives of firms having significant actual or potential trade involvement with Czechoslovakia. It seeks to establish a channel of direct communications between key commercial decision makers of the United States and Czechoslovakia.

Emergency Committee for American Trade (ECAT)
1211 Connecticut Ave., N.W., Suite 801
Washington, DC 200036
Telephone number: (202) 659-5147

The Emergency Committee for American Trade was founded in 1967 and has sixty-five members. It is made up of major U.S. corporations and supports liberal international trade and investment policies and opposes trade and investment restricting legislation, such as import quotas and capital controls. It publishes periodic membership lists.

Finance Credit and International Business
    and National Association of Credit Management (FCIB/NACM)
520 Eighth Avenue
New York, NY 10018
Telephone number: (212) 947-5368

The Finance Credit and International Business and National Association of Credit Management was founded in 1919 and has one thousand members. It works with companies and financial institutions in the area of international credit. It also does periodic surveys and makes credit reports on various foreign companies and countries. FCIB/NAMC publishes *FCIB Country Credit Report,* a periodic international bulletin, which appears monthly, and other publications.

Federation of International Trade Associations (FITA)
1851 Alexander Bell Drive
Reston, VA 22091
Telephone number: (703) 391-6106

The Federation of International Trade Associations was founded in 1985 and has 150 members. It conducts conferences and seminars on international trade and maintains a resource library. It publishes an annual membership directory and periodic newsletters.

Forest Industries Telecommunications (FIT)
871 Country Club Road, Suite A
Eugene, OR 97401
Telephone number: (503) 485-8441

Forest Industries Telecommunications was founded in 1947 and has 1,800 members. It represents the forest products industry in communications matters before the Federal Communications Commission. The FIT publishes a quarterly magazine.

Forest Industries Council (FIC)
1250 Connecticut Ave., N.W., Suite 320
Washington, DC 20036
Telephone number: (202) 463-2460

The Forest Industries Council was founded in 1943 and has nine members. It is the policy-coordinating organization of representatives of paper, pulp, pulpwood, and lumber industries. It publishes an annual report/summary of proceedings.

Grain Equipment Manufacturers Council
410 N. Michigan Avenue
Chicago, IL 60611
Telephone number: (312) 321-1470

The Grain Equipment Manufacturers Council was founded in 1986 and has thirty members. It is composed of several former associations representing such farm equipment as grain bins, portable augers, and elevators.

Greenhouse Suppliers Association (GSA)
224 Maple Avenue
Bird In Hand, PA 17505
Telephone number: (717) 397-4271

The Greenhouse Suppliers Association was founded in 1980 and has ten members. It is composed of companies supplying equipment and other supplies to greenhouses.

Group of 33
1225 19th Street, N.W., Suite 600
Washington, DC 20036
Telephone number: (202) 466-7720

The Group of 33 was founded in 1978 and has thirty-three members. It is an ad hoc labor-industry trade coalition of twenty-eight industry trade associations and labor unions organized to advocate changes in import trade remedy laws. It focuses on the multilateral trade negotiations, subsidies code, and trade regulations.

Hardwood Research Council (HRC)
P.O. Box 34518
Memphis, TN 38184
Telephone number: (901) 377-1824

The Hardwood Research Council was founded in 1953 and has 1,300 members. It works in every area of the growing of, harvesting of, and utilization of hardwood in the United States and abroad. It also researches forestry practices, lobbies legislatures in the United States and Canada and does public-relations work on behalf of this arm of the forestry industry. It publishes *Hardwood Forestry Business*, which appears monthly.

International Trade Club of Chicago (ITCC)
203 N. Wabash Ave., Suite 1102

Chicago, IL 60601
Telephone number: (312) 368-9197

The International Trade Club of Chicago was founded in 1919 and has five hundred members. It is made up of individuals who are involved in international export and import operations for their firms and representatives of allied service fields. It seeks to expand international trade by eliminating the barriers to such trade. Hosts of other education and public-relations activities. The ITCC publishes a monthly periodical, *INTERCOM,* an association newsletter for business executives.

International Trade Council (ITC)
1900 Mt. Vernon Avenue
Alexandria, VA 22301
Telephone number: (703) 548-1234

The International Trade Council was founded in 1976 and has 850 members. It is made up of companies and organizations that import and export products, commodities, and services in three hundred major industries, including agricultural commodities, livestock, food, farm implements, and food machinery, and agencies dealing with health and medicine, housing, energy, communications, transportation, forestry, water, and sanitation. It seeks to promote free trade. The ITC has many publications, including an annual membership directory, a newsletter, weekly research reports, etc.

International Traders Association (IT)
c/o The Mellinger Company
6100 Variel Ave.
Woodland Hills, CA 91367
Telephone number: (818) 884-4400

The International Traders Association was founded in 1947 and has fifty-three thousand members. It represents individuals and firms engaged in the import/export business and/or mail order business. Its objectives are to promote world trade and international business between members and to educate foreign suppliers, manufacturers, and governments on the traders' role in the marketplace through publications and personal visits.

Its publications include: *Inside Mail Order,* which appears monthly, *Trade Agreement Catalogs Book,* which is published semiannually, *Trade Opportunities Magazine,* which is published monthly, and others.

Industrial Chemical Research Association (ICRA)
1811 Monroe Street
Dearborn, MI 48124
Telephone number: (313) 563-0360

The Industrial Chemical Research Association was founded in 1985 and has 3,251 members. It represents manufacturers, marketers, researchers, formulators, salesmen, and suppliers of industrial chemical products. It publishes the *Industrial Chemical Research Association,* a newsletter that appears periodically.

Industrial Specialty Chemical Association (ISCA)
c/o Sigmund Domanski
1520 Locust Street, 5th.Floor
Philadelphia, PA 19102
Telephone number: (215) 546-9608

The Industrial Specialty Chemical Association was founded in 1983 and has thirty members. It represents manufacturers of specialty chemicals for industrial sale. It plans to publish a newsletter soon.

India Engineering Export Promotion Council (EEPC)
333 N. Michigan Avenue, Suite 2014
Chicago, IL 60601
Telephone number: (312) 236-2162
Telex: 254638 EEPCCGO

The India Engineering Export Promotion Council has six thousand members. It represents manufacturers of engineering products in India. It aids members in sales and product promotion, marketing research, advertising, and importation of engineering products in the Canadian and American markets. It also provides services to importers in the United States on the selection and choice of products from India. It publishes the *Directory of Indian Engineering Exporters,* which appears triennially, and *Indian Engineering Exporter,* which is published quarterly.

Inland International Trade Association (IITA)
P.O. Box 417418
Sacramento, CA 95841
Telephone number: (916) 334-4161

The Inland International Trade Association was founded in 1979 and has one hundred members. It represents individuals and corporations involved in or interested in the import/export business in the Northern California and Nevada area, though memberships are not restricted to that area.

Industrial and Construction Equipment Division (ICED)
c/o Tim Metzger
Farm & Industrial Equipment Institute
410 Michigan Ave.
Chicago, IL 60611
Telephone number: (312) 321-1470

The Industrial and Construction Equipment Division was founded in 1959 and has 115 members. It represents manufacturers of industrial wheel tractors, log-skidders, backhoes and loaders, etc.

International Silo Association (ISO)
712 Broadway, Suite 605
Kansas City, MO 64105
Telephone number: (816) 421-4594

The International Silo Association was founded in 1907 and has fifty members. It represents manufacturers of silos, crop processing equipment and containers, and related storage structures for agricultural products. Its purpose is to extend the use of ensilage through education and research. Its publications include an annual membership directory and a bimonthly newsletter.

Irrigation Association (IA)
1911 N. Ft. Meyer Drive, Suite 1009
Arlington, VA 22209
Telephone number: (703) 524-1200

The Irrigation Association was founded in 1949 and has 1,100 members.

It represents manufacturers, wholesalers, and contractors of irrigation equipment. It is the primary organization in the field. It publishes a membership directory, research papers, technical papers, etc.

Milking Machine Manufacturers Council (MMMC)
410 N. Michigan Ave.
Chicago, IL 60611
Telephone number: (312) 321-1470

The Milking Machine Manufacturers Council is a council of the Farm and Industrial Equipment Institute. It publishes *The Modern Way to Efficient Milking*.

Metalworking Trade Association (MTA)
9300 Livingston Road
Ft. Washington, MD 20744
Telephone number: (301) 248-6200

The Metalworking Trade Association was founded in 1982 and has forty-six members. It represents thirty-three independent trade associations representing the metal parts industry and thirteen supporters of the industry. The MTA works to obtain governmental cooperation and action to assure fair trade between the United States and its world trading partners. It publishes a periodic bulletin and a periodic press release.

Master Furriers Guild of America (MFGA)
370 Seventh Ave., Suite 216
New York, NY 10001
Telephone number: (212) 244-8570

The Master Furriers Guild of America was founded in 1929 and has 825 members. It represents retailers of custom furs; associate members represent allied branches of the fur industry. It works to foster and maintain uniformity and equity in the customs and trade practices and ethical standards of advertising and selling in the retail branch of the fur industry. It publishes *The Master Furrier* six to nine times per year.

Men's Fashion Association of America (MFA)
240 Madison Avenue

Wantagh, NY 11793
Telephone number: (212) 833-5665

The Men's Fashion Association of America was founded in 1955 and has four hundred members. It represents textile mills, apparel manufacturers, yarn producers, converters, suppliers, mill and manufacturers' agents, and retailers of men's and boys' apparel.

National Association of Blouse Manufacturers (NAMB)
450 Seventh Ave., Room 2304
New York, NY 10123
Telephone number: (212) 563-6390

The National Association of Blouse Manufacturers was founded in 1933 and has 150 members. It represents manufacturers of women's blouses.

National Association of Fashion and Accessory Designers (NAFAD)
2180 E. 93rd St.
Cleveland, OH 44106
Telephone number: (216) 231-0375

The National Association of Fashion and Accessory Designers was founded in 1949 and has 240 members. It represents persons engaged in the field of fashion design and other allied fields. It fosters the development of the black fashion designer and encourages integration of members in all phases of the fashion industry through the extension of educational and economic opportunities. Its publications include an annual membership roster and a semiannual newsletter.

National Association of Hosiery Manufacturers (NAHM)
447 S. Sharon Amity Road
Charlotte, NC 28211
Telephone number: (704) 365-0913

The National Association of Hosiery Manufacturers was founded in 1905 and has three hundred members. It represents manufacturers who knit and otherwise process men's, women's, and children's hosiery. It develops standards in the field and sponsors annual National Hosiery

Week for public-relations purposes. It publishes *Annual Hosiery Statistics*, *Hosiery News*, which appears monthly, and others.

National Association of Men's Sportswear Buyers (NAMSB)
500 Fifth Avenue, Suite 1425
New York, NY 10110
Telephone number: (212) 391-8580

The National Association of Men's Sportwear Buyers was founded in 1953 and has one thousand members. It sponsors trade shows for buyers of clothes for men's wear stores. It also conducts media interviews to discuss men's wear and distributes fashion video tapes. The NAMSB publishes a monthly newsletter.

National Association of Milliners, Dressmakers, and Tailors
c/o Harlem Institute of Fashion
157 W. 126th St.
New York, NY 10027
Telephone number: (212) 666-1320

The National Association of Milliners, Dressmakers, and Tailors was founded in 1966 and has four hundred members. It represents designers, dressmakers, tailors, milliners, fashion commentators and coordinators, and others engaged in the fashion industry. Its publications the *Directory of Black Fashion Specialists*, which appears periodically, a newsletter, which appears monthly, and *Pride*, a semiannual magazine.

National Association of Uniform Manufacturers and Distributors
   (NAUMD)
1156 Avenue of the Americas
New York, NY 10036
Telephone number: (212) 869-0670

The National Association of Uniform Manufacturers and Distributors was founded in 1931 and has five hundred members. It represents manufacturers and distributors of military, police, post office, industrial, and other uniforms and uniform caps and embroidery houses and distributors; associate members are textile mills and fabric distributors. It publishes an association and industry newsletter.

National Sporting Goods Association (NSGA)
Lake Center Plaza Building
1699 Wall Street
Mt. Prospect, IL 60056
Telephone number: (312) 439-4000

The National Sporting Goods Association was founded in 1929 and has eight thousand members. It represents retailers, manufacturers, wholesalers, and importers of athletic equipment and sporting goods supplies. It provides a multiplicity of services for sporting goods businesses. It publishes *Sporting Goods Market,* which appears annually, research studies, and other publications.

National Customs Brokers and Forwarders Association of America
(NCBFAA)
One World Trade Center, Suite 1153
New York, NY 10048
Telephone number: (212) 432-0050

The National Customs Brokers and Forwarders Association of America was founded in 1897 and has five hundred members. It represents treasury-licensed customs brokers and FMC-licensed independent ocean freight forwarders, CNS-registered air cargo agents, and associate members in twenty-five foreign countries. Telecommunications services: Easy Link 6266720; Fax: (212)432-5709; Telex: 888259. Its publications include *NCBGFAA Bulletin,* which is published monthly, and periodic reports on legislation, regulation, and tax codes affecting the industry.

National Federation of Export Associations (NFEA)
1511 K St., Suite 825
Washington, DC 20005
Telephone number: (202) 347-0966

The National Federation of Export Associations was founded in 1984. It represents the National Association of Export Companies, the Overseas Sales and Marketing Association of America, the Export Managers Association of California, and the Florida Export and Import

Association. These associations, in turn, represent 850 trading and service companies. The NFEA publishes a quarterly newsletter.

National Foreign Trade Council (NFTC)
100 E. 42nd St.
New York, NY 10017
Telephone number: (212) 867-5630

The National Foreign Trade Council was founded in 1914 and has 550 members. It represents manufacturers, exporters, importers, foreign investors, banks, transportation lines, and insurance, communication, law, and publishing firms. The NFTC works to promote and protect American foreign trade and investment. Its publications include *NOTICIAS: Latin American Report,* which appears weekly, *Policy Declaration,* which appears annually, *Washington Report,* which appears periodically, and materials on laws, regulations, etc.

NCITD—The International Trade Facilitation Council
350 Broadway, Suite 205
New York, NY 10013
Telephone number: (212) 925-1400

NCITD—The International Trade Facilitation Council was founded in 1967 and has two hundred members. It represents exporters, importers, air and ocean carriers, banks, insurance underwriters, forwarders, custom brokers, port authorities, and communications/computer software service companies. It is dedicated to simplifying and improving international trade documentation and procedures, emphasizing electronic processing and exchange of trade data information. It has a research library and implementation brochures. The NCTID publishes an annual report (advertising is accepted).

National Electrical Manufacturers Association (NEMA)
2101 L Street, N.W.
Washington, DC 20037
Telephone number: (202) 457-8400

The National Electrical Manufacturers Association was founded in 1926 and has six hundred members. It represents companies that manufacture equipment used for the generation, transmission, distribution, control, and utilization of electric power. It publishes a periodic *Directory of Member Companies* and manuals, guidebooks, and other material on wiring, installing equipment, lighting, and standards.

National Electrical Manufacturers Representatives Association
   (NEMRA)
222 Westchester Ave.
White Plains, NY 10604
Telephone number: (914) 428-1307

The National Electrical Manufacturers Representatives Association was founded in 1969 and has 1,100 members and 41 regional groups. It represents electrical sales representatives and manufacturers who use independent representatives. It offers professional development programs in business management, sales training, and computer systems and sponsors educational and scholarship programs It publishes the *Annual Locator of Electrical Manufacturers' Representatives,* which appears every twelve to eighteen months, and periodic industry news.

National Rural Electric Cooperative Association (NRECA)
1800 Massachusetts Ave., N.W.
Washington, DC 20036
Telephone number: (202) 857-9500

The National Rural Electric Cooperative Association was founded in 1942 and has one thousand members. It consists of rural electric cooperative systems, public power districts, and public utility districts in forty-six states. Its activities include: management institutes, professional conferences, training and consulting services women's and youth programs, legislative representation, energy and regulatory expertise, insurance and safety programs, international programs, and wage and salary surveys. The NRECA maintains a library of twenty thousand volumes. It publishes *Management Quarterly* and miscellaneous literature related to electric power.

National Agricultural Chemicals Association (NACA)
1155 15th St., N.W., Suite 900

Washington, DC 20005
Telephone number: (202) 296-1585

The National Agricultural Chemicals Association was founded in 1933 and has eighty-nine members. It represents firms engaged in producing or formulating agricultural chemical products including agricultural fumigants, agricultural scalicides, chemical plant sprays and dusts, defoliants, soil disinfectants, weed killers, and similar fungicidal, herbicidal, insecticidal, and rodenticidal products used to protect against agricultural fungus diseases, insect pests, rodents, and weeds; it also represents producers of ingredients of agricultural chemical products. Its publications include: *Actionews,* which appears bimonthly, a periodic bulletin, and manuals.

National Association of Chemical Distributors (NACD)
1615 L Street, N.W., Suite 925
Washington, DC 20036
Telephone number: (202) 296-9200

The National Association of Chemical Distributors was founded in 1971 and has 285 members and five regional groups. It was formed to promote professionalism in the business of distributing chemical products, to promote safe practices, to educate managers, to exchange ideas, and to inform other sectors of the chemical industry of the role of distributors. Its publications include: *Action Bulletin,* periodic. Newsletter. *Government Affairs Update,* periodic.

National Forest Products Association (NFPA)
1250 Connecticut Ave., N.W., Suite 200
Washington, DC 20036
Telephone number: (202) 463-2700

The National Forest Products Association was founded in 1902 and has five hundred members. It represents the forest industries on national issues concerning the growing of timber and the manufacture, distribution, marketing, and use of wood products. It bestows awards and compiles statistics. The NFPA publishes *In Focus,* which appears bimonthly, and booklets, designs for buildings, etc.

National Family Business Council (NFBC)
60 Revere Drive, Suite 500
Northbrook, IL 60062
Telephone number: (312) 480-9574

The National Family Business Council was founded in 1976. Members are family-owned firms. It serves as a resource center on family-owned businesses. It maintains a library of books, periodicals, and articles. It also offers consultations, a speakers' bureau, and other communications with other family businesses. The NFBC publishes *Family Business Newsletter,* which appears periodically, and *Resource Guide to Family Business,* which also appears periodically.

National Nurses in Business Association (NNBA)
4286 Redwood Highway, Suite 252
San Rafael, CA 94903
Telephone number: (707) 763-6021

The National Nurses in Business Association was founded in 1988 and has three hundred members. It represents nurses in all types of businesses, including medical and legal consulting and quality-care assurance. It promotes the growth of health-related businesses owned and operated by nurses. It also provides computerized networking services to members and maintains a speakers' bureau. The NNBA publishes the *Bulletin on Non-Traditional Careers,* which is issued quarterly, *Directory of Nurses in Business,* which appears annually, *The Nurse Entrepreneur Exchange,* which appears bimonthly, and a newsletter.

National Trust Closely Held Business Association (NTCHBA)
c/o Howard F. Nichols
Bank of Boston
Mail Stop 01-07-10
P.O. Box 1890
Boston, MA 02105
Telephone number: (617) 434-3622

The National Trust Closely Held Business Association was founded in 1976 and has 150 members. It serves representatives of trust departments from 60 banks. Its purpose is to discuss problems associated with closely held businesses that are in trust or estate.

National Women's Economic Alliance (NWEA)
1440 New York Ave., Suite 300
Washington, DC 20005
Telephone number: (202) 393-5257

The National Women's Economic Alliance was founded in 1983 and has 1,500 members. It represents executive-level women and men. It promotes dialogue among men and women in industry, business, and government. In particular, it focuses on professional, economic, and career concerns and how to address these issues within the framework of the free-enterprise system. It conducts leadership seminars, offers placement services, maintains biographical archives, and bestows awards. The NWEA publishes the *Directory of Women Serving on Corporate Boards*, which appears annually, *NWEA Outlook*, which appears bimonthly, and policy papers, which appear periodically.

North American Association of Inventory Services (NAAIS)
1609 Holbrook Street
Greensboro, NC 27403
Telephone number: (919) 294-2216

The North American Association of Inventory Services was founded in 1982 and has forty-four members. It represents independent inventory services, individuals interested in inventory services, and individuals outside the industry who have performed notable service. It promotes all activities related to the industry. It publishes *NAAIS Newsletter*, which is issued quarterly.

National Clay Pot Manufacturers (NCPM)
P.O. Box 485
Jackson, MO 62557
Telephone number: (314) 243-3138

National Clay Pot Manufacturers was founded in 1956. It represents manufacturers of red clay flower pots.

National Greenhouse Manufacturers Association (NGMA)
c/o Dr. Harold E. Gray
P.O. Box 567
Pana, IL 62557
Telephone number: (217) 562-2644

The National Greenhouse Manufacturers Association was founded in 1958 and has eighty-five members. It represents manufacturers and distributors of greenhouses and supplies to greenhouse manufacturers. It also provides continuing education. It publishes structural, cooling and ventilating, heating, glazing, and retrofit standards.

North American Equipment Dealers Association (NAEDA)
10877 Watson Road
St. Louis, MO 63127
Telephone number: (314) 821-7220

The North American Equipment Dealers Association was founded in 1900 and has 8,200 members and is made up of thirty-one regional groups. It represents retailers of farm machinery, implements, light industrial machinery, tools, vehicles, outdoor power equipment, and related supplies. It conducts programs on management training and governmental and trade relations. It publishes the *Cost of Doing Business Study,* which is issued annually, *Farm and Power Equipment Dealer,* which appears monthly, and other publications.

National Association of Export Companies (NEXCO)
17 Battery Place, Suite 1425
New York, NY 10004
Telephone number: (212) 809-8023

The National Association of Export Companies was founded in 1965 and has one hundred members. It represents established independent export firms acting as representatives and distributors for manufacturers in the United States, export trading companies, and export management companies. It promotes expansion of U.S. trade. It encourages U.S. manufacturers to use export management and trading companies as export departments. It publishes *News Alert,* which is issued monthly.

National Association of Foreign Trade Zones (NAFTZ)
1825 I Street, N.W., Suite 400
Washington, DC 20036
Telephone number: (202) 429-2020

The National Association of Foreign Trade Zones was founded in 1973 and has 253 members. It represents foreign trade zone grantees, operators and users, law firms, automobile manufacturers, port authorities, customs brokers, industrial firms, chambers of commerce, magazine and newspaper firms, development corporations, and concerned individuals. Its purpose is to promote, to stimulate, and to improve foreign-trade zones and their utilization as integral and valuable tools in the international commerce of the United States (Foreign-trade zones are sites within the United States where foreign and domestic merchandise may be bought without formal customs entry or payment of duties. Merchandise entering a zone may be stored, destroyed, displayed, sampled, re-exported, and salvaged, and it may be subject to various other procedures. Goods exported from the United States are not entitled to customs duty or excise tax.) The NAFTZ publishes *Zones Report,* which appears periodically, a newsletter, brochures, special reports, and handbooks.

Overseas Sales and Marketing Association of America (OSMA)
P.O. Box 37
Lake Bluff, IL 60044
Telephone number: (312) 234-1760

The Overseas Sales and Marketing Association of America was founded in 1964 and has thirty-five members. It represents export management and export trading companies. Its purpose is to serve the common interests of independent exporters. Its publications a periodic directory and a periodic newsletter.

Pacific Cooperative for Export (PACE)
21 Tamal Vista Blvd., Suite 106
Corte Madera, CA 94925
Telephone number: (415) 924-2442

The Pacific Cooperative for Export was founded in 1972 and has twenty members. It serves firms involved in the exportation and overseas marketing of agricultural products. It negotiates rates and terms with carriers and monitors legislation concerning antitrust immunity. It also compiles export statistics.

Presidents Association (PA)
135 W. 50th St., 8th Floor
New York, NY 10020
Telephone number: (212) 586-8100

The Presidents Association was founded in 1961. It is a division of American Management Association. It represents presidents, board chairmen, and chief executive officers of private and public sector organizations. It also conducts courses and seminars on professional management and other topics of interest. It publishes *The President,* which is issued monthly, a newsletter, and research papers.

Recreational Industries Council on Exporting
200 Castlewood Road
North Palm Beach, FL 33408
Telephone number: (407) 842-4100.

The Recreational Industries Council on Exporting was founded in 1979 and has ten members. It represents sporting goods associations seeking to promote the sports and recreation equipment industry worldwide. It maintains a speakers' bureau and compiles statistics.

Ski Council of America (SCA)
600 Madison Ave., 26th floor
New York, NY 10022
Telephone number: (212) 874-3030

The Ski Council of America was founded in 1964 and has 229 members. It represents suppliers to the retail ski market. It also promotes snow skiing, functions as central source of information on snow skiing, and disseminates information to trade and consumer media sources. It publishes the *Snow Show Directory* every year.

Ski Industries America (SIA)
8377B Greensboro Drive
McLean, VA 22102
Telephone number: (703) 556-9020

Ski Industries America was founded in 1954 and has 264 members. It serves manufacturers, distributors, and importers of ski apparel, equipment, footwear, and accessories. It also bestows Ski Retailers of the Year awards. Its publications include *Ski Industry Advisor,* which appears quarterly, *Ski Rep Newsletter,* which appears quarterly, and *Trade Show Directory,* which appears annually.

Soccer Industry Council of America (SICA)
200 Castlewood Drive
North Palm Beach, FL 33408
Telephone number: (407) 842-4100

The Soccer Industry Council of America was founded in 1985 and has forty-five members. It represents manufacturers, suppliers, and retailers of soccer equipment, and others involved in the soccer industry. It is affiliated with the United States Soccer Federation. It publishes *Soccerline,* which is issued six times per year, and a newsletter.

Sporting Goods Manufacturers Association (SGMA)
200 Castlewood Drive
North Palm Beach, FL 33408
Telephone number: (407) 863-8984
Fax: (407) 863-8984

The Sporting Goods Manufacturers Association was founded in 1906 and has 1,500 members. It represents manufacturers of athletic clothing, footwear, and sporting goods, and it compiles statistics. It publishes many publications, including a newsletter.

Sell Overseas America, The Association of American Export (SOSA)
2512 Artesia Blvd.
Redondo Beach, CA 90278
Telephone number: (213) 376-8788
Telex: 662272

Sell Overseas America was founded in 1980. This is a for-profit organization that promotes American exports and fosters broader U.S. participation in international trade. It publishes *Showcase, USA,* which is issued quarterly, and *Showcase USA Buyers' Guide,* which is issued annually.

Services Group (SG)
1815 N. Lynn St., #200
Arlington, VA 22209
Telephone number: (703) 528-7444

Services Group was founded in 1980 and has two regional groups. Its purpose is to provide assistance to free-trade zones and free ports in starting up and in operations. It offers workshops and technical services and maintains a 2,500-volume library. Its publications include *Caribbean and Central American Free Trade Zone,* which appears annually, *Free Trade Zone Update,* which appears quarterly, a newsletter, and others.

Shoe Suppliers Association of America (SSAA)
Nine Hillside Avenue
Woburn, MA 01801
Telephone number: (617) 923-4500

Shoe Suppliers Association of America was founded in 1968 and has fifty-two members. It also includes state groups. It represents suppliers to the American shoe industry.

Trade Reform Action Coalition (TRAC)
c/o Stanley Nehmer
1225 19th St., N.W., Suite 210
Washington, DC 20036
Telephone number: (202) 466-7720

The Trade Reform Action Coalition was founded in 1983. It represents companies, trade associations, unions, and workers in industries that produce a variety of items, including textiles, apparel, footwear, leather products, valves, nonferrous metals, steel, forgings, chemicals, and industrial and agricultural equipment. It seeks to create more equitable international trade through changing legislation.

Trade Relations Council of the United States (TRC)
c/o Stewart Trade Data
808 17th St., N.W., Suite 580
Washington, DC 20036
Telephone number: (202) 785-4194

The Trade Relations Council of the United States was founded in 1885 and has forty members. It represents manufacturing, mining, and agricultural interests, and trade associations. It publishes *Employment, Output, and Foreign Trade of U.S. Manufacturing Industries, 1958–84,* which is now in its seventh edition.

USA-Republic of China Economic Council (USA-ROCEC)
1737 H St. N.W.
Washington, DC 20006
Telephone number: (202) 331-8966
Fax: (202) 331-8985

The USA-Republic of China Economic Council was founded in 1976 and has 375 members. It represents American states and firms engaged in business activity with Taiwan. It seeks to promote business relations for members. It holds business conferences and seminars to promote understanding of business opportunities, government policies, laws and regulations, and means for achieving technological transfer. It also serves as a liaison between business and government. USA-ROCEC publishes an annual conference report, a periodic membership list, an annual progress report, *Taiwan Economic News,* which appears periodically, and other publications.

U.S.-China Business Council (USCBC)
1818 N Street, N.W., Suite 500
Washington, DC 20036
Telephone number: (202) 429-0340

The U.S.-China Business Council was founded in 1973 and has 325 members. It represents American companies engaged in trading with and investing in the People's Republic of China. It was established to facilitate the development of U.S.-China commerce. It hosts delegations to and from the People's Republic of China. It also assists companies in making contacts with mainland China and provides business advisory services. In addition, the U.S.-China Business Council maintains a library and conducts market research for member firms. It publishes *China Business Review,* which appears bimonthly, and many other publications.

[U.S.-U.S.S.R.] Trade and Economic Council
805 Third Avenue, 14th floor
New York, NY 10022
Telephone number: (212) 644-4550

The Trade and Economic Council was founded in 1973 and has 350 members. It represents U.S. industry and foreign trade groups from the former USSR devoted to facilitating trade expansion between the two. It supports tourism, banking, insurance, shipping, aviation, and approved technology transfer between the U.S. and the former USSR. It is responsible for market development and individual trade development for members. It maintains binational staffs of trade and economic specialists and offers business support facilities.

U.S.-Yugoslav Economic Council (USYEC)
1901 N. Fort Myer Dr., Suite 303
Arlington, VA 22209
Telephone number: (703) 527-0280
Fax: (703) 527-0282

The U.S.-Yugoslavia Economic Council was founded in 1974 and has 254 members. It serves industrial, financial, and commercial firms. It represents firms in the United States in the development of trade and investment with all six republics of Yugoslavia. It publishes *Business News,* which is issued monthly and available to members only.

United States Council for International Business (USCIB)
1212 Avenue of the Americas
New York, NY 10036
Telephone number: (212) 354-4480

The United States Council for International Business was founded in 1945 and has three hundred members. It serves as the U.S. National Committee of the International Chamber of Commerce. It enables multinational enterprises to operate effectively by representing their interests to intergovernmental and governmental bodies and by keeping enterprises advised of international developments having a major impact on their operations. It also serves as the U.S. representative to the International Organization of Employers, among other duties. It is open for communications with individuals, companies and governments. It publishes the Corporate Handbook Series, which appears periodically, *IGO Report,* which appears monthly, and many other publications.

World Business Council (WBC)
2000 Pennsylvania Avenue, N.W., Suite 5400
Washington, DC 20006
Telephone number: (202) 452-6200

The World Business Council was founded in 1970 and has 1,100 members and 20 local groups. It represents corporate executives, all of whom are former members of the Young Presidents' Organization. Its purpose is to serve as a graduate school for former YPO members. It publishes an annual report to members, *World Business Council Communique,* which appears quarterly, and other publications.

World Export Processing Zones Association (WEPZA)
P.O. Box 986
Flagstaff, AZ 86002
Telephone number: (602) 779-0052

The World Export Processing Zones Association was founded in 1978 and has fifty members. It represents export-processing zones and industrial parks, public and private, and others who are interested. (EPZs and EIPs are zones and regions, generally within Third World countries, where materials are brought in to be assembled or used in the manufacture of other products. These zones are customs-controlled, allowing for inexpensive production, and later exportation, of goods. EPZs and EIPs are found throughout the world.) WEPZA publishes *Journal of the Flagstaff Institute,* which is issued semiannually, and quarterly newsletter.

Western International Trade Group (WITG)
c/o Ronald A. Ingersoll
P.O. Box 29774
Phoenix, AZ 85038
Telephone number: (602) 271-6361

The Western International Trade Group was founded in 1946 and has 208 members. It is made up of 7 regional groups. It represents officials of companies manufacturing for export, export sales managers or agents, importers, shippers, investment house or bank officials, publishers, officials of chambers of commerce, and foreign trade associations or other organizations engaged directly or indirectly in international trade, investment, or travel.

World Trade Center of New Orleans (WTCNO)
Two Canal Street, Suite 2900
New Orleans, LA 70130
Telephone number: (504) 529-1601

The World Trade Center of New Orleans was founded in 1985 and has 3,300 members. It represents U.S. and foreign business leaders united for the promotion of international trade, friendship, and understanding. It programs visits for VIPs and sends trade and cultural missions of business and civic leaders abroad each year. It offers instruction in sixteen languages and maintains a library of 10,000 books. It also offers periodic seminars. It publishes *Louisiana Trade Directory,* which is issued biennially, and *Trade Winds,* which appears periodically.

World Trade Center Association (WTCA)
One World Trade Center, Suite 7701
New York, NY 10048
Telephone number: (212) 313-4600

The World Trade Center Association was founded in 1968 and has 186 members. Regular members are organizations substantially involved in the development or operation of a world trade center; affiliate members are chambers of commerce and organizations sponsoring world trade center clubs, libraries, exhibit facilities, and other trade-center related activities. The World Trade Center Association seeks to encourage expansion of world trade, to promote international business relationships, and to increase participation in world trade by developing nations. It publishes *WTCA News,* which is issued monthly, and other publications.

Brief Biographical Sketches of Twenty Management Specialists and Their Specific Contributions to the Art and Science of Management

Introduction

Although the industrial scene has changed dramatically since the beginning of the twentieth century, people who occupy that scene have not. Management always has been and always will be people centered. Managers must deal with time and motion, with new technology, and with ever-changing products, but the key to all of this is the people who make things happen in production.

The future of management faces two problems. One, the manager will have to manage high-tech workers who have vast stores of knowledge of rather narrow fields of endeavor. Two, the manager will have to manage people in the service industry whose production is difficult to quantify, and who may indeed resent attempts at quantification.

One thing seems sure. If managers ever settle on a reasonably successful theory of management, it will be when the experts truly recognize what human beings are, and how they can be motivated to work with some degree of peace and productiveness with other people. This remains the whole reason for the study of management.

Chester I. Barnard 1886–1961

Chester I. Barnard was one of those rare people who, while holding a high position in industry, developed a sound philosophy of management.

While developing his philosophy, Barnard was president of the New Jersey Bell Telephone Company, later spent some time at Harvard, and then became president of the Ford Foundation.

Barnard did not take sides between management and labor, which was against the tendency of management theorists of his time. Instead, he looked upon an organization as a place of cooperation among all concerned, and he looked upon the efficiency and profitability of an enterprise as a cooperative effort. Workers and managers were to complement one another and work together harmoniously. He proposed that it was not the goals of an enterprise that caused conflict, but rather inappropriate means used in attaining those goals.

For example, should an enterprise make a goal of profit maximization, giving little regard to the methods used to attain that goal, conflict was sure to occur. Neither managers nor workers would submit themselves to serfdom in order to maximize profits, nor should they.

Barnard entered into the current discussion of value-oriented institutions, such as churches or schools, that still sometimes attempted to pass judgments on business enterprises. It was his belief that no theology had been developed to that time that could offer proper guidelines to industry.

While he remained in industry, Barnard was not able to do much to change management thinking. His theories were misunderstood and not popular. Even colleagues at Bell Telephone looked upon his thinking as a personal hobby, to which they attached little importance.

Barnard, along with Mary Parker Follet, also deserves credit for being among the first to study the process of decision making in organizations, the relationships between formal and informal organizations, and the role and function of the executive. Barnard analyzed and stressed the socio-psychological and ethical aspects of managerial organization and function. He viewed organization as a social system.

As stated earlier, Barnard's view supports a high degree of cooperation on the part of the manager as opposed to authority and order-giving; the relegation of economic factors as motivators to a secondary role; the individual's identification with the organization based on a strong belief in its codes, as opposed to compliance imposed from without. He was also among the first to emphasize the communication responsibilities of executives, to analyze the role of status in organizational endeavor, and to develop a system of analysis of incentive programs in organizations.

While still with Bell, Barnard asserted that a leader's role is to harness the social forces of an organization in order to shape and guide values. He once described good managers as value shapers concerned with the informal social properties of organizations. He contrasted such managers with mere manipulators of formal rewards and systems, who dealt only with the narrower concept of short-term efficiency. So, without unduly modifying Barnard's views, it appears that the real role of the executive is to manage the values of the enterprise.

After retiring from Bell, Barnard went to Harvard where he wrote his famous book, *The Function of the Executive* (Cambridge, Mass.: Harvard University Press), in 1938. The book is dense, and most difficult to read but does try to make clear the fundamental management theory of the author. His stated purpose in the book was to provide a comprehensive theory of cooperative behavior in formal organizations. Cooperation, he avers, originates in the need for an individual to accomplish purposes to which he is by himself biologically unequal. Although few other people were thinking as he was at the time, Barnard, with top executive experience, fixed the responsiblity on the top executive to see that all of the proper things happened in the organization. His book has been referred to as a complete management theory.

It may be difficult for some to imagine how revolutionary his management concepts were. Even after World War I, management practices were still quite primitive, although management theories were tending more toward the human relations school of thought.

The most important concept propounded by Barnard was his insistence that the top executive was responsible to see that the enterprise ran efficiently, with every human component being cooperative because the values and practices of the enterprise were fair to all concerned.

Ralph Courier Davis 1894–

Ralph Courier Davis headed the management department at General Motors Institute in Detroit from 1927 to 1930, and he was professor of business organization at Ohio State University from 1936 to 1965.

He was the first American to identify and differentiate the functions of management, which he saw as "creative planning, organizing and controlling the work of others." He defined management as ". . . a function of executive leadership." His classic book (written with Alten Baker), *Fundamentals of Top Management* (New York: Harper & Row, 1951) was used for more than twenty years as a basic textbook, and it is still widely used in management research.

The following statements stand out in the preface of that book. "A sound philosophy of management is necessary for the continuance of the free enterprise system. It is a requisite, therefore, for the continuance of a high standard of living and other material benefits of a highly developed industrial economy." And:

> A distinction can be made between a business mechanic and a professional executive. The former may be defined as one who has learned his executive trade in the "school of hard knocks," by the process of trial and error. He may be able at present to do an effective job. His effectiveness may decline rapidly when broad, basic changes in economic, political and social conditions render much of his practical experience obsolete. The professional executive is one who has developed, in addition, a sound philosophy of management. He is accordingly one who has a broad, fundamental basis for effective thinking in the solution of managerial problems.
>
> He should be able to exercise an effective leadership with respect to organizational groups under his command. He should be able to exercise a leadership of ideas concerning business and management, with respect to the community and the social groups of which he is a part. A superior business leadership without a sound philosophy of management is unlikely.

Undoubtedly, Davis's greatest contributions to the art and science of management were his books, widely used in colleges and universities, and his own teaching in the classroom. In addition to the classic mentioned above, his other books are *Principles of Factory Organization and Management*, 1928, 3d ed., 1957; *The Principles of Business Organization and Operation*, 4th ed., 1937, reprinted in 1973; and *Principles of Management*, 1962.

William Edwards Deming 1900–

More than any other individual, Williams Edwards Deming was responsible for turning Japanese industry into the finely tuned machine it is today. Therefore, he directly or indirectly affected management all over the world.

Deming put the emphasis on "the best" and felt assured that the worker would follow any reasonable scheme if what he produced was the best. He once said to Rafael Aguayo that "quality is pride of workmanship." And, throughout his teaching, he affirmed that quality is integral to the product or service, and thus quality is an integral part of the management process. Deming's concern for management was real, just as his knowledge of the needs of management was real.

He was born on October 14, 1900, in Sioux City, Iowa. Shortly thereafter the family moved to Wyoming, where Deming stayed until a year after he finished college. He graduated in 1921 with a major in physics, but remained for a year to assist in teaching math and engineering. He taught two years at the Colorado School of Mines and from there was encouraged to go on to Yale. There he graduated with his Ph.D. in mathematical physics in 1928. While studying for his Ph.D., he worked summers at the Western Electric Hawthorne Plant in Chicago, doing research on telephone transmitters. There he came into contact with Walter A. Shewhart who later would become famous for the statistical control of quality.

Few have lived as long as Deming, a period which encompasses all the years from the flowering of the industrial revolution in the United States to the present. He still lectures. Thus, few would know more about the needs of management or the foibles of management than he.

It cannot be said that Deming was contemptuous of either management theory or theorists. Nor was he without feeling for the human-relations side of management. He simply seemed to feel that often "the cart was gotten before the horse." In fact, he was more contemptuous of the practice of management than he was of the theory of management.

Deming was primarily a statistician who used that science to create quality as it was used in conjunction with dedicated workers. In the late 1930s, the United States Census Bureau began considering the idea of sampling, rather than relying on a full count. Deming was asked to join them. In 1939 he became head mathematician and advisor on sampling. The results obtained from these first experiments with sampling have made what was then a revolutionary practice into something we use every day.

It was at the Census Department that Deming began using quality-control methods in a nonmanufacturing environment. The results were astounding, and the Census Bureau is still considered by many a model government agency.

In 1946 Deming left the Census Bureau to establish a private consulting practice in statistical studies. At the same time he joined the Graduate School of Business Administration at New York University.

As a consultant to the War Department, Deming first visited Japan in 1947, and he returned in 1950, 1951, 1955, and 1956. He became not only a consultant to industrial Japan but also a demigod who forever will be revered there.

Yet, despite his success, Deming was still not recognized widely in the United States. In 1980, at the age of eighty, Deming did an NBC white paper on the subject "If Japan Can, Why Can't We?" This work brought him attention that allows him to conduct seminars, keeps him teaching at NYU, and permits him to run clinics for statisticians. But, at age ninety, Deming cannot expect to go on much longer, and over the first eighty years of his life the United States and her managers virtually ignored him. What he did for Japan he might have done for the United States, had we been wise enough to listen.

Deming was sold on quality. Anything less than the best possible was unacceptable to him. Further, he did not suffer fools gladly, and he frankly felt that much U.S. management was foolish at best and fatal at worst.

The use of statistics in manufacturing was not something Deming dreamed up. But he did put it into practice first in Japan, and his ideas about how to apply statistics to manufacturing were later influential, to a degree, in the United States For him, mathematics is a tool to reduce the tolerance levels in manufactured products or to refine procedures in service industries.

Nor did Deming forget about the line worker, who, in the final analysis, was the quality-control expert. He promoted "quality-control circles" and the participation in management of such groups. In these things he was very much ahead of his time in management theory.

Deming's objection to U.S. management is much like the objections many of us have made over the years. He felt that management was too "bottom-line conscious." He felt that too many legal people and financial people, who knew little about what was going on in the plants, had found their way into top management. These managers seemed uncaring of the companies they worked for, so long as the "bottom line" looked good at the end of each quarter.

He was not unaware of the absolute need for a company making a profit in the long run, but he felt that profit was best gained by building a quality product in the short run. To him, there was no substitute for quality, a spirit which he felt U.S. industry had all but abandoned.

In 1955, Deming was awarded the Shewhart Medal, which is awarded annually by the American Society for Quality Control.

Up until this time, Deming's scientific papers number 170; he has written 7 textbooks, and his articles, speeches, etc., are innumerable. The following two works provide more information on W. Edwards Deming: Rafael Aguayo, *Dr. Deming, the American Who Taught the Japanese about Quality* (New York: A Lyle Stuart Book, published by Carol Publishing Company, 1990) and David Halberstam, *The Reckoning* (New York: William Morrow & Company, Inc., 1986). Read all of this book even though only pages 311–18 are devoted specifically to Deming's work.

Peter F. Drucker 1909–

One approaches with a degree of trepidation any attempt to describe the life and work of Peter F. Drucker. Suffice it to say that he stands as a giant not only in the field of management but also in economics and philosophy. It is impossible in a volume such as this one to do justice to his many works. The reader is urged to investigate Drucker's works more thoroughly.

Several scholars have described him as the founding father of the discipline of management. Kenneth Boulding called him "a foremost philosopher of American society." Drucker is the most prolific writer among the management authorities of the twentieth century. He now has about twenty books to his credit, a few of which we shall list at the end of this piece. He writes often for many magazines, and he is an editorial columnist for the Wall Street Journal.

Peter F. Drucker was born in Vienna, Austria, in 1909. He was educated in Austria and England. He migrated to England in 1929 and became a news correspondent and an economist for an international bank in London.

In 1937 he moved from England to the United States, where, for a time, he was an economist for a group of London banks and insurance companies. His first book was *The End of Economic Man* (New York: John Day and Co., 1937).

From 1942 to 1949, Drucker was professor of philosophy and politics at Bennington College. From 1952 to 1972 he was professor of management at the Graduate Business School of New York University, and since 1972 he has been Distinguished University Lecturer at New York University. Since 1971 Drucker has been Clarke Professor of social sciences at the Claremont Graduate School, Claremont, California. Moreover, from 1942 on, Drucker has served as a consultant to the U.S. government and many major domestic industries. He also has consulted with governments in the Free World, notably Japan and Canada. In addition, he has consulted with many multinational industries in the United States and other countries.

Drucker lives with his wife in Claremont, California.

It should be understood that Peter Drucker is not just an authority in the field of management. He is learned in all of the social sciences, and his writings also reveal a broad knowledge of psychology, ethics, and logic.

Since Drucker's book, *The Practice of Management* (New York: Harper & Row, 1954), is usually considered his best, some citations from it may provide some insight into the basic beliefs of this multifaceted man.

The manager is the dynamic, life-giving element in every business. Without his leadership the "resources of production" remain resources and never become production. In a competitive economy, above all, the quality and performance of the managers determine the successes of a business, indeed they determine its survival. For the quality and performance of its managers is the only effective advantage and enterprise in a competitive economy can have.

The emergence of management as an essential, a distinct and a leading institution is a pivotal event in social history. Rarely, if ever, has a new basic institution, a new leading group, emerged as fast as has management since the turn of the century. Rarely in human history has a new institution proven indispensable so quickly; and even less often has a new institution arrived with so little opposition, so little disturbance, so little controversy.

Management, its competence, its integrity and its performance will be decisive both to the United States and to the free world in the decades ahead. At the same time the demands on management will be rising steadily and steeply.

. . . [T]he hostility to capitalism and capitalists is moral and ethical. Capitalism is being attacked not because it is inefficient or misgoverned but because it is cynical. And indeed a society based on the assertion that private vices become public benefits cannot endure, no matter how impeccable its logic, no matter how great its benefits.

The Practice of Management, even though it was published in 1954, has truths that continue to hold. A second very valuable book is *Management: Tasks, Responsibilities, Practices* (New York: Harper & Row, 1973). Here are some citations from it:

It is fashionable today to talk of a revolt against authority and to proclaim that everybody should "do his own thing." This, then, I have to admit, is a most unfashionable book. It does not talk about rights. It stresses responsibility. Its focus is not on doing one's own thing but on performance.

If the institutions of our pluralistic society of institutions do not perform in responsible autonomy, we will not have individualism and a society in which there is a chance for people to fulfill themselves. We will, instead impose on ourselves complete regimentation in which no one will be allowed autonomy. . . . Tyranny is the only alternative to strong, performing autonomous institutions.

But it is managers and management that make institutions perform.

Performing, responsible management is the alternative to tyranny and our only protection against it.

While management is a discipline—that is, an organized body of knowledge and as such applicable everywhere—it is also a "culture." It is not a value-free science. Management is a social function and embedded in a culture—a society—a tradition of values, customs and beliefs, and in governmental and political systems. Management is—and should be—culture-conditioned; but, in turn, management and managers shape culture and society.

But a leadership group needs not only to function. It needs not only to perform. It also has to have legitimacy. It has to be accepted in the community as "right."

"Legitimacy" is an elusive concept. It has, in effect, no real definition. Yet it is crucial. Authority without legitimacy is usurpation. And the leadership groups of society—and this means the managers today—have to have authority to perform their functions.

At the same time, none of the traditional grounds of legitimacy will do for the managers. Birth or magic are just as unsuitable for them as popular election or the rights of private property. They hold office because they perform. And yet performance by itself has never been sufficient grounds for legitimacy.

What managers need to be accepted as legitimate authority is a principle of morality. They need to ground their authority in a moral commitment which, at the same time, expresses the purpose and character of organizations.

Almost three centuries ago the English pamphleteer Mandeville in a didactic poem "The Fable of the Bees" laid down what became, a century later. the principle of capitalism. "Private vices make public benefit." Blind and greedy profit-seeking, Mandeville laid down, advances the public good through the "invisible hand." In terms of performance, history has proved Mandeville remarkably right. But morally his principle was never acceptable. And the fact that capitalism has become the less acceptable the more it succeeded—as the great Austro-American economist Joseph Schumpeter pointed out repeatedly—has been the weakness of modern society and modern economy.

If he is to remain—as he should—the manager of an autonomous institution, he must accept that he is a public man. He must accept the moral responsibility of organization, the responsibility of making strengths productive and achieving.

These brief quotations will acquaint you somewhat with the breadth and depth of Drucker's thinking.

Among Drucker's many other books are: *Technology, Management and Society,* 1958; *Managing for Results,* 1964; *The Age of Discontinuity,* 1968; *Men, Ideas and Politics,* 1971; *Managing in Turbulent Times,* 1980; *Innovation and Entrepreneurship: Practice and Principles,* 1985. All the books listed were published by Harper & Row Publishers, New York. Drucker's major book, *The Concept of the Corporation,* was first published by the John Day Company, New York, in 1946, and was reissued in 1972.

Mary Parker Follett 1868–1933

Mary Parker Follet was a political and social philosopher whose primary contribution to management was the application of psychological insight and social science findings to industry.

Follet began lecturing to leaders of American industry about 1924, and she continued to lecture in the United States and England until her death in 1933. Her writings serve as a bridge from the scientific management concepts of Frederick Taylor to the later behavioral approach, which is still much in vogue today.

Follet devised what she referred to as the "Law of the Situation." Her method sought to depersonalize order giving and unite all concerned in a study of the situation in order to discover the "Law of the Situation" and obey it. In short, instead of a manager being an order giver, whom all must obey, the orders were to have been worked out in group discussions until every person related to the project was, in fact, an order giver, and the manager was the one who began the process of discovering the law. (This approach was much ahead of its time.)

When the word "conflict" was used as related to management—and it often was used with the rise of unionism—Follet had this to say: "What people often mean by getting rid of conflict is getting rid of diversity, and it is of the utmost importance that they not be considered the same. We may wish to abolish conflict, but we cannot get rid of diversity. We must face life as it is and understand that diversity is its most essential feature. . . . Fear of difference is dread of life itself. It is possible to conceive of

247

conflict as not necessarily a wasteful outbreak of incompatibilities but a normal process by which socially valuable differences register themselves for the enrichment of all concerned"*

Follet looked upon disagreement and conflict as being the result of incongruities in perception (what A sees so vividly, B cannot see at all). Follet along with Barnard first studied the process of decision making in organizations and the role and function of the executive.

Her books include: *The New State* (New York & London: Longmans, Green and Company, 1921) and *Dynamic Administration: The Collected Papers of Mary Parker Follet*, edited by Matcalf and Urwick (London: Pitman, 1941).

Henry Laurence Gantt 1861–1919

Henry Laurence Gantt was a pioneer American industrialist and management engineer. He was a contemporary of the "father of scientific management," Frederick Taylor, and a sometime colleague. From 1887 through 1901, he held important positions in industry. He then became a consultant to industry, a career that he pursued until 1917, when he went into government service to assist with the war effort.

He was one of the earliest management specialists to give attention to the human relations aspects of industry, as distinguished from Taylor's emphasis on financial incentives. He was enamored with further training for workers, and he insisted that such training was the responsibility of management.

Before Taylor introduced his wage-incentive plan, Gantt had already introduced his "task and bonus" wage system, which was little more than assigning a task to a worker and then rewarding him as the task was completed. His plan, unlike that of Taylor's, did not pit one worker against another, but rather sought to draw out the best in every worker according to his ability.

Gantt became well known for introducing the "Gantt Charts" to industry, which are still used with modifications. The charts, in whatever form, are management-control devices, developed during World War I.

---

* *Creative Experiences* (New York: Longmans, Green & Co., 1924), pp. 300–01.

They are composed of linear calendars on which future time is spread horizontally and the work to be done is indicated vertically. The Planning Chart showed graphically the things that had to be done, entered in symbols and descriptions under the portion of the calendar in which it was planned to do them. The Progress Chart, used in production control, depicts cumulative work against time in relation to schedules. Incidentally, one can see a distinct relationship between Gantt's work and the Project Evaluation and Control Technique (PECT) used in World War II.

Gantt was considerably more forward looking and philosophical about management than most of his contemporaries. He pioneered a democracy-in-industry approach, and helped to humanize the science of management. While he agreed with Taylor that management should be approached scientifically, rather than haphazardly, he did not try to reduce people to objects of science. He further proposed equal opportunity in industry, years before it was given serious thought by others.

The scope of his writing was great; he had more than 150 books and white papers to his credit. Three of his better known works are: *Work, Wages and Profit* (Engineering Magazine Company, 1910); *Industrial Leadership* (New Haven, Conn.: Yale University Press, 1916); *Organizing for Work* (New York: Harcourt, Brace and Howe, 1919).

Frank Bunker Gilbreth 1868–1924
Lillian Evelyn Moller Gilbreth 1878–1972

This husband and wife team must be studied together, since they formed probably the most influential team in the history of the study of management. Frank Gilbreth was an engineer, a management consultant, and a contemporary of Frederick Taylor and H. L. Gantt. He was of the school of "scientific management" and did his first important work in the field of "motion study."

Although he may be best known for his work in motion study, he also worked continuously in the field of general management, first applying his theories to his own company. There he delineated lines of authority and responsibility.

While motion studies are often thought to be scientific means for getting greater productivity out of the worker, Gilbreth related motion studies to the greater comfort of the worker and sought means of gaining greater productivity with less stress on the worker. The emphasis was upon "wasteful and unproductive" movements that also made tasks more difficult for the ones performing them. When applying this concept to brick laying (in his own company) he simplified the motions from 18 to 5, and the number of bricks laid from 175 to 350.

Gilbreth gave up his contracting business in 1912, and he spent the remainder of his life studying the science of motion. Frederick Taylor's emphasis had been primarily on the external forces affecting the worker. Gilbreth looked first at the worker, applying available knowledge from the social sciences to increase the worker's capacity to produce in ways less physically draining on him. Gilbreth was a pioneer in developing management as a social science, with the human factor being the focal point of concern.

Lillian Evelyn Moller Gilbreth was a psychologist and a teacher prior to her marriage to F. B. Gilbreth. During his lifetime she collaborated with her husband in all his work, and she took over the work after his death in 1924.

She may be best known for her writings in her later years, which were directed to increasing the efficiency of physically handicapped women as homemakers.

Gilbreth's Principles of Motion Economy*

Gilbreth's twenty-two Principles of Motion Economy are still considered vital in increasing the efficiency of work and decreasing fatigue in manual labor. Although all twenty-two principles cannot apply to every situation, each applies to some situations.

Use of the Human Body:

1) The two hands should begin as well as complete their *therbligs* (the elements of human motion, and Gilbreth spelled backwards) at the same instant.

*W. C. Zinck, *Dynamic Work Simplification* (New York: Van Nostrand Reinhold, 1962).

2) The two hands should not be idle at the same instant except during rest periods.

3) Motions of the arms should be in opposite and symmetrical directions, instead of in the same direction, and should be made simultaneously.

4) Hand motions should be confined to the lowest classification with which it is possible to perform the work satisfactorily.

5) Momentum should be employed to assist the worker wherever possible, and it should be reduced to a minimum if it must be overcome by muscular effort.

6) Continuous curved motions are preferable to straight-line motions involving sudden and sharp changes in direction.

7) Ballistic (rhythmic) movements are faster, easier, and more accurate than restricted (fixed) or "controlled" movements.

8) Rhythm is essential to the smooth and automatic performance of an operation, and the work should be arranged to permit easy and natural rhythm wherever possible.

Arrangement of the Workplace:

9) Definite and fixed stations should be provided for all tools and materials.

10) Tools, materials, and controls should be located around the workplace and as close to the point of assembly or use as possible.

11) Gravity feed bins and containers should be used to deliver the material as close to the point of assembly or use as possible.

12) Drop deliveries should be used wherever possible.

13) Materials and tools should be located to permit the best sequence of therbligs.

14) Provisions should be made for adequate conditions for seeing. Good illumination is the first requirement for satisfactory visual perception.

15) The height of the workplace and the chair should preferably be so arranged that alternate sitting and standing at work are easily possible.

16) A chair of the type and height to permit good posture should be provided for every worker.

Design of Tools and Equipment:

17) The hands should be relieved of all work that can be performed more advantageously by the feet or some other parts of the body.

18) Two or more tools should be combined wherever possible.

19) Tools and materials should be pre-positioned wherever possible.

20) Where each finger performs some specific movement, such as in

typewriting, the load should be distributed in accordance with the inherent capacity of the fingers.

21) Handles such as those used on cranks and large screwdrivers should be designed to permit as much of the surface of the hand to come into contact with the handle as possible. This is particularly true when considerable force is exerted to use the handle. For light assembly work, the screwdriver handle should be so shaped that it is smaller at the bottom than at the top.

22) Levers, crossbars, and handwheels should be located in such positions that the operator can manipulate them with the least change in body positions and with the greatest mechanical advantage.

Some of Frank Bunker Gilbreth's books include: *Concrete System* (New York: Engineering News Publishing Company, 1908); *Field System* (New York: Myron C. Clark, 1908); *Motion Study* (New York: D. Van Nostrand, 1911); in collaboration with L. E. Gilbreth, *Primer of Scientific Management* (New York: D. Van Nostrand, 1912).

Some of Lillian Evelyn Moller Gilbreth's books, in addition to works on which she collaborated with her husband, include: *Psychology of Management* (New York: Macmillan, 1912); in collaboration with Alice Rice Cook, *The Foreman and Manpower Management* (New York: McGraw-Hill, 1947); in collaboration with O. M. Thomas and Eleanor C. Clymer, *Management in the Home* (New York: Dodd, 1954; rev. ed., 1959).

Samuel Gompers 1850–1924

No list of management authorities would be complete without a prominent name from the ranks of organized labor. It is for this reason that the name of Samuel Gompers is included. Of all the individuals who have played a major role in the life and progress of organized labor, Samuel Gompers' name stands head and shoulders above all the rest.

Samuel Gompers was born in London in 1850, the son of a Dutch cigar maker. In 1863, when Gompers was thirteen, the family migrated to the United States, settling on the east side of New York City.

His formal schooling ended when he was ten years of age, but he continued to study on his own and supplemented his education by attending evening lectures in New York's Union. From this he attained a broad education. While very young he had achieved a prominent position in the American labor movement, being active in the Cigar Makers Union.

In 1881, along with Adolph Strasser of the Cigar Makers Union, he formed the Federation of Organized Trades and Labor Unions. In 1886 this became the American Federation of Labor, with Gompers as its president. He was re-elected every year, save one, until his death in 1924. In this one year (1885) he was supplanted by a Socialist candidate, but that did not last long.

For those who have a stereotyped concept of what a labor leader looks like and acts like, Samuel Gompers would quash that concept. He was a mild man and was as fully aware of the needs of business and industry as he was of the needs of labor. He simply felt, and correctly so, that workers, in general, were underpaid, overworked, and had no one to represent them.

As is the case with many managers, Gompers' views were subject to alteration over time. In 1879 he helped frame a constitution that contained the following words: "We recognize the solidarity of the whole working class to work harmoniously against the common enemy—capitalists—united we are a power to be respected; divided we are the slaves of the capitalists." This sounds much like the Socialist doctrine of that time.

In 1903, however, while addressing the convention of the AFL, Gompers castigated the Socialists: "I declare to you that I am not at variance with your doctrines, but with your philosophy. Economically, you are unsound; socially, you are wrong; industrially, you are an impossibility." During the last twenty years of his life, Gompers spent as much time combating the influences of Socialism in the unions as he did combating the "capitalists."

He had a specific view of unions, and this view was to form the framework for the AFL. He believed that every trade or craft should be represented by a union. Then he believed that union power could be multiplied by bringing these unions together in a federation which could serve as a common voice for all of them.

Although Gompers did not know of Galbraith's concept of "counter-vailing power," he likely would have been an advocate of it. Simplistically, this concept states that both business and labor need sufficient power to deal properly with each other, and that both should conduct all their business in a manner to protect the public interest. Government was to have sufficient power to assure that this was true of business and the unions.

Gompers never forgot that business was "the goose that lays the golden egg" and was not to be killed. While he constantly pushed for "more," that is, more of the fruits of the labor of workers, he also recognized the need for business to make a profit, and he did not push union demands to the point where they became dangerous to the business.

He was throughout his career widely recognized by both business and government. While he had generally opposed war, after the outbreak of World War I, he opposed any pacifist tendencies in the unions belonging to AFL. He organized the War Committee on Labor. He was a member of the advisory commission of the U.S. Council of National Defense in 1917, and he represented the AFL at the Paris Peace Conference, 1918–19. There he was named chairman of the Peace Conference Commission on Labor Legislation.

Although as a labor leader Gompers was often passionately hated by sectors of American industry, it could not have been otherwise in that era of the developing American economy. It is still held that Gompers had those qualities necessary for being a great manager of management and union relations.

Before his death in 1924, the AFL had a membership of more than five million. It was not to hold that high position very long.

Gompers was also proficient as a writer. Some of his works include: *Seventy Years of Life in Labor* (New York: E. P. Dutton, 1925), his autobiography in two volumes; *Labor in Europe and America* (New York: Harper & Bros., 1910); *American Labor and the War* (New York: Geo. H. Doran, 1919); *Labor and the Common Welfare* (New York: E. P. Dutton, 1919); with W. E. Walling, *Out of Their Mouths: A Revelation and an Indictment of Sovietism* (New York: E. P. Dutton, 1921).

Frederick Herzberg 1923–

Frederick Herzberg is a clinical psychologist who spent most of his career at Case Western Reserve University and the University of Utah. As a psychologist, he became interested early in his career in the relationship between a meaningful experience at work and mental health. He spent many years of research and experimentation on his belief that man has two sets of needs: 1) to avoid pain and 2) to grow psychologically. Out of this came his well-known theory, the Motivation-Hygiene Theory.

Herzberg suggested that those factors related to a positive attitude toward the job, called "satisfiers," were motivational factors and were directly related to the "content" of the job. The "dissatisfiers," or negative factors related to a job, had more to do with the "context" of the job, or the conditions with which the job was surrounded.

Those satisfiers, which are motivators on the job appear to be as follows: 1) achievement, 2) recognition, 3) work itself, 4) responsibility, 5) advancement, and 6) growth. The satisfiers work together when the work itself is interesting, challenging, and gives a feeling of achievement when finished. The satisfiers also work together when the job, when done well, offers the possibility of advancement to even more challenging work.

The dissatisfiers, or the job context, or the hygiene factors, might include anything such as salary, company policy and administration, supervision, working conditions, and interpersonal relationships on the job. Example: the rest rooms may be perpetually unclean, or the supervisor may be overbearing and tyrannical. Correcting a dissatisfier does not mean that the worker will be satisfied, since satisfaction is not supposed to emerge from the hygiene side. It will simply mean that his dissatisfaction will be lessened.

The three key principles propounded by Herzberg are:

1. The factors involved in producing job satisfaction are separate and distinct from the factors that lead to job dissatisfaction.
2. The opposite of satisfaction on the job is not dissatisfaction, it is merely no job satisfaction.

3. The motivators have a much longer-lasting effect on sustaining satisfaction than the hygiene factors have on preventing dissatisfaction.

Herzberg would have to be considered a part of the human relations school of management, and he particularly emphasized job enrichment.

Some citations from Herzberg, Mausner, and Snyderman's *The Motivation to Work* (New York: John Wiley and Sons, 1959) may be helpful:

> For industry to operate successfully it is essential that efficient procedures be used to the maximum. This necessity has presented management with what appears to be mutually exclusive positions: It believes it cannot be both efficient and human. Because it is imperative that efficiency be maximized, the management process tends to overlook certain fundamental human needs—and, as is starkly evident today, to overlook environment and social welfare. For many years American management has believed that anarchy will result if work is humanized to the extent that good mental health is made operative. But the problem of humanizing job content must be solved in order that social needs as well as industrial needs are met. Management, in short, must be efficient, but at the same time it must be human.
>
> This concept [Maslow's needs hierarchy] has led many people to feel that the worker can never be satisfied with his job. How are you going to solve the dilemma of trying to motivate workers who have a continuously revolving set of needs? Since each individual may present at any one time a different scramble of his psychological need list, a systematic personnel practice hoping to cater to the most prepotent needs of its entire working force is defeated by the nature of the probabilities. Forgetting for a moment the individual "needs hierarchies" it can be argued that there is sufficient homogeneity within various groups of employees to make for a relative similarity of "need hierarchies" within each group. Even so, the changes in prepotency for the group will occur, and personnel administration will have to keep up with them. For some who hold to this point of view personnel administration is reduced to the essential of labor-management bargaining. For others it means that personnel programs must be geared to be sensitive to the changes that are continually taking place in the needs of the employees. And since this can be done only by supervisors, the training of supervisors in understanding human motivation, the factors underlying it, and the therapeutic or manipulative skills with which to cope with it is the most essential ingredient to any industrial relations program."

Another well-known book by Herzberg is *The Managerial Choice* (Homewood, Ill.: Dow Jones-Irwin, 1976).

Rensis Likert 1903–

Dr. Rensis Likert was director of the Institute for Social Research, University of Michigan, from 1948 to 1972. From this advantageous position he conducted highly significant humans relations research. Likert is from the human relations school of management, which was quickly taking root by the time he took a research position at the University of Michigan.

Like most men of his time who were concerned with work and workers, Likert took exception to "Taylorism." He viewed scientific management as being contrary to the nature of workers, and, while it did indeed increase production, it did so at the expense of overworked employees.

In fairness to Taylorism, it should be said that Taylor did what needed to be done in his time. Workers, treated as "warm bodies," were bunched together in workplaces that were not designed for productivity, and the work itself was generally systemless. Taylor worked out systems for each job, figured the time and motions necessary to do jobs, and thus made the worker a more productive individual.

Likert took issue with the idea that high worker morale would always result in higher productivity. While he believed that to be true, he thought it too simplistic. He considered that the following two concepts were valuable to productivity: 1) supervision which is supportive as opposed to threatening and 2) participative as opposed to hierarchically controlled management.

Here is an example of Likert's thinking from *New Patterns of Management* (New York: McGraw-Hill Book Company, Inc., 1961):

> The supervisors and managers in American industry and government who are achieving the highest productivity, lowest costs, least turnover and absence, and the highest levels of employee motivation and satisfaction display, on the average, a different pattern of leadership from those managers who are achieving less impressive results. The principles and practices of

these high-producing managers are deviating in important ways from those called for by present-day management theories.

The high-producing managers whose deviations from existing theory and practice are creating improved procedures have not yet integrated their deviant principles into a theory of management. Individually, they are often clearly aware of how a particular practice of theirs differs from generally accepted methods, but the magnitude, importance, and systematic nature of the differences when the total pattern is examined do not appear to be recognized.

Likert was referring to various human relations theories and practices, including supportive supervision and participation in management.

In an article, "Motivation and Increased Productivity" in *Management Record* 18 (April 1956) Likert discusses the two major trends in management philosophy. The first was scientific management (Taylorism), and the second, beginning after World War I, was the human relations school of thought.

According to Likert, the speedup in production due to scientific management, while increasing both production and productivity, eventually resulted in harassed workers, and unrealistic production goals. It was a habit of management to believe if a worker could produce 100 "gizmos" in a day, with a bit of pressure, he could produce 110. When pushed to do this, however, the worker often rebelled and actually began to produce less, even while doing piece work.

The increase in production and productivity was desirable, but not at the expense of the good will of the workers. It was evident that pushing the worker was not enough, and some industrialists began to consider this problem after World War I. In order for a worker to consistently produce more, he needed both good technology and the high morale which comes with supportive supervision and participation in management.

Likert and dozens of his peers bridged the gap between the values of scientific management and the human relations school that was just emerging.

In the 1960s and 1970s, the human relations school was still scorned in many places. Deciding to "humanize" the worker was not a popular concept, even then. Suffice it to say that Likert and others planted some good seeds, and in many places they have taken root. However, one still finds glaring examples, even in big companies, where the truth that the human relations approach holds has not as yet been learned.

Another vital book, besides the two publications already mentioned, is *The Human Organization: Its Management and Value* (New York: McGraw-Hill Book Company, Inc., 1967).

Karl Marx 1818-1883

Karl Marx may seem a strange selection for a listing of management theorists. No person in the history of humanity has influenced public and private administration as much, and in such a negative manner, as has Karl Marx.

The father of revolutionary communism, Marx was born in Trier, Germany, in 1818, the son of a lawyer. He studied law in Berlin and Bonn, but finally rejected the law for the study of philosophy and history that was to give him the foundation for further study in economics and politics.

As did many people of his time, Marx despised the social conditions around him. Poverty was the lot of nearly 90 percent of the population of any given country, and the start of the Industrial Revolution had not yet resulted in the creation of a stable middle class. There were essentially the two classes, the rich and the poor, and the plight of the poor was abject. It did not require the sensitivity of a saint to feel empathy for these people. And, what was worse, even following the revolutions in America and in France, the conditions appeared to be fixed; there seemed to be little hope for change.

Marx moved often, usually because of persecution by the governments for his virulent writings, which were boldly revolutionary. In 1842 Marx became editor of a paper, the *Rheinische Zeitung,* which was forced out of publication in a year due to its inflammatory nature. He moved to Paris in 1843, but was expelled in 1845, again because of his writings. He then settled in Brussels where, in collaboration with Frederich Engels, a

German Socialist, he reorganized the Communist League, which met in London in 1847. Jointly Marx and Engels produced the *Communist Manifesto* in 1848, which advocated monumental institutional changes for the emerging industrial society. Upon the publication of the *Manifesto,* Marx was asked to leave Brussels.

Having participated in the revolutionary social upheavals in the Rhineland in the late 1840s, Marx settled in London, where he would spend the rest of his life pursuing his dream. He spent most of his time in private study, while his family lived in an impoverished state. Engels, the son of a wealthy textile manufacturer, gave Marx financial aid, but it was seldom enough. Engels' role is unique in that he prospered as a member of the very class communism sought to destroy.

With Engels' help Marx published the first volume of *Das Kapital* in 1867. Volume II was published by Engels in 1885, two years after Marx's death, and the third volume came out in 1895.

Marx's theories did not take management into consideration, neither in government nor in industry. He had argued that the "proletariat" would eventually rise up and throw off the shackles of oppressive government, that then would come a stage called "the dictatorship of the proletariat," when apparently all people would live in a classless society, in complete harmony, with no one to manage them. Marx never got beyond this chimerical concept.

In the real world, however, there is somebody to manage everything. When revolutionary communism came into full fruition, as it did in Russia in 1917, management took on a new and hideous look. The "manager," after the revolution, was theoretically the Communist Party. Managers in government were party members who often knew nothing of what they were supposed to manage. Managers in industry were puppets, again often knowing little about what they were supposed to do, and they were generally devoted to protecting their own positions.

Marx's plan, which excluded management, was eventually to manage more than two-fifths of the world's population.

Abraham Maslow 1908–1971

Two decades after his death, Abraham Maslow remains a recognized giant in the area of management theory and motivational theory.

Maslow was a clinical psychologist. As a young man he broke with the traditional schools of psychological thought, propounded by Sigmund Freud (1856–1939) and John B. Watson (1878–1958). He was not contemptuous of traditional schools of psychology, but he felt that both fields approached humanity from the wrong perspective.

Maslow was disturbed by the fact that Freud drew most of his conclusions from his experiences with the insane, the neurotic, and the irrational. He wondered how Freud could find the "normal" *Homo sapiens* in this atmosphere. The work of Freud was called the "First Force," a term probably coined by Maslow's friend, Frank Goble. And, while Maslow never underestimated the pioneering work of Freud, he departed from it almost altogether in his own work.

The "Second Force," or behaviorism, was formulated by John B. Watson. While Freud's theory was developed primarily from listening to his patients and from his subjective interpretation of their neuroses, the behaviorists concentrated on a strictly objective, "scientific" approach. And, while Freud placed the major emphasis on deep inner drives and urges, the behaviorists placed the emphasis upon external, environmental influences.

Watson argued that "personality is the sum of the activities that can be discovered by actual observation of behavior over a long enough period of time to give reliable information. In other words, personality is but the end product of our habit systems."*

Generally, the behaviorist is not interested in morals except as a scientist, because he believes that human beings are flexible, malleable, and passive products of their environments, which determine their behavior. While Maslow never openly disavowed either Freud's or Watson's theories, he viewed them as inadequate to understand people as they are and as they might become.

*John B. Watson, *Behaviorism* (Chicago: University of Chicago Press, 1930).

Maslow's theory, now called the "Third Force," was encapsulated in his "Hierarchy of Human Needs." He planned his hierarchy in this ascending order:

1. Basic physiological needs, such as food, drink, sex, etc.
2. Safety, security needs.
3. Love and belongingness needs.
4. Esteem needs: self-esteem and the esteem of others.
5. Self-actualization needs (Self realization).

While this book will deal with these concepts superficially, Maslow did not. He spent years in the laboratory, in the classroom, and in industry, testing his hypothesis.

A major contribution of Maslow was the emphasis he placed on the "sameness" of people, as opposed to the differences among people. If people, indeed, are alike in some fundamental ways, then we have a firm foundation from which to launch any motivational program. Maslow's hierarchy is a method of understanding all people, to some degree, rather than depending on a small sample of the entire population.

Maslow's ideas opened the door to managing people, under any circumstances, to understand the people better and come more nearly achieving their goals as a result.

Simplistically, Maslow's theory is that these same five levels of needs exist in all people, everywhere. And, although there is a natural overlapping of the needs, one need is dominant at any point in time and will remain so until reasonably satisfied, at which time the individual will move up to the next area of need.

With regard to motivation, the theory states that human beings can be motivated in the area of their dominant needs at a given time. Thus, if a manager were aware of the basic need of the person at the time, the manager would have greater knowledge as to how that person could be motivated.

Basic physiological needs are rather obvious and need no discussion in the context of this volume. Safety and security needs relate to any life experience that is a threat to the person, and against which the person desires to be protected. It will be remember that no sooner had labor unions gotten the pay and fringe benefits they wanted for the present than they began to push for a guaranteed annual wage. In short, the unions claimed to be doing well, but they wanted safety for the future. Love and belongingness needs appear after security needs are met. Persons want to feel a part of a group, and they want to be accepted and appreciated for themselves. Esteem needs come next, and both self-esteem and the esteem of others are regarded as important. The "self-actualization" area is somewhat difficult to explain briefly, since it may refer to one who is already mature, or it can refer to one on a continuum toward maturity, in which the individual is constantly striving to become all he or she can be.

Maslow was the father of humanistic psychology, and this expression needs to be examined in some detail. Humanistic psychology seeks to show what people can become starting with where and what they are. The almost infinite capacity for human development is recognized. In Maslow's hierarchy, individuals are neither the victims of inner drives nor of their environments, but they enjoy a relative freedom in which to grow and develop.

If Maslow's theory is true then wherever a manager manages, the people will be basically the same. And, in our new world economy, this knowledge could be invaluable to an international manager.

Some of Maslow's writings are: *Motivation and Personality* (New York: Harper & Row, 1954); *Toward a Psychology of Being* (New York: Van Nostrand, 1962); *Euphyscian Management* (Homewood, Ill.: Irwin-Dorsey, 1965). A book about Maslow that every student of management should read is: Frank Goble, *The Third Force* (New York: Grossman Publishers, 1970).

G. Elton Mayo 1880–1949

Mayo is best known for his participation in the Hawthorne Experiments, conducted at the Hawthorne plant of the Western Electric Company in Chicago during the period from 1927 to 1932. The experiments had begun at Hawthorne in 1924, but Mayo, with the help of a research staff from the Harvard Graduate School of Business, joined the work in 1927 and continued to the end in 1932.

Until this time, speaking generally, scientific management, led by

Frederick Taylor, had viewed management and organization purely from an engineering perspective. While it is true that some of Taylor's contemporaries, including H. L. Gantt, had given serious thought to what we now term "human relations," no serious study had been done on such a subject.

The Hawthorne studies were preceded by, and built upon, a series of experiments on the effects of illumination on employee efficiency, which were conducted in cooperation with the National Research Council of the National Academy of Sciences from 1924 to 1927. These studies led, over time, to a more thorough understanding of human relations in industry and also resulted in many changes in personnel management.

The Hawthorne Studies were divided into three phases: 1) Test Room studies; 2) Interviewing studies; and 3) Observational studies. Each phase grew out of, and added dimensions to, the preceding phase.

The review presented here is obviously simplistic, and serious students should pursue the matter further.

Illumination Test Room Studies, 1924–27

These studies developed from a series of controlled experiments that extended over three winters and dealt with the relationship between variations of the intensity of illumination and the efficiency of shop workers.

After many experiments with lighting, which yielded many strange and contradictory results, these two following conclusions were drawn: 1) Illumination was only one, and not the most important, factor affecting output; 2) There was no simple cause-and-effect relationship between the single variable, illumination, and operator efficiency.

Interviewing Studies, 1928–31

These studies concentrated on the attitudes employees had toward their jobs, working conditions, and supervision. About 21,000 interviews were done.

The experiment was not a resounding success. The responses followed no well-defined patterns. However, it was established that there was value in talking to an employee and listening to problems. And, as a result of this conclusion, clinical psychologists became a part of industrial life, and many companies established employee counseling programs.

Observational Studies, 1931–32

This study grew out of the recognition that workers in the work place cannot be studied alone, but they must be studied as an integral part of their total work situation. This last phase of the experimental programs highlighted some of the social factors important in the motivation of a worker.

Fourteen men and their supervisors were studied. The findings of the study made it clear that the work group constituted a complex social organization with established norms of conduct and shared sentiments above and beyond those required by the formal organization of their work.

Summary

Out of all the studies one thing became apparent: the worker was something other than an "economic man". That is, he did not work for money alone, and thus could not be motivated by money alone. Another discovery was the importance of the supervisor's role in motivation and productivity. Moreover, a group spirit was found to be of primary importance in the work situation.

G. Elton Mayo wrote two important books: *The Human Problem of an Industrial Organization* (New York: Viking, 1933) and *Social Problems of an Industrial Organization* (Cambridge: Harvard University Press, 1945).

Douglas McGregor 1906–1964

Douglas McGregor did most of his work while teaching and researching at the Massachusetts Institute of Technology. He was also president of Antioch College where he continued his work in behavioral psychology. In short, he believed that to understand the worker one had to understand what people are and what moves them to act in specific ways.

Most experts agree that McGregor's work was not original, which he affirmed, but it built upon rough ideas that were never fully developed by other thinkers.

McGregor wrote on all areas of the work environment, including leadership, motivation, personnel functions, etc. His best-known theory however, is encompassed in the Theory X, Theory Y concept of the worker.

Far into the development of the Industrial Revolution in the United States, the notion prevailed that workers really do not want to work, that they viewed work as a kind of punishment, and that if made to work they will do as little as they can.

This concept of the worker, which is still very much alive in the less-developed areas of the United States, was the concept that McGregor attempted to refute with Theory X and Theory Y. In his book, *The Human Side of Enterprise* (New York: McGraw-Hill, 1960), he described the worker, according to Theory X, in this manner: people are lazy; they dislike and shun work; they have to be driven to work; and they need both the carrot and the stick. Theory X assumes workers to be immature people who do not really want responsibility and who yearn to be looked after. (This type of worker would do well under a system of paternalism.) Theory Y asserts that human beings seek maturity, that people like responsibility, and that they seek, as Maslow would have said, self-actualization.

Although McGregor wanted to present Theory X and Theory Y as alternatives, he made it clear, as did many other writers, that his fundamental belief about workers was that they fit the characterization of Theory Y. The fact is that one can hardly accept Theory Y without reservation if empirical evidence is closely considered. One can, in the average workplace, find both those who seem to be Theory X workers and others who represent Theory Y.

Many of McGregor's peers, such as Maslow and Drucker, fundamentally believed in the Theory Y concept but felt that it left something to be desired as an overall explanation of the average worker.

Maslow, in fact, who experimented for a year with the Theory Y characterization in a small company in California, came to believe that

Theory Y could not stand alone, inasmuch as many workers were not yet at the stage of self-motivation that Theory Y requires, nor were they visionary as far as work was concerned. They needed a strong guiding hand, and indeed many felt lost without it. He found that the business world was not peopled with mature adults but with many who were still immature, some of whom might remain that way.

Both Maslow and Drucker (Drucker had essentially presented a Theory Y conception some years before, but his was more restrained) came to be of the opinion that, while Theory X was not acceptable, Theory Y could be envisioned as too permissive, which would put great pressure both on workers and on managers. Maslow probably could have seen Theory Y as compatible with his "self-actualizing" worker, but not his worker still straining to meet safety and security needs.

Despite its limitations, McGregor's theory retains a lot of truth. By the time of McGregor's writing, however, it had become all too evident that two views of the average worker were wrong. One was the ancient, but still existing, idea that men are indeed lazy, non-innovative, and in need of being driven to do their work. The second was that the paternalistic system which followed closely on the heels of Theory X (not called by that name) was sufficient. In fact, it appeared that while both Theory X and Theory Y were right in part, both were incomplete as a total explanation of the average worker.

In spite of the weaknesses to be found in this theory of Douglas McGregor's, he did point the way to higher ground for those who would both study and follow him. As a pioneer in the human-relations school of management, he did call attention to weaknesses existing in man's view of his fellow man. And he did make managers of that age, and for many years after, reconsider their views.

In later years, William Ouchi, in *How American Business Can Meet The Japanese Challenge* (Reading, Massachusetts: Addison-Wesley Publishing Company, 1981) came out with the Theory Z concept of management. It suggests that an involved worker is the key to greater productivity. Again, the so-called Theory Z concept did not originate with him. But his emphasis upon the aspects of Theory Z did come at a time when the United States needed help. Productivity was lagging, and foreign competition was becoming very real. But, upon investigation, one finds that Theory Z does not have all the answers either.

It is quite possible that one will find, after reading most of the management concepts that are well known in the trade, that no single theory works in all cases, but that many theories combined do work in most cases.

The two books for which Douglas McGregor was best known are *The Human Side of Enterprise* (New York: McGraw-Hill, 1960) and *The Professional Messenger* (New York: McGraw-Hill, 1967).

George S. Odiorne 1920–1992

Odiorne, who did most of his work at the University of Michigan, is included in this list not because he is a pioneer in management theory, but because he has done much to publicize the concept of management by objectives (MBO). This concept, Odiorne thought, would be the management "savior" of the 1980s and beyond. There is much to commend in MBO, but the theory leaves much to be desired.

As early as 1954, Peter Drucker discussed management by objectives, but not necessarily in a positive light. He put the emphasis upon "self-set goals," which is not the thesis of MBO proper.

The primary program of MBO is this: each management "pair," that is, a manager at any level and his immediate superior, following a formal procedure, periodically reach mutual agreements on specific and measurable goals or objectives that the subordinate manager is supposed to attain in the subsequent period. Usually there are periodic measurements taken to see how the plan is progressing, and then there is an evaluation at the end of the period to see if the goals were actually reached.

No one, I think, opposes MBO per se. Many arguments have raged about this concept, and they usually focus on who is setting the objectives and who is carrying out the steps to reach the objectives.

Some positive aspects of MBO are: 1) it encourages top managers to do long-range planning; 2) it encourages all managers, at all levels, to be aware that certain objectives in the enterprise must be met; 3) it encourages better communications between levels of management; 4) it encourages goal-orientation throughout the enterprise; 5) it quantifies the goals so that measurements can be taken to judge the success or failure of the plan.

Some negative aspects of MBO are: 1) its tendency to draw critics who like to stick pins in the latest balloon and who like to point out that top managers "wheel and deal" and often give little thought to long-range planning; 2) its "top-down" characteristics; 3) its vulnerability to some unions' belief that MBO should not be used to judge the merits of workers; 4) its allowance for some deterministic criticism which scorns all long-range planning, averring that "what will be, will be."

It is the judgment of this author that MBO can only be seriously criticized where planning is done without consulting those who actually do the work, i.e., the line people. Example: Suppose that a vice-president for production calls in his top supervisor and together they plan production for the next quarter. The goals are set, and the top supervisor then hands the orders down to line supervisors, who are supposed to hand them down to the people working on the line. But 70 percent of the line workers declare that they are already producing at top levels given the technology they have to work with. So, in a situation like this, MBO breaks down. Moreover, using MBO in a case like this could result in further problems. The line people might well ask why they were not consulted about the new goals. If there is a union in the plant, the union people complain that too much pressure is being put on the workers. It would appear at this point that the vice-president of production erred when he did not include line workers in the planning. After all, he is not going to achieve the goal, nor are his supervisors. The line people are ultimately charged with achieving the goal, and they should be consulted about how to go about it.

Also, I have been in year-end sales meetings in which the sales manager stands up, shows the graphs for last year, and then declares enthusiastically, "Let's all agree that we will increase our sales by 10 percent next year." Here is a goal, albeit a rather hazy one. If this is to be a goal, it cannot be taken out of thin air and thrown at the salespeople. If a 10 percent increase is to be a workable goal, all the people involved should discuss the matter, and then work out the steps necessary to reach the goal.

So there appears to be nothing basically wrong with MBO, but there can be a lot of things wrong with how the matter is worked out in specific situations. The often-asked question, "Whose goals?" remains valid.

Other books by Odiorne include his first book on MBO, *Management Decisions by Objectives* (Belmont, Calif: David S. Lake, Pub., 1965), *Personnel Administration by Objectives* (Homewood, Ill.: Richard D. Irwin, 1971), *How Managers Make Things Happen* (Englewood Cliffs, N.J.: Prentice-Hall, 1961).

Robert Owen 1771–1858

Robert Owen, a Scotsman, is listed in many books as a socialist, and that is probably strictly true. When one reviews his life and work, he comes across as one who was not only a humanitarian, but also one who understood human relations in management long before anyone else had.

What Owen ultimately became famous for conceiving was what is now known as "paternalism," which we now eschew and for good reason. But the good he accomplished should not be forgotten.

By the time Owen went to work in industry, the Industrial Revolution had long since started in England and Scotland. This period was marked by flagrant child-labor abuses, long working hours, low pay (often theoretically related to the concept of "the iron law of wages"), hovel housing, and virtually every human indecency one can imagine. There were the "haves" and the "have nots," and this came to seem like a divine decree with people, similar to the notion of the divine right of kings, which had been so prevalent in the centuries preceding the Industrial Revolution. Despair was generally the lot of working people, but it always had been their lot.

Robert Owen began as a textile mill employee, and by dint of hard work and a superior intelligence he ultimately became the managing director of a group of textile mills in New Lanark, Scotland. He pursued this career from 1800 to 1828.

Textile mills were among the worst examples of the evils that existed through much of the Industrial Revolution. Child labor was widely used;

often the children were no more than eight or nine years old, and they were sometimes chained to their machines, and loosed only occasionally to relieve themselves or eat a scanty lunch. The factories were ill-lighted and ill-ventilated.

Furthermore, most workers, both children and adults, lived in hovels, not homes, which were poorly heated if they were heated at all, and where subsistence rations alone were available to eat. The so-called "iron law of wages" decreed that workers would only be paid enough to allow them to subsist and to procreate so that another generation of workers would be available. All of these galled the young Owen, and he determined to do something about it.

Students of human relations in industry do not like to call Owen's experiments "human relations" experiments. But, whatever one chooses to call these experiments, they immediately made life better for workers, and that was Owen's primary concern. Owen set out first to improve working conditions in the mills by cleaning them up, including the grounds around them. He then turned to improving the domestic lives of the workers by putting in streets, building company houses, and setting up company stores where goods could be bought by the employees at cost. Mills were equipped with facilities for serving meals where the workers could be freed for a time from their machines and could be fed nutritious meals.

The minimum working age for children was introduced, along with restrictions on the number of hours a child could work. Children were also helped by the setting up of schools and school reforms, which gained worldwide attention.

Owen virtually built a small city that he looked upon as a model industrial town.

Another area of management explored by Owen was personnel. He felt that the personnel department of a company should not be totally subordinated to management but rather a part of the management structure that would look after the needs of employees.

Owen is also looked upon as the father of the modern cooperative, working both in the industrial and the agricultural fields. He believed that individual character is molded by environment and can be improved in a society based on cooperation. This is common socialistic philosophy.

Owen's contribution can be summarized by saying that he introduced "paternalism" into the industrial world. In Owen's time, any kind of help for workers was important, and Owen gave help that others were not inclined to give.

The writings of Robert Owen are virtually impossible to come by, but one which is representative, though it, too, is difficult to find, is *A New View of Society*, edited by G. D. H. Cole (London: Everyman, 1927).

Frederick Taylor 1856–1915

Taylor is known as the "father of scientific management." In spite of the fact that his views are often looked down upon by modern managers, his theories opened up a whole new concept of work and management for industry.

In 1878, during a prolonged depression, Taylor joined the Midvale Steel Company as a day laborer. He was a diligent worker, perhaps because of his Quaker background, and he also had an avid curiosity and above-average intelligence. Within three months, he had become the gang boss of the lathe section. Over the next three years, he was involved in a long, hard struggle with his workers. Although they were on piece work, they did not seem to want to work hard or efficiently. He was convinced that they were underproducing. As well as being a hard-working man, Taylor was a tough man to work with or for. During his period as gang boss, he belabored his men to work better, but usually without result. He hired and fired at will, but, without the social graces he needed, he did little but antagonize his men.

After three years as a gang boss, Taylor became a foreman, and continued his work to make his people produce more and better products. He wanted to serve his company well; yet Taylor could see that the workers were not doing as well as they might, and he could also see that there were many weaknesses in the company's management.

In his effort to solve some of the problems of industrial work and the problems of workers, he found himself leaning more toward methods than he did toward understanding workers. He believed, for example, that the workers were not the only culprits in the nonproductivity that marked the industries of his day. For whatever reason, the workers did not work as well as they should have, and it seemed that management did not really understand how productive a worker should be in a day. While managers were constantly pushing for more production, they could not tell anyone how to improve production. So, generally, workers were merely admonished to "work harder."

Before leaving Midvale Steel Company in 1890, Taylor rose to the rank of chief engineer. He had earned a degree in 1883 by going to night classes. In 1886, Taylor gave his first scientific paper before the American Association of Mechanical Engineers. This group continued to provide the forum for his developing ideas. Taylor spent time, after his stint at Midvale, with a number of different firms, but the last fourteen years of his life he spent consulting and developing his scientific management theories, which he propounded to industry.

Taylor's basic approach to work was to 1) plan work and 2) execute work. He saw a vast difference between the two, even though they were absolutely complementary. For plans to be effective, the planner had to know how to execute work. For work to be properly executed, some idea of the planning method and purpose was necessary.

Taylor conceived the idea that if planned work were ever to be effective, it had to be broken down into many component parts, with time and attention given to every part. Thus, his studies came to be called "time and motion" studies. In short, he addressed the question of how much time was needed for each component of an operation, and what motions were needed to make it the most efficient operation.

To many managers that followed Taylor, his studies seemed cold and devoid of human understanding. To a degree, this is true. Taylor was certainly not schooled in human relations. But, in budding industries, his scientific management did make workers more productive, and, in fact, Taylor's approach was generally used by the Ford Motor Company to enhance its first assembly lines. Labor costs became lower because of scientific management, while wages went up. The quality of the products might not have been better, but the products did come off the assembly lines at much lower prices than before.

It is believed by many experts that the work of Frederick Taylor opened the door to seventy-five years of increased productivity and production in the United States, and gave the working masses an opportunity to share in the lower-cost production.

Taylor's critics point out that his theories led to specialization so minute that work became pure monotony for assembly line workers. And there is much truth in this, though had Taylor lived to see it, he may very well have opposed the type of specialization that ultimately appeared in industry.

Most experts, who see both sides of Taylor's work, see him as a laudable pioneer who appeared on the industrial scene at exactly the right time. It would be left to others to refine what he did and to add those nuances of which we are aware in industry today.

Taylor wrote many scientific papers. His best known book is *Principles and Methods of Scientific Management* (New York: Harper & Bros., 1911).

Ordway Tead 1892–1972

The name of Dr. Ordway Tead will not be as well known to the average reader as will others. This is not because his work is less important, the contrary is true, in fact, but because his major work was done prior to the post–World War II boom in management theory. He was known primarily for his work in the field of personnel administration, though he did work, in a pioneer fashion, in virtually all fields of management theory.

He was an avid proponent of democratic principles in management long before this concept was popular. His work in this field, though early, is as up-to-date as anything now existing in the field.

Tead taught personnel administration, and at Columbia, 1917–18, he was in charge of war emergency employment management courses at the War Department.

He continued at Columbia as a lecturer in personnel administration from 1920 to 1950. From 1951 to 1956 he was adjunct professor of industrial relations. He was, in addition to his other work, a faculty member of the department of industry at the New York School of Social Work from 1920 to 1929.

Some citations from his writings will serve to clarify some of his views. The first is from *The Art of Administration* (New York: McGraw-Hill Book Company, Inc., 1951), p. 198:

> Those who approach participation in business direction from the point of view preponderantly of "banker management," or of what Veblen called "financial capitalism," are not usually those who are deeply interested in or necessarily skilled in administration in the sense here conceived. There are still those in business who are playing for high stakes and quick results, who see industrial enterprises as pawns in a game of financial manipulation, who are not unfairly spoken of as "business buccaneers." Promoters and "entrepreneurs" of this caliber do not tend to have administrative interests. They do not usually possess the patience, the human sensitivity and the public outlook to administer well in the constructive, long-range way today required. Fortunately the demands and occasions of present-day economic adventure lie much less in the field of financial manipulation that in the field of the more sober and steady building of productive unity on foundations of cooperative effort.

Tead believed that the corporation was an organization not to just make a profit, which he knew was necessary, but to deal with social problems that arise in any human organization. He also believed that people of higher intelligence should occupy administrative positions, especially the top ones. At the same time, Tead was not an elitist. A lot of his writing has to do with democratic policies in the corporation, but he did believe that the top administrator should have the intelligence to occupy the position for the long term and work for the long-term growth of the enterprise, rather than putting all the emphasis on the bottom line for the next quarter.

In recent years we have seen the negative results in virtually all areas of American industry when financial men occupy the top administrative spots. The same kind of problems have occurred when wheeler-dealers, posing as administrators, strip a company and then ride off into the sunset. In fact, it has been proved in our time, *ad infinitum, ad naueseam,* that such false administrators can literally wreck an industry. One need only consider the state of the savings and loan industry to see a prime example.

As for effective leadership, Tead wrote in *Human Nature and Management* (New York: McGraw-Hill Book Company, Inc., 1929), p. 149, that: "Leadership is the name for that combination of qualities by the possession of which one is able to get something done by others, chiefly because through his influence they become willing to do it." Likewise, in the same place he wrote that organizational morale, or esprit de corps, is: "that attitude which results from the mobilizing of energy, interest and initiative in the enthusiastic pursuit of a group's purposes."

Other important books by Ordway Tead are: *The Art of Leadership* (New York: McGraw-Hill Book Company, Inc., 1935) and with Henry C. Metcalf, *Personnel Administration: Its Principles and Practices* (New York: McGraw Hill Book Company, Inc., 1933).

Leonard D. White 1891–1958

Leonard D. White was another management pioneer who is not well known in many circles because his primary contribution to management was in the area of public personnel administration. In spite of this fact, his work won international fame, and has, no doubt, provided the framework for public administration personnel policy around the world.

White is credited with a number of "firsts" that indicate the breadth and depth of his work. He was the author of the first text on public administration. He was the first educator to teach public administration in a university classroom. He started the Junior Civil Service Examiner Examination, which attracted liberal arts and social science majors to careers in the federal government. While he taught a class in public personnel administration at the American University, the idea was born to establish the Society for Personnel Administration.

In recent years as tasks of government at all levels have multiplied, public administration as a discipline has not prospered as much as might be expected. Still, the tasks ahead in public administration are ever-growing. One should only recall that the federal government, through various departments and agencies, administers about one-fifth of the Gross

National Product, or one trillion dollars annually, to realize the need for effective public administration.

If people who are expected to fill these positions are not deserving of a branch of the management discipline which deals specifically with their problems, it's hard to imagine who would be. There are, of course, many problems related to public administration that are worth examining.

The situation surrounding public administration changed radically during the late 1970s and the 1980s. The number of government jobs, at all levels, proliferated. City managers or administrators began to take over even small town governments. And the Freedom of Information Act made government more aware of its obligation to communicate with citizens.

New knowledge entered the arena of public administration and fell into a number of categories. First, much of the new knowledge was mathmetical and quantitative, demanding new administrative skills. Second, information became more concerned with interrelationships and the managing of people in a group context. Third, the new knowledge had to deal with new concepts of public management, many of which clashed with long-held ideas. (One does not have to go back many years to find that "public administrators" really did not believe that what they did and how they did it was the business of the public.) Fourth, communications and the need for communications accelerated, as files, by law, were more open, and as most meetings became open to the public. Fifth, participation by citizens, particularly in municipal government, became a fact that many public administrators found hard to deal with.

There is also the strange admixture in public administration of management and law. While this exists in all fields of management, it is a paramount matter for consideration in the public field.

White dealt with many of these problems in his studies, but quite naturally he could not foresee the vast growth of government and the need for so many public administrators. But he and a few others in the 1920s and 1930s did open the door to a field that continues to grow in importance.

White's most famous writing was the book, *Introduction to the Study of Public Administration,* 4th ed. (New York: Macmillan, 1955). Other writings include: *The City Manager* (University of Chicago Social

Science Studies, Number 9, 1927) and *Prestige and Value of Public Employment* (University of Chicago Social Science Studies, Number 14, 1929).

William Foote Whyte 1914–

William Foote Whyte did most of his work as professor of industrial relations at the New York State School of Industrial and Labor Relations, Cornell University, where he began teaching in 1948. Although Whyte is usually listed as a member of the human relations school of management, his research ranged over virtually every aspect of the management field. His book, *Men at Work* (Homewood, Ill.: Richard D. Irwin, Inc., 1961), is one of the most quoted books in management literature.

One of the primary contributions of Whyte was his untiring re-evaluation of theories as they actually worked in the real world of work. An example of this practice is his report, "Human Relations Theory: A Progress Report," *Harvard Business Review* Vol. 34, No. 5 (Sept.–Oct. 1956). In this article, Whyte gives an outline of the progess of the human relations school of thought since the 1933 edition of Mayo's *Human Relations of an Industrial Civilization* was published (the 1933 edition was published by The Macmillan Company in New York; the 1946 edition was published by the Division of Research, Harvard Business School, Boston). The outline of progress of human relations theory is as follows:

1. Staking out the claims—Since 1933 the human relations school has been established as having a permanent place in management theory and practice.
2. Following the leads—The human relations school is now working more on the positive side, rather than just deciding what is wrong in a given situation.
3. Developing a new pattern—Since early thought was generally centered on finding out what was wrong with human relations in a given situation, the newer research takes a more positive direction.

Whyte's thoughts on the progress made since Mayo's groundbreaking work:

1. We know how to use money more effectively as an incentive.
2. We have gone beyond the simple "work group" concept to discover some of the different forms of group behavior actually to be found in industry.
3. We are learning how the structure of the organization can affect morale and productivity.
4. We have learned some of the limitations of human relations training—a necessary step in the development of more effective action.

One area which Whyte attacked as being incomplete is the area of supervisory training in human relations. Beginning in the 1950s, this type of training proliferated, and continued through most of the 1970s. It was finally discovered that supervisory training did little good to train first line supervisors, if the management higher up remained either ignorant or opposed to the idea. (This writer lectured in dozens of places in the 1960s and early 1970s in the area of human relations. It was still relatively new idea in the "hinterlands." One night after a lecture, two men from the same company came forward and said, "We liked the lecture, but you are talking to the wrong group. Unless you sell this to top management our knowledge is not going to mean much." Unfortunately, this was the pattern all over the country.)

Whyte also discovered, as did others, that good human relations is a function of relatively stable patterns of interaction, both in the frequency of the contact and the balance in those who initiate contact. Closely related to this insight is Whyte's thought that the contacts made by subordinates to superiors is vital in human relations in that it gives the subordinate the feeling that he is in charge of a given situation, and could speak his mind freely to the superior.

In exploring areas generally referred to as the managerial mind, Whyte gave the following example:

One Sunday morning on the twelve to eight shift, the crane broke down. My shift foreman called the mechanical department and asked them to repair the crane immediately. The mechanical people said they could not do the job, that they would have to call in the millwrights, pipefitters and so on. They said, "We cannot do that without the approval of our superintendent." He said, "You call those men right away because this crane is stopping the production, and I can't afford to lose that production." There was some reluctance from the mechanical people to do that, but my foreman insisted that he was taking upon himself the whole responsibility of this decision. Finally, the mechanical people decided to call the repair crew and the whole thing was repaired before eight in the morning.

A major aspect of the managerial mind is the ability to accept responsibility.

Other books by Whyte are: *Pattern of Industrial Peace* (New York: Harper and Brothers, 1951) and *Money and Motivation: An Analysis of Incentives in Industry*, written with others, (New York: Harper & Row, Publishers, Inc., 1955).

Conclusion to Biographical Sketches

In spite of all the progress that has been made in the study of management over the past one hundred years, it is going to be necessary to begin again in many areas, both in terms of management theories and in terms of dealing with business throughout the world.

For example, how are those managers in communist countries, which are now seeking the freedoms of more democratic forms of government, going to be trained or retrained after decades under systems that made a shambles of management theory? Likewise, how will a developed economy, as in the United States, regain the momentum it once had in any industrial field?

The prize for management knowledge and practice still awaits the nation that will take the time to understand humanity and to find those ways that will make human beings work productively with one another.

World Dictionary of Management

A

abandonment *insurance* A term describing goods that have been covered by insurance, or the remains thereof, which have been taken over by the insurance company in return for a settlement for the total loss of the goods.

abandonment, of a product or business Sometimes the result of poor management, but often the open door to innovativeness and profitable opportunity.

ABC method A way of categorizing a range of items that must be analyzed by putting them into A, B, and C groups. Each group then will be dealt with as the need requires.

ability The aptitude or the propensity in a person to perform certain tasks well.

ability, synergic An ability to operate in the synergic mode (synergy literally means "working together") in a specific area. (*See* synergetics)

ability to follow instructions test A test used by the National Institute of Industrial Psychology (UK) to determine the fitness of a person for the engineering apprenticeship.

above-the-line promotion *Marketing* Monies used in sales promotions in the press, in radio and television, or in some other media outlet. The converse, promotion below-the-line, indicates monies spent in reduced-price special offers, coupons, point-of-sales displays, etc.

absenteeism to be away from one's place of employment. Absenteeism tends to be about 35 percent higher among women workers than among men workers, in part because many newly formed jobs for women are low-skill, low-paying jobs. When comparisons are made between men and women in the same job classifications, the rates of absenteeism are much closer.

abusive dismissal The dismissing of an

employee in a manner that is legal, but which makes use of managerial tactics and power that are distasteful and unfair. (In some nations, abusive dismissals are illegal.)

Academy of Management An association of professional academicians in the United States, teaching primarily general business and management.

accelerated depreciation 1. A method of decreasing assets in a more rapid manner than usual in order to speed up the recapture of capital. Methods of depreciation must fit the laws of any given nation. 2. Any type of depreciation method that produces larger deductions for depreciation in the early years of a project's life.

accelerated vocational training Classroom teaching of a vocation that is supplemented by actual work in a factory or in some work situation matching the classroom instruction.

acceptance criterion Any minimum standard of performance in investment analysis.

acceptance house A financial institution, often called a "merchant bank," that specializes in lending money on the security of bills of exchange or in adding its name as an endorser to a bill drawn on another person or institution. (*See* bill of exchange)

acceptance of others The ability, in the work situation, to behave toward other people constructively so as not to be an impediment to goal achievement.

acceptance sampling A form of statistical quality control in which the quality of a sample of a product determines the acceptance or rejection of the entire lot of a product.

Accepting Houses Committee A body in the United Kingdom that safeguards the standards of the seventeen leading merchant banks that compose its membership.

accessions rate of labor The total number of employees, part-time or full-time, that are added to the payroll of a firm in a given period of time.

accidents, analyzing Methods for both examining accidents to discover their causes and for preventing accidents.

accommodation party A person who signs a bill of exchange as a guarantor in the event the acceptor fails to pay at the proper time. (*See* bill of exchange)

accomplishment and hard work No direct relationship has been proved, nor should be assumed, between accomplishment and hard work. Presuming that there is a direct relationship between accomplishment and hard work has been labeled the "buckets of sweat syndrome."

accomplishment/cost procedure A technique developed at Stanford University for accurately comparing and contrasting results of large-scale projects. It is essentially an information system that assists management in the effective control of large projects.

accord and satisfaction A legal term for the making and completion of an agreed-upon variation of a contract. The word "accord" means there must be agreement on the variation, and "satisfaction" means the contract must be completed according to the variation.

account executive In advertising, the members of the advertising firm who have the responsibility for dealing with the accounts established between the firm and its clients in all aspects of those accounts.

account period An accounting for time followed by the London Stock Exchange, which operates on twenty-three two-week periods and two three-week periods each year. Generally, buyers and sellers in the market are expected to settle their accounts at the end of each period. However, some exceptions to this rule do exist.

accountability The act of taking responsibility for one's actions to a superior.

accountability, for delegated responsibility The person delegating responsibility is still ultimately responsible for what he has delegated. The top manager must always remember that "the buck stops with him."

accountable management The action of making work units responsible for performance in a manner which is as objective as possible, with the cooperation of the units themselves.

accountant's return A term synonymous with return on capital or rate of return. (*See* rate of return, return on capital)

accounting Principles and techniques used in establishing, maintaining, recording, and analyzing financial transactions.

accounting, human-asset *See* human-asset accounting

accounting income An economic agent's realized income as revealed by financial statements. (*See* economic income)

accounting, international A true international accounting system is a goal rather than a reality due to the wide differences in bookkeeping, in standards, and in auditing. It is not probable that a true system of international accounting will emerge in this century.

accounting, measure of organization performance Accounting provides a measure of the performance not only of a total organization, but also of various departments and top management individuals within an organization. The direct responsibility for profit falls to the general manager, president, or other top official by whatever name. Cost accounting points directly to the production manager, and living within a prescribed budget falls to sales and service personnel.

accounting period A period of time, of some specific length, at which a summary of financial condition and costing information is prepared and a new period begun. The period should be sufficiently short to reveal any problems that should come to the attention of management.

accounting rate of return Annual average cash inflow divided by total outflow. (*See also* internal rate of return)

accounts receivable financing Pledging accounts receivable funds to financing institution as a basis for financing. Such a pledge usually entails periodic turning over of invoices to the financial institution. As invoices are paid, money is turned back to the financing institution, with a discount fee being paid. This kind of agreement is set up as a legally binding agreement. The financing institution may reject any suspect invoices at will.

accounts receivable management The act of keeping accounts receivable in proper ratio to sales, volume of credit sales, seasonality of sales, rules for credit limits, collections policies, etc.

accretion The growth of a fund, such as a pension fund, as a result of new contributions and/or the interest building on the principal.

accrual accounting A method of accounting in which revenue is recognized when earned and expenses recognized when incurred without regard to timing. (*See also* cash accounting)

accrual method A technique used in accounting to enter the income into the accounts during the period in which the sales are made, yet recording expenses only when incurred.

accuracy in communications The achievement of imparting truth in communications, often by making communications two-way or manifold so that more people can evaluate the information being imparted.

ACER speed and accuracy test A clerical aptitude test in which names and numbers, in pairs, are checked against each other under the pressure of a time limit.

achievement analysis The act of examining a project by specific stages, sometimes called milestones. (*See also* PERT)

achievement motivation In simple form, achievement motivation is established by having high goals, having a positive attitude toward ultimate success, instituting programs that reward achievement, and putting together a team that can work together toward goals.

achievement, need for A basic need existing in most people that is acquired by positive reinforcement.

achievement, personal The attainment to something that has specific and positive meaning to the individual.

achievement test A term used for psychological tests in the United States that measure achievement in a specific occupation as opposed to general potential or aptitude.

acid test A measure of liquidity defined as current assets minus inventories divided by current liabilities. (*See also* quick ratio.)

acid test ratio The ratio of total cash, accounts receivable, and the market value of saleable investments to current liabilities. (*See also* liquid ratio)

acquisition The obtaining of companies or property. The short-cut way for a business to get more raw material, diversification, or a broader market.

across-the-board settlement A pay increase agreement that gives each employee the same proportionate pay increase.

AC test of creative ability A psychological test originating in the United States designed specifically for engineers. Known also as the "Purdue creativity test."

Act for International Development of 1961 United States Congress legislation establishing the Agency for International Development to administer overseas economic aid programs.

action and feeling An act that occurs in response to one's feelings about a specific person or subject at a specific point in time.

action-centered leadership A "packaged" course on leadership developed in the United Kingdom by The Industrial Society and based on the concepts of John Adair. It is closely allied to T-group training. (*See* T-group training)

action principle The act of deciding on a plan or an alternative and getting on with the job without undue expenditure of time.

action research A program of research that combines the investigation of a specific problem within an organization and then follows up on the implementation and evaluation of the proposed procedures.

action skill The ability to effectively carry out the type of behavior required by a specific situation.

active learning A type of learning that allows for discussion by students as opposed to a lecture only situation in which students are passive.

active listening Listening that conveys the impression that the listener understands what is said but makes no judgment on it (i.e., listening while not adding to, nor taking from, what has been said).

active money Money actually in circulation or being used in business transactions.

activism A mark of many successful companies that includes free-flowing communications, openness between labor and management, and a determination to get the job done more quickly and better than the competition.

activities The various behaviors of people in an organization, such as designing, making, selling, keeping books, engineering, bargaining, etc., that are supposed to add value to the original product.

activities analysis One of three programs devised by Peter Drucker to establish the key activities of a firm. (*See also* decision analysis, relations analysis, Drucker, Peter)

activities management A traditional view of management, i.e. emphasis upon the things that had to be done, with the manager having the power over people as to what was to be done and how. The emphasis is now placed on results, with their achievement being assured by the participation of the people with management.

activity chart A graphic presentation of the breakdown and composition of a series of activities, or a process plotted against a time scale.

activity, defined The multiplicity of systems used to achieve goals.

activity rate (for working-age population) The proportion of working-age persons in a population who may be working or seeking work at a given time.

activity ratio A comparison of budgeted output with actual output for a specific period of time. Expressed as:

$$\frac{\text{Standard hours of budgeted output}}{\text{Standard hours of actual output}} \times \frac{100}{1}$$

activity vector analysis, AVA A psychological test developed in the United States for use in temperament and personality testing. It has not fared well as related to personnel selection.

acts of bankruptcy The voluntary admission, or a declaration by a court, that one cannot discharge his financial obligations. There are many rules governing bankruptcy that the student or manager may wish to review.

ACTU Australian Council of Trade Unions.

actual market volume The sum total of suppliers' sales made at a specific price, or a given price range, to a specific market segment.

actualization, individual The achievement of those goals that are of primary importance to an individual, and upon which he tends to place the greatest personal value.

actuals Commodities or goods that are physically ready to be bought or sold immediately (that is, on the spot market) as opposed to futures trading. (*See also* futures)

actuarial return The return on a project or enterprise using the discounted cash flow technique. (*See also* internal rate of return)

actuary One who specializes in measuring risk in insurance. (*Cf.* risk economist)

actuating functions of management Those necessary steps to be taken by management, after planning and organizing has been done, to achieve whatever the goal of the organization is.

adaptability test An intelligence test, used primarily in the United States, for personnel selection.

adaptive control A method of computer control of the production processes in a plant in which the computer makes calculations, based on past experience, to change procedures which may make the plant more productive.

adaptive program A flexible form of programmed learning in which the sequencing of frames depends upon the responses of the student (e.g.,

slower sequencing for slower students, etc.).

adaptivizing patterns One aspect of planning that allows a company to adapt to either long-run or short-run goals, under a variety of circumstances.

ADB Asian Development Bank.

addendum An addition made at the end of a report or the addition to a motion in a formal meeting. (*See* amendment)

additive opportunity An opportunity that exists within the business to produce an additional good or a different kind of service without changing the structure or nature of the business.

Adelaide Stock Exchange One of the six-member Australian Association of Stock Exchanges.

add-on-sales Continuing sales made to a customer who is already a regular and satisfied customer.

adhocracy The principle of achieving results through various ad hoc committees. Such a principle can be fruitful if the ad hoc committees are few and super-active, but it can kill a company if the committees are numerous and indecisive.

adjournment, motion for Essentially a gesture to end a meeting, which must have a second and a majority vote to pass, and is not debatable. This motion can be acted upon even if there is another motion on the floor at the time.

adjustment The adaptation to circumstances that leaves the individual reasonably content in a work situation.

Adler, Alfred (1870–1937) An Austrian pioneer in "Individual Psychology" (i.e., that psychology of the individual that differentiates him from others). Adler was one of the teachers under whom Abraham Maslow studied. Acknowledged as one of three "founding fathers" of modern psychiatry, Adler argued that the essential foundations of character are set by age four. Adler also argued that once people recognize who and what they are, they have the task of accepting other people for who and what they are. Adler was convinced that people could not change essentially, and that, in the absence of their ability to change, they would have to accept both themselves and others.

administration An area of management that is concerned with interpreting company policy and implementing it by effective executive action.

administrative costs Costs allocated to a branch or department of a firm for its proportionate share of total company administrative costs.

Administrative Management Society (AMS) An organization in the United States concerned with general office management that offers seminars and consulting services in that area.

adolescent values A period in one's life when one needs a positive sense of self. Often this aim is served, in part, by an acceptable job.

ADR European Agreement on the International Carriage of Dangerous Goods.

ad valorem A tax levied on the basis of the value of the property involved.

advance factory (UK) A kind of factory built by the United Kingdom in underdeveloped areas that is rented to

a company wishing to set up business in that area, with the enticement of attractive rates.

advancement, cohesion as a factor in The more the opinions of the subordinate are similar to those of the superior, the greater the opportunity for advancement within the company.

adversarial society A theory that every human being is to be in competition with everyone else, and thus sees little chance for loving, caring, or mutual helpfulness.

advertising One aspect of marketing, the goal of advertising is to build company image or call attention to a product or service for the purpose of attracting purchasers.

advertising agency A firm that handles advertising for other firms for a fee, which is usually based on a percentage of the business handled.

advertising control The periodic survey of any advertising program, by management personnel who have the authority to control it, to determine its cost-effectiveness to the firm.

advisory staff authority An advisory (consulting) staff person who usually has little authority and must use "moral suasion" to sell ideas to line managers.

AE *Anonymous Etairia,* a Greek form of joint stock companies.

AfDB *See* African Development Bank.

affection needs One of Maslow's "hierarchy of human needs" which is often referred to as "belongingness, or love needs." This basic need, which Maslow averred was present in all people, requires that the individual consider himself to be acceptable to family or friends to be satisfied in the work situation.

affidavit A written, sworn statement.

affiliated company Usually, a company owned by another company.

affiliation needs A term in psychology denoting a need for acceptance by one's peers.

affiliation-centered government The general posture of government, especially state government, which is usually more politically centered than objectives centered.

affluence, abuse of The proliferation of material wealth of an individual or as a nation. Both the United States and many individuals in the country have been accused of abusing the growing affluence of the 1950s and 1960s by building lives of "quantity" rather than of "quality."

affluence, psychology of A mood, widespread in the early 1970s, that the nation had forever put behind it the hardships and required self-denial of the 1930s and had embarked upon a sea of affluent tranquility to which there would be no end. The "energy crunch" of 1973–74 dealt a crushing blow to the idea that economic prosperity would continue indefinitely.

AFL *See* American Federation of Labor.

AFL-CIO *See* American Federation of Labor-Congress of Industrial Organizations.

African Development Bank (AfDB) An association of more than thirty African nations that was established in 1964 under the guidance of the United Nations Economic Commission for Africa. Address: BP 1387, Abidjan, Ivory Coast.

after-acquired property clause The act of putting into a mortgage bond indenture the stipulation that all subsequently acquired property will also serve as security for the bonds.

aftertax cash flow Operating income after tax, plus the tax rate times depreciation.

age, cultural variability The expectations of particular age groups evidenced in the multiple social strata usually based upon wealth and/or income. It has been noted that age is less of a factor in expectations than is social class.

Age Discrimination Act of 1967 As amended, "prohibits job discrimination against workers between 40 and 70 years of age." The act also forbids an employer to operate a seniority system or employment benefit plan that requires or permits the involuntary retirement of an employee under age 70. (As "age" as an employment concept continues to be less meaningful, this will be an area to watch for further change.)

age-pattern analysis An analysis of the age distributions among the different strata of employees in a firm, which can be important in future manpower planning.

age roles The changing roles forced on both men and women by advancing age, the leaving home of the children, and the forced retirement of men, women, or both.

Agency for Economic Development A United States agency that oversees American foreign economic aid programs.

agent A person or company empowered to act on behalf of another.

agent de change A stockbroker on either the Brussels Stock Exchange, the Paris Exchange, or one of the Swiss exchanges.

agent de change correspondent A stockbroker who may deal through the Brussels Stock Exchange, but can do so only through an Agent de Change.

agente de cambio y bolsa A Spanish stockbroker.

agenti di cambio Stockholders who trade on the floors of the Italian Stock Exchanges.

aggregate supply of labor The total labor force in a nation, or available in a locality to local industry, without distinguishing between types of workers.

aggression 1. A type of hostile behavior that may be directed at a person or a problem that is external in nature, or which may be inward in the sense that the hostility of the person is aimed at himself. 2. Hostile behavior, though sometimes masked, that is believed by some to be inherent in every human being. This view has been countered by the fact that few people actually take a hostile attitude toward the world.

agreed procedure An agreement between management and labor as to how grievances will be handled.

agribusiness All businesses that deal primarily with agriculture, whether they involve production, marketing, processing, storage, or transportation. In all developed countries, those employed in agribusinesses in its many forms far outnumber those directly engaged in agriculture.

Agricultural, Horticulture and Forestry Industry Training Board Established in 1966 under the Industrial Training Act, 1964. UK. Address: 32/34 Beckenham Road, Beckenham, Kent BR3 4PB.

Agricultural Revolution An extended period of time in which new technology replaced much manual labor connected with the agricultural industry. This was the result of amassing and exchanging ideas about technology. It vastly increased the ability to produce and relieved workers of much back-breaking labor.

AH4 Test In psychological testing, a verbal and non-verbal general intelligence test that also measures some aspects of numerical aptitude.

AH5 Higher level version of AH4 Test.

Ahmadabad Share & Stockbrokers' Association One of seven major stock exchanges in India.

AIDA Abbreviation for attention, interest, desire, and action, which are four key requirements for effective selling. Often used as a backdrop for sales seminars.

aided recall A market-research technique used to assist interviewees to remember products or services by reminding them of associated events.

AIIE *See* American Institution of Industrial Engineers.

AIM *See* American Institute of Management.

aiming A term used to describe a psychomotor skill, which reveals an individual's ability to perform quickly and accurately a series of movements demanding eye-hand coordination.

Aksjeselskap A Norwegian joint-stock company.

Aktiebolaj A Swedish joint-stock company.

289

Aktiengesellschaft (A/G) A joint-stock company under Austrian, German, and Swiss company law. Also known in Switzerland as Société Anonyme (SA).

Aktieselskab (A/S) A Danish public company or corporation.

ALGOL An acronym for Alogrithmic Language, a computer language.

algorithm A logical sequence of deductions for problem solving, which tends to reduce the problem solving task to a simple series of steps, and which does indicate the order in which the steps should be carried out.

alienation in the work place A situation that grew up, primarily in the auto industry, from the early 1950s into the 1970s, in which workers were so disenchanted with management that absenteeism, alcoholism, and other impediments to good work proliferated. Quality suffered immeasurably.

alienation of workers A situation in the workplace that causes the workers to develop a hostile attitude toward management and the job, and which hinders personal motivation and thus production.

all-fours A lawyer's term for a direct legal precedent.

all-in rate A wage that incorporates all extras, such as bonuses, in addition to the basic wage.

all-union shop *See* closed shop.

Alliance for Progress An agreement made in Uruguay in 1961 between the United States and most Latin American Countries with the objective of improving the economies of Latin American countries. The United States carries this out through the Agency for International Development.

alliances, effect on implementing MBO Alliances between departments or divisions of an organization can either make or break the concept of Management by Objectives. The need for total organization cooperation with the concept of MBO may make individuals or departments feel threatened. MBO is indeed a threat to "empire building" within an organization, and thus numerous individuals and some departments may become impediments to MBO progress.

allocated costs Costs systematically allocated among specific products or departments.

allocation The use of quantitative methods for allocating available men and other resources to obtain optimum results.

allonge A slip of paper attached to a bill of exchange to give more room for endorsements once the back of the bill has been filled.

allowed time The time needed to complete an assignment at the standard performance rate, including rest periods, etc.

alongside date The date on which a ship is supposed to be at the dock and ready to accept cargo.

alternating shift A work situation in which employees change shifts periodically.

alternative cost The cost incurred when a firm decides to take one of several specific alternatives. (*See also* opportunity cost)

alternative road A method of learning through applications rather than through more traditional methods, such as the study of principles.

alternatives, examination of The act of playing a devil's advocate by promoting an alternative to a matter under discussion without taking responsibility for being contrary.

altruism, synergic An unselfish working together.

AMA *See* American Management Association.

ambiguity, area of An area in the work life of a manager that is not well structured, and which increases in scope as the manager moves up the corporate ladder. How the manager is able to fill these unstructured hours will determine his effectiveness.

ambivalence An attitude of indecisiveness in a person in which he does not particularly love a person or situation or hate a person or situation. Since most relationships in business and in other facets of life require a degree of decisiveness if one is to have a successful relationship, ambivalence can become an unsuccessful force.

amendment A change in a motion before any legislative body in a formal meeting that seeks to clarify a point in the original motion or make the wording of a motion more acceptable. The original mover of the motion and the seconder must approve the amendment before it can be accepted, and then the motion is ready to be voted upon by the body.

American Bankers Association An organization established in 1875 to which most banks in the United States belong. Address: 1120 Connecticut Ave., NW Washington, DC 20036.

American culture, economic shading of A belief, held by several prominent sociologists and psychologists, that economic competitiveness in the United States prevented the cultural advancement one might have expected in the wake of the affluence experienced from the 1950s through the "energy crunch."

American culture, introspective thinking in A reference to that period in the 1970s when, having been astounded by the "energy crunch," people began to rethink their lives with respect to who they were, what they wanted to do, and where they wanted to go. Since introspection is by nature a selfish action, it produced the "me decade," but solved few personal or corporate problems.

American Federation of Labor (AFL) An association of trade unions in the United States and Canada, established in 1881, which includes most of the craft unions.

American Federation of Labor/ Congress of Industrial Organizations (AFL/CIO) A labor organization formed in the United States and Canada from a merger of the AFL and the CIO. Address: 815 16th St., NW, Washington, DC 20006.

American Institute of Management This organization appraises the management of enterprises by a comparative audit or examination. The ten basic categories used are: economic function, corporate structure, health of earnings growth, fairness to stockholders, research and development, directorate analysis, fiscal policies, production efficiency, sales vigor, and executive evaluation. There is a total of ten thousand points possible in the evaluation, proportioned among the ten points according to the supposed value of each function.

American Management Association (AMA) A professional nonprofit organization, formed in 1923, which provides research, training, and publications on a wide range of management subjects. Address: 135 West 50th St., Washington, DC 20036.

American Psychological Association A professional organization that assists business and industry by devising and making recommendations for psychological testing for occupational and industrial psychologists.

amiable social style One of four "social styles" that makes the one who has it more responsive to other people and less assertive. Amiable people feel more empathy for others and are usually helpful in interpersonal problem solving. (*cf.* analytical social style.)

amortization The consummation of a debt by full payment, often when the debt has been discharged by making periodic payments.

AMS American Management Society.

Amstel Club A group of major European and British banks that has a reciprocal agreement for financing imports and exports between their countries.

Amsterdam Stock Exchange (Vereeniging voor den Effectenhandel) The principal stock exchange of the Netherlands, which dates back to the seventeenth century. It has as members individual stockbrokers and corporations, such as banks.

Amtlicher Markt The official market for trading in securities on German stock exchanges.

analog computer A computer that processes data in the form of physical quantities, and which performs high speed and complex calculations. It is used often in simulation. It does not have the capacity to store large quantities of data.

analog models Models used in education and management to simulate business or industrial situations.

analysis and intrinsic creativity The minute examination of intrinsic (internal, already existing) innovative programs, which may provide the key for change based on the adoption of new technology.

analysis and synthesis, principle of The act of breaking down a problem into its several component parts, and, in contrast, combining various entities under consideration in order to establish the relative importance of each.

analytical estimating A technique used in production and works management to break down estimated times or costs for a job between the various components in order to build a reasonable estimate of the job cost and time.

analytical job evaluation A technique by which common features of a specific job are compared.

analytical social style Exhibits a high level of emotional self-control and a low level of assertiveness.

angle of incidence The angle at which the sales revenue line crosses the total cost line on a break-even chart.

angle of peripheral vision The extreme areas in which an individual is aware of movements and objects while his vision is focused on something directly in front of him.

animal trainers Managers who look

upon employees as "animals" who can be motivated by a "carrot on a stick" technique. Such an approach often prevents managers from coming to a deeper understanding of the needs of employees.

annual premium costing *pensions* A situation where the cost of a total premium is expressed as a level annual premium payable each year until retirement.

annual report to employees A part of the formal communications of many companies through which an annual report especially designed for employees gives the employees news and statistics of particular interest to them.

annual strategic goals statements One of three events in a year followed by companies using the MBO concept to determine progress. There are four sets of questions answered in the statements: 1) What is the posture of your area now, and what strengths and weaknesses are discernable? 2) What trends are visible, and what alternatives would you follow in the future? 3) What is your mission? What are you in business for, and are you achieving that goal? 4) What new strategies could be considered that would make the goals more achievable, and what are their costs.

annual wage audit A system of regular, intensive reviews of the wages and fringe benefits structure of a company. This audit may alert a company's management of possible labor objections, or it may alert managers to over- or under-spending of a company on salaries.

annuity A level stream of payments, usually for a limited number of years.

anomie A term used by sociologists to describe the disunity and disarray that follows when norms collapse and people come to believe there are no rules or believe that observing rules makes no sense because those who comply with them end up empty handed while those who flount the rules are rewarded.

anonymity A state in a growing industry in which the individual becomes a non-entity as the number of employees grows and the employee becomes distanced from top management. This feeling of nonexistence is a major problem in current times and requires the understanding and action of management to keep it under control.

anonymity, independence fostered by The notion that the more nearly one can remain anonymous, the more independent one can be in fostering an idea, particularly an idea that is contrary to those common in a company.

Anonymous Etairia (AE) A Greek joint-stock company in which shareholders are liable only to the extent of their investment, as is true with a U.S. corporation.

antagonists Persons who stand opposed to each other with respect to a particular point of view.

anthropology, culture as viewed in ". . . refers to both to the physical and intangible contents of the human habitat: the values, shared meanings, social norms, customs, rituals, symbols, arts and artifacts, ways of perceiving the world, life styles, behavior and ideologies by which people participate in organized society." (Daniel Yankelovich, *New Rules* [New York: Random House, 1981], pp.13–14.)

anthropology The scientific study of human beings—their origins, their cultures, and their beliefs—a discipline that is now widely used by management in its study of human behavior.

anticipation (UK) A practice of a customer (not a business, necessarily) paying a bill before its due date in order to receive a discount.

anticipation, management by A term that describes those goal-setting actions required of staff departments—such as personnel departments, accounting departments, legal departments, finance and controller departments—in advance of budget making for the coming year.

anticipation stock raw materials inventory, partly finished goods, or finished goods purchased, etc., in anticipation of greater demand, a rise in prices, and other economic factors.

anti-intellectualism An attitude common among blue-collar workers and white-collar managers when it comes to dealing with difficult social problems they do not wish to confront, such as hiring of minorities and allowing them to rise in business.

antipoverty legislation Acts passed since the beginning of the Great Depression to help alleviate poverty. Such legislation has encouraged management to provide certain basic needs for employees, including health insurance, and other benefits.

antiquarian A person who is reluctant to look into the future and who tends to base all present and future decisions on things in the past.

anxiety 1. A state of being troubled or worried that may spring from a deep-seated neurosis or simply be a short-term reaction to an unpleasant work situation. In either case, the state of mind should not be ignored. 2. The pressure managers build up in themselves when they feel unsure as what they are doing or whom they trust.

APEX (UK) Association of Professional, Executive, Clerical, and Computer Staff.

applied research The application in the real work place of truths revealed in basic research.

appointments, handling of One of the most important areas of an executive's task. Ineffective handling of appointments can ruin an entire day. It is generally recommended that the secretary handle appointments under strict guidelines.

appraisal interview A technique for analyzing the past performance of an employee and the employee's future potential in making a salary review.

appraisal method A method of calculating depreciation in which asset values are determined by making a judgment at the beginning and end of each accounting period. This method is used mainly for depreciating small tools and minor but necessary equipment.

appraisal test (the Kostick Profile) A test developed by Max M. Kostick to assist the executive in appraising him or herself in the areas of perception and preference.

appreciation training A method devised to give background information or a generalized understanding of a subject rather than to convey detailed knowledge.

apprentice Generally a younger person

who is employed in a training position by an employer for the purpose of learning a specific trade. While this practice dates back to the guilds, there is strong evidence that the practice will be revived as specific technical skills become more in demand, and as young workers decrease in number in the developed countries.

apprenticeship A method of developing expertise in trades by beginning one's training in the most basic tasks and increasing the importance of the work over time until the person is considered expert. This same method is being used (wisely) in developing management personnel.

approval, need for A basic need apparent in all people, a part of which must be satisfied in the workplace. It is closely allied with Maslow's "esteem" need.

approximation of laws In Articles 100–02, of the Treaty of Rome, 1957, it is recommended that the laws of individual members of the European Economic Community be made to harmonize with the general objectives of the Community.

aptitude tests 1. Tests that are used prolifically by firms to try to avoid filling staff positions with incompetents. These tests are usually designed by psychologists. While no such measure is exact, the tests can be useful. 2. Tests devised to ascertain the skill levels of an individual and the propensity of that individual for performing certain tasks effectively.

APU occupational interest guide An interest inventory test used in personnel selection to indicate the primary interests of the candidate.

Arbeitsgemeinschaft der deutschen Wertpapierbörsen The Federation of German Stock Exchanges.

arbitrage Simultaneous buying and selling of stocks, currency, bills of exchange, etc., in order to profit from different prices and rates.

arbitration agreement An agreement between two parties that any dispute between them will be given to an arbitrator for solution.

arbitration A procedure, either prescribed, as in a labor contract, or simply desirable, in which a problem between two parties is given to a third party for consideration and solution.

Argentinian central bank Banco Central de la Republica Argentina.

Argentinian stock exchanges The principal exchange is the Bolsa de Comercio, Buenos Aires. There are other exchanges in Cordoba, Mar del Plata, Mendoza, Rosario and San Juan.

Aristocratic ethic The attitude of an aristocrat who feels that the affluent should use part of their wealth to help the poor. This attitude was supposedly exemplified in President Kennedy.

arithmetic average A statistical measure of central tendency obtained by summing the items under consideration and dividing by the number of items. (e.g., avdding 10, 12, 20 equals 42, which divided by 3 equals 14.

arithmetic unit A part of the central processing unit of a digital computer.

arm-hand steadiness A type of psychomotor skill, e.g., dexterity of arm and hand displayed by a person.

arm's-length market price The stated price prior to negotiations.

array The systematic grouping of a number of values by magnitude, usually from the smallest to the largest.

art of management The part of management that is art is revealed in this definition of art: ". . . the bringing about of a desired result through the application of skill."

art vs. science in management Management is an art in the sense that its "laws" are not absolutes, and erudition is required to deal with people as individuals. It is a science only in the general sense that certain things do seem to apply in more than one situation.

Arusha Agreement A pact that associated four British Commonwealth countries—Kenya, Nigeria, Tanzania and Uganda—with the European Economic Community prior to the entrance of the British.

ASA American Standards Association. A federation of technical societies, trade associations, and federal government agencies, the aim of which is to establish a group approach to common standards problems.

asbestosis A form of dust disease of the lung (pneumoconiosis) caused by prolonged inhalation of asbestos dust.

asceticism In early America, spurred by the beliefs of the Puritans and the Quakers that one was supposed to work for the glory of God and eschew worldly luxuries and pleasures.

Asian Development Bank (ADB) Established in 1966 under the auspices of the United Nations Economic Commission for Asia and the Far East. There are some thirty-five member countries, and the address is: Commercial Center, POB 126, Makati, Rizal, D-708 Philippines.

aspiration, level of The degree of ambition evidenced by an individual which usually determines how often the individual may expect promotions, and how far up in the organization he/she may expect to go.

aspirational groups A type of status group brought together to examine consumer buying habits. In such groups, the individual consumer is brought into contact with people who buy what he aspires to be able to buy.

assembly The official term used in documents of the European Economic Community to refer to its meetings.

assembly line A mass-production technique used in the assembling of automobiles and of many other products. In many instances the work is dirty, the pace is fast, and it is often found to be disagreeable to workers. The situation is a difficult one in which to motivate workers. The assembly-line concept has allowed wages to go up dramatically, and management has often assumed that high wages offset the monotony of the work.

assembly-line production Mass production of items that are highly standardized. In this type of production, the worker carries out some small task on each item passing him on a line.

assertiveness A personality trait that makes a person seem to others as being forceful and directive.

assertiveness scale A graphic description of the degree of assertiveness exhibited by a person.

assessment center A place and process

of evaluating personnel with managerial ability. Such a procedure may be conducted within the company or by a consulting firm from outside the company.

asset Property, either tangible or intangible, owned by a company or by an individual.

asset stripping An action of acquiring a company to strip it of all possible assets in order to strengthen the acquiring company, with no regard for the acquired company or its personnel.

asset structure Refers to the left-hand side of the balance sheet, i.e., the firm's resources that must be financed.

asset turnover rate A broad measure of asset efficiency, defined as net sales divided by total assets.

assign The act of transferring property to another, or any right in property, often to serve as collateral for a debt or as surety for a promise made.

assignment A technique for liquidating a debtor and yielding a larger amount to the creditor than might be recovered in bankruptcy. Three types of assignment are: common law assignment, statutory assignment, and assignment plus settlement.

assistant to the manager A staff position best described as "personal assistant to the manager" since the position tends to carry no real authority, as the position of "assistant manager" would. However, the "assistant to the manager," who carries out certain staff duties for the manager, can often have a lot of authority derived from his proximity to the manager.

Assisted Area (UK) An expression denoting an economic development area in the United Kingdom.

Associacao Commercial de Lisboa Portuguese chambers of commerce, established in 1834. Address: Rua das Portas de Santo Antao 89, Lisbon.

Associated Chambers of Commerce and Industry of India The central organization for Chambers of Commerce in India. Address: Royal Exchange, Calcutta.

association agreement A preferential trade agreement between Common Market states or associated states.

assurance A term synonymous with insurance, particularly in the United Kingdom.

Athens Stock Exchange Although founded in 1876 and modeled after the Paris exchange, this organization is not very active, since nominally public companies remain, for the most part, in private hands in Greece.

atmosphere, creative An atmosphere in a business firm that encourages innovativeness, but does so not by merely asking employees to be creative, but by requiring that they be so, and by rewarding them when they are.

atmosphere of an organization The environment or "mood" of an organization. Atmosphere is usually established by the feelings, either positive or negative, people in the organization have toward each other and toward the operation in general.

"atta boy" The attitude of a supervisor who seeks to motivate his workers by hype, or certain "hygiene factors," because the work itself is not conducive to being highly motivated.

297

attainment test A test that measures knowledge in a specific field or attainment in a specific skill. Also known as an achievement test.

attendance bonus *money* Money earned above the normal rate for regular attendance at work.

attestation The act of witnessing the signature to a document.

attitude(s) 1. A predisposition to act or think in certain ways. 2. The mental or bodily comportment of an individual, consisting of two parts: expectations and anticipations. 3. The way a person tends to feel, see, or interpret a given situation. Since attitudes tend to be intangible in themselves, they are usually revealed by the actions of a person.

attitudinal changes The changes in attitudes forced upon people by the changes in society around them when, psychologically, it is impossible for people to change quickly. Such changes produce stress in individuals, which is then translated into a stressful society. (*See* Alvin Toffler, *Future Shock* [New York: Random House, 1970])

attribution error, fundamental The tendency in people to overestimate their own weaknesses and to underestimate situational factors with respect to burnout.

attrition A process by which average salary levels in an organization tend to decrease over time as older workers retire and newer workers take their places.

audio aids Such instruments as record players, tape recorders, etc., used in education and training.

audit The action of verifying the validity of procedure and the statistical accuracy of a firm's accounting records.

audit cycle The period of time over which all sectors of a firm or organization are audited by rotation.

audit of philosophy An analytical review of a company's objectives, which clearly sets out its motivating spirit.

audit of social responsibility action This type of audit, which has not yet been perfected, attempts to put a dollar value on training programs, health-maintenance programs, child-care programs, etc., that, in part, discharge the responsibility of the firm toward employees and the general public.

audits *management* A periodic assessment of how management is carrying out the duties of planning, organizing, actualizing, and controlling, compared to some accepted norm.

Australia Associated Chambers of Commerce An organization founded in 1901, the members of which include chambers of commerce from Adelaide, Brisbane, Darwin, Hobart, Ingham, Launceston, Melbourne, Newcastle, Perth, Sydney, and Tamworth, together with state federations. Address: Brisbane Avenue, Barton ACT 2600.

Australian Associated Stock Exchanges An organization established in 1937 with six member exchanges: Brisbane, Adelaide, Hobart, Melbourne, Perth, and Sydney.

Australian Institute of Management A professional organization for management personnel in industrial and commercial organizations. Main address: National Centre, 476 St.Kilda Road, Melbourne, Victoria 3000.

autarky A condition of national economic independence, without reliance on trade with other countries.

authenticity, self-fulfillment as
Defined by some as "being one's own person." In this age of "meism," authenticity has often been translated into selfishness.

authoritarian personality A personal trait that presents an excessive need for control, which often means the control of everything and everyone related to a given situation. This personality type, strong as it appears to be, is prone to burnout.

authoritarian theory An attitude toward work and workers that deems workers to be lazy, indolent, and unco-operative, and thus requiring strong-handed control in order to achieve goals.

authority 1. The ability or power con-ferred upon a certain position to make decisions important to the total work situation. 2. The degree of power that accrues to a specific job or position that gives the holder the right to carry out the responsibilities of his job and make whatever decisions necessary.

authority, acceptance of The tendency to accept authority as a trade-off for the promise of security.

authority and dependency in organi-zations Organizations require author-ity at the top, and generally this authority is diffused as one goes down through the levels of the organization. Authority creates dependency—the lower levels require the support of the higher levels—and if an individual feels insecure about this dependency, ambivalence will usually result.

authority and responsibility The power, in a business situation, to give orders and require that they be carried out within the scope of normal busi-ness operations. On the other hand, responsibility is the obligation of an individual, manager or otherwise, to carry out assigned tasks to the best of his or her ability. Responsibility must always be accompanied by the author-ity to do what is being required. In business and industry, the giving of responsibility without concurrent authority is the root of many problems.

authority of middle managers Middle managers are given broad responsibili-ties, often with little authority to carry them out. Authority of middle man-agers must be consistent with the responsibilities they have. This has been a major problem in industry for many years.

autocratic control The tight personal control of a company or department by the chairman or the manager. Sometimes called "Caesar manage-ment."

autocratic theory of leadership A the-ory that features commands, enforce-ments, and arbitrary actions on the part of the leader toward subordinates. The autocrat seems to believe that he is all-wise, that employees are unwise, and that the objectives of the firm are almost totally dependent upon him for their achievement. (It is interesting to note that some employees like auto-cratic leaders, since the employees are not required to think for themselves and are always sure about what is expected of them.)

autokinetic effect The effect of thought convergence that is brought about by the continual comparison of one per-son's ideas with others' ideas in a peer group.

automation The use of machines, often of a highly technical nature, to replace manual and mental labor.

automatism A state of acting mechanically and without thinking.

automistic competition *economics* pure competition and direct competition, without any intervention by government or any other agency.

autonomous social character A combination of the rugged individualism of the past, when people were primarily in the process of conquering nature, and the "other-directed" culture of today when most people work for others and become, in part, cogs in an economic and social wheel.

autonomous work groups A form of worker's participation in management in which the work group plans its production schedule and sometimes its training.

autonomy of subordinates The authority subordinates may have in a specific firm to implement known goals without further permission from superiors. Academic people in management have long argued that subordinates should have as much autonomy as possible. What is possible, and effective, however, must be dictated by the structure of the organization and the dependability of the subordinates.

autonomy-entrepreneurship The freedom the risk bearer has in departing from well-established models in management and tending toward new and potentially more efficient paths.

availability policies Rules designed to discourage people from making themselves available for anything, at any time, related to their jobs. Such policies are designed to protect employees who are constantly volunteering to work overtime, refusing days off, shortening vacations to get back to the job, thinking only of the job while off from work, etc. Workers with this tendency can be the most highly respected professionals or the lowliest workers on a job. This type of person can burn out more quickly than others.

average adjuster An insurance official skilled in assessing average, i.e., the value of damage or loss at sea.

average collection period An alternative ratio for measuring the accounts-receivable turnover. Simplistically, one can divide annual sales by 365 to get the average daily sales and then divide daily sales into accounts receivable to determine the number of days' sales tied up in receivables.

avoidance The tendency of a worker to refrain from doing or saying certain things in order to avoid the unpleasantness he knows it will cost him.

awareness An enhancement of rationality and of the feelings people have toward activities and persons around them.

B

baby boom A period of time in which the number of babies being born is considerably greater than normal. This happened in the United States after World War II, when between 1947 and 1949 the number of live births increased 50 percent. This can have a positive effect on an economy that is growing rapidly, such as that of the United States, and a negative effect when more population is not needed and the depths of poverty are increased.

baby bust A period of time in which the number of live births in a nation drastically declines. Beginning in 1960, the rate in the United States fell about 30 percent and has continued in that vein. This bodes ill for a growing nation in which labor needs are increasing.

BACIE British Association for Commercial and Industrial Education.

background criteria selection approach A method of personnel selection on the basis of the background of the individual, specifically with respect to having a college degree.

back selling The act of stimulating sales to the end consumer through some part of the sales chain; e.g., the manufacturer makes it possible for the retail outlet to increase sales through some promotion, which obviously increases sales at each point in the sales chain.

"Back to Basics" management A type of management that includes a knowledge of techniques and technology, but puts great emphasis upon understanding individual employees.

"Back to Basics" management, foundation blocks A set of guidelines for "Back to Basics" management, as follows. Foundation block 1: understanding, commitment, and discipline. Foundation block 2: effective communication. Foundation block 3: interpersonal relations.

back-up style Predictable, style-based behavioral changes in response to stress.

backward integration 1. Method of either concentrating or diversifying the total firm structure. 2. Consolidation of a business from the market to manufacturing or from manufacturing to raw materials.

backwash effect Divergence in productivity between developed countries' exports, which are mainly manufactured goods, and those of underdeveloped countries, which consist mainly of raw materials.

bad vs. good recipients Those people in the workplace who may demand more of another person than is just, and thus are "bad" for workers' progress vs. the "good" people who are more interested in giving than taking and can be a positive forces in the lives of other people in the workplace.

bailment A transaction contemplating no transfer of ownership whereby A (bailor) transfers to B (bailee), or B rightfully retains possession of personal property, usually for a special purpose. Such property is to be returned upon the accomplishment of the purpose of the transaction.

bail out In the United States, methods used by firms to use corporate funds to provide payments to shareholders that are taxable at favorable capital gains rates.

balance of payments A country's balance sheet of wealth going out of the country and coming back into the country for a given period. The accounts are divided between capital accounts (payment on loans, etc.) and current accounts (payments for imports, etc.).

balance sheet equation Assets = liabilities + capital.

balance sheets, comparative A balance sheet showing comparisons of the current year with past years.

balancing time A change in working hours, with no reduction in hours worked. Similar to "flextime" work.

Banca d'Italia Central bank of Italy, formed in 1893. Address: Rome, Via Nazionale 91.

Banco Central de Brasil Central bank of Brasil, established in 1965. Address: Avda, Presidente Vargas 84, Rio de Janeiro.

Banco Central de la Republica Argentina Central bank of Argentina, established in 1935. Address: Reconquista 266, Buenos Aires, Argentina.

Banco de España Central bank of Spain, established in 1829. Address: Madrid 14, Alcala 50.

Banco de Portugal Central bank of Portugal, established in 1846. Address: Rua do Commercio 148, Lisbon.

band curve chart Also known as a cumulative band chart, which is a graphic display of the component parts of a whole plotted on one graph, one above the other, with the curve areas shaded differently to show the composition of the whole.

Bangladesh Bank The central bank of Bangladesh, established in 1972. Address: Dacca, Bangladesh.

bank draft A draft drawn by one bank on another bank.

Bank for International Settlements (BIS) An organization that promotes cooperation between various central banks and provides back-up financing for them. Address: 7 Centralbahnstrasse, CH 4002, Basel, Switzerland.

Bank of Canada Central bank of Canada, established in 1934. Address: 234 Wellington Street, Ottawa, Ontario.

Bank of England The United Kingdom's central bank, which was set up as a joint-stock company in 1694. It acts as the government's bank and assumes a similar role to the Federal Reserve in the United States. The bank was nationalized in 1946. Address: Threadneedle Street, London EC2R 8AH.

Bank of Ghana Central bank of Ghana, established in 1957. Address: POB 2674, Accra.

Bank of Greece The central bank of Greece, formed in 1928. Address: East Venizelou Avenue, POB 105, Athens.

bank rate The rate of interest at which the central bank of a country is prepared to loan money to other banks. In the U.S., the Federal Reserve calls this the discount rate.

banker's acceptance A draft for the price of goods drawn on and accepted by a bank.

Banque Nationale de Belgique The national bank of Belgium, established in 1850. Address: 5 boulevard de Berlaimont, 1000 Brussels.

Banque Nationale Suisse The central bank of Switzerland, called the National Bank, and organized in 1905. Address of head office: Zurich, Borsenstrasse 15.

Banque of France The central bank of France, established in 1800 and nationalized in 1946. Address: 1 rue de la Vrolliere, Paris 1e.

Barcelona Stock Exchange one of the principal stock exchanges of Spain. Also known as Bolsa de Barcelona.

bar chart A graphic presentation of data in terms of frequencies and magnitudes with rectangles drawn to scale. The bars can be either vertical or horizontal, and may be developed in many ways to include multiple data, using various shadings, etc.

bargaining range A term in industrial relations denoting the wage range within which a wage claim is apt to be settled.

bargaining scope The range of items that may be covered in collective bargaining between labor and management.

barratry *law* A willful misdemeanor committed by a ship's captain or crew which is contrary to the best interests of the owner or the charterer of the ship.

barriers of communicating According to George Terry they are as follows: 1) The identity and the interpretation of facts by the giver (sender). 2) The willingness and ability of the receiver to perceive the communication. 3) The attitudes of the giver (sender) and the receiver toward each other, their superiors, their peers, their subordinates, and the communication subject. 4) The general view taken by the giver (sender) and the receiver toward the situation in which the communication occurs. 5) The mutual acceptance of the communications medium by the giver (sender) and the receiver.

barriers to communications Events or states of mind that prevent proper transmitting and receiving of information. Two broad barriers stand out, namely, mechanical barriers and psychological barriers. Among these are dozens of impediments to good communications, all of which may be experienced at one time or the other in the workplace.

barriers to entry In the opinion of many chief executives, the greatest barrier to market entry is getting everyone in the company completely tuned in to company goals and delivering the product or service with zero tolerance for mistakes.

barrister A qualified advocate in the United Kingdom who is a member of one of the Inns of Court and can plead law cases in higher courts. An advocate does not deal directly with a client, but through the client's solicitor.

base period A reference point in time that always equals 100 percent, and from which base comparisons can be made with times past and with predictions about the future.

BASIC An introductory computer language named after All-purpose Symbolic Instruction Code that combines many of the facilities of more advanced languages.

basic needs Usually defined as physiological needs, such as food, water, warmth, etc.

basis, synergic The purpose for synergy is goal-oriented activity; i.e., activity with a good purpose. Goal orientation supposedly releases a flow of synergy in the mind, activating a variety of mental processes.

basketball team analogy Theory Z is likened to a basketball team with respect to the teamwork, the flexibility of the organization, and the dependence upon the entire team as opposed to one or two people. (*See* Theory Z)

Bayesian formula ". . . the knowledge of a certain probability of an event occurring can be modified should additional evidence which seems to differ from the first be obtained."

Bayesian statistics A type of statistical analysis developed for translating subjective forecasts into mathematical probability curves.

bear A person who sells shares of stock in the belief that the market will be going down.

bearer bonds Bonds made payable to their holder that are negotiable.

bed and breakfast deal A type of stock swapping in which investors establish tax losses to offset capital gains by selling shares and then buying them back in a separate transaction.

behavior and habit Behavior is related to habit, since habits are the ways things are customarily done and behavior constitutes acts and attitudes.

behavior, assertive The degree to which a person's behavior is seen by others as being forceful or directive.

behavior changing An attempt on the part of a manager to change the behavior of an employee by decree or by force. While this approach might work occasionally in the short-term, changing behavior in the long term can only be accomplished by creating a work atmosphere of which the employee will want to be a part and for which the employee will change behavior to become a part.

behavior, group A somewhat indefinable notion that asserts that the way that a collection of people acts is different than the sum of the behavior of individuals within the group.

behavior modeling in training A term denoting a systematic way of developing the skills desired in human interactions, utilizing well-established learning principles.

behavior, norms and A person within a group will often tune his behavioral patterns to the norms accepted by the group, since failure to do that will often result in his exclusion from the group. (I.e., the employee who tends to work more diligently than others may be disapproved by the group unless he is willing to adjust to their norms.)

behavior study A statistical technique used in market research to assess the behavior patterns and opportunities existing in a particular market.

behavior, viewpoint of organization In any organization with its hierarchy of positions and tasks, there is constant change occasioned by the behavior of individuals within the group.

behavioral change When the behavior of a person is not what is expected by the organization of which he is a part, he is expected to change. However, he is often expected to change himself, with no change in the environment around him.

behavioral modification 1. Conceived as a four-part process, it can be summarized in the formula G + N + R = PPG = goal (whether a business goal or a behavioral goal). The letter N equals needs (tangible and intangible), R equals rewards (what's in it for me), and PP equals productive performance (performance that is highly motivated, enthusiastic, effortful, determined, vigorous, sustained, and productive). 2. The opinion once held by William Irwin Thompson that industrial society was drifting toward an authoritarian system controlled by big industry and big labor, and to which power the individual's behavior would be expected to conform.

behavioral objectives A statement of responses required of a trainee after instruction or training.

behavioral science Psychological and sociological theories relating to analyzing and explaining the activities and ways of acting of individuals and groups.

behavioral science and management knowledge The behavioral sciences have enlarged the body of knowledge management needs to understand itself, but the primary emphasis of knowledge in management still must be on the actual work of managing. No sphere of study outside the realm of management will ever completely duplicate the activities of management itself.

behaviorism A general theory developed by John B. Watson (1878–1958), professor of psychology at Johns Hopkins University, who sought to reduce human behavior to chemical and physical terms.

behavior theory in management Every person who deals directly with other people in the workplace, especially in a superior/subordinate relationship, already has or soon develops a basic assumption about the behavior of people. The superior may take the Theory X view, the Theory Y view, or some combination of both, such as

Theory Z. The theory with which a manager attempts to manage other people will largely determine his success or failure. (*See* Theory X, Theory Y; Theory Z)

belief A representation of reality that is accepted by the individual as true or valid and is a basis for action.

belief systems Systems that express explicitly what the company is in business for and which beliefs motivate the people in the firm to be the best.

belongingness vs. individualism The conflict between the commonality a person wants to express by being an accepted member of a group, i.e. a church, a family, etc., and the individualism a person wishes to express through achieving personal psychological well-being relying only on inner resources.

below-the-line promotion A marketing term used to denote special promotions such as reduced prices, premiums, coupons, etc.

belt and braces "If the belt does not keep the trousers up, the braces will." A term denoting two separate courses of action, one of which should achieve the desired goal if the other fails.

Benedict, Ruth (1887–1948) A professor of anthropology at Columbia University who sought to show that the concept of cultural relativity, popular at the time, did not reveal enough about human beings. She set out to compare various societies as unitary wholes or as systems. She settled on two types of society that she chose to call "high synergy" and "low synergy" societies. High synergy societies tended toward more cooperation, a more just distribution of wealth, and fewer social problems within the society. Low synergy societies were marked by aggression, selfishness, often slave labor, and unjust distribution of wealth.

benefit method of selling An approach to selling that emphasizes the benefits that will accrue to the buyer if he indeed buys a good or service.

benefit plan document The official description of welfare and pension plans for employees that the employer files with the Department of Labor. It is becoming more popular to couch these documents in language that the average employee can understand rather than in the legalese that has historically been used.

benefits communicated by "bank books" A small book, resembling the old-fashioned savings-account book issued by banks to customers that sets out the type of benefits the employee has and the value of each for the individual employee.

benefits communicated by booklets Most companies do issue booklets explaining employee benefits. Many of them, however, are written by insurance companies or other firms that play a role in the benefits and are not always easy to read. Where possible, booklets should be issued by companies and written in the language of the average employee.

benefits communicated by cases The employee benefits communicated to employees by the use of a case study of one employee and his use of medical insurance, his benefits at retirement, etc.

Better Business Bureaus A type of agency in the United States and a few other countries that has a dual purpose: 1) to be a self-regulatory force for private enterprise within a nation 2) to demonstrate a real and visible concern for consumers.

bill of exchange (B/E) In legal terms, this is defined as a signed and unconditional order in writing addressed by one person to another requiring the person to whom it is addressed to pay on demand, or at a fixed future time, a sum certain of money to, or to the order of, a specified person, or to a bearer of the bill. Used often in international trade, since bills of exchange resemble transfers of cash.

bill of lading (B/L) The documentation related to a consignment of goods transported by ship.

biofeedback A method of controlling mental reactions and physical functions that normally are involuntary by the use of electronic monitoring devices.

black-leg A worker who continues to work during a strike, or who comes in to take a striker's place. Also known as a scab.

blame in norm-shifting process In the discussion of a norm, and some radical departures from it, people tend to blame "others" until there has been time for a full discussion of the matter and an emptying of the preconceptions of the participants. Once this process runs its course, the old norm may again be approved, with a much greater chance of success, or a new norm may be established.

blind spots, executive The tendency of an executive to be unaware of the feelings others around him have of him, whether they are superiors or subordinates.

block check An accounting or auditing term denoting the minute examination of a specific and key account of a company.

block design *psychological testing* A type of test in which a subject is given several blocks of different colors and is instructed to build a specific design from them.

blocked currency A law in a country forbidding currency from being taken out of the country.

blue-collar blues A state of mind of blue-collar workers resulting in disillusionment with their jobs. It is marked by decreased productivity, hostility toward the company, and perhaps alcoholism or drug addiction.

Board of Directors A formal group of people, created by the papers of incorporation, and empowered to exercise the powers of the corporation, limited only by any conditions that may be set out in a corporation's bylaws.

Board of Education (Sweden) An organization that oversees three hundred basic industrial training courses at many different levels of expertise at special training centers. The courses are used by the Labor Market Board.

body language The "silent language" that deals with gestures, tones of voice, and the entire environment.

Boehm-Bawerk's Law A rigorous theorem of economics that proves that existing means of production will yield greater economic performance only through taking greater risks.

Bologna Stock Exchange One of ten Italian stock exchanges.

Bolsa de Barcelona Barcelona stock exchange, one of the principal exchanges in Spain.

Bolsa de Comercio Buenos Aires stock exchange.

Bolsa de Comercio de Caracas The principal stock exchange in Venezuela.

Bolsa de Comercio de Lima Lima, Peru, stock exchange.

Bolsa de Commercio Bogota Bogota, Colombia, stock exchange.

Bolsa de Lisboa Lisbon stock exchange.

Bolsa de Madrid Madrid stock exchange.

Bolsa de Porta Oporto, Portugal, stock exchange.

bond Long-term publicly issued debt that is a fixed-income investment vehicle.

bond rating An appraisal by a recognized financial organization of the soundness of a bond as an investment.

bonuses 1. Incentives used by many companies to help motivate executives and lower-level management personnel. 2. Payments, above base pay, usually predicated on performance.

boodle United Kingdom colloquialism for counterfeit money or money obtained by corrupt dealings.

book value The value at which an item is reported in financial statements, and is normally the cost of the asset.

book value per share In managerial finance, book value is said to be merely the historical investments that have been made in the assets of the company.

boom One phase of a business cycle in which business is good, businessmen are optimistic, inflation occurs as prices rise more rapidly than real income, and productive resources are often scarce.

boomerang effect The act of reverting to a past state of mind by an employee after the first effects of a hygiene-motivated act have been performed by management.

boredom That feeling of disillusionment among workers, both blue-collar and white-collar, that what they do is not significant and that they themselves are not significant. Boredom occurs when the people involved perform virtually the same tasks day after day, without being able to see beyond the task to the larger things that are being accomplished.

borrowing allocation The limit set on a company or organization as to its ability to borrow to meet capital expenditures. The limit is usually set by the board of directors.

Borsa Valori di Firenza Florence stock exchange.

Borsa Valori di Genova Genoa stock exchange.

Borsa Valori di Milano Milan stock exchange, which is the principal one in Italy.

Borsa Valori di Napoli Naples stock exchange.

Borsa Valori di Palermo Palermo stock exchange.

Borsa Valori di Turino Turin stock exchange.

Börsenagent A trader on one of the Swiss stock exchanges.

boss syndrome A fear on the part of many management people that they will lose their power to control the firm, thus causing the firm to fail.

bottom-up approach In determining objectives for results management, this approach entails beginning at the bottom of the organization chart with the lower echelon submitting objectives to the next level, and so on until the highest echelon has all the objectives in hand which it can quickly modify and merge into the firm's objectives.

boundaries of planning The use of "premises and constraints" by the manager in the planning procedures.

Box-Jenkins approach to forecasting Simplistically, a method of prediction that utilizes model building with time series.

brain drain The loss of skilled manpower or professional people through immigration to other countries or other regions of the same country.

brainwashing The act of subjecting another person to propaganda that is so intense and so relentless that the person is ultimately made to think in the same patterns as the person performing the act. Some ill-advised managers have been known to try this on employees.

brand differentiation, as a barrier to entering the market A corporate brand, when it achieves positive recognition in the market, is a formidable barrier to overcome when trying to break into the market with a new product.

breakdown maintenance Repairing machinery that has broken down but for which arrangements had already been made by having spare parts, skilled mechanics, etc., available.

break-even analysis 1. A formal profit-planning approach based on established relations between costs and revenues. It is a device for determining the point at which sales will just cover total costs. 2. The level of sales at which a firm, or product, will just meet costs.

breakthrough opportunity The opportunity an existing business may sometimes encounter that offers the chance, but only at great risk, to multiply the wealth-producing capacity of the entire business. It may be the introduction of a new product or the acquisition of another company.

Bretton Woods system The system under which gold was pegged at thirty-five dollars an ounce. The collapse of the Bretton Woods system resulted in inflation and the devaluation of the U.S. dollar.

brick areas Sales territories that are broken down into segments having similar marketing potential.

brick-by-brick forecasting An informal method used in sales and marketing forecasting that is done by talking with the people involved and weighing different ideas.

bridging A person evaluates areas of agreement between himself and some other person, and uses that agreement to overcome any other gap between them.

B-risk Portfolio risk that cannot be diversified away. Also known as systematic risk, nondiversifiable risk.

"British Disease" A prolonged state of economic stagnation.

British Institute of Management A group in the UK similar to the Business Round Table in the United States. This organization attempts to direct the formation of economic policy, along with social policy. Members are primarily top management people from major industrial firms.

British Overseas Trade Board (BOTB) Established in 1971 as the British Export Board, the name was changed in 1972. The purpose of the organization is to make export promotion relevant to the real needs of business and industry. Address: 1 Victoria Street, London SWIH OET.

broad-banded salary structure A salary structure in a firm with a relatively small number of grades.

brokers' contract notes Signed confirmation to principals from their brokers that their buying or selling orders have been carried out.

Brownlow Committee A committee that reported to President Franklin D. Roosevelt and which was charged with planning and implementing management techniques in public administration. The committee is quoted as reporting: "Good management will promote in the fullest measure the conservation and utilization of our national resources and spell this out plainly in social justice, security, order, liberty, prosperity, in material benefit and in higher values of life."

Brown-Spearman formula *psychological testing* A method of validating an intelligence test, particularly when the length has been increased and the validity of the longer test needs to be confirmed.

bucket shop An old colloquial term denoting a brokerage house of doubtful respectability.

309

Budget Treaty 1970 A treaty to be effective after the full implementation of the Treaty of Rome, 1957, which gave the control of the common budget of the Common Market to the European Commission.

buffer stock A marginal quantity of goods or raw materials kept in stock to safeguard against unexpected shortages.

building society A type of financial institution in the United Kingdom in which persons invest money that is then lent to home buyers. Much the same as the original "building and loan" companies in the United States.

built-in obsolescence Lack of quality that is part of the design and building of a good that will insure that it will have to be replaced after a given period of time. Consumer durables have allegedly been in the forefront of built-in obsolesence.

Bulgarska Narodna Banka Bulgarian National (Central) bank, established in 1879. Address: 9th September Square, Sofia.

bull weeks A colloquialism denoting weeks in industry when absenteeism is low and productivity is high.

"bullet train" The "shinkansen," or high-speed train, of Japan.

bulletin boards The primary vehicle in most plants to communicate with employees. Obviously such communications must be impersonal and brief, but most employees will visit the bulletin boards, at least once a day, experience has shown.

Bureau of Standards A U.S. government agency attached to the Department of Commerce and established in 1901. It is concerned with all facets of pure and applied measurement and the establishment of standards of performance.

Bureau of the Census An agency in the Department of Commerce that collects and publishes a wide array of data on all aspects of American life. A census of population is taken every ten years and now includes much social and economic data. A census of business is taken every four to five years, as is the census of manufacturers.

bureaucracy Originally, this term denoted an organization that worked with great efficiency. However, when the term was attached to governmental operations, it came to be an expression denoting an organization burdened with official routine and inefficiency.

bureaucratic organization A term originated by Max Weber to describe the typical organization of government. However, the same type of organization is found in many industries, and the characteristics are as follows: 1) vertical authority pattern, 2) marked degree of specialization, 3) strict job descriptions defining duties, privileges, and latitude, 4) maximum use of rules, 5) impersonal administration of staff, and 6) employment usually for a lifetime, especially for management personnel.

bureaucratic roles Roles that must be played in organizations that are bureaucratic in nature, i.e., much official aggrandizement, tasks which must be done in a very specific way, the discouragement of innovativeness, and the emphasis upon "sameness."

business One of the best definitions of business is offered by Peter Drucker: "A process that converts an outside resource, namely knowledge, into outside results, namely economic values." (Peter Drucker, *Managing for Results* [New York: Harper & Row, 1964], p. 5.)

business and forward projection The action of looking to the future of a business by the consideration of two things that might be done or should be done: 1) The replacement of present products or services that may be good, but which could be better; 2) The development of innovation.

business, burden of The primary burden of business, which includes all others, is economic survival.

business by-products Those products which remain after the primary product has been extracted from the raw materials.

business cost accounting The practice of using cost accounting to determine, with as great exactness as possible, the true cost of every unit of product sold, taking every aspect into consideration that contributes to the manufacture and sale of a product.

business cycles A theory put forward by Joseph Schumpeter that the businessman himself is the cause of changes in business success, as he innovates and forces change into the total business activity.

business, diagnosis of A four-stem process of analysis that should give a good picture of the business: 1) analysis of results, revenues, and resources 2) analysis of cost centers and cost structures 3) marketing analysis 4) knowledge analysis.

business enterprise, profit objective While a business enterprise must make

a profit to remain in business, to use profit as the ultimate goal is short-sighted, and may well cause a company to show a profit one year and losses thereafter. Perhaps it is better to say that the objective of a business enterprise is to make growth an ongoing concern, which includes the making of a profit.

business forecasting, economic rhythm in A method that forecasts a time series. A time series is defined as a collection of readings belonging to different time periods of some variables or composites of variables, such as the production of steel, per capita income, gross national product, etc.

business game A computer game designed to assist business students in decision making, and in showing them the quick results of their decisions. Team play is common in most schools, and competition often occurs between schools.

business-government relations A necessary relationship in today's complex world that is established, in the United States, by businesses that have a presence in Washington, including lobbying headquarters, paid lobbyists, or any other presence that has access to the powers in the capital.

business humanitarianism Acts or feelings of goodwill toward employees, which may or may not be genuine or deep seated, and which are usually parts of "packages" sold by social psychologists and others to industries under the guise of motivation.

business indicators Periodic statistical data on sectors in the economy, which point to factors likely to have an effect on the economy. Indicators are called leading indicators, lagging indicators, and coincidental indicators.

business intelligence, sources of information Government agencies, trade associations, the U.S. Chamber of Commerce, private research and information agencies, and a host of other persons and places, most of which can be found in periodicals dealing with specific matters are the best sources of information. Three major sources long used by this author are periodicals from the Federal Reserve System, the Economic Report of the President, and the Statistical Abstract of the United States.

business investment in managerial ego The tendency on the part of a business to keep pushing a product even when it is known that the product cannot be successful. This approach tends to massage the combined egos of management, but does the company great harm. A classic example is the Edsel automobile.

business leadership position A business must have a leader, but that leadership is usually transitory, and the person leading is extremely vulnerable.

business mergers A business's attempts to expand its resource base, its product base, or its market base. Currently, mergers are widespread.

business oligopolies Limited competition between a small number of manufacturers or suppliers. (In modern business, getting into an industry may be cost-prohibitive, thereby encouraging oligopolies.)

Business Periodicals Index (BPI) A major bibliographic tool of business research that indexes titles widely held in U.S. libraries.

business practice The scope of a business specifically as it relates to specialization and diversification.

business purpose Defined by Peter Drucker as "to create a customer."

business risk 1. Risk in business due to uncertainty about investment outlays, operating cash flows, and salvage values, without regard to how investments are financed. 2. A potential danger to all, or part of, a business enterprise. While risks are real in all businesses, if one attempts to operate a business on the basis of the fear of risk, failure is almost assured.

business trust An arrangement in which the legal ownership of property is held by one party for the benefit of someone else.

business vulnerability The danger that a business may fail or be weakened because of certain economic facts of life that govern it. While all businesses are vulnerable, the refusal to recognize vulnerability is the greatest danger.

business waste Those human or nonhuman resources that are not used to full capacity in operating a business.

"Business X-ray" A process dealing with the concepts related to a business, and one which allows the viewer to look at the entire business at one time not just at one department or at one product. The process was named by Peter Drucker.

but what have you done for me lately syndrome According to Frederick Herzberg, originator of the "hygiene" approach to management, the act of making a one-time improvement for an employee, such as facilitating his "clocking out" of the plant, which will satisfy him temporarily, after which resentment builds quickly if other improvements are not made.

buzzword Words that emerge from business discussions, and which become, for a time, a part of business jargon, i.e., management by objectives,

accountable management, optimizing the market, etc.

byssinosis A lung disease similar to silicosis that is found in workers with long tenure in plants manufacturing cotton products.

C

cable TV, as an advertising medium A useful medium for two reasons: 1) cable TV reaches where conventional signals are not available and 2) Local businesses can advertise on cable TV within their own marketing areas.

CACM Central American Common Market.

Caesar management A type of management with all authority concentrated in one person.

cafeteria system A general type of fringe benefits system in which an employee is allotted so many dollars that he can spend on his fringe benefits, and he may pick and choose as he will until his dollar amount is exhausted.

CAI or CAL Computer-aided instruction or learning.

Cairo Stock Exchange (la) Bourse de Valeurs de Caire. One of two principal Egyptian stock exchanges.

calculus A fundamental branch of mathematics which allows calculations of the rate of change in a dependent variable in relation to a change in an independent variable.

Calcutta Stock Exchange Association Limited One of seven major Indian stock exchanges.

Calgary Stock Exchange One of six major Canadian stock exchanges.

California Psychological Inventory (CPI) Developed in the United States for use in personality and temperament tests, CPI is derived in part from the Minnesota multiphasic personality inventory and covers eighteen components divided into four classes: 1) measures poise, ascendancy, and self-assurance; 2) measures sociability, maturity, and responsibility; 3) measures achievement potential and intellectual efficiency; 4) measures intellectual and interest modes.

Calvinism, profit making and The Puritan ethic, an off-shoot of Calvin's theology, gave its blessing to profit making so long as profit was accompanied by hard work. Theology from ancient times until the time of Calvin had condemned profit making, since it was usually made by lending money or by trading both of which were considered theologically suspect.

Canadian Central Bank Bank of Canada.

Canadian Forces School of Management A school operated in Montreal for the military forces that did a study on time management a few years ago and named some impediments to good time management. These impediments include unclear objectives, poor information, postponed decisions, procrastination, etc.

Canadian Manufacturers' Association The national organization of employers' associations, established in 1871. Address: 67 Yonge Street, Toronto, Ontario.

Canadian stock exchanges Canadian Stock Exchange, Montreal; Calgary Stock Exchange; Montreal Stock Exchange; Toronto Stock Exchange; Vancouver Stock Exchange; Winnipeg Stock Exchange.

CAP Common Agricultural Policy of the European Economic Community (EEC).

capacity The ability to discharge a debt when it is due.

capacity loading Planning a work schedule, often on a specific project, that will cause all the machines to be manned and a full complement of workers to be on the job.

capacity loading and schedule system (CLASS) A computer software package developed by IBM for factory shop floor control, including measuring value of work in progress.

capital 1. Assets used in a business enterprise. 2. Simplistically, the amount of money invested in a business venture.

capital allowance The allowances for writing down assets in lieu of depreciation.

capital appropriation A sum of money set aside by a business for further capital expenditure at a given time.

capital budget A list of planned investment projects, sometimes running

throughout a ten-year plan, but often confined to one budget year.

capital consumption adjustment The adjustment made to historic cost depreciation to correct for understatements made during a period of inflation.

capital consumption allowance A charge against the Gross National Product for the depletion of capital goods over the previous year. The deduction from GNP equals Net National Product.

capital cut-off point The point at which a company can no longer acquire capital cost effectively.

capital employed All fixed and current assets employed in a business.

capital expenditure Normally, money spent on fixed assets, otherwise known as capital goods, or money spent on goods used in the production of other goods.

capital formation, drop in rate of Capital formation is dropping in most developed nations, in part because of inflation. Capital formation is one of the four absolute needs in economic growth and development.

capital gains tax A tax on the profit accruing from the sale of a capital interests and assets. This tax was changed by the Tax Reform Act of 1986, and the reader would be well advised to watch the recurring changes in this tax.

capital intensive firm A business having a high degree of capital assets or a high level of mechanization for use in production rather than a large number of manual laborers.

capital rationing A shortage of capital that forces a company to choose between planned capital projects.

capital transfer tax *See* gift tax.

capital-output ratio The relationship between capital investment and the flow of goods and services.

capitalism, the failure of Several prominent economists have predicted the demise of capitalism, as we now know it, because of the roadblocks erected by security-minded middle managers. An oft-used, paraphrased quote is as follows: "The vast wastelands of passive and dependent people in middle management positions and the concept of the administrator as the person who by situation and temperament prevents things from happening bore within them the seeds of capitalism's downfall. Far more deleterious than the rants of radicals, or the conspiracies of bomb-throwing Marxists, were the blockers on the corporate payroll, the security-minded managers." (George S. Odiorne, *MBO II* [Belmont, Calif.: David S. Lake, Pubs., 1979], p. 37.)

capitalism, the rational nature of Joseph Schumpeter, although sometimes inconsistently, generally believed that capitalism, by the forces within it, would ultimately become a "march into socialism." Four rational concepts would bring this about: 1) the success of business in creating a new high standard of living for society breeds its ultimate control by political forces through its own bureaucratization; 2) the rational nature of capitalism spreads rational habits of mind, and free contacts between superior and subordinate tend to destroy a system based

solely upon satisfying individual short-run utilitarian interests; 3) because business managers concentrate on the technology of managing plants and offices, a political system and an intellectual class independent of, and hostile to, the interests of corporate business has emerged; and 4) the value system of capitalism has bred counter values of security, equality, and regulation that must ultimately overwhelm it.

capitalism, welfare Capitalism, as a system that allows the accumulation of capital and the private use thereof, makes no specific provision for social welfare. Government has stepped into this breech, aided somewhat by social programs undertaken by many companies.

capitalization The sum of all long-term sources of financing to the firm, or simplistically the total assets minus current liabilities.

capitalization standard A formulation of a debt standard as it relates to capitalization, taking into consideration the magnitude of the risk and any other pertinent matter that will leave a company in a reasonably safe position.

CAPS Computer Assisted Placement Service, used by universities and technical schools in the United Kingdom.

career ethic A perception of "rightness" that guides the individual in the pursuit of a career and career goals.

careerism The push by students to make good grades and to settle on a well-paying career, which emerged after the rebellious decade of the 1960s.

career, need for second The need for a second career stems from two areas of personal life: 1) often a worker, particularly a "knowledge" worker, will want to have different experiences, rather than staying with one job for many years and 2) Many "knowledge" workers find that retirement is not acceptable, and they often must pursue a different career to fulfill their need to be productively occupied.

career paths The various routes one may take to achieve a career goal.

careers teacher A school teacher with the special responsibility of advising students on career choices in the United Kingdom.

Caribbean Employers' Confederation An organization set up in 1960 with the special interest of industrial relations. Address: 9 Dere Street, Port of Spain, Trinidad.

Caribbean Free Trade Association (CARIFTA) Set up in 1967 to work towards custom unions and the free movement of labor between Antigua, Barbados, Belize, Dominica, Grenada, Guyana, Jamaica, Montserrat, St. Christopher-Nevis-Anguilla, St. Lucia, St. Vincent, and Trinidad and Tobago. Address: Georgetown, Guyana.

carriage trade A type of consumer trade that is generally isolated and in which trade is carried on in a relatively small area. Usually, the trade is also confined to a specific type of consumer.

carrot-and-stick approach A "promise of something later" type of management that holds little appeal to today's employees.

carrying costs Costs related to doing business, such as holding inventory, warehouse space, depreciation, insurance, etc.

cartel International business agreements

between firms or countries that attempt to monopolize the market for certain products or services. At one time, countries would create cartels for favorites "of the court," and these organizations sometimes lasted for many years.

cartogram A map-graph, shaded, often in various colors, to provide graphic information to business people. Sales density could be so marked, as could sources for raw materials, locations of warehouses, etc.

case history An industrial situation, whether real or hypothetical, used for study and analysis in training situations, such as at colleges or during in-house training.

case law Law which is based on prior case histories and precedent, rather than statutes and legislation.

case method A form of study wherein a case history of a firm, or some segment thereof, is given and then analyzed to find the strong and weak points of that history. This approach is widely used in graduate schools and in in-plant studies.

case study A presentation of a situation involving problems to be solved that is basically descriptive rather than analytical.

cash accounting A system that recognizes cash receipts only when they are actually received. (*See also* accrual accounting)

cash budget A projection of cash receipts and a plan for the use of those receipts.

cash cow A company, subsidiary, or product that generates more cash than can be profitably used to support the company, subsidiary, or product, thus making it available for other developments in the firm.

cash flow 1. The amount of cash received and disbursed over a specific period of time. 2. The amount of money required to finance operations during a week, month, or year.

cash-flow cycle The periodic transformation of cash through working capital and fixed assets back to cash.

cash-flow forecast An estimate made in advance of anticipated revenues and the uses for those revenues.

cash flow from operations Cash generated or consumed by the productive operations of a firm over a specific period of time (profit after tax plus noncash changes minus noncash receipts).

cash-flow principle A principle of investment evaluation that states that only actual movements of cash are relevant and that they should be listed on the date they move.

cash-flow statement A statement enumerating all sources of cash received and disbursed by categories.

cash forecast A schedule of money that will be needed in a business to pay salaries, to pay normal operating expenses, and to pay for capital investment.

cash provided by operations All cash generated by the productive activities of a firm over a period of time, including changes in current assets and liabilities required to support changing levels of sales volume.

cash ratio 1. Ratio of a bank's cash holdings and liquid assets to its total deposit liabilities. 2. Ratio of a firm's liquid assets to its current liabilities. (*See also* liquidity ratio)

casting vote In some countries, and in some situations, the chairman of a meeting may cast a vote in case of a tie, even though he has already used his regular vote.

categorization of people The tendency on the part of managers to ignore the uniqueness of people and cast them all into one mold.

category analysis A market research technique to determine whether conditions are right to introduce a new product or service.

causal models The attempt to create highly sophisticated forecasts based on historical data and detailed analysis, which allows the explicit relationships between the factor to be forecast and other factors, such as related businesses, economic forces, and socioeconomic factors to be made manifest.

causative thinking Emphasizes the shaping of future events and achievements instead of waiting for destiny to decide them.

caveat emptor A principle of common law that dictates that a consumer should exercise caution in buying a good or service, since, should the consumer later sue the firm, the courts may not support him.

caveat subscriptor A common law principle that advises the signer of a document, such as a contract, to exercise caution, since he will likely be held to the terms of the document.

CBA Cost-benefit analysis.

CBD Cash before delivery.

CBI Confederation of British Industry.

CCT Common Customs Tariff of the Common Market.

cd Cash discount.

CEI Council of Engineering Institutions in the United Kingdom.

census survey A market research action, or other kind of survey, that involves the investigation of an entire market by the use of a random sampling of that specific universe.

Center for Interfirm Comparison (CIFC) Organized in 1959 as an independent, non-profit firm by the British Institute of Management in association with the British Productivity Council to conduct interfirm comparisons.

Central American Common Market (CACM) An organization formed in 1960 that includes Costa Rica, Guatemala, Honduras, Nicaragua, and El Salvador. The General Treaty on Central America Integration was designed to establish a free-trade area within a common external tariff and to facilitate consultation on monetary policy. (*See also* Latin America Free Trade Association, LAFTA)

central bank A type of bank, often owned by the country in which it operates, that serves as the banker's bank and as a national bank with authority over monetary policy.

Central Standard Time (CST or CT) Local time in the United States at the 90th meridian.

centralization A situation in a business organization whereby decision making and responsibility are generally left to the very top managers, with authority and formal activities concentrated in fewer and fewer managers.

ceremonies One way Japanese management conveys to employees the philosophy of the firm. Ceremonies within a firm tend to become fixed, and thus they become an expected part of the lives of the employee.

certainty-equivalent A guaranteed amount of money that a decision maker would trade for an uncertain cash flow.

certificate of origin Document sent with exported goods for the information of customs officers.

certiorari A higher court writ served on a lower court requesting a transcript of case proceedings so that the condust of the case can be reviewed.

CET Common External Tariff of the Common Market.

CETA The Comprehensive Employment and Training Programs.

Ceylon Former name of Sri Lanka.

CF Cost and freight.

C/F Carry forward.

CFI Cost, freight, and insurance.

chain of command A formal line of communications in a company or other organization denoting proper lines to follow in communicating upward, downward, and laterally.

Chambre de la Bourse de Geneve Geneva Stock Exchange, the principle one in Switzerland.

Chambre Syndicale des Agents de Change An organization that publishes the official list of securities of the Paris stock exchange and implements its rules and regulations in collaboration with the Commission des Operations de Bourse.

Chancellor of the Exchequer A United Kingdom cabinet minister, head of the Treasury, with the specific responsibility for national policy and performance, including the annual budget and the Finance Bill.

channel money Interim payments made to a seaman prior to the "settling up" that is done at the end of the voyage.

channels of organizations The tying and relating of the organization units by means of delegation of authority set forth in channels or avenues along which formal authority is exercised over the activities of each unit.

character disorders In business, those defects in moral character that lead to the "success at any cost" syndrome. The business community should disdain these defects.

characteristics of management The major characteristics are listed as follows: 1) management is purposeful, in that it deals with the achievement of a specific objective; 2) management makes things happen; it is active; 3) management is accomplished by, with, and through the efforts of others 4) management effectiveness demands the use of certain types of knowledge, skills, and practices; 5) management is an activity, not a person or group of persons; 6) management is aided, not replaced, by the computer; 7) management is usually associated with efforts of a group; 8) management is an outstanding means for exerting real impact upon human lives; 9) management is intangible; 10) Those practicing management are not necessarily the same as owners. Taken from George R. Terry,

Principles of Management (Homewood, Ill.: Richard D. Irwin, Inc., 1972), pp. 11–14.

chart, activity A graphic presentation of a specific position outlining the responsibilities a position has in achieving some specific objective.

chart, organization A graphic presentation of the formal job organization of a firm, with each position occupying a place relative to all other positions with respect to function, authority, responsibility, and communications. Generally, the chart will flow from the top down, according to the relative importance of the job or function.

chartered company A type of company in the United Kingdom that was incorporated by the British royalty, particularly in the seventeenth, eighteenth, and nineteenth centuries. Included among these are the Hudson Bay Company (1670), Bank of England (1694), and the British South Africa Company (1889).

check-off agreement A clause in a union-management contract that allows the employer to deduct union dues from the pay of the employee. This clause assures the union that the members' dues will be paid.

checkups, preburnout The wisdom on the part of a person to get a medical (perhaps psychological, also) checkup if there are any signs of burnout, such as intolerance for the job, subtle changes in mood, and general malaise.

Chilean stock exchanges The two Chilean stock exchanges are in Santiago and in Valparaiso.

chi-square A statistical test to discover whether a difference between the findings of two surveys has any significance.

chose-in-action A legal term for a right to the possession of a particular property or a sum of money in the event of a certain contingency, with the right of possession being enforceable in a court of law.

Christ Church Stock Exchange One of four major stock exchanges in New Zealand.

CIA Cash in advance.

circular flow of income A graphic presentation that illustrates how, in a private-enterprise economy, resources are sold to businesses and payments are made by the businesses to the consumers, who then spend their money for the products or services produced by the resources, thus keeping the incoming flowing in the circle. Leakages from the flow can exist in the form of taxes or savings. Savings go to financial institutions, which inject them back into the economy by making loans. Government, the recipient of a large income in the form of taxes, gets these monies back into the flow via transfer payments and expenditures for goods and services.

City of London A square mile of London in which national and international financial expertise and institutions are concentrated, including the Bank of England, the Stock Exchange, Lloyds, the commodities markets, the Baltic Exchange, etc.

Civil Rights Act of 1964 1. Legislation designed to reduce and ultimately eliminate racial discrimination in the United States. 2. Title VII, a vitally important bit of this legislation, pro-

hibits an employer from discriminating against an employee or applicant for employment on the basis of race, color, religion, sex, or national origin.

Civil Service Assembly of the United States and Canada Formerly the National Assembly of Civil Service Commissioners (1906) with headquarters in Chicago, Illinois.

class market A market designed for wealthy people, often contrasted with the "mass market," which is for all consumers.

class system, British management and the The insistence, on the part of some students of management, that British lack of productivity is based on the old class system, which produced a contempt for workers by management and contempt for management by workers.

classical administration A theory of Henri Fayor, a French contemporary of Frederick Taylor, stating that classical administration, as opposed to scientific organization, focuses upon the organization as a whole and not upon a single segment of it.

Clean Air Acts of 1956 and 1968 United Kingdom acts of Parliament designed to ultimately eliminate industrial and domestic smoke in London. These acts were particularly inspired by the deaths, in 1952, of four thousand London residents due to smog.

clearlook An expression used in the study of synergetics that generally means an objective analysis of all data as opposed to emotional responses to these data. Three aspects of the "clearlook" are: 1) objective, precise appraisal (OPA), i.e. the individual carefully separates what he wants to see or fears to see from what is actually there; 2) semantic discrimination, i.e., the individual continuously makes a distinction between word and referent, between verbal map and territory represented; 3) Information force, i.e., every individual is confronted in the course of his life with an enormous variety of input data. In order to handle the data efficiently, he assigns it to categories. This organizes the data and enables him to respond economically and in an organized way. From N. Arthur Coulter, M.D., *Synergetics: An Adventure in Human Development* (Englewood Cliffs, N.J.: Prentice Hall, 1976), pp.99–100.

clerical aptitude test Tests used in personnel selection to determine the ability of a person to check and classify words, figures, symbols, etc., skills which will be a part of clerical duties.

clerical cost burden The share of the total clerical costs divided by the total number of shipments for the shipping route served. (In essence, certain clerical functions are required by any shipment regardless of its relative size. The clerical cost burden, then, is the total of all clerical costs related to shipping goods.)

clerical work evaluation (CWE) A work-study technique developed in England to measure the work done by indirect labor in offices.

client relationship A relationship that an employee has either with a superior in the company or with some external person or force, with whom he must develop a relationship that is satisfactory to the client and to rewarding to him.

"client responsibility" approach in burnout Many psychologists agree that the "burnout client" must be given a number of simple responsibilities for his own welfare, thus avoiding overdependence on his physician or others.

climate, organizational That general personal and technical atmosphere in the plant (or firm) that is most conducive to reaching the firm's goals.

close off the top Financial jargon that means to exclude the possibility of further debt financing.

closed shop A factory or business operating under a contractual arrangement between a labor union and the employer by which only members of the union may be employed.

closure, compulsion to The quality that motivates a manager to complete a task.

CLU Chartered Life Underwriter.

cluster analysis A technique used in market research to sort out categories of items, people, etc., for further and closer study.

C/N Credit note.

coaching In a personal problem-solving situation, the "coach" is the person who assists the troubled person, often by listening and making suggestions and often by changing roles and relating his own problems and solutions in a way that makes the first person recognize himself and his own problems.

coaching by middle managers A major responsibility of middle managers is to coach their subordinates. Though the jobs of these people may often call for hands-on work, in the main they are in their positions to coach others to do the work and to do it effectively.

COBOL Acronym of Common Business Oriented Language.

cobweb theory A theory developed by N. Kaldor, H. Schultz, and J. Tinbergen in an attempt to explain business cycles as they are specifically related to commodities.

COD Cash on delivery.

co-determination laws, in West Germany Laws that enhance the position of the employee in a company by giving him more social, political, and participative power in the company. These laws are being enacted in some measure in Sweden, also.

CODOT Classification of Occupations and Directory of Occupational Titles.

cohesion, groupthink resulting from the drawing together of people because they like each other or their views coincide tends to result in a "groupthink" situation in which individuality is absorbed in the adherence to the wishes of the group.

COI Central Office of Information of the United Kingdom.

coincident technique A technique used in market research interviewing in which a consumer, specifically a user of a product in question, is asked about what he is doing at the time of the interview.

cold call In sales, an unannounced call upon a client or prospective client by a salesperson.

collaboration 1. The intentional cooperation of a group in the work of problem solving, or any other need, of the firm. 2. The positive personal interaction within a firm that tends to cut "red tape" and facilitate the attainment of objectives.

collection period A ratio measure of control of accounts receivable, and defined as accounts receivable divided by credit sales per day.

collective bargaining rights The statutory rights of labor and management to negotiate all facets of working conditions ostensibly for the protection of the employer, the employee, and the general public.

collectivism A philosophy in Japanese industry that all good things happen in a firm as the result of teamwork, and little attention is given to individual effort.

colleges and managerial values Belief that standards of values can be taught in colleges, and often are, but lasting standards are more apt to be learned by the person on the job, primarily from superiors.

collision clause A clause in Marine insurance indemnifying a shipowner against liability for damage caused to other ships in collisions.

Colombo Plan An organization started in 1950 by British Commonwealth countries and others to promote economic cooperation in south and southeast Asia. Original member states were Afghanistan, Australia, Bhutan, Burma, Cambodia, Canada, Sri Lanka, India, Indonesia, Japan, South Korea, Laos, Malaysia, Nepal, New Zealand, Pakistan, Iran, Philippines, Thailand, the United Kingdom, and the United States. This organization raises funds from the members and from the

International Bank for Reconstruction and Development. Economic concerns, public health, agriculture and industry, plus scientific research and development are included in the work of the organization. Address: 12 Melbourn Ave. P.O. Box 596, Colombo, Sri Lanka.

Columbia Executive Program for Management One of twenty-seven different management programs offered annually by Columbia University to top managers.

COMECON (Council for Mutual Economic Assistance) This organization was formed in 1949 to promote economic cooperation in Eastern Europe between Albania, Bulgaria, Czechoslovakia, East Germany, Hungary, Mongolia, Poland, Romania, and Russia. Albania withdrew in 1961.

comfort zone of Amiables The need for a person who is slow-paced and amiable to become more fast-paced, and goal-oriented in the presence of more self-determined people.

comfort zone of Analyticals Persons who are analytical by nature may find it profitable to become more decisive when conferring with others to prevent inducing stress by slowness of decision making.

comfort zone of Drivers By making a concerted effort to listen to others, drivers will yield a degree of comfort to the slower-paced amiables and analyticals.

comfort zone of Expressives This type of person, who is verbally expressive and prone to quick decisions, may lessen stress on others and himself by slowing the tempo, checking the facts

again and again, and listening patiently to others in the group.

Commanditaire Vennootschap A limited partnership under the laws of the Netherlands.

commanditaire A type of partner in certain forms of partnerships in Belgium or France that allows a partner to be liable only to the extent of his participation in a project.

commando sales team A special sales force assembled for the promotion or introduction of a new product or service.

commercant Official designation for a trader under French commercial law.

commitment, ethics of A moving away from self and a moving toward others in all aspects of life.

committed costs Those costs to which a firm will be almost irrevocably committed once the project or enterprise has begun.

commodity The term is used most specifically to denote foodstuffs and raw materials such as grain, rice, tea, coffee, sugar, rubber, tin, lead, etc. Also defined as goods or products being transported to a manufacturer or consumer.

common budget The budget to which all Common Market countries contribute and from which common projects are financed.

common carrier Generally a type of carrier who undertakes to transport for hire, from one place to another, the goods of anyone who employs him.

Common Market Term for the European Community, which was formed by the Treaty of Rome in 1957. The members were France, West Germany, Italy, Belgium, the Netherlands, and Luxembourg. The Treaty of Accession, 1972, expanded the market to include other countries. While it was first looked upon as a "customs union," Europe wanted an organization that could compete with the United States and that might deter any further European wars. (*See also* EC)

Common Industrial Policy An industrial policy the Common Market countries are attempting to work out for future relationships. Since the markets are supposed to be tariff free, this approach will require that countries coordinate their widely differing industrial practices so as to be able to trade on some common ground. Legislation will also be needed to guide the multinational companies. It is possible that if all other plans for the market work out, industries will be partially allocated to the areas that are best suited to accommodate them.

Common Labor Market Articles 48 and 49 of the Treaty of Rome (1957) proposed the free movement of labor among the Common Market countries. Generally, these articles have been carried out. Only with respect to government employees are the member nations supposed to give priority to nationals.

common law An English form of law based on prior decisions and the doctrines underlying them, including custom and usage, rather than on statutory, or codified, law.

Common Social Policy In Articles 117–28 of the Treaty of Rome, social policies of the Common Market countries were addressed. Early action introduced vocational training and redeployment of workers, and later policies dealt with health policies, social security, industrial health and safety, plus equal pay for men and women doing the same work.

common standards Common industrial policies in the Common Market.

Common Taxation Policy Articles 95–99 of the Treaty of Rome were written to insure that one country did not impose higher taxes on the goods of other countries than the taxes on its own goods. In time, all tax policies in the Common Market countries are to be harmonized.

Common Technological Policy It was the ambition of the Common Market to develop a common technological policy. Since the market was comprised of about 250 million people, essentially the size of the United States, it was desired to adopt policy in computers, nuclear energy, meteorological forecasting and materials that would make the market competitive with the United States and Russia.

Common Transport Policy Article 3 and Articles 74–84 of the Treaty of Rome dealt with transport policies, including waterways, rails, and roads. Ultimately, the framers of the Treaty of Rome knew that the transportation policies would embrace air and sea transportation. A consultative committee exists to advise the Common Market ministers.

Commonwealth Chambers of Commerce, Federation of Organized in 1911, this body changed its name and constitution in 1960. It exists to promote trade among the Commonwealth countries and with other countries outside the Commonwealth.

Commonwealth Development Corporation Established in 1963, this organization was originally known as the Colonial Development Corporation. It was originally set up by the Overseas Resources Development Act of 1948. It is supposed to stimulate trade among Commonwealth countries and make loans to less-developed members.

Commonwealth Industries Association Ltd Organized in 1926 as the Empire Industries Association, its name was changed in 1967. The aim of the organization was to strengthen commonwealth relations through mutual preferential trade, investment, cooperation in technology, etc. Commonwealth countries usually have a 10 percent tariff advantage over non-commonwealth nations, making competition extremely difficult. Address: 60 Buckingham Gate, London SW1.

Commonwealth Institute The information and education center of the Commonwealth. Established in 1887 as the Imperial Institute, the name was changed in 1958. Address: Kensington High Street, London W8.

Commonwealth of Nations A voluntary association of nations once a part of the British Empire. It was inaugurated in 1931 by the Statute of Westminister. Address: Commonwealth Secretariat, Marlborough House, Pall Mall, London SW1.

communicating A continuing and thoughtful process dealing with the transmission and interchange with understanding of ideas, facts, and courses of action.

communications, free Within the limits of sound business practices, there must be free-flowing communications among company personnel at all levels. This does not assume that normal lines of communication will be forgotten, but that in proper circumstances each level of personnel will talk to other levels about matters vital to the success of the business.

communications modes The ways in which one communicates, namely face to face, by memo, by phone call, etc., all of which are appropriate in certain situations and inappropriate in others.

communications, technological changes in Communications, once severely limited by the necessity of a face-to-face meeting or limited by slow mail exchanges, have now changed due to technology to the point where people can carry on a meeting, literally around the world, not alone by voice, but by video as well.

community An evoking of the thought that "this is where I belong, these are my people, I will look out for them, and they for me; I am on familiar ground; I am home."

community action A term denoting actions of a town, community, or region that sets an objective of its own, such as to reduce the crime rate, depending upon its own resources and programs to accomplish the goal.

community integration A theory that workers are less strike-prone when they live in integrated communities and more strike-prone when they live in segregated communities.

community laws A term denoting the regulations, directives, decisions of the Council of Ministers and the European Commission of the Common Market. Most rules are in the area of customs duties, etc., but they may touch on anything, including the free movement of labor, transportation policies, the status of monopolies, etc.

Companies Acts In the United Kingdom, acts governing limited liability companies, passed respectively in 1856, 1948, and 1967.

company director In the United Kingdom, a person appointed to a board that directs the activities of a company by its shareholders. A director may or may not be a shareholder, but in any case, directors usually are more active in the UK than the United States.

company policy and administration A policy and practice within an organization that recognizes an individual as an "Adam," i.e., as human, and as an "Abraham," i.e., a human who seeks self-satisfaction and growth. (Frederick Herzberg, *The Managerial Choice* [Homewood, Ill.: Dow Jones-Erwin, 1976], pp. 60, 61.)

company schools Such schools proliferated in the 1970s and were supposed to continue into the 1980s and later. They worked in both the technological fields and in human relations areas.

comparative advantage The ability to produce a good at a comparative cost lower than that of other nations producing the same or a similar good. (*See also* counter-purchasing)

comparative estimating A form of analytical estimating that depends largely on similar jobs or projects carried out in the past.

compensating rest A period of relaxation after a prior period of arduous work.

compensation, in conglomerates While the way of measuring pay to managers may be less than ideal, historically the compensation of managers in conglomerates is based on the profit picture of that particular manager's profit center.

compensatory demands The demands an employee may make on a spouse at home to compensate for lack of job satisfaction.

competence motivation An atmosphere in a plant or firm that is marked by a feeling of confidence in the skills of personnel, thus positively impelling them forward on any given project.

competition 1. Simplistically, a vying for mastery. In the opinion of some experts, who say that the United States is becoming an "adversarial society," competition among persons can become a major source of stress and thus can become unhealthy. 2. Vying for prominence in one's industry is supposed to be at the very heart of the private enterprise system, yet business often belies this by attempting to either thwart or eliminate competition.

competition, conflict with cooperation Whereas competition may appear to rule out cooperation in the firm, this is not true. While competition is encouraged by use of bonuses, etc., the end of competition should be cooperation among all personnel to achieve the goals of the firm.

competition, the European view The

Europeans and, in large measure, the Japanese look at competition from the standpoint of staying technologically ahead of other nations. In both the European and Japanese markets the need to export goods demands that this notion of competition be considered carefully throughout the world.

complementary opportunity An action that changes the structure of a business by adding something to it that supports other actions of the business and that will increase its effectiveness and profitability.

component bar chart An ordinary bar chart on which various components of the data are illustrated by various bar colorings, shadings, etc.

compounding The growth of principal over time when the interest earned periodically is added to the principal and reinvested.

computer program Instructions, written in computer language, to a computer to carry out certain tasks.

computer programmer A person who translates a task, or certain instructions, into computer language.

computer store Also known as memory, that part of a computer into which information can be fed, stored, and retrieved.

computer terminal An input or output point linked to a source computer, though located some distance from the computer.

concentration analysis A development of the Pareto concept, in which the emphasis is placed on areas of major significance for the business, namely customers, vendors, key products, inventory, etc. (*See also* Pareto's Law)

concentration by economic results The action by the management of a business to concentrate on the product, or number of products, that makes it most cost effective and profitable.

concentration, principle of Focusing efforts on the task most critical and continuing to do so until the task is finished.

conditioned reflex An action of conditioning in which, through use of repetitive exercises, the person or animal in question will automatically respond in the accepted manner to certain stimuli.

conditions of employment The situation under which an employee works, including health and safety conditions, hours per week, rate of pay, general working conditions, job security, chance for promotions, fringe benefits, etc. In a union contract these conditions are usually spelled out specifically.

Conference Board A non-profit organization, formerly known as the National Industrial Conference Board, financially supported by more than four thousand industrial associates. The Conference Board does research and publications in economic and management matters that concern business and industry. Organized in 1916. Address: 845 Third Avenue, New York, NY 10022, USA.

conference, stand-up In an impromptu interview, usually unplanned, to remain standing should signal the unexpected visitor that his time is severely limited.

conflicts of interest Those activities of a manager that may not be right for all people with an interest in the activities, or activities that may be perceived as not being right.

conformity and nonconformity

While the top administrator in a firm may look upon the interests of a company as the overwhelming concern, it is unlikely that employees will. It is a task of management to induce from employees sufficient conformity to assure company success and enough nonconformity to allow each employee to retain individuality.

conformity and creativity

Since conformity usually has people going along with each other to avoid "rocking the boat," creativity, which is ultimately individualistic, will usually clash with conformity.

conformity, dynamics of

In a conforming group, which may be set upon by a deviant, the usual procedure is to isolate the deviant until he surrenders his deviant opinion or have him removed from the group.

conglomerate diversification

The ownership of a number of businesses, often producing completely unrelated products or services. (At one time ITT had 250 profit centers in the world, with about 25 totally differentiated product lines.)

conglomerates

A large, diversified corporation with multiple divisions, producing multiple products and services.

conscientious objector

A name given to an employee in the United Kingdom who refuses to join a union or pay union dues because of matters of conscience, such as religious prohibitions.

consequences analysis

A type of project evaluation in which the effects of alternative outcomes are weighed with regard to major management decisions as compared to the entire company operations. The object is to ascertain how much effect, positive or negative, a given decision would have on the total operations of the firm.

conservatism

In business as elsewhere, conservatism means the temporary renouncing of change. Conservatism is slow to see the need for change and often openly resists proposed changes. It depends for its strength on calmness and rationality.

consortium

A joint project undertaken by a number of companies in tandem, since one company might have insufficient resources to attempt a project on its own. These arrangements are normally found in the area of research.

consortium project

A project undertaken by a number of companies in tandem, with each company contributing expertise and financial help in proportional amounts. An example is the tunnel now being built under the English channel.

constant dollar accounting

A method of accounting during a period of inflation in which historical cost items are restated to adjust for changes in the purchasing power of the monetary unit.

constant purchasing power

The amount of a monetary unit needed at any point in time to purchase the same basket of goods, services, or assets.

constructive dismissal

A legal term denoting a situation in which it appears the employee has voluntarily terminated his employment with a firm when in reality management has made the task intolerable to force resignation. Such an action is usually subject to litigation.

consultants Outside advisors, knowledgeable about the business of the firm, can often offer constructive advice about company goals because of the greater degree of objectivity they can bring to a problem.

consumer disposable A good designed to be consumed immediately (such as a candy bar), or one which is to last only a short time, such as a roll of hand towels.

consumer durables Goods designed to be consumed in the long term, such as kitchen appliances or furniture. Industry has been accused of building obsolescence into these products to assure their re-purchase in a shorter-than-necessary length of time.

consumer goods Products to be directly used by the buyer, as contrasted to capital goods, which are used in the manufacture of other goods.

consumer price index (CPI) An index measure of inflation in which the index year is always 100 percent, and prior or subsequent years are compared by purchasing the same consumer items and giving a proportionate weight to each item. The total of all items will then be compared to the base year to analyze for total inflation or deflation and item by item inflation or deflation.

consumer promotions Sales marketing technique directed to the end consumer, either through discounted prices, coupons, trading stamps, etc:

consumer society 1. A society whose members desire better lives through the accumulation of more goods and services. 2. A term denoting an economy,

and perhaps social values, based on the assumption that man is primarily motivated by material goods and services.

containerization A technique used in transportation, most often ocean transport, where the goods are put into large containers of uniform size to making shipping easier and to give greater protection to the goods.

contingency management The act of defining goals and targets clearly and then allowing more latitude in the ways employees try to reach those goals.

contingency planning Plans which are arranged in advance to meet some unknown, but possible, abnormal incident.

contingency theory The four assumptions that make up this theory are: 1) human beings bring varying patterns of needs and motives into the work organization, but one central need is to achieve a sense of competence; 2) the sense of competence motive, while it exists in all human beings, may be fulfilled in different ways by different people depending on how this need interacts with the strengths of the individuals' other needs—such as those for power, independence, structure, achievement, and affiliation; 3) competence motivation is most likely to be fulfilled when there is a fit between task and organization; 4) sense of competence continues to motivate even when a competence goal is achieved; once one goal is reached, and new and higher goal is set.

contract of service The conditions of employment, usually of a high ranking official in the firm.

contributed value Term defined by Peter Drucker as "[T]he difference between the gross revenue received by a company for the sale of its products or services, and the amount paid out by it for the purchase of raw materials and for services by outside suppliers. . . ."

contribution coefficient The ability of a product to generate revenue as its volume goes up or down.

contributory pension scheme A pension plan to which contributions are made by both employer and employee, with the employee participating usually at a percentage of gross salary, up to a maximum amount.

control and behavior change Changes in behavior cannot be controlled by any person other than the one who needs the changes. The leader, or controller, can only provide an atmosphere in which change can occur.

control theory in management The pragmatic theory that every step in the production process must be tightly controlled.

controlled circulation journal A magazine financed by advertising revenue and sent free of charge to a select group of readers.

controller In the United States, a senior financial official in a company charged with the control of all financial transactions and reports.

controlling function of management Determining what is being accomplished, that is, evaluating the performance and, if necessary, applying corrective measures so that the performance takes place as planned.

convenience foods Usually prepared foods, which are quick and convenient to prepare and consume.

convergent/divergent One of three spectra on which people are measured in temperament and personality testing. At the convergent end of the spectrum are personality types that concentrate on the job at hand, while at the divergent end are types whose interests and quests for solutions extend beyond their own fields and tasks.

conversion ratio The number of shares of common stock that will be traded for a convertible bond at any point in time.

convertibility The extent to which one currency is exchangeable for another currency or for gold.

cooling-off period The legal, injuncted postponement of a strike to allow both sides to assess their positions and perhaps to give a mediator time to work with both groups. The cooling-off period was designated as eighty days by the Taft-Hartley Act of 1948.

cooperative advertising A situation in which a manufacturer shares advertising costs with a distributor or with a retailer.

copyright The exclusive right to reproduce specific literary, musical, or artistic material.

Corn Exchange A two-hundred-year-old commodities exchange designed to conduct cereals trade in the UK between millers, merchants, brewers, manufacturers, etc. Address: Mark Lane, London EC3. (A corn exchange in Liverpool deals in futures.)

corporate amorality Forces such as personal greed, selfishness, "success at any price", etc., within an organization can often render it unethical, even when the company philosophy coming from the CEO. is moral.

corporate identity program In the United Kingdom, a special design or other kind of image that is easily recognizable to the public and used by firms to keep their names and products before the public.

corporate planning The act of extrapolating a company's growth into the future with respect to products, revenues, etc., usually on one-year, five-year, or ten-year bases.

corporate "weight control" The act of throwing off a corporate activity that is nonproductive to take on a new program that should be productive.

corrective advertising Advertising designed to rectify an incorrect prior claim with respect to a product, often required of a firm by the Federal Trade Commission.

correlation *statistics* a measure of the relationship between two numerically valued random variables.

correlation coefficient The measure of the comovement of two variables.

cost analysis One of various methods for computing the expense of a product or service. Cost analysis is often viewed as simple, but it is often highly complicated since it must account, in some manner, for every aspect and every type of cost of a product or a service, from the raw beginnings to total utilization by an ultimate consumer.

cost-benefit analysis An analytical technique that makes a monetary assessment of the total costs and revenues of a project, most often including social costs and benefits that do not usually appear in a cost analysis.

cost center A department, a subsidiary firm, or any other area where significant costs occur in producing the products or services of the firm.

cost-effectiveness An analytical technique first introduced by the U.S. Department of Defense that attempts to establish whether a specific expenditure or an alternate one would produce more benefits, or whether the same results could be obtained with less spending.

cost-effectiveness analysis The quantitative examination of alternative ways to accomplish public goals as to their benefits to be gained and the costs to be incurred for the purpose of identifying a preferred alternative.

cost insurance and freight basis A method of computing a nation's balance of payments, considering the value of invisible exports and imports such as finance insurance, shipping services, etc. This term is used primarily in the United States.

cost of equity The return investors expect to earn by holding shares in a company as compared to what they might have earned by making an alternative investment.

cost plus pricing The calculation of the price of a specific project by adding a percentage to the estimated cost.

cost-push inflation Price increases occasioned by the rising prices of factors of production which go into the production of goods and services.

cost reduction programs Any plan to lessen the expenses involved in producing a good or service while maintaining the quality of the good or service produced.

cost structure A breakdown into component parts of the costs of producing a good or service, which, if a company is efficient, will tend to be proportional over time.

cost-volume-profit analysis A microeconomic technique used for measuring the functional relationships between the major factors affecting profits and for determining the profit structure of the firm.

Council of Ministers The supreme decision-making body of the European Community and all of its satellite councils and commissions, as decreed by the Treaty of Rome, 1957. Ministers representing different countries usually rotate as president of the Council at six-month intervals.

counseling The managerial function of giving personal guidance to troubled employees relating to on-the-job problems and, in some companies, family problems as well.

counterculture A state of mind, or an action opposed to, that which is usually accepted in society.

counter-purchasing The action of placing an order with one country with the stipulation that that country place a similar dollar-amount order with the first country. Often, the one country will buy manufactured goods and sell, in return, raw materials or goods with which the second country has a comparative advantage. (*See also* comparative advantage)

countervailing duty An import duty imposed to counteract the influence of an export subsidy on the goods of another country. A type of anti-dumping action.

countervailing power A theory of the economy, contributed by John Kenneth Galbraith, that states that the overwhelming power of one sector of an economy can best be combated by increasing the power of other sectors. A case in point is that when industry is powerful, government and labor must also be powerful to offset the power of industry.

country of origin That country from which goods are being exported in a specific situation.

coupon rate The interest that is specified on the coupons attached to the bonds.

covenant (protective) A provision in a debt agreement requiring the borrower to do, or not to do, a specific thing.

coverage analysis A technique used to ascertain that level of inventory that is most cost-effective, yet which adequately supplies the inventory need, either raw materials or finished goods.

craft ethic The spirit of "what was right" that once pervaded all the crafts in America. This belief was both a practical view and a spiritual view, in that if the craftsman did not produce good products, he would soon be forsaken by customers. By virtue of this belief, "doing right by others" was engrained in many of the early Americans.

creative problem solving The utilization of the ability to evolve new and workable ideas and to implement them.

creativity The use of innovative strategies to find a role to achieve goals that brings inner satisfaction to the innovator.

creativity, extrinsic The introduction of new ideas from outside the company, as from an outside consultant.

creativity, intrinsic In-plant discovery of new ways, combinations, methods, or systems for doing the present job.

credit The practice by a firm of making noncash sales to customers, with payment being made at pre-agreed upon times. (The extension of credit also has a "cost" that must be considered in a total cost analysis.)

credit interchange The action of exchanging credit information between firms, sometimes informally, and sometimes through the use of a credit agency.

credit mobilizer A plan or plans for utilizing the financial assets of a community or country to assist start-up businesses and expanding businesses. In modern times this is usually done through financial institutions where individuals and businesses make deposits, and where those needing capital can borrow.

crisis decisions The decisions a manager makes when an emergency arises.

crisis management vs. planning A mark of a good manager is one who will not be forced into a position of constant urgency, but, rather, will be so well coordinated in his planning that few things become crises.

criterion behavior A term used in connection with programmed learning specifying what is expected of a student after the training or regarding a specific part of the training.

critical incident technique 1. A group-training technique in which individual students recount incidents that presented them with problems. 2. A technique devised by J. C. Flanagan that involves the analysis of critical incidents of successful or unsuccessful job behavior, and which gives a guideline for assessing total job performance.

Critical Path Method (CPM) A mathematically ordered system of planning and scheduling for program management, often using electronic data processing, that makes possible a balanced, optimum, time-cost schedule to assure timeliness and minimum use of resources.

cross-charging The charging by one department of a firm for services rendered to another department.

cross-subsidization The action of using profit from one sector of an organization to offset losses from another sector.

cultural relativism The conviction in a culture that there is no absolute "right" or "wrong" action.

cultural revolution A "new story in human affairs" as it relates to shared meanings, i.e., those things which are generally accepted by society.

culture As defined by Daniel Bell, culture is "[T]he effort to provide a coherent set of answers to the existentialist situations that confront human beings in the passage of their lives."

culture, in Japanese industry This includes all of the life of the firm, whether economic in nature, in the workplace, or elsewhere. Each employee is seen as a part of the firm as a whole, and his or her actions are guided by the underlying and comprehensive philosophy of the firm.

culture, technology and For good or for ill, the Technological Revolution brought with it the greatest impact upon all of man's culture that history has ever revealed. A number of changes that have affected man directly are: 1) less manual labor, 2) the ability to communicate more readily, and 3) the ability to span distances in communications and travel with ease.

cumulative preferred stock A type of preferred stock that requires the payment of a dividend every year, and, if this is not done in one year, the cumulative dividend must be paid the next year before any dividends are paid on common stock.

current asset Any existing asset that will probably be turned into cash within one year.

current portion of long-term debt That portion of long-term debt that must be paid in the current year.

current ratio A measure of liquidity defined as current assets divided by current liabilities.

curve, general esteem A graphic presentation of the two-way relationship between a person and individuals or groups and the esteem they have for each other.

custom A practice, honored by time, that may be followed in business or in any organization and that has been acceptable to the majority of people in those organizations.

customer The ultimate buyer of a good or service without which no business could exist.

cybernetics The science of communications and control in human resources and in machines.

cybernetic system Inputs, activities, and outputs, defined as follows: 1) inputs are the resources committed to an idea to make it a tangible, important concern. They include capital, labor, and materials; 2) activities are the behaviors of people—designing, making, selling, keeping books, engineering, bargaining, and the like—that presumably add value to the inputs; 3) outputs are the goods and services that come out of the system. These outputs are more valuable than all the inputs used in their making, and a value added can be computed.

cyclical indicators The guidelines used in business forecasting. They are referred to as leading, lagging, and coincidental.

D

D-group A work group used in training and development in which the trainer tries to relate group behavior to the participants' own work experience.

Danish income tax State income tax, or indkomstskat til staten, a progressive tax charged by the state on total income, in addition to a flat rate dividend tax.

Danmarks Nationalbank Denmark's National Bank, or central bank, first established in 1818. Address: 17 Holmens Kanal, 1093 Copenhagen K.

Data logging The use of a simple form of computer to record the performance of a plant or equipment. The computer, however, does not control the activity of the plant.

Datel service A service that transmits data to home and overseas addresses using normal telecommunications facilities in addition to special terminal equipment at the recipient's end.

day release The release for a day from employment and without loss of pay for attendance at a training course related to industrial employment and training.

debentures An unsecured bond which does not constitute a lien against company assets.

debt capacity The total amount of debt a company can assimilate, given its earnings expectations and its equity base.

debt/equity decision factors These factors comprise the pragmatic approach to debt/equity decisions: 1) flexibility, 2) risk, 3) income, 4) control, and 5) timing.

decasualization A process by which workers on probationary status with a company are switched to full employment status.

debt-to-equity ratio A strict measure of a firm's financial leverage, defined as debt divided by shareholder's equity.

decision analysis One of three programs developed by Peter Drucker to establish the key activities of a firm. (*See also* activities analysis, relations analysis, Drucker, Peter)

decision making Conceived as five distinct phases: 1) defining the problem; 2) analyzing the problem; 3) developing alternative solutions; 4) deciding upon the best solution; 5) converting the decision into effective action.

decision making, unilateral The decisions made by a manager without the input of a work group. While some managers see this as the only way to go, the action creates worker resentment and tends to reduce productivity.

decision theory A series of mathematical techniques for forecasting that which cannot be predicted so that forecasting errors are kept to a minimum.

decision tree 1. A graphic representation of a number of possible future events that may effect a future decision. 2. A type of flow chart, or visual aid, that summarizes the various alternatives and options that can be followed in a complex, often multishaped, decision process.

decisional management school A school of thought that believes the decision maker is the manager.

decisional problem solving A school of thought that accepts the making of a decision as the first step in problem solving.

decisions Primarily, decisions are value judgments, made in the light of all facets of a situation and its history and in the context of the decision maker's personality.

decisions, key Decisions made that tend to set the course of a business, assure its capitalization, define its product or service line, and assure its marketability.

deductive reasoning The act of coming to a conclusion through the process of reasoning from a premise.

deductive thinking A process of reasoning that proceeds from the whole to the parts of a problem.

deed A sealed legal document by which one person conveys some asset to another, with the asset often being real property.

default premium The higher return required by investors on certain debt instruments as compensation for the possibility that the company may default on its obligations.

defeat, characteristics of The tendency to respond to defeat in a discussion, either by an individual or by a group, is to express less enthusiasm about the project. It behooves the manager to end a discussion making all concerned feel that they have won, to one degree or another.

defense mechanisms, ego The three categories are 1) identification, or the process of behaving like someone else; 2) sublimation, or the process by which basic drives are refined and directed into socially acceptable paths; 3) the third group is composed of mechanisms that can be called into play when necessary for a situation, namely, denial, rationalization, projection, idealization, reaction formation, substitution, and compensation.

deferred compensation Compensation that is due to the employee currently, but which is deferred for later payment, often at retirement, and usually for reasons of taxation.

deferred shares or capital A rare type of stock share on which a dividend is paid only after a specified rate of dividend has been paid to ordinary shares. It is an obviously more speculative share, which may bring in high dividends during very good times and nothing at other times.

deferred tax liability A future tax liability that will become payable on income already earned, but which is not as yet recognized for tax purposes.

definite supervisory channels For any given enterprise, the various formal organization units should be connected by a determinate hierarchical structure.

deflation The part of a downward trend in the trade cycle where there is a marked downturn in economic activity, purchasing power, and national income, accompanied by lower employment and general sluggishness in the economy.

delayed call A provision in a security that gives the issuing company the right to call a security in, but only after a stipulated period of time has elapsed and proper notice has been given. Also known as a call provision.

delegate 1. One who has the power to act for others, usually in some type of formal meeting. 2. The act of giving such authority to a person.

delegation The "passing down or along" authority to carry out a given task, or accomplish a certain goal, in the business situation. (It is noted that the act of passing the authority down or along indicates that with such authority the recipient will be better able to accomplish the goal.)

delegation of authority The action on the part of top management (as related to the tasks involved) to grant and confer authority to a person to accomplish certain tasks. Delegation must nearly always be done in order to facilitate task accomplishment.

Delphi approach A method resembling brainstorming that is often used in technological forecasting, involving a panel of experts from a number of different scientific fields.

delusion of decisiveness The appearance of making decisions that is nothing more than avoiding decisions by quick answers, confrontational disagreement, and smoothing over areas one does not wish to discuss.

demand An economic term for a want for which there is concurrent purchasing power, and the purchasing power must be active for the want to become demand.

demand analysis The identification and measurement of forces at work in the marketplace that will affect sales of a product or service.

demand elasticity The percentage of change in demand occasioned by a percentage of change in price.

demand inflation Often called "demand pull" inflation, which is the condition of "too many dollars chasing too few goods."

democratic theory of leadership A granting of almost complete freedom to workers to accomplish tasks assigned to them with a bare minimum of interference. This tends to sound better than it works, under most conditions.

demographics The study of the characteristics of human populations, with respect to size, growth, density, distribution, and vital statistics such as age groups and mortality.

denial, psychological concept of A form of mental repression in which individuals reject reality by refusing to act as the situation in the real world demands.

Department of Education and Science In the United Kingdom, the department responsible for planning and implementing the national education policy. The national department works with local departments in this planning and implementing.

Department of Employment In the United Kingdom, the department responsible for manpower planning, labor relations, conciliation services, etc. Address: St. James Square, London SWI

Department of Energy In the United Kingdom, the department with responsibilities for the demand and supply for all types of energy, particularly coal and oil. The Department of Energy was established in 1974. Address: 1 Victoria Street, London SWIH OET.

Department of Health and Social Security In the United Kingdom, this department is charged with the operation of national insurance, the National Health Service, paying social security benefits, etc. Address: Alexander Fleming House, Elephant and Castle, London SEI.

Department of Industry Until 1974, the Department of Industry was a part of the Department of Trade and Industry in the United Kingdom. It is responsible for regional and other industrial development. Address: 1 Victoria Street, London SWIH OET.

department of managerial planning A separate department in a business organization charged with planning for management leadership over an extended period of time. Example: if a company has a ten-year plan for growth, coexistent with this must be a plan for providing managers for this growth.

Department of the Environment In the United Kingdom, this department is responsible for policies affecting industry and management, which include building planning, road freight, international transport, and road transport. Address: 2 Marsham Street, London SW1P 3EB.

Department of Trade In the United Kingdom, this department is responsible for all matters pertaining to commerce. Address: 1 Victoria Street, London SW1H OET.

dependence, pathological A type of dependency that develops in an employee whose major concern is for "hygiene" matters, which, even when met, will not yield him satisfaction.

dependency and authority in organizations The fact of authority in the business organization naturally creates a dependency evolving from the lower echelons to the upper echelons. Yet, dependency can evolve into ambivalence that the organization cannot tolerate. So the manager faces the problem of creating a proper atmosphere of both authority and dependency in which indifference to the goals of the organization does not arise.

depersonalization, of chief executive role The subconscious act of turning the chief executive into whatever kind of role model the employee may need at any given time; i.e., father figure, mother figure, protector, etc.

deposition A written testimony given under oath by a witness in a law case for use in court.

depreciation The amount by which capital assets decrease in value over time as a result of use or of obsolescence.

depreciation, accelerated A method of decreasing assets by taking larger deductions in early years and smaller ones in later years. The process does not increase the total depreciation amount, but spreads it differently over time.

depreciation, straight line The decrease in value of an asset by the same amount each year until it is totally depreciated.

depression *psychology* In the business situation, depression is an indication of anger with oneself, originating in anger toward another, and, in Freudian terms, reflects the attack of the superego on the ego. The usual result is a feeling of self-guilt and self-blame.

depth interview Also called an "extended interview." A technique most often used in market research wherein the interviewee is given time to express his opinions at length and in his own way.

Design Centre In the United Kingdom, an organization run by the Council for Industrial Design to give publicity to designs that appear to have unusual promise in the industrial field and which are both innovative and technologically successful. Address: 28 Haymarket, London SW1.

design factor A term describing the level of reliability and efficiency of a sample used in a survey in market research.

de-skilling The modification of a task to reduce the skill level necessary to perform it.

desk training Clerical and commercial training that is done on the job; i.e. learning by doing.

destructive drives Psychological propulsions within an individual that produce hostility, hatred, and aggressiveness.

Deutsche Bundesbank The central bank of West Germany, formed in 1957, when the central banking system was reorganized. In the organization there are also eleven Land Central

Banks. Address: 6 Frankfurt am Main 1, Taunusanlage 4-6.

Deutsche Mark The basic unit in the German currency.

devaluation An official reduction by a country of its monetary unit as it relates in exchange value to the monetary unit of another country.

developing countries Countries that have not as yet combined the basic factors of production, such as land, labor, and capital, with proper management that would translate the other factors into greater production and higher standards of living.

development The action by a company to plan for, test, produce, and market a new product or service.

Development Area In the United Kingdom, a type of economic development that is being assisted with funds from the government.

development of managers The application of planned efforts to assist in maintaining and improving managers at or intended for the middle and top organizational levels in order that they can more effectively attain the objectives of the enterprise.

developmental objectives In the study of management Theory Z, it is noted that development objectives should not consider financial objectives alone, but should include the rate of technological advance and service to customers.

deviation *See* standard deviation.

devil's advocate One who seeks to encourage examination of an alternative point of view while taking no responsibility for it.

dexterity Agility in the performance of certain tasks achieved through the coordination of physical and perceptional skills.

diagnosis The action in the work situation that may exist at any level of attempting to figure out why an individual acts as he does and what it might take to change that person.

diagnostic ability A degree of sensitivity in which one is able to perceive with a high degree of accuracy the relationships between people, concepts, and situations.

dichotomous question A term used in marketing surveys that describes a question designed to produce one of two possible answers, such as yes or no.

diffusion index A statistical device for summarizing the direction of movement of a number of statistical series in one figure.

digital computer A computer that handles data in digital, or numerical, form using binary notation. (Binary is a numbering scheme with the base of 2.)

dilemmas The often contradictory problems a manager faces in carrying out his role as a manager while at the same time assuming his role as a family man, a concerned human being, etc.

dilution *stocks* The reduction in earnings per share, or book value per share, occasioned by the increase in the number of shares outstanding through a new issue or conversion.

dimensions of management There are three functions, equally important but essentially different, that management must perform to enable the institution with which it is charged to function and perform its social contribution:

1) the specific purpose and mission of the institution, whether business enterprise or other organization; 2) making work productive and the worker achieving; 3) managing social impacts and social responsibilities. (Taken, in part, from: Peter Drucker, *Management: Tasks, Responsibilities, and Practices* [New York: Harper and Row, 1973.]

diminishing return A point in production in which the addition of factors of production do not yield proportionate increases in output.

diminishing returns industry An industry in which production becomes progressively more difficult and expensive. This often happens in extractive industries such as mining.

Diploma in Management Studies (DMS) In the United Kingdom, a national award for completing specified series of studies in management that is awarded and approved by the Department of Education & Science or the Scottish Education Department.

direct cost Costs which are directly related to the production of a specific product.

direct-mail selling A type of selling that utilizes the mail to advertise certain products or services and which normally will enclose a postage-paid reply card or form for use by the recipient. Catalog selling can be classified as direct mail selling, since no shop is involved.

direct-response promotion The direct promotion of a product or service to a prospective customer that usually seeks to elicit a response from the recipient by including a reader's reply card or form.

direct selling 1. The selling of a company's goods or services to customers by the company's sales force. 2. The selling of goods or services directly to the consuming public without the use of a shop.

directedness of behavior The concept that behavior is consciously altered and aimed toward a particular mood or situation that encourages goal achievement.

Disabled Persons (Employment) Acts of 1944 and 1958 Legislation in the United Kingdom with the force of criminal sanctions that all employers having not fewer than twenty employees should employ a quota of disabled workers. The acts exempt certain small businesses and also provide for the training of disabled workers.

disablement benefit A part of the United Kingdom's National Insurance (Industrial Injuries) Acts, which states that disablement benefits may be payable to an employee if claimed within 156 days following an accident at work that leads to loss of physical or mental faculty irrespective of whether the employee is incapable of work. (Many other provisions are included.)

disciplinary action A managerial process for conditioning individual and group behavior to bring them in line with the policies and goals of the organization.

discounted cash flow A method of evaluating long-term projects that takes into account the time value of money.

discount rate The interest rate used to calculate the present value of future cash flows.

discretionary income The cash available after "necessities" have been paid for.

discretionary time The time available not needed to make a living and to get the necessary rest, i.e., time available for leisure, recreation, education, etc.

discrimination test A term used in market research describing a situation in which the informants are exposed to a number of products or packages and asked to describe the differences between them.

disinflation A part of the down phase of a business cycle in which there is a marked downturn in economic activity, purchasing power, and national income, but not a sufficient downturn to endanger full employment.

dispatching The action on the part of top management of withholding information and directives from lower echelon employees until such time as their actions on those directives will properly coordinate with the other actions on the total project.

dispersion Statistical values that measure the concentration or spread of items in a frequency distribution.

displaced plant (or equipment) A plant or equipment which is shut down prior to the time it was anticipated to be shut down, usually due to new technology that makes the plant or the equipment or both obsolete. (This practice has been prevalent in the automobile industry in the past decade.)

displacement of aggression The action of substituting a more socially acceptable action or frame of mind for aggression.

disposable income The cash remaining after taxes and other normal deductions are taken from one's paycheck.

dissatisfiers Factors in the environment of an employee that may result in the dissatisfaction of that employee.

distributed centers of power In the study of management Theory Z, it is recommended that power be distributed throughout the company by forming worker's councils, quality circles, etc.

distributive channels In short, the end customer. The place where the product or service will finally be used.

Distributive Industry Training Board In the United Kingdom, a board established in July 1968 under the Industrial Training Act of 1964. Address: MacLaren House, Talbot Road, Stretford, Manchester.

diversifiable risk That risk that can be eliminated through diversifying a portfolio, i.e., by adding certain other assets to it. Also known as B-risk or Beta-risk. (*See also* B-risk)

diversification A company policy designed to expand the number of products or services produced, usually to avoid too great dependence on one or a few products or services.

diversification by mature industries Mature industries often seek to diversify their product line after they find themselves in trouble relative to what is already being produced. Thus, diversification may well either come too late to rescue the firm, or it may be done too quickly to assure a degree of success.

diversity and conflict The presence of differences of opinion in the work situation are normal, but since such differences are often really a mark of diversity, which is much needed in the workplace, they must, through proper communications, evolve into a positive rather than a negative situation.

dividend payout ratio Simplistically, dividends divided by earnings.

dividend policy The actions by a company to distribute earnings to stockholders. A young and growing company usually will retain most of the earnings to assure continued growth, and a mature company may become known for paying high dividends on a regular basis.

division of labor The dividing up of the various facets of an operation in production so that each employee can specialize in, and become proficient at, a particular task, which will usually result in greater efficiency.

dollar The name of the basic unit of currency in the United States, Canada, Australia, New Zealand, Mexico, Hong Kong, and other countries. (*See* Section VII)

dollar diplomacy Economic interchange between countries motivated by financial interests.

dollar gap A negative balance of payments in a nation with a dollar currency unit.

domestic credit expansion (DCE) The measure of a change in the domestic money supply, usually expressed as a plus or minus percentage after adjustment to allow for the effects of changes in foreign exchange reserves and government foreign borrowing.

doomsday strike A labor strike that usually occurs about the time one contract is running out and a new contract is to be negotiated.

dotting test *psychology* A psychological test designed to measure fatigue and the ability to concentrate.

double call A marketing term describing a sales call where the salesperson is accompanied by another person, such as a distributor or area agent.

double pricing A marketing technique where the price actually offered to the consumer is compared to a price, usually higher, which is the "recommended" price of the good. Usually the consumer does not know whether this recommended price is genuine or not.

double time A payment of wages at double the day or hourly rate, usually as a bonus for working overtime or on a holiday.

double-headed monster A name given to highly trained professionals that modern business organizations must have, but who, as a rule, are more dedicated to their professions than to an organization. It is the task of the manager to blend these professionals into the organization so that the proper goals may be achieved.

Dow Jones Index An index of stock share prices on the Wall Street Stock Exchange published by Dow Jones & Co., Inc. Address: 30 Broad Street, New York, NY 10004.

downtime A period when a plant, or specific equipment within a plant, is not being used productively.

downward communication Realistically one can only send commands downward; one cannot communicate downward anything having to do with understanding or motivation. The recipient must possess the ability to receive "with understanding" and be "motivated" by it.

drive A term denoting physical and mental energy that usually marks a leader, as contrasted with the less-energetic non-leader.

drives, management by The tendency of management to zero in on a specific problem and to begin a concerted effort to get rid of it. This short-term view often results in decisions that are more costly in the long term.

drive to maturity stage That stage in the economy of a nation when it is using its resources to raise standards of living consistent with available resources and is therefore reaching toward economic maturity.

Drucker, Peter A consultant, academic, author, management specialist, and lecturer who helped to popularize the concept of Management by Objectives (MBO). (See: Section IX.)

DT Statistics and Market Intelligence Library In the United Kingdom, a Department of Trade service that provides information for firms on export markets and the Common Market. Address: Export House, 50 Ludgate Hill, London EC4M 7HU.

dumping *foreign trade* The action of selling goods on the export market at prices below domestic prices, which makes for unfair competition in the foreign market. GATT (General Agreement on Tariffs and Trade) has an anti-dumping code

dustbin check A technique used in market research wherein the testing company will ask a household to retain all discarded packages, etc., so the testing company can survey them periodically to obtain knowledge on what is being used, how often certain products are used, etc.

dutch auction The action of putting an object up for sale at a certain price and gradually reducing that price until it is sold.

duty A government tax, usually on imports.

duty free Foreign goods allowed to come into a country tax free.

dynamic organizations Five important considerations are usually a part of a forward-moving, changing organization: 1) maintain an environment in which uncomfortable questions can be asked; 2) utilize the changes to motivate personnel; 3) have a program for recruiting and developing; 4) combat vested interests and procedural red tape; 5) concentrate on what the organization can become, not on what it is or has been.

Dynamic Programming (DP) A plan designed to achieve utilization of the optimum decision at every stage of a multistage problem.

dysfunctions The characteristics or aspects of formal organization that cause unintended or unanticipated behavior.

E

E & OE "Errors and omissions excepted." Sometimes used on bills of lading, invoices, etc., as a disclaimer for any errors that might appear.

earnings/dividend ratio The ratio of company profits to dividends declared.

earnings drift The extent to which wages and salaries may rise above national rates in certain regions due to a shortage of labor, overtime worked, or union bargaining.

earnings yield The earnings per share divided by stock price.

earthquake approach to organizational change A sudden decision to make changes in the company before anyone has a chance to object.

East African Community (EAC) A form of common market set up in Africa by Burundi, Ethiopia, Kenya, Somalia, Tanzania, Uganda, and Zambia, and patterned after the European Economic Community.

Eastern approach to management An approach that embraces the statement "man is the measure of all things." Eastern managers are more heavily human-relations oriented than Western managers and less bottom-line oriented.

EC European Economic Community or Common Market. Is also used to indicate "communities" including the EC proper, the Euratom, and the European Coal and Steel Community. Also known as EC. (*See also* Common Market)

EC/EFTA Information Unit In the United Kingdom, an agency established by the Department of Trade as a source of information for general inquiries about the European Economic Community and the European Free Trade Association. Address: EC/EFTA Information Unit, 1 Victoria Street, London SWIH OET.

eclectic-process approach management A term indicating that the best has been taken from other schools of thought to add to one's own theories.

ecological school of management thought A somewhat limited school of thought whose theory begins with basic units—customers, students, or soldiers—and then adds the elements of operations required to accomplish goals.

ecology The scientific study of the management situation in all of its various relationships.

econometrics A quantitative branch of economics concerned with applying mathematical and statistical methods in establishing relationships, if any, between economic variables.

Economic and Social Committee A Common Market consulting committee established under the Treaty of Rome (1957), Articles 193–98. This committee has representatives from all walks of life and should be consulted by the Council of Ministers or the European Commission in matters relating to the entire community.

economic and monetary union After realizing a full customs union between the member states of the Common Market, the EC then planned to achieve the free flow of capital, goods, labor, services, traffic, etc., as an economic union.

economic batch determination (EBD) A term used in production management and control for the analysis of batch production size of various orders or projects.

Economic Commission for Africa (ECA) One of four regional economic commissions of the United

Nations. It was established in 1958 at the following address: African Hall, Addis Ababa, Ethiopia.

Economic Commission for Asia and the Far East (ECAFE) One of four regional economic commissions of the United Nations. Its primary concern is with developing the areas economically, industrially, and socially. It was established in 1947 at the following address: Sala Santitham, Bangkok, Thailand.

Economic Commission for Europe (ECE) Established by the Economic and Social Council of the United Nations. Its objective was to stimulate economic activity and cooperation in and with Europe. Address: Palais des Nations, Geneva, Switzerland.

Economic Commission for Latin America (ECLA) One of the four regional economic commissions of the United Nations. Address: Santiago, Chile.

economic dimension The economic problems faced by a manager as he seeks to achieve the goals of the company: 1) he is faced with the internal limitations of the business and 2) he is faced with the external economic limitations placed upon his company and his product.

economic forecasting A primary task for managers of on-going concerns who must, with a degree of accuracy, predict the economic, technological, social, and political trends of the future.

economic growth The rate of real production or income experienced by a nation's economy (usually in a year) and usually measured as a percentage of the preceding year.

economic income The amount an income agent could spend during a period of time without affecting his or her basic wealth.

economic man theory A school of thought based on the concept that employee motivation is based almost entirely on financial incentives.

economies of scale One of six major barriers to entry, the manager must be aware of the economies of scale before pushing his firm into a specific industrial climate. The other barriers to entry are the barrier of product differentiation, the barrier of capital requirements, the barrier of cost disadvantages independent of size, the barrier of access to distribution channels, and the barrier of government policy.

The Economist Famous economics journal published in the United Kingdom, established in 1843. It deals with worldwide news of business and industry along with economic theory.

educational factors The general attitude toward education, the literacy level, and the practicality of education offered, as they relate to the needs of managers in any given era and any given situation.

education and burnout The theory that people with college and postgraduate education show less evidence of burnout than do less-educated people, with lower "burnout" levels for those with postgraduate work than those with an undergraduate degree.

education shift The trend away from going to work at a very young age and remaining in school until past twenty-two years of age, in many cases. This development affects directly the number of workers in the labor force in different age categories.

345

education, managerial A type of training, whether in school or outside of it, that exposes the prospective manager to real situations in which risks must be taken and results evaluated.

Eenmanszaak Name for a sole proprietorship under Netherlands law.

efficiency in stagnant industries Achieving and maintaining profitability through sensible cost cutting, increased productivity, and innovation.

efficiency, the myth of The assumption that the most efficient manager is also the most effective one.

efficient market *finance* A market in which asset prices immediately reflect new information.

effort/result ratio The amount of effort that must be put forth to achieve a given result. The lower the effort relative to the result, the lower the cost of production.

egalitarian ethic The concept that "equality" should exist among people in the work situation.

egalitarianism, Theory Z Implies that each worker can apply discretion and work autonomously without close supervision, inasmuch as management feels he can be trusted.

egocentricity The state of self-centeredness that prevents people from considering others as they consider themselves; a state of overwhelming self-centeredness.

egoistic needs An industrial psychologist's term for the remuneration a worker receives in addition to his pay. This may include self-esteem, the esteem of others, status in the plant, etc.

eighty-twenty rule An empirical law that denotes the common tendency in a business that 20 percent of the items produced yield 80 percent of the income.

Einzelfirma A one-man firm under German and Austrian laws.

elastic demand The effect a change in price has on the demand for goods and services. If the percentage change in demand is less than the percentage change in price, the change is said to be inelastic. If the percentage change in demand is greater than the percentage change in price it is said to be elastic. Example: if a 10 percent change in price evokes only a 4 percent change in demand, it is inelastic. If a 10 percent change in price evokes a 15 percent change in demand, it is elastic.

Eldridge-Green lantern tests A form of color vision test given to subjects that includes a number of different colors and different degrees of brightness.

electronic data processing (EDP) The use of computer systems for processing data.

elitism and leadership development A practice of choosing those people in a firm with a given college degree, or given personality traits, and attempting to develop them as leaders to the exclusion of others.

emergency situations The manager must make critical decisions in crisis situations, but afterward the people related to the situation should have a complete explanation of why the decision was made.

emotional maturity The mark of a good manager that encompasses the traits of dependability, persistency, and objectivity.

emotional stress In the business community, stress is the feeling of being pressed to hard to accomplish certain things that may be evidenced by impatience, short temperedness, psychosomatic diseases, etc.

empathy The ability on the part of a manager to identify with a person or a situation and therefore be more able to understand the feelings, emotions, and problems of employees.

empire building 1. An action on the part of a manager to sublimate his own need for power and influence to the broader need to increase the power, influence, and profitability of the company. 2. The activity of a manager who seeks to build his own private empire within the company structure.

empirical reality A reality that the evidence of our senses confirms.

empirical school A management school of thought that observes how better managers have done a thing in the past and copies their methods.

employee communications Good communications from the manager to the employees develop a good rapport with them and influences productive actions positively.

employee relations department A term usually synonymous with personnel department, though the concept has been greatly broadened over the past two decades.

employees, centralization of The term designates the concentration or dispersion, respectively, of employees and physical facilities.

employee's contributory negligence The contributory negligence on the part of an employee will reduce the possible damages awarded him against his employer under laws in the U.K. Other nations have similar laws.

Employee Stock Ownership Plan (ESOP) A widely used plan for getting equity capital for companies by allowing employees to buy stock in the companies. On the positive side, this practice makes the employee an owner and ostensibly motivates him to do things in the best interest of the company. On the negative side, the company may fail, leaving long-tenure employees with nothing to show for many years of work.

employer's association Organizations in some countries that meet to discuss questions of employment and industrial relations as distinct from commercial matters, which most trade associations promote.

employment costs Compensation paid to employees, plus the cost of fringe benefits. Some firms also include per capita overhead costs.

employment, inventory of A statement of the available and required number of employees, in different categories, within a firm.

end price support A part of the Common Market's efforts to subsidize small farmers, such as dairymen, who might not be able to stay in business otherwise. The subsidies, however, since they are not restricted to small farmers, give larger farmers much greater returns than normal.

energy, principal of dissipation of The concept that the poorest user of time in the business will tend to drag associates down to his level, thus partly dissipating the productive energy of all.

English Tourist Board The agency responsible for promoting tourism in the United Kingdom. Address: 4 Grosvenor Gardens, London SW1W ODU.

engross The proper preparation of a legal or official document.

enlargement of jobs The action of increasing the desirability of a job by enhancing technology (such as replacing a typewriter with a word processor in an office) or by giving the job an aura of importance that it has not had before.

enrichment of jobs The action of enhancing the job of an employee by giving it more status. The job therefore becomes a greater challenge to the worker.

Ente Nazionali Idrocaburi (ENI) The Italian agency that coordinates state involvement in the petrochemical industry.

entrapment The feeling of being trapped in a job because one does the same monotonous tasks every day, or because one is exposed constantly to people who need to be kept satisfied all the time and who show scant empathy with the person seeking to please them.

entrepreneurial drive The need among managers to innovate and take risks in order to maintain the firm as an on-going concern.

environmental factors Five such factors influencing the manager are economic, political and legal, social, technological, and educational factors.

Equal Pay Act of 1970 In the United Kingdom, an act enforceable from December 29, 1970, to eliminate discrimination between men and women with respect to pay and other terms of employment.

equilibrium planning and budgeting All future plans must achieve an equilibrium between "reach" and "reality," i.e., what the firm would like to do as contrasted with what it is safely able to do.

ergonomics The study of man in relationship to his occupation, including man's physiology, psychology, and the equipment and environment of his job.

error-avoidance philosophy A concept that to avoid mistakes is a primary goal of a worker.

escrow agreement A general term for a written agreement that does not become effective until specific conditions are fulfilled by the grantee.

esteem needs The need in the work situation for a person to have self-respect, achievement, and recognition by others.

ethical standards in business The study and practice of moral obligations in the business arena.

ethics The study of personal conduct and moral duty that concerns itself with human relations and right and wrong actions. It deals with the behavior of individuals and the standards governing the interrelationships between individuals.

Euratom Treaty An agreement signed in Rome in 1957 to establish the European Atomic Energy Community (Euratom). The agreement was signed at the same time the treaty was signed establishing the European Economic Community. The Euratom Treaty was preceded by the 1951 Treaty of Paris, establishing the European Coal and

Steel Community (ESCS). Essentially, these three treaties established the Common Market. These three communities were then combined under the Council of Ministers and the European Commission by the Merger Treaty of 1967. With these agencies in place, a common budget was arranged through the Budget Treaty of 1970. The Treaty of Accession took Denmark, the Irish Republic, and the United Kingdom into the Common Market on January 1, 1973.

Eurobonds EC bonds negotiable within the Common Market.

Eurocrat A term designating civil servants who work for the Common Market, which number about 10,000, who work primarily in Brussels and Luxembourg.

Eurodollar, Eurocurrencies Generally defined as an American dollar owned by a non-American and on deposit outside the United States. Actually, Eurodollars or Eurocurrencies can be owned by anyone and deposited anywhere.

Eurodollars 1. Dollar credits that are circulated in the Common Market but not restricted to that area. They are designed to facilitate business transactions. 2. Sometimes the term denotes U.S. dollars held in foreign banks, primarily in Europe. 3. The term also indicates a paper promise to pay interest on loans in U.S. dollars.

Eurofrancs Francs that are traded and dealt outside of France but within the Common Market.

Euromarks Marks traded and dealt outside West Germany but within the Common Market.

European Agricultural Guidance and Guarantee Fund A fund coming from the common budget of the Common Market that is used to do support buying of agricultural products, make modernization grants, etc.

European Commission A civil-service type of body located in Brussels and Luxembourg which administers the business of the Common Market. (A more complete explanation of the agencies of the EC are to be found in Section IV.)

European Coordination Office An agency that receives monthly employment reports from EC countries and circulates the information to facilitate the mobility of labor.

European Free Trade Area (EFTA) A group formed in 1959 as an answer to the EC. The nine founding members were Denmark, Sweden, Norway, Switzerland, Austria, Portugal, Finland, Iceland, and the United Kingdom. Denmark and the UK ultimately went over to the EC. The EFTA is not a customs union, but there are no tariff walls between the member nations. Address: 9-11 rue de Varemb'e, 1211 Geneva 20, Switzerland.

European Investment Bank An agency established by the EC under Articles 129 and 130 of the 1957 Treaty of Rome to make grants and loans to developing areas within the market.

European Nuclear Energy Agency (ENEA) An agency operated by the Organization for Economic Cooperation and Development (OECD) to promote the peaceful use of nuclear energy. There are some eighteen countries holding membership, with some associate members, including the United States. Address: 38 Boulevard Suchet, Paris 16e, France.

European Parliament (or Assembly) A major Common Market institution that meets in Strasbourg and Luxembourg and is composed of delegates from each of the member states of the EC.

European Units of Account A trade unit devised in Luxembourg as an alternative to using national currencies for trading within the Common Market.

evaluated maintenance programming (EMP) A planned program of preventive maintenance in a plant based on the analysis of past performance and records of costs.

event A term used in critical-path planning and network analysis for a specific stage reached in a complex project and denoted in the network by a numbered circle.

evolutionary operation A new program based on the use of computers in industry that allows for constant changes in operating methods by simply changing computer settings.

ex ship In a foreign sale contract, this term denotes the fact that the buyer must pay the costs of having the goods removed from the ship.

exchange control A type of control over the domestic currency of a nation, concerned with the ways the domestic currency may be exchanged for the currencies of other countries.

Exchange Control of 1947 Legislation in the UK to give government control over the outflow of gold and currency from the sterling area.

Exchange Equalization Account An account managed by the Bank of England for the Treasury to offset major fluctuations in the exchange rate of the pound. Established under the Finance Act of 1932, the account has as assets gold and foreign exchange reserves and sterling invested in treasury bills.

exchange rate The rate at which the currency of one nation can be exchanged for the currency of another nation.

excise duty A tax levied on certain goods in the nation of origin or manufacture.

executive High-level administrator who makes decisions, guides their implementation, and bears the responsibility for results.

existing use value A price placed on property assuming that the property will continue to be used as it is now being used.

expansion demand A term used in marketing to denote new consumer demand related to new consumers entering the market for a specific type of product.

expected return The average of possible returns measured against the probability of returns.

exploitation, of labor The attempt to require or induce people to contribute as much as or more than can reasonably be expected of them in the work situation while returning to them less than they have a right to expect.

exponential smoothing A mathematical technique used to improve the quality of forecasting by weighting it to take the most recent trends into account.

export finance house A financial institution specializing in making or arranging nonrecourse financing for exporters. (*See* nonrecourse financing)

export house An agency that facilitates exports by purchasing the goods and reselling them to the foreign client or, as is usually the case, by acting as an export agent for the exporter.

Export Services Division In the United Kingdom, a division of the Department of Trade that provides information for UK firms on export opportunities, licensing, customs, and tariffs regulations, etc. Address: Export Services Division, Department of Trade, Export House, 50 Ludgate Hill, London EC4M 7HU.

export subsidy (or restitution) Under the Common Agriculture Policy of the EC, the European Commission pays an export subsidy or restitution to cereal grain producers selling to non-member states, with that subsidy bridging the gap between world market prices and the EC intervening price.

exposure A term used in marketing and public relations denoting how much and how long a person or product stays in the public eye through the media and public appearances.

extrapolation A statistical term denoting the use of historical data in forecasting future trends.

extrinsic creativity The introduction of new ideas from outside the company.

F

Fabians English Socialists of the early twentieth century.

face-to-face group A type of reference group that is brought together to discuss consumer buying motives. The group is small so that each individual can openly express opinions on the matters at hand.

face-to-face influence The most direct way of influencing people once a viable relationship has been established with them.

face value The nominal value of a share of stock as opposed to its market value.

facilities, as a company resource A firm's physical facilities that enable it to carry out production, and which makes production a going concern. (Technical people frequently look upon facilities as the all-in-all of the company and tend to leave out physical resources, while financial people look upon facilities as a necessary evil, if they look only at the bottom line.)

facility visit A PR term for a press visit set up for a group of journalists who wish to gather materials and perhaps conduct an interview for a specific story.

FACT *See* Factor analysis chart technique.

FACT assembly test A mechanical comprehension test of one's ability to visualize how mechanical parts fit together.

FACT coordination test A test of psychomotor skills, i.e., the speed and accuracy in the coordination of eye and hand.

factor A commission agent, or one who receives goods from a manufacturer to sell on behalf of the owner. Often the goods are sold in the name of the factor, and the name of the producer of the goods remains unknown.

factor analysis chart technique (FACT) A job evaluation method of determining the relative worth of a management position within a specific salary structure. Points are assigned to the major elements of the job.

factorial sample design A term used in marketing research to determine what factors about a product or service influenced the consumer to make a purchase. The major factor is of importance to the total test.

factor rating A type of job evaluation in which the manager is rated on the various factors important to his duties. Usually the factors are weighed according to their importance in the total task accomplishment.

Factories Act 1961 In the United Kingdom, a combined piece of legislation covering the following headings: 1) health, general provisions; 2) safety provisions; 3) welfare, general provisions; 4) health, safety and welfare; 5) notification of industrial accidents and diseases; 6) employment of women and young persons; 7) special applications and extensions; 8) domestic system (home work); 9) wages; 10) notices and returns; 11) administration; 12) criminal sanctions; 13) and 14) application and interpretation of the act.

factoring The business of buying

accounts receivable from a firm at a discount and then attempting to make collections. More often, perhaps, the firm, for a fee, farms out the collecting of receivables.

factors of control The four factors of control are production, sales, finance, and personnel.

Factory Inspectorate In the United Kingdom, factory inspectors are charged with the periodic evaluation of factories. They have broad authority to enter, inspect, and evaluate factories with respect to their compliance with the Factories Act of 1961.

failure toleration The willingness on the part of industry to undergo lack of success, particularly in bringing out a new product, in order to earn greater profits when the product is perfected.

Fair Trading Act 1973 In the United Kingdom, legislation that covers mergers, monopolies, fair trading, and the promotion of competition in industry and in retail business.

Fairs and Promotions Branch A part of the Export Services Division of the Department of Trade in the United Kingdom, this agency is responsible with overseas trade promotions. Address: Hillgate House, 26 Old Bailey, London EC4M 7HU

fall-back pay A guaranteed minimum level of pay provision that is sometimes written into a pay-by-results, piece work, or some other variable wage agreement.

false positive A situation where a test may show an individual is unfit for a job when actually that person is fit, but the test is less than accurate.

Far East Exchange, Ltd. One of two Hong Kong Stock Exchanges.

FAS Free alongside ship.

Fayol, Henri (1841–1925) 1. A French management specialist who did his work combining theory and personal experiences with French industrial and mining operations in nineteenth-century France. His major book was *General Principles of Management* (1916). 2. His four general concepts have been followed since that time by many management experts. Fayol argued that a manager must be involved in 1) planning; 2) organizing; 3) coordinating; and 4) controlling.

fear of promotion An unrealistic fear of moving upward in the organization, usually with the individual thinking he is not capable of meeting all of the demands of the new job. Psychology has long since learned that one can be more afraid of success than of failure under certain circumstances.

feather bedding A term used in the United States to denote restrictive labor practices. In the main, the term refers to the keeping on of employees who are no longer needed for the operations being performed. This was particularly true in railroading.

federal decentralization The organizing of activities into autonomous business divisions, each with its own product(s), markets, and profit and loss responsibilities. Original concept has been linked to Peter Drucker.

Federal Deposit Insurance Corporation (FDIC) That insurer in the United States with which national banks must have their deposits insured and state-chartered banks nor-mally have their deposits insured by choice. Maximum insurance per account is currently one hundred thousand dollars.

Federal Reserve Note A type of U.S. paper money issued by Federal Reserve banks. At the time of their founding, these notes had to be backed by 25 percent gold and 75 percent government securities. The gold backing is no longer required, and most assets held by the Fed can be used as collateral. These notes constitute cost of the currency in the nation.

Federal Reserve System The central banking system of the United States. (*See* Section VII)

Federal Trade Commission (FTC) *See* Section III.

Federation Nationale des Chambres de Commerce et d'Industrie de Belgique Translated into English as the Federation of the Belgian Chambers of Commerce, this organization was established in 1875. Address: 40 rue de Congress, 1000 Brussels.

Federation of German Stock Exchanges English translation of Arbeitsgemeinschaft der deutschen Wertpapierbörsen. Address: Berliner Allee 10, 4000 Dusseldorf 1. (*See* Section VII)

Federation of Greek Industries This organization was formed in 1907. Address: Odos Xenophon 5, Athens 118.

Federation of Stock Exchanges in Great Britain and Ireland Originally established in 1965 to coordinate the work of the London Stock Exchange, the UK provincial exchanges, and the Irish Stock

353

exchange. It was replaced in 1973 by the United Stock Exchange that united all trading floors of the exchanges. (*See* Section VII)

feedback The difference between what is done—performance—and the standard—what is expected.

feedback concept A method of checking the performance of a system or process against certain standards and reporting any variations so that future performances can be improved.

fictitious assets Items that may appear on a financial statement or balance sheet, but which are less than tangible and for which there may be little or no value. Goodwill can often be included in this group of items.

fiddle In the United Kingdom, the action of restricting production to a given level by informal agreement. The term "quota restriction" is often used in the United States.

fidelity insurance A type of insurance policy taken out to protect a company in the event of fund embezzlement by an employee.

fiduciary issue Currency not backed by silver or gold.

fiduciary loan A loan granted with no security except the word and signature of the borrower.

FIFO Accounting method where the costing or valuing of stocks assumes that the first items purchased or produced are the first items sold. (*See* LIFO)

fight-or-flight response A situation in which a person appears to be reduced to two alternatives: 1) stay and fight or 2) flee the situation.

figure of merit A number that summarizes the investment value of a project.

figurehead role The role every manager must play as the ceremonial leader of the particular group.

Financial Times Daily newspaper published in the United Kingdom focusing on news from business and industry. It was founded in 1888. Address: Bracken House, Cannon Street, London EC4.

filter question A market-research technique in which the one doing the questioning only asks a further question if the answer to the preceding question was as desired. Example: Do you drink coffee at breakfast? If the answer is yes, the next question likely will be what brand?

final demand Demand for a product that will immediately be followed by consumption: the product has reached the point of satisfying the demand for which it was made.

Finance Corporation for Industry Ltd. In the United Kingdom, an organization established under the umbrella of the Bank of England, leading insurance companies, investment trusts, and clearing banks to provide loans of at least two hundred thousand pounds sterling for industrial developments that are in the best interests of the nation as a whole. Address: 4 Broad Street, London EC4M 9BD.

Finance Houses Association In the United Kingdom, an organization whose members include banks and finance houses. Address: 14 Queen Anne's Gate, London SW1H 9AA.

finance policies Actions that govern the financial dealings of a company, namely, utilizing long-term creditors for sources of capital, practicing paying out a stable dividend rate, investing capital not needed for immediate operations, and, extending credit to rated firms only.

financial accounting Composed of two main financial reports, the balance sheet and the profit and loss statement, and made up primarily for shareholders.

Financial Accounting Standards Board (FASB) The official rule-making body of the accounting profession.

financial flexibility The concern that today's financial decisions will not jeopardize future financial concerns nor future opportunities for growth.

financial intermediary A financial services institution that receives deposits from individuals and firms and invests them in various kinds of income earning assets so that the savers do not have to make separate investments and yet may earn an income on their savings.

financial leverage A technique for increasing the returns to owners of the business and involves the viable substitution of fixed-cost debt financing for owner's equity in the hope of increasing equity returns.

financial manipulations, danger of The temptation for a firm to replace viable management with financial manipulations. This practice almost always leads to disaster, since finance is a tool of management, not a master of it.

financial markets, and the cost of new issues The dollar cost to the issuer of getting the new issue of securities on the market, which will generally involve two things: 1) the cost of attorneys, investment bankers' fees, printing, etc.; 2) a second cost may be the selling of the new issue for less than the market price of existing stock to make it more attractive to buyers.

financial planning A vital aspect of continuing company life usually involving three actions: 1) the consideration of the alternatives a firm has; 2) departmental and divisional activities that will affect future financing; 3) the planning on a departmental or a divisional basis, which is then translated into financial needs.

Financial Times Industrial Ordinary Index An indicator in the United Kingdom of the level of business on the UK Stock Exchange (similar to the U.S. Dow-Jones Index). Based on the average prices of thirty blue chip shares. It is published daily in the *Financial Times*. Address: Bracken House, Cannon Street, London EC4.

financial year 1. A government's fiscal year. 2. In the United Kingdom, name for fiscal year, the formal annual accounting period.

fine control sensitivity A type of psychomotor skill relating to an individual's ability to make controlled movements with the fingers.

Finnish Central Chamber of Commerce Suomen Keskuskaupakamari.

Finnish Foreign Trade Association This organization was established in 1919 to encourage foreign trade. Address: Helsinki 13, E. Esplanadikatu 18, Finland.

Finnish income tax The Finnish income tax includes: 1) state income tax, or *valtion tulavero,* which is charged on total income from all sources; 2) local income tax, *or kunnallisvero,* together with a church tax, or *kirkollisvero,* which is levied at a flat rate on members of the Orthodox and Evangelical Lutheran churches; 3) state new wealth tax; 4) Seamen's tax, or *merimiesero,* deducted from source of a seaman's income, in lieu of income tax.

fire engine decisions Crisis decisions often the result of lack of planning.

FIRO Fundamental interpersonal relations orientation. A theory of interpersonal behavior containing three basic notions about the needs of individuals 1) need for inclusion; 2) need for control; 3) need for affection.

firsthand distribution (FHD) A method of wholesale selling in very large quantities which can be either a consignment sale or an outright sale.

fiscal drag The period between a governmental decision on fiscal policy and the time that decision begins to directly affect the economy.

fiscal measures A term denoting government actions related to taxing, spending, and debt management that are taken to try to achieve and maintain equilibrium in the economy.

Fisher effect The concept that the nominal rate of interest should be approximately equal to the real rate of interest plus a premium for expected inflation.

Fisher equation An equation devised by economist Irving Fisher, so designed as to include the rate of inflation when making a loan (in = (ir + ip) - 1). In is the nominal rate of interest, ir is the real rate of interest, and ip is the expected rate of inflation.

Five "W's" and the "how" question of planning Basic question related to planning, namely, 1) why must it be done? 2) what action is necessary?

3) where will it take place? 4) when will it take place? 5) who will do it? and 6) how will it be done?

five-fold grading schemes A type of personnel selection interview action introduced by John M. Fraser under the following headings: first impressions, qualifications, motivation, abilities, and adjustment.

fixed assets The capital equipment of a company, such as buildings, machinery, etc., which is used in the production of other goods and is depreciated over time.

fixed assets to tangible net worth ratios If the ratio is too high, it indicates that too much of the capital of the firm is tied up in fixed assets, indicating that capital (cash) may be short at any given time.

fixed cost A cost that remains constant (usually over a specific period of time) regardless of the level of business activity in the firm.

fixed exchange rate A value rate that is set according to the monetary unit of a country as it relates to all other monetary units in the world. (*See* floating exchange rate)

fixed expenses The expenses of a firm that remain the same regardless of the level of business activity.

fixed-income security Any investment vehicle that promises an unvarying payment stream to the holder over its life.

fixed-price contract One which the contractor must honor for a completed job, which was the original agreed-upon price between the parties.

flash of inspiration A moment in the process of creative thinking when one "sees" the image of what he has been considering. This approach to thinking can be differentiated from "emotional" responses to difficult problems in that the creative thinker has already been deeply immersed in the facts of the case and is seeking a plausible answer.

Flexibel Arbestid A Swedish term denoting a system of employment emphasizing flexible working hours.

flexible budget One that is flexible enough to accommodate different volumes of production and sales or multivolume budget Also known as a multivolume budget.

flexible working hours (fwh) A system in which most employees are allowed to choose their own hours for work, as long as a given number of hours are put in daily. Usually, there is a period of time, known as a "core" time, when all employees will be working, with all remaining hours being flexible.

flexing In the process of budgetary control, this is a method of adjusting the budget to various levels of production and/or sales.

floating asset A current asset.

floating exchange rate The valuing of a nation's monetary unit as it relates to all other monetary units of the world, which allows fluctuation in exchange as the purchasing power of the various units increase or decrease, or as demand and supply causes the values in exchange to change.

flow chart A graphic representation of the interrelationships between the various stages of a production program, etc.

flow charting A method used by auditors to follow the internal control system of a firm.

flow diagram A graphic design used in work flow study to show the locations of activities, personnel, and materials. Also known as a route diagram.

flow line production A method of organizing work used in mass production industries in which each successive stage carries the product from the beginning to the end, all in the same direction and usually without interruption.

fluctuation price contract A type of contract, often called "cost-plus" in the United States, where the end cost is allowed to vary from the original estimate if costs of doing the complete job increase during the operation.

FOB Free on board.

focused interview A method used in market research in which the interviewer attempts to elicit answers from the interviewee without actually asking questions.

Follet, Mary Parker (1868–1933) A social worker born in the United States who was also an early management theorist. She was concerned with vocational guidance, leadership in industry, and the importance of personal and group relationships in the work situation. She also developed the concepts of "creative conflict" and "Law of the Situation." (*See* Section IX)

Food and Agriculture Organization (FAO) An agency of the United Nations with the responsibility of fighting poverty, hunger, and malnutrition throughout the world. Address: Viale delle Terme di Caracalla, Rome, Italy.

Forbes An important business periodical (called a "capitalist tool" by the publishers) published biweekly except weekly during two weeks in October by Forbes, Inc., 60 Fifth Avenue, New York, NY 10011.

forced-choice approach 1. In the performance appraisal of a staff person, evaluations are made by providing other staff people with selected phrases, and they are to choose the phrase(s) that seems best to fit the staff person. Such a plan is obviously shot through with subjectivity; 2. A method of conducting a market survey in which the interviewees are given an attribute or attributes of a product or brand and asked if it describes the brand. This is obviously "suggestive" in nature and may produce erroneous results.

forcing conversion A strategy used by companies with outstanding callable securities that "forces" owners to convert the security by calling it in at a time when its call price is below its conversion value.

forecasting The attempt to assess the future using historical data and taking into account current trends.

forecasting, economic The action of management looking into the future to discern the economic posture of the nation or of an industry. (Political and technological forecasting must attempt to reasonably predict the future in those fields.)

formal organizing "Organizing is the establishing of effective behavioral relationships among persons so that they may work together efficiently and gain the personal satisfaction of doing selected tasks under given conditions for the purpose of achieving some goal or objective." (George R. Terry, *Principle of Management* 6th ed. [Homewood, Ill.: Richard D. Erwin, Inc., 1972], p. 299.)

form and substance In management language, "substance" is the detail of goals and performance that is needed to reach certain objectives, while "form" is interpersonal relationships that must be used in getting the goals accomplished.

FORTRAN Acronym for Formula Translation.

Fortune A U.S. business periodical that is considered by some to be the Cadillac of all business periodicals. In the main, it deals with big companies and broad trends in economics and business. Address: Time & Life Building, Rockefeller Center, New York, NY 10020-1393.

Fortune 500 An annual listing in *Fortune* magazine of the five hundred major industrial corporations in the United States, reporting on sales, profits, assets, stockholders' equity, market value, profit as a percentage of sales, assets, and stockholders' equity, earnings per share showing also the ten-year growth rate, and total return to investors, again with a ten-year average. Firms are ranked from one to five hundred in each category.

forward integration The action of a company acquiring businesses that takes the company closer to the end consumer than did the original firm. Example: A manufacturer of men's clothing decides to buy or to build a chain of men's stores selling directly to the consumer.

Foundation for Management Education (FME) In the United Kingdom, a registered tax-exempt foundation set up in 1960 to promote management education at the university level.

founder's shares Now relatively uncommon, at least by this name, these shares were once issued to the original subscribers to company stock and carried with them certain privileges not available to later holders of stock. The term is used most widely now in the United Kingdom.

frame Graphic information presented at one time in a text of programmed learning.

franc (Belgian) Basic unit of Belgian currency.

franc (French) Basic unit of French currency.

franchise The permission, or license, to manufacture or to market products or services, usually because the brand name is well known and will attract immediate business. The franchisee pays a fee for this privilege and usually participates in advertising programs with the mother firm.

free alongside ship (FAS) A situation in which the seller of a product is responsible for transporting the product to the ship's side, but the buyer is responsible for getting it on board.

free choice of products A type of market-survey tool in which products are presented to respondents and they are asked which brand is superior regarding one or more specific attributes. (Examples: Taste is a common attribute tested, though it is obviously highly subjective.)

free economy A laissez faire economy.

free movement of capital 1. The unregulated flow of capital between countries with no exchange control or any other form of government intervention. 2. In the 1957 Treaty of Rome,

Articles 67–73 loosely set out the conditions for the free flow of capital between Common Market countries. (*See* Section IV)

free movement of labor In the 1957 Treaty of Rome, Articles 48–49 generally set out the provisions for the free movement of labor in the Common Market countries. (*See* Section IV)

free on board (FOB) A situation in which the seller or supplier of goods is responsible for delivering the goods to be transported on board a ship.

free on rail (FOR) A situation in which the seller or supplier of goods is responsible for delivering the goods onto the rail cars for transportation.

free port 1. A port in which imported goods can be held and/or processed for re-export with no customs duties charged. 2. A harbor where port facilities are open to all commercial vessels on equal terms.

free trade A vital concept in international trade that would dispose of all customs duties and tariffs and allow free interchange of goods and services between the nations of the world.

free-market argument The contention that the forces of supply and demand, when there is no government interference, are sufficient to stabilize the economy.

freie Makler Free brokers or dealers on either the Vienna Stock Exchange or one of the German stock exchanges.

freight forwarder A company that serves exporters by arranging for the shipment of goods. Virtually all paperwork and contracting for shipping space is done by this company; they are vital forces in international trade.

frequency distribution A statistical method of condensing a large quantity of data by arranging it in groups or categories and then showing the relative frequency with which members of groups have the same or similar values.

frictional overhead A term used collectively for persons who serve as aides to top executives, either as full-time employees or as consultants. Peter Drucker sees this as a part of the "malorganization" of certain companies.

frictional unemployment A type of short-term unemployment occasioned by inclement weather, breaks in production levels, and other random variables.

fringe benefits Those benefits offered employees by employers over and above their normal compensation, which includes health-care programs, group life insurance, discounted goods, etc.

frozen convertible A convertible security that has been outstanding for several years and cannot be forced to convert because its conversion value is below its call price.

frozen pension A paid-up pension. Often a pension in existence when an employee leaves a firm that will remain with the firm until such time as the employee reaches retirement age and begins to draw upon it.

Fukuoka Stock Exchange One of five main stock exchanges in Japan. (*See* Section VII)

full employment An economic term denoting the fact that there is little unemployment. Full employment is measured differently by different nations. In the United States, 4 percent unemployment has historically been considered full employment. In the United Kingdom, 3 percent unemployment is considered full employment.

functional controls Controls that are exercised in the four major categories of production, sales, finance, and personnel.

functional decentralization One of two distinct principles advocated by Peter Drucker as vital in an organizational structure. Denotes an organization that has integrated units with maximum responsibility for a major and distinct stage in the total business process.

functional strategy The planning for each department and division of the firm in the area of functions that must be performed to carry out the total objectives of the firm's program for the future.

fundamental design method (FDM) An approach to engineering design and other creative work developed by E. Matchett in the United Kingdom.

funded debt to net capital worth ratios When this ratio is too high, it may indicate that the cash fund has been depleted to pay debt. A ratio of 40 percent of funded debt to working capital would not be excessive.

funds statement A type of financial statement used by some firms to reveal their sources of investment funds during a specific accounting period.

funnel interviewing technique A type of market research that is generally unstructured, but in which the interviewer tries to guide the interviewee toward a specific subject of research.

fusion of drives The joining together of human motivations and interests toward the solution of a problem.

fusion theory of organization The theory that the firm uses the employee to further its goals and the employee uses the firm to further his goals. This is simplistic, but the best working conditions exist where companies and employees understand each other's needs and work to fulfill them to the greatest possible degree.

futures Contracts to buy or sell securities or commodities at a fixed price at some time to come.

G

gains from trade The increase of output and income in a nation that is generated by the increased efficiency resulting from specialization in trade.

gains to net debtors The increase in a debtor's wealth due to a decline in the purchasing power of liabilities.

galloping inflation A colloquialism for rapidly spiraling inflation.

game theory 1. A teaching technique used in many schools that applies mathematical techniques to problem solving through the use of model building. Normally the game is played by two or more persons who apply alternate strategies to attempt to find the solution to a problem, which is often maximizing returns and minimizing losses. 2. The concept that decision-making events can be of two types: 1) the win/lose situation (the zero-sum game) or 2) the win/win situation in which everyone making a decision comes out a winner.

gamesmanship, subordinate Where specific activities of the company are being carried out by different groups at various levels, this is the action of moving a problem or suggestion from a lower level to a higher level until it reaches the president or CEO. Usually this is done with the agreement of each succeeding level.

Gantt chart A bar chart devised by Henry Gantt that is widely used in planning and scheduling the work in specific projects.

Gantt, Henry L. (1861-1919) *See* Section IX.

gap analysis A market-research term denoting statistical methods and other techniques to identify holes in market coverage or market saturation.

GATT General Agreement on Tariffs and Trade. (*See* entry below)

Gaussian curve A symmetrical or bell-shaped curve, often called the "normal curve," which represents the normal frequency distribution when analyzing data based on a large-scale sample of the population or the whole population.

GAW Guaranteed annual wage.

GCA Group capacity assessment.

GDP Gross domestic product.

geared incentive scheme A type of payment-by-results plan in which the incentive pay goes up in increments rather than in exact proportion to output.

gearing Term in the United Kingdom for "leverage" in the United States. The extent to which the money capital of a company is divided between fixed interest or fixed dividend capital and equity or ordinary shares where the return is not guaranteed.

gearing ratio The ratio of preference and outside loan capital to ordinary capital and reserves.

General & Municipal Worker's Union An affiliate of the Trade Union Congress in the United Kingdom that has about one million members. Address: 'Ruxley Towers,' Claygate, Esher, Surrey KT10 OTL.

General Agreement on Tariffs and Trade (GATT) A somewhat informal international body established in Geneva in 1947 for the purpose of promoting free trade. Nations supporting the plan are responsible for 80 percent of the world's trade. The periodic meetings are called "rounds" (such as the Kennedy rounds). Usually the rounds deal with specific problems. The 1964–67 negotiations, for example, related to tariff reductions on cereals and the anti-dumping code. In 1955 GATT set up the Organization for Trade Cooperation as its administrative body. Address: 154, rue de Lausanne 1211 Geneve 21, Switzerland.

general clerical test Developed in the United States, this three-part psychological test measures verbal, numerical, and organizing skills.

General Confederation of Labor Confederation Generale du Travail (CGT). Confederation of French trade unions.

general creditor An unsecured creditor.

general equilibrium A situation in which all of the markets in the economy are simultaneously in balance. (A theoretical notion that is never realized in the real world.)

general learning ability test In the United States, this term denotes a general intelligence test as opposed to a specific skills test.

General Strike (1926) The historic strike in the United Kingdom that began with miners and spread quickly to other industries until a general strike ensued. The Trade Disputes Act of 1927 outlawed general strikes until it was repealed in 1946.

Geregelter Freiverkehr The regulated free market on the Vienna Stock Exchange for securities that are permitted on the trading floor, but which are not registered and therefore not on the official list.

German federal companies Forms of business partnerships and companies: 1) one-man firms, *Einzelfirma*; 2) general partnership, *Offene Handelsgesellschaft* (OHG); 3) limited partnership, *Kommanditgesellschaft*; 4) sleeping partnership, *Stille Gesellschaft*; 5) combined limited partnership and limited liability company, *Gesellschaft mit beschrankter Haftung & Kommanditgesellschaft* (GmbH & Co KG); 6) limited partnership with shares, *Kommanditgesellschaft auf Aktien* (KG a A); 7) limited liability company, *Gesellschaft mit beschrankter Haftung* (GmbH); 8) joint-stock company, *Aktiengesellschaft* (AG).

Gesellschaft mit beschrankter Haftung (GmbH) A limited liability company under Swiss, Austrian, and German company law.

Gesellschaftsteuer The company capitalization tax on the initial acquisition of shares in Austrian companies. On the Vienna Stock Exchange, there is a securities tax, or *Wertpapiersteuer*, on bonds when they are issued for the first time.

Gestalt psychology This theory, with its beginning in Germany in the early twentieth century, is now used extensively in psychological testing and personnel selection. The basic thesis of this theory is that a distorted and incomplete picture of mental and psychological processes is obtained if these processes are analyzed without considering the complete personality and the manner in which the processes interrelate. It gives credence to the significance of nonverbal communications.

g factor A concept developed by Charles Spearman that claims that human beings possess an underlying basic intelligence, or "g" factor, along with many special abilities, called "s" factors.

Ghana National Chamber of Commerce Established in 1961, this organization's address is POB 2325, Accra, Ghana.

Ghana Trades Union Congress Established in 1945, this organization's address is Hall of Trade Unions, POB 701, Accra, Ghana.

gift tax A tax paid by an individual on gifts to others above a certain value on an annual basis. This tax seeks to discourage wealth transfer for the purpose of tax avoidance. Also known as a capital transfer tax.

Gilbreth, Frank B., and Lillian Gilbreth *See* Section IX.

Gilbreth symbols *See* therblig.

Giles-Archer lantern tests A form of color-recognition test in which the student is shown several different colors with variations of brightness.

gilt-edged A term describing securities, often U.S. government securities, that pay interest or dividends regularly, and in which the risk of loss is very low.

GIRO A system used by many European countries to transfer money via the postal system. It was accepted by the United Kingdom in 1968.

Glacier project A research project conducted by Elliot Jacques, associated with the Tavistock Institute of Human Relations, and used in the management reorganization of Glacier Metal Co., Ltd. Topics of interest were methods of payment, measurement of responsibility, joint consultation, etc.

glamour issues Stocks representing companies presumed to have a bright future, and more specifically those companies dealing with new technology or other attractive products or services.

Gleitzeit A term used in Germany to denote flexible working hours.

GMT (GT) Greenwich Mean Time.

GNP price deflator The price index number used by the Bureau of Economic Analysis of the Department of Commerce in the United States to decrease gross national product figures to eliminate the effect of inflation.

GNP Gross National Product. (*See* entry below)

go-slow The action of slowing down the production rate of a company by employees (usually organized) who wish to send a message to management that they have grievances.

goal achievement The attaining of objectives by pointing every decision in the direction of those objectives.

goals, corporate Those goals, which must include making a profit, that are considered to be the sum total of all things the corporation must be to all people.

goal identification A task of the leader with the input of subordinates. Such identification must be made plain to all subordinates to elicit their complete cooperation in goal achievement.

goal obsession A term used in T-group training indicating too great a concern for goal achievement and too little concern for current behavioral patterns. (*See also* T-group training)

goals Specific statements of achievements that are marked to be accomplished by specific deadlines.

goblet issue A topic of any importance that gives one member of a group the opportunity to hear and to size up other members of a group.

'going public' The action of a privately held company to offer stock to the purchasing public. This action must have SEC approval, and, according to the size of the company, the company will trade its stocks (after the sale of the initial issue) through some or several stock exchanges.

gold and foreign-exchange reserves Gold and foreign currencies held by a nation to settle debts that are called in and to guard against deficits in its balance-of-payments account.

gold certificate Currency that is backed by and convertible into gold. None is in circulation now.

golden handshake A colloquialism denoting the severance pay awarded to a top executive at the termination of his contract; generally such pay is awarded in cases in which the termination is on friendly terms.

gold standard An international monetary system in which all currencies bear a direct relationship to gold.

golden rule fallacy The erroneous view, sometimes found in T-group training, that there is one correct way for all people to interact in all situations. (*See* T-group training)

good-faith bargaining A term denoting that the parties in labor negotiations are sincerely trying for a viable plan, acceptable to both parties, that will allow them to continue to work together in relative peace.

goods *economics* Anything people find useful and desirable and are willing to pay money for.

goods for process Goods imported for further processing in the United Kingdom. This importation is free of customs duties. Normally the goods will be destined for re-export after the processing is finished.

goodwill A term denoting the assumed favorable light in which a firm is held, either because of selling a well-known product, because of giving superior services, or because of having a backlog of good and regular customers. This is an intangible asset, but it is often set into the financial statement of a company in order to be included in a selling price. The practice of measuring goodwill is highly suspect and should be carefully researched by a prospective buyer.

goon squad A term once used in the United States to denote people related to labor unions who were used to "rough up" those who opposed them in an attempt to gain the opposition's support or at least to discourage the opposition.

Gopertz curve A graphic presentation of a curve that shows the actual or potential sales of a new product over time. The curve usually reveals three stages: a growth period, a plateau period, and a period of decline.

Gordon personal inventory and profile A psychological inventory test used primarily in the United States. The test requires only about fifteen minutes to complete and measures cautiousness, original thinking, personal relations, vigor, and provides a total score.

government broker A stockbroker appointed by the government in the United Kingdom to deal in government securities on the floor of the London Stock Exchange. The Bank of England operates through the government broker.

government securities 1. In the United States, debt instruments issued by the Department of the Treasury, including Treasury bills, notes, and bonds. 2. In the United Kingdom, investment vehicles issued by the government that comprise part of the national debt.

Government Training Centres Programs operated in the United Kingdom by the Training Opportunities Scheme of the Training Services Agency for the Department of Employment. At the outset, six-month courses were offered in engineering, construction, etc., but these have been somewhat expanded in later years.

grade creep The action of regrading or reclassifying certain people in a company in order to increase pay.

graduated benefits (or supplement) and contributions A program introduced by the National Insurance Act of 1961 in the United Kingdom that provided retirement pensions in addition to the flat-rate benefits and contributions that formed the basis of the original National Insurance Act.

grants-in-aid Term usually refers to money given by the federal government to some lower level of government.

grapevine An informal type of communication in which information is transmitted verbally, usually with no official documented fact to back it up. Such communications can be useful to management when used to test opinions in an informal manner.

graphic break-even point problem solution A graphic presentation revealing the break-even point at various sales and revenue levels.

graphic method of linear programming A simple straight-line method of linear programming that simplifies the problem of getting material across to viewers.

gray-area occupations A new term denoting types of jobs that may be classified either as blue-collar or white-collar jobs depending on the situation.

Great Society A social welfare program initiated by President Lyndon Baines Johnson that was generally an offshoot of the New Deal, the Fair Deal. One aspect of the Great Society program came to be known as the War on Poverty.

Greek companies Several types of business partnerships and companies exist by law in Greece, but only one is listed on the Athens Stock Exchange, *Anonymous Etairia* (AE), which is a form of joint-stock company.

green revolution A name given to the monumental agricultural breakthroughs of the 1960s and 1970s, including the introduction of rapid growing, high-yielding plants.

Greenwich Mean Time The local time at Greenwich in southeast England, which is on the zero meridian. Used as a world datum time for international air travel and simultaneous meteorological reports.

Gresham's Law "Bad money drives out good money." When currency becomes less valuable, it tends to drive "hard money," such as silver and gold, out of the market and into hiding.

grid theory A theory of management that states that there are three universals in any business organization: 1) people, 2) production of goods or services, and 3) the management hierarchy.

grievance procedure A procedure negotiated in a labor contract between management and labor outlining how grievances are to be handled.

gross business product That part of gross national product produced by businesses.

gross income *income tax* term denoting all income of an individual from all sources before deductions are made for qualified allowances.

gross investment Total annual investment of a company prior to deducting depreciation.

gross margin percentage Revenue minus cost of goods sold divided by revenue.

gross national product (GNP) The sum total of all final goods and services produced in a nation in a year stated in terms of dollars or some other monetary unit.

gross profit (or margin) That amount by which revenue from sales exceeds the production costs of the goods and services sold.

group action, MBO The actions of any group, operating within the framework of the company, in which Management by Objectives is paramount. The more people with input, the more problems are apt to be found before they have a chance to hurt the company.

group behavior The study, still relatively new in management, that considers the group as a whole with its behavioral patterns as contrasted with the consideration of individuals.

group, development of Conceived of as a three-phase action, individuals go through interpersonal phases of inclusion, control, and affection.

group dynamics The study of the behavior patterns of groups and the behavior patterns of individuals as they interact with other individuals in the group.

Group Export Representation Scheme A program in the United Kingdom that assists groups of exporters who produce complementary products to jointly sponsor a trade representative. The agency that oversees this program is the Special Export Services Branch of the Department of Trade. Address: Special Export Services

Branch, Export House, 50 Ludgate Hill, London EC4M 7HU.

group influence The power of an organization to influence the thinking and the actions of the organization. A group tends to be more than the sum of the individuals that make it up.

group life assurance policy *Insurance* A blanket policy taken out by an employer under which all employees, and sometimes their dependents, are covered for specific amounts. Group personal accident policies are handled essentially in the same way, except that there is no coverage for dependents.

group project training Programs in which students undertake a task as a group, rather than as individuals. This "team" approach is popular in many schools of business.

group selection techniques A method in personnel selection in which individuals are evaluated while performing as part of a group.

group technology A type of management in which the plant involved in the manufacture of a given product will bring together related groups, often with the possibility of occasional job rotation. This approach is used to allow all workers to become aware of different tasks within the plant, which is supposed to reduce the monotony and increase motivation.

group test A psychological test taken by a group, rather than one taken by individuals.

growth companies, profits of In a growth company, the estimate of the next year's profits are usually an extrapolation from the past year's profit.

However, relative to profits, growth companies tend to pay lower dividends as they plough the profits back into the business. Shareholders receive the capital growth of shares in lieu of larger dividends.

growth cycle In the growing process of a company, usually from small to large, when the large number of changes may demand different leadership at different junctures and perhaps a complete reworking of the organizational structure periodically.

growth, economics of Growth is required of a company, since zero growth elicits both complacency and leads to unprofitability as the business already held is taken by more energetic, imaginative firms.

growth enterprise, changes in The changes that occur as the company experiences development, including more levels of management, more employees, the need for better communications, etc.

growth industry and self-deception The deceptive concept that any industry will be in a position of ascendency forever. No matter how long-lasting an industry may appear to be, changes in technology will ultimately render any company obsolete.

growth planning A continuing program of both short-range planning (SRP) and long-range planning (LRP) must play a major role in an on-going business enterprise.

GTC Government Training Centre in the United Kingdom.

g (test) A nonverbal intelligence test used in vocational guidance and personnel placement.

guaranteed annual wage (GAW) An unrealized concept on the part of labor that employees will be guaranteed some minimum wage whether or not they work the year around.

guest worker A term used in the Common Market to denote a foreign worker who is able to work in the country, but not to move a family there.

guide-chart profile method A method of job evaluation built around the factors of know-how, problem solving, and accountability in the context of a specific salary bracket.

guide price In the Common Market, this term is used to refer to a target price set for beef and veal. Producers are helped to achieve this price by subsidies or by import controls.

guild socialism A form of syndicalism advocated in the United Kingdom in the early twentieth century, the aims of which was to restore some of the medieval guild ideas.

guilder Basic unit of currency in the Netherlands. Also spelled gilder.

Guilford-Zimmerman temperament survey A test devised in the United States to measure temperament and personality.

guillotine A method in meetings of closing debate on a specific theme once the time allotted to it has expired. It is used principally in the House of Commons in the United Kingdom.

guilt feelings and aggression In Freudian terms, an aggressive or hostile spirit produces guilt feelings in the individual as the superego condemns the individual for these feelings. This guilt may then lead to depression.

guilt feelings and superego In Freudian terms, the superego emerges from the culture in which one lives and refuses to accept any undesirable traits. When an individual discovers these traits and brings them to consciousness, the individual experiences feelings of guilt.

guns vs. butter An expression denoting the trade-off between the production of military goods and consumer goods. Since resources can be easily be overburdened, decisions often have to be made between military hardware and consumer goods.

H

habitual movements *motion study* Movements that, through constant, precise repetition, can be performed without thought.

hall test A tool of market research wherein individuals are brought together to test their reactions to specific products.

Hall, Douglas Helped develop the theory that if an employee fails to meet performance expectations that are close to his own expectations, he will lower his standards, and his performance will continue to drop off. (David E. Berlew and Douglas T. Hall, "The Socialization of Managers: Effects of Expectations on Performance," *Administrative*

Science Quarterly [September 1966], p. 208.)

halo effect 1. The tendency of a boss to favor an employee because of the following: 1) effect of past record; 2) compatibility; 3) a single strong asset; 4) the blind-spot effect (i.e., the boss does not see the person's weaknesses because they are the same as his own); 5) the high potential effect; 6) a no-complaint bias. 2. The end result of an interviewer looking favorably upon a candidate because of one characteristic; i.e., physical appearance, education, etc.

Halsey Plan An early form of payment-by-results in which the employee is compensated for work finished above the target amount, but not in proportion to the increase in production.

hammered The "three strokes of the hammer" on the stock exchange floor denoting that some broker or trader is unable to meet his debts.

Hancock, John Chairman of the Jewel Tea Company in 1931. He pioneered the idea of bringing into the company bright young people and "giving them their heads" to learn and to innovate.

hand-over pay A payment made to shift workers who remain a short time after their shifts are over to orient the next shift to what has occurred and to what is expected.

Hanley, John W. A former top executive at Proctor and Gamble who resigned after the CEO promoted another man over Hanley because he thought Hanley to be too aggressive and too willing to innovate. This occasioned many studies regarding how a chief executive could better evaluate a valued employee before taking actions

that might send him off into the arms of a competitor.

hard-boiled manager An autocratic type of manager who seems satisfied with nothing less than complete subservience on the part of his people.

hard-core control That small group of top officials in a company who plan long-term strategies for a firm.

hard information Information based on solid facts rather than on emotion or speculation.

hard sales promotion A promotion concerned with increasing sales and consumption of a product, usually carried out through reduced prices or increased package size.

hardware A term denoting the physical structure of a computer as opposed to programs, codes, etc., that comprise the software of a computer.

harmonization A term denoting the Treaty of Rome (1957) requirements on balancing employment needs, social concerns, etc., in Common Market countries.

Harvard case method Developed by the Harvard Business School, this teaching technique consists of using case studies of real companies from which students can learn the discipline of management.

Hawthorne Effect The instinctive propensity of employees to group together, either formally or informally, to improve performance or change behavior while being observed.

Hay Clerical Battery A three-part psychological test, developed in the United States, which contains three parts, each taking four minutes:

1) number perception, 2) name finding, and 3) series of numbers.

Hayes Pegboard Test A test of psychomotor skills, taking only about three minutes, measuring hand and arm coordination for the left hand, right hand, or both hands.

headhunter An executive search consultant, who may work independently of any organization, but who works with organizations and business firms in seeking top executive personnel.

hedge fund A fund the object of which is to maximize capital appreciation, but at the expense of substantially increased risk. Such a fund, therefore, is inherently speculative. In the quest for maximum appreciation, speculators involved with hedge funds may use such aggressive investment techniques as financial leverage or short sales and options, in addition to more conventional investment methods. Also known as leveraged funds.

hedging A method of minimizing risk, particularly in the commodities market, by buying large quantities of commodities for actual delivery at some future time. Such purchases insure the buyer against unfavorable changes in the price of such commodities by entering into compensatory arrangements or by counterbalancing transactions on the other side.

Her Majesty's Customs and Excise An agency working under the Department of Trade that is responsible for control of imports and exports, including commercial interchange with the European Community, the collection of customs duties, excise duty, and the value-added tax. The agency also supervises the manufacture of dutiable goods.

heredity factors in behavior A concept that an individual is moved to behave in certain ways because of inherited traits.

"heroic materialism," age of A name given to the post–Second World War period by British art historian, Kenneth Clark, who argued that there were several stages in this development of the psychology of affluence, including "we-expect-more-of-everything" complex; acquiring more of everything is an entitlement, not just a hope; the economy will function more or less automatically; and the turning upon its head of the self-denial ethic.

heuristic computer programs Programs that aid in the discovery of new uses that can be made by banks of computer data.

heuristic models Making use of mathematical models while including practical considerations in getting work done.

hidden assets Assets that cannot be seen in a cursory reading of a balance sheet. Often these assets include property that is still on the books at the purchase price, though the value may have increased several times over.

hierarchical assignment of work The position one occupies in a firm's hierarchy dictates what kind of work the individual performs.

hierarchy of needs See Abraham Maslow entry in Section IX.

hierarchy of objectives The allocating of priorities to the many things that must be done through a business organization.

hierarchy of position and tasks A term denoting the formal organizing of a business structure, sometimes set out in a "table of organization" in which positions, and the tasks to be performed within the context of those positions, are briefly outlined.

high school graduation, post–World War II The number of high school graduates in the period following World War II grew quickly, from 50 percent prior to the war to 75 percent soon afterward. This movement was directly connected with the knowledge that the way to a white-collar job was through education.

high-level language A sophisticated "human-like" computer language used to write programs for many types of computers and for complex applications.

hire purchase An installment purchase, one which is paid out over time with periodic payments.

histogram A bar chart representing frequency distributions using the X axis for class intervals and the Y axis for frequencies. (*See also* frequency distribution)

historical-cost depreciation A depreciation schedule based on the original cost of an asset.

historical costing The recording and analysis of costs after they have been incurred.

hoeklieden Stockjobbers on the Amsterdam Stock Exchange.

holding company 1. A "parent" company that controls other companies (subsidiaries) by owning a majority of the voting stock of such companies. 2. A corporation specifically incorporated to hold the stock of other companies. New Jersey was the first state to pass

enabling legislation in 1889, which helped stem the proliferation of such companies. The movement then gained impetus when, in 1890, the Sherman Act was passed, which prohibits combinations or collusion in restraint of trade.

holding companies, leverage in The ability of a holding company to invest a dollar and control perhaps a thousand dollars worth of another company.

holistic development A type of individual development that emphasizes the importance of the whole person and the interdependence of his parts.

home audit A type of market research in which homes are checked to see what products are to be found and to check on the volume of those products used by the household.

homeostasis In mathematical models, the retaining of an attribute without change.

Homeowners' Insurance Basic fire policy endorsements, comprehensive liability policy, and personal theft coverage develops a package known as "Homeowners Insurance." Types are HO-1, HO-2, HO-3, HO-4, HO-5, HO-6, HO-8. (For the interested user of this volume, these types can be investigated with any agent selling property and casualty insurance.)

horizontal gaps An area within an organizational level that is not connected with any supervisory channel.

horizontal growth in an organization The in-house lateral growth experienced in a growing company when it finds that one worker cannot function alone with the responsibilites he has and others are added to help carry the load. This growth can result in more

371

efficient work, or the presence of more people than are necessary to accomplish goals can burden the firm with oversized human-resources costs.

horizontal integration The acquisition or merging of homogenous business units, which were formerly separate entities, for the purpose of gaining leverage in the market. (*Cf.* vertical integration)

horns effect The reverse of the halo effect (see above), which contains the following elements: 1) the boss is a perfectionist and therefore expects more of people than he should; 2) the employee is contrary because he disagrees with the boss; 3) the oddball effect, resulting in conflicting personalities; 4) membership on a weak team; 5) the guilt-by-association effect, which occurs when the employee tends to be seen with the "wrong" crowd; 6) the dramatic incident effect, which occurs when a recent mistake wipes out good work; 7) the personality trait effect, which occurs when people seem either too cocky, too timid, etc.; 8) the self-comparison effect, which occurs when the boss remembers how he once did a job, and compares himself with how the current jobholder is doing it. (G. S. Odiorne, *MBO II* [Belmont, Calif.: David S. Lake, Pubs., 1979], pp. 248–49.)

Hospital and Medical Expense Association An association such as Blue Cross/Blue Shield, usually started by a physician or someone related to health care delivery, which is formed as a nonprofit plan to sell certain hospital care and medical care services for a monthly fee. Usually the association will deal directly with a hospital that will provide the services and then be idemnified by the association.

hostility and love Every human relationship contains both love and hate. However, since this is not always understood, guilt feelings can arise because individuals feel hostile toward someone they are supposed to love. Only the knowledge that the hostility, up to a point, is natural can relieve the pain of this paradox.

hot money Money that is attracted to a country by interest rates that are more favorable, or money that is moved because of currencies that holders want to move quickly since they fear that the current exchange rate is unrealistic and that devaluation may be imminent. Foreign exchange speculators are sometimes accused of making a currency "hot."

house journal An in-house magazine or paper published primarily for employees of a firm, but sometimes also distributed to customers, shareholders, etc.

House United Kingdom House of Commons, or the London Stock Exchange, are each so known.

human-asset accounting In the United Kingdom, a method and practice of evaluating the human factor in business in an attempt to identify the economic and social impact of company policies on employees and, subsequently, on the company itself.

human behavior school of management A school of thought derived from the social sciences, such as psychology and social psychology, where the individual is viewed as a sociopsychological being who has needs, which, when discovered, can provide the foundation for human understanding and motivation.

human element in controlling That part the function of control, which is a part of the manager's task, that governs how people are understood and how their efforts can be directed to the achievement of the goals of the organization.

human relations department A relatively new term in management denoting the department that deals with the human resources of a company. It tends to be more comprehensive than a personnel department.

human-relations school A school of management thought that generally began in the United States in the 1930s and 1940s. It was led at first by Elton Mayo. The general theme of this approach is that better relationships between all human resources contribute to a more settled and productive company.

human relations, big issues in Those aspects of human relations that appear to be required if a program is to succeed. The issues include the understanding and compliance of top executives, an atmosphere open enough that vital communications can take place, and a basic integrity that marks the whole organization.

humanist psychology A school of psychological thought, which developed prolifically in the 1950s, that essentially propounded that man, within himself, could achieve anything he wanted to without the intervention of a higher power or an outside force. This notion, according to Erich Fromm, gave man the power to become god and an end within himself. (While Abraham H. Maslow is credited with propounding the idea of "self-actualization," he should not be saddled with extraneous ideas later proffered by those who followed him, which were often diametrically opposed to Maslow's intentions. (*See* Abraham Maslow entry, Section IX)

hunches Nonquantitative human feelings that contribute, whether recognized or not, to decision making.

Hungarian Chamber of Commerce Organization was Formed in 1968. Address: Budapest v, Rosenberg v 17, Hungary.

hurdle rate *finance* The minimum acceptable rate of return on an investment.

hygiene factors *See* Herzberg's theory in Section IX.

hypermarkets A new type of retail merchandising entity even larger than the general supermarket. These new markets are normally more than 100,000 square feet in size, with mammoth parking lots, and they sell many kinds of merchandise.

hypothesis A tentative explanation of a problem, which is a vital part of problem solving.

IAEA International Atomic Energy Agency.

IANEC Inter-American Nuclear Energy Commission.

IATA International Air Transport Association.

IBRD International Bank for Reconstruction and Development (World Bank).

ICAO International Civil Aviation Organization.

ICATU International Confederation of Arab Trade Unions.

ICC International Chamber of Commerce; Interstate Commerce Commission.

ICFC Industrial and Commercial Finance Corporation Ltd.

ICFTU International Confederation of Free Trade Unions.

ICMA Institute of Cost and Management Accountants.

iconic models Laboratory simulations of real-life situations, particularly in the field of engineering.

ICOR Incremental capital-output ratio.

ICTU Irish Congress of Trade Unions.

id In Freudian terms, the unconscious, unorganized source of all instinctual drives and the directive force towards amoral, immediate gratifications; i.e., that part of the psyche that, more or less, effectively stimulates the ego and the superego to act.

IDB Industrial Development Bond; *see* Inter-American Development Bank.

idea fluency An ability to put together numerous ideas about a specific problem on the premise that the more ideas are investigated, the greater the chance of finding the right one.

idea traps Places where the crux of ideas can be jotted down when they occur to a person, such as in a notebook, on note cards, etc.

idle time Situation in a plant when neither capital resources nor human resources are being utilized productively. Also known as down time.

IDP Integrated Data Processing.

IFC International Finance Corporation.

IFF Institute for the Future.

ILA International Longshoremen's Association.

ILGWU International Ladies' Garment Workers Union.

illegal contracts Contracts that cannot be considered legal because they exist for an unlawful purpose, such as circumventing antitrust legislation, conspiring with a foreign enemy, etc.

image study A study of consumer attitudes toward a company and/or its products.

IMF International Monetary Fund.

IMM International Monetary Market of the Chicago Mercantile Exchange.

immaturity, psychological 1. In Freudian terms, the inability to act on the basis of the "reality principle." 2. The inability to consider the long-range consequences of decisions.

impact testing A method of evaluating the effectiveness of an advertising program by testing to see how much of it people recall.

impingement pay In the United Kingdom, a term used to denote holiday pay in the printing industry.

import duty A tax on imports. (*See also* tariff)

imposta communale sull'incremento di valore degli immobili In Italy, a municipal or communal tax charged on capital gains from the transfer of real property and also chargeable every ten years on capital appreciation of properties held by property companies.

imposta complementare progressiva sul reddito complessivo In Italy, a complementary tax, or progressive surtax, levied on an individual's total income.

imposta di ricchezza mobile sul reddito In Italy, a moveable wealth tax charged as a proportional tax.

imposta sul reddito agrario In Italy, an agricultural income tax levied on income from agriculture and assessed on such bases as value or property, investment, number of employees, etc.

imposta sul reddito dominicale dei terreni In Italy, a form of income tax charged on land according to its rental value.

imposta sul reditto dei Pabbricati In Italy, a type of income tax in the form of a building tax charged on annual rental value after the deduction of 25 percent of maintenance costs.

imposto complementar In Portugal, a complementary tax charged as a progressive surtax on total income.

imposto de capitais In Portugal, a tax on income from moveable capital assets.

imposto de mais-valias In Portugal, a capital gains tax.

imposto profissional In Portugal, a professional tax on earned income.

impot a forfait In Switzerland, a graduated tax levied on the incomes of certain foreigners in place of the national defense tax paid by nationals.

impot des personnes physiques In Belgium, an income tax, progressive in nature, levied on all income for all sources.

impot federal pour la defense nationale In Switzerland, the federal national defense tax levied on all income for Swiss nationals.

impot foncier In Luxembourg, a local tax levied on the capital value of all real property, whether developed or not.

impot sur la fortune In Luxembourg, a capital tax levied on investments in agriculture, forestry, real property, industry, business, professions, and movable capital.

impot sur le revenu The principal income tax in both Luxembourg and France, progressive in nature, levied on all types of personal income, including capital gains.

imprecision, art of The ability of a manager never to become committed to any specific set of objectives.

imprest An advance or loan. Term used in denoting petty cash that is replenished every accounting period against the vouchers issued by the fund.

impuesto general sobre la renta de las personas fisicas In Spain, a general, progressive income tax levied against all income.

impuesto sobre actividades y beneficios commercailes e industriales In Spain, the industrial tax.

impuesto sobre las rentas des capital In Spain, a tax levied on unearned income.

impuesto sobre los rendimeintos del trabajo personal In Spain, a tax levied on income from personal work.

imputed costs Costs not directly associated with the main conduct of business, but with inevitable expenses associated with any business, such as interest payments.

in-basket exercises A type of training exercise wherein the trainee has a number of different items placed in his "in-basket" and the time is gauged as to how long it takes him to work through the items and to come up with viable answers.

in-company training Personnel training programs carried on in-house, sometimes by in-house people, and sometimes by outside consultants.

incentive engineer In the United States, a term denoting one who establishes the rates paid by a firm for "payment-by-results" programs, or any program in which rates for labor may fluctuate from a given base.

incentive merchandise Name-brand products given to salespeople or others as a reward for positive action.

incestuous share dealing The actions between companies of buying and selling each other's stock with the objective of avoiding taxes or of gaining other financial benefits.

inclusion phase of group development That time in the development of a group when individuals believe they have found a place within the group and are a part of it.

income elasticity of demand The relationship between the level of income and demand (or sales volume) for a given product or service.

income statement *See* profit and loss statement.

income tax A tax levied on income by the government of a nation, which may take several forms, such as direct taxes on earnings, capital gains taxes, etc. Most countries now have some kind of income tax because it is a relatively easy tax to collect. In the United States, the Constitution was changed in 1913 to allow for an income tax. Corporations, as well as individuals, have their incomes taxed.

income, circular flow of *See* circular flow of income.

incomes policy A government policy designed to control incomes, particularly during a crisis, such as war, galloping inflation, etc. An incomes policy can be a part of far-reaching wage-and-price controls.

increasing returns to scale Normally larger plants or firms can produce more efficiently and at a lower cost than smaller ones. As the size of the plant or the firm grows, the output, or returns per unit of input, increases. The long-term average total cost curve slopes downward. In pursuing the "economies of scale" however, a point of diminishing returns can be reached, and any further increase in size will simply become more costly to the producer, and the total cost curve will begin an upward swing.

incremental capital-output ratio (COR) The increase in capital stock (goods used in the production of other goods) divided by the increase of goods and services produced during a specific period of time, usually a year.

incremental cost A term sometimes used in business in place of marginal cost or revenue. Also known as incremental revenue.

incremental costing *See* marginal costing.

incremental payment system The granting of pay increases based on some specific attribute such as tenure, increased productivity, etc. These pay increases are usually on some predetermined schedule.

incremental profitability An increase in the profitability of a firm due to nonquantifiable measures, such as the increased efficiency of workers, for whatever reason, or the bringing in of more skilled workers.

indemnity fund In the United Kingdom, a fund set up by employers' associations to compensate member firms for losses incurred in labor strikes, etc. (In the United States, strike insurance is the method used for indemnity in labor disputes.)

indexation Adjusting various prices and incomes on the basis of changes in the general price level, as indicated by the "consumer price index."

index linking A method of price adjustment during a period of inflation to assure that loss is not incurred by keeping prices low as inflation increases. In labor contracts, this price adjustment is often written in so that workers get a cost-of-living increase adjusted to the rate of inflation.

index number A number showing the percentage of change between a "base year" (always 100 percent) and the year to be compared to the base year.

Indian Central Bank Reserve Bank of India. (*See* Section VII)

Indian National Trade Union Congress (INTUC) Established in 1947, this umbrella organization covers all Indian trade unions. Its members include approximately two thousand unions and nearly three million individuals. Address: 17 Janpath, New Delhi.

Indian Stock Exchanges *See* Section VII.

indicative planning Otherwise known as "participative planning," i.e., planning by agreement rather than by edict.

indifference curve A graphic presentation revealing the combinations of two goods that would yield equal satisfaction to the consumer.

indirect cost Any cost incurred by a company that is not directly linked to the productive process. However, indirect costs usually are allocated, through accounting procedures, to each product on a pro rata basis.

indirect demand Demand that is occasioned by the demand for another product. There is, for example, an indirect demand for gasoline by builders of internal combustion engines. Also known as derived demand.

indirect labor Labor in a company not directly engaged in the manufacture of the company's product. The sales force of a company, for example, is not engaged in the manufacture of products.

indirect review The review of a company's product that comes either in the form of compliments or complaints from the users of a product.

indirect tax Sales taxes, excise taxes, luxury taxes, import duties, value added taxes (VATS) are all considered indirect taxes.

individual expectancy chart A graphic presentation of what may be expected of an individual following psychological testing as he moves into the workforce and begins to achieve degrees of success.

indkomstskat til staten In Denmark, a state income tax that is progressive and levied on total income, upon which is added a flat-rate dividend tax. There are also wealth taxes, church taxes, various local taxes, etc., in Denmark.

induction training An introductory training for new employees designed to acquaint them with a company, its products, and its goals.

inductive thinking A type of thinking that reasons about parts of a problem until the parts fall into place as the ultimate whole.

indulgence pattern A tolerant style of management.

Industria A monthly business and industry magazine established in 1905 and published in Sweden. Address: Fack, 104 25 Stockholm 22.

industrial action In the United Kingdom, any action on the part of employees designed to voice some grievance, which can result in slow downs, strikes, etc.

Industrial and Commercial Finance Corporation Ltd. (ICFC) An agency in the United Kingdom that provides long-term loan capital and share capital for small- and medium-sized businesses; these funds are not obtainable through conventional banking institutions. Address: Piercy House, 7 Copthall Avenue, London EC2R 7DD.

Industrial and Commercial Policy Division (DT) An agency in the United Kingdom that provides information to firms on monopolies, consumer protection, etc., Address: Industrial and Commercial Policy Division 3, Department of Trade, 1 Victoria Street, London SW1H OET.

Industrial Bankers' Association A confederation of banks and other financial institutions in the United Kingdom concerned with promoting high standards in industrial banking and small finance houses.

industrial democracy A general term denoting the increase of worker participation in decision making in the workplace.

Industrial Democracy Bill Legislation passed in the United Kingdom to try to guarantee more worker participation in companies.

industrial development certificates (IDCs) In the United Kingdom, a permit granted to a firm to accompany an application for planning permission to erect a building of a specified size. Not all areas of the UK require this certificate.

industrial engineer A type of engineer specifically schooled in production planning, methods study, and work management techniques.

industrial espionage The actions on the part of one company to illicitly obtain secrets of another company, either through "agents" or through "inside assistance" by an employee of the other firm.

Industrial Health and Safety Centre An agency of the Department of Employment in the United Kingdom that gives advice to companies on health and safety in industry. Address: 97 Horseferry Road, London, SW1.

Industrial Injuries Fund Established under the United Kingdom's National Insurance Acts of 1946, 1965, 1966, and 1967, this is the fund from which workers who suffer industrial injuries are paid.

Industrial Location Advisory Service (DI) A division of the Department of Industry in the United Kingdom charged with advising industry on the most favorable conditions for regional development or expansion.

industrial market research A branch of market research concerned with finding market potential for industrial goods.

industrial policy, common *See* common industrial policy.

industrial property rights *See* patent.

Industrial Relations Act, 1971 Legislation in the United Kingdom that came into being by stages from October 1971 to February 1972 and was designed to make collective bargaining more enforceable. This act was repealed in 1974 by the Trade Union and Labour Relations Act.

Industrial Revolution A historical period beginning in the middle of the eighteenth century when factories began to utilize more machinery, when specialization became common in the performance of work, and when more scientific methods were used in factory work.

Industrial Safety Advisory Council An agency of the Department of Employment in the United Kingdom that advises on all aspects of industrial safety. Address: Department of

Employment, St. James Square, London SW1.

Industrial Society A nongovernmental agency in the United Kingdom that was founded in 1918 as the Industrial Welfare Society. Its purpose is to provide to industry advice on personnel and welfare matters, organizing training courses, etc. Address: Robert Hyde House, 48 Bryanston Square, London WIH 8AH.

Industrial Training Act, 1964 A United Kingdom law with three main objectives: 1) to help assure an adequate labor force at all levels of industry, 2) to assure an improvement in the quality and efficiency of industrial training, and 3) to share the cost of training more equally among firms. This act was modified somewhat by the Employment and Training Act of 1973.

Industrial Training Service An independent, non-profit agency in the United Kingdom sponsored by the Department of Employment and the Training Services Agency to consult with industry and the Industrial Training Boards.

industrial union An organization that is open for all people engaged in work in a specific industry, regardless of differences in tasks performed.

industrialism and society The age of industry in the United States has separated people into two distinct groups: 1) those who manage other people and 2) those who are managed. Without considerable modification, this situation robs a great portion of working society from being creative and from receiving the satisfaction therefrom.

Industry Act, 1972 Law enacted in the

United Kingdom that provided for regional development through specific attention to Special Development Areas, the Development Areas, the International Areas, and Northern Ireland.

industry-based student Courses in the United Kingdom at the college or university level in which the student spends some time in classes and some time in the industrial work situation. (Similar to Cooperative Education in the United States.)

Industry Week A publication in the United States dealing with basic problems in economics and business. The journal was established in 1882. Address: Penton Publishing Company, Penton Plaza, Cleveland, Ohio 44114.

industry-wide agreement A union agreement covering all employees in one industry in which the union has the right to represent the workers.

inelastic demand 1. The quantities of a good demanded following a decrease or increase in price are less than are the changes in prices. In short, demand does not fluctuate much even when prices fluctuate. Example: Wheat bread decreases 10 percent in price, but the demand does not change at all. 2. A situation in which a percentage change in price results in a lesser percentage change in demand.

inferior good Products that people will buy fewer of as income increases. Example: Low priced, prepared food products may be almost ignored by a consumer once his income is sufficiently large to buy more attractive food.

inflation A condition of rising prices in an economy that may stem from one of two basic problems: 1) The supply of money is increasing faster than the supply of goods and services; there is, in other words, too much money chasing too few goods, which is called "demand pull" inflation. 2) The prices of basic resources—those resources going into production of goods and services—are increasing, and the increases must be built into the ultimate selling price; this is called "cost push" inflation.

inflation accounting Financial accounting that takes into consideration the increases in prices and the effects they may have on costs, revenues, and profits.

informal organization A type of organization that grows up where people are congregated together for a common purpose, but which bears no relationship to the formal structure of the organization.

infrastructure The vital foundation structure of a nation, such as roads, bridges, ports, airports, hospitals, housing, educational institutions, etc. These foundation institutions vitally affect the economy both directly and indirectly. For example, a poor transportation system may well impede the economy, while a sufficient system might encourage its growth. Some of the items in the infrastructure may well affect the economy for many years into the future.

inhibition Restraints imposed upon individuals by culture and local social mores.

injection Payments, in any form, entering the circular flow of income through the expenditures of governments.

Obviously, other injections are made by foreign buying (exports), consumer spending, and investment spending.

injunction An order from a court requiring that an individual or an organization either perform or not perform a specific action until further notice.

injury benefit Under National Insurance industrial injuries provisions in the United Kingdom, injury benefits may be made to an employee for up to 156 days when he or she is unable to work because of a disease or injury sustained on the job.

ink blot test *See* Rorschach Test.

inkomstenbelasting In the Netherlands, a progressive income tax levied on total net income, along with a flat-net-rate wealth tax on property.

Inland Revenue An agency of government in the United Kingdom charged with assessing and collecting income tax.

innovation The development and introduction into the market of new products or of new techniques in the production process.

innteksskatt til statskassen The state progressive income tax in Norway that is charged on a scale on total income from all sources.

inntektsskatt til kommunen A local income tax in Norway that is levied on total net income.

input question The vital economic question of what combination of inputs will be used to produce each product.

input, control of Input in production is the physical obtaining of the resources needed for production and is often controlled by space, but it is more often controlled by determining the quantity of the various inputs that are necessary on site at any given time.

input-output analysis A technique in market research for tracing the purchases and sales between industries.

INSEAD European Institute of Business Administration

insertion charge A payment to be made to a newspaper or periodical for carrying an advertisement or an insert.

insider trading Trading in the stock market, in their own company's stock, by top officials of a firm, including in some cases the board of directors. Sometimes these traders use inside information unknown by outsiders. This is patently illegal in the United States, but it happens at times anyway.

insolvency The inability on the part of an individual or a company to pay debts as they come due.

Institute for the Future (IFF) An American non-profit, tax-exempt research organization, founded in 1968 to develop comprehensive computer oriented systems and models to assist in forecasting and "controlling" the future. Address: Middletown, Connecticut.

Institute of Administrative Management (IAM) A professional body in the United Kingdom, formerly known as the Institute of Office Management. Address: 205 High Street, Beckenham BR3 1BA.

Institute of Chartered Accountants The major professional and qualifying body of accountants in the United

Kingdom. Address: Moorgate Place, London EC2.

Institute of Cost and Management Accountants A professional body of accountants, which has more than ten thousand members, which is concerned with developing management accounting practices in the United Kingdom. Address: 63 Portland Place, London WIN 4AB.

Institute of Directors An organization of company directors in the United Kingdom, numbering more than fifty thousand. Address: 10 Belgrave Square, London SWI.

Institute of Export An agency in the United Kingdom that provides export sales services and conducts specialized courses and examinations on exports, a major factor in the economy of the United Kingdom.

Institute of Freight Forwarders A professional group to provide advice on shipping and freight forwarding. Address: Suffield House, 9 Paradise Road, Richmond Surrey.

Institute of Linguists A professional body in the United Kingdom established in 1910. Among the services it provides is supplying the names of translators able to deal with business correspondence and commercial paper for firms doing business with foreign countries.

Institute of Management Consultants A professional body in the United Kingdom dealing with the problems of management consultants. Address: 23 Cromwell Place, London SW7.

Institute of Marketing A professional marketing organization and examining body in the United Kingdom. It offers sales and marketing courses at its College of Marketing. Address: Marketing House Cookham, Berkshire SL6 9QH.

Institute of Personnel Management This agency offers a wide range of services both to government and to private business and industry in the United Kingdom. Its monthly publications are *Personnel Management* and *Digest.* Address: Central House, Upper Woburn Place, London WC1H OHX.

Institute of Public Relations A professional organization for public relations officials in the United Kingdom. Address: 20 Lambs Conduit Street, London WC2.

institution 1. An establishment holding a marked degree of public concern in the culture in which it is expected to function. 2. A term used on the British stock exchange to denote large organizations with large holdings in various public companies, which, when they decide to buy or sell stock, can greatly influence the market.

institutional expectancy chart A graphic presentation sometimes used after the psychological testing of an individual or a group to attempt to predict how well the people tested may do on specific jobs.

instruction *law* Oral or written information related to a specific matter designed to aid the one receiving it to accomplish whatever it is he has been charged with.

Insurance and Companies Department, DT An agency in the United Kingdom that provides companies with company legislation and insurance other than export-credit insurance.

Address: Insurance and Companies Department, Department of Trade, Sanctuary Buildings, 16-20 Great Smith Street, London SW1P 3BT.

insurance broker One who arranges business contracts between insurance companies and individuals and between companies and organizations, acting as an agent for the insurance company.

intangible assets Items that may appear on a balance sheet that are not real (i.e., not visible or touchable), but which are listed on the balance sheet as having value; e.g., goodwill, etc.

integrated person One whose intuitive and rational capacities are both highly developed.

integration A term used in the Common Market countries to denote a leveling of differences in terms and conditions of employment for blue-collar and white-collar workers. (*See also* harmonization)

intellectual skills Denotes skills involving conceptual and rational processes as contrasted with manual skills.

Inter-African Labour Institute Established in 1953 as an information and research center on labor relations in Africa. Members represent some thirty countries. Address: BP2019, Bazzaville, Zaire.

Inter-American Development Bank (IDB) Established in 1953 to promote economic and social development in part through the provision of technical assistance. Original members include: Argentina, Barbados, Bolivia, Brazil, Chile, Colombia, Costa Rica, Dominica, Ecuador, El Salvador, Guatemala, Haiti, Honduras, Jamaica,

Mexico, Nicaragua, Panama, Paraguay, Peru, Trinidad and Tobago, the United States, Uruguay, and Venezuela. Address: 1300 New York Avenue, Washington, DC, 20577.

interactive skills The art of interacting with others in a group and making the group perform better through the development of social sensitivity in individuals.

interest test or inventory In personnel selection, such an evaluation is used to discover outside, off-the-job interests, which may relate to some area where the person might excel on the job.

interest yield The effective rate of interest that an investor receives on an investment. In the case of a bond, the effective yield is based on the face value of the bond, the coupon rate, the purchase price, the intervals between interest payments, and the length of time until maturity.

interface Equipment that links two parts of a computer system.

interfirm comparison A technique for comparing two or more companies in a number of different areas by collecting data on all of them and charting the data, or putting it into a computer, to make comparisons.

interlocking directorate A situation in which board members of one firm are also on the boards of other, sometimes competing, firms.

intermediate product Any product that is not in the "final use" stage, and which will be used as an input in further production.

internal audit An in-house audit that keeps management continually aware of the condition of the company.

internal rate of return (IRR) A return on a project or enterprise using the discounted cash-flow method. (*See also* actuarial return)

internal revenue The revenue a government generates within the confines of the country through various forms of taxation.

International Court of Justice Established at the Hague in April 1946 as the primary judicial body of the United Nations, this court serves as an international tribunal between nations.

International Finance Corporation (IFC) An agency of the United Nations that is connected to the World Bank and the International Development Association. The role of the IFC is to stimulate private investment and enterprise in the developing countries. Address: 1818 H Street, Washington, DC 20433.

International Management Council Address: 291 Broadway, New York, NY 10007.

intervention price The price at which the European Commission of the Common Market buys surpluses of cereals to help producers in the member states achieve target prices.

intrinsic value The inherent price of a resource before it has been acted upon by some manufacturing process.

introversion/extroversion One of the areas of concern in temperament and personality testing.

intuition The basic process of all human understanding which is composed of cultural experiences, inherent strengths and weaknesses, and a multiplicity of emotions.

investment In economics, a term denoting the spending of current income on stocks and on fixed capital.

investment appraisal The analysis of the return on an investment of money. However, such analyses can be made on any type of investment, including human resources, equipment, etc.

investment bank The selling agent for firms that want to market a new issue of securities. In very large issues, the primary agent may put a syndicate of investment banks together to conduct the sale. Sometimes the banks buy the issues and resell them; at other times, they simply act as agents. In the United Kingdom, such a bank is called an issuing house, or a merchant bank.

Investment Counsel Association of America This organization represents firms that invest client's funds for a fee. Address: 20 Exchange Place, New York, NY 10005.

investment in the economy Expenditures on new capital goods (goods used in the production of other goods), such as plants, machines, inventories, etc.

Investment multiplier *See* multiplier .

invisible exports Export of services, such as insurance, banking, tourism, shipping, etc.

invisible hand A concept propounded by Adam Smith in his book, *Wealth of Nations* (1776), which says that a businessman pursuing his own self interest will direct those activities in such a way as to benefit society in general. Example: The entrepreneur, opening a manufacturing plant, will end up hiring many people to work in the plant, thus benefitting society as a whole through employment.

IPO Initial Public Offering.

IQ Intelligence quotient. A measurement of intelligence expressed as a ratio of mental age to chronological age.

IR investor relations.

IRA Individual Retirement Account.

IRB Industrial Revenue Bond.

IRC Internal Revenue Code.

Irish Association of Chambers of Commerce Formed in 1923. Address: 7 Clare Street, Dublin 2.

IRR *See* Internal Rate of Return.

irregular (industrial) action short of a strike A term included in the Industrial Relations Act of 1971 in the United Kingdom.

irrevocable documentary acceptance credit A "letter of credit." In international trade, an importer will open credit with a bank in the country of the exporter to guarantee payment for the purchase of the imported product.

IRS Internal Revenue Service.

ISBN International Standard Book Number.

isocost curve A straight-line curve on a graph indicating different combinations of inputs having an equal cost. The curve is negatively sloped, and the slope represents the price ratio between the two inputs.

isoquant curve A negatively sloped curve showing equal quantities of output that could be produced using different combinations of the two inputs shown on the axes of a graph. Where the isocost curve is tangent to the isoquant curve, that indicates the least cost combination of these two inputs for producing the quantity of output indicated by the isoquant curve.

ISSN International Standard Serial Number.

issue by tender Tenders that are invited for shares in a company, with the shares often being sold to the highest bidder.

Istituto per la Ricostruzione Industriale The Italian state company, a government institution under which major parts of Italian industry have been nationalized.

ITC Investment Tax Credit.

ITS Intermarket Trading Service.

J

Jamaica Stock Exchange Limited *See* Section VII.

Japanese Central Bank *See* Section VII.

Japanese Stock Exchanges *See* Section VII.

jawboning Efforts of government to get labor and industry to do certain things without any law to force such action.

jerque note A document issued by a customs officer certifying that a ship's cargo is in order.

jet lag The mental and physical effects on a person who travels at high speeds through time zones.

job The sum of the tasks carried out by a person in the work situation, but, in a wider context, the social and physical environment in which he works.

job analysis A complete survey of the components of a specific job, often for the purpose of time motion studies. etc.

job-and-finish A job situation in which the worker is free to leave as soon as a certain amount of work has been completed (rarely used in United States).

job centres A new type of employment exchange in the United Kingdom, performing a variety of services for both employed and unemployed.

job clinic A technique used most often in sales training in which two or more people recount problems they encounter on their jobs, and together they try to find solutions.

job core A basic operation on a job upon which all other actions must rest.

job cover plan A method of assessing jobs in order to determine the training needs of workers.

job description A written document setting forth the various duties and responsibilities of a job.

job design The redesignating of the various activities of a job after a job analysis.

job dissatisfaction The feeling an employee has when his job does not give him a keen sense of personal achievement, particularly in an atmosphere where things to dislike are more prevalent than are things to like.

job engineering Changing the responsibilities, methods, and equipment of a job, which also changes the skill level needed to do the job.

job enrichment 1. Taking the necessary steps to make a job more satisfying to a worker. 2. The addition of psychological aspects to a job that give the employee a greater feeling of accomplishment.

job evaluation Assessing the worth of a specific job to the total job hierarchy.

job, extrinsic aspects of Factors revolving around the environmental setting of a job.

job factor comparison An analysis of the factors of a specific job as they relate to the same, or similar, factors in another job.

job, fractionated A situation in a job that does not give the worker opportunity to use all of his skills and talents.

job grading Stratifying jobs in the order of their importance to the firm and in terms of the skill level required in order to properly adjust pay scales.

job, ingredients of a good 1) direct feedback; 2) a client relationship; 3) a learning function; 4) the opportunity for each person to schedule his own work; 5) the use of unique expertise; 6) control over resources; 7) direct communication; 8) personal accountability. (Frederick Herzberg, *The Managerial Choice* [Homewood, Ill.: Dow Jones-Irwin, 1976], p.114.)

job, intrinsic aspects of The content of a job and the actual doing of a job.

job knowledge test An achievement test related to a specific job or skill.

job loading, horizontal Adding factors to a job to make it appear better, but which really add meaningless activities.

job loading, vertical The provision on the job of motivating factors.

job price contract A method of paying a predetermined price for a finished job, no matter how long it takes to complete it.

job production The making of a product to precise specifications as contrasted with batch production.

job requirements The attributes of a worker deemed necessary to perform a certain job.

job rotation A method of switching employees from job to job periodically, usually for one of these reasons: 1) to relieve the boredom of doing one job continuously, 2) to teach workers the requirements of a number of different jobs, and 3) to help train a manager who needs to be acquainted with many of the jobs he may supervise.

job satisfaction 1. Gaining from one's job personal growth and a feeling of personal worth. 2. The degree to which an employee is satisfied with the content of his job or is displeased with the same.

job security The extent to which an employee can be sure of the continuation of his job from year to year.

job specification A statement, based on job analysis, detailing the physical and mental requirements of a job.

job spoiler A term used to describe an individual in a work group who does not conform to the standards necessary to do the job well.

Johannesburg Stock Exchange *See* Section VII.

joint and last survivor annuity Income is payable throughout the lifetimes of two or more annuitants, continuing until the last survivor dies.

joint and last survivor income option Insurers pay the cash value or proceeds of a life insurance policy as income payable until the death of the last survivor of two persons.

joint life and last survivor pension A pension, often paid for by the employer, that provides for an employee and for the employee's spouse.

joint products Products that, when the quantity of one is increased, the quantity of another is automatically increased. Example: The production of T-bone steaks results in the production of more beef roasts and hamburger.

joint regulation The theory that management and labor can achieve a balance of power by agreeing jointly to certain aspects of the way a firm is run. Usually this is some type of agreement between a labor union and management. The theory is considered to be more plausible in theory than it is in practice.

joint tenancy with right of survivorship if one of the owners dies when two or more people own property in joint tenancy, interest in the property passes automatically (by operation of law) to the other joint owner(s).

journal *accounting* A book of original entry in double-entry bookkeeping. Also known as a day book.

journeyman A skilled tradesman who has finished his apprenticeship and is employed in that trade by an employer.

Junta Sindical A Spanish stock exchange committee composed of members of the exchange's stockholders' association, *Colegio de Agentes de Cambio y Bolsa.*

jurisdictional dispute A dispute between labor unions as to which union has control in a given situation.

K

Kaiser Plan A plan once adopted by the American Kaiser Steel Corporation and the Steelworkers Union to guarantee employees against possible loss of earnings or loss of employment due to changes in technology.

Kapitalertragsteuer The capital-yields tax on dividends and other distributions of company profits in Germany, Luxembourg, and Austria.

Karachi Stock Exchange Limited Pakistan's stock exchange, established in 1947.

Keller Plan In the United States, an instruction system or course structure developed in higher education. Stress is placed on the tutorial system and programming instruction for individual students. Students work on a self-paced basis. This system has been used primarily in engineering and science. Also known as Personalized System of Instruction (PSI).

Kelly repertory grid A method used in market-research interviews designed to determine informants' opinions on competing products and brand images. Three or more products are presented to the informants, and they are asked to select the product that is different from the others and to describe how it is different.

Kennedy round A particularly important meeting in the series of meetings held under the aegis of the General Agreement on Tariffs and Trade (GATT). The meeting resulted in general tariff reductions negotiated between members of GATT from 1964–67, on the initiative of former President John F. Kennedy. This round also produced a cereals agreement and an anti-dumping code. (*See also* General Agreement on Tariffs and Trade)

Kenya Stock Exchange *See* Section VII.

keyed advertisement One that is coded so that the response from each advertising vehicle can be tabulated. Example: If the ad is placed in several periodicals, each one will be assigned a code number, such as Dept. ABC. As the responses come in, the number of responses from each periodical will be known. (One will often see something like the following in an ad: "When responding to this ad, please include the department number.")

keyman An employee who is considered to be important to a specific project or to the running of a department, shift, etc.

Keynesian economics The macroeconomic theories propounded by John Maynard Keynes in the decade of the 1930s. Essentially, his theories were "demand side," since he focused his attention on the determinants of total spending. One view he brought to the United States in 1933 was that government should promote spending in times of recession through government sponsored programs which would increase aggregate demand.

Keynesian National Income and Spending Graph A graph showing national spending and income, the consumption function, and the effect of spending injections on the equilibrium level of the national income. Also known as the Keynesian Cross.

Keynesian-Monetarist debate, the The classic disagreement about macroeconomic theory and policy. Basically, Keynesians believe in fiscal actions (taxing, spending, and debt management) to try to achieve and maintain economic equilibrium. Monetarists, usually led by Nobel laureate Milton Friedman, take the position that equilibrium can best be achieved in the economy through the control of the money supply. Monetarists also tend to want to let the forces of the market work with as little government intervention as possible.

key points/factors Those important aspects in a job analysis that stand out as being vital to the completion of a task and are thus due special notice.

key ratios of total activities Many managers exercise control through the use of various ratios relating to the enterprise, such as sales to inventories, current assets to current liabilities, etc.

key task That specific duty in a multiplicity of job tasks that determines the success of the related tasks in the full completion of the job.

key task analysis An examination of important jobs to be performed in the operation of a total project, including levels of performance and methods of checking real results against standards. Such analysis is used in training supervisors and managers.

Key Workers Scheme A plan run by the Department of Employment in the United Kingdom to give assistance when an employer needs to transfer employees, either permanently or temporarily, to a new plant in a Special Development Area, a Development Area, or an Intermediate Area. Subsidy grants are usually made to the firm involved to move the employees and to get them started in the new locations.

KG *Kommanditgesellschaft.* A limited partnership under German company law.

KGaA *Kommanditgesellschaft auf Aktein.* (*See* German federal companies)

kibbutz A commune, usually agricultural, in Israel, occupied by men and women, young and old, and often by the children of families. The workers specialize, but, unless they are in a managerial position, usually all workers are treated the same. Some have become models of good management.

kickback A secret payment made to a person who is able to influence another person or a company to complete a business deal, which might not have been made otherwise. Often this is an unlawful action or at least an unethical practice.

kicked upstairs A colloquialism denoting a person who has been promoted to remove him from a job in which his inefficiencies have become intolerable. Tradition has it that this term was first used in the United Kingdom to denote a person who was moved up from the House of Commons to the House of Lords.

kinked demand curve A demand curve as seen by an oligopolist seller. (An oligopoly is a situation in the market in which there are few sellers of goods or services.) The kink is at the existing price. The kinked demand curve assumes that if the seller raises prices, other sellers in the oligopoly will not. But if the seller lowers prices, all other sellers will do the same. The curve is highly elastic for a price increase and inelastic for a price decrease.

kirkeskat A church tax levied in Denmark.

kirkollisvero A church tax in Finland levied on members of the Orthodox and Evangelical Lutheran churches at a flat rate. This is in addition to other types of income taxes.

kitchen cabinet A term apparently first used to describe the men close to President Andrew Jackson, who, it is believed, assisted him more in policy making than did the real cabinet. The term is now used to denote people who are close to the CEO, or another top-level manager, and advise him, even though they do not have official status.

"knee of the curve" That point on the production curve where the increments of output begin to decrease rapidly; the point of diminishing returns.

Knights of Labor A labor union that originated in Philadelphia about 1869 that was designed to include workers of all types. It was heavily populated by industrial workers. Women and blacks were included in the membership.

Some of the aims of the union were: an eight-hour work day, abolition of child and convict labor, and equal pay for equal work. It eventually became a nationwide organization with more than seven hundred thousand members. Due to poor management and some labor riots at the end of the century, the union was virtually extinct by 1900.

Kobe Stock Exchange One of nine Japanese stock exchanges.

Kobenhavns Fondsbors Copenhagen Stock Exchange. (*See* Section VII)

Kolbe Conative Index (KCI) A recent psychological test devised by Kathy Kolbe comprised of thirty-six multiple-choice questions designed to measure what a subject will or will not do.

Kollektivgesellschaft A general partnership under Swiss company law. Also known as *Société en Nom Collectif.*

Kommanditaktiengesellschaft A limited partnership under Swiss law. Also known as *Société en Commandite par Actions.*

Kommanditgesellschaft auf Aktein (KgaA) A limited partnership under German company law.

kommunal indkumstskat A local or county income tax in Denmark.

kommunal inkomstskatt A flat-rate local income tax in Sweden.

Konossement German bill of lading.

Korea Stock Exchange *See* Section VII.

KPRO *See* Kuder Preference Record.

krona The basic unit of currency in Sweden.

krone The basic unit of currency in Denmark and in Norway.

Kuala Lumpur Stock Exchange A stock exchange in Malaysia. (*See* Section VII)

Kuder Preference Record (KPRO) A test used in personnel selection that indicates interests of a prospective employee.

kunnallisvero Local income tax in Finland. It is paid in addition to other income taxes.

kupongskatt A flat-rate tax levied by the Swedish government and paid by Swedish companies on dividends paid to nonresidents and certain residents.

Kyoto Stock Exchange One of nine in Japan. (*See* Section IX)

L

labor One of the four "factors of production" that includes all human effort used in the production of goods and services. Human resources is the term most used currently.

Labor Day The first Monday in September, set aside to honor the workers in the United States and around the world. Celebrated on May 1 in much of the world.

labor force In a nation, the number of people in the total population who are either working or looking for work at any given point in time.

labor hoarding The retention on a company payroll of more workers than necessary for current production to guard against the possibility of needing them soon. (This has been done at times in the past as full employment was being approached, but Communistic countries are accused of labor hoarding consistently, along with retaining unnecessary inventories.)

Labor Market Board A public corporation financed by government revenue in Sweden that is responsible for implementing the government's manpower policy and its industrial training program.

labor market An economic theory that the size and the skill level of the labor force in the nation generally decides wage rates and other terms and conditions for labor. This notion is based on a pure law of demand and supply.

labor participation rate The percentage of the population that is included in the labor force.

labor relations The study of the interpersonal relationships of management and labor. Sometimes, more specifically, this term refers to the way that unions are seen by the unions or by government.

labor turnover The leaving of workers and the hiring of workers in a given period of time, usually stated as a percentage of the total number of workers employed in a plant. If the percentage is high, it can usually be assumed that there are serious problems with relationships within the plant.

labor unions, membership trends The membership in labor unions quadrupled from 1935, when the National Labor Relations Act was passed, and the end of World War II. Since that time the trend has generally gone down, with minor upturns occurring at times. In 1945, the membership was 35.5 percent of the labor force, and this figure dropped to 16.8 percent by 1988. The trend downward has been continuous for fifteen years. This trend reversal can probably be attributed to two factors: 1) the continuing problem of fraudulent activities on the part of union leaders and 2) more enlightened management has been more willing to share with labor the fruits of production.

labor, division of The dividing up of the various facets of an operation in production so that each employee can specialize in, and become proficient at, a particular task, which will usually result in greater efficiency.

labor, free movement of *See* Section IV.

labor-intensive firm One where more labor is used in the production process and there is less capital investment, usually because this is the lowest-cost way of producing.

Labor-Management Relations Act (1947) In its Title I, it rewrote the Wagner Act to restrain excesses of labor, as the Wagner Act had opened the door for freer labor activities. One specific provision, the so-called "right to work," was widely hailed by management and widely hated by labor and gave to the various states the right to have or to refuse to have the "closed shop"; i.e., a situation in which no person can work in a union establishment without becoming a member of the union.

Labor-Management Reporting and Disclosure Act (1959) By this time in the history of the labor movement, labor had become, at the top, both powerful and corrupt. This act was aimed at eliminating or preventing improper practices on the part of labor organizations, employers, labor relations consultants, and their officers and representatives that tended to distort and defeat the intents of the Labor-Management Relations Act of 1947.

labor-only subcontracting A contractor, particularly in the construction industry, who furnishes all materials but obtains labor by subcontracting it to someone else.

Laffer curve A curve that illustrates the relationship between tax rates and revenues collected. It shows, graphically, the assumption that higher tax rates discourage productivity and encourage people to use tax loopholes, so that beyond some point, the higher rates will produce lower revenues. A concept developed by Arthur Laffer.

LAFTA *See* Latin American Free Trade Association.

Lagos Stock Exchange *See* Section VII.

lags A term denoting the required "response time" following some economic policy change. Example: Raising the discount rate by the Fed can help control inflation, but the desired result does not happen immediately.

laissez faire Literally, "let things alone." A French term denoting no intervention of government in the economy.

laissez-faire economy An economy in which the market forces are allowed to work without intervention. This is a concept that has never been worked out in any nation in a practical way. There is always and always has been, to one degree or another, the intervention of government.

lame duck In the United Kingdom, a term used in two ways, one denoting a defaulter who has been thrown out of the stock exchange, and the other denoting an industrial enterprise about ready for bankruptcy.

land bank In the United Kingdom, a lending institution that makes long-term loans on residential housing. (roughly equivalent to S & L's in the United States).

land office A term denoting a government office in the United States that records sales or transfers of public land. Few of these offices still remain.

land-grant The Morrill Act of 1862 in the United States allowed the federal government to make grants of land to state colleges that offered courses in agriculture and mechanical engineering.

land One of the four factors of production, the term includes actual land and those so-called "free gifts of nature" that come from the land.

language laboratory Technical laboratories used by schools at all levels to teach various languages and to correct pronunciation by using standardized tapes and listening to one's own efforts. Foreign languages are taught using this method quite often.

lateral integration *See* horizontal integration.

Latin American Free Trade Association Formed by the Montevideo Treaty (Uruguay) in 1960, the founding members were Argentina, Brazil, Colombia, Chile, Ecuador, Mexico, Paraguay, Peru, Uruguay, Venezuela and Bolivia. Different countries signed at different times. Bolivia was the last signer in 1967. The general notion behind LAFTA was to form a free-trade area, but this was impeded by the great variation of economies in the group. As of 1974, only 6 percent of the trade done by these nations was conducted under the provisions of the original treaty. In 1980, LAFTA gave way to the Latin American Integration Association. The two principal vehicles of LAIA are negotiated partial agreements and regional tariff preferences. (Prolific information about Latin American trade is contained in the Inter-American Development Bank's publication, *Economic and Social Progress in Latin America,* 1984.)

Latin square design A term in market research denoting a scheme that measures the effect on sales of a number of different factors at one time. The results pertaining to each factor are then plotted, giving a graphic of the results that is easily read.

lattice work organizational patterns Grid or matrix departmentation.

Lausanne Stock Exchange One of eight Swiss stock exchanges. (*See* Section VII)

law merchant In past times, this term denoted commercial and trade regulations based on merchants' customs.

Law of 20/80 There is a normal and natural maldistribution among possible causes or focal points of trouble and the dispersion of effects of the trouble. This "rule of the vital few and the trivial many" among the causes of specific results. For example: 1) 80 percent of the complaints come from 20 percent of the customers; 2) 80 percent of the quality errors are made by 20 percent of the operators; 3) 80 percent of the grievances are filed by 20 percent of the employees; 4) 80 percent of the orders come from 20 percent of the customers; 5) 80 percent of the scrap is caused by 20 percent of the operators (machines); 6) 80 percent of the downtime occurs on 20 percent of the machines. In any situation where past results point to a management problem, the opportunity for improvement lies in concentrating effort on the vital 20 percent of the factors concerned. (George S. Odiorne, *MBO II* [Belmont, Calif.: David S. Lake, Pubs., Inc., 1979], pp. 160–61.)

law of demand The economic principle that people will buy less of a good when the price is high and more of a good when the price is low.

law of effect A theory of learning and motivation originally propounded by E. L. Thorndike. It essentially states that when various responses are made to the same situation, those which are accompanied by or closely followed by satisfaction will, other things being equal, be more closely related to the situation, so that when the situation recurs, the responses will be likely to recur. When a response is accompanied by discomfort, its relationships with the situation will be weakened, and is less likely to recur. In short, the greater the satisfaction the greater is the strengthening of the bond between a situation and the responses to the situation.

law of the situation A concept developed by Mary Parker Follett stating that solutions resulting from conflict situations should be dictated by the logic of the facts of the situation and not by the exercise of superior power by either party. Further, Follett believed that problems of organization

or management should be solved in the light of situational demands, rather than in terms of universal principles or laws. (*See* Section IX)

laws, approximation of *See* approximation of laws.

lay day A day that a ship is allowed to stay in port without paying fees.

LC Library of Congress.

L/C Letter of credit.

LDC's Less developed countries. Countries in which the per capita income is low. Afghanistan, for example, has a per-capita income of about 220 dollars. (There is no strict rule about what level of per-capita income would indicate an LDC.)

Lda An abbreviation for *Sociedade anonima de responsabilidade limitada,* a joint-stock company under the laws of Portugal.

lead time That period of time that is used in the completion of a job.

leader An integrated person whose intuitive and rational capacities are both highly developed, and one who is able to communicate such powers to others not for self-aggrandizement but for the good of the total organization.

leader and publicity The leader operates in an arena of public inspection, and it is most difficult to hide either his strengths or his weaknesses. The leader must be able to handle this situation, if he is to be successful.

leader, effectiveness of, In studies done by Fielder, three dimensions were used to measure the leader's effectiveness: 1) the degree of confidence his followers have in him, 2) the degree to which the followers' jobs are routine or are ill-structured, and 3) the degree of power inherent in the leader's position.

leader, role of A leader achieves a role by inheritance, through personal power, through appointment by peers, by being elected by peers, or by being recognized by subordinates.

leadership 1. The action of getting a specific project finished with the help of the team and satisfying the task needs, the group maintenance needs, and the needs of the individuals in the group. 2. Simplistically, leadership is the relationship in which one person, the leader, influences others to work together efficiently on related tasks to attain what the leader, or the body that appointed him, desires. 3. *psychology* The theory that the primary role of the leader is to develop the best possible motivation system. 4. *sociology* The view that leadership is made up of work efforts that facilitate the activities of followers and strive to reconcile any organizational conflicts between followers.

leadership, bureaucratic A self-perpetuating type of authoritarian leadership that impedes innovation and discourages creativity.

leadership, employee-centered A type of leadership that recognizes the value of human resources (employees) and seeks to include them in the phases of the tasks in which they are best prepared to be of assistance.

leadership, fundamentals of Usually some adaptation of these five points are considered fundamental: 1) recognizing the complex relationship concept; 2) recognition that the leader's role, and the degree to which it is accepted by employees, conditions leadership; 3)

recognizing that the degree to which jobs are described in detail plays a significant role; 4) recognizing that the leader has the power to decide what actions will best accomplish the goals of the group; 5) recognizing that leadership style and the situation in which the leading takes place affect the results obtained.

leadership, spiritual qualities of Those qualities of the leader that put much emphasis upon the importance of the individual in the organization and upon his being able to "self-actualize" within the organization. Such a leader is not, per se, an "easy" leader, but is one who accepts difficult challenges in the belief that they provide the best fields of action for himself and those people whom he attempts to lead.

leaders, obsessional Persons in positions of leadership who use in their public performances the mechanisms of defense that originate in their private conflicts, such as hyper-rationality, the isolation of thought and feeling, etc.

leaders, personality types The two types are referred to as the "once-born," who is a person at home with himself and his ideas, and the "twice-born," for whom the sense of self derives from a profound feeling of separateness.

leakages Withdrawals from the income spending flow. These can be in the form of savings, taxes, etc.

leap-frogging A situation in which a pay increase to some employees, or to some department, in a plant will soon result in demands for increases by other employees.

learning curve Also known as "a skill-acquisition curve," this graphically depicts the progress of a trainee.

learning plateau A flattened area on the learning curve that indicates that the trainee has reached a point where he needs greater challenges, or where he is in a period of assimilating what has already been presented to him.

learning resource center A central depository where all types of learning materials (books, tapes, graphs, etc.) are available for those who wish to use them.

learning, critical period of Those early years in an organization when a young employee can be deeply influenced by the organization's leaders and concepts.

learning, peer training The concept that peers learn from each other, particularly in group situations where there is a free exchange of ideas. Some experts dispute this concept with the claim that most learning is gained by a lower group, or person, from a higher group, or person.

least-squares A statistical method developed by Legendre, a French mathematician, that states that a trend best fits a given set of values when the constants of the equation are chosen so that the sum of the squares of the deviations between the original data and the corresponding trend values are at a minimum, and that the data can be used to predict the future based on the past.

ledger account A summary of all financial transactions with a customer. At this point in time, most accounts are kept on computer rather than written in a ledger.

Leeds Stock Exchange One of a number of provincial stock exchanges in the United Kingdom.

legal factor The laws under which a business must operate, with which the leader must deal.

legal reserve Monies that financial institutions and quasi-financial institutions, such as insurance companies, must keep on reserve as a security in the conduct of their business.

legal tender 1. Any type of money that a government decrees must be accepted in the payment of debts. 2. Currency approved by a central government that must be accepted as payment of debts.

legitimate power The power that is derived from the leader's position in the organization.

lender of last resort One function of a central bank wherein it lends money to the banking system of its country, which will influence both interest rates and the money supply.

letter of credit A document issued by a financial institution guaranteeing that a borrower can draw on it to satisfy a specific debt. Example: A foreign buyer establishes a letter of credit with a bank in the country of export origin to guarantee the seller that the debt will be promptly discharged.

letters of administration A legal document issued by a probate court instructing the court-appointed administrator to proceed with the settling of the estate of a deceased person.

letter(s) of marque A document granted by a government to an individual authorizing the seizure of goods or of citizens of another nation, or an authorization to arm a ship to attack enemy ships.

leverage The use of borrowed money to attempt to make more money. Known as "gearing" in the United Kingdom.

liability Any form of debt owed to others. Usually, current liabilities are short-term debts to be repaid within twelve months. Long-term liabilities can run from one year to forty years. Secured liabilities have assets of the firm backing them to ensure the payment of the debt.

liaison role of manager The role of meeting with and communicating with various groups in an organization, both subordinates and superiors.

liberal studies Studies introduced into a degree program, often as a "minor," that tend to broaden the knowledge of the student.

libido In psychology, the constructive drive in man that is the source of feelings of love, creativity, and psychological growth.

Library of Congress (LC) The official library of the United States, founded in Washington, D.C., in 1830.

Liege Stock Exchange *Bourse de Fonds Publics de Liege.* A provincial Belgium stock exchange.

lieu days Days taken as holidays in the United Kingdom when overtime pay is not forthcoming.

LIFO *accounting* last in, first out. A method of costing that assumes that whenever an item is sold, it should be costed as though it were the last one purchased. (*See* FIFO)

Lille Stock Exchange *Bourse des Valeurs de Lille.*

Lima Stock Exchange *Bolsa de commercio de Lima.* Peru's stock exchange. (*See* Section VII)

limited liability A term often used, but not exclusively, to denote the fact that stockholders in a corporation are liable only to the extent of the worth of their holdings in the company. Shareholders are not held liable for any debt of the company beyond their own holdings, in the event of a liquidation.

Limited Liability Act of 1855 The first legislation in the United Kingdom to limit the liability of a shareholder in a stock company to the amount of stock owned. This act, and others to follow, naturally stimulated the growth of stock companies everywhere.

Lincoln Incentive Management Plan, The Established in 1934 by James F. Lincoln in the Lincoln Electric Company, Cleveland, Ohio, which produced welding equipment and supplies. It is primarily a combination of a profit-sharing and incentive plan. It rewarded suggestions that would make work easier and more efficient. It is possible, under the Lincoln Plan, for a worker to receive bonuses at the end of the work year larger than his wages, and these wages were much better than the average at the time. The plan has been copied over the years, in whole or in part, by many other companies.

linear program A type of programmed instruction in which a series of frames, or steps, are presented to the student in a progression in terms of difficulty that would most likely fit the average student in a specific population.

linear programming A technique of mathematical programming established by George Dantzig and his associates in 1947. Programming, in this sense, means to plan for the best use of scarce resources in situations in which there are many alternative uses for them and therefore more than one possible solution to management problems. Obviously, the necessity of choosing between alternatives is not new, but Dantzig stated the problem in mathematical terms and developed a systematic method of solution that was named the "simplex method." The building of a linear programming model of a management decision-making problem involves the following: 1) a definition of the operating area in which choices can be made and identification of all the alternatives available; 2) quantifying the economic and physical consequences of choices; 3) quantifying external, uncontrollable circumstances that restrict the scope of choice; and 4) quantifying the criteria for evaluating alternative choices; that is, defining the criteria for optimal success.

Linear Responsibility Charting (LRC) A graphic method of analyzing and recording: 1) organizational structure, job content, and functional operating responsibilities, and 2) a procedure and the distribution of responsibilities for this procedure, which usually crosses a number of departments. This technique was introduced to the United States in the early 1950s by Serge A. Birn Company. It is an outgrowth of an earlier and more complex technique developed by a Netherlands consultant, Ernst Hijmans, which was called the Hijmans Chart.

linear thought processes The systematic, sequential processes that must be used by a manager in the planning process.

Line of Balance (LOB) A technique devised by a group headed by George E. Fouch in 1941 to monitor production at the Goodyear Tire and Rubber Company at the beginning of that company's war efforts. In essence, LOB is a management control procedure for collecting, measuring, and presenting facts relating to time cost and accomplishment, all measured against a specific plan. LBO is a graphic device; it reveals the progress, status, background timing, and phasing of intra-project activities, giving management the means to: 1) compare actual progress with projected performance; 2) examine only the deviations from established plans and gauge their degree of variance with respect to the remainder of the project; 3) receive timely information related to trouble areas and indicate areas where appropriate corrective action is required; 4) forecast future performance.

line-of-balance technique A method of scheduling that graphically displays the progress of a project, or it displays a stage in manufacturing comparing what is actually happening with what was supposed to happen at a specific point of time.

line of credit A privilege usually extended to a company to enable the company to draw on a specified credit limit over a period of time, usually, one year. In most such accounts, the recipient is supposed to "clear up," or balance, the account at least once a year.

line-staff relationship A line organization is one that is actually doing the work that is primary in the total mission of the company. A staff organization unit is any unit that is helping the line do its work or making it possible for the work to be done, but is not actually engaged in the production work per se.

linking pins A concept developed by Rensis Likert that describes the organization of most firms, universities, and institutions as a series of "linking pins" in which the leader of a lower group is also a member of the next highest group.

Lipsey Equation Developed by R. G. Lipsey in the United Kingdom in about 1960, this mathematical technique was designed to relate money wages to the level of employment, but also taking into account changes in retail prices over a past year. It resembles the Phillips Curve. (*See also* Phillips Curve)

liquid assets Cash or investment vehicles that can be readily turned into cash.

liquidation A legal action by order of a court of law in which a business is required to close down, liquidate assets, and pay off creditors.

liquid ratio The ratio of current assets minus stocks to current liabilities. (*See also* acid test ratio)

liquidity 1. The degree to which an individual or a company can convert assets into cash without loss of principal. 2. Sometimes used to denote the ability of an individual or a business to meet financial obligations when such obligations are due.

liquidity preference The desire on the part of an individual or a firm to hold cash rather than to hold investments, which might be difficult to convert to cash.

liquidity ratio *See* cash ratio.

lira Basic unit of Italian currency.

Lisbon Stock Exchange *Bolsa de Valores Lisboa.* (See Section VII)

list building The process of creating mailing lists for direct-mail selling. Lists can be compiled from many sources, or they may be purchased from companies that compile them.

list renting The renting for a one-time use of a list of names, usually from a firm doing business in various listings.

Liverpool Cotton Exchange A United Kingdom provincial exchange.

Lloyd's, Corporation of (Lloyd's of London) A worldwide insurance representative, known for its purported ability to insure almost anything. Lloyd's, however, does not insure anything itself, but conducts its business through syndicates of Lloyd's Brokers and Underwriters. This now-famous business had its beginning in a London coffeehouse in the late seventeenth century. The first, and still primary, interest was in marine insurance. This company probably has more information about maritime shipping, including specifics on literally every vessel afloat, than any organization in the world.

Lloyd's Register A comprehensive record of all oceangoing ships throughout the world, kept in London by Lloyd's.

LMT Local mean time.

loaned capital In the United Kingdom, capital invested in a company that constitutes a debt on the company books and that receives a stated rate of interest paid periodically. It is often represented by bonds issued by the company or by a mortgage on company assets.

loaned employee A term not often used in the United States, but denoting an employee who has been sent to work by one company to another for a period of time. This often takes place in highly technical fields.

loan shark A person who, working alone or representing an organization, makes loans at exorbitant rates of interest, often at illegal rates. Organized crime makes this a fertile field of operations.

Local Enterprise Development Unit An agency in Northern Ireland that provides technical and marketing advice for small firms, usually those with fifty employees or fewer. There is a specific emphasis on those firms with export potential. Address: Chichester House, 64 Chichester Street, Belfast, BT1 4JX.

localization A term used by LCD's that denotes the replacement of expatriate (foreign) workers with native workers.

localization of function The concept that each separate part of the brain is concerned with one single psychological function.

local option A law giving communities the right to decide certain issues on a local basis without appeal to a higher level of government.

lock-out A situation in which the management of a plant will shut the doors of the plant and prevent the workers from coming in. It usually occurs when there are unsettled labor problems.

logic Theory dealing with the procedures of valid thought and with the ways of demonstrating the accuracy of thought processes.

Lohnsteuer A wages tax in Germany and Austria, which, along with the capital gains tax, generally comprises the income tax.

Lombard Street A street in London originally named for the money changers and bankers who came over from Lombardy, but it is now known as the financial street of London, much as Wall Street is in New York.

London Fruit and Wool Exchange A specialist commodity exchange. Address: Brushfield Street, London E1.

London Metal Exchange A specialist commodity exchange dealing in copper, tin, lead, zinc, etc. Address: Whittington Avenue, London EC3.

London Stock Exchange *See* Section VII.

long run A period of time long enough to make all factors of production variable so that all of the adjustments required to achieve "long-term equilibrium" can be made.

long-run equilibrium The hypothetical "model condition" in a market (or an entire industry) in which all adjustments to demand and cost conditions have been made, all excess profits (or losses) have been eliminated, and there are no existing conditions in the market (or the industry) that would induce any further change to occur.

long-service death benefit A type of

group life insurance where the death benefit is related to the length of service of the employee.

long-term liabilities Those that will usually not have to be discharged for at least three years.

longitudinal method The studies by tests, measures, and observations of the responses of the same individual over time.

loneliness of workers The tendency, in Western countries, to look upon an employee as a part-time human resource and as only one part of a system in which there is little room for individuality. This attitude often results in making the employee feel isolated and lonely.

looking-glass self The concept of the self that is developed through observations of the responses of other persons to oneself.

Loop The central business district of Chicago.

Lorenz curve A curve depicting the percentage of total income that is being received by each of the various income groups in a society.

loss leader A product, often sold for a period of time at less than cost, to entice customers into a store, where presumably they will make other purchases as well.

loss ratio *Insurance* A term for the ratio between the total of the premiums paid the insurance company and the total value of the claims settled by the company in a year.

lot tolerance percent defective (LTPD) The point in statistical quality control where it is decided how many items in a lot should be inspected to determine if the entire lot should be accepted or rejected.

love In interpersonal relationships, a force that neutralizes aggression and impedes hostility.

love, need for In all areas of life, there is need for esteem and belongingness, which are aspects of love. Since people spend about 35 percent of their lives in some work situation, it seems probable that love needs must be satisfied there as well as at home and in society generally.

loyalty, unit Employees tend to give their primary loyalty to the smallest unit of which they are a part, instead of to the entire organization.

Ltda An abbreviation of *Sociedade anonima de responsabilidade limitada,* a joint-stock company under the laws of Portugal.

lump labor Labor, particularly in construction, in the United Kingdom that is paid a lump sum daily. Such workers are regarded as independent contractors.

lump-sum death benefit Payment to the dependents of a deceased employee, in one lump sum as opposed to monthly or annual payments. Such payments are normally tax free.

Lutine bell A ship's bell, originally taken off the vessel *Lutine,* which went down in the North Sea in 1799. Now used at Lloyd's of London to signal news of importance, two rings for good news, and one for bad news.

Luxembourg Declaration of 1965 A declaration of former President de

Gaulle of France that France held the right to veto any Common Market decision made by the Council of Ministers that affected the vital interests of France. This was considered to be contrary to the provisions of the 1957 Treaty of Rome, and was declared to be illegal. However, the power of veto has continued informally and was re-affirmed by Heath and Pompidou in 1971.

Luxembourg income tax *impot sur le revenu or Einkommensteuer* Composed of the following: 1) A tax assessed on total income; 2) A graduated withholding tax on wages, salaries, and pensions; 3) A flat-rate capital gains tax on dividends, etc.; 4) A flat-rate tax deducted at source from specified income of nonresidents.

Luxembourg Stock Exchange *Bourse de Luxembourg.* (*See* Section VII)

Lyon Stock Exchange *Bourse des Valeurs de Lyon.* (*See* Section VII)

(m) In the United Kingdom, coding for mechanical comprehension tests in the engineering apprentice test battery of the National Institute of Industrial Psychology.

M1 The money supply of the nation described as the total dollar amount of currency in circulation, plus demand deposits in commercial banks, savings and loans, credit unions, savings banks, and all outstanding traveler's checks.

M2 The money supply of the nation described as M1, in addition to money-market funds, savings deposits, and a few other highly liquid assets.

M3 The money supply of the nation described as M2, in addition to large-denomination time deposits, such as certificates of deposit (CD's) and a few other liquid assets.

Maatschap A civil partnership under law in the Netherlands.

Machiavellian A belief that disowns any moral or ethical standards and holds that the end justifies the means, however ruthless. Machiavelli was an early sixteenth-century Italian political leader and theorist.

machine ancillary time Production time lost by a machine when it is being set-up, cleaned, or otherwise prepared for continued efficient production.

machine down time Production time lost by a machine do to its breakdown or due to scheduled maintenance.

machine-hour rate For costing purposes, the rate at which a machine is charged for production.

machine idle time Production time lost due to lack of materials, etc., even though a machine is operating properly.

machine investments, return on What a company may expect in terms of annual percentage return on an investment in a machine. This is obviously an indirect return, depending upon the depreciation schedule, the annual hours the machine works, and maintenance costs, etc. In an indirect way, a machine should earn for a company at least as much if the same amount of money had been put into a security of some type. Also, many machines still are operative after having been depreciated out.

MacQuarrie test for mechanical ability A psychological test originating in the United States. While it chiefly deals with mechanical comprehension, it also tests elements of spatial ability and psychomotor skills.

macro Prefix from the Greek meaning large.

macrocosm The universe, or society, at large.

macroeconomic policy Government policies designed to try to achieve economic equilibrium—relatively full employment, stable prices, reasonable economic growth—through the combined use of monetary and fiscal policies. Macro (meaning large) refers to the "national look" at the economic picture as contrasted to micro (small) view of an individual industry or business.

macroeconomics The large-scale study of the rates of flow in the economy (income, employment, output, consumer spending, investment spending, etc.) and of the factors that influence the flow of these rates.

Madison Avenue The street synonymous with advertising in the United States.

Madras Stock Exchange One of seven Indian stock exchanges. (*See* Section VII)

Madrid Stock Exchange *Bolsa de Commercio de Madrid.* (*See* Section VII)

magnetic ink character recognition (MICR) A type of character recognition system, often used on documents such as bank checks, to feed specific

and prerecorded data into a computer. (The ink on the input devices is impregnated with magnetized particles, and the letters are then read by the head of the computer.)

magnetic memory or store Computer data storage devices that operate electromagnetically. Common forms are magnetic core storage, disks, and tapes.

Magyr Nemzeti Bank National Bank of Hungary, established in 1924. (*See* Section VII)

maieutics The method of instruction used by Socrates, who believed that learning is actually a matter of reviving memories.

main question In a formal meeting, run according to *Robert's Rules of Order,* the original motion (main question) must be debated and decided upon before another main question comes to the floor. If amendments are made to the main question, they can be considered. Also, a substitute motion on the same general topic can be made and considered. If it passes, the original motion must still be acted upon, but the conclusion is foregone after passage of the substitute motion.

maintenance factors *See* Herzberg's theory, Section IX.

make-work practices A practice unions sometimes are accused of, namely, following restrictive work practices to make a job last longer.

make-work Busy work. Work that occupies the time of employees after a job has been finished, or when there is no other productive work to do, to allow them to get in their allotted number of hours.

Makler A stockbroker on a German stock exchange.

Maklerkammer The Association of German stockholders.

maladroit Clumsy.

malaise A vague but general feeling of weakness, illness, or discomfort.

Malaysia Stock Exchange *See* Section VII.

malingerer One who pretends to be ill or weak in order to gain a personal advantage.

malorganizations, symptoms of Organizations that are not well adjusted in their industry, and often reveal ill-defined goals, unneeded layers of management, and a failing market structure.

Malthusian problem The theory of the Englishman, Thomas R. Malthus (*An Essay on the Principle of Population,* 1798), that population would tend to grow more rapidly than our ability to produce food, thus bringing the world to the ultimate point of starvation. Malthus believed that the population would tend to grow geometrically, while the production of food would grow arithmetically.

man-profile A statement containing the attributes required of a person under consideration for a position. Usually a job description will already exist and will serve as a guide to determine the attributes necessary for a position.

managed change technique (MCT) An approach developed by Westinghouse Electric Corporation in the United States concerned with getting the involvement of both management and workers in implementing the changes needed in a company. The plan involves considering all proposals for changes, analyzing them thoroughly,

and then devising the means to get them properly implemented in the company.

managed costs Those costs of a project, or for a budgeted period—such as one year—over which management has some control. While many costs are fixed and will not vary much, other costs give management room to make discretionary decisions (not the same as variable costs).

managed currency A term, not often used, denoting a situation in a nation that is not on a gold standard and thus has its money managed by a central bank or by some agency of government. In this situation, the currency is usually fiat money, which can lose purchasing power quickly if the economy does not remain stable.

management 1. Management is a specialized process consisting of planning, organizing, actuating, and controlling, and it is designed to achieve goals through the use of people and other resources. 2. Generally, those people responsible for directing the affairs of a company.

management accounting A branch of accounting designed to provide management with periodic financial reports on the company to assist managers in making ongoing decisions. Such reports usually are not for public view but for the exclusive use of management.

management, art of Management is considered an art, at least in once sense, since it includes the application of certain known skills to produce desired results.

management audit An ongoing systematic appraisal of all management personnel of a company, related to training, personal development, salary status, potential for future growth, and virtually every other facet of a manager's personal and professional life. Often such appraisals are done by objective, outside agencies, though they can be done in house when human resources are present and able to be totally objective. (Such an ongoing appraisal is desirable for a growing company, in which human resource plans should be at least as long term as the other plans the company has.)

management board *Vorstand.* One section of the two-tier structure of corporate boards in Germany. There is usually a supervisory board (*Aufsichtsrat*), which would probably be equivalent to a board of directors in the United States. The management board, appointed by the supervisory board, runs the everyday operations of the business and usually includes representatives from blue-collar workers. (The European Commission, a leading body of the European Community, has looked upon this structure with favor, thus it may become widespread in Western Europe.)

management by correction A type of management that is able to adjust to the times and make whatever adjustments are necessary in the workplace to keep employees motivated and reasonably happy.

management by crisis An unstructured form of management that uses hastily thought-up programs to meet unexpected events in the company as they arise. This is a weak and dangerous form of management. Unfortunately, more of it is done than is wise for business firms.

management by custom school A

school of management thought that emphasizes the study of past management people of stature and often bases current decisions on those practices that worked in the past. While such an outlook is to be commended and can surely help any manager, the rapidly changing times probably demand more of the manager.

management by exception A somewhat generalized type of management wherein employees carry out the everyday operations and seek management help only when an exceptional situation arises where higher authority may be needed.

management by mission It incorporates participative management or any other approach that will achieve desired results. Also known as Management by Objectives and results management.

Management by Objectives (MBO) A type of management that assigns goal performances to every level of management so that both they and their superiors have an objective and quantifiable way of evaluating those performances.

management by process school A prominent school of thought, led by George Terry, wherein management is looked upon as a process in which the following facets are emphasized: 1) visualizing and determining all of the proposed managerial actions; 2) the effectual utilization of people working in groups; 3) assisting people to be satisfied on the job and becoming members of a satisfied group; 4) making periodic checkups to be sure that the goals are being achieved.

management, characteristics of The following may be considered characteristics of management, though they may be added to or amended: 1) management is activity with a purpose; 2) management makes things happen; 3) management accomplishes goals through the use of people and other resources; 4) management requires the application of knowledge, gained skills, practice, and vision; 5) management is always active; 6) technology, particularly computers, enhances management but cannot replace the human aspects of it; 7) management is always associated with groups of people and additional resources; 8) management, in a measure, is intangible.

management development An ongoing plan for the development of management personnel. Two facets of this plan should be: 1) the development among blue-collar personnel of those who have management potential and 2) the further development of those already in management positions in order to fill those higher positions that will ultimately be open. Such training should be consistent, not hit-or-miss, and be planned as carefully as production is planned.

management discretion Those areas in which a manager uses personal judgment and has freedom to make changes.

management failure of America The recent years of economic decline in the United States have often been attributed to the machinations of OPEC, the unfairness of Japanese competition, or a host of other things. The truth is, none of these culprits can account for the United States' decline in productivity, its declining product quality, and the continually rising prices. In its failure to see the changing times and make solid plans to deal

with them, bad management must eventually be singled out as the culprit.

management game A type of business game used in many colleges and universities that simulates real-life situations and tests the student's ability to make proper decisions.

management information systems (MIS) Systems, usually computerized, that supply the manager with many facts deemed necessary for proper decision making.

management prerogative A traditional system in which complete authority is exercised by management, unless qualified by government regulations, union contract provisions, etc.

management ratios Normally refers to ratios that relate management costs and activities to more direct costs related to the production of the company's products or services. These ratios can both keep management informed about every aspect of the business and can also reveal the contributions of management and the cost of management, as contrasted with the direct costs of the firm.

Management Review A publication of the American Management Association in the United States.

management styles Broadly broken down into two categories, authoritarian and democratic. Some modification of these two categories marks the management style of most managers.

management succession The vital function of planning for the filling of management positions when they are vacated by retirement or job-changing. The development of succession should be another ongoing concern for any successful company.

Management Today A monthly publication of the British Institute of Management.

management threshold That period in the development of a non-management employee when he is about ready to step into lower-management ranks.

management trade union A union whose members are white-collar personnel as contrasted with the traditional blue-collar unions. This concept is growing modestly, as blue-collar unionism decreases.

managers and "pseudo-professionalism" The advance of financial people into top corporate posts in recent years has left technological expertise an unrecognized force in industry. Thus, many "professionals" in corporations really know little about the business, per se. This "pseudo-professionalism" has dealt harshly with many companies and will continue to do so until businesses put things into proper order again.

manager's letter Under the concept of Management by Objectives (MBO) this letter constitutes a statement of the manager's responsibilities. Usually this is not as detailed as is the job description of other employees.

managers, job attributes of Among many skills, managers should have analytical ability, specialized knowledge of a number of fields, sensitivity in social fields, open-mindedness, emotional stability, good communications, and the ability to empathize with others.

managers, obsolescence of The dynamics of the organization and the technological dynamics of the times may make certain managers obsolete.

They can either be brought up to date, if that is possible, or be moved to some other spot in the organization while a new manager is brought in.

managing director In the United Kingdom, a position roughly equivalent to the position of president in a U.S. company.

Managua Stock Exchange *Camara de Comercio,* Nicaragua's only stock exchange.

Manchester Stock Exchange A provincial stock exchange in the United Kingdom.

Manila Stock Exchange The largest stock exchange in the Philippines.

mannerism Specific idiosyncrasies of people, often manifested in their postures or in the way they walk or talk.

manpower analysis A complete survey of all existing manpower in a plant made in preparation for manpower planning.

manpower deficit A term describing a situation in which jobs available are more numerous than are people to fill them.

manual dexterity test A psychomotor skills test designed to measure muscular control and coordination between perception and manipulation. Such tests tend to measure existing abilities with no regard for future development.

manual worker Colloquially, a "blue-collar" worker; one who works with his hands.

marginal A "marginal unit" is an additional unit of something. (In teaching economics, I found this to be a difficult concept for students to grasp.

I instructed them to think of marginal as "last", i.e., the marginal product of a plant is the last unit produced; the marginal cost is the cost added to total cost as a result of producing one more unit, etc.)

marginal accounts Those sales accounts served by a firm which are financially weak, and which may need more severe controls than the average account.

marginal cost The cost of increasing the rate of production by one unit of output, etc.

marginal costing Simplistically, an accounting for variable costs.

marginal efficiency of capital The expected return from an investment in an additional unit of capital equipment.

marginal loss *See* marginal profit.

marginal physical product (MPP) The additional output, measured in units, that is produced as a result of adding one more unit of variable input.

marginal profit The profit added to total profit that results from the production and sale of one more unit of production. Profit indicates that the marginal revenue from the last unit produced is greater than the marginal cost of that unit.

marginal propensity to consume (MPC) That part of an increase in income (normally expressed as a fraction) an individual would spend for consumer goods.

marginal propensity to save (MPS) That part of an increase in income (normally expressed as a fraction) an individual would save.

marginal rate of substitution The trade-off between two goods from which one would get equal satisfaction; how much of good A must I get to equal the loss of satisfaction from the loss of good B. The slope of the indifference curve at each point indicates the marginal rate of substitution between two goods at a given combination of goods.

marginal rate of transformation A ratio showing how much of one product (product A) must be given up in order to release the inputs necessary to produce one more unit of product B. Graphically, this curve shows the opportunity cost of a unit of each good in terms of the other goods.

marginal revenue The revenue added to total revenue that results from increasing the output by one unit and by selling that unit.

marginal tax rate That tax rate that applies to the last unit of income earned.

marginal utility That satisfaction (usefulness) realized by the consumption of an additional unit of some good or service.

marginal value product (MVP) The additional revenue received when one additional unit of the variable factor is employed and the marginal physical product of that unit of the variable factor is sold.

margin of safety The degree to which the sales revenues of a company exceed the break-even point as depicted on a break-even chart.

market 1. That place (real or in concept) where things are bought and sold. It is the place where demand and supply interact and exert their influence on the price, and where buyers and sellers react to the changing price levels. 2. The area, and the consumers of the area, that any business may reasonably expect to reach with its products or services.

market and sales forecasting The act of projecting possible sales into the future through the use of statistical techniques and in light of the existing market.

market assessment The systematic evaluation of all factors affecting a market that a firm serves, or desires to serve. Factors include: 1) identifying the market and the characteristics of customers, direct or indirect; 2) identifying the market's size and structure; 3) identifying those external factors that could affect the market, including competition (domestic and foreign), demographics, government policies, etc.; 4) comparing the market share held by the firm and that held by competitors and any factors that could change the status quo.

market changes Changes in the market for the goods or services produced by a company, which require that a manager be flexible enough to challenge those markets and continue to be effective. In recent years, adapting to a one-world economy has been the challenge and will continue to be.

Market Council Colloquial name for the Council of Ministers of the European Community.

market diversification Any action taken by a firm to acquire a different range of buyers, a different product mix, or a new market segment.

market dominance, dangers of The "lulling to sleep" of a company that dominates the field it is in that occurs when the company begins to believe that it can never be successfully challenged by anyone.

market economy 1. An economic system in which the decisions of what to produce, how to produce it, and who will get it after it is produced are answered by the actions in the market of demand, supply, prices, etc., with a minimum of intervention. (Usually contrasted with a "planned market" situation as one would find under communism.) 2. An economy advanced beyond the stage of producing for oneself and one's family; an economy that sustains itself by producing goods and services for profit.

market equilibrium price The price at which the supply is exactly equal to the demand. There are no surpluses or shortages, but the equilibrium price may be for the short term only.

market factor derivation A technique used in market research that specifically seeks out those aspects of a product that might be expected to cause or increase demand for a given product.

market follower As distinct from a new, or pioneer, product, a product that is introduced to compete with existing products.

market identification The process of identifying existing or potential customers for a specific product.

marketing The integrated use of all company resources to aid the firm in supplying wanted goods and services at a profit to the company. (Peter Drucker believes that the term "marketing" is so all-encompassing that it cannot be used to describe one department of a business, and it may be, in fact, the most important facet of every business.)

marketing and population myth The error of believing that because the population is growing and consumers are more numerous, a company no longer has to be innovative nor has to keep the customer firmly fixed in mind.

marketing, customer-oriented Every company that wants to achieve continuing success must remember that it is producing goods and services primarily to satisfy a customer.

marketing research All surveys of and examinations of a market that will assist management to make correct decisions on what should be produced and how it should be marketed.

marketing research vs. market research Market research refers to that grass-roots surveying of the specific local markets in which the sales people will do their work. Marketing research is corporate in nature and explores the whole spectrum of products, services, and markets where it might be possible to sell those goods.

marketing vs. selling In brief, selling looks to the needs of the seller, while marketing looks to the needs of the buyer. In our age of mass production and the need to move products quickly, this difference is often overlooked.

market intelligence The composite of all market information gathered in market research.

market leader A firm that controls the largest share of the market for a specific good or service.

market mechanism The way in which demand, supply, and prices direct the market economy. Also known as the price mechanism.

market order Instructions given to a broker to buy or to sell stocks or commodities at the current market price.

market penetration The percentage of the market for a specific good or service that is controlled by one company.

market planning, direction and definition Essentially, deciding with top management the direction a company wants to take and planning a strategy to accommodate those plans. (This approach certainly does not rule out proper attention to customer wants and needs, since it is assumed that those things are already well known by the marketing people.)

market potential The demand for a product or service at a given price, at a given time, and within a given segment of the total market.

market power The power that one seller can exercise over a market and over a price. Also known as monopoly power.

market price In a true market economy, the name for a price arrived at by the unimpeded workings of the laws of demand and supply.

market process That force that guides a laissez-faire economy, in which supply, demand, and prices determine most of the economic decisions that are made.

market share The market share of an individual business is its dollar sales in a given period of time, expressed as a percentage of the sales in the market served by the business.

market share and low performance It is a documented fact that a strong company, even with a low market share, can be profitable on an ongoing basis, usually because it discovers "niches" for itself in the market and is small enough and agile enough to serve them well.

market structure The physical characteristics of the market, including such things as the relative size of businesses, the size and income strata in the population, the degree of product differentiation, the ease of entry and exit from the market, etc.

market value The price at which an item can be sold.

mark-up With respect to price, the difference between the price charged for a good and the price for which the good is ultimately sold to the end consumer.

Marseille Stock Exchange *Palais de la Bourse Marseille.*

mass action In social psychology, the vigorous protest of a group against whatever is perceived to be frustrating the satisfaction of their needs.

mass production The production of products on a mammoth scale. Normally, such products have essentially the same specifications. This type of production often involves employees in rote jobs, which can become monotonous and debilitating. Many companies use job rotation as a partial cure for the malaise that can accompany mass production.

mass unemployment One symptom of a severe recession or depression in the economy, which may last for several months and even years in rare instances. Mass unemployment in the 1990s would probably translate into double digits. Currently, 6 percent unemployment is generally being recognized as a "full employment," so 10–12 percent would likely be considered mass unemployment. In the Great Depression of the 1930s, unemployment reached 25 percent and was lingering at about 15 percent in 1940.

master activity programming (MAP) One approach to the analysis and simplification of office procedures generally based on historical observation and obvious needs resulting from such observation.

master clerical data (MCD) A form of clerical work measurement in the United States covering twelve major types of office work, including calculating, machine operation, reading, writing, communicating, etc.

master sample A statistical sample of a specific population that can be used frequently.

master scheduling A plan that incorporates every function of a company's production for several months ahead, or perhaps a year or more.

master Used in the context of the "master and servant" relationship under common law in the United Kingdom, this term describes a wide range of duties and remedies in cases of industrial labor unrest.

mastery motive The need to overcome difficulties and to achieve control over conditions; to self-actualize.

materials handling The application of analytical methods and sophisticated equipment design to the problems of moving products and materials in any form in a prescribed sequence and to desired locations. This approach has added to the efficiency of both production and warehousing.

mathematical models Models symbolizing real-life situations and used to experiment symbolically with alternatives in producing, etc., without incurring the expense of trial and error.

matrices That framework within which a thing develops, such as a non-verbal intelligence test, or a psychological test, which may involve the completion of squares, etc.

maturity stage A term used by some economists to denote the high point in a business cycle, at which time there is little unemployment and consumers are most active in the market.

maturity 1. Legal adulthood in a person; the full development of a contract such as a loan or insurance contract. 2. The realization of the fullest potential for development; adulthood.

maximization of profits A concept long held by economists and others that the maximization of profits is the primary goal of the company. This concept is false, since the primary goal of the company is to satisfy the wants and needs of as many customers as possible, after which the needed profits will come naturally.

maximum working area The working area used by an employee either sitting or standing, where full full-length arm and shoulder movements must be made to reach tools, materials, etc.

maximum/minimum An inventory term in which regularly used items are reordered up to the prescribed maximum levels when stocks drop to the prescribed minimum levels.

May Day Synonymous with Labor Day in the United States, the day set aside to honor socialist labor.

MBA Master of Business Administration.

MBO Management by Objectives.

MBO and group action A thoroughgoing MBO program demands the involvement of the entire concerned group with respect to the work to be done, how it will be done, who will evaluate the work, and what caused the successes or failures, etc. In short, MBO requires group action as a fundamental concept of the whole plan.

MBO and "ideal" process Inasmuch as Management by Objectives and performance appraisal are irrevocably related, the "ideal process" would probably proceed in these steps: 1) a discussion by the worker with his superior about how the worker would describe his own job; 2) the establishment of short-term goals; 3) occasional meetings by the worker(s) with the superior to discuss progress; 4) the establishment of progress check points; 5) the discussions with a superior by a subordinate at the end of the project to make evaluations.

MBO and motivational assessment An assessment to determine whether the manager seeks to force his workers, by one means or another, to reach the required goals, or whether he is willing to achieve a real partnership with them to reach those goals.

MBO and personal goals If the manager, along with the workers, is given consideration in setting the goals of the company, then probably those goals will coincide to one degree or another the goals of the manager and workers.

MC = MR Marginal cost equals

marginal revenue. That point at which profits for a company are maximized. Until this point is reached, the company is profitable, because revenues always exceed costs. However, the profits are not maximized because profits can still be made by continued production, though at diminishing returns. When the point is passed where marginal cost and marginal revenue are equal, units produced begin to cost more than the revenues they produce.

measurement systems World principal systems of measurement, including: the British Imperial System (BIS), the International System (IS) of metric units, and the U.S. Customary System.

mechanical aptitudes tests and mechanical comprehension tests Respectively, tests designed to measure the ability to understand mechanical movements and tests designed for personnel to determine operative aptitudes.

mechanistic organization Denotes bureaucratic structure.

mechanization The trend toward alleviating ordinary manual labor with the use of machinery, a trend which actually began with the Industrial Revolution and has accelerated since that time, until we now have what may be called the age of robotics.

media analysis An analysis of advertising, often done by giving the ads in different periodicals a different code number, so that responses must be directed to that number. Example: When answering this ad, please include Dept. #XYZ.

media of communication, formal The manager has many avenues of communication open to him, including personal interviews, departmental meetings, mass meetings, company newspapers, company handbooks, bulletin boards, etc.

Medicare A medical aid program for those on Social Security in the United States. Several annual publications make people aware of the provisions of Medicare, since they do change periodically. One source is the annual publication, *All About Medicare,* published by The National Underwriter Company, 420 East Fourth Street, Cincinnati, Ohio 45202.

mediocrity, safe The false sense of security, often prevalent in a company, that one cannot be fired no matter what one's performance record is. Mediocrity is ofttimes considered safe because, while it does little good, it does little harm.

medium-term liabilities Normally, those obligations that must be discharged in about three years.

Mehrwertsteuer A German term denoting a value-added tax.

Melbourne Stock Exchange One of six Australian stock exchanges. (*See* Section VII)

meliorism The view that the gradual, day-by-day efforts to improve one's personality, organization, or social order are more effective than an all-or-none perfectionist method.

member bank A commercial bank that is a member of the Federal Reserve System. Nationally chartered banks must be members, and state-chartered banks may become members if they qualify.

memo-motion study A technique of filming segments of the various tasks of a job and then reviewing the film in an effort to improve a situation.

memorandum of association A document in the United Kingdom setting out the reasons for which a company is formed, and naming the various types of share capital. Somewhat like the "red herring prospectus" in the United States combined with the constitution and bylaws of the company.

memoriter That which is learned by rote, not understanding.

memory A broad term that includes learning, retaining, recognizing, recalling, and relearning.

memory span The amount of unrelated or meaningful material that, after a single presentation, can be correctly reproduced.

mensualization A term, French in origin, used normally to denote the fact that blue-collar workers are to be paid on a period basis (by the week or month), as are white-collar workers. This does not necessarily mean that the blue collars will be considered staff employees, but it does indicate an attempt to bring into closer harmonization the two groups of employees.

mercado a plazo A forward settlement market on Spanish stock exchanges. (*See* Section VII)

mercado de contado The spot market on Spanish stock exchanges. (*See* Section VII)

mercantile agent A person or company with the authority to transact certain types of business for his principal. Often this is an international agreement, where an agent is appointed in one country by a company in another for the care and sale of goods.

mercantile credit A term used primarily in the United Kingdom to denote the line of credit extended by the manufacturer to the wholesaler. Also known as commercial credit.

merchandise balance Balance of trade accounts between nations that exclude intangible exports or imports.

merchandising The methods used in marketing goods, which might include advertising, personal calls, special promotions, etc.

merchant bank A type of bank in the United Kingdom granting long-term venture capital loans, as contrasted with the short-term loans granted by commercial banks.

merger Normally denotes a friendly uniting of two or more companies, often producing similar goods, in an attempt to strengthen the capitalization of the entire company, to broaden the market, and to seek a larger share in the market.

Merger Treaty The 1967 treaty that formally brought together the European Economic Community (EEC), the European Atomic Energy Community (Euratom), and the European Coal and Steel Community (ECSC) under the Council of Ministers and the European Commission of the European Community. (*See* Section IV)

merit good A good or service produced by government and given to society "free" since it is for "the public good." Example: Public education.

merit rating A technique of classifying

according to skill levels. Workers perhaps perform the same jobs, but they show different abilities to do the job well, and thus such a technique could help strengthen the company.

meta system A general term used in the United Kingdom that indicates an overall view of an industry or a system that takes into consideration every facet of that industry or system.

Meteorological Office The government office in the United Kingdom responsible for forecasting the weather and for gathering multi-year data on the same.

method A prescribed way of doing any given task, with due consideration given to the end objective, to the facilities available, and the expenditures of time, talent, and money.

methods engineer Usually synonymous with industrial engineer, this term denotes one skilled in production techniques.

metric ton 1,000 kilograms or 18 kilograms lighter than an Imperial ton. (*See* Appendix E)

metrication The process of changing to the metric system from some other system of weights and measures, such as the U.S. Customary System. While a complete switch to the metric system has been encouraged all over the world for many years, it has not factually transpired.

Mexico Stock Exchange *See* Section VII.

MG Managerial grid.

MICR Magnetic ink character recognition.

microeconomics A term used in a number of different ways to describe a market system in which demand, supply, and prices answer many economic questions. As contrasted with macroeconomics (national income economics), microeconomics puts more emphasis on the individual actions of business firms, consumers, etc.

microfiche A small section of microfilm carrying the equivalent of several pages of a book or other document. A special reader is necessary to magnify the print.

microfilm Film containing reduced-size print, graphs, pictures, etc.

Midlands & Western Stock Exchange A provincial stock exchange in the United Kingdom. (*See* Section VII)

Midwest Stock Exchange A U.S. stock exchange in Chicago. (*See* Section VII)

migrant worker In the European Community, term indicates a worker from one country who is temporarily working in another Common Market country. In the United States, the term indicates workers who generally work during the fruit and vegetable harvests and migrate from place to place as the need for harvesters dictates.

Milan Stock Exchange *Borsa Valori di Milano.* (*See* Section VII)

mind The sum total of all psychological contents or functions.

minimal cue The smallest stimulus that can evoke a response.

minimum lending rate (MLR) In 1972, this rate succeeded the so-called "bank rate" as the rate at which the Bank of England was prepared to lend to UK banks.

minimum manufacturing quantity (MMQ) The minimum quantity of a specific product that can be produced economically by a company.

Ministers Council of Ministers of the European Community.

Ministry of Labor Created in the United Kingdom in 1916, its name was changed to the Department of Employment and Productivity in 1968. Its name changed a second time to the Department of Employment in 1970.

Minnesota Clerical Test A two-part psychological test used in the United States and designed to measure number comparison and name comparison skills.

Minnesota Engineering Analogies Test (MEAT) A psychological test designed for engineers and engineering students in the United States, this test has achievement and intelligence test aspects.

Minnesota Multiphasic Personality Inventory (MMPI) A psychological inventory, set up in questionnaire form and designed to measure personality and temperament traits. It is more attuned, however, to clinical psychology than to industrial psychology.

Minnesota Rate of Manipulation Test A test of psychomotor skills, measuring the speed and accuracy of finger, hand, and arm movements.

misdirection The mistake, often made by a manager, of failing to make necessary changes in personnel to meet the needs of the times. Meeting new challenges can often be accomplished by putting the people in question into new jobs fitting their technological expertise instead of firing them, which has the effect of lowering morale throughout the company.

misfeasance The improper and unlawful commission of an act that is, itself, lawful.

missionary selling The "missionary" salesperson sells for the direct customers of the company, while the trade-force salespeople sells through the direct customers. In the food industry, for example, much of the selling is done through brokers, but the missionary force undergirds the brokers, makes personal appearances for them, and attends trade shows with them, all in an attempt to assist them in sales.

mixed economies Economic systems that have varied degrees of free enterprise and Socialism. At this point in time, this type of system includes most of the economies of the world.

MLR Minimum lending rate designation in the United Kingdom.

MMO Minimum manufacturing quantity.

MMPI *See* Minnesota Multiphasic Personality Inventory.

MO Mail order; money order.

models A multidimensional representation of an object, or a collection of objects, which would not be possible to view in its actual size. Example: A building (mall, hospital, etc.) is often represented by a scale model to allow people a reasonable idea of what the finished product will look like.

modus operandi Methods used by an organization in its operations.

monadic product test Term used to denote market research on a single product.

monetarist economics A school of economics most often associated with Milton Friedman that places emphasis on the money supply as the principal factor in achieving and maintaining equilibrium in the economy.

monetary asset Any asset that has a value defined in dollars or in other units of currency.

monetary measures Actions by government to combat either inflation or deflation by manipulating the money supply.

monetary policy The control of the money supply and interest rates as means of achieving economic equilibrium.

monetary union A situation in which two or more countries share a common currency and a common monetary policy. It is the hope of the Council of Ministers that EC countries will share currencies following the fruition of the Common Market in 1992.

money Anything that has value and can be used as a medium of exchange.

money broker A financial institution that specializes in dealing in foreign exchange, in gold, and in short-term securities and loans.

money manager An individual or organization that manages the assets of individuals or organizations.

money market The market in which short-term lending and borrowing takes place.

money purchase plan *pensions* A plan whereby a company—and an individual employee if the plan is contributory—pays into a plan to assure the pension of the employee upon retirement. The payment is a fixed amount, and the ultimate pension is whatever that money would buy. Usually the amount of the payments is based on some percent of the salary of the individual. Inflation can severely cut the purchasing power of such pension payments.

money shop a small location in the United Kingdom, often in a shopping area, that offers some financial services to consumers, such as small loans. (Often called "finance companies" in the United States.)

money supply 1. Simplistically, the amount of coin and currency in circulation plus demand deposits (checking accounts). There are other measures listed elsewhere in this volume. (*See* M1, M2, M3, etc.) 2. The number of "spendable dollars" (or other monetary units) that exist in an economy at any given point in time.

Monopolies and Mergers Commission The Monopolies and Mergers Commission in the United Kingdom was established by the Monopolies and Mergers Acts of 1948 and 1965. Its responsibilities also extend to the Restrictive Trade Practices Act of 1966 and the Fair Trading Act of 1973. This Commission is appointed by the Department of Trade and carries out those tasks that the names imply.

monopolistic competition A market situation in which several firms sell essentially the same products, but which are differentiated usually by a brand name.

monopoly 1. A market situation in which there is one seller of a product. 2. In the United Kingdom, under the Monopolies and Mergers Acts of 1948 and 1965 a monopoly is defined statutorily as a situation in which at least one-fourth of a local or national market is controlled by one person or one company or a group of people collaborating together.

monopoly power the power to control the market for a product and its price by exercising control over the supply of the product.

monopsony A market situation in which there is one buyer.

Montevideo Stock Exchange *Rincone Missiones,* a stock exchange in Uruguay.

Montreal Stock Exchange One of six major Canadian stock exchanges. (*See* Section VII)

moonlighting Carrying a second job in addition to a primary job.

moral suasion Generally, a tool of monetary policy in which the Fed urges the buying or selling of government securities, even though it has no power to enforce such an action. This tool is used often by the Open Market Committee of the Fed when it wants to reduce or expand the money supply.

morale The degree of enthusiasm for purposeful endeavor, whether in personality development or in group participation.

mores Social customs evaluated from the standpoint of ethics.

morphological research A term sometimes used by marketing people to denote an exploratory approach to technological research through a thorough study and analysis of the varied parameters of the design, materials, and function of a product. Developed in the United States by Professor Zwicky of the California Institute of Technology.

Morrisby Compound Series Test A nonverbal intelligence test involving problems with bead patterns and matrices.

Morrisby GAT-N Test A thirty-five-minute numerical aptitude test.

Morrisby GAT-V Test A verbal intelligence test having three parts. Norms exist for the general population, for schools, and for school graduates.

Morrisby Mechanical Ability Test A mechanical aptitude test that uses a wide range of practical mechanical problems.

Morrisby Shapes Test A spatial aptitude test taking about fifteen minutes to complete.

Morrisby Speed Test Designed to measure clerical aptitude, it pairs numbers with names against a time limit of ten to fifteen minutes.

mortmain *law* Or "dead hand." Deals with the ownership of real property by institutions, such as churches, where there exists nontransferability and perpetual ownership.

motion In a formal meeting, the prescribed manner of getting a matter for discussion before a group. After the original motion is made and seconded, it can then be discussed. While amendments to the motion can be made, and if they are accepted by the mover of the original motion, they can be included in the motion for vote. No other motion, except a substitute motion, can take precedence over the original motion. It must be acted upon or tabled.

motivation The providing of reasons for acting in the way desired by a supervisor or manager. All true motivation is self-motivation to some extent, and thus managers do not motivate people per se, but rather they establish situations in which workers can be self-motivated

motor skills Skills related to muscular coordination and control.

Mountain Standard Time (MST or MT) Local time at a place in the United States at the 105th meridian.

moving average An average computed from part of a series of items, progressively adding unused items as items already used are eliminated.

MPA Advanced college degrees in Public Administration or Public Accounting.

MSL Mean sea level.

multigrade salary structure A company's salary structure that contains a large number of grades.

multinational company A domestic company that has usually majority interests in companies in other countries. The formation of these companies is destined to grow under the one-world economy concept now developing.

multilateral foreign aid Any program of foreign aid in which several nations participate.

multiple bar chart A bar chart that includes a grouping of bars distinguished by different colors or shadings that may represent the same entity or several entities.

multiple regression analysis A statistical technique for investigating the relationships between a number of independent and dependent variables and evolving an equation for predicting the latter in terms of the former.

multiplier As most often used in economics, the term refers to the ratio of the change in national income resulting from a change in investment. Another oft-used multiplier is the deposit multiplier, which refers to the amount of increase in the money supply that can result from an initial increase in bank reserves.

Munich Stock Exchange *Bayerische Börse in München.* One of eight German stock exchanges. (*See* Section VII)

Murphy's Law A tongue-in-cheek "law" declaring that if anything can go wrong, it will.

mutual fund Open-end investment fund.

mutual insurance An insurance company ostensibly owned by the policyholders, who pay into a common fund and who are indemnified from that common fund.

mutually exclusive alternatives Two or more projects that accomplish the same end so that only one alternative will be used.

N

Naamioze Vennootschap (NV) A joint-stock company under Netherlands law. Most companies in the Netherlands are still privately owned and are not quoted on the stock exchange.

NACED National Advisory Council on the Employment of the Disabled.

NAF *Norsk Arbeidsgiverforeing.* Norwegian Employer's Association.

Nagoya Stock Exchange One of five stock exchanges in Japan. (*See* Section VII)

Nairobi Stock Exchange Stock exchange of Kenya. (*See* Section VII)

naive forecast A forecast made from projections of past trends and not a foolish or childish forecast, as the term might imply.

named vote A vote in a formal meeting that is tabulated by the name of the voter.

name screening A market-research technique that attempts to measure the effectiveness of a product's name and the image it will create.

nanosecond One-billionth of a second.

Naples Stock Exchange *Borsa Valori di Napoli.* One of ten Italian stock exchanges. (*See* Section VII)

narcissism In psychoanalysis, the direction of libidinal energy toward the self as the object-choice.

narcosis The state of deep stupor caused by drugs.

narcotism The addiction to stupor-producing drugs.

Narodna Banka Jugoslavije Central Bank of Yugoslavia, first established in 1883. (*See* Section VII)

Narodowy Bank Polski Central Bank of Poland, established in 1945. (*See* Section VII)

NASA *See* National Aeronautics and Space Administration.

National Advisory Council for Education for Industry and Commerce An agency in the United Kingdom that advises the secretary of State for Education and Science concerning facilities for technical and commercial education, including management training.

National Advisory Council on the Employment of the Disabled (NACED) An agency in the United Kingdom created by the Employment Acts of 1944 and 1958, reporting to the secretary of State for Employment.

National Aeronautics and Space Administration (NASA) A U.S. government agency responsible for research and development in space flight and exploration.

national agreement In labor/management relations, the negotiating of a contract on a nationwide basis in one industry.

National Association of Accountants A U.S. national accounting association with overseas chapters, established in 1919 and headquartered at 919 Third Avenue, New York, NY 10022.

National Association of Manufacturers (NAM) The major employer's association, once known for its ultra-conservatism, but now more moderate. Established in 1895, this organization is headquartered at 1776 F St. N.W., Washington, DC, 20006.

National Association of Purchasing Management This group was established in 1915 and is headquartered at 11 Park Place, New York, NY 10010.

National Association of Securities Dealers (NASD) The prime regulator of the market in securities that are not listed on an exchange.

National Association of Securities Dealers Automated Quotation System (NASDAQ) An automated price quotation system for over-the-counter securities.

National Bank Examiner A top employee of the Office of the Comptroller of the Currency, whose task it is to see to the auditing or examining of banks on a periodic basis. The examinations focus on the financial strength of the banks and upon their adherence to banking regulations.

National Bank Surveillance System (NBSS) A computer system used to collect and monitor data that is maintained in the office of the comptroller of the Currency. It provides the information that may reveal vital changes in the condition of a specific bank or in the banking system as a whole.

national bank A name often applied to the central bank of a nation. Used in the United States to denote a federally chartered bank, which, because of its charter, is a member of the Federal Reserve System.

National Banking System The system of nationally chartered banks that existed in the United States from the Civil War until the Federal Reserve Act

of 1913. At that time, all nationally chartered banks were required to join the Federal Reserve, and they still are required to join the Federal Reserve today.

National Chamber of Trade Established in 1897 in the United Kingdom, this organization includes local chambers of trade and trade associations. Address: Enterprise House, 3 Hyde Park Place, London W2 2LD.

national character An integrated pattern of habits and values that supposedly differentiate one nation from another, and which are passed on by the old teaching the young.

national claim In the United Kingdom, a union demand for more pay or better working conditions, introduced by one union, but the precursor for nationwide claims by the same union.

National Colleges In the United Kingdom, colleges that offer courses related specifically to certain industries' needs or to technological fields.

National Credit Union Administration (NCUA) The regulatory agency for federally chartered and federally insured credit unions. The NCUA administers the National Credit Union Share Insurance Fund.

national debt A debt owed by the central government of a country, usually made up of long-term and short-term debt instruments, such as bills, notes, and bonds.

national development Developing countries require expert management to handle the loans, aid grants, or whatever resources come into their hands.

National Economic Development Council (NEDC) A nongovernmental body established in the United Kingdom in 1965 that is concerned with economic development of Great Britain and the world. Serves as a sounding-board for government policy makers.

National Economic Development Office (NEDO) A government agency that measures the economic condition of the nation on behalf of the government. Address: Millbank, London sw1, UK.

National Flood Insurance Act An act establishing a program to provide flood insurance to homeowners located in specially designated flood areas, which is administered by the Federal Insurance Administration.

National Foundation for Educational Research A research establishment in the United Kingdom that studies education and learning, and which produces psychological tests. Address: 2 Jennings Bldgs., Thames Avenue, Windsor, Berks.

National Grange A farmer's group established in the United States in 1867. Much better known fifty years ago. Address: 1616 H Street nw, Washington, DC 20006.

National Health Services A creation of Parliament in the United Kingdom in 1946 to provide all residents free and fair medical treatment, as well as preventive medical care. It is run by the Employment Medical Advisory Service and the Factory Inspectorate, both of which answer to the secretary of State for Employment.

national income This term is essentially the same as Gross National Product, except that capital depreciation is subtracted from the GNP.

national income and product account The Gross National Product accounts that show the income and product flow of the nation and indicate the rate at which the economy is running.

National Industrial Recovery Act (NIRA) An act passed by Congress in 1933, after it was pushed through by President Roosevelt, giving the president great power to regulate trade, industry, labor, and prices through appointed agencies. In 1935 it was declared unconstitutional on two counts: 1) Congress cannot delegate its legislative powers; 2) Congress cannot legislate intrastate commerce.

National Industrial Relations Court (NIRC) Organization established in the United Kingdom under the Industrial Relations Act of 1971 and designed to adjudicate complaints related to organizations rather than individuals.

National Institute of Industrial Psychology (NIIP) Organization established in 1921 to perform work in psychological testing, etc. Ceased to function as a separate organization in 1973, when its work was taken over by the National Foundation for Industrial Research.

national insurance In the United Kingdom, a government-operated insurance designed to cover unemployment and/or sickness. It is closely akin to the Workman's Compensation program in the United States.

National Insurance Acts A series of acts beginning in 1946, outlining the benefits for unemployment, disability, and survivors' benefits in the event of the death of the wage earner, etc.

nationalization The confiscation or purchase of private industry by the state, after which the state runs the industry.

National Labor Relations Act Also known as the Wagner Act, this U.S. legislation of 1935 gave greater latitude to organized labor by requiring the employer to recognize collective bargaining and other concessions. This was the act that opened the door for organized labor, which was strong until the Labor Management Relations Act of 1947, which sought to equalize the powers between labor and management.

National Labor Relations Board (NLRB) An independent agency established by the National Labor Relations Act of 1935 that advises on labor/managment matters in all details of such relationships.

National Reference Library of Science and Inventions In the United Kingdom, the major library for the physical sciences, engineering, and technology, with a collection of a half-million volumes. It operates under the Department of Trade. Address: National Reference Library of Science and Invention (Holborn Division) 25 Southampton Building, London WC2A IAY.

National Research Development Corporation (NRDC) In the United Kingdom, an independent agency responsible to the secretary of State for Industry and responsible for developing research findings and inventions into useable instruments in industry. At times, financial assistance is given to individuals or firms engaged in innovation that is in the national interest and that has specific export potential. Address: P.O. Box 236, Kingsgate House, 66-74 Victoria Street, London SW1 6SL.

National Union of Mine Workers The trade union for mine workers in the United Kingdom, affiliated with the Trades Union Congress. There are about 250,000 members in the National Union of Mine Workers. Address: 222 Euston Road, London NW1 2BX.

National Union of Railwaymen A trade union in the United Kingdom affiliated with the Trades Union Congress. It is an amalgam of the Amalgamated Society of Railwaymen, the General Railway Workers Union, and the Pointsmen and Signalmen's Society, established in 1913. It has about 200,000 members.

NATO *See* North Atlantic Treaty Organization.

NATO codification system A coding system based on the American Federal Supply classification that is used by NATO countries to facilitate store numbers for parts and equipment used by the Organization. It consists of thirteen digits indicating the country of origin, identification number, type of equipment, etc.

natural guardian The parent of a minor, either father or mother. This designation applies to the parents of a minor only.

natural law A body of moral principles dictated by reason or conscience and thought to be innate within human beings and human societies.

natural monopoly An industry in which the most efficient firm is one that is large enough to supply the entire market.

natural movement On-the-job physical movements that make the best use of the parts of the body used most on that job. Related to time/motion studies.

natural selection The Darwinian theory that favorable variations in heredity facilitate, and unfavorable variations impede, the survival of a species.

natural wastage In the United Kingdom, the term for reducing the number of employees in a company by not hiring new people when others quit or retire. In the United States, "reduction by attrition" would likely be the term used to indicate the same process.

nature-nuture controversy The arguments surrounding whether heredity or environment plays the larger role in growth and development.

NBS National Bureau of Standards.

NCW *Netherlands Christlijk Werkgeversverbond.* A Dutch employers' confederation.

ne exeat *law* Latin expression "that he should not leave." A writ enjoining a person from leaving the jurisdiction of the court.

near cash Short-term investment vehicles that can be turned into cash in a relatively short time.

NEDC *See* National Economic Development Council.

Nederlandsche Bank N.V. Central bank of the Netherlands. (*See* Section VII)

NEDO *See* National Economic Development Office.

needs and wants Those things human beings must have to survive or things they desire to have for self-satisfaction. Needs and wants provide the backdrop for motivation and for consumer choices.

negative acceleration Descriptive of a frequency curve that rises rapidly and then flattens into a plateau.

negative adaptation A learned indifference to a stimulus.

negative carry 1. A situation in which the revenue created by an asset is not sufficient to pay interest on the money borrowed to buy the asset. 2. The cost incurred in excess of income when borrowing to finance the holding of securities.

negative cash flow A situation in which cash is flowing out of an organization more rapidly than it is flowing in. Ultimately this situation demands some kind of cash injection if the organization is to remain in business.

negative factor or value With regard to the Equal Opportunity Act, this is some bit of information, either qualitative or quantitative, that casts a less favorable light on a prospective debtor than the information the creditor already has.

negative income tax An income tax system that collects taxes from those above a specified income level and makes payments to those individuals below a specified income level.

negative motion A motion made in a formal meeting that has the intent of putting the meeting off course; e.g., a motion, totally negative in content, that could add nothing to the meeting and that is probably out of order.

negative pledge clause A covenant in an indenture stating that a corporation will not pledge any of its assets unless the notes or debentures outstanding under the particular indenture are at least equally secured by such a pledge.

negative practice The continual practice of an error with knowledge of what is wrong and how the act ought to be performed.

negative transfer A reduction of efficiency because what was learned from one performance is carried over to another activity.

negotiable instrument An order, without condition, to pay an amount or money, which is easily transferable from one person to another. The Uniform Commercial Code requires that for an instrument to be negotiable, it must be signed by the maker or drawer, must contain an unconditional promise or order to pay a specific amount of money, must be payable on demand or at a specified future time, and must be payable to order or to the bearer.

negotiating rights A situation in which a union has the authority to enter into full negotiations with a company.

neoclassical economics The accepted basic theories of microeconomics that made up most of the field of economics prior to the development of the Keynesian economic theories beginning in the 1920s.

nervous breakdown A colloquialism denoting physical debilitation and mental tiredness, mental malaise, and sometimes accompanied by anxieties.

net Term used on an invoice to indicate that a fee is payable at the full amount

either immediately or at some short-term future date.

net amount at risk *insurance* The difference between the face amount of an insurance policy and the reserve held against the policy.

net book value The value of an asset on the company books after allowing for depreciation.

net charge off The gross amount charged to bad debts minus recoveries received during a specific period.

net cost *insurance* The total premiums paid on a policy minus the dividends received and the cash-surrender value as of the date the net cost is determined.

net current assets Current assets minus current liabilities.

net effective distribution A marketing term denoting a product survey measuring how many stores in a physical survey actually had the item(s) in stock at the time of the survey.

net investment Capital investment minus depreciation of equipment and stocks.

net margin *See* net profit.

net monetary creditor An economic agent having monetary assets in excess of liabilities.

net monetary debtor An economic agent having monetary liabilities in excess of assets.

net national product The Gross National Product minus depreciation of capital goods.

Net Operating Income (NOI) Earnings before interest and taxes.

net present value method (NPV) A measure for the assessment of a project or of an enterprise based on discounted cash-flow techniques.

net profit Gross profits minus cost of administration, marketing, and finance.

net regression coefficient *statistics* in multiple correlation, the coefficient of each independent variable in a regression equation is the net regression coefficient. The term "net" indicates that the relation of the dependent variable to that particular independent variable is free of associated influences of the other independent variable or variables upon the dependent variable. The term partial regression coefficient is used by some for the net regression coefficient.

net rentable area A term usually applied to an apartment building or to an office building that denotes the space available for rent after counting out stairwells, elevator shafts, etc.

net reproduction rate The ratio of the number of females (daughters) who will become mothers to the number of females (mothers) who reproduced them. If the ratio is 1 to 1, the population is static. If it less than 1 to 1, the population is declining. If it is more than 1 to 1, the population is increasing.

net tonnage Net tonnage is gross tonnage minus space for the crew, machinery, and fuel.

net wealth tax A tax on wealth applied to wealth beyond a specified level.

net working capital ratio Current assets related to current liabilities. A desirable ratio is 2 to 1.

net worth Total assets minus current liabilities.

Netherlands Bank *Nederlandsche Bank N.V.* (*See* Section VII)

Netherlands companies Types of companies that can exist under Netherlands law: 1) proprietorship, or *Eenmanszaak*; 2) general partnership, or *Vennootschap onder Firma,* usually found in medium-sized firms or family firms; 3) limited partnership, or *Commanditaire Vennootschap*; 4) civil partnership, or *Maatschap*; 5) limited partnership with shares, or *Commanditaire Vennootschap op Aandelen*; 6) joint-stock company, or *Naamloze Vennootschap (NV)*; 7) Private or Closed Limited Company, or *Besloten Vennootschap (BV).*

Netherlands income tax *Inkomstenbelasting.* A progressive tax charged on net total income. In addition to this, there is a flat-rate net wealth tax on property.

Netherlands Industry, Federation of *Verbond van Nederlandsche Ondernemingen.*

Netherlands stock exchange *See* Section VII.

network analysis/planning A range of "critical path planning" techniques in which specific events in the life of the project are represented by circles and the activities needed to reach those events are represented by straight lines.

neurophysiology A science concerned with the relationships between the functions of the nervous systems and health.

neurosis In psychoanalytic terms, a functional disorder that is more complex than a simple personality maladjustment, but is regarded as more benign than a functional psychosis.

neurotic inventory A list of questions or problems, which are usually self-reported, that indicate whether any given pattern of neurosis is present.

neurotic One who is inclined to have excessive anxieties accompanied by unusual behavior as a result of the anxieties.

neutral equilibrium *economics* A condition that, once achieved, will continue indefinitely unless one of the variables (economic or noneconomic) is altered. Then the economic system will come to rest or a new equilibrium will emerge, with new and different adjustments.

neutrality *taxes* A situation in which a tax does not cause the economic choices of either businesses or individuals to change—production and consumption patterns remain the same.

New Deal The name most often given to the social and economic programs introduced during the first term of Franklin D. Roosevelt in the United States.

new issue Securities that are being issued for the first time, usually by an investment house or a syndicate of the same.

new money The additional amount of money generated by a new issue in excess of the amount necessary to redeem maturing or refunded issues.

new product introduction and time use The time required to get a new product through all stages from inception to acceptance on the market is generally about thirty-six months. (This figure must be seen as a rough average.)

New Town In the United Kingdom, a term used to denote towns built under the New Towns Acts of 1946–66, which are financed by the central government. Ultimately, the new towns become self-governing. (Some similar, but generally private, towns have been built under the government's supervision in the United States.)

New York Clearing House Association (NYCHA) The clearing association for New York banks.

New York Stock Exchange The largest stock exchange in the United States. (*See* Section VII)

New York Times New York newspaper noted for its financial section. It has extensive stock market reports, currency reports, commodities reports, etc. Address: 229 West 43rd Street, New York, NY 10036.

New Zealand Associated Chambers of Commerce A confederation of about fifty local Chambers of Commerce. Address: POB 1071, Wellington, New Zealand.

New Zealand Central Bank Reserve Bank of New Zealand. (*See* Section VII)

New Zealand Federation of Labor (NZFL) The central trade union confederation in New Zealand. Address: 25 Trades Hall, Wellington C2, New Zealand.

Nigerian Association of Chambers of Commerce Confederation of several local Chambers of Commerce. Address: POB 109, Lagos, Nigeria.

Nigerian Employers' Consultative Association Established in 1961, this organization is the headquarters of a number of employers' associations. Address: POB 2231, 31 Marina, Lagos, Nigeria.

Nigerian Stock Exchange Established in Lagos in 1960. (*See* Section VII)

Nihon Keieisha Dantai Renmei (NIKKEIREN) The Japanese Federation of Employers' Associations. Address: 4-6 Marunouchi 1-chome, Chiyoda-ku, Tokyo.

NIIP *See* National Institute of Industrial Psychology.

Niitmash system A Soviet classification and coding system for components.

NIKKEIREN *Nihon Keieisha Dantai Renmei.* The Japanese Federation of Employers' Associations.

Nippon Ginko Central Bank of Japan. Address: 2-2-1 Hongoku-cho, Nihonbashi, Chuo-ku, Tokyo. (*See* Section VII)

Nippon Shoko Kaigi-sho Japanese Chamber of Commerce and Industry. The mother organization of nearly five hundred local Chambers of Commerce. Address: 2-2-3-chome, Marunouchi, Chiyodaku, Tokyo.

NOBIN (not otherwise indexed by name) *transportation* A freight classification that applies if no specific class exists.

no par value stock Shares issued with no nominal value mentioned.

noegenetic principles Those principles arising from pure reason, independent of sensory bases.

nolle prosequi *law* The dropping of a case at the request of the prosecuting attorney.

nolo contendere *law* A plea by an accused in a criminal case that he does not wish to contest the matter and thus implies that he would otherwise be found guilty and convicted.

nominal capital The sum total of the nominal value of the shares in a company.

nominal damages *law* Damages awarded when the plaintiff proves his case but the damages are negligible.

nominal value The value of a share when it is issued, if such value is printed on the certificate or is logged in the company's final prospectus. This value is ethereal, in that it may not coincide with the price the market is willing to pay for it.

nominal yield The rate of return specified in a security.

nominee holdings Stock holdings in the name of another person or organization with real ownership residing in the purchaser of the stock.

nomothetic method A procedure that leads to general laws or principles on the basis of detailed observations of the behavior patterns of many individuals.

nonanalytic job evaluation The evaluating and grading of jobs done from observation and private decision rather than by scientific means.

nonassessable insurance Insurance in which the liability of the insured is limited to the premium he pays and no assessment can be made against him.

non compos mentis *law* Incapable of conducting one's own affairs; psychotic.

noncontributory pension plans Pension plans to which the employee makes no contributions, all such being made by the employer.

nondirective counseling A client-centered procedure in which the counselor serves merely to help by permissive acceptance and clarification, not by assuming responsibility for solving a problem.

nondirective interview A technique used in market research and in personnel selection in which the interview is conversational in nature, rather than being structured around predetermined questions.

Nondiscretionary Investment Agency A relationship in which the trust department does not take title to the assets of a trust, but serves as an agent to the trustee, who dictates his own investments. The agent, however, may recommend investments and make periodic reports.

nonemployed person A person who is not employed and not available for employment. (*See also* unemployed person)

nonexempt employee An employee who is not exempt from the provisions of the Fair Labor Standards Act, and thus must receive proper compensation for overtime hours worked, usually one and one-half times the normal hourly rate.

nonfeasance The omission of an act that one ought to do or that one is required by law to do.

nonfinancial incentives Rewards that may include recognition, prestige, pride of accomplishment, etc. Such incentives tend to be more productive than monetary incentives after a cer-

tain level of monetary compensation has been achieved.

noninsurable risk A risk, the occurrence of which is not measurable by actuarial science and hence is noninsurable. Examples are: Changes in demand for a product, inventions, social changes, etc.

nonlegals Securities that do not conform to the statutory requirements in some states concerning investments for savings banks and trust funds.

nonlinear correlation Any correlation based on regression lines that are not straight lines, such as parabolas and hyperbolas.

nonliterate society A people who have no written form of communication. In our industrial society, the term refers to people unschooled in the basics of reading, writing, and arithmetic.

non-notification plan A lending arrangement wherein a dealer will sell his installment sales contracts to a bank, but will not so inform the customer, who will continue to make his payments to the dealer.

non obstante verdicto Latin for "notwithstanding the verdict." After a jury has rendered a verdict, the judge may give judgment to the contrary if there is no evidence from which a jury could have arrived at its decision or for other reasons specified by statutes.

nonparametric statistics Procedures that do not assume that the true arrays of all data are distributed according to the frequency curve of theoretical probability but, instead, that other types of distributions may occur.

429

nonparticipating policy *insurance* A policy for which the insured is charged a premium approximating the anticipated cost but with no provision for refunding of part of the premium in the form of a dividend.

nonperforming loan A loan on which interest payments are not being paid.

nonprice competition Actions taken by sellers to increase sales without lowering prices. Advertising, special promotions, etc., are some examples.

nonprofit endowment assurance A type of insurance policy in the United Kingdom in which the policyholder does not participate in the profits of the company.

nonprofit enterprises Generally, the objective of such projects is to provide services that are needed and that are socially acceptable. The government often grants tax relief to such organizations because they provide services the government might otherwise have to provide.

nonrecourse agreement A type of retail dealer financing wherein the dealer has no liability for the paper sold to a bank in case of default, except for honoring the warranty, affirming the genuineness of the paper, the terms of the sale, and the title.

nonrecourse financing A loan raised in such a manner as to leave the applicant with no responsibility to repay. In international trade, an exporter may be helped by the finance house giving credit directly to the importer, leaving the exporter without responsibility for a loan.

non sequitur A conclusion which does not logically follow from the premises adduced to support it.

nonstochastic model A model using no random variables.

nonsuit *law* A judgment against a plaintiff who has failed to prove his case or has defaulted.

nontariff barriers Obstacles to international trade that do not involve direct duties imposed on imported products. Unrealistic product specifications, quotas, licenses, etc., are examples.

nonverbal test A test that uses pictures, manipulative materials, or hypothetical situations in order to measure intelligence.

nonvoting stock Shares that do not give the holder a right to vote at corporate meetings.

Nordic council An advisory body consulting with Denmark, Iceland, Finland, Norway, and Sweden on social and economic matters.

Norges Bank Central bank of Norway. (*See* Section VII)

Norges Industriforbund A federation of Norwegian industries. Address: Bankplassen 4, Oslo, Norway.

norm Usually considered an "average" whether referring to the behavior of a person, a testing scale, or a base for the comparison of people or things.

normal curve *See* Gaussian Curve.

normal distribution *statistics* The curve expressing the relationship between the frequency (measured on the Y axis) and the deviations (positive or negative) from the mean (measured on the X axis) of a series of measurements. Over 99 percent of a normal distribution will lie within a range of three standard deviations on either side of the arithmetic mean, 95 percent will lie within a range of two standard deviations on either side, and 68 percent within a range of one standard deviation on either side.

normal personality A broad concept defined statistically as the most common type in a group, defined evaluatively as an ideal type, and often defined as an individual free from defects or disorders, especially psychiatric ones.

normal price A price just large enough to cover the cost of production and to yield the producer a reasonable profit.

normal-realistic objectives To give people a sense of accomplishment in achieving objectives, objectives must be realistic, but rigorous enough to bring out the best in people.

normative economics That part of the study of economics that concerns itself more with what ought to be than what is, which is "positive economics." Normative economics seeks to analyze and evaluate programs as to their social cost, etc.

Norsk Arbeidsgiverforening (NAF) Norwegian Employers' Confederation. Address: Oslo 23, Kr Augustgst.

North Atlantic Treaty Organization (NATO) A military alliance established in 1949 by Belgium, Canada, Denmark, France, Great Britain, Iceland, Italy, Luxembourg, the Netherlands, Norway, Portugal, and the United States. Greece, Turkey, and West Germany joined later, in 1952 and 1956 respectively. The original aim was to protect Western Europe from the Soviet Union and the Eastern Bloc. NATO policies are coordinated through the North Atlantic Council, Brussels, 1110, Belgium. Three commands are included in the structure

of NATO: European Command (SACEUR), the Atlantic Command (SACLANT), and the English Channel Command.

Northern Stock Exchange A provincial stock exchange in Manchester. (*See* Section VII)

Norwegian Central Bank *Norges Bank.* (*See* Section VII)

Norwegian chambers of commerce Includes about twelve chapters in all. Address: Oslo Chamber of Commerce, Drammensveien 30, Oslo 2.

nostro account A term meaning "our account with you" that denotes an account maintained by a bank with a foreign correspondent.

note of hand term for a promissory note in the United Kingdom.

note, United States A type of U.S. currency issued by the Department of Treasury. Such notes are no longer in circulation.

notice of motion In formal meetings, an action in which it is required that a proposed motion be placed on the formal agenda for consideration.

notice to creditors A newspaper notice placed by the executor or administrator of an estate that creditors should present their claims for payment. It is also taken as a notice that debtors of the estate should come forward and make payments.

notification plan The act of pledging accounts receivable as security for a loan and then notifying the customers maintaining the accounts receivable of such action. Usually the creditors will then make their payments directly to the party making a loan.

NOW account A savings account on

which interest is paid, but which can also be used as a checking account, sometimes on a limited basis.

NPV Net present value method.

nuclear complex In psychoanalysis, the Oedipus complex, which is regarded as the forerunner of later maladjustments if not properly resolved.

nudum pastum Literally, a naked promise. A promise that has no force in law because there is no consideration.

null hypothesis The assumption of the opposite of the hypothesis being investigated.

number completion test A test requiring the subject to continue a series of numbers according to the primary guiding principle. Used sometimes in psychological testing.

number factor One of the primary mental abilities; facility in dealing with numbers and number concepts.

numeraire A commodity chosen as a standard of value when dealing with multiple exchange to avoid the special problems raised by the peculiar characteristics of money, such as liquidity.

nunc pro tunc *law* Latin for "now as well as then." The phrase indicates that the decision of a court is effective retroactively.

nursery finance A type of financing made available in the United Kingdom to ongoing private companies that are planning to go public in the near to intermediate term.

nurture The sum total of all the environmental factors that influence growth and development, as opposed to heredity.

NV *Naamloze Vennootschap.* A joint-stock company under Netherlands law.

NZEF New Zealand Employers' Federation.

NZFL New Zealand Federation of Labor.

O

O In structural psychology, the observer or trained introspectionist.

OAPEC Organization of Arab Petroleum Exporting Countries. An organization established in 1968. The members are Algeria, Bahrain, Iraq, Kuwait, Libya, Qatar, Saudia Arabia, Syria, and the United Arab Emirates. Egypt was suspended from the group in 1975. This organization is a separate association from OPEC.

OAS *See* Organization of American States.

OASI Old Age and Survivors' Insurance.

oath A pledge or promise by which a person swears that a statement made, or about to be made, is true.

obiter dictum Latin for "what is said in passing." A statement or opinion by a court not necessary to the decision of a case and therefore not so binding in authority as a proposition necessarily involved in a decision.

objectives The specific aims of an organization.

objectives, commitment A positive and clearly defined method of stating, in writing, the objectives of an enterprise that suggests ascending levels of excellence.

objectives, inadequate Stated objectives that do not clearly convey to the reader or hearer what the manager intends, and thus may produce results less than the manager intends.

objectives of management 1. A managerial objective is the proposed goal which prescribes a definite scope and suggests a direction to apply to the efforts of the manager. 2. The activities involved in achieving the goals of the organization to which one is attached. Sometimes worded like this: "The achievement of goals through the use of people and other resources." These goals will vary widely, however, and the level of management where one is will generally dictate the immediate goals of the manager.

objectives of management, definiteness of 1) should be clearly defined and preferably quantified and measurable; 2) should be realistic in that they are attainable with some degree of difficulty and determination; 3) should be reasonably specific and known by all members of the business affected by them.

objectives of management, determination of Objectives are usually determined by top management personnel, often in concert with the individual manager involved, and sometimes with the input from lower echelon employees as well.

objectives of management, profit and While the objective of many enterprises is the making of a profit (tempered by many other objectives) not all enterprises seek a profit, such as churches, some hospitals, etc.

objective test A standardized, impersonal type of test often taking the form of true-false, completion, multiple choice, or matching items.

objectivism In philosophical psychology, the point of view which emphasizes empirical, verifiable inquiries of an impersonal nature.

objectivity and MBO Under certain circumstances objectivity seems to disappear under the MBO program, inasmuch as any failure will be judged subjectively, with nearly all people looking for other people to blame.

obligation The act of obliging; that which obligates; the binding power of a vow, promise, oath or contract. The origin of the word is found in the Latin term *obligato*, meaning "tying up".

obliterate To blot out, cancel, or cross out.

oblivescence Material in a state of partial or complete loss through forgetting.

oblivious The condition of having a thought extinguished from one's mind.

obscure Not clear, full, or distinct; clouded; imperfect.

obsessional neurosis The presence of vague anxieties and forebodings as disruptive, persistent ideational components; a maladjustment marked by troublesome fixed ideas.

obsolescence That condition or process by which anything gradually ceases to be useful or profitable, often because of changed conditions.

obsolescent managers Managers at any level can become obsolete by failing to stay abreast of the changing times or by being so emotionally unable to change that they become useless in the firm.

433

obsolescence of functions Changing objectives also call for changes in functions to achieve those objectives, thus rendering some old functions useless.

obstruct To hinder or to prevent progress, or to retard the progress of or make accomplishment difficult and slow.

obstructing justice Interference with the orderly process of law.

OBU Offshore banking unit. A foreign bank usually handling foreign exchange.

obvious Easily discovered, seen or understood, or readily perceived by the eye or the intellect.

occupancy ratio The percentage of available housing units fit for occupancy that are occupied. In hotel, motel, and hospital operations, the occupancy ratio is vital.

occupation 1. A trade or profession or a group of jobs with a large number of tasks held in common. 2. A vocation, calling, or profession in which one is usually or occasionally engaged. With regard to real estate, occupation denotes possession.

occupational analysis The identification of those main tasks of specific jobs to cause them to be grouped under one occupational description.

occupational description Setting out the main characteristics and responsibilities of a job. Also known as a job description.

occupational guidance Counseling with individuals with regard to the occupation(s) for which they seem best suited.

Occupational Guidance Scheme Set up by the Department of Employment in the United Kingdom and developed further by the Employment Service Agency, this organization was designed to assist people in choosing a career or making a career change.

occupational profile An analysis of all skills and occupations present in a specific industry and often expressed in ratios or proportions.

occupational psychologist A type of psychological practitioner who majors in psychological testing, ergonomics, job enrichment, job satisfaction, programmed instruction, etc.

occupational structure The pattern of occupations, usually in an entire nation, but sometimes confined to one industry.

occupational therapy Planned activities designed to facilitate the rehabilitation of the convalescent patient.

ochlophobia A morbid fear of crowds or crowded places.

O'Conner finger dexterity test A pegboard test of psychomotor skills, originating in the United States. The test involves sorting out small brass pins and placing them in groups of three holes.

odd dates Deals in foreign exchange and money markets in periods other than the regular market periods.

odd-lot doctrine *insurance* In the context of disability insurance, the doctrine is that although a worker can be physically capable of performing some work, because of lack of skills and intelligence or because of advanced age, it is practically impossible for him to find suitable work. In such situations, a court may find for permanent and total disability.

odd-lot dealers Members of a stock exchange who handle transactions in less than the usual trading unit of one hundred shares.

Odiorne's law "Things that do not change will remain the same." (George S. Odiorne, *MBO II* [Belmont, Calif.: David S. Lake, Pubs., Inc., 1979], p. 299.)

odium Hatred and dislike. Ill feelings toward a person.

OEM Original equipment manufacturer. A term denoting goods sold to or by a manufacturer as an entire unit, as opposed to a manufacturer selling or buying parts.

Offene Handelsgesellschaft General partnership under both Austrian and German company laws.

offer A promise or proposal made by one party to another with the intention that a legal relationship be created upon acceptance by the other party. Essentially, an offer is an essential ingredient for the formation of a contract.

offer curve *See* price-consumption curve.

Office of Management and Budget An agency of the U.S. federal government that advises on the annual budget, on federal programs, and on how money is being spent by other departments and agencies. Address: Executive Office Building, 17th Street & Pennsylvania Ave. NW, Washington, DC 20503.

Office of Manpower Economics (OME) An independent, nonstatutory body established in 1970 in the United Kingdom to counsel with government on wages, etc.

official exchange rate The ratio that is applied by the monetary authority of one country in exchanging its money for that of another country in the absence of free-floating exchange rates.

Official Journal of the Communities A publication of the European Community, published in Dutch, English, French, German, and Italian that provides regular reports on secondary legislation and other activities of the European Community.

ogive 1. A curve of frequency distribution (with frequency on the Y axis and the measured magnitude on the X axis) that is cumulative so that at any given point on the curve, all items of that value or less are included (or that value and more, if the ogive is to run in the other direction). 2. A curve representing a cumulative frequency distribution of scores.

OHG *See Offene Handelsgesellschaft.*

oligarchy A form of government in which the supreme power is vested in a few people.

OME Office of Manpower Economics in the United Kingdom.

omission The nonperformance of a duty required of a person with an awareness on his part that the performance is required or needful. Also refers to the nonperformance of a duty required by law.

omit To pass over, let alone, take no notice of, fail to do.

omnibus clause *insurance* In auto liability insurance, the clause providing that insurance protection also extends to those persons (other than owner) who are using a car with the consent of the insured and within the conditions of the policy.

omnibus motion A motion placed before a formal meeting that contains a number of different subjects that probably should be separate motions.

omnibus survey A type of market survey in which a lot of different information is sought for a number of different clients.

on account Used in relation to a debt, the term means a partial satisfaction of an account as contrasted with payment in full.

on arrival A phrase used in relation to drafts and bills of exchange, requiring the collecting bank to present the same for payment on the arrival of the goods to which the draft relates.

on call An obligation is said to be "on call" when it is to be met or becomes payable when demanded.

on line The description of a part of a computer system that is directly under the control of the central processing unit as opposed to off-line activities that take place in the computer system but not under the control of the central processing unit.

on-line storage A situation in which a computer data store is directly controlled by the central processing unit of a computer.

on stream A term describing a part of a complete line in a continuous production process.

Ondernemingsrad A "works council" that is a legal requirement in the Netherlands for firms with more than one hundred employees.

one hundred percent reserve money A somewhat antiquated way of referring to a plan to require commercial banks to hold legal reserves equal to their deposits. Thus no loans could be made by a commercial bank except to the extent of the bank's net worth. The purpose of such a plan is to prevent changes in the volume of bank credit.

one-man, one-boss concept It is generally conceded that no person can successfully answer to two managers, so one boss alone should deal with one subordinate and the employee should know to whom he should be committed.

"1-2-3 bank" An institution in the United Kingdom that carries a higher status than a finance company, but does not have the standing and proved resources of a commercial bank.

opcentiemen A Belgium local tax that is part of the income-tax structure.

OPEC *See* Organization of Petroleum Exporting Countries.

Open Accounts Scheme A plan operated in the United Kingdom under which the Export Credits Guarantee Department guarantees to an exporting firm's bank the financing of short-term transactions made on open account.

open bid An offer to perform a contract together with the price of the materials or work but with the right to reduce the price to meet the price quoted by others for the same job.

open contract A contract in which the parties, the subject of the contract, and the consideration are all ascertained, leaving the other terms to be implied by law.

open-door policy 1. A policy followed by some top managers to allow employees access to them in order to make suggestions, air grievances, etc. 2. The policy of admitting citizens of foreign countries to a country to trade on equal terms with the country's own citizens.

open-end credit plan A plan prescribing the terms of credit transactions which may be made thereunder from time to time and under the terms of which a finance charge may be computed on the outstanding unpaid balance from time to time thereunder.

open indent An importer's purchase order to an exporter, which may be filled with goods from any manufacturer or firm provided the goods meet the proper specifications.

open insurance policy A policy in which the maximum limit of the insurer's liability is set forth in the policy obliging the insurer to pay the actual value of the loss up to the maximum limit. Such a policy is called an "unvalued policy," and usually fire insurance policies are examples of this type.

open letter of credit A letter of credit without special conditions. (*See also* letter of credit)

open listing A contract between a real estate agent and a seller wherein anyone selling real estate will receive a commission.

open-market operations The buying and selling of securities in the open market by a central bank, such as the Bank of England. As in the U.S. with the Federal Reserve, central banks use open market operations to control the money supply. (*See also* Federal Reserve System, Section VII)

open-market rate The interest or discount rate for commercial paper on the open market.

open-office planning A new type of office plan that emerged some thirty years ago, where few offices were private and where most people worked at a station in a large, open office. This was tried by many industries, including banking, but was less than successful. Such a plan is most adaptable to a firm that has large amounts of similar work of a repetitive nature going on at all times.

open order In finance, an order to buy or sell securities on a stock exchange at, above, or below a stated price whenever the order can be filled.

open policy *insurance* A policy covering a risk for a specified time or stated value, but permitting interchange of the goods insured. Often used in transportation.

open stock Stock of a particular type of merchandise such as silverware or china that is kept to fill in broken or missing pieces in a set.

Open University An educational system set up in the United Kingdom in 1969 by Royal Charter that is designed to offer correspondence courses, along with radio and television courses, for people unable to attend conventional schools.

open-circuit television (OCTV) In the United Kingdom, a broadcast transmission of television signals to an unrestricted audience, as contrasted with closed circuit television by cable.

437

open-end company The technical name for what is usually called a mutual fund; a company incorporated under the Investment Act of 1940. Such a company continuously offers its shares for sale, as opposed to a "closed-end" company, where the number of shares remain static after the original offering. An open-end company redeems its own shares.

open-end contract A contract that permits a buyer to order additional units upon the same terms without additional consent by a seller.

open-end investment trust An investment company that sells and rebuys its own stock at book value plus a handling charge.

open-end mortgage A mortgage which allows additional sums to be borrowed, and usually providing that at least the stated ratio of assets to the debt be retained.

open-ended An approach to learning that leaves students free to follow a number of different solutions rather than one predetermined solution.

opening price The price at which the first sale on an organized market is made on a particular day.

operate To act on or function, especially with force, influence, or control. To control the workings or function of a machine, motor vehicle, etc.

operating assets Assets that contribute to regular income from the operations of a business.

operating costs Cost of goods sold plus production expenses.

Operational Research Society A professional association in the United Kingdom designed to promote operational research studies and standards. Address: 64 Cannon Street, London EC4.

operational stocks Work-in-progress stocks or buffer stocks.

operations, influence of values on Values held by top managers that usually affect the total enterprise more than is known. Three values seem to dominate and to be most important: 1) the most important human relationships are those influencing directly the organization's objectives; 2) knowledgeable approaches to problems are to be emphasized; emotional responses are to be played down; 3) human relationships are influenced most effectively through unilateral direction and control, as well as through rewards and penalties that sanction all three values.

operations research Consists of collecting available data on a problem, processing the data, and from them resolving quantitative reports on the relative merits of various alternative actions.

operative supervision The question of how many operators can successfully be supervised by a superior. The number six is often used as an ideal, but this would vary widely according to the operations in which the operatives were engaged.

operator/operative In the United Kingdom, terms that indicate a worker who labors at a repetitive task, usually doing the same operations over and over, as contrasted with a craftsman, who is able to perform many tasks.

opinion *law* A conclusion or belief held with confidence after an analysis of the facts and the law relating to the matter. Used synonymously with the term judgment.

Oporto Stock Exchange *Bolsa de Porto,* or Portuguese stock exchanges.

opportunities in management The chances that one might be able to have a career in management depend upon several factors: 1) how fast the economy is growing; 2) the rate of technological change; 3) the type of work prominent in the region or nation in question. (It is currently believed that the opportunities in management are almost endless for those people who remain abreast of technology and of human understanding.)

opportunity cost *economics* The dollar amount that would be derived from the employment of a factor of production in the best alternative use. (*See also* alternative cost)

optical character recognition (OCR) A type of character-recognition system used in certain input devices to feed specific and prerecorded data into a computer.

optimism The belief that life is essentially and basically good.

optimization A balancing out of the various variables and parameters in an entire business operation, or an entire department, to attempt to achieve the optimum efficiency.

optimization of input-output One feature of the quantitative school of management thought, "optimization" includes all aspects of the enterprise, and a certain number of people is called the "optimum population".

optimum population In any given state

of the art and accumulation of capital, there is a certain number of people whose labor will produce the largest possible per capita product from a given territory.

option 1. A contract, which must have all the characteristics of a contract to be legal, giving a party rights with respect to property, usually the right to buy or sell the property. 2. The privilege existing in one person to buy or sell certain merchandise or specified securities, if he chooses, at any time within an agreed period at a fixed price.

optional date The time at which a municipality or corporation has the right to redeem its obligations under certain conditions.

option dealing In general, the dealing in rights to buy or sell property that is granted in exchange for an agreed-upon sum. If the option right is not exercised at the end of a specified period, the option buyer forfeits money.

order A mandate, precept; a command or direction given with authority.

"order paper" With regard to negotiable instruments, a document that is in such form as to require endorsement by the payee or endorsee. "Order paper" can be converted to "bearer paper" by a blank endorsement.

order to show cause *law* An order by a court to bring a question on for a hearing. The order states that the party served with the order is directed to show cause on the date set why the action desired by the party bringing the order should not be taken.

ordinal utility theory The proposition that economic analysis must proceed from a ranking of pleasurable alternatives since there is no unit for measurement of pleasure.

ordinance A subordinate legislation promulgated with the authority of a properly established body of government, such as a city or town.

ordinary shares A term usually synonymous with "common stock" in a company, which is an equity investment. Usually common stock has voting rights, but not always. Usually the most prolific type of stock.

ordinate The Y axis of a graph.

organic populism Ad hoc organizations or groups, such as task forces, project management group, etc., that assist in keeping change before the people without destroying the basic organizational structure.

Organisation Commune Africaine, Malgache et Mauricienne (OCAM) An organization established in 1965 to promote political and economic cooperation between Cameroon, the Central African Republic, Chad, Congo, Dahomey, Gabon, Ivory Coast, Madagascar, Mauritius, Niger, Rwanda, Senegal, Togo, Burkina Faso, and Zaire. Address: BP 437, Yaounde, Cameroon.

organization chart 1. A pyramidal chart depicting the organization of a firm from the top man down, usually to line supervisors in the case of manufacturing industries. Ostensibly, the chart should show where each person functions and his relationship with those above and below him. It is often used to denote channels of communications and lines of authority. At best, such a chart cannot draw the fine distinctions that people depicted on the chart would like to see. Example: The "Assistant to the President" may be shown on the top of the chart next to the president, but may have no authority over the people below him. Some firms have discarded the chart altogether, since, in the midst of change, the chart tends to become outdated before it is printed. 2. One of the tools of formal organization, which is functional in nature. Usually it is accompanied by a personnel and job manual, a job description, and various other details designed to acquaint the employee with the company and with his job. Also known as organization tree.

organization chart, procedural flow chart and A combined organization chart and the procedural flow chart for a specific procedure that makes clear the functions of personnel in that specific procedure.

organization climate The atmosphere in a business firm or other organization, which is often a reflection of top management philosophy. Some of the prominent indicators of this atmosphere might include: 1) the degree to which there is cooperation and teamwork; 2) the extent to which people in the organization are committed to its success; 3) the effectiveness of communications; 4) the degree to which innovativeness is encouraged; 5) the way internal conflicts are resolved; 6) the degree to which lower-echelon employees participate in decision making; 7) the degree to which the organization runs on mutual trust between various echelons of employees.

organization development (OD) The continuing evolution of a business firm or some other organization in the light of continuing change. This often means the periodic change of aims, along with all the other changes necessary to meet new goals. Successful companies usually make this evolution a priority in everything they do; less successful companies or failing companies often neglect to evolve.

Organization of American States (OAS) Established in 1948 to promote cooperation in economic activities between the member states, which are: Argentina, Barbados, Bolivia, Brazil, Chile, Colombia, Costa Rica, Dominica, Ecuador, El Salvador, Guatemala, Haiti, Honduras, Jamaica, Mexico, Nicaragua, Panama, Paraguay, Peru, Trinidad and Tobago, the United States, Uruguay, and Venezuela. Canada has observer status within the organization. While this organization has been helpful, it has yet to achieve the goals set out in the beginning, due primarily to conflicting national interests. Address: Washington, DC 10006.

Organization of Petroleum Exporting Countries (OPEC) Formed in 1970, OPEC is a cartel made up of petroleum-exporting nations. The purposes of OPEC are to maintain stable oil prices for exports of its members and to promote economic trade interests with the industrialized oil-consuming nations.

organization structure 1. The framework within which managerial tasks are performed. 2. The dividing up of various operations in the total operation of a company, with the proper number of workers and management personnel in each division. To make the structure effective, there must be utmost cooperation between working groups, such as divisions or departments, promoted by good communications.

organization structure, functional A situation where the structure of the organization is built around functions.

organization tree *See* organization chart.

organization, behavior approach This approach views management as a system of cultural interrelationships, is sociologically oriented, and stems from the development of behavioral sciences as applied to management.

organized exchange A place where goods or property rights are bought and sold according to recognized rules. Examples are the stock and bond markets and the commodity markets.

organizing function of management The work of allocating tasks, establishing relationships, and maintaining relationships in the work situation.

organizing function of management, social requirements of The concept that the organizing function can no longer be looked upon as merely an economic and logical one, but also as a social function.

original cost theory of rate making In public utility and railroad rate making, original cost is the cost of the property at the time it was first devoted to public service minus accrued depreciation.

original motion A motion made in a formal meeting in its original form before any amendments are made.

original nature The totality of traits and characteristics due wholly to heredity.

O'Rourke Mechanical Aptitude Test Originally an achievement test, but now often used as a mechanical aptitude test.

Osaka Securities Exchange One of the major Japanese stock exchanges. (*See* Section VII)

Osgood scales A market-research tool invented in the United States by Osgood that consists of multiple-choice questions or precoded questions for use in market-research interviews. The participant must choose answers from the answers proposed in the multiple-choice questions.

Oslo Bors Oslo Stock Market, Section VII.

ostensible agency *law* An agency under the law when a principal causes a third party to believe another to be his agent, whether he is in fact an agent or not.

ostensible authority The apparent authority of an ostensible agent.

Österreichische Nationalbank Austrian central bank (*See* Section VII)

Otis Self-Administering Tests of Mental Ability intelligence tests designed in the United States that were originally intended for schools, but are now used in industry as well.

ought The term in a strict sense denotes an obligation that may or may not amount to a legal duty, depending upon the context. The term is synonymous with "must" if other contexts require such an interpretation.

ouster Dispossession. Generally a wrongful dispossession in respect to which the aggrieved party becomes entitled to pursue legal action.

outlay In governmental accounting, expenditures that occur in the acquisition of fixed assets. Also known as capital outlay.

output 1. As related to a cybernetic system, outputs are the goods and services, hardware and software, that come out of a system. These outputs are more valuable than all of the inputs used up in their making, and added value can be computed. 2. *taxes* The name given to that phase of production that has just been finished, with the VAT levied against the new wealth created by that phase of production. It should be remembered that the VAT is added to each phase of the production and the total amount is included in the price of the finished product.

outstanding Remaining undischarged, unpaid, or uncollected. Existing as an adverse claim.

outstanding bonds Bonds that have been issued and sold to the public and that have not as yet been redeemed.

outward trade mission Term used in the United Kingdom to refer to trips to trade fairs and to other meetings to "hawk" exports from Great Britain. In the United Kingdom, these are often financed by the Fairs and Promotions Branch of the Department of Trade.

outwork The practice of some businesses in recent years of allowing certain employees to do some work at home. Usually this consists of simple work such as addressing envelopes, putting simple parts together, or using a home computer to work on reports.

overachievement A performance that exceeds the level predicted by tests or other measuring techniques.

overall impression A "method" sometimes used in personnel selection when there are several applicants for one job, wherein the interviewer will get reactions from the interviewees and perhaps select an applicant from those reactions.

overall managerial controls A method of control that looks at the whole of the enterprise and provides simple but effective benchmarks for measuring and evaluating performance in all major areas.

overall market capacity The ability of an entire market to absorb production of a product, with no measurements made of differing sectors of that market.

over-bought 1. In securities or commodities, a term denoting that a price is too high; 2. Generally, a term denoting excessive inventory, especially in retailing.

overcapacity The presence of more firms in an industry with the ability to produce more output than can be sold at prices high enough to realize a profit.

overcapitalize To place too high a value on property; to place an unreasonably high value on the nominal capital of a company; or to provide an enterprise with more capital than it can assimilate.

overdetermined system *econometrics* A system of equations (even though consistent and independent) such that the number of equations is greater that the number of variables and different solutions are obtained, depending on which variable is eliminated first.

overdraft A term in banking parlance meaning any adverse balance in a customer's account, whether the balance was created by writing checks or by debiting past-due bills and notes to that account.

overdue A negotiable instrument, such as a check, is said to be overdue when it has been in circulation for an unreasonable length of time.

overextended A term in business denoting a high ratio of liabilities to assets.

overhead An indirect cost. In the generic sense, the term means any cost not specifically associated with production, such as administrative costs.

overinsured A term denoting that an individual is carrying more insurance than is necessary for the desired protection.

overlapping debt In municipal finance, that portion of the debt of government units for which the residents of a community are responsible.

overlapping procedures, principle of A minimum amount of time required to perform a number of successive tasks to produce one product is obtained by performing the same kinds of tasks at the same time.

overmanning Having more employees in a plant than are necessary for efficient operation.

overpopularity and demarketing A situation in which a certain product or service is extremely popular, but the producer does not wish to appeal to all segments of the market, and thus the producer attempts to eliminate those unwanted segments of the market.

overrule To supersede, annul, make void, or reject by subsequent action or decision.

oversaving An excess of saving in a given period than can be profitably used in maintaining the current scale of investing.

oversaving theory of the business cycle A term denoting that oversaving, and thus underconsumption, can result in a downturn in the economy.

Overseas Projects and Technology Division (DT) An agency in the United Kingdom designed to provide information for UK firms on overseas projects, etc. Address: Department of Trade, 1 Victoria Street, London SW1.

over training The act of training a person to a higher level than is needed for his or her job. This practice often results in dissatisfaction for the worker, who may grow bored in a task that is not demanding enough. Although people often debunk the concept of "over-qualification," it is a very real problem in industry.

overvaluating A term frequently used in psychological testing to indicate that too much trust is being placed in the test results.

owner one who possesses; one who possesses property, which confers rights.

Oxbridge tutorial system A type of instruction used traditionally at Oxford and Cambridge, where instruction is done in small groups and attendance is voluntary.

P

PABLA Acronym for "problem analysis by logical approach." Devised by the UK Atomic Energy Authority.

pacers Name for workers in the United Kingdom who set the pace that management considers should be the norm for all plant workers.

Pacific Coast Stock Exchange A regional stock market in the United States.

Pacific Standard Time Local time at a point at the 120th meridian.

package courses Courses that include books, slides, films, etc.

package tour A vacation tour the price of which covers all the expenses of the trip, except personal expenditures.

packaging Methods and materials companies use to enclose products for handy marketing. This has become an expensive practice, and one which directly affects the environment.

pack test *marketing* A technique for checking the effectiveness of a product's packaging.

paid-in surplus A surplus that is paid to stockholders and does not arise from profits. Often, in opening a bank, a surplus is paid in at the time of organization. Also, the sale of stock shares above the par price results in a paid-in surplus.

paid-up additions *insurance* In life insurance, units of single premium insurance bought by application of the dividends on a policy under the insured's option concerning the disposition of dividends.

paid-up insurance Insurance for which the policyholder has completed the payments, but the policy has not as yet matured. Or a case in which the insured has stopped paying premiums and uses the cash value of the policy to pay up a certain percentage of the face value of the policy.

Palais de la Bourse, Marseille Marseille stock exchange. (*See* Section VII)

palletization Warehousing and transporting goods on wooden frames or pallets that are so constructed as to be easily handled with forklifts.

Pan-African Workers Congress (PAWC) Established in 1959 by the uniting of several trade union confederations. Address: BP 8814, Kinshasa, Zaire.

panacea in everyday parlance, a cure-all.

panel interview A personnel selection process in which a panel does interviewing rather than just one person.

panic *economics* A sudden, intense, overwhelming fear. Often related to wide swings in the stock market or other economic phenomena.

panoramic office planning (POP) Term in the United Kingdom for open office planning.

pansophy Universal, encyclopedic knowledge.

pantophobia Irrational fear of anything or everything.

pantry check A market-research term describing surveys designed to show what consumer goods a homemaker actually has.

paper profits The profit that would be realized on stock shares or any other assets which have appreciated in value if they were sold.

paper standard A monetary standard that has no commodity such as gold or silver behind it.

par value Nominal value of stock. (*See also* face value, nominal value)

PAR Program Analysis and Review.

paradigm A model or schematic representation.

paradox of thrift The concept that if the people of a nation save more than they should, economic activity will fall off, unemployment will increase, and a recession, or a depression, will occur. This development could ultimately mean that people out of jobs would not have money to save, thus the savings rate would decrease, and there could be an upswing in the economy after a given amount of time. Essentially, the teaching from this concept is that what is good for individuals in an economy may not always be good for the economy as a whole.

parallelism The concept that mind and body are totally different entities that function simultaneously but that have no causal relationship.

paralogism Fallacious reasoning.

parameter 1. *econometrics* A constant or the coefficient of a variable in a model or system of equations. 2. The property or quality of an infinite number of data, from which the sampling has been drawn; hence, popularly, the graphic representation of the data in the form of a curve with corrections for true probability.

parent company *See* holding company.

Paretian optimality A condition in which no further improvement of one's total utility can be achieved without taking utility away from someone else.

Pareto's law 1. A generalization regarding the distribution of income in a population. A frequency distribution of incomes at different times and places will show a high degree of stability. A frequency distribution of income sizes would be highly skewed toward the low-income group. 2. In most business activities a minority of the total produces the most problems, costs, profits, or whatever area one wishes to measure. This has been dubbed the law of the trivial many and the critical few. The moral of this law is that firms should give greater amount of attention to the areas that can be called critical, and less attention to those areas termed trivial.

pari materia *law* Latin for "same subject." All language in legal statutes or contracts treating the same subject is supposed to get at the meaning so that one consistent meaning is applied throughout the statutes, wherever possible.

pari passu *law* Latin for "by the same step." Refers to situations calling for equal treatment of those with equal rights.

Paris Bourse Paris stock exchange. (*See* Section VII)

Paris Treaty A term referring to the 1951 Treaty of Paris, which established the European Coal and Steel Community (ECSC).

parity price 1. The concept that prices received by farmers for their products should, over time, equate with the general price levels of the products they must buy. 2. In the United States, the price of an agricultural commodity that gives a commodity the purchasing power, with respect to articles farmers must buy, equivalent to that price which the product had in a base period, usually August 1909 to July 1914, a period of relatively high prosperity for farmers. Parity prices are published monthly on some commodity prices and semiannually on others.

Parkinson's Law "Law" of business formulated by Professor Northcote Parkinson: "Work expands to fill the time available."

parliamentary law That body of rules governing the internal procedure of a legislative group. *Robert's Rules of Order* is used in Congress and form the backbone for rules governing most formal bodies.

parol contract An oral agreement.

parol evidence A verbal statement offered in evidence in a court of law.

parsimony, law of The economy or simplicity of assumptions in logical formulation. In management theory, the attempt to make simple highly complex theories.

partial correlation The net relationship of a dependent variable to one or more independent variables after the effect of one or more other independent variables has been held constant statistically.

partial equilibrium An equilibrium reached from a consideration of only a few indigenous variables while other economic variables are held constant.

participating loan A loan in which several banks participate, either because the loan is too large for one bank or because the risk of the loan needs to be spread among several banks.

participating policy *insurance* A policy for which the insured is charged a premium greater than the anticipated cost with the excess to be refunded in the form of dividends.

participating preferred stock Preferred stock that entitles the owner, after receiving the regular preferred dividend, to share in the profits declared as dividends with the holders of common stock, either immediately or after a stipulated amount has been paid to the holders of common stock.

participation 1. In business, a general term denoting methods used to get workers more concerned with the overall success of the company. One method popular now is "participative management," in which workers are given an opportunity to participate in some decision making. 2. The psychological and physical involvement of an employee to contribute to the decision-making process, with emphasis upon those areas in which the employee has a personal interest and in which the employee can assume his share of responsibility for the decisions made.

participative theory of leadership The concept that people can best be led when they have a part in outlining the direction they will take.

particular average *insurance* In marine insurance, any loss resulting from an accident other than normal perils of the sea is not apportioned among the shippers but borne by the particular owner of the damaged goods.

partnership An ancient form of business enterprise in which each partner historically had full responsibility for the business actions of other partners. This has been modified some so that there are now limited partnerships in which

partners are limited to the amount of their investment, should the business fail.

party plan A method of selling, now widely used in the United States, in which the salesperson holds a party for invited guests and presents and demonstrates, if necessary, the products to be sold. Usually the party will be held in the home of some well-known person, who does the actual inviting to the party. This is done so refusals can be held to a minimum. Each guest is given a small gift and is expected to make a purchase. The host is given a larger gift for his or her services. During the party, each person present may be given the opportunity to hold his or her own party, thus compounding the good for the product that can be done in one meeting. While many people look askance at this method of selling, it is widespread and apparently successful.

passive Lacking in assertiveness; inactive.

patent 1. In common law, the grant of some privilege, property, or authority by the Crown (government) to one or more individuals. 2. In the United States, the rights granted to an inventor under Federal Statutes relating to patents to exclude all others from making, using, or selling the registered invention. A patent confers a statutory monopoly for a given number of years. 3. The legal securing of valuable property rights on inventions, etc. The U.S. Constitution provided for securing these rights, which gave the United States a firm foundation for further innovation.

Patent Office and Industrial Property and Copyright Department (DT) In the United Kingdom, the office of the Department of Trade that handles and registers patents, trademarks, and industrial property rights. Address: Patent Office & Industrial and Copyright Department, Department of Trade, Southampton Buildings, Chancery Lane, London WC2A 1AY.

patents, foreign All nations have patent rights and patent laws, and many of them are similar to those of the United States, particularly those of Western Europe. Most major nations have treaties covering patents that may affect other countries.

paternalism A long-used method of managing in which the boss assumes the role of a father and the workers assume the role of his children. The boss assures the employees that he will take care of them, and they, in return, are to give him their full loyalty. Some management experts look upon this method as thinly disguised authoritarianism.

Paterson method A method of job evaluation designed by T. T. Paterson of Strathclyde University, Scotland. The assumption of the method is that all jobs can be analyzed by the degree of decision making involved in a job, along with policy making, etc.

pattern interview An interview based on two different techniques: 1) the interviewer puts the same questions to a number of people and looks for the emerging continuities in their responses; 2) the interviewer analyses the answers received and uses these results to project the prospective employee's behavior in the future.

patterned decisions Decisions that are made when the people involved are presented with no alternatives, and the

whole process becomes a "follow-the-leader" situation.

Pauschalsteuer A graduated tax levied on incomes of certain foreigners in Switzerland instead of the national defense tax. Also known as *impot a forfait.*

PAV Potential acquisition valuation.

PAWC *See* Pan-African Workers Congress.

pay-as-you-earn (PAYE) A withholding tax levied on income and deducted from paychecks at the source.

pay-as-you-go A situation in which retirement pensions are paid out of contributions currently being made into the plan, as contrasted with the payments coming from a fund contributed to by the pensioner and perhaps by the employer as well.

payback *See* rate of return.

payment-by-results Another term for performance-related pay.

payment pause A temporary freezing of wages and salaries by government order.

payment system Refers to one of two systems generally used for employees who work by the hour: 1) performance-related pay or 2) per-hour wages.

pay-out ratio The ratio of dividends to earnings in a given year.

PBR Payment by results.

PDG In France, President Directeur General, or Chief Executive, of a limited liability public company.

PDM *See* Physical distribution management.

P/E ratio *See* Price earnings ratio.

peaceful picketing The picketing done by workers during a labor dispute that is nonviolent in nature. The objective of the picketers is to call attention to the dispute.

peak absences Points in a demand cycle in which the workload is relatively light due to decreased demand.

peak loads Points in a demand cycle in which demand increases greatly and in which employment is high.

pecking order A term indicating the dominance-submission relationships in a situation. Such relationships are revealed in the lines of authority controlling the members of a group.

peer An equal; people who live and work in similar ways and do similar jobs.

peer rating In the United States, a method of rating students in some business schools in which levels of attainment are checked at intervals and qualitative judgments are made concerning the progress of the student.

pegboard test A test of manual dexterity in which pegs are put into specially designed holes within given time limits.

penetration pricing A method of pricing often done when launching a new product. The market is saturated with the product at very low prices and then the price is raised slowly as the product gains acceptance.

penny stock A low-priced and often speculative stock that sells for a dollar or less.

pension a regular payment made to a retired employee either by his company or by a firm entrusted with the pension fund by the company. Most firms also have disability clauses in their pension plans, as well as death payments to beneficiaries of employees.

pensionable salary All of the earned income of an employee that is considered when calculating entitlement to a pension.

pensionable service Those years of an employee's service that are considered when calculating entitlement to a pension.

people, ideas, resources, and objectives (PIRO) A basic concept that these are the resources with which the manager works.

per curiam *law* Latin for "by the court." Applied to a court opinion that is not credited to one individual judge but rather is the expression of a group of judges.

per my et per tout *law* French for "by the half and by the whole." This is the mode of description for property held in joint tenancy. For possession and survivorship, each joint tenant holds the whole; for purposes of conveying, each owns half.

per stirpes Latin for "through the branches." A rule for descent of property in which a person dies without a will. The presiding probate judge will rule as to how the property is divided, using the "family tree" as a guide.

PER The Professional and Executive Recruitment Service of the Department of Employment in the United Kingdom.

percentile curve *statistics* An ogive in which the scores within each interval are distributed in terms of their percentages of the total distribution. (*See also* ogive)

percentile rank The relative position of each score in a distribution as arranged on a scale of one hundred. (Thus a percentile rank of 80 indicates that 79 percent of the scores lie below the given raw, or obtained score.)

perception A process by which a person becomes aware of the significance of events.

perceptive Capable of making sharp and accurate discriminations among sensory or ideational data or concepts.

perceptual distortion A term used in market research to denote that an interviewee's opinion of a product may be skewed by interests and value systems.

perceptual speed A primary mental ability that is measured by tests of quick, accurate grasping of visually presented items or of similarities and differences among them.

perfectionism A neurotic obsession with achieving unattainable lofty goals, even when working at tasks of minor importance.

perfectly elastic demand A situation in which a small price change results in a much larger or unlimited increase in the quantity demanded. This situation also applies to supply.

perfectly inelastic demand A situation in which a small price change results in virtually no change in demand This situation also applies to supply.

performance test A measure, often making use of manipulative materials,

that involves a minimum of verbal instructions or no instruction at all.

performance tolerance The degree of error that can be tolerated in an employee's performance, particularly if this employee is working on a machine with a well-defined ability to produce.

peril point The limit beyond which reductions in tariffs would substantially injure domestic industries. At times in our history, Congress has instructed the U.S. Tariff Commission to arrive at this point regarding many different products.

perks A shortened form of perquisites. Fringe benefits, often of an informal kind, that are usually confined to top management personnel.

perpetual inventory The determination of what is on hand by starting at a specific point with a physical count and thereafter adding acquisitions and deducting disbursements so that the amount on hand can always be determined.

personal accident policy *insurance* A policy that pays a lump sum upon the accidental death of the policyholder and pays usually lesser sums on the loss of limbs, etc. Normally, the face payment is higher when the holder is traveling in commercial transportation. People who travel extensively often carry such policies, since the premiums are quite low.

personal goals and MBO The MBO process generally ignores the personal goals of the individual, which can be a weakness unless some means are found for combining the two.

personal holding company A holding

company that under income-tax law derives at least 80 percent of its gross income from royalties, dividends, interest, annuities, and sales of securities, and in which over 50 percent of the outstanding stock is owned by not more than five persons.

personal income That part of national income that flows to individuals.

personal preference criteria Most managers have personal biases that might determine whom they hire to work and whom they reject. While federal non-discrimination laws have limited these biases to a marked degree, such biases are still present and will often be followed by a manager when he can get by with them.

personal property Movable property, such as furniture, as contrasted with real estate.

personal qualification inventory A combination of education and personal traits that may well point to probable success or failure in a specific task.

personal representative *law* The term applied to the person carrying out the disposition of the estate of a decedent. This person is called an executor if named in the will, and an administrator in case there is no will, and he is named by the court.

personal savings That part of personal income not spent on personal consumption expenditures and not paid in personal income taxes.

personal selling This action is defined by marketing personnel as creating a desire in the buyer to purchase goods, which is more important to buyer than the time or money spent.

personal-behavior theory of leadership A concept that a leader can be understood through his personal qualities and through his personal actions as a leader. It is agreed that the leader's behavior will not be the same under all circumstances, but will be modified according to the situation.

personality promotion A market promotion in which a celebrity will make an appearance on behalf of a company and perhaps visit with the people buying the product the company produces.

Personnel Classification Test A rapid screening device that appraises verbal reasoning and number facility.

personnel department The department in a company that deals directly with the problems of personnel, from hiring to firing. Often called the department of human resources.

personnel policies Broad guidelines by which a company deals with its human resources.

personnel specification The description of the kind of employee required for a specific job.

PERT Program (Project) Evaluation and Review Technique. A technique first used in WW II. to judge the critical paths followed in the activities and events of a specific project.

PERT-COST That part of the Program Evaluation and Review Technique that deals with costs rather than time.

Perth Stock Exchange One of six Australian stock exchanges. (*See* Section VII)

Peru Stock Exchange *See* Section VII.

peseta Basic unit of currency in Spain.

Peter Principle "In a hierarchy every employee tends to rise to his level of incompetence." First verbalized by Dr. Lawrence J. Peter, in his book by the same name. (*See* Section VI)

phantom stocks A type of bonus plan in which participants receive partial or complete financial benefits from stock share ownership, while not actually owning the stock. Books are kept on the plan with complete exactness.

phi coefficient An index of the degree of association between two arrays of discrete scores.

Philadelphia-Baltimore-Washington Stock Exchange *See* Section VII.

Philadelphia lawyer A colloquialism denoting a shrewd lawyer who is adept at finding loopholes in the law.

Phillips Curve 1. A chart devised by A. W. Phillips in the United Kingdom in 1958 to depict changes in money wage rates to the percentage of the labor force that is unemployed. The Lipsey Equation further refined this two years later. 2. The strong inverse relation between the rate of the money wage increase, as it is plotted on one axis, and the unemployment rate, which is plotted on the other axis. The curve for the United States suggests that with 5 to 6 percent unemployment, prices will remain fairly stable; if unemployment is reduced to 3 percent, however, rising prices would quickly result. (*See also* Lipsey Equation)

phobias Highly exaggerated fears or overwhelming compulsions to do certain things or to refrain from doing certain things. Example: Most workers enjoy a clean working atmosphere, but this can become a phobia when the person involved is overly sensitive about even modest disarray in the workplace.

phototelegram service Essentially a fax service offered by the post office in the United Kingdom. Address: Electra House, Victoria Embankment, London WC2R 3HL.

physical distribution management (PDM) An integrated approach to all movement of raw materials and finished goods related to the enterprise of a firm.

physical inventory The physical counting, at intervals, of all items to show exactly the stock on hand.

physiocrat school A school of economic thought holding that only land is value creating in its product, which is called the "produit net." Another basic tenet of this school is that economics should analyze transactions in terms of flows of income to get at the changes in relationships. This was done by a chart called *tableau economique,* which was attributed to many French economists of the seventeenth and eighteenth centuries.

physiological age The level of glandular, muscular, and skeletal development an individual has attained as compared to the normal level of any given chronological age.

pictogram A diagram depicting figures or products printed in different sizes, usually to denote quantity. These diagrams may represent numbers of employees, production units, etc. A key normally accompanies the pictogram at the bottom of the design.

piece work A term not used much currently denoting payment-by-results. In short, one is paid for the amount of work.

pie chart A circular graph divided into various sized "slices" to indicate the sectors of an enterprise being depicted. Sales, for example, might be so depicted with respect to the regions of the country where the sales were made. Or the total revenues of the firm might be depicted with respect to how they were divided.

piggyback service The loading of semi trailers on railroad flat cars for line haul, with the pick-up and delivery being done by the semis. This system has improved work for the railroads, while relieving many long hauls for the truckers.

pignorative contract In European law, the pledging of property as security, which is the American equivalent of a mortgage.

Pigou effect The proposition that a fall in a price level will cause an increase in consumption due to lower prices; the increase in consumption is supposed to be sufficient to prevent a fall in employment.

pilot production The initial production of a product under shop-floor conditions to test the best methods for proceeding into full production.

pilot study A brief and relatively simple trial before an extensive experiment or investigation is begun.

pink-tea picketing A somewhat archaic U.S. term denoting perfunctory, nonviolent picketing, usually set up simply to attract the attention of passers-by.

pioneer product A totally new product in design or function as contrasted with a product designed to compete with existing products.

piscary The right to fish in another's waters.

planned economy An economy in which the basic resources are owned or controlled by the central government that makes plans for their use in production. This planning is almost universal in a Communist government and exists in some degree in Socialist governments.

planned investment The spending done by business to purchase capital equipment and inventory, which constitutes the active demand for capital goods.

planned learning experience Experiences planned for an employee by his firm that will complement all experiences he should have leading to the ultimate employment on a specific job.

planning blight A situation in which an urban area begins to decay, and no one wants to improve the property since it is known that there is planned development for that area.

planning function of management Managing is the drawing of conclusions, relating them to all other facts, and the use of assumptions related to the future to get a mental picture of the activities believed necessary in achieving specific goals.

planning, programming, budgeting system A program first initiated by the U.S. Department of Defense, this is a method to promote greater efficiency by developing more rational approaches to decision making.

plat A map or chart of a given area of real estate, usually prepared by a surveyor, showing the size and location of various parcels of real estate, as well as streets, alleys, easements, etc. Such a plat is often recorded in the register of deeds and is referred to in conveyances of such parcels for accuracy and convenience.

plateau The stage of no apparent progress on a typical learning curve, occurring between rapid progress at first and a slow ascent to the end.

platykurtic curve A frequency distribution curve that is "flat-topped" by comparison to a normal curve.

pleadings *law* The written complaint of the plaintiff or the answer of the defendant or subsequent written statements dealing with the last preceding written statement by either party.

pliopoly A situation in which there is a high probability that more sellers of a product are likely to appear when an industry making a product becomes especially profitable.

Plowden Committee on the Control of Public Expenditure A committee report for the chancellor of the Exchequer in the United Kingdom that made recommendations that led to management reforms for public expenditures. The employment of proper management techniques and efficiency was recommended.

pluperfect market A market in which the price, or terms of trade, increases as the quantity exchanged increases.

plural executive Two or more executives, usually with line authority, at the top levels of an organization. This practice is used to promote shared decision making.

pluralistic theory A concept often accepted by industrial psychologists that, while there are natural areas of divergence between labor and management, there are also many areas of common interest, and, if these areas are properly explored, there should be less friction between the two.

PMA The primary mental abilities. (*See* Primary Mental Abilities Test)

PMAT Purdue Mechanical Adaptability Test.

PMTS Predetermined Motion-Time Study.

P/N Promissory note.

point of order In a formal meeting, should a participant decide that a meeting is straying from the proper course or perhaps violating proper rules of order, a "point of order" can be called for and suggestions made for returning to proper procedures.

point of personal explanation In a formal meeting, if the mover of a motion or anyone engaged in the debate feels his proposal has been misunderstood, he can request permission from the chair to further explain his point.

point-of-sale material Display materials stationed near a product designed to promote its sale.

police power The power, reserved to the states by the U.S. Constitution, to regulate activities in the interest of the safety, morals, health, and welfare of the people.

policy A verbal, written, or implied overall guide that establishes parameters that supply the general limits and direction in which managerial action will occur.

Polish Central Bank *Narodowy Bank Polski.* (*See* Section VII)

Polish Central Council of Trade Unions *Centralna Rada Zwaizkow Zawodowych (CRZZ).*

Polish Chamber of Foreign Trade *Polska Izba Handlu Zagranicznego.*

political economy A synonym for economics, generally adopted after politics began to play an increasing role in the world of economics as government began to intervene more and more in economic activities.

political fund That part of the dues paid by trade unionists in the United Kingdom that can be used for political purposes.

political science One of several social sciences that managers draw upon for help in the management process.

poll tax A flat tax that some states and local governments levy on persons regardless of wealth or income. At one time this was a favorite tax in the southern United States, where the tax had to be paid in order to vote. Most poor voters (including many minorities) could not pay the tax, and thus did not vote.

Polska Izba Handlu Zagranicznego Polish Chamber of Foreign Trade. Address: Warsaw 1, Trebacka 4.

polytechnic institute A school devoted to a number of fields in applied sciences and arts.

POP Panoramic office planning.

population The total number of people represented in a statistical area or realm.

portfolio management The management of a securities portfolio owned by an individual or an institution.

Portuguese Central Bank *Banco de Portugal.* (*See* Section VII)

Portuguese companies Different forms under Portuguese laws: 1) Incorporated Partnership, *Sociedade em nome colectivo;* 2) General Partnership, *Sociedade em comandita simple;* 3) Partnership Limited by Shares, *Siciedade em comandita por accoes;* 4) Cooperative, *Sociedade Cooperativa;* 5) Joint Stock Company, *Sociedade anonima a Responsabilidade Limitada* (Lda, Ltd, Ltad.); 6) Limited Liability Company, *Sociedade per cotas.*

Portuguese stock exchange *See* Section VII.

POSDCORB Acronym for general terms that are often accepted as the functions of management: planning, organizing, staffing, directing, coordinating, reporting, and budgeting. Often identified, as George Terry suggests, as planning, organizing, actuating, and controlling.

position analysis A semiscientific survey of all management positions in an organization, with the end of planning for the filling of those positions as people retire or change jobs.

positive cash flow A situation in which more cash revenues are flowing into an enterprise than are flowing out.

positive economics That "pure" study of economics that concerns itself with causes and effects in the economic world. Analyzes "what is" in the world of economics and does not concern itself much with what "ought to be."

post 1. A horseshoe-shaped enclosure on the main floor of a stock exchange, around which trading in certain stocks takes place. 2. In accounting, the transfer of an entry from a journal to a ledger.

postdoctorate Academic work, usually research, that is done after a doctorate has been earned.

post test A test after a marketing promotion to check its effectiveness, or a test at the end of a training program to check its results.

postulate An assumption or inference that needs to be tested empirically.

posture An attitude or mindset.

potential acquisition valuation method (PAV) A systematic method consisting of ten stages to evaluate investment proposals. (*See also* rate of return)

potential demand The demand that will probably evolve for a specific product or service. This demand is governed by many variables such as the ability of the good or service to satisfy consumer needs, pricing, personal income, consumer priorities, etc.

pound sterling Basic unit of currency in the United Kingdom.

poverty trap When a country makes social welfare payments to low-income people, the poverty trap appears when a rise in the wages of an individual are offset by the decrease in social welfare payments. This trap has made appearances in many countries, to the extent that many jobs are no longer done because such jobs do not pay people enough to do the work and to lose certain welfare payments.

power and authority Authority denotes the legal right to command the actions of others, while power denotes the ability to command such actions, though there may be no particular legal authority present. Groups tend to give certain individuals power, though it may be an unofficial power.

power and game playing The fallacy that if one is in a position of authority in a company, he can "push through" almost anything he wishes. Actually, the better executives are are reluctant to undermine plans or to use their personal authority to derail plans that have been carefully made.

power figure A person who represents, consciously or unconsciously, the possession of a high status or authority.

power of attorney A document executed to enable one person to act on behalf of another in legal transactions.

power of mind The concept that "we become what we think," with positive and constructive thinking being a great force to move people in the direction of successful goal achievement.

power test A type of intelligence test, or other psychological test, in which the questions are worded in such a manner as to defy the abilities of some people and which often inhibits the testees from completing the test.

PR Public relations.

precatory trust A trust established by words of desire rather than the usual form of written declaration.

preceding year basis A situation in which the income tax in a new year is predicated on the income from last year. In the US, where self-employed people pay income tax quarterly, this is normally the basis used to estimate the payments to be made in the new year.

precoded question Multiple-choice test questions in which answers are inscribed so that when the testee marks a certain square or circle the test can be graded automatically.

preference test A measure of vocational or avocational interests or aesthetic judgments by requiring the testee to make forced choices between members of paired or grouped items.

preference theory A technique used in decision making that has to do with the risk-taking attitude of the management of a company.

preference-expectation theory of human need A theory set forth by Victor Vroom in 1964, with two basic premises: 1) a person subjectively assigns values to the expected outcomes of various courses of action and therefore has preferences among the expected outcomes; 2) any explanation of motivated behavior must take into account not only the ends that people hope to accomplish but the extent to which they believe that their actions are instrumental in producing the outcomes they prefer. (Victor Vroom, *Work and Motivation* [John Wiley and Sons, Inc., 1964], pp. 17–33, 121–47.)

preferential tariff A tariff that is lower for goods from certain preferred countries than for the same goods from other countries.

preferential trade agreement Trade agreements that can be made with states that are associated with the European Community, but not with members of the organization.

preferred creditor A creditor whose claim by law enjoys priority in bankruptcy with respect to a mortgage, a wage claim, or a tax claim.

preferred stock A special issue of stock, often sold in the early life of a corpora-

tion to raise much-needed capital, which holds privileges that common shares do not have.

preliterate culture A culture that has not as yet developed a system of writing.

premie makelaars Specialists on options on the Amsterdam Stock Exchange.

premise 1. Assumptions that provide background against which the actuating, planning, organizing, or coordinating of objectives will take place. 2. In logic, either of the two propositions from which a conclusion is drawn in the syllogism.

premium 1. *insurance* An amount paid periodically for an insurance policy. 2. An amount paid as a bounty. 3. *finance* An amount paid for a loan either in lieu of, or in addition to, interest. 4. The difference between the established, normal, or nominal price of an article and the price at which it can be purchased. 5. *commodities* The excess of a cash commodity price over a futures price or of one futures contract price over another.

present value The value at the present time of money that will be paid at a future date. The present value will be less than the future value because it must be discounted at some given interest rate.

presentment *law* The requirement in the law of negotiable instruments that in order to bind endorsers on their liability, the instrument must be presented to the maker or other party primarily liable for payment as specified on the document. Failure to do so promptly discharges the liability of the endorsers for the default of the drawer or acceptor.

president of the Council of Ministers This position as head of the EC Council of Ministers is usually held by the foreign ministers of the member states for a period of six months.

president Usually the title of the chief executive of a U.S. company.

prestige Having an enviable role and status in a group; having the power to make suggestions that will be listened to and the ability to change attitudes.

Price Commission An agency established in 1973 under the Counter-Inflation Act in the United Kingdom. It was set up to monitor prices in accordance with the government's anti-inflation policies. Address: Cleland House, Page Street, London SW1P 4DW.

price-consumption curve *economics* An indifference curve plotting quantities of commodity A on one axis and quantities of commodity B on the other axis; reveals all the combinations of the two commodities that will yield equal satisfaction to the individual. Also known as offer curve.

price discretion A situation in which a salesperson has the authority to alter normal prices in order to make a sale.

price discrimination Selling the same goods or services to different people for different prices, often called "charging what the traffic will bear." This practice cannot succeed in the long-term.

price earnings ratio (P/E ratio) The market price per ordinary share divided by earnings per ordinary share, after taxes.

price fixing Collusion of leading producers in a market to keep costs to

consumers artificially high. (*Cf.* price stabilization)

price index A percentage number showing the degree of change in a price, or an average group of prices, as compared with the prices in a "base year." The base year always equals 100%, and the prior or subsequent years some degree of that base.

price leadership: In some industries with similar products, a major producer often sets a price which is followed by other producers, though, ostensibly, there is no collusion between the companies.

price stabilization The regulation by law of the price of one or more commodities. The commodities so regulated usually have relatively inelastic demand so that slight changes in quantity demanded would cause disproportionate changes in the absence of regulation. Often known as price fixing.

price supports Government guarantees on agricultural commodities to prevent them from falling to unprofitable levels. This program usually entails the government's buying up the surplus commodities at a lower price.

prima facie *law* Latin for "at first sight." In law, the term refers to evidence that will carry the verdict in favor of one party if nothing of substance is presented in rebuttal.

primary beneficiary *insurance* The person named in a life insurance policy to receive the benefits upon the death of the insured. Usually a secondary beneficiary is named in the event the primary beneficiary dies before the insured.

primary boycott An action sometimes taken during a labor strike in which the striking union urges people to refuse to buy the products of the company against which the strike is being conducted.

Primary Mental Abilities Test A test of the following abilities, measured by factor analysis: Spatial, Perceptual, Number, Verbal, Word Fluency, Memory, and Reasoning. Appeared as a test in 1938.

principle A general truth, law, doctrine, or motivating force, which may be derived from empirical observations, that provides a guide for thought and action.

probability Generally denotes the relative frequency with which a specific event occurs when the event is repeated many times.

probability analysis The use of historical data to ascertain what the probabilities are for a company's prospects in every aspect of the company's operation.

probate court *law* A court with jurisdiction over wills and inheritance from those dying intestate. Usually this court also has jurisdiction over guardians and their wards.

probate of a will Establishing the validity of a will through court proceedings.

problem analysis A problem is a deviation from some standard that the manager considers normal and that is important enough to be solved, and to which people are committed to finding a solution.

problems of decision making The major problem in decision making is the absolute necessity for making a choice from what may be several alternatives.

problem-solving development In management trainees, the method most used involves a case study, either real or hypothetical, that demands managerial action.

procedendo *law* A writ by a higher court directing a lower court to proceed to final determination in a case in which the grounds for bringing the case before the higher court cannot be established.

producer's cooperative An association of producers, quite often of farm products, who pool capital for advertising and marketing a given product or products. Often a single brand name will be adopted. Profits are realized on a pro rata basis by members.

product differentiation The development of any difference, real or imaginary, that can make one product preferable over another, though they may be quite similar in nature. This is a common marketing practice for many products. It is incumbent upon the producer to build an image for the product which will allow the product to gain a higher price or perhaps to capture a greater share of the market. Aspirin is a good example. Although all aspirin is chemically essentially the same, some brand names have sold at high prices for many years, and, without regard for physical evidence, some people will still buy only those brands of aspirin.

product homogeneity A situation in which a given product of one producer is considered in the minds of buyers to be identical with the same type of product from other producers.

459

Commodities, generally, are sold on this premise, although various categories do exist.

production coefficient With respect to a given factor of production, this is the quantity of that factor necessary to produce one unit of product. The assumption can be made that the quantity of the factor is fixed or that it is variable and this will result respectively in a linear or curvilinear relation.

production controls One aspect of managerial control, others being inventory control, maintenance control, quality control, salary control, sales control, advertising control, and cost control.

production orientation A company that ostensibly emphasizes the making of products rather than being people oriented.

production possibility curve A curve showing the maximum output combinations of two goods that can be produced with the limited inputs available. The curve reveals the opportunity cost of each good in terms of the other. Also known as transformation curve.

production unit method of depreciation The original cost of a capital asset minus its probable salvage value. The difference is divided by the number of units produced in a specific period or the projected number of units which will be produced in the working life of the asset. Depreciation can then be established on a per-unit-produced basis.

productivity 1. Output per working hour, with quality of working life being considered. Increased productivity is seen by many as the primary objective of every business enterprise, and pro-ductivity consists of the new wealth created by an hour's work. 2. Probably the most vital statistic in all the production process, since it ultimately determines the amount of a product that will be available and the price for which it will sell. Productivity, in the long-term, determines the standard of living the nation has.

produit net The net product of extractive industries such as mining, forestry, fishing, etc. This term was popular in the Physiocratic school of economic thought.

profit Total revenue minus total cost. In economic theory, total cost will include a cost to cover the "normal" profit. Anything above that may be referred to as excess profit.

profit á prendre *law* The right to take soil, gravel, minerals, etc., from the land.

profit and loss statement An accounting statement for a business that shows the sources of revenue, the various costs that have been incurred, all taxes and other payments that have been made, and what is left over, which is profit. Also known as an income statement.

profit centers A segment of an enterprise with a designated manager responsible for its income or revenue, expenses, and assets used to sustain operations.

profit sharing A method of sharing company profits related to the profits earned and to the salary base of each participant. This practice is considered good since it does not commit the firm to an annual payment, yet it motivates workers.

pro forma Latin for "for the sake of form." A term describing accounting, financial, and other statements or conclusions based upon anticipated facts rather than historical facts.

program A comprehensive plan that includes the projected use of different resources in an integrated pattern and establishes a chronological sequence of required actions and time schedules in order to achieve objectives.

project market strategies (PIMS) A program designed to identify and measure the major determinants of return on investment in individual businesses. By the year 1973, this project had revealed thirty-seven key profit influences, of which the most important is market share. Others are economies of scale, market power, and management quality.

proletariat People of the working class who own no capital goods and are completely dependent upon wages earned. This term was used by Karl Marx, but it is now used widely, and not always related to communism.

propaganda Carefully planned means designed to influence the attitudes and actions of other persons. Often, this term is used in a negative sense.

propensity to consume The ratio between consumption and income for an individual or for a country.

propensity to invest The relation between new capital formation and national income.

propensity to save The ratio between the income not consumed and national income, or, in the case of an individual, the ratio of income not spent on consumption to total income.

propensity A natural tendency or driving force toward some specific type of action.

proportional tax A tax that takes the same percentage of each worker's income, whether large or small.

propria persona *law* Latin for "in his own person." A person is entitled to conduct his own suit personally and need not be represented by an attorney.

pro rata Latin for "in proportion." In a partnership, for example, either profits or losses fall proportionately upon the partners according to the investment of each.

Protectionism A concept of foreign trade that would protect domestic industry from foreign competition by keeping the products of other countries out or by raising import taxes so that prices could not be competitive.

Protestant ethic The concept that one is required by a religious life and practice to work hard. This concept was strong among the Puritans and marked the early years of the history of the United States.

proxy A written authorization by a stockholder designating another person to vote for him.

prudent man rule *law* A rule that permits a trustee to step outside a legal list for investment of trust assets provided the trustee acts prudently. Most such rules limit the percentage of the trust assets permitted outside the legal list.

pseudoscience A term often used to describe management to contrast it to the so-called "hard sciences." Management is, in fact, a general or social science, with some of the characteristics of a science, but some characteristics of an art.

461

psychic income 1. The amount of satisfaction a buyer receives from a good or service bought, with no way of quantifiably measuring them. 2. The amount of satisfaction a worker may get from his job apart from monetary compensation, again with no way of measuring that satisfaction.

psychological determination The doctrine that no behavior occurs by chance, but that there is always a cause, whether conscious or unconscious, for each action.

psychological environment The sum of all the perceptual and the conceptual data that at any given moment are operative in directing the behavior of a person or of a group.

psychological needs and MBO The psychological needs of an employee may be ignored in pushing the MBO program, particularly if the employee cannot see how meeting company objectives are going to help him meet his personal objectives. (*See also* Management by Objectives)

psychological test Standardized procedures for comparing the performances of two or more persons in abilities, aptitudes, achievements, and the like. The test itself is classified according to its purposes, the method of administration, and the manner in which it is standardized.

psychological theory of the business cycle A way of explaining business cycles that puts the emphasis on how optimistic or pessimistic people feel at any given time. Actions, in either case, can trigger a budding boom or a recession.

publications monitoring The exploration of pertinent literature in a field

that the wise manager will constantly keep advised of.

public choice economics A comparatively new way of studying economics that emphasizes how economic decisions are either made or strongly influenced by the political process.

public domain 1. After expiration of a copyright or patent, the ideas involved may be exploited by anyone. 2. Land owned by the government.

public monopoly A firm, such as a public utility, that is allowed a monopoly in a given area because it would be impossible to allow competition under circumstances that have always existed. Some modifications are now being made to the public monopolies, and more modifications are likely to be made in the future. Also known as a legal monopoly.

pump priming The theory, introduced by John Maynard Keynes, that production, and thus employment, can be increased during a serious downturn in the economy (a depression) by having the central government pour money into projects or directly into the hands of people.

punitive damages Damages awarded in a lawsuit over and above the actual damages suffered to make an example of the offending party. Such damages are usually allowed when the action has been malicious or reckless. Sometimes the damages awarded are of little value, but they are awarded to emphasize the malicious guilt of the convicted person.

purchasing power of money Measures the real value of money in the actual purchasing of goods and services. It varies inversely with the general level of prices.

purchasing power parity theory A theory devised to explain the relationship between two currencies, neither of which is on a commodity standard. In this event, the domestic purchasing power of each currency determines its value as related to the other, and thus establishes an exchange rate.

pure competition A situation in which no individual buyers or sellers in the market can influence the market, especially the prices in the market.

pure economics The theoretical study of economics, which is the study of economics under certain conditions and with certain assumptions being made.

pyramiding 1. *finance* The lessening of the amount of capital needed to control a company through the use of holding companies and through the use of the principal that ownership of 50 percent of the voting stock of a corporation gives control of the firm. 2. *stocks* an increase of holdings of a particular stock financed out of the margin created by an increase in the price of shares already owned.

pyrrhic selling A sale that may help the company in the near term, but hurt it in the long term.

Q

Q The quartile deviation.

Q-charts Quantitative charts. Revises an organizational chart to assign quantitative values to each subunit on a chart. Boxes are sized proportionately.

QSE's Shortened name for "qualified scientists and engineers" in the United Kingdom.

Q sort A technique used in making an inventory of personality by sorting statements into piles, with each representing the degree to which a given characteristic applies to a person being studied.

quadrant One of four areas on a graph; an area bounded by a Y-axis and a X-axis at the point of their intersection on a graph.

quadratic mean A value obtained by squaring all the values of items in a series, then adding these squares and dividing the total by the number of items, and finally extracting the square root of this result.

quadratic programming An operational research technique used for problems having nonlinear relationships.

qualified acceptance 1. Referring to a bill of exchange, a variation of the terms by the acceptor. The holder can then treat the bill as dishonored. 2. *contracts* A qualified acceptance is not really an acceptance, but a counter offer.

qualified endorsement Words contained in an endorsement indicating that the endorser does not agree to the full liability of a typical endorser. This does not free the endorser completely, however, since he is still liable for the other warranties listed under the endorsement, but is freed of the warranty that the instrument will be paid at maturity.

qualified pension, profit sharing and stock bonus plans Plans set up by employers for employees that meet the requirements of IRS Section 401, so that the employer contributions are deductible for income tax purposes.

qualified report *accounting* A report by a CPA that does not certify that everything in the report is correct, but the report is accompanied by a statement claiming that, while proper methods were used, some transactions have not been examined nor verified.

qualified stock option plan A privilege granted by a corporation to an employee to purchase shares of the capital stock of a company under conditions prescribed by IRS codes. The general conditions are: 1) the option plan must be approved by stockholders; 2) the options are not transferable; 3) the "exercise price" (the price at which the shares are finally bought) must not be less than the market price at the time the options were issued; 4) the grantee may not own more than 5 percent of the company's voting power or 5 percent of the value of all outstanding stock (this goes up to 10 percent if the equity capital is under one million dollars); 5) no income tax is paid when the options are issued, nor when they are exercised. When the stock is sold, the capital gains tax is paid, which, beginning in 1988, paid at the same rate as the individual rate. (Readers should note that there has been a constant push in Congress to again set up special rates for capital gains. Capital gains rates were made the same as individual rates by the Tax Reform Act of 1986.)

quality control The absolute command of a company over the standards of

materials going into a product and the standards of the end product.

quality control and reliability The techniques used to insure that the quality of materials used in a product falls into proper tolerance and that the finished products do the same.

quality control in marketing strategy Excellence in a product, from the outset, will largely determine marketing strategy, and certainly it will do so in the long term.

quality market An existing market for a good or service that puts more value on excellence than it does on price.

quality protection Those methods used to insure the value of a product, often when there is no complete quality control program.

quality, management With regard to market share, good management will result, ultimately, in a larger share.

quality, power of buyers and The buying power of customers will ultimately determine the value and price of the products to be marketed in certain areas or among certain categories of customers.

quantify The conversion of data into numerical equivalents for statistical analysis or evaluation.

quantity theory of money Classical theory that holds that the level of prices in the economy is directly proportional to the quantity of money in circulation, so that a given percentage change in the money supply will cause an equal percentage change in the price level. The theory assumes that the the income velocity of circulation of money remains fairly stable, and that it always tends toward full employment.

quartering A system of clocking-in in the United Kingdom that penalizes an employee fifteen minutes if the employee is five minutes late.

quasi-public corporation A corporation, the stock of which is held by private individuals, but which is operated by public servants in whole or in part, such as the Federal Reserve System.

quasi Prefix from Latin meaning in a sense or a to a certain degree; similar. Seemingly, but not actually.

Queen's Award to Industry Established in 1965 in the United Kingdom to award firms that increase exports or that do superior work in innovations. Those winning awards are allowed to display the Queen's Award emblem for the next five years. Address: Office of the Queen's Award to Industry, 1 Victoria Street, London SWIH OET.

question, putting the, or calling for the In formal meetings, when a motion is under discussion, anyone from the floor can "call for the question" to be acted upon. The chairman will allow the call if there is no objection. The chairman's act is called "putting the question."

queuing theory The analysis of waiting lines and waiting times.

quia timet *law* Latin for "because he fears." In law, a writ or bill in equity seeking protection against anticipated injury.

quick asset ratio The ratio of cash or near cash to current liabilities.

quick asset Usually considered as cash, marketable securities, accounts receivable, and other assets that can quickly be turned to cash.

quickie strike A term sometimes used for a wildcat strike, an unauthorized strike, often called with little or no notice given to the firm.

quid pro quo Latin for "one thing for another." In law, a term used to refer to the fact that a legal contract demands consideration.

quick ratio *See* acid-test ratio, liquid ratio.

quiet title, action to A legal remedy by which the party who believes itself to be the owner can clear up the defects in the title to the land.

quintile A point that divides an array of scores into fifths.

quitclaim deed A deed in which the grantor (party giving the deed) signs away whatever rights he may have in the property involved, but makes no claim that he has any rights at all.

Quito Stock Exchange Stock exchange in Ecuador. (*See* Section VII)

quit rate The turnover in employees that is not the result of firings or of having too many employees, but the result of deliberate quitting by employees.

quo warranto Latin for "by what authority." A suit to test the authority of a person in office or the authority of a corporation over its franchise or charter.

quorum With regard to formal and legal meetings, the term indicates the number of people who must be present (in person or by proxy) to conduct a valid meeting.

quota agreement An agreement made between members of a cartel (such as OPEC) to determine how much production will be allocated to each member.

465

quota buying When the best reorder size is determined, this is divided into annual sales to get the size of each periodic reorder. Also known as buying to the minimum inventory.

quota restriction A nation may place a limit, or quota, on a specific import, or, when supplies of a product are limited, a firm may give quotas to customers proportionate to their normal buying pattern.

quota sample The separation of a population (or universe) into categories with common characteristics, with samples taken from the categories weighted according to size. Some population categories could be age, sex, national origin, etc.

quota share reinsurance A reinsurance contract providing that there will be reinsurance of a quota amount or percentage of all insurance falling within the terms of the agreement.

quotations The current published price of a share of stock or a commodity. Often two prices are given, namely "bid" and "asked".

quotient The number obtained when one divides one number by another number.

R

R A symbol for the unconditional response, or just response.

R & D Research and Development.

rabble hypothesis A concept, usually found under this title in the United Kingdom, that people always pursue their own self-interests, a view somewhat challenged by the human relations school of management.

Race Relations Act, 1968 Legislation in the United Kingdom making race discrimination illegal in industry as elsewhere, and also establishing the Race Relations Board and the Community Relations Commission.

racial memory Those ideas and impulses supposedly having their origin in the dim past of the human race, and thus being a part of every person's mental equipment.

racial unconscious Old memories that the psychologist Jung assumed resided in the unconscious and derived from the race's accumulated experiences.

rack jobber A type of wholesaler who services merchandise racks in supermarkets and other stores.

rack rent The term for maximum obtainable commercial rent in the United Kingdom.

radius clause A clause in an employee's contract under which, should the employee leave, he agrees not to take employment with a competing employer within a certain radius of his original job.

rain check A colloquialism denoting a delay in a decision.

RAMP *See* Review Analysis of Multiple Projects.

random error 1. An error that is not biased in any way and therefore the distribution of items has a mean or other equally acceptable measure of central tendency at zero or some other central point. 2. Chance error or unsystematic error.

randomize To select on a chance basis.

random movement A movement for which the observer cannot determine a definite cause.

random numbers Tables of numbers arranged at random in rows and columns for use in unbiased assignment of subjects to groups in experiments.

random sample A number of persons, numbers, or objects drawn by chance from a larger universe, usually on the assumption that they will be representative of the larger group.

random sampling A method of drawing a sample from a population in which each individual or item in the population has an equal chance to be drawn.

random walk A market research technique in which the market researchers walk along a specified route and make calls, either at random, or specified, in order to interview the householders.

range 1. The difference between the largest and smallest values in a distribution. 2 The total dispersion of a frequency distribution, or the highest value minus the lowest value in the distribution. 3. *real estate* a length of six miles running north and south in the United States as established by the U.S. survey and used as a basis in land title descriptions.

range-of-earnings chart A graph that relates earnings per share to earnings before interest and taxes using alternative financing options.

ranges In using the MBO concept, it is good to state objectives in "ranges" (in terms of upper and lower limits) rather than trying to be too specific.

rank correlation The degree of agreement between the rankings of two statistical series.

rapport An empathetic relationship between two individuals characterized by mutual confidence.

ratchet effect As applied to income and expenditures, and using the analogy of an automobile jack, this term denotes the action of a consumer gaining more income and increasing spending proportionately. As applied specifically to the consumption function, the concept is that a change in the absolute level of income is associated with a change in the marginal propensity to consume.

ratebuster A piece worker in a piece work situation in which the rates are "loose" who takes advantage of that situation to produce as much as possible and earn as much as possible. Plausible as this approach may seem, it upsets the routine of other workers who generally set a norm for themselves and expect all workers to abide by it. (The tendency is for the ratebuster to encourage the company to reduce the money earned on each unit produced.) In the United Kingdom, such a worker is called a job spoiler.

rate changing Actions taken by a company that pays piece work rates to change such rates because they are perceived as being either too tight or too loose.

rate cutting An action of management to cut piece work rates because they appear too loose. This is the type of situation that encourages workers to hold down the production effort.

467

rate discrimination The charging of different rates for the same service furnished to two or more customers.

rate fixing The action of a company in the United Kingdom to fix piece work rates on the basis of the productivity of workers who have performed the task before and are considered to be average workers.

rate of change The difference between the amount of change in a variable and the value of the variable before change.

rate of exchange The rate at which one currency can be exchanged for another currency in the international monetary market. Usually, this exchange is guided by the laws of supply and demand, undergirded by the purchasing power of the currencies in question.

rate of return 1. Yield obtainable on an asset. 2. *public utilities* Percentage by which the rate base is multiplied to provide a figure that allows a public utility to collect revenues sufficient to pay operating expenses and attract investment.

ratification 1. *law* A general doctrine concerning the approval or acceptance by a party of the responsibility for, or benefits from, an act after it is done. May be expressed or implied. 2. The approval of treaties between nations by representatives having the authority to do so. In the United States, the U.S. Senate has such authority.

rating An estimate, made on some systematic basis, of the presence or absence of some trait, characteristic, or quality of a person, place, or thing.

rating bureau *insurance* An agency that collects experience on risks in an area and establishes rates based on data it has collected.

ratio A relation of numbers, amounts, or degrees.

ratio analysis 1. *finance* In analyzing financial statements, the ratios between various balance-sheet figures or between profit-and-loss statement figures. Some examples are: acid test ratio, capital-output ratio, preferred stock ratio, etc. 2. *accounting* The process of determining the relations of selected items in accounting statements.

rational Based on reason, or having the capacity to reason.

rationale The underlying reason or theory on which a particular belief or action is based.

rational expectations theory A relatively new theory that contends that government cannot successfully undertake stabilization policy because there is no way of eliciting assured public response to government policies.

rationalization The act of giving socially acceptable or plausible reasons for one's actions or beliefs, usually with the intent of avoiding the real or true reasons. 1. Reorganizing into a more efficient structure. 2. A psychological term denoting the process of attempting to justify one's beliefs or behavior in a fashion deemed reasonable.

rational working hours A Ferman workplace innovation in which hours of work are varied according to the workload.

rationing function of prices The use-limiting conserving function that prices perform. Normally, the higher the price, the less of a product will be demanded, and the lower the price, the more the product will be demanded.

rationing of exchange Governmental

control of foreign exchange through the forced surrender of exchange by exporters for domestic currency at the government rate, and the subsequent allocation of such exchange to importers according to a government ration schedule.

ratio-trend forecasting Mathematical technique used in planning for manpower needs based on current activity in the plant and forecasts of activity for the future.

Raven's progressive matrices A nonverbal intelligence test complicated enough to need to be administered by an industrial psychologist, but which has proven to be quite effective. The test is in matrix form, takes about thirty minutes to administer, and has norms for various age groups.

raw test score A basic score made on an intelligence test before it is adapted to the appropriate norm.

REA The chief duty of the Rural Electrification Administration, created in the Department of Agriculture in 1935, was to make loans to finance the cost of putting electricity and telephones into rural areas.

reaction The integrated pattern of responses to a situation.

reaction curve or function In the economic theory of duopoly, the reaction curve is the locus of all the points of maximum profit for each firm for each corresponding quantity of a good that its rival may produce.

reaction psychology An orientation emphasizing behavior as reaction-to-stimulus, which is especially concerned with motor activity.

reaction time The interval between stimulation and response.

readiness The sum of an individual's intellectual, sensory, and motor development, needs, and acquired abilities and ideas, as a result of which the individual is more likely to respond in one fashion rather than another.

Reading rule *insurance* A situation in which a blanket policy covers two items also insured by two specific policies, one on each item, and the blanket insurance is apportioned between the two items in proportion to the values of the items insured by it. The usual contribution applies to both the blanket policy and each specific policy in the ratio of the face values of the insured items.

Reaganomics A colloquialism denoting the economic policies of President Ronald Reagan and his administration in the 1980s. Supply-side economics formed the base of Reagan's economic program, and its goals were to reduce inflation and increase productivity in industry.

real estate mortgage bonds The bonds of a corporation, or sometimes of an individual, that are secured by a mortgage upon its real property.

real income Total earned wages after factoring out inflation; i.e., the purchasing power of wages or salaries.

real interest rate The nominal interest rate adjusted for inflation.

real investment The expansion of the infrastructure of a company.

realism A tendency to face facts and be practical rather than imaginative or visionary.

realism and reach in planning The planning of a company revolves around what the company can do given the resources available and the future projections and desires.

reality-based person One who has the highest tolerance for ambiguity, and who does not demand that every situation be cut and dried.

reality principle In Freudian terms, that part of the ego structure that operates to achieve satisfaction of instinctual drives while regulating behavior in accordance with the demands of one's environment.

realization 1. The disposal of assets for cash. 2. *taxes* In income taxation, the tax is not levied until the income is definite enough to tax.

realized income The earning of income (actually coming into possession, or constructive possession) related to a transaction as contrasted with "paper gain," which is the increase in value as yet unrealized since the vehicles of investment have not been sold.

real national income The national income measured in terms of unchanging purchasing power. It is normally measured by dividing current dollar national income by a price index.

real property Essentially, land and rights to land and improvements to land.

real wages Money wages expressed in terms of purchasing power at any given point in time.

recall The bringing to mind of a representation of something previously experienced.

recall method A technique of measuring retention by requiring the subject to reproduce material previously learned.

recapitalization A voluntary readjustment of the types of securities a corporation issues, which does not indicate any kind of financial weakness in the corporation.

recapitalization surplus Additional capital resulting from readjustment of securities within a company, usually arising out a reduction in the par value of stocks and the exchange of bonds for securities of lesser value.

receiver's certificate A short-term note issued by a receiver after approval by the court that appointed the receiver for the purpose of carrying out orderly liquidation or reorganization of a company.

receivership *law* A proceeding involving the appointment by a court of a person (the receiver) to administer the affairs of a person or firm unable to meet its debts as the debts mature. If the final decision is to liquidate, the receiver's title is changed to "trustee in bankruptcy."

recession A mild form of depression; a mild turn downward in the business cycle.

Rechnungsrevisoren Zurich Stock Exchange auditors.

reciprocal demand A concept developed by John Stuart Mill that essentially says that reciprocal demand is one country's demand for a second country's product, measured in terms of the first country's product.

reciprocal exchange *insurance* An unincorporated association writing insurance for its members.

reciprocal laws Laws that provide that one state will extend to the citizens and corporations of another state the same rights as the second state is willing to give to the first. This occurs frequently in tax and insurance laws.

reciprocal trade agreement An executive agreement between countries allowing for the interchange of goods and services at mutually lowered tariffs, or other advantageous provisions.

reciprocal trading An action of the supplier of a good or service receiving, in turn, orders for goods or services from his customer.

reciprocity principle The granting of concessions in return for concessions received.

recognition The awareness of things or people that one has known or has experienced at some time in the past.

recognition dispute A dispute over which labor union has the right to negotiate with a company or industry.

recognition method A technique for measuring retention in which the subject is required to select items previously presented.

recognition span The number of words or numbers a person can perceive in a single glance.

recognizance *law* An obligation entered into by a person before a court to do a specified act, such as making an appearance on a set date. This may or may not be supported by a bail bond, though it usually is not.

Recommendations Proposals handed down by the Council of Ministers of the EC that do not have binding force. (*See also* Regulations)

RecomPension A recognized company pension in the United Kingdom.

reconsignment *transportation* Any change, other than a change in route, made before arrival of goods at the destination when the change is made under conditions permitted by the rules of the carrier.

Reconstruction Finance Corporation (RFC) Created by Congress in 1932 at President Hoover's urgent request, this organization was designed to bring back prosperity by loaning money to corporations suffering because of lack of capital. The loss ratio on the loans was low. During World War II, the RFC was converted into a wartime loan agency.

record date In corporate matters, the date established by the board of directors as the closing time to establish the schedule of stockholders to receive a dividend, to set voting rights for a specific meeting, or to provide some other benefit.

recourse 1. The right of a holder of a negotiable instrument to collect from parties who previously held the document if the primary party obligated to pay does not pay it. 2. The right of the purchaser of accounts receivable to look to the seller for a deficiency in any account. (This provision must have been agreed upon in advance.)

recruitment of management members, biographical data This is the first means used in appraising a candidate and may contain the following elements: 1) the total number of dependents; 2) specific work done in recent years; 3) whether applicant is presently employed; 4) length of present or last employment; 5) organizations of which the applicant is an active member; 6) offices held in such organizations;

7) approximate net worth; 8) minimum monthly living expenses needed by the applicant and his family; 9) amount of life insurance carried. (In recent years, because of rapidly changing technology, the mobility of the labor force, and the frequent need on the part of an employee to look for another job, there has been the tendency to believe that if the applicant was not employed at the time of application, perhaps the applicant was not a good employee. This is a fallacy, and all recruiters must be abreast of the times, and realize that there are a lot of competent people out of work through no fault of their own.)

rectilinear coordinates Two straight lines, or axes, intersecting one another at right angles; units on both axes are used to locate points representing values with respect to both axes.

recursive system A system in which a causal chain of events is established on the assumption that only one endogenous variable at a time is the dependent variable.

"red herring" *Finance* The advance copy of the statement or prospectus to be filed with the Securities and Exchange Commission prior to the issue of a new security. The copy is marked in red ink on the cover to identify it as a "red herring."

Redcliffe-Maud Report on the Management of Local Government A 1967 report made to the government of the United Kingdom by a committee chaired by Lord Redcliffe-Maud, on the subject of local-government entities in the UK, and the best methods of keeping responsible and competent people in government.

redemption price The price at which a corporation may at its option require the surrender of a bond or a preferred stock before maturity, providing the security is issued carrying such a provision.

redeployment Mobility of labor is often required after the introduction of technological changes in industry. Structural unemployment may be kept to a minimum by retraining workers and by giving assistance in relocating workers.

rediscount The resale of a promissory note or bill of exchange by one who has purchased such a document. This action goes on constantly between Federal Reserve banks and member banks.

red-tape crisis and coordination The over-sized bureaucracy that often grows up in an organization results in much time being given to useless bureaucratic words and actions that inhibit true communication.

reduced form equation *econometrics* the equation(s) resulting from a reduction of the size of a model by reducing the number of equations in the model or system.

reducing balance method A method of spreading the cost of a fixed asset over its estimated useful life. The amount of depreciation charged each year decreases over the life of the asset.

reductionism The theory that the more elemental components of a complex phenomenon are real, and that the whole is completely explainable in terms of these elemental parts only.

Redundancy Fund Established by the Redundancy Payments Act of 1965 in the United Kingdom. In cases in which employers are required to make payments to former employees who were laid off because of new technology or difficult economic times, this fund reimburses employers, in part, for those payments.

redundancy The dismissal of an employee in the United Kingdom whose specific job may have fallen victim to new technology or changes in the economy. Most companies attempt to fit the employee into another position, particularly if the employee has several years of service.

re-education *psychology* In psychological therapy, the process of aiding an individual to relearn appropriate and efficient behavior patterns that have been temporarily forgotten.

referee A person appointed by a court of equity (chancery court) to investigate and report to the court, usually about complicated factual matters.

reference back A situation in which a full committee refuses to accept a report from a subcommittee and returns the report to the subcommittee for further study.

reference consequences The two ends of a preference curve.

reference groups A term used in marketing research denoting a situation in which a number of people are called together, usually following a specific structure, for the purpose of discussing consumer buying motives.

reference tariff A tariff or scale of charges among EC members that is not restricted to the upper and lower limits of a a bracket tariff, but which must be published if it is outside the proper brackets. Such tariffs are usually used for inland waterways and bulk transport under the common transport policy of the Common Market.

referent power The identification of a follower with a leader who is admired and held in high esteem by the follower. In this case, the leader's "power" emerges from the regard in which he is held by the follower.

reflation 1. An economic term denoting a situation in which the general income level of a community is increasing with a positive stimulating effect on employment and real incomes. 2. The process of managing currency for the purpose of restoring a previous price level.

reflex effect The tendency for markets in the real economic world to return to balanced conditions following any attempt to mandate the price either too high or too low.

refund annuity An annuity policy that provides that upon death of the annuitant the difference between the purchase price of the annuity and the total of payments to the heirs of the annuitant will be paid in a lump sum or in continuing periodic payments to the person designated by the annuitant.

regimen A style of living that ostensibly promotes health.

regional development grants Grants made to sections of a country to stimulate economic development, a practice which is common in the United Kingdom, in the United States, in the EC nations, and in many other countries of the world. Also, the International Bank for Reconstruction and Development (World Bank) makes loans at a low rate of interest to developing countries. Some developed countries, such as the United Kingdom and the United States give grants to developing countries, but to date it is difficult to define the specific progress that has been made because of such grants.

Regional Employment Premium Contributions to labor costs to companies in special development areas of the United Kingdom as a special incentive to locate in special development areas and stay there. These contributions are commonly given to labor-intensive industries.

Regional Industrial Development Division A government agency in the United Kingdom that provides industry with information on regional development projects and policies. Address: Regional Industrial Development Division, Department of Industry, Millbank Tower, Millbank, London SWIP 4QU.

registered bond A bond entered on the books of the issuing corporation or of its transfer agent in the name of the purchaser. The name also appears on the face of the bond.

register of deeds An office, usually in each county or parish of a state in the United States, in which documents affecting the titles to land are recorded. The same offices may also register other documents affecting property rights.

Registrar of Business Names A directory of names of businesses, business owners, managers, etc., in the United Kingdom. States, and sometimes regions, in the United States have similar directories.

Registrar of Friendly Societies A registry of trade unions in the United Kingdom established under the Trade

Union Acts of 1871–1964 and the Friendly Societies Act of 1896.

Registrar of Restrictive Trade Agreements A registry of exempt trading agreements in the United Kingdom under the Restrictive Trade Practices Act of 1956 and the Resale Prices Act of 1964. In 1973, the Fair Trading Act replaced the Registrar with the Director-General of Fair Trading.

registry *marine law* The listing of a ship under the law of the nation whose flag it flies, without regard to the citizenship of the ship's owners. In the United States registry of a ship has much stiffer requirements than in some other countries.

regression 1.*statistics* A method for determining relationships between variables by exposing an approximate functional relationship between them, and often using regression lines calculated by the use of the least squares method. 2. *psychology* The practicing of immature behavior after the person has already revealed maturity, often because of frustration, stress, or repression.

regression analysis *statistics* The development of average relationships between variables by means of the least squares method or correlation.

regression coefficient *statistics* The coefficient associated with an independent variable when a line of average relationship (regression line) has been fitted to the observed values of a dependent variable and one or more independent variables. A coefficient is a multiplier.

regression equation *statistics* The technique for determining within the limits of probability the most likely value of Y from the known value of X; also the formula for drawing straight lines (curves) adjusted to the means of any array of values in a two-way (or double entry) table. A standard formula is: Y = a + bX.

regression line *statistics* Any line that describes the average relationship between two or more variables. The line is usually developed by the least squares method or correlation.

regressive tax 1. A tax on income or property in which the rate of taxation diminishes with increases in the base. 2. A tax the effect of which is to take a decreasing percentage of income.

Regulations (EC) Binding rules applying to all members of the EC that are made by the Council of Ministers of the EC. (*See also* Recommendations)

regulatory policies and distribution The impact that ever-changing regulations have upon the bringing in of raw materials and the taking out of finished goods.

rehypothecation *stocks* The repledging of a security by a broker or dealer to whom the security has been pledged. Technically, this is not a repledge, since possession is not surrendered to the broker or dealer, but the right to order sale on default is.

reinstatement test Any measure of retention that requires the learner to recall, recognize, relearn, or repeat what was previously learned, with special reference to retention for rote material.

reinsurance The sharing in risk by two or more insurance companies when the risk assumed is considered too much for one company.

rejection, fear of In business, this emotion is most often related to weaknesses the individual believes he has and the underlying anxiety that he will be "found out" by superiors, who will lose respect for the individual.

relations analysis A technique, identified by Peter Drucker, to be used in deciding the organization structure suitable for a company. This technique based on intracompany relationships between managers and management relationships. (*See also* activities analysis, decision analysis)

relative average deviation The average deviation divided by the median.

relative income hypothesis The saving ratio (saving/income) does not depend upon the level of income, but on the relative position of the individual on the income scale, i.e., an individual's income compared to the average income for all individuals. Dusenberry expresses the saving ratio as a function of the ratio of current income to the highest level of income previously attained.

relative priority The priority given to various kinds of debt in the event a company is forced into liquidation. Usually the oldest debt has the greatest priority rating.

relative quartile deviation The quartile deviation divided by the median.

relative skewness The difference between the mean and the mode divided by the standard deviation.

relativism *social psychology* The theory that folkways and mores are established within a group at a given time or in any given area and that, consequently, there are no absolute standards of behavior.

relaxation allowance Time allowed workers by the company for "compensating rest" (coffee breaks, etc.).

relaxation therapy A method of reducing tension levels by relaxing muscles, one by one.

released rate Formerly, with respect to a commodity varying greatly in value, a released rate is an agreement by a shipper to set a limit to the value of a shipment in return for a concession in rate. This practice is now illegal under the Interstate Commerce Act, except for baggage, special livestock, and other specific exemptions.

relevance trees The process of identifying and evaluating various inputs, in order of priority, in order to better achieve a specific goal. Process is of military origin and is also called "relevance analysis."

reliability *statistics* The degree to which repetition of the same test produces the same results.

reliction The addition to a piece of land by the withdrawal of a river or of the sea.

remainder A future interest in land in a party other than the grantor. A period of time must elapse between the present and the time when the person granted the remainder comes into possession of the land.

remedial program *education* Instruction that tends to fit the needs of the student who is having difficulty in a specific discipline.

remisiers People who sell securities at Italian stock exchanges, known as non-bidding dealers, who are not permitted to bid on the trading floors.

remittitur of record An order issued by a court of appeals sending a case back to a lower court after the lower court's decision has been reversed or modified.

remonitization 1. "Legal" remonitization when a nation removes a type of currency from its legal tender list. 2. "Factual" remonitization occurs when the price of precious metal falls below the mint price and metal that had been melted down from its coined state is returned to money use.

remuneration A comprehensive term denoting all of the benefits, including salary or wages, received by a worker for his employment with the company. Includes all fringe benefits.

rendu price An import delivered price; the price of an imported good including all charges for tariffs and freight.

rent A stated return for the temporary possession or use of a house, land, or other property, made, usually at regular intervals, by the tenant or user to the owner.

rentes A French interest-bearing bond without a maturity date.

rentier Originally, one who derived the bulk of his income from the renting of land. Often used to denote one whose income is largely derived from the investment of previously acquired capital.

reopener clause An agreement between labor and management denoting that negotiations can be reopened when the cost of living reaches a given point, rather than having cost-of-living adjustments built into the original agreement.

reparations As normally used, this term refers to money, goods, or services paid by one nation to another as compensation for damages incurred in war. Historically, reparations are seldom paid in full, if at all, since the "losing" nation is usually economically bankrupt following a war.

repeat demand *marketing* A term in denoting continual demand for often-purchased consumer goods.

repertoire The complete panorama of all the responses, learned and unlearned, that an individual is capable of making.

replacement cost *insurance* The price of restoring property lost or damaged to its condition prior to the loss. Paying this cost is now one of the most common types of homeowner's insurance.

replacement demand Demand occasioned by the wearing out or growing obsolete of consumer durable goods or producer capital goods.

replacement theory *accounting* A technique in accounting relating to discounted cash flow, which is designed to identify the optimum points in time at which to replace either a plant or equipment or both.

replevin *law* A remedy at law by which one party can have a sheriff take specific property from another party pending a decision concerning who has the right to possession of the property. The party getting possession usually will have to post bond.

replication *law* The reply by a plaintiff in a lawsuit to the defendant's answer.

reporting by responsibility A term used in connection with the concept of "management by exception." The plan seeks to give the manager all the information he needs to do his job, but to see that the manager is not encumbered with unnecessary information.

reports A written or oral factual presentation of information that is directed to

a particular audience for a specific purpose.

representational rights Generally, the right of a trade union to consult with management on everyday problems, but not the right to negotiate contracts.

representative firm A theoretical device devised by Alfred Marshall for economic analysis. Marshall defines it as "a firm that has its fair share of those internal and external economies which pertain to the aggregate scale of production in the industry to which it belongs." Not to be looked upon as "average" in a statistical sense.

repressed inflation An action taken to forestall inflation when the economy is at full employment and aggregate demand is great by placing some kind of controls on wages and prices.

reproduction new cost theory of rate making In making payment schedules for transportation and public utilities, reproduction new cost is the current cost of reproducing the present facilities minus accrued depreciation, and the rates will reflect this base.

reprographics Denotes the technology of the reproduction of printed material through photocopying, off-set printing, etc.

reproof A type of negative reinforcement, such as a reprimand, or attaching blame for a specific action.

repurchase agreement *finance* The sale of securities, usually government bills, to an investor with excess temporary funds subject to the agreement of the seller to buy back from the buyer at a specified time. The agreements may last only twenty-four hours.

477

required actions Social mores, translated into actions, that are made mandatory by the group to which one belongs.

required bank reserve The amount that a member bank of the Federal Reserve is supposed to have deposited with the Fed or in the bank vault at any specific period of time. Based on a percentage of time deposits and a percentage of demand deposits.

Resale Prices Act of 1964 Legislation in the United Kingdom generally abolishing retail price maintenance for a wide variety of goods and services, contending that manufacturers do not have the right to dictate prices to retailers. Similar to fair trade laws in the United States.

rescind *law* To revoke an action or an agreement. This can always be done with the consent of both parties and can sometimes be done, depending upon the controlling law, without the consent of both parties.

rescript A duplicate of a document.

research The application of scientific methods, and often mathematical techniques, to entities with the ultimate goal being the discovery of meaningful relationships and universal social and physical laws regarding human beings and their environment.

reserve *Common Market* A part of the Agricultural Policy of the EC in which producers of fruits and vegetables may fix a price for each commodity, and, when necessary, may call upon the Community funds to assure that the commodity gets its fair price. Also known as fall-back price.

reserve price A price below which the vendor is not prepared to sell, particularly at an auction or at a sale. Also known as floor price or upset price.

reserve ratio *banking* The primary reserve ratio relates to the balance of a member bank at the Federal Reserve Bank, plus money in the vault. A secondary reserve ratio is the ratio of government securities held by a bank to its demand deposits. There is also the time deposit ratio, which is a primary ratio that is related to time deposits instead of demand deposits. Reserves required for time deposits are much lower than those required for demand deposits.

Resettlement Transfer Scheme A program in the United Kingdom that sometimes provides financial assistance for people moving to a new job in some other part of the country.

res gestae *law* Latin for "the things done." Statements or acts made under the pressure of the situation so that there is little likelihood of lying. Such statements constitute an exception to the hearsay rule, which bars testimony by a witness in response to statements made by another that are offered to prove the truth of what is stated.

residual income security A security that has last claim on company income, usually common-stock shares. This security, however, is the primary beneficiary of the capital growth of a company.

residual profits Defined as income minus the annual cost of the capital invested in a profit center. This serves as an alternative to return on investment as a measure of profit-center performance.

residual theory of wages A general concept that labor is the last claimant to the product of industry after all capital costs have been paid. This is regarded as a somewhat antiquated theory.

residuary legacy A provision in a will leaving all property not otherwise disposed of in the will to one called the residuary legatee.

res inter alios acta *law* Latin for "acts done between others." The rule barring admission into evidence of declarations or other acts of those who are mere strangers to each other.

res ipsa loquitur *law* Latin for "the matter speaks for itself." A doctrine that in certain situations, usually negligence cases, mere proof of what happened establishes a presumption sufficient to carry the case unless evidence to the contrary is produced.

resolution A motion that has been passed or carried at a formal meeting or conference.

resource appraisal A management technique designed to keep all the resources of a company under review in order to make vital information that is necessary for their decision making available to top management.

respondeat superior *law* The rule that a principal or master is liable for the acts of his agent or servant done in the furtherance of the principal's business.

respondentia A combination of money lending on the cargo of a ship and insurance of that cargo so that if the cargo of the ship is lost, the lender cannot recover the money lent. Also known as bottomry.

response budgeting A two-tier budget in which two figures are used for key control areas, with the object being to achieve higher input results and lower expenditures.

response orientation A technique used to ascertain an individual's ability to select and make the correct response from among alternatives in the work situation. A psychomotor skill.

responsibility The obligation an individual has for carrying out assigned duties to the extent of his ability.

restraint equation *econometrics* An equation stating technological or institutional limitations, such as a production function or tax laws.

restricted commitment A situation in which the CEO proposes a plan of action, but communications are limited, thus allowing subordinates to give only limited commitment to the project.

Restrictive Practices Court An agency set up in the United Kingdom to monitor complaints and trading agreements under the Restrictive Trade Practices Act of 1956 and the Resale Prices Act of 1964 and to revoke agreements not considered to be in the best interests of the public. The work of this court was expanded by the Fair Trading Act of 1973, which replaced the Registrar of Restrictive Trading Agreements with the Director-General of Fair Trading.

restrictive labor practice A term denoting labor's attempt to control productive practices and the introduction of new technology in order to assure job security, worker benefits, etc.

results management A type of management that emphasizes consequences rather than activities and tends to give a worker a sense of accomplishment when goals are achieved.

479

retail audit A technique used in market research that involves a study of retail establishments to get information on sales, stocks, advertising presentations, point-of-sale displays, etc. Known as a shop audit in the United Kingdom.

retail method of inventory A method of approximating inventory through records kept at retail prices.

Retail Price Index Official measure of the change in the value of the monetary unit in terms of consumer purchases in the United Kingdom. A report is printed monthly by the Department of Employment. Similar measures are called the wholesale price index and the BLS Consumer Price Index in the United States.

retained earnings The amount of the earnings of a company that is retained and invested in the business rather than being paid out in dividends. Also known as earned surplus.

retainer The fee paid to a professional person to engage his services.

retention money A part of the agreed-upon price of a building contract in the United Kingdom that is withheld until the purchaser has the opportunity to inspect and approve the building.

retenue d'impot sur les revenues de capitaux A capital gains/capital yields tax, which is part of the Luxembourg income tax. It is a flat-rate tax deducted at the source on dividends, interest, etc., but with a lower rate for certain incomes. Also known as *Kapitalerstragsteuer.*

retenue d'impot sur les revenues echus a des contribuables nonresidents A form of Luxembourg income tax consisting of a flat-rate tax

deducted at the source from specified income of nonresidents. Also known as *Steuerabzug von Einkunften bei beschrankt Steuerflichtigen.*

retenue d'impot sur les tantiemes A flat-rate director's tax deducted at the source from directors' fees in Luxembourg. Also known as *Steuerabzug von Aufsichtsrats-Vergutungem.*

retrocession *insurance* The reinsurance of a risk by a reinsurer with yet another company.

retrogressive consumer *marketing* A term denoting a consumer with the propensity to economize on a purchase who probably could not be persuaded to buy a better product at a higher price.

retrospective payment The payment of wages in the United Kingdom as a result of an agreement to backdate a new wage agreement or system of payments.

return on assets managed (ROAM) One measure of the efficiency of a company's management that expresses sales minus the cost of goods sold as a percentage of assets managed minus liabilities.

return on assets (ROA) One measure of the productivity of assets, defined as income divided by total assets.

return on capital (ROC) When profits are projected for a new plant or enterprise, this is expressed as a percentage of the capital employed in that enterprise.

return on equity (ROE) A measure of the efficiency with which the shareholder's equity is employed in carrying out the activities of the enterprise, which is defined as income divided by equity.

return on investment (ROI) The efficiency or productivity of a profit center or an investment, defined as income divided by book value of the investment or profit center.

return on machine investment ratios A ratio related to how production is being done, either by human labor or by machines. Since human labor will normally be used until it is inefficient to do so, the return on machine investment should always be greater than the return would be without the machines.

returned work Products considered inferior that have been returned by buyers. A method of inspection, denoted as the "indirect review" method, which depends largely on complaints and returned products.

returns to scale Comparing the returns of an enterprise, if all factors of production are proportionately increased or decreased, to the scale of operations.

revalorization The action of restoring the former value of a monetary unit.

revaluation 1. The act of writing up the value of an asset to its current market value. 2. The change made by a government in the official rate at which its currency will be exchanged for the currency of another country. Revaluation is the term used when the currency is valued upward, and devaluation is the term used when the currency is valued downward.

revenue The result of turning a company's real assets into cash.

revenue account In the United Kingdom, the account of a company's revenues and expenditures made against those revenues, not including capital accounts.

revenue bond A bond, usually state or municipal, which is designed to be paid off by revenues from the project funded by the bond issue.

revenue center A department, for example, where the manager does not have the authority to alter prices to increase revenues and possibly profits.

revenue sharing The collection of tax revenues by a higher level of government (usually the federal government) and the sharing of the money collected with lower levels of government, usually through grants of some type.

reverse split Upon the action of the board of directors of a corporation, one new share of stock will be exchanged for two or more shares already held.

reverse take-over bid A situation in which the acquiring company plans to give management responsibilities and perhaps name preference to the acquired company because of that company's proven ability to grow and be profitable.

Review Analysis of Multiple Projects (RAMP) A techno-factor plan that deals with a multiple of related projects rather than one, as does PERT.

Revised Minnesota Paper Form Board A much-used and highly regarded spatial ability or aptitude test that takes about twenty minutes to complete.

Revised Operational Procedures (ROP) After an organizational audit, this new set of guidelines describes the changes that must be part of the operations of the new organization.

revocable credit Credit that can be cancelled or withdrawn without the consent of the person in whose favor the credit is given.

revolving credit Credit established by a bank (or some other financial institution) permitting a borrower to make new withdrawals equal to payments made on prior accounts.

reward power Power bestowed when rewards are given for compliance with the superior's actions and wishes.

reward system Any type of plan designed to provide incentives and awards to employees.

rework The action of redoing work that was not properly done at the outset.

Rheinisch-Westfalische Börse zu Dusseldorf Dusseldorf Stock Exchange. (*See* Section VII)

rhochrematics A techno-factor dealing with the management of material flow, which includes the concept of integrating the management of all material flow from its original source through production facilities to final consumers.

Rhodesian stock exchanges Situated in Bulawayo and Harare. (*See* Section VII)

rhythmical movements A series of movements that produce a natural rhythm, which has important consequences in time-motion studies.

Ricardian theory of rent The concept that land is usually valued according to its productivity, with the productive land being high-priced and the marginal land very low-priced.

Ricardo effect An assumption that a rise in real wages will encourage capitalists to substitute machinery for human labor.

rider 1. *insurance* A form attached to a policy adding special provisions to the regular terms of the policy, which may include double indemnity, waiver of premium, etc. 2. *government* An unrelated addition to a legislative bill.

right of recourse The right to recover a bad debt, such as a bill of exchange that has been rejected.

right of search *international law* The "right of visit and search" is a recognized right of a nation at war to stop neutral vessels on the high seas and search for contraband.

right of way *real estate law* The right of a person to pass over the property of another person.

rights issue An action taken by a company that is bringing out a new issue of stock. It consists of an offer to those who already own shares in the corporation the first chance to buy the new issue of stock.

rights of absolute priority A specification in a bankruptcy proceeding stating that each class of claimants with a prior claim on company assets be paid in full before junior claimants receive any payment at all.

right-to-work laws Provisions in some state constitutions or state statutes prohibiting closed-shop labor practices even in cases in which a labor union represents the employees of a plant. (*See also* closed shop)

Riksbank Sweden's central bank. (*See* Section VII)

Rio de Janeiro Stock Exchange *See* Section VII.

riparian rights *law* The rights of an owner whose land abuts water to the land under the water. Laws differ from state to state, and they also differ if the water is a river or stream, a lake, or an ocean.

risk aversion Defined as the unwillingness to bear risk without proper compensation or as the psychological dislike of risk that only reasonably safe, fixed-income securities will be bought.

risk capital Capital invested in high-risk companies, usually new ventures. There are investment firms that specialize in this type of investment, and they usually make loans at a high rate of interest.

risk economist An economist who measures the chance of failure in a venture in insurance terms, using a wide range of possible variables.

risk manager Usually an officer in a company who handles the insurance problems, keeps abreast of the possible at-risk situations in the company, and keeps the company adequately protected.

risk premium The increased return on a security required to compensate investors for the risk borne. It is a stated precept in investing that the higher the risk, the greater must be the return to persuade the investor to invest.

risk ratio banking The ratio of the total risk assets to total capital accounts.

risk-adjusted discount rate A discount rate that includes a premium for risk.

rival unionism Actions between labor unions that are vying for members in the same industry or company. There has been much such competition since the beginning of the decline of unionism.

Road Transport Training Board An agency established in the United Kingdom in 1966 under the Industrial Training Act of 1964. Address: Capitol House, Empire Way, Wembley, Middlesex.

Robert's Rules of Order A well-known book on parliamentary procedure.

Robinson-Patman Act, 1936 A part of the large quantity of antitrust legislation passed in the United States since 1890.

robot In technology, an automaton programmed to perform skills as a human being does.

ROGBY A personality assessment technique devised by William Isbister in the United Kingdom that is based on the concept that the individual is a "confused mass of colors" that can be broken down into the basic colors, such as red, blue, green, yellow, etc., which will, combined with biographical material, give a reasonable view of what the person is, what the person's judgments will be, etc.

rogue product Term used in the United Kingdom to refer to a product, inferior in construction, that has the reputation of breaking down repeatedly.

role 1. A characteristic form of behavior imposed upon a person because of status within a group. 2. The function or task the employee performs in an organization.

role conflict A situation that often occurs in industry in which a person must occupy two jobs, but finds that one does not fit with the other.

role perception How an employee perceives his place in the organization among other employees.

role playing A teaching technique in which students assume different functions in the organizations they represent.

roll back The reduction of wages or prices to a previous level; normally, this is action undertaken by a government of some sort.

roll-call vote In a formal meeting, a vote taken by calling out the names of individuals present and getting their response (often "yea" or "nay").

rolling plan In the United Kingdom, a long-term type of plan that is reviewed periodically and changed if necessary.

rolling stock *transportation* Movable property, such as trucks, freight and passenger cars, locomotives, etc.

Romanian central bank Banca Nationala a Republicii Socialiste Romania. (*See* Section VII)

Romanian Chamber of Commerce Established 1949. Address: Bd. Nicolae Balcescu 22, Bucharest.

Rome Stock Exchange *Borsa Valori di Roma.* One of ten Italian stock exchanges. (*See* Section VII)

Rome Treaty A term often used to describe the Treaty of Rome, 1957, which established the European Economic Community.

root-mean-square deviation *See* standard deviation.

Rorschach Test A test with ten basic cards, each with a symmetrical inkblot, to which the subject is asked to attach meanings, which, in turn, are supposed to reveal characteristics of the subject's personality.

rotating shift A work schedule designed to allow employees to change shifts periodically, if they choose, rather than working the same shift all of the time. (*See also* alternating shift)

rote learning A type of learning that requires little understanding, but a lot of repetition.

Rothwell-Miller interest blank Interest or inventory test used in personnel selection. The blank consists of nine sets of twelve job titles, with the candidate ranking them in order of preference. Interest categories include outdoor, mechanical, computational, musical, clerical, etc.

Rotterdam Stock Exchange *Vereeniging van Effectenhandelaren.*

round lot A trading-unit term on the New York Stock Exchange denoting either one hundred shares of stock or a one-thousand-dollar par value in the case of bonds.

roustabout In the United Kingdom, an oilfield worker associated with the drilling. Usually called a roughneck in the United States. A deck or wharf laborer.

routine problem solving Problem solving by traditional means.

routing Establishing the path materials will take through the plant in the production process.

Royal Aeronautical Society A member organization of the Council of Engineering Institutes in the United

Kingdom. Address: Royal Aeronautical Society, 4 Hamilton Place, London WI.

Royal Society of Arts An agency in the United Kingdom that cooperates with the London Chamber of Commerce in administering the Ordinary National Certificate in business studies.

Rubber Exchange A specialist commodity exchange in the United Kingdom dealing in both cash and in futures. Address: Plantation House, Mincing Lane, London EC3.

Rucker Plan A cash-incentive plan that relates payroll costs to the sales value added by the manufacturer.

rugged individualism A type of management philosophy that puts great emphasis upon the power and the acumen of the leader, usually the founder of the company. Henry Ford is an apt example of a manager who lead according to a principle of rugged individualism.

rule against perpetuities *law* The common-law rule that a future interest in land must vest within the time period of lives in being at the time the interest is created plus twenty-one years. The term "vest" means that the person to enjoy the interest must be identified within this time period and any conditions attached to the taking of the interest must have been resolved. Any attempted interests beyond that period are void.

rule against suspension of the power of alienation As an alternate or a supplement to the rule against perpetuities, some states by statute have a rule limiting the period during which the power to deal with land can be suspended in order to avoid the social problems involved with the non-saleability of land.

rule against unreasonable accumulations *law* A rule in some states that income from a trust cannot be accumulated without distribution for a period of not longer than the minority of a beneficiary or some similar period. Legislation similar to this began in England with the Thelusson Act and was designed to deal with a large estate that, if permitted to accumulate, might have resulted in that estate's total acquisition of English property in a finite time.

rules of competition Article 85 of the Treaty of Rome prohibits restrictive practices that distort competition in trade between the member states of the EC. Restrictive practices include price fixing, market sharing, etc.

running-down clause *marine insurance* A type of "collision clause" in marine insurance.

running with the land Something related to land that is considered part of the ownership of the land.

rupee Basic monetary unit of India.

S

SA *Société Anonyme.* French and Belgian companies.

sacrifice tax theory A theory of taxation that says the burden of taxes should fall in such a manner as to require the same degree of sacrifice from all tax-payers.

saerlig indkomstskat A special flat-rate income tax levied by the government of Denmark on certain capital gains and lump-sum payments in lieu of the ordinary progressive income tax, or *indkomstskat til statem.* Denmark also has church taxes, local taxes, and net-wealth taxes.

SAF *Svenska Arbetsgivareforeningen.* The employer's confederation of Sweden.

safety factor *finance* The ratio of inter-est on funded debt to net income before taxes but after such interest has been deducted.

safety fund system A system of bank insurance used in New York in the nineteenth century.

salary club An informal group of employers in the United Kingdom who occasionally meet to discuss wages, fringe benefits, etc.

salary increment Periodic increases in salaries, often written into work con-tracts.

salary sacrifice *insurance* A situation in a company whereby the employee has a part of his salary withdrawn every pay period to cooperate with the employer in the purchase of insurance, usually life insurance, or in the purchase of an endowment.

SALC South African Confederation of Labor.

sale and leaseback The sale of an asset to a vendee who immediately leases the asset back to the vendor. Usually this is undertaken for the purpose of freeing the cash of the vendor for other pur-poses.

sale on approval A transaction of the sale of goods wherein the seller retains ownership until such time as the pur-chaser completely approves of the goods and agrees to pay for same.

sales budget The projected annual bud-get for the sales department of a com-pany.

sales chain A process though which a product passes from the producer to the ultimate consumer.

sales charge A fee demanded by some investment companies to cover the expense of commissions to paid sales-persons and other initial costs of start-ing a new account.

sales contour If selling costs are put on one axis and output prices on the other axis, an indifference curve will trace all combinations of selling costs and out-put prices, which will enable a seller to dispose of a given quantity of output. There will be a different curve for vari-ous levels of output.

sales control Any activity of a firm can be regulated with respect to any or all of the following production factors: 1) quantity, 2) quality, 3) time use, 4) and cost. Sales control will have to do, pri-marily, with the quantity of sales and the cost of sales.

sales control units Geographical areas that can be separately identified as con-trol areas.

sales depth test *accounting* All of the steps taken in processing an order from a customer, from the receipt of the order until proper collection is made.

sales finance company A company the principle business of which is to buy the accounts receivable of other com-panies. There is commonly recourse between the finance company and the seller in the event the buyer defaults on payments.

sales for the account *stock exchange* A sale of stock contemplating future delivery.

sales line *economics* If selling costs are put on one axis, and out prices on the other axis, one indifference curve (sales contour) will trace all combinations of price and selling cost enabling a seller to sell a given quantity of output.

sales manual A booklet prepared by a company for its sales staff relating to every aspect of the company's policies on sales, along with sales suggestions to the salesperson.

sales order processing The process all sales orders go through from the time they come to the company, either by mail or phone or fax, to the time they are processed, delivered, and collected.

sales policies Those rules that apply specifically to the sales functions of a firm.

sales potential The possible sales of a commodity or a service in a given market in a given period of time. Historical trends, changes in the demographics of an area, population changes, etc., all contribute to possible sales. Above all, the sales potential for an area should never be looked upon as static, since all regions change rapidly, given the changeableness of both industry and labor.

sales promotion Actions usually accompanying direct selling, and having to do with all aspects of selling and making prospective customers aware of a product or a service.

sales-purchase curve With price on the Y axis and quantity purchased on the positive of the X axis and quantity sold on the negative side of the X axis, the sales-purchase curve traces the quantities that an individual is able to buy or sell at various prices. In a perfect market the sales-purchase curve would be horizontal; in an imperfect market it would be an ascending curve; in a pluperfect market—a market in which the price increases as the quantity exchanged increases—it would be a descending curve.

sales revenue That revenue that flows into a business by the sale of goods or the provision of services.

sales target A predetermined goal for an individual salesperson, an area, or for the company as a whole.

sales tax A tax levied and collected on goods at the point of sale. Sales taxes on some items, such as liquor or cigarettes, are often called luxury or excise taxes.

sales territory The area to be covered by a salesperson on behalf of the company, and within which the salesperson will be credited with all sales, whether the salesperson makes the sales or not. If the team concept is used, it is necessary to carefully divide the territory.

Salt Lake City Exchange One of twelve exchanges in the United States. (*See* Section VII)

sample *statistics* 1. A limited or finite number of items of data from a universe or population. 2. *marketing* One or more units of a product given free (or sold at a price much below market) in order to induce buyers to try the product and perhaps become regular users of the product.

487

sample reliability *statistics* The reliability of the arithmetic mean of a sample can be judged by dividing the estimated standard deviation of the items in the universe by the square root of the number of cases in the sample.

sample survey A survey for any purpose based on an examination of some representative part of the entire population.

sampling *statistics* An approximation of the nature or magnitude of some characteristics of a universe arrived at through actual measurement of some of the individual units or elements of that universe, called a sample, which may be chosen at random or by other methods.

sampling frame The data assembled on a population that is used in defining and gathering a sample of that population.

sampling orders Orders sent, usually free, for the inspection of a prospective customer. When this action is directed to the consumer, usually "trial sizes" of the product are made available.

Samuelson Substitution Theorem *input-output analysis* The proposition that even when variation of input proportions is possible, it will never be advantageous to vary input proportions when there are constant returns to scale, only one scarce input, and no joint products.

Samuelson-Stolper Effect A proposition stating that under free trade, goods may serve as a partial substitute for immigration of labor into a labor-scarce economy and hence that real wages might fall under free trade. In other words, the relative and absolute share of labor might go down although real national product would go up under free trade in such a situation.

San Francisco Stock Exchange One of twelve in the United States. (*See* Section VII)

Sanborn map *fire insurance* A map locating the risks in large cities with the insurance carried on the various locations.

sanctions Rewards resulting from a willingness to respond favorably to a directive, or penalties exacted for failure to accept and act upon a directive.

sandwich courses College courses, usually at the undergraduate level, that are alternated with periods of practical work in a specific industry.

sandwich lease When land is leased to a lessee, who in turn releases the land to another, the relessee, the first lease is called a sandwich lease.

sane *law* A legal concept denoting a person free from symptoms of grave mental disorder and therefore responsible for behavior.

sanguine temperament A temperament characterized by cheerfulness, optimism, and hope.

Santiago Stock Exchange *La Bolsa de Commercio.* One of two Chilean stock exchanges. (*See* Section VII)

Sao Paulo Stock Exchange *Bolsa de Valores de Sao Paulo.* One of two Brazilian stock exchanges. (*See* Section VII)

Sapporo Stock Exchange One of nine Japanese stock exchanges. (*See* Section VII)

sarkild sjomansskatt A tax levied on the income of seamen in Sweden.

satiation effect 1. The tiring effect a long test may have on the testee, which tends to lower the final score. 2. The tiring effect of long hours on the job, which may result in lower-quality work in the waning hours.

satisfaction of judgment A document stating that payment has been received and signed by a judgment creditor and filed in the same court or courts where the judgment is docketed.

satisfier The outcome of a response that is gratifying, and thus may be repeated.

save as you earn: (SAYE) A savings plan that allows employees in the United Kingdom to have periodic sums deducted from their paychecks to supplement a savings plan.

savings Popularly, the difference between disposable income and consumption.

savings bond A non-transferable registered bond issued by the federal government in the United States.

savings withdrawal ratio A measure to compare inflow and outflow of savings. The ratio is savings received in a period divided by savings withdrawn in that period.

Say's law of markets Designed by Jean Baptiste Say (1767–1832), a French economist, this law holds that aggregate demand price of output as a whole is equal to its aggregate supply price for all volumes of output. It states that there can never be general overproduction because every supply creates equivalent demand. The law assumes that liquidity preferences do not change.

scalar principle The concept that subordinates should communicate with their superiors only through designated channels.

scale In psychological testing, a series of items experimentally arranged from easy to difficult.

scale effect The effect on the size of output of each firm in an industry caused by a change in the price of a factor of input or by a change in the price of the product.

scale line *economics* If quantities of one factor of production are put on one axis, and quantities of another factor put on the other axis, one indifference curve (the iso-outlay curve) traces all combinations of the two factors that can be purchased for the same amount of money.

scalp *stock exchange* A short transaction made in contemplation of closing out at a profit.

Scandinavian Institute of Administrative Research A center of management and business research in Stockholm.

Scanlon Plan A cash-incentive plan devised by Joseph Scanlon in the 1930s and 1940s that allowed employees to share in savings made by more efficient production.

scarce currency *finance* Describes a situation in which the demand for one country's currency threatens to exhaust the available supply at current exchange rates.

scarce Not available in sufficient quantities to satisfy the wants of everyone without cost.

scatter The variability of scores around the measure of central tendency in a frequency distribution.

scatter diagram *statistics* A graph with one variable measured on the X axis and the other variable on the Y axis, and each item of a distribution is plotted on the graph. If there is a reasonable relationship between the two variables the plotted points will tend to follow a diagonal line.

scattergram A graphic portrayal of individual items that are by nature variable, and which may represent test scores or any other series of variable items.

scenario A term used in corporate planning to broadly describe the position the company might assume in the future.

schedule 1. Almost any orderly array of information. 2. In economic analysis, the tabular arrangement of prices and quantities or other similar data.

scheduling The assigning of time values, either by clock or by calendar, for carrying out the various operations of a firm in an orderly and synchronized manner.

scheduling of reinforcement The manner in which a reward is given, perhaps at fixed intervals, for the amount of work done.

schema A logically organized plan or outline.

schools of management thought 1) management by custom; 2) scientific management; 3) human behavior school; 4) social system school; 5) systems management school; 6) decisional management school; 7) quantitative measurement school; 8) management process school. (Designers, or proponents, of these management schools will be found in Section IX of this volume.)

Schweizerischer Gewerkschaftsbund Swiss federation of trade unions, established in 1880.

Science Research Council (SRC) UK An agency responsible to the Department of Education and Science for pursuing the following: 1) the carrying out of research and development in science and technology; 2) encouraging such research among individuals and firms; (3) providing and operating equipment or other facilities for common use in such research; 4) making grants for postgraduate instruction; 5) disseminating knowledge of such research. Address: State House, High Holborn, London WC1.

science 1. Any organized body of knowledge of general significance. 2. A body of knowledge dealing with phenomena having such a constant relation that there can be precepts known as laws. 3. More narrowly, denotes only the natural sciences. (Note: management can be called a "science" only in the sense of the first definition above. The discipline has produced a mountain of literature and some generalizations that might be construed as giving structure to the discipline as a science. However, management most nearly seems to be an art.)

scienter *law* Denotes knowledge on the part of one who has made false representations.

scientific management school A school of thought, generally attributed to Frederick W. Taylor (1856–1917), that is based on four principles: 1) the development of the best method of doing a job; 2) the development of workmen for that job; 3) the relating and bringing together of the right methods and the right workers; 4) the cooperation of managers and workers. (*See* Section IX)

scientific method The use of thorough investigation, controlled experimentation, and careful interpretation of data; such an approach provides a reliable basis for the determination and evaluation of new facts used by managers.

scire facias *law* Latin for "you may cause to know." An order of a court directing recognition of a public record unless reason can be shown to the contrary. This writ is used to revive an unexecuted judgment or to investigate the compliance of a corporation with its charter.

Scitovsky double criterion *welfare economics* A change in the economy is an improvement only if 1) those who gain evaluate their gains at a higher figure than the value that the losers set on their losses, and if 2) at the same time, the return move from the new position to the old position will not result in those who gain evaluating their gains at a higher figure than the value at which the losers set their losses.

Scottish Business Education Council (SCOTBEC) A professional and examining body. Address: 22 Great King Street, Edinburgh, EH3 6QH.

Scottish Education Department The government department responsible for public education in Scotland. Address: Sr. Andrew's House, Edinburgh, and Dover House, Whitehall, London.

Scottish Electrical Training Scheme Ltd. (SETS) A training course designed for graduate apprentices in electrical engineering.

Scottish Export Committee Motivates, directs, and coordinates Scottish export/import business. Address: Scottish Export Committee, Scottish Council Development and Industry, 1 Castle Street, Edinburg 2.

Scottish Stock Exchange Provincial stock exchange based in Glasgow. (*See* Section VII)

Scottish Tourist Board Promotes and advises on tourism in Scotland. Address: Rutland Place, West End, Edinburgh, EH1.

Scottish Trades Union Congress A federation of trade unions in Scotland, most of which are also members of the London-based Trades Union Congress. Address: Woodlands Terrace, Glasgow C3.

SDR's Special Drawing Rights. A new kind of monetary unit created for international use by the International Monetary Fund.

sealed bid A bid submitted in a sealed envelope, usually a price on a contract for construction, a sale of some major machine, etc. The sealed bid is supposed to eliminate collusion.

seasonal index The seasonal pattern of a business. In order to arrive at an annual average for sales, revenues, etc., an average figure is used for each month, with the averages being totaled at the end of the year and divided by twelve.

seasonal variation The fluctuation in any series of economic data during a year that recurs consistently from one year to the next. Simple averages are often used to make comparisons.

secondary bank reserve High-grade securities that are readily convertible into money.

secondary banking sector Special, but lesser, banks in the United Kingdom that do carry out some of the duties of commercial banks, but are not as important as commercial banks, credit banks, etc.

secondary distribution *finance* The reselling in smaller lots of a large block of securities purchased for such resale from existing stockholders and not from the issuing corporation.

secondary evidence rule *law* The rule admitting copies (or other secondary evidence) when sufficient explanation is offered as to why the original (or other primary evidence) is not available.

secondary goal One which is acquired through learning, as contrasted with a primary goal, which satisfies primary needs.

secondary group *social psychology* A number of persons who have a community of interests, but who do not have a face-to-face relationship, such as political parties, veterans' groups, etc.

secondary legislation Legislation, or other directives, handed down by the Council of Ministers, by Parliament, etc., of the EC that are are directly related to the provisions in the Treaty of Rome, and previous and subsequent treaties related to the European Common Market.

secondary picketing A form of picketing against a firm in which no labor dispute exists by a firm that is related and in which there is a dispute. The goal is for the picketing firm to bring pressure on the management of the related firms to make peace with labor.

secondary reinforcement The action of strengthening a response by use of a stimulus associated with another stimulus that has primary reinforcement value.

secondary strike A strike that spreads to firms that furnish materials to the "struck" firm.

seconder In a formal meeting, one who seconds the motion of another person. A motion and second are necessary before formal discussion of a matter can take place.

sectional tariff *transportation* A tariff made in sections, with each section containing different rates between the same points with provisions for alternative application.

sector accounts Dividing the economy of a country into four sectors, business, government, personal (consumers), and the rest of the world for the purpose of analyzing the flows between the sectors.

sector graph An arrangement of scores in a circle, the circumference of which includes all the scores.

secular stagnation theory The theory that the economy has reached "maturity", and the frontiers are gone, the rate of increase in population is declining, and vital discoveries are lacking. In such a stagnated economy, long periods of recession or depression predominate, and the periods of prosperity are shorter.

secular trends Related to the business cycle, denoting the average course that would be followed by economic activities over a period of several cycles. The trend may be calculated by fitting a line by the least squares method to the deseasonalized data.

secured creditor A creditor whose obligation is obtained by the pledge of some asset. In liquidation proceedings, the secured creditor receives the money from the sale of the pledged asset.

secured liability Debt that is secured by specific assets.

securities A cover-all name for written instruments, such as mortgages, bonds, stocks, bills of exchange, bills of lading, warehouse receipts, etc.

Securities and Exchange Commission (SEC) The U.S. federal agency that regulates securities markets.

Securities Exchange Act of 1934 The act provides for the regulation of securities exchanges and over-the-counter trading through the Securities and Exchange Commission in the United States. Also provides a source of information on companies whose securities are listed on the exchanges.

Security Council Permanent council of the United Nations responsible for peace keeping, which has five permanent members and ten elected members.

security issue tax A tax levied on the initial issue of stock by a corporation. Both federal and state taxes are levied.

security of tenure The ability of a tenant to maintain his tenancy, or the ability of an employee to maintain his tenure.

seigniorage The profit a government makes on the minting of money. This was an important source of revenue for princes and kings in the past, but is generally excluded in modern times.

seizin The possession of premises under claim of ownership of a freehold estate.

selection consultant A person or firm that specializes in seeking out personnel, usually at some top level of management, for other companies, generally for a specific position. Also known as a headhunter.

selective credit controls Controls that try to make some kinds of loans more difficult to obtain than others.

selective perception Emphasizing some aspect of a situation, while neglecting other aspects, resulting in a distortion of the total situation.

selective selling A policy of selling to a limited number of accounts in a specific area.

self All that a person means when the person says "me" or "mine". The awareness of one's being and functioning.

self-abasement Deferring to others in the extreme because of a strong attitude of personal inferiority.

self-administered test A test with instructions that are so explicit that the test can be taken without assistance or further explanation.

self-completion questionnaire A questionnaire usually sent to people through the mail, which they are supposed to fill out and return to the company.

self-deception In some personality theories, rationalizing as a defense mechanism.

self-esteem The degree to which individuals think well of themselves and of their ability to accomplish the goals that they and others have set.

self-fulfilling prophecy A forecast that the individual or the firm helps to come true by applying time and energy to achieve it.

self-insurance Denotes a firm establishing a reserve fund to pay for losses rather than taking out an insurance policy. Some companies do not set up a reserve fund and still take the chance of not insuring against loss.

self-liquidating An investment or loan, taken out for a specific purpose, that is supposed to yield enough return to retire the principal and interest.

self-report inventory A listing of items to be checked honestly by the testee, even though the patterns of responses may indicate deviation from the normal or the desired personality organization.

self-selection store Much like self-service, except that there are usually salespeople to offer some assistance if needed and to answer questions about products

self-service store A convenience store in which the selections are comparatively few and in which the customer picks out his goods and pays for them at a check-out point.

sellers' market A market in which the scarcity of goods makes it possible to sell goods without much effort and perhaps raise prices.

selling against the box Denotes a practice, usually carried out by a large stockholder who desires to shield his selling of shares, of "selling short" and delivering borrowed certificates rather than the shares the seller holds.

selling group *finance* The group working for underwriters of a stock or bond issue in selling to customers. Usually the selling group serves only as an agent and turns back any unsold shares.

selling platform The predominant theme of an advertising campaign.

selling short An agreement to deliver at some future date a security or commodity that the seller does not own, but which he hopes to buy later at a lower price.

semantic differential A term used in market research for the use of precoded questions put to the interviewees to learn their attitudes toward certain products, etc.

semiaverages method of fitting a straight line The division of data into two equal parts, an upper half and the lower half, with the arithmetic mean to be established for each group. A straight line drawn through these two means is an approximation of a linear regression line.

semi-interquartile range Half the distance between the 25 percentile and the 75 percentile, used as a measure of the dispersion of scores about a midpoint.

semilogarithmic chart A graph in which one axis is scaled in logarithms and the other axis is scaled arithmetically.

seminar A short course of study or a conference, usually pinpointing a certain topic of general interest at the time. Often such conferences last only a few hours or a day.

semiskilled labor Often defined as work that requires less than one year of either formal or informal training.

semistrong efficient market A market in which all publicly available information is supposedly instantaneously reflected in prices.

semivariable cost A cost that varies indirectly with changes in the level of production, but not proportionately. Electric power is usually a good example, since more power is used in further production, but usually grows proportionately less as more units are produced.

senior creditor Any creditor who has a claim on income or assets ahead of the claims of any general creditors.

seniority Length of service to a firm or an organization, sometimes used as the primary criterion in considering promotions, etc.

Sensale Public officials who must pass examinations and be nominated by members of the Stock Exchange, and who serve as official brokers on the Vienna Stock Exchange

sensitivity analysis The analysis of the impact of a change in an input variable on a specific plan.

sensitivity training A method of increasing one's awareness of one's effect on others and of increasing awareness of subconscious motivations. (*See also* T-groups, T-group training)

sentence completion A type of question often used in market research in which the respondent must complete a sentence. The response reveals to the researchers how the respondent feels about the product or service being researched.

sentence-completion test A sentence that becomes meaningful when a particular word or phrase is used to complete the sentence. The word or phrase used implies basic personality dynamics in the testee.

Seoul Stock Exchange The Stock Exchange of South Korea. (*See* Section VII)

separation of powers Denotes the division of the functions of government, which in the United States, are divided into the executive branch, the legislative branch, and the judicial branch.

separation rate In personnel management, denotes the ratio of the number of employees terminating work during the month to the average working force in the month. Those terminating are divided into three groups: quit, discharge, and layoff.

sequence analysis The study of the causal connection of the economic events of one period with those of the succeeding period or periods.

sequential analysis A sampling method in which a final decision depends more upon the successive observations of the population than on the size of the sample. As each item is tested, a decision is made on the basis of the observed values up to the point where the question of whether to continue the sample or to terminate the sample is raised.

sequestration *law* A writ installing representatives of a court to compel performance of a court order.

serial bonds Bonds issued at the same time, but with different maturity dates. The interest rates usually differ according to the length of time to maturity.

serial correlation 1. A situation in which two different time series are correlated when the values of one series are lagged by a fixed time interval with the values of other series. 2. Techniques in forecasting, based on past experiences, but using fewer data and thus less accurate than time series forecasting.

series bonds Groups of bonds usually issued at different times with different maturities but under the authority of the same indenture.

service mark A mark, such as a trademark or design, which is used in the United Kingdom to represent a product or service, and which may become part of the company image.

set *psychology* Term denoting the predisposition for acting in a certain manner under certain circumstances.

settlement options *life insurance* The right of the beneficiary of a life insurance policy or an endowment policy to select the payment method the company will follow in paying out the principal fund.

settlor One who creates a trust.

seven point plan A technique for personnel selection, with the potential of individuals assessed under these headings: attainments, general intelligence, special aptitudes, health, interests, disposition, and circumstances.

s-factors In Spearman's theory of intelligence, those psychoneural elements that account for successes in certain tasks, as contrasted to the general (g-factors) basic to all related performances.

's-Gravenhage Stock Exchange *Bond Voor den Greld-en Effectenhandel in de Provincie Tès-Gravenhage.* One of three Dutch stock exchanges.

shadow price *See* opportunity cost.

shake-out The action of making employees unneeded, by whatever means.

share-draft accounts Deposits in credit unions that can be transferred by check.

Share Incentive Scheme One of the provisions of the Finance Act of 1973 in the United Kingdom. Full-time employees are able to contribute a specified sum per month; the funds are used to buy shares in the company at 70 percent of the market value without immediately incurring tax on the benefit. The shares, when sold, are subject to capital gains taxes.

share reinsurance Reinsurance in which the reinsured participates on a share basis with the insurer in any losses.

sharecropping A method of farming wherein a tenant farmer works the ground and gives part of the crop to the owner as rental payment.

shareholder's equity The worth of the assets owned through shares in the corporation of the corporation's assets.

shelf registration A plan of the SEC under which a corporation can file a general-purpose prospectus describing its possible financing plans for up to two years, including any proposed new issue of securities. This eliminates the time lags for new public-issue securities.

shell company Term used in the United Kingdom for a company that exists only on paper. A company that is registered, and then sold to someone who is needing a company name and registry.

sheriff's sale A public sale of real or personal property carried out by the sheriff on orders from the court.

Sherman Antitrust Act A law passed by Congress in 1890 with the purpose of prohibiting acts or contracts in "restraint of trade" or "tending to monopoly." It provides for recovery of up to triple damages upon conviction. Subsequently amended by several acts, such as the Clayton Act, the Robinson-Patman Act, etc.

Shindica Method An analytical approach to anticipating and isolating potential problems in a complex operation, so that management can be reasonably well prepared for an emergency should it occur.

Shipbuilding Industry Training Board Established in the United Kingdom in 1964 under the 1964 Industrial Training Act. Address: Raeburn House, Northolt Road, South Harrow, Middlesex.

shipping and forwarding agent Term used in the United Kingdom for what is called a freight forwarder in the United States. One who assumes the responsibility for the paperwork and all other logistical matter related to an export.

shock and error model *econometrics* A system of equations containing random disturbances of the variables and errors in specific equations.

shock model *econometrics* A system of equations containing random disturbances of variables in contrast to a system in which the variables are subject to errors of observation.

shop talk A colloquialism denoting the continuance of talk about work in a nonwork situation.

short circuiting The gradual elimination of superfluous responses, particularly in motor skills, as a result of learning.

Short Employment Tests A grouping

of three psychological tests for clerical workers developed in the United States that measure verbal, numerical, and clerical skills.

short interval scheduling Assigning tasks and work assignments that cover a short period of time, with the thought that any inefficiencies or problems can be observed and understood in a short-term situation.

short rate *insurance* The charge made for insurance canceled before the expiration of the term of the policy. The rate is somewhat higher for this period than it would be for a matured policy

short run 1. A time period that is too short for the fixed factors of production to be changed. 2. *economics* The period of time during which some of the costs of a particular firm are fixed and cannot be changed substantially, such as plant size, etc.

short-time working Term in the United Kingdom for working only part time, or at somewhat reduced hours, generally on a temporary basis.

short ton two thousand pounds.

shortage A situation in which buyers are trying to buy more at a specific price than sellers are willing to sell.

SIAR Scandinavian Institute for Administrative Research.

SICOVAM *Société Interprofessionalle pour la Compensation des Valeurs Mobiliers.* The clearing house for the settlement of accounts on the Paris Stock Exchange.

sigma 1. The capital Greek letter Σ denotes the sum of a number of items. 2. The small Greek letter σ denotes the standard deviation.

significance *statistics* In the statistical analysis of data, the probability that in the universal array of scores the obtained score would occur beyond chance.

silent or sleeping partner A colloquialism denoting a partner who invests in a partnership but does not participate in its management. Unless this partner qualifies as a "limited partner," he is exposed to the same liability as any other partner.

silicosis A progressive and nearly always fatal disease caused by breathing silica in coal mining, quarrying, etc.

silver standard A monetary system under which money is convertible into silver at a specified rate and vice versa and free shipment of silver internationally is permitted.

simple average An average in which the individual items are not weighted.

simple interest A method of calculating interest that does not compute interest on interest past-due.

simulation model A model involving a dimension of time so that the results of a preceding period can be incorporated in the new period.

simultaneous equations A system of equations designed so that the same value for each variable will satisfy each equation.

Singapore International Chamber of Commerce Established in 1837. Address: Denmark House, Raffles Quay, Singapore.

Singapore National Trades Union Congress Includes about 150 trade unions with approximately 120,000 members. Address: Trade Union House, Shenton Way, Singapore.

Singapore Stock Exchange One of two Malaysian stock exchanges. (*See* Section VII)

single life pension A pension that ceases all payments when the one beneficiary dies, since there is no provision for anyone besides the one individual.

single status A situation in which both blue collar and white collar workers in a firm have the same status. This is sometimes the case in the United Kingdom and is widely approved.

single tax A proposal by the economist Henry George that the government appropriate all of the unearned increment of land by means of a tax, in the belief that this tax alone would yield sufficient revenues so that the government could abolish all other taxes. (Henry George was a Fabian Socialist who was appalled by the vast wealth held by a few people and the poverty in which so many people lived. He wanted to find an answer to that deplorable situation, and he finally concluded that ownership of land was a primary cause of the unequal distribution of wealth. He thus proposed to take all of the unearned increment of the land annually as a one-tax measure that would allow the government to forego all other taxes.) (*See also* unearned increment)

sinking fund A fund set aside by a company to finance some future obligation. With regard to bonds, the fund is a payment of cash to bondholders, thus retiring the bonds to some degree.

sit-in A labor situation in which the employees do not leave the factory, but remain in it twenty-four-hours a day and refuse to leave. This action prevents a lock-out by managers. This type of "strike" became popular in the United States in the 1930s.

situational theory of management The concept that leadership must be multidimensional, flexible, and able to adjust to different situations.

situationism A principle that says as situations change, there are changes in roles, and hence changes in personality.

Six M's of management Men, materials, machines, methods, money, and markets.

Sixteen Personality Factor Questionnaire (16PF) One type of personality test based on a theory of personality structure devised by R. B. Cattell of the United States. It is designed to measure sixteen primary personality factors, plus a number of secondary factors

sjomannsskatt A tax levied on seamen in Norway in place of the regular income tax.

skewness The degree to which a frequency curve lacks symmetry; a frequency distribution of scores that bunches up on one side of the mean and tails out on the other.

skill A systematic and coordinated pattern of physical and mental activities, some of which are categorized as perceptual, motor, manual, intellectual, social, etc.

skill dissipation The loss or partial loss of a skill, usually from lack of use.

skilled labor Work that requires skills gained through education or through apprenticeships, which usually take more than one year to complete.

skilled worker An astute craftsman in a specific occupation who is able to apply a wide range of techniques and knowledge to his work with a minimum of direction or supervision.

skimming Term used in the United Kingdom to indicate the action of putting a product on the market at a high price and lowering that price as necessary and by degrees until the market is saturated.

slander An untruth that is spoken about a person that is sufficiently negative to cause damage to the reputation of the person being spoken about.

slave unit A part of a system that is controlled by a master unit in the system. Often this part of the system replicates the work of the master unit but depends upon the master unit.

sliding-parity *exchange rates* Essentially a "crawling-peg," which is a compromise between fixed exchange rates and free-floating exchange rates.

sliding-scale tariff A tariff in which the duty varies with the price of the goods, whether the duty is ad valorem or specific.

slope The slope of a curve at a point is the change of the dependent variable (Y axis) divided by the change of the independent variable (X axis). The slope of a straight line is the same at all points.

sluice-gate price The price of agricultural commodities fixed each quarter by the European Commission of the European Community on certain products being imported into member countries.

slump Usually the lowest point (trough) in a business cycle.

slumpflation United Kingdom term for

the U.S. term stagflation. A combination of unemployment, slow economic growth, and inflation.

Small Business Administration (SBA) A federal government agency created in 1953 to advise, protect, and make loans to eligible small businesses. Address: 1441 L Street, Washington, DC 20416.

Small Industries Council for the Rural Areas of Scotland An agency covering all but seven counties in Scotland that makes loans, gives advice, and suggests technology for firms employing fewer than twenty skilled workers. Address: 27 Walker Street, Edinburgh EH3 7HZ.

Smith-Connally Act A 1943 federal law enacted in the United States as a war measure, justifying government seizure of plants affected by labor strikes and forbidding strikes unless thirty days' notice was given. This legislation was part of an integrated wartime program that included wage and price controls as well.

smoothing *statistics* The application of formulas to remove irregularities from an array of data, without losing any essential characteristics of the data.

social accounting The economic evaluation of projects, which includes social costs.

social age The development of a person expressed in terms of age at which any given series of social adjustments are typical.

social audit The study of the social impact of a company on national policies, which includes such categories as the employment of disabled workers, pollution, utilization of resources, health and safety considerations, etc.

social dynamics Those conditions that relate to social progress.

social facilitation The enhancement of behavior through the presence of co-acting or observing groups.

social increment The enhancement of output when other persons are present, as compared with output when one is working alone.

social insurance Compulsory insurance in the United States, or any country, that protects the worker against unemployment, industrial accidents, and old age.

social investment Those investments made in the infrastructure of a nation that are funded from tax monies at some level of government, which might include roads, bridges, hospitals, among many other services and institutions.

social participation The willingness and ability of a manager to meet and to talk with people of all types, to know their strengths and weaknesses, and to be able to relate to them so that the manager gains their trust.

social psychology The science of psychology as it relates to interpersonal relationships, which includes the workplace and the people and experiences related to the workplace.

social sanction Those activities of an individual or of a group that are acceptable in the society of which they are members.

Social Science Research Council (SSRC) An agency in the United Kingdom responsible to the Department of Education and Science that is designed to promote, by all means possible, researching and teaching in the social sciences. Address: SSRC, State House, High Holborn, London WCI.

social sciences 1. The study of human beings as members of a group. 2. All sciences that relate to group activities, such as history, economics, psychology, sociology, etc.

Social Security Act of 1973 Legislation in the United Kingdom that provided that all employees be introduced to the State Reserve Pension Scheme by April 1975, except where a recognized company pension is in place. The object of the act was to provide every employee with a secondary pension.

social status The relative position of one in the group, colloquially referred to as the "pecking order".

Socialism Socialism exists in many forms. Revolutionary socialism, called communism, requires that all capital resources be owned by the state and administered by the state "on behalf of the people." Democratic socialism emerges in a nation by vote of the people, and under this system the government may own some basic industries, but private enterprise is often encouraged. Under socialism, taxes must always be high to support social programs administered by the government.

socialized communication A situation in which another person's point of view and interests are taken fully into consideration. Also known as adapted communication.

Sociedad anonima de responsabilidade limitada Abbreviations: Lda., Std., or Ltda. A joint-stock company in Portugal, formed either by private or public subscription.

Sociedad anonima A joint-stock company under the laws of Spain.

Sociedad cooperativa A cooperative formed under the laws of Portugal.

Sociedad de responsabilidad limitada Limited liability company in Spain.

Sociedad em comandita por accoes A limited partnership formed under the laws of Portugal.

Sociedad em comandita simple A general partnership formed under the laws of Portugal.

Sociedad em nome colectivo An incorporated partnership under the laws of Portugal.

Sociedad per cotas Under the laws of Portugal, a limited liability company.

Societa a Responsabilita Limitata Under the laws of Italy, a private limited liability company.

Societa cooperative A cooperative under Italian law.

Societa di Fatto A "partnership in fact" under Italian Civil Law. While effectively it is a partnership, there is no contract making it so.

Societa in Accomandita per Azioni Under the Commercial Code of Italy, a partnership limited by shares.

Societa in Accomandita Semplice A Limited Partnership under the Italian Commercial Code.

Societa in Nome Collettivo A General Partnership under the Italian Commercial Code.

Societa irregolari Under Italian Civil

Law, this is an "irregular partnership"; all proper legal formalities required for establishing an ordinary partnership have not as yet been completed.

Societa non Azionarie Under Italian commercial code, a nonstock company.

Societa Semplice A private partnership under the Italian Commercial Code.

Societas Europea (SE) *See* The European Company concept.

Société á Responsabilite Limitée A private limited company in France or Luxembourg. Partners must number between two and fifty, and each shareholder's liability is limited to his investment. Shares can be transferred only with the agreement of those holding 75 percent of the capital.

Société Anonyme (SA) A joint-stock company in which shareholders are liable only to the extent of their investment in France, Switzerland, Luxembourg, and Belgium. Under the laws of each country, the qualifications for forming such a joint-stock company differ.

Société Cooperative A business cooperative under the laws of both Belgium and Luxembourg.

Société de Personnes a Responsabilite Limitée A private limited company under Belgian law, the shares of which are non-negotiable and may be held only by individuals.

Société en Commandite par Actions Under Swiss law, a partnership limited by shares. Also known as *Kommanditaktiengesellschaft.*

Société en Commandite par Actions (SCA) A partnership under the laws of Belgium, France, and Luxembourg

that is limited by shares. The *commandites,* or general partners, are liable for the debts of the partnership, with other shareholders being liable only to the extent of their investments. This type of partnership is seldom used in France.

Société en Commandite Simple (SCS) A limited partnership under the laws of France and Luxembourg. In France, some of the partners (*commandites*) are jointly and severally liable for all the debts of the partnership, while regular shareholders are limited by the amount of their investments.

Société en Commandite A limited partnership under Swiss law. Also known as *Kommanditgesellschaft.*

Société en Nom Collectif (SNC) Under the laws of Switzerland, France, Belgium, and Luxembourg, a limited partnership in which all partners are jointly and severally liable for the debts of the partnership. In France, the shareholders are also liable to the full extent of their personal assets, and all partners are "commercants" unless the statutes state otherwise. Shares are not negotiable without the agreement of all the other partners.

Société Interprofessionnelle pour la Compensation des Valeurs Mobilieres (SICOVAM) The clearinghouse for the Paris stock exchange.

Société Simple (Einfache Gesellschaft) A simple partnership under Swiss law.

Society for Advancement of Management (SAM) A nongovernment organization devoted to the perfection of management practices, in part through the selection of terms related to management which can become known and used on a universal scale.

socioeconomic status 1. The relative class position of an individual evaluated from the standpoint of income, family background, occupation, organization memberships, etc. 2. In the United Kingdom social grades under which households are commonly divided (such as A, B, C1, C2, D, and E). Grades represent income status as well as worker or professional status.

sociodyne Some inhibiting factor in society that works contrary to synergy in a society.

sociological theory of leadership A view that leadership is made up of work efforts that facilitate the activities of followers and strive to reconcile any organizational conflicts between followers.

sociology 1. The science dealing with social groups and institutions, their origins, their characteristics, etc. 2. Conceived broadly, it is the most general of all social sciences. It bears the same relation to the special social sciences, such as economics and politics, that biology has to botany and zoology. It is concerned with the origin, development, functions, and structures of all human relationships. 3. More narrowly, sociology is the social science that deals with social relations not already covered by the older social sciences such as economics and politics, and it deals particularly with problems such as family relations, poverty, criminology, etc.

soerskatt til utviklingshjelp A special tax levied in Norway on incomes to finance aid to developing countries.

soft goods Nondurable consumer goods.

soft sales promotion A type of promotion that does not direct attention to the product itself, nor does it try to prove that the product is superior, or any such usual promotion. Rather, by use of some well-known personality or some gimmick, the product is surreptitiously revealed with the hope that it will be remembered. Usually, this is a low-budget promotion that does not produce much.

software Programs with codes that guide the computer to do certain things, as contrasted with the hardware itself.

Soil Conservation Service (SCS) An agency created in 1935 to aid in eliminating soil erosion and to aid in flood control. (The agency came into being during the so-called Dust Bowl days and is considered to be one of the wisest moves ever made for the benefit of agriculture and the nation as a whole.)

sole proprietorship The most simple form of business organization, owned and controlled by one person.

solicitor Term for a lawyer, attorney in the United Kingdom.

solidarism A doctrine of mutual dependence stating that each individual has economically justifiable obligations to less-fortunate individuals.

solus position An advertising position in a newspaper usually not used for ads, such as the editorial section. Advertising placed in such a position is usually more expensive, but is more successful than ads in the usual advertising pages.

solvency The ability to pay debts as they come due.

somandsskat Special income tax levied on seamen in Denmark.

SOP Standard operating procedure.

SOPC Sales operations planning and control.

sources and uses statement A type of financial statement that shows the sources of all revenues and the purposes for which those revenues were spent. It entails separating the changes in the balance sheet accounts into those areas in which cash was brought into the company and those areas in which expenditures took money out of the company.

South Africa stock exchanges *See* Section VII.

South African Association of Chambers of Commerce An affiliation of Chambers of Commerce in South Africa with about 120 members. Established in 1892. Address: POB 566, Cape Town and POB 694, Johannesburg.

South African Confederation of Labor (SACL) The central organization for white workers' trade unions. Address: POB 31105, Braamfontein, South Africa.

South African Reserve Bank Central bank of South Africa established in 1920. Address: Church Square, Pretoria. (*See* Section VII)

SpA *Societa per Azioni*, or joint-stock company under Italian law.

span of authority The number of immediate subordinates that report to a manager.

span of managerial responsibility Peter Drucker made this statement,

which is generally accepted: "the extent to which assistance and teaching are needed" by subordinates.

Spanish Central Bank *Banco de España*. (*See* Section VII)

Spanish companies General types of companies under Spanish law: 1) limited liability company, or *Sociedad en commandita*; 2) partnership, or *Compania collectiva*; 3) limited liability company, or *Sociedad de responsabilidad limitada*; 4) joint-stock company, or *Sociedad anonima*.

Spanish Employers' Federation *Confederacion Patronal Española*.

Spanish income taxes 1) a progressive income tax charged on all income from all sources, or *impuesto general sobre la renta de las personas fisicas*; 2) an urban land tax, or *contribucion territorial urbana*; 3) agricultural land tax, or *contribucion territorial rustica y pecuaria*; 4) industrial tax, or *impuesto sobre actividades y beneficios commerciales e industriales*; 5) tax on earned income from personal work, or *impuesto sobre los rendimientos del trabajo personal*; 6) Tax on income from capital, or *impuesto sobre las rentas del capital*. (The reader should remember that tax laws change, sometimes rapidly, in all countries. This information is consistent with the latest information available.)

Spanish stock exchanges *See* Section VII.

special abilities test A test that measures proficiency in selected fields, such as clerical, mechanical, etc.

special agent an agent whose power to act on behalf of his principle are strictly limited.

special aptitudes test A test that measures the likelihood of success in a specialized field, usually after training, and may include everything from music to nuclear physics.

special assessment A payment imposed on property by government when some special benefit financed by government enhances the value of the property, such as widening a street, etc. Such payments are usually the cost of that part of the project that directly affects the property.

special assessment bond *finance* A bond issue that will be paid off by the revenues coming from special assessments against specific property.

special deposits Reserve monies clearing banks are required to deposit with the Bank of England, which limits the clearing banks' ability to lend.

Special Export Services Branch A part of the Export Services Division of the Department of Trade in the United Kingdom. Address: Special Export Services Branch, Export House, 50 Ludgate Hill, London EC4M 7HU.

special verdict *law* A verdict that makes separate findings on a number of issues in a case as well as a final finding for one party or the other. A special verdict must be consistent in all of its parts.

special warranty deed Similar to a quitclaim deed, inasmuch as the grantor states he will defend the grantee only against acts of himself and persons claiming under himself.

specialist *finance* A member of the stock exchange who handles orders with limits above or below the current market price for other brokers, and who may deal for his own account. The specialist usually devotes attention to making a market for one or two stocks.

specie Coin, usually gold or silver; hard money.

specific commodity sales tax Virtually the same as an excise tax.

specific deposit Not a general deposit, but a deposit made for a particular purpose, such as bond coupons deposited for collection only.

specific legacy The provision in a will leaving specific property to a particular named person. In the event the grantor disposes of the property before death (i.e., the legacy is adeemed), the named person receives nothing.

specific performance The right to have a contract specifically enforced according to its terms rather than the mere recovery of damages. This right exists in law where damages provide an inadequate remedy.

specific unemployment Unemployment existing in specific industries that can be quickly and accurately tabulated.

speculation The buying and selling of goods or services in the hope of making a profit from the change in price. Thus a "stock speculator" will buy stocks that may be of questionable value in the hope of making profit when the price goes up.

speculative risk All risk that is inherent in operating a business enterprise.

speed test A type of intelligence test in which the number of questions answered in a specific time period is of importance.

spendthrift trust A trust in which the

terms bar creditors from reaching the income or principal of the trust.

spiral omnibus test A psychological test consisting of an admixture of types of items that are arranged in ascending levels of difficulty.

split-income A provision of the federal income-tax law that says that the incomes earned by a married couple may be considered as earned one-half by each, when a joint return is filed. This essentially lowers the total tax for all people except those in the lowest income-tax bracket.

spontaneous sources of cash Those areas that produce revenues automatically, such as the accounts payable to the company, without further action and in the ordinary course of doing business.

spread 1. Simplistically, the difference between the production cost and the selling price to consumers, i.e., the mark up. 2. *underwriting* The difference between the buying price of the underwriter and the selling price to the public. 3. *stock exchange* The difference between the present or spot prices and present prices for future delivery. 4. *stock exchange* A combination of a call and a put, so that the purchaser of the spread may at his option demand delivery from or make delivery to the seller of the spread. The put and the call are for different prices, else the transaction would be called a straddle. 5. The difference between asking prices and bid prices. 6. *investment banking* The difference between the issue price of a new security issue and the net amount paid to the company.

Springer-arbeiter A term used in German industry denoting a person who possesses a number of skills and can fill any job on an assembly line.

spurious correlation *statistics* An association that appears mathematically to indicate a relationship, but which actually is the result of uncontrolled factors in the study.

squatter's right The acquiring of land through adverse possession. The right to acquired land by one who has continuously occupied the land, without recognition of the rights of the owner, for a period required by law, usually twenty years.

SRA clerical test A three-part psychological test covering five minutes of vocabulary, five minutes of arithmetic, and five minutes of checking.

SRA mechanical aptitude tests Psychological tests of mechanical comprehension originally used with service personnel during World War II.

SRA nonverbal test A general learning ability test designed by Science Research Associates for use in psychological testing.

SRA tests Psychological tests and measures designed and copyrighted by Science Research Associates in the United States.

Srl *Societa a Responsabilita Limitata.* A limited liability company under the laws of Italy.

stability/neurosis spectrum One of three scales on which people are measured in temperament and personality tests. The other two spectra are convergent/divergent and introversion/extroversion.

stable equilibrium *economics* A condition that, once achieved, will continue indefinitely unless there is a change in some noneconomic conditions.

staff authority The word "staff" indicates the support function provided by staff members, with the primary emphasis upon the assistance a staff member gives to workers to accomplish the tasks assigned to them.

staff status The terms and conditions of employment and compensation. In the United Kingdom, as well as in the European Community. There has been an attempt at leveling with respect to hourly workers and staff positions, by calling both "staff" positions. This is a socialistic concept that does not appear to substantively change actually working conditions or pay.

stag A term sometimes used on the stock exchange, mainly in the United Kingdom, for a speculator who buys a lot of shares of a new issue of stock not for holding, but for selling soon at a profit.

stagflation A situation in which inflation and economic stagnation exist at the same time. Economists once believed this situation to be impossible.

stagnation An economic situation in which per-capita real income is static or declining.

stagnation thesis The original proposition, related to the 1930s, that real per capita income would not rise in the future because of: 1) a declining rate of population growth; 2) the disappearance of the geographic frontier; 3) the growth of the absolute volume of savings; and 4) the tendency of new techniques of production to be capital saving rather than capital using.

stamp trading The use of retailers of trading stamps, which are given for so many dollars spent and which are usually redeemable for prizes, etc. This is a dying business in the United States since competition is so stringent that profits are difficult to make.

standard A unit of measurement established as a criterion or level of reference.

standard deviation *statistics* 1. A term denoting to what degree figures tend to cluster around an average. A measure of the variability of a distribution. 2. The square root of the deviations squared from the mean of the distribution (in a normal frequency distribution, the middle 68.34 percent of the scores).

standard deviation of return A measure of variability. It is the square root of the mean squared deviation from the expected return.

standard error *statistics* Any one of a number of statistical procedures used to indicate the difference between an obtained and a true (or theoretical) distribution of scores.

Standard Industrial Classification Classification of industries by numbers in the United Kingdom. The system is compatible with the International Standard Industrial Classification.

standardization The establishment and use of specific sizes, types, styles, etc., based on accepted norms.

standard of living The necessities and luxuries that are accepted by a particular social group or economic group as necessary for its well-being.

standard time 1. The time it takes to complete a job at "standard performance," which includes rest breaks, etc. 2. Local time in any one of the twenty-four time zones in the world.

Standard Weights and Measures Division Provides UK industry with weights and measures of the European Common Market. Address: Standard Weights and Measures Division, Department of Industry, Abell House, John Islip Street, London SW1 4LN.

standing committee In a formal organization, a subcommittee of an executive committee, or a council, which is normally permanent, with well-defined duties and authority.

Standing Joint Industrial Council A joint committee of employers and employees who meet to discuss wages, salaries, working conditions, procedures for settling disputes, etc.

standstill agreements *international economics* A term referring to external debt payment and denoting the agreement of creditors to permit temporary freezing of their credits.

stare decisis *law* The doctrine that principles of cases already decided will be applied to a new case. The departure from previously applied principles are called overrulings.

start-up costs Expense involved in starting up an enterprise or a project.

state bank A bank chartered by the state in which it will operate. It may become a member of the Federal Reserve System and the Federal Deposit Insurance Corporation if it can qualify under the two sets of regulations.

statement of changes in financial position A financial statement that shows all the sources and the uses of working capital for a specific period of time.

static equilibrium *economics* A term denoting that the population of a country and its composition, stocks of capital and its composition, consumption and its composition, prices, the quantity of money, and other economic variables are constant.

statics *economics* The consideration of economic situations without regard to changes over time.

stationary state *economics* An economy in which factors are assumed not to change independently, but only as a result of an assumed change in one of the factors. Specifically, population is constant in numbers and composition, the rates of production and consumption of commodities are constant, prices are constant, and there is no net saving or capital accumulation.

statistical quality control A system of quality control, highly mathematical in nature, used to obtain information on the costs of eliminating faults in a product and on the value to the company of a fault-free product.

statistics The application of the techniques of mathematics to the classification and organization of data as a basis for conclusions and predictions.

statlig formgenhetsskat Net wealth tax levied by the state in Sweden on the capital value of individual assets at the end of the year minus net liabilities. The tax is progressive in nature.

statlig inkomstskatt In Sweden, the progressive state income.

Statni banka ceskoslovenska Central bank of Czechoslovakia. (*See* Section VII)

statute law A rule governing the conduct

of persons established by the legislature and stated in a code.

statute of frauds *law* Originally enacted in England in 1677 and now enforced in all our states as well. It could be more precisely called a statute requiring written evidence in the proof of certain classes of contracts in which the opposite party insists on that sort of proof. Contracts in the following areas are covered by this statute: 1) real estate; 2) guarantees; 3) mutual promises to marry; 4) executor's contracts; 5) contracts for more than a specified amount (usually from fifty dollars to five hundred dollars) unless there is part performance.

statutes of limitations Laws in states that make rights legally unenforceable after a certain number of years on the grounds that the party waited too long to try to enforce such rights. The length of time a right can endure differs with the right.

statutory minimum wage A minimum wage set by state, province, or national law.

stereotyped An oversimplified and usually biased classification of people or things.

Steuerabzug von Einkunften bei beschrankten Steuerpflichtigen In Luxembourg, a flat-rate tax deducted at the source from the specified income of nonresidents. Also known as *retenue d'impot sur les revenus echus a des contribuables non-residents.*

sticker An employee in the United Kingdom who is not looking for a promotion and who frequently will turn it down if it is offered.

Stille Gesellschaft A "sleeping (or silent) partnership" under Austrian or German company law.

Stilling Tests A type of color vision test.

Stirling Stock Exchange Provincial stock exchange in Scotland.

stochastic *statistics* a variation that is random as opposed to determined or biased.

stochastic process A sequence involving many variables that strives for some degree of assurance, but not certainty, in knowing what the order will be.

stock insurance company An insurance company with stockholders, as opposed to a mutual company, that acts as any other corporation in the marketplace.

stockjobber Commission broker in the United Kingdom. The stockjobber sells to the public and buys from a floor trader.

stock market chartist A stock market analyst who tracks the history of the market and investigates possible trends in the future.

stock option A privilege, usually given to senior executives of a corporation, granting the holder the right to purchase a specified number of shares of stock at a specified price for a specified period of time. Stock options are often used to attract an executive to the company.

stock warrant A document evidencing a right to buy stock.

stock Common stock, i.e., shares denoting equity in a corporation.

Stockholm Fondbors The only stock exchange in Sweden. (*See* Section VII)

stock, preferred A special issue of stock, often sold in the early life of a corporation to raise much-needed capital, which holds privileges that common shares do not have.

stoppage in transit rights The right of an unpaid seller to repossess goods while they are in transit if the buyer becomes insolvent.

straight bill of lading A nonnegotiable bill of lading, providing for delivery of merchandise by a carrier to the person named in the bill.

straight letter of credit One in which the issuer (e.g., a bank) recognizes only the person named (e.g., an exporter) as authorized to draw drafts under the letter for advances to the named person for whose benefit the letter is issued.

stratification *marketing* Dividing up a population according to categories such as age, occupation, race, etc.

stratified sampling A random sampling of the population divided into proportions representing each class.

street-name stocks Term used in the United States to denote negotiable bonds drawn on brokerages rather than on individuals.

Street Colloquialism for Wall Street in New York.

stress interview An appraisal made of an interviewee that gives insight into his ability to cope with problems, such as discouragement, anger, etc.

striking price The fixed price for which a stock can be purchased in a call contract or sold in a put contract. Also known as exercise price

Stromberg dexterity test A psychomotor skill testing both speed and accuracy.

strong-form efficient market A market in which the prices ostensibly instantaneously reflect all information on the firm involved, whether public or private.

structural determinants of behavior Environmental factors that play a leading role in shaping the attitudes and actions of people as individuals and as working groups.

structural equation *econometrics* An equation stating the relationship between variables in an economic system.

structural unemployment Unemployment that occurs when the industrial structure of a nation changes.

structural-functionalist school A term used in industrial psychology in the United States that denotes the opinion of a specific school of thought that believes that stability and equilibrium are the norm in society and in industry, and that all people have shared values that make society stable.

study of values A test developed in the 1950s in the United States as an interest and inventory test, which helps to determine whether workers' personal interests would assist them in performing well in particular types of work.

Stuttgart Stock Exchange *Die Wertpapierbörse in Stuttgart.*

style of life According to Alfred Adler, the manner in which a person strives to attain the goal of superiority (as he sees it), which determines what the individual learns, perceives, and feels to the neglect of all else.

SUB Supplemental unemployment benefits. Payments provided in a labor contract that are in addition to unemployment compensation provided by law.

subculture A grouping of persons according to special customs that bind them together, though they may be, at the same time, members of the larger society of their regions or nations. Examples are some religious groups, such as the the Mennonites and Seventh-Day Adventists, and nationalistic groups.

subjective That which exists in a person's mind that may not be discernable to another person, but which belongs to the person alone.

subliminal That which exists below the threshold of normal sensory awareness.

submarginal land Land so poor that it cannot pay back the cost of cultivation.

submissiveness An attitude of compliance, nonassertiveness, and yielding to other persons.

subordinated creditor A creditor who holds a debenture that has a lower chance of being paid than do other company liabilities.

subpoena *law* A court order demanding the appearance of a person in court to testify as a witness. Defiance of such an order is looked upon as constituting contempt of court, which can result in a fine or imprisonment or both.

subpoena duces tecum *law* A court order directing a person to appear in court as a witness that also requires that the witness bring certain named documents or items with him.

subrogation *law* A doctrine entitling a third party to be substituted for one of the original parties to a transaction.

subsidy A payment by government to help support some desired economic activity, ostensibly in the best interests of that activity and of society in general.

subsistence theory of wages The theory held by some classical economists in England, from about 1775 to 1840, that wages in the long run would be at the level just sufficient for the working population to maintain and reproduce itself. (subsistence here does not refer to the minimum standard for maintaining physical life, but rather the level of wages that would discourage people from having more children.)

substantive motion A motion that has been amended and is ready to be voted upon, as contrasted with an original motion that has not as yet been discussed or voted upon.

substitutes Two goods, each of which can be used as a substitute for the other. If the price of one goes up, buyers may immediately switch to the other, which because of increased demand may cause the price of the substitute to go up.

substitution effect The action of buyers switching to a second good when the price of a similar good goes up. Often buyers switch back again when the price of the first good goes back down.

successive approximations One feature of the mathematical technique of iteration, in which successive approximate results are examined and recalculated until they approximate an exact answer.

suggestion scheme Any method that allows employees to make suggestions for the consideration of the company without trying to take such suggestions through the channels of communication.

sui juris *law* Latin for "of his own right." Denotes one who is competent to act.

sumptuary law A law devised to help prevent the consumption of goods considered harmful to the health and welfare of society.

sunk(en) cost A prior outlay of capital that cannot be changed by any current or future action.

sunspot theory A theory of the business cycle that contends that the activities of sun spots affect the weather, which affects agriculture, and which thus affects the entire economy.

Suomen Ammattiliittojen Keskusjarjesto (SAK) Confederation of Finnish Trade Unions, established in 1907. Address: 00530 Helsinki 53, POB 53161, Finland.

Suomen Keskuskauppakamari The central Chamber of Commerce in Finland, which is associated with all the local chambers. It was established in 1918. Address: Helsinki 10, Fabianinktua 14, Finland.

Suomen Pankki Central bank of Finland, established in 1811. (*See* Section VII)

Suomen Puunjalostusteollisuuden Keskusliitto Central Association of Finnish Woodworking Industries, established in 1918. Address: 00130 Helsinki 13, Etelaesplanadi 2, Finland.

Suomen Teollisuusliitto The Federation of Finnish Industries, established in 1921. Address: Helsinki 13, Etelaranta 10, Finland. Woodworking industries have their own federation.

superego *psychoanalysis* The ideals or standards introjected from parents or parent surrogates that making up the ego-ideal and the conscience; the sum total of self-critical, self-judgmental functions that are partly conscious but mostly unconscious.

supernormal intelligence A mental ability above that which is exhibited by about 80 percent of the general population, as measured by standard intelligence tests, by the rate of progress through a school curriculum, or by the judgments of qualified persons.

supersedeas *law* A writ staying the proceedings. Originally, an order by a court of equity to a court of law. Now used by an appellate court in emergency situations.

superstore A somewhat ethereal designation of a large retail establishment, usually situated on the outskirts of town and yet smaller than a hypermarket.

supertwangles A situation in which two or more members of a group whose ideas are so diametrically opposed to each other that the synergy is virtually brought to a standstill.

Supervisory Board *Aufsichtsrat.* The upper tier of the two-tier board of directors structure in German industrial firms.

supply The amount of a good a seller is willing to sell for a specified price in a specified market.

supply curve A graphic presentation of supply with dollars on the Y axis and quantity on the X axis. Where the two curves intersect is the amount of a good the seller will supply at that price.

supply-side economics An economic theory stating that a nation should attempt to increase the supply of goods and services through more capital investment.

supply-side tax cut A tax cut designed to increasing productivity and output in the economy, which eventually should also increase government revenues.

supportive leadership A concept of the human relations school of management that recommends the building up of good social relations in an organization.

surety bond A written promise by the insurer to reimburse the party named in the bond against the failure of performance of obligations or duties undertaken for another party.

surplus A quantity supplied in excess of the quantity demanded at a specific price.

surrender value *insurance* Cash value of an insurance policy at any given point in time; i.e., the cash the insurer will pay the insured upon surrender of the policy.

surrogate *law* A deputy of a court of equity. Often applied to a probate court.

survey A tentative inquiry or a sampling.

survivorship The right of a surviving partner or joint owner to the outright ownership of property that was previously jointly owned.

suspense account An account that temporarily debits or credits items until they are directed to the correct permanent account.

sustainable growth rate 1. The rate of increase in sales a company may expect to attain without changing its margin of profit, assets-to-sales ratio, debt-to-equity ratio, or dividend-payout ratio.

2. The rate of growth a company may expect to attain without excessive borrowing or without the issuing of a new series of equity instruments.

Svenska Arbetsgivareforeningen (SAF) Swedish Employers' Association. Address: Blasieholmshamnen 4A, POB 16120, 103 23 Stockholm 16.

Sveriges Industriforbund A Federation of Swedish Industries. Address: Storgatan 19, Box 5501, 114 85 Stockholm.

Sveriges Riksbank: Central Bank of Sweden.

SVIB In psychological testing, a strong vocational interest.

Swedish budget A type of central government budget that is balanced over a period of years rather that for each specific year.

Swedish Central Bank *Sveriges Riksbank.*

Swedish chambers of commerce There are about twelve in Sweden, including one in Stockholm, called Stockholms Handelskammare, V, Storgatan 8, Jonkoping, Stockholm.

Swedish companies Forms generally are trading partnerships, limited partnerships, and cooperatives. The joint-stock company is the only permitted type of industry based on shares.

sweetheart contract A labor contract that appears to be in the interest of the employer and union representatives, but which may not be in the best interest of the employees.

Swiss stock exchanges *See* Section VII.

Swiss Trade Unions *Schweizerischer Gewerkschaftsbund.*

SWOT analysis The analysis of an organization's strengths, weaknesses, opportunities, and threats.

syllogism 1. In logic, the deduction that where A implies B, and B implies C, then A also implies C. 2. The formal expression of an act of deductive reasoning from a major premise through a minor premise to a conclusion, which may then be proved or disproved by the rules of logic.

symmetallism A monetary standard under which a government buys and sells gold and silver in fixed proportions in order to maintain the weighted average price of gold and silver.

syndicalism A movement, particularly strong from 1900 to 1920, advocating workers' ownership of industries.

syndicate Most often denotes a group of underwriters who have formed an organization to underwrite a new issue of stock or bonds.

syndicated research Research funded by a group of firms, usually when the cost is too great for one, and each firm benefits proportionately from the findings.

synergese Terms, usually coined, related to the study of synergetics.

synergetics The art and science of producing synergy (working together) and reducing dysergy (the failure to work together) in a complex system.

synergetics, group The art and science of producing synergy and reducing dysergy in small groups.

syntality The characteristics of individual behavior that are shared by the group as a whole in a consistent, predictable manner.

Syntalk I A "language" developed by proponents of synergetics.

systematic error 1. *statistics* An error that is in some sense biased as distinguished from a random error. 2. *management* The measure of difference of individual raters of individual traits from the mean of all raters.

systematic sample The arrangement of a population in some order, and then choosing particular items throughout the population for study.

systems An organized whole made up of parts, related in some fashion, and directed toward the accomplishment of some goal.

T

t The ratio of a score to its standard error.

tableau economique A device showing the flow of income graphically, which is used by many members of the French Physiocratic school of economic thought. Income-receiving groups are divided into three categories: 1) the productive class, namely

the class of workers in agriculture and mining; 2) the owning class, i.e., those who own property; 3) the sterile class, namely servants, merchants, and manufacturers. Quesnay of France was a Physiocratic leader and had a primary interest in the development of the profitability of agriculture. Agriculture was becoming more profitable in

England, and it was desired in France, especially by the wealthy landowners. Agriculture was considered by this school to be the basic and most noble of occupations. This school of thought was popular during the late eighteenth century.

taboo Something forbidden by social mores.

tachistoscope 1. A device used in sales promotion and marketing research that works out the optimum time for displaying advertisements, slogans on TV, flashing signs, etc. 2. A machine for the rapid presentation of visual stimuli.

tactical planning Short-range, and single focus planning, such as planning for a product or for an advertising campaign, as contrasted with planning for the entire enterprise, which is called strategic planning.

tactics Detailed plans for carrying out decisions; the best methods of achieving results.

tactile Pertaining to the sense of touch or pressure.

tactus The sense of touch or pressure.

Taft-Hartley Act of 1947 An amendment to the National Labor Relations Act of 1935, based on the theory of equalizing the bargaining power between labor and management. Major provisions are: 1) specification of unfair labor practices by labor; 2) granting individual workers the right to prosecute for unfair labor practices by union or company officials; 3) anti-Communist provisions; 4) restriction of the closed shop.

tainted goods Goods that have been blacklisted by a union. Also known as blackened goods.

take-home pay Pay actually left to an employee after deductions for taxes, insurance, etc., have been taken out.

take-offs The effects, positive or negative, that can result from using sales agents in export markets.

take-off stage *economics* That period in the economy of a nation when the traditional economy is being abandoned and the new industrial society is attempting to get started.

takeover bid The attempt by one company to assume control over another by an offer of money, often made directly to the shareholders themselves. If the target company is private, nothing can transpire except an offer by the prospective acquiring company.

tale quale Latin for "in such shape as it is." Term used in commodity transactions.

tall organization An organization with many management levels.

tallyman Term for a records keeper, or one who makes collections periodically from customers without the formality of giving them a receipt in the United Kingdom. The payments are made in the tallyman's "tally" book. (At one time in the United States, insurance premiums were collected in this way.)

tangible assets Assets that are real and touchable, but are not for sale, such as capital assets.

tangible asset turnover Net sales divided by tangible assets.

tangible net worth The net worth of a firm excluding such intangible assets as good will, patents, etc.

tangible personal property Movable

wealth, such as furniture, farm machinery, automobiles, jewelry, etc.

tare weight The weight of a container and the material for packing, or the weight of a vehicle exclusive of its contents.

target population *statistics* A term denoting the whole of a group that is being targeted for a specific survey.

target price Under the Common Agricultural Policy of the Common Market, the European Commission sets a specific price for cereals, which is supposed to be an average price and is not a guaranteed price. The Commission assists producers to achieve the target price by setting a threshold price as a minimum for imports from nonmember states and an intervention price at which cereal surpluses are purchased by the Community.

target pricing The policy of placing a value on products so as to earn a set rate of return on capital invested in the production and sale of goods.

tariff Tax on imports.

tariff barrier Import duties imposed on other nations with the intention of improving the trading status or economic status of the country receiving such goods.

Tariff Division An agency in the United Kingdom providing information for firms on antidumping tariffs, on countervailing duties, and on import licensing. Address: Tariff Division, Department of Trade, Kingsgate House, 66-74 Victoria Street, London SWIE 6SJ.

tariff war The use of tariffs to further the competitive position of a country, usually in retaliation for tariffs another country has levied.

task Major elements, or combination of elements, of a job.

task analysis examining a job to find possible trouble spots that may require specific training techniques to overcome.

task-based appraisal The report of a superior on a subordinate that outlines the strengths and weaknesses of the accomplishments of that individual in a specific job. The "score" may be compared to a norm or to previously planned and agreed-upon objectives.

task-based participation A type of participative management related to specific tasks.

task bonus system Payment-by-results system in which bonuses are paid on the basis of savings made in the production process.

task description A written description of a specific task, including techniques, decisions, and procedures.

task method of budgeting *marketing* Term denoting the act of making budgeting as real as possible by basing it on a detailed description of the how money is to be used in the jobs to be performed.

TAT *psychological testing* 1. Thematic apperception test. 2. The Murray-Morgan Thematic Apperception Test.

Tavistock Institute of Human Relations An advisory organization in the United Kingdom involved in research in human relations in the workplace and in the home. Address: Tavistock Centre, Belsize Lane, London NW3 5BA.

tax A compulsory payment to government to defray the expenses of government and to perform services presumably for the benefit of all of society.

tax abatement The reduction of a tax because the tax was improperly levied or because of a legislative directive.

taxable income That income remaining when all credits, exemptions, and deductions have been allowed and deducted.

tax assessment The valuation placed upon property in order to levy a tax on it is called assessed valuation. Applying the tax rate to this valuation produces the tax.

Taxation Policy, Common *See* Common Taxation Policy.

tax avoidance A legal means of avoiding the payment of a tax, contrasted with tax evasion, which is an illegal means of avoiding the payment of a tax.

tax base The value or unit to which the tax rate is applied to determine the tax due. For example, in property taxes, the base is the assessed valuation.

tax carryback and carryover A provision that is often in American corporation income and excess profits taxes to the effect that losses (or in the case of an excess profits tax, unused credits) can be carried over to apply against a preceding or following year's income. The general effect is to level the income over the years for tax purposes.

Tax Court of the United States A special federal court that hears appeals from the decisions of the Bureau of Internal Revenue concerning almost all federal taxes except tariffs. Formerly called the U.S. Board of Tax Appeals.

Appeals from this court go to the U.S. Court of Appeals. Address: 400 Second Street, Washington, DC 20217.

taxe á la valeur ajoutée (TVA) Value-added tax (VAT) in France.

taxe anticipe *Verrechnungssteuer,* or anticipatory tax. A proportional tax in Switzerland, deducted at the source from interest, dividends, etc.

taxe communale additionelle In Belgium, an additional tax within the income tax system.

tax effect Technically, the result in the output change caused by a tax change.

tax exemption 1. The total freedom from taxes, which is enjoyed in the United States by educational, charitable, religious, and other nonprofit organizations. 2. The partial freedom from taxes, which includes the personal exemptions in the federal individual income tax.

tax-exempt securities Securities issued by state and municipal governments that are generally free from federal income tax.

tax-free exchange The trading of goods between parties that is considered an "even trade" and thus produces no recognition of gain or tax on gain. When "boot" is paid by one party, there is the possibility of recognition of gain, and of taxes on that boot.

tax holiday A temporary relief from taxes sometimes granted to a new industry in an area, both in the United States and in the United Kingdom.

tax incidence 1. In general, the final resting place of a tax once all the "shifting" is over. 2. Technically, the price change resulting from a tax change.

taxiplane Planes in the United Kingdom available for charter on short flights.

tax limit A constitutional or statutory limit placed on the kind of tax or maximum tax rate that a political subdivision can impose.

tax loophole A weakness in a tax law that allows some taxpayers to escape a tax that they probably should pay.

tax pyramiding The situation in which a tax imposed on one is added to his cost and the customary markup is applied to this total.

tax rate The ratio of the tax to the tax base.

tax roll A list, usually computerized, of all taxpayers in a given jurisdiction, with a statement opposite each name of the total tax assessment and the amount of tax due on that assessment.

tax sale The forced selling of property with delinquent taxes to satisfy the tax bill from proceeds of the sale.

tax shield In capital budgeting, some expenditures that are deductible for income tax purposes, such as start-up costs for a new plant, are recognized as reducing, or shielding against, income taxes that would otherwise be due.

tax shifting The process of passing a tax from the one who pays the tax to a consumer, such as the one who buys or uses the taxed article or service. For example, gasoline taxes are added to the per-gallon cost, and the full cost shown on the pump includes the taxes.

Taylor, Frederick Winslow (1856–1915) One of the first management experts to apply scientific principles to the solving of factory and production problems. He pioneered time and motion studies and payment-by-results compensation. (*See* Section IX)

TCD Total cost approach to distribution management technique.

"t" curve The adaptation of the Gaussian curve or normal distribution to small samples. (*See* Gaussian curve)

TE Trial and error.

Tea Auctions Specialist commodity exchange in the United Kingdom. Address: Plantation House, Mincing Lane, London EC3.

team selling A method used in some companies, often technical firms, of having several company representatives call on the customer, with each one having a special field of expertise.

technical authority That authority possessed by the person who understands computer programming and output and is able to interpret such in managers' meetings. Also known as computer authority.

technical communication Communications among people who work with computers.

Technical Help to Exporters An agency in the United Kingdom offering assistance to exporters and prospective exporters on all aspects of export trade to virtually all the countries of the world. Both legal and technical assistance is offered. Address: British Standards Institution, Marylands Avenue, Hemel Hempstead, Herts.

technical selling Increasing company sales by giving the customer technical guidance before and after the sale.

technical societies Organizations that grow up around different technical groups for the promotion of common interests. Sometimes these societies band together into federations, such as the American Standards Association (ASA), which includes technical societies, trade associations, and some agencies of the federal government.

technician A specialist in some technical field, such as a computer technician, or a technician in any field.

Technician Education Council Established in 1973 by the secretary for Education and Science, in the United Kingdom for the purpose of setting up and maintaining a unified system of technical courses for all areas of enterprise.

Technological Policy, Common *See* Common Technological Policy.

technological trend extrapolation A statistical technique of forecasting the future of technology from historical data and from the present data available on technology or on a product.

technological unemployment Unemployment ostensibly caused by the introduction of new technology into industry.

technology The entire body of machines and methods used to achieve goals in industry.

Tel Aviv Stock Exchange *See* Section VII.

Telefonverkehr Unregulated and unofficial market for trading in securities on Germany's stock exchanges. Most of such trading is done by telephone.

teleology The theory that natural processes are intelligently and purposefully directed toward ends.

teleselling Term for selling via telephone in the United Kingdom.

Telex A telegraph service yielding instant printed communications between subscribers.

temp Colloquialism for a temporary employee, often hired from a company specifically designed to provide temporary help.

temperament and personality tests Often are question-type psychological tests that give clues relative to introversion, extroversion, etc. The introvert has the tendency to be self-sufficient (i.e., not ask for help), solitariness, shyness, sensitivity, etc. The extrovert tends to be gregarious, impulsive, and adventurous. Most people will be somewhere in between the two extremes, and it is often the task of the plant psychologist to determine if the personality revealed will fit the tasks available.

temperament The enduring quality of affective functions and/or constitutional determinants.

temporary exports Goods usually taken to international exhibits on which no duty is charged.

tempos In Synergetics, one of four "broad bands" through which it is possible to expand one's consciousness.

tenancy as to duration A lease or right to occupy property for a specified period of time.

tenancy by the entirety Ownership as husband and wife. In most states, the term is equated with joint tenancy.

tenancy in common Ownership by two or more people of property in common, with the interest of the one dying passing to his heirs and not to his co-owners.

tenement *law* Anything of a permanent nature with regard to land or its income.

tenendum clause *real estate law* A clause in a deed no longer having meaning but originally describing the tenure by which the land was held.

Tennessee Valley Authority A government corporation established in 1933 in the United States to construct and operate the dams, hydroelectric plants, and the flood control systems of the Tennessee River Valley.

tenor *finance* The period of time between inception and maturity of a debt obligation.

term of court *law* The specified periods a court sits in a year.

term shares A somewhat antiquated term used in London to refer to land banks or building societies in which shares were bought, representing deposits made, and were not available upon demand because of the nature of the loans made from them.

terms of trade The relation of export and import prices. Terms of trade are considered more favorable when imports fall in price in relation to exports.

terotechnology Term used in the United Kingdom to refer to technology that is supposed to reduce the costs related to long-term maintenance, including the plant installation, maintenance, replacement or removal of plants or equipment, using feedback information.

test age The score on any given test interpreted by reference to a table of age norms, thus indicating the chronological age at which the average person achieves a similar score.

test battery 1. A group of tests administered one after the other in order to obtain a total or average score, which may indicate a person's fitness, aptitude, or achievement with respect to a particular task. 2. A wide range of complementary psychological tests designed to measure a wide range of abilities for the general purpose of personnel selection, vocational guidance, promotability, etc.

test ceiling The highest level of difficulty represented by the items comprising a test or measure.

test floor The easiest problems on a test that, presumably, all who take the test are able to pass.

test groups *marketing* Generally, highly mobile people who are at least somewhat aware of the changes going on around them, who are willing to try new things, and who thus provide a test market for new products and new methods.

test town *marketing* A town or area chosen for a testing site in marketing a product or a service.

test Any vehicle or technique for validating or invalidating a hypothesis. In the measurement of mental capacities, any task or series of tasks that yields a score that may be compared with scores made by other individuals.

testament Same as a will.

testamentary capacity A trust created by a decedent in his will.

testator A person who has died leaving a will.

T-groups Sensitivity training groups.

T-group training A technique of training a group in human relations skills that directs the attention of the individuals in the group to interpersonal events and relationships.

TGWU Transport and General Workers Union in the United Kingdom.

Thematic Apperception Test (TAT)
1. The Murray-Morgan Projective Technique, consisting of a series of pictures that evoke fantasies or stories expressive of the needs of the teller. 2. A projective technique type of personality test in which the person is presented with a set of about twenty pictures and required to write a story based on those pictures. What the pictures revealed to the subject and what the subject writes about them supposedly reveals basic personality traits.

theory A coherent explanation or unifying principle that has undergone some validation, and which may be applied to some data, but which does not have the status of a law, but usually more status than a hypothesis.

theory of concentration One tenet of Marxism that says large capitalists will swallow up small capitalists and thus concentrate wealth in fewer hands.

Theory X, Theory Y Theories devised by Douglas McGregor. Theory X classifies people do not like work, and will do as little as they can to get by and generally will resist change. Theory Y takes an opposite position, and avers that people like work and have the capacity for doing many things in the workplace if they have sympathetic management. (*See* Section IX)

Theory Z A notion of worker motivation and personality developed by William Ouchi following Douglas McGregor's lead. It suggests that an involved worker is the key to greater productivity.

therapeutic Palliative or curative.

therblig Anagram of Gilbreth, who coined the term to describe eighteen types of movements in the workplace, e.g., select, grasp, transport, assembly, inspect, use, etc. These concepts are used in time and motion studies.

thinking A general and broad term variously defined as reasoning, creativity, as-if behavior, implicit speech, ideational activity, problem solving, judging, planning, etc.

thinking, deductive Thinking for the "whole" to the "part" in dealing with a problem or concept.

thinking, free association technique and Another term for "brainstorming," which denotes a free flow of ideas in a meeting uninhibited by an agenda.

thinking, inductive Denotes reasoning based on building up to a general principle or conclusion from various specific data.

thinking, problem solving A judicial type of thinking that considers all alternatives and then decides on a course of action.

thinking, self-programmed In synergetics, tracking, or a short sequence of mental operations.

Thorndike theory of intelligence The teaching that intelligence actually consists of specific abilities.

threat Any situation, real or imagined, present or anticipated, that arouses fears and tensions.

three-position promotion plan A plan used by some industries in which a promotable employee is doing his own job, learning the job just above, and training a person just below to fill in when the employee is promoted.

threshold agreement An agreement between management and labor wherein wages will increase as the cost of living index increases by a predetermined amount.

threshold price Under the Common Agricultural Policy of the Common Market, the European Community sets a standard price for the import of cereals from nonmember states in order to help producers in member states achieve the target price.

thruster A manager or a firm in the United Kingdom, the policy of which is to act aggressively, to be dynamic, and to exploit opportunities.

Thurstone Temperament Schedule A psychological inventory covering seven different components and used for testing temperament and personality. The seven components are vigor, impulsiveness, activity, dominance, stability, sociability, and reflectiveness.

tied indicator *marketing* A term denoting a product whose success may be tied to the success of other products.

tight rate A situation in the United Kingdom where piecework production has been made so stringent by the fixer of rate that it is difficult if not impossible to earn a bonus.

time and motion study A "scientific" study of the various operations involved in doing a given task and of the time involved in doing each one of the operations.

time deposit A deposit that, historically, had to remain on deposit for at least thirty days, and which drew interest when demand deposits did not. Financial institutions seldom hold time depositors to the thirty-day rule now; instead, they use other vehicles, such as certificates of deposit, to assure a time element.

time-indifference curve Using an indifference map with consumption expenditure in year one on the X axis, and consumption expenditure in year two on the Y axis, this type of curve traces all the combinations of consumption expenditures in the two-year span of time that give equal satisfaction.

time-limit test Speed test. Often made up of relatively simple questions, wherein the participants are judged by the number they finish answering and the number they answer correctly.

time note Promissory note, or a similar document, that has a specific date or dates of payment.

time-power test A type of testing in which the items are arranged in order of difficulty, from the easiest to the hardest, with a time limit also imposed.

time preference *economics* This term refers indirectly to interest rates in that it attempts to measure the degree to which a consumer might wish to have a product right now as opposed to a later time. If the consumer's desire is to have the product immediately, the consumer will be willing to pay interest on money borrowed to buy it.

time preference theory of interest An explanation of interest as the price people are willing to pay (i.e., the interest on a loan) for the privilege of having immediate possession of goods as opposed to future possession.

time-related payment scheme A term generally denoting a day-rate payment plan, as contrasted with an hourly plan.

time reversal test *statistics* A method of testing the mathematical validity of an index number.

time sampling A situation in which the instructor notes meticulously the times when the participants speak out in T-group sessions.

times burden carried A coverage ratio measure of financial leverage, defined as earnings before taxes and interest, divided by interest expense plus principal payments grossed up to their before-tax equivalent.

time series Data with time as the independent variable and some other factor as the dependent variable, as contrasted to a frequency distribution in which the data are presented without regard to the time factor.

time-series data Observations of the values of economic variables over a series of successive time intervals.

time-series forecasting *statistics* Techniques that take into account seasonal differences and other types of fluctuations in the past and forecast the future in light of this information.

time-served worker A worker in the United Kingdom who has completed a formal apprenticeship.

time sharing A term currently in use to denote the sharing of a computer by various departments of a firm.

times interest earned A common measure of the earnings protection

that a bond has. The number of times the interest requirement of a business was earned in a period, and therefore a measure of the degree of safety which the owner of debt (bond) has. Computed as the amount available to pay interest to all creditors divided by the interest requirements of all debts with equal or prior standing.

time span of discretion A term not widely used denoting how long a manager can function without appealing for help from his superiors.

TIR Carnet Transport International Routier Carnet. In road transportation in the United Kingdom, the container or vehicle is sealed by customs before export and can then be carried abroad with a minimum of customs examination and documentation in the countries passed through en route, with the intermediate countries waiving the payment of deposits or duties. Such TIR shipments must have the approval of the whole system.

Tjanstemannens Centralorganisation (TCO) Central Organization of Salaried Employees in Sweden, a white-collar trade union independent of the Swedish Trade Union Congress. Address: Liannetatan 12-14, 114 47 Stockholm.

Tokyo Stock Exchange *See* Section VII.

tolerance The deviation from the norm that can be allowed in a finished product and still be acceptable.

top hat pension scheme A plan providing for especially attractive pension plans for senior executives in addition to the regular company pension plan in the United Kingdom.

top-down approach An approach by the president of a company to those

523

who work under him in trying to determine the success of a year's work or any other similar matter.

Toronto Stock Exchange *See* Section VII.

tort *law* A wrongful act against another person that may result in court proceedings.

total cost approach to distribution (TCD) A management technique in the United States that is used to identify and collect the more obscure distribution-related costs as well as the more common ones. It is used particularly by large, complex companies in their continuing search for cost-cutting measures.

total cost line *See* break-even analysis.

total loss control A training and security program designed to reduce and, if possible, eliminate all factors that cause loss, using measures to control accidents, fire, industrial health, pollution, etc.

total population *statistics* The total number in a group to be surveyed for whatever purpose. A population may be surveyed according to age groups, nationalities, sex, or any other defining characteristic.

total remuneration concept The total package of fringe benefits that may be offered to the employees of a firm. In some instances the "cafeteria" plan is used, in which there are numerous benefits available, and an employee is allowed to chose from several options within a certain cost limit.

total retirement benefits The totality of all benefits given to a retiring employee, which may include the pension, continuing group insurance paid by the company, etc.

Totalact In Synergetics, focusing on the goal and exerting an all-out effort to achieve it.

totalitarian group An organization that does not tolerate dissenters or minorities.

township In surveys of U.S. public lands, an approximate square area of land consisting of 36 sections with each section consisting of 640 acres.

track record A term used in the United States to denote past performance; often used when considering the promotability of an employee.

tract book A book containing plats of the land parcels in given areas.

trade acceptance A trade bill that has been signed by the buyer to show his obligation to make payment as outlined in the bill of exchange.

trade association A voluntary organization encompassing all firms in a given business or industry. Usually such organizations require annual dues, proportioned to the size of the business, and an executive director is hired to run the day-to-day work of the association. The association promotes all of those things pertinent to the industry involved.

trade barrier Customs tariff or import duty.

Trade Bill An Act of the U.S. Congress in 1974 promoting "a more open and equitable" economic order with its worldwide trading partners.

Trade Descriptions Act of 1968 A UK bill designed to reduce "misdescriptions of goods, services, accommodation and facilities provided in the course of trade," along with misleading information on prices. Penalties may run from fines to imprisonment or both.

trade discount A sum deducted from the price of a product by the manufacturer or by the wholesaler for the trader who deals with direct consumers. This usually allows the retailer to offer discounts or other incentives to trade.

trade dispute A term used in the United Kingdom to denote a labor/management dispute.

Trade Disputes Act of 1906 An act in the United Kingdom that defined trade dispute and gave trade unions, their officers, and members immunity in tort for the consequences of strikes and other industrial actions.

Trade Disputes Act of 1965 An act designed to re-establish the immunity from tort allowed by the 1906 act, which had been done away with in a case known as *Rookes v. Barnard,* which had held that labor unions, officials, and members could be liable for tort.

trade dollar A special silver coin minted by the United States from 1873 to 1885 with more silver content than the standard silver dollar that was used for trade with the Orient.

Trade Expansion Act Legislation that had protected U.S. industries by the erection of tariff barriers. When the act expired in June 1967, it opened the way for the Kennedy round of the General Agreements on Tariffs and Trade. (*See also* General Agreements on Tariffs and Trade)

trade fair or exhibition An event organized to give producers an opportunity to show off their goods, sometimes on an international level.

trade magazine A periodical devoted to the ongoing activities of a specific trade or industry.

trademark A symbol, wording, or any other thing that specifically identifies a given product or service so that over time the symbol comes to represent the product or service everywhere it is sold. Such symbols can be registered with the federal government and by some states in the United States.

trade mission Usually a journey from one country to another designed for the purpose of promoting a country's goods and eliciting trade.

trade name Often part of a trademark; i.e., the name under which a product or service is marketed.

trade-off The act of considering alternative ways of reaching an objective and discarding the undesirable ones for the best one.

trade promotions Almost any method that may be used to elicit sales, e.g., price cuts, coupons, free samples, etc.

Trade and Industry A journal providing weekly information on the procedures and practices of the Common Market.

trades council A term in the used in the United Kingdom to refer to local representatives of the labor unions in different areas.

Trades Union Congress (TUC) The central federation of trade unions in the United Kingdom, established in 1868. The organization represents about 10 million workers out of a labor force of about 25 million. In recent years, the growth in unions has mostly been among white-collar workers. Address: Congress House, Great Russell Street, London WC1B 3LS.

trading limit 1. Prices above or below

which trading is not permitted in any one day. 2. The maximum quantity of commodity futures that may be purchased or sold by one person or on any one trading day. These limits are fixed by the Commodity Exchange Commission.

trading on the equity The act of borrowing funds for a business in anticipation of making more on the borrowed money than the interest costs.

traditional society stage *economics* A period just prior to a surge in the growth of an economy, when old, traditional ways are relegated to the past and new technology takes over.

train To impart skills, often by example; a sequence of related responses. Distinguished from education, which is an accumulation of knowledge over a period of time.

trainability test A test designed to measure an individual's potential for assimilating training.

training function Conceived of in four steps: 1) identifying training needs in terms of both jobs and people; 2) the formulation of a training policy for the consideration of top management; 3) implementing the policy using the most effective means; 4) assessing training policy effectiveness.

training levy Normally a percentage of the payroll levied against firms covered by the Industrial Training Board in the United Kingdom.

trait Any distinctive physical or psychological characteristic of an individual or a group that may be shared or may be unique.

trait theory of leadership The doctrine

that certain traits are to be found in most successful leaders.

tramp steamer A ship that does not operate on a regular schedule, but has its schedule determined by the cargo it picks up and delivers. Such a ship may be out of its home port for months at a time.

transactional psychology The systematic exposition of facts and principles that emphasize the interpersonal relationships or the exchanges that take place in behavior.

transaction time ratio Divide average inventory for a specific period, such as a year, by net shipments for the same period.

transferability The ability to transfer title or ownership.

transfer by generalization The gains in skills or knowledge that may be carried over to a new assignment because of the broad application possessed by the knowledge gained.

transfer in contemplation of death When some transfer of assets is made by a person before death and in expectation of it, the rule of law looks upon this transfer as a transfer at death.

transfer income Income usually received from some level of government for which there has been no work done during the period. Veterans' pensions, welfare payments, social security payments, etc., qualify as transfer income.

transfer journal A book kept by a corporation or by a representative of a corporation to show stock certificates issued, transferred, and canceled.

transfer pricing the pricing of a product

or of a service between departments of the same firm.

transformation curve *economics* As applied to a nation's economy, using a graph with military goods on the Y axis and civilian goods on the X axis, the transformation curve traces all the combinations of both types of goods that the economy can produce in a year.

transformation functions Those functions that limit the attainable positions to which a firm can move in light of the structure of its assets, liabilities, and other variables.

transhipment Goods in transit that will be handled by more than one carrier.

transit number The number on a check that identifies the bank on which it was written under the national numerical system. The number has three parts: 1) a number designating the location of the bank; 2) a number indicating the bank's name; 3) a number indicating the Federal Reserve District and area within the district.

transitory action *law* A matter that can be tried anywhere that jurisdiction can be obtained over the person of the defendant. Not all actions in law are transitory.

Translators' Guild A branch of the Institute of Linguists in the United Kingdom, which is composed of expert translators and interpreters.

transplacement An error caused by moving all digits to the right or left of the proper columns without changing the order of the digits.

transportation ratio *railroad transportation* The ratio of transportation

expense to operating revenues. This figure includes the cost of moving trains but not depreciation, repairs, and maintenance of trains.

transposition In Gestalt psychology, the transfer of a previously achieved configuration or set of relationships to a new situation.

traveler's check A check payable on sight and used to facilitate cashing the check by eliminating any question whether there are sufficient funds on deposit to clear the check and by giving the one accepting the check the opportunity to verify a counter signature against an authentic signature.

Treasury bill A debt obligation of the U.S. government with a maturity date of less than one year. The bill does not pay interest, but it is sold at a discount.

Treasury bonds 1. Issued bonds that have to be reacquired by the corporation from bondholders. 2. Bonds issued by the U.S. Treasury Department. 3. Authorized but unsold bonds still held by the treasury of a corporation.

Treasury certificate An obligation of the U.S. Treasury, usually with a one-year maturity. These certificates pay interest through coupons.

Treasury notes A debt instrument of the U.S. Treasury, with a maturity of from one to five years of date of issue.

treasury stock 1. Issued stock that has been acquired by the corporation from stockholders. 2. Sometimes refers to stock that has not as yet been issued and is still in the corporate treasury.

Treasury A government department responsible to the chancellor of the

Exchequer in the United Kingdom for coordinating national economic policy and overseeing public expenditures.

Treaty of Accession Amended the Treaty of Rome of 1957, which created the European Economic Community, to provide for Denmark, the Irish Republic, and the United Kingdom to join the EEC starting January 1, 1973.

Treaty of Paris, 1951 A document that created the prototype of the Common Market, the European Coal and Steel Community, which included France, West Germany, Italy, the Netherlands, Belgium, and Luxembourg.

Treaty of Rome, 1957 A document that created the Common Market (EC), whose founding members were France, West Germany, Italy, the Netherlands, Belgium, and Luxembourg. Also signed in Rome in 1957 was the European Atomic Energy Community (EURATOM) Treaty. (*See* Section IV)

trend A prevailing tendency, e.g., continuing unemployment over an extended period, price increases over an extended period, etc.

triadic product test *marketing* A test in marketing research in which participants are given three products, two which are identical, and asked to identify the one that is different.

trial-and-error The gradual reduction in those responses that bring pain or annoyance, and the tendency to repeat those which bring a reward, as the basic explanatory principle in the learning process.

trial balance *accounting* Checking to see whether all the debit and credit items in a double-entry ledger are in balance.

trial runs Going through the process of producing a product, using sample installations, so that the actual process can be reviewed without an undue expenditure of capital.

triangular trade The pattern of trade between three countries.

tribology The science and technology of the interaction of surfaces by rubbing, rolling, etc., and relates to the design of bearings, lubricants, etc.

Trieste Stock Exchange Italian stock exchange. (*See* Section VII)

trigger To release a response, the vigor of which has no direct relation to the strength of the stimulus.

trover and conversion A type of action in common law to recover damages for personal property wrongfully appropriated.

truck farms A name usually given in the United States to a small farm that raises vegetables, melons, etc.

true bill *law* The verdict of a grand jury that there is sufficient evidence to warrant a trial.

trust company A corporation, often a bank, that manages trusts for individuals or organizations.

trustee in bankruptcy The person or persons appointed by a court to liquidate the assets of a bankrupt firm or to supervise reorganization of a firm, although those charged with performing the latter function are more often called the receivers.

tuning In Synergetics, the ability to focus on those individual qualities that promote synergy and to avoid those qualities that are dysergic.

Turin Stock Exchange *Borsa Valori di Torino.* (*See* Section VII)

Turkish Central Bank *Türkiye Cumhuriyet Merkez Bankasi.* (*See* Section VII)

Turkish Chambers of Commerce The central organization is: Union of Chambers of Commerce, Industry and Commodity Exchange of Turkey, 149 Ataturk Bulvari, Ankara.

turnover in labor The number of employees lost by quitting or discharge during a specific period of time. This is often a key to the ability of a manager.

TVA *Taxe á la valeur ajoutée,* or value-added tax.

twanglemakers In Synergetics, one who pays lip service to a group goal, but whose actions are dysergic.

twangles In Synergetics, chain reactions between two or more members of a group.

twig-benders In Synergetics, those people who "capture" children when quite young, and attempt to bend them in the way they want them to go.

twisting *insurance* Somewhat antiquated term for persuading a policyholder to drop one policy (usually with another company) and take out another. (With the drastic changes in the insurance industry, changes are often beneficial to the client, and twisting no longer has the popularity it once had.)

two-tier monetary system A situation in which a country has two separate exchange control sets of rules as a part of its strategy to protect its currency and its balance of payments.

typology The doctrine that all persons may be fitted into a few clearly defined and differentiated biosocial or psychological categories.

U

UAW Acronym for a U.S. confederation of labor unions that includes the United Auto Workers and the United Auto, Aircraft and Agricultural Implement Workers.

UCATT Union of Construction, Allied Trades and Technicians.

UDC Universal Decimal Classification.

UGTAN Union Generale des Travailleurs d'Afrique Noire.

UIL *Unione Italiana del Lavoro.* An Italian trade union confederation.

UK central bank Bank of England. (*See* Section VII)

Ulrich's International Periodicals Directory A directory listing all the periodicals and journals of concern to people in business and industry. In two volumes and indexed.

ultimate facts *law* The vital facts put in issue as distinguished from the evidentiary facts designed to establish the ultimate facts.

UMW United Mine Workers, a union in the United States.

UN United Nations.

unaccrued Income resulting when payments are made that are not as yet due, such as a payment of rent before it is due.

unassociated variance *statistics* The sum of the squares of that part of the deviation of a variable from its arithmetic mean represented by the distance from a line of least squares to the actual values of the variable divided by the number of items.

unassociated variation *statistics* The unassociated variance multiplied by the number of items.

uncalled capital That part of the capital of a corporation that has been authorized, but that shareholders have not been asked to subscribe.

unconfirmed letter of credit A letter of credit for which a credit has been established but on which the advising bank does not guarantee payment.

unconscious motivation Desires that cannot be fully analyzed.

uncontrolled variables Factors that disrupt an experiment because they cannot be controlled, counteracted, measured, or anticipated.

UNCTAD United Nations Conference on Trade and Development.

undercapitalized A business with insufficient capital for the level of business it is trying to carry on.

underconsumption theory of the business cycle A term used in explaining the depression of the business cycle as a result of a failure of consumption to keep pace with the growth in savings.

underemployed A situation in which a worker is employed but at a lower skill level than the worker is capable of performing. This situation is often found during a recession or a depression or during a time when there is structural unemployment.

underground economy All of a nation's economic activity that does not show up in the national income statistics and on which no taxes are paid.

underinsurance Insurance written for less than the value of the item insured.

underlying bonds That bond issue, in the case of a company with several bond issues, which stands first in line in payment of income.

underlying mortgage A mortgage prior in claim to another mortgage.

undermanning A situation in which a plant has too few employees to operate at maximum efficiency.

undertaking *law* An engagement by one party guaranteeing some performance.

undistributed profits Profits earned but not paid to stockholders.

undivided right The right of one person to property owned jointly by several persons.

UNDP United Nations Development Program.

unearned charges A term denoting obligations incurred, but not covered by earnings. Interest on bonds during a loss period is a prime example.

unearned income Income from interest and dividends from investments.

unearned increment The increase in

the value of property that does not result from any effort or action of the owners.

unemployed person One who has previously been employed, but has no work now and is actively looking for work and probably is receiving unemployment compensation.

unemployment benefit A payment made to a person who is unemployed and is legally qualified to draw unemployment compensation.

UNESCO United Nations Educational, Scientific, and Cultural Organization.

unfavorable balance of trade A situation in which the cost of imports exceeds the cost of exports.

UNICE Central employers' organization in the European Community.

UNIDO United Nations Industrial Development Organization.

unified tax system A system of personal income tax introduced in the United Kingdom in the 1973–74 tax year, with the rate starting at a basic 30 percent.

unimodal A frequency distribution with only one mode.

union label A label attached to some inside part of a garment and other products identifying them as produced by a company with a recognized union.

Union of Construction, Allied Trades and Technicians A major trade union affiliate to the Trades Union Congress in the United Kingdom. Address: 9-11 Macaulay Road, Clapham, London SW4 0Q2.

Union of Shop, Distributive and Allied Workers A major trade union affiliated with the Trades Union

Congress in the United Kingdom. Address: 'Oakley' 188 Wilmslow Road, Fallowfield, Manchester M14 6LJ.

union shop *See* closed shop.

Unione dei Comitati Derettivi delle Borse Valori Italiane Union of the Management Committees of the Italian stock exchanges.

Unione Italiana delle Camere di Commercio, Industria, Artizianato e Agricolture Italian Union of Chambers of Commerce, Industry, Crafts and Agriculture. Address: Piazza Sallustio 21, 00187, Rome.

unique-product production One of three major systems of production defined by Peter Drucker. The other two are mass production and process production.

unique selling point (USP) A feature of a good or service that makes it valuable in marketing, usually by differentiating it from other similar products.

unitary elasticity A situation in which a change in price produces the same percentage change in demand.

unitary system A system of management in the United Kingdom with the power concentrated in one individual or in a small group.

unit bank A bank with only one location for business.

United Engineering Center An organization in the United States with research facilities shared by the American Institute of Consulting Engineers, the American Institute of Mining, Metallurgical and Petroleum Engineers, the American Society of

Civil Engineers, the American Society of Mechanical Engineers, The Engineering Foundation, and others. Address: 345 E. 47th St., New York, NY 10017

United Nations (UN) Created as a replacement for the League of Nations, which was established after World War I. The UN was established on October 24, 1945, with 51 founding members. Membership now includes about 157 nations. The aims were outlined as: 1) to maintain international peace and security; 2) to develop friendly relations between nations; 3) to cooperate internationally to solve international economic, social, cultural, and humanitarian problems and to guarantee fundamental freedoms; 4) to become a center for harmonizing the actions of nations in realizing these common ends.

United Nations Capital Development Fund (1966) Associated with the UN Development Program and designed to make low-interest loans and grants-in-aid to developing countries.

United Nations Conference on Trade and Development (UNCTAD) (1964) Designed to deal with the problem of the widening gap in the standards of living of developed and developing countries. Address: Palais des Nations, Geneva, Switzerland.

United Nations Development Program (UNDP) (1965) Agency set up to assist developing countries through economic and social programs. Address: New York, NY 10017. USA.

United Nations Educational, Scientific and Cultural Organization (UNESCO) (1964)

Its responsibility is to "work for peace and security by promoting collaboration among the nations through education, science and culture in order to further universal respect for justice, for the rule of law, and for human rights and fundamental freedoms which are affirmed . . . by the Charter of the United Nations." Address: 7 and 9 place de Fontenoy, Paris 7e, France.

United Nations Industrial Development Organization (UNIDO) (1967) Established to mobilize international resources to the development of undeveloped and underdeveloped countries.

United States Chamber of Commerce Established in 1912. About four thousand members from across the United States. Address: 1615 H Street NW, Washington, DC 20006.

United Steelworkers of America (USWA) Founded in 1936, this organization has about 750,000 members. Address: 5 Gateway Center, Pittsburgh, PA 15222.

unity of command A concept that "one man have only one boss."

univariate analysis The analysis of values of one variable, such as the determination of standard deviation.

Universal Decimal Classification (UDC) A system derived from the Dewey Decimal System, this system organizes printed matter into ten main branches and then into many subclassifications. It is used by librarians and information services for classifying books and other literature. It is also used in filing and retrieval systems to a lesser degree.

Universal Postal Union (UPU) A UN agency charged with promoting international cooperation in developing international postal services. Address: 3000 Berne 15, Switzerland.

universe *statistics* A total population. The total of all items, or persons, included in a specific survey.

Universities Central Council on Admissions (UCCA) A central clearinghouse for all applications to all UK universities.

unlawful detainer In common law, a remedy by which a landlord can have a tenant evicted when the tenant has overstayed his term or has broken the terms of the lease.

unlisted security a security that is not traded on a recognized stock exchange.

unloading An action of trying to sell a large amount of goods quickly by lowering the price of such goods. Looked upon as "dumping" in foreign markets.

unplanned investment The value placed on goods that have been produced but have not been sold, and thus remain in inventory. Keeping goods in inventory normally causes a slowdown in production and ultimately unemployment.

unproductive labor The expenditure of the factor of labor on the production of something that has no economic value.

unsecured creditor One who is owed money but has collateral to insure payment.

unsocial hours A term in the United Kingdom for out-of-the-ordinary hours of work that may interfere with the person's social life. Many services, such as hotels, etc., come under this category.

unsocialized Not having acquired the folkways and the mores of the group.

unspaced practice Continuous repetition of techniques to be learned without any interpolated activities or rest periods.

unstable equilibrium *economics* A condition which once achieved will continue indefinitely unless one of the variables (economic or noneconomic) is changed, and then the system will not return to the original equilibrium and will not come to rest unless there is further alteration of a variable.

upset price The price below which an item is removed from sale, either at an auction or at a public sale.

upstanding wage In the United Kingdom, a guaranteed work week and, therefore, a guaranteed wage.

UPU *See* Universal Postal Union.

usury laws Laws of the states that limit the amount of interest lenders can charge borrowers on loans.

utility 1. The ability of a material good or service to satisfy a need. 2. Colloquialism for public utility. 3. The satisfaction received from the consumption of goods.

utils A fictitious name for a measure of utility.

Utopia An imaginary place where political and economic arrangements are approximately correct. Used by Sir Thomas More in 1516 to describe such a state in a book entitled *Utopia*.

V

vacancy ratio The number of housing units fit for occupancy, but unoccupied.

validity *statistics* The degree to which a test measures the object it is intended to measure.

valorization scheme The direct government intervention, or cartel intervention, to maintain the price of a product in the world markets. A good example is the Brazilian valorization scheme for coffee.

valtion tulovero State income tax in Finland.

value 1. The amount of money a consumer is prepared to pay for a good or service. It may bear little relationship to cost or to market price. 2. The utility of a good weighed by its price.

value-added tax (VAT) A tax on consumption that is levied on each stage of production according to the value added in each stage. The tax per stage is totaled in the end product and added to the sale price, thus making it a consumption tax to buyers.

value added The difference between the cost of raw materials and the price of the finished product.

value analysis A technique using a systematic, creative approach to identify unnecessary costs in a product or service and subsequently substituting different materials and methods to obtain equal performance at lower costs. The three basic steps in value analysis are: 1) identify the function; 2) evaluate the function by analysis; 3) develop valuable alternatives.

value-analysis engineering Methods of evaluating existing design, production, and marketing of products to assure the utmost efficiency of cost in each stage.

value date *banking* The date on which a deposit is recognized as effective, due to the time needed for the collection of checks.

value of money The actual purchasing power of money.

value satisfactions *marketing* The multiplicity of reasons why a consumer may buy a specific good or service.

valued policy *insurance* A property or casualty coverage in which a value is placed upon each item of the property covered.

values, function of Values tend to dictate, to a marked degree, our actions both in the workplace, in the home, and in society in general.

Vancouver Stock Exchange *See* Section VII.

variable annuity An annuity contract that invests in equities, thus making the annuity payments vary as the return on the equities varies.

variable cost A cost that changes with the level of production. Such a cost is sometimes proportional to the level of production, but the cost is often less than proportional to the level of production.

variable expenses Expenses that change with the level of production.

variable factor programming (VFP) A management technique using work study to improve the efficiency of clerical workers.

variable working hours *See* flexible working hours (fwh).

variable A magnitude whose value changes.

variance *statistics* 1. The measure of dispersion of a frequency distribution. 2. The square of the standard deviation of a number of items.

variance analysis A mathematically based method for analyzing the effect, influence, and importance of different parameters in a complex business situation.

variate The mathematical value assigned to a unit of performance.

variation The variance multiplied by the number of items.

variety reduction A scientific method of simplifying product range and raw materials through more standardization.

variometer an apparatus that exposes words, pictures, etc., for a fraction of a second, used to increase reading speed and to test memory. Also known as a tachistoscope.

VAT *See* value-added tax.

Veblenian school *economics* One of the schools of institutional economics. Thorstein Veblen coined the terms "leisure class" and "conspicuous consumption." His economic theories, as the coined terms imply, were sociological in nature, as he sought to reveal the differences in incomes, the nonproductive nature of the leisure class, etc.

Vece Saveza sindikata Jugoslavije Council of the Confederation of Trade Unions in Yugoslavia. Address: Belgrade, Trg Marksa i Engelsa 5.

vehemence Neurotic or psychotic impetuosity and fury.

velleity A condition of minimal volition or drive in making choices.

velocity of circulation The average number of times in a year that a dollar serves as income.

Venezuela Stock Exchange *Bolsa de Commercio de Caracas.* (*See* Section VII)

Venice Stock Exchange *Borsa Valori di Venezia.*

venier The name of a writ by which a jury is summoned.

Vennootschap onder Firma Under Netherlands law, a general partnership.

verbal aptitude or intelligence tests Tests facility in the use of words in oral and written communication.

Verband Osterreichischer Banken und Bankiers Association of Austrian Banks and Bankers.

Verbond van Nederlandse Ondernemingen (VNO) One of two federation of Netherlands industry. Address: VNO, The Hague, POB, 2110.

Vereeniging van Effectenhandelaren Rotterdam Stock Exchange. (*See* Section VII)

Vereeniging voor den Effectenhandel Amsterdam Stock Exchange. (*See* Section VII)

verification The fourth stage in creative thinking, in which the illumination is tested realistically.

Vermögensteuer Net wealth tax levied on the citizens of Austria and Luxembourg.

vernacular One's mother tongue. The language an individual acquires from the earliest years of life.

Verrechnungssteuer *Taxe anticipe* or anticipatory tax, levied in Switzerland on interest and dividend income.

vertical combination A combination that unites under one ownership a number of plants that are engaged in successive processes or stages of production and marketing.

vertical integration Industrial integration that moves to take in the various stages in the industry. An automobile company, for example, might buy a steel or glass company or merge with them. Through this practice, a firm hopes to pick up various stages in the industry and own them, thus being assured a supply of goods that can probably be purchased at a lower price.

vested remainder *law* An interest in property to take effect and be enjoyed at some time in the future, after another property interest is determined.

vested rights That proportion of a company's pension fund that belongs to an employee who quits the company, dies, or is fired. Usually plans are set up to vest a proportionate amount after the employee has worked a given number of years. Sometimes the funds can be drawn out by the employee upon termination; sometimes there is a waiting period; and sometimes the funds are frozen in the account and cannot be withdrawn until age sixty-five or some other specified age. All of this pension information must be made available to the government and to employees who participate in the plan.

vested 1. *law* A term used to identify a right of immediate enjoyment of a right or a future enjoyment that cannot be altered without the consent of the person having the right. 2. *real estate law* A future interest in land that has been finalized by the determination of what individual is to take the property and the accomplishment of any conditions attached to that interest.

vestibule training Training of an employee by the employer in the employer's own school before beginning actual work experience.

VFP *See* variable factor programming.

vicarious liability A situation in which a company becomes liable for the wrongful actions of an employee who is acting within the scope of his employment.

vice propre French for "inherent vice."

Vienna Stock Exchange Wiener Börse. (*See* Section VII)

Vincent Mechanical Diagrams Test A mechanical aptitude test developed in the United Kingdom with the assistance of the National Institute of Industrial Psychology. Test takes about thirty minutes to complete.

Vineland Social Maturity Scale A standardized developmental schedule, from birth to twenty-five years of age, indicating an individual's level of ability in taking care of needs and accepting responsibility for behavior, both personal and social.

virtue A trait of personality highly valued from an ethical or theological point of view. Plato stated that the four cardinal virtues are wisdom, temperance, courage, and justice.

visible exports Tangible exports.

visible items of foreign trade The goods, money, and other tangible items entering foreign trade.

Vision A French business magazine, published monthly in four languages. Address: 52 rue Taitbou, Paris 9e.

vital statistics Statistics on births, deaths, marriages, divorces, etc. Usually kept by a state Bureau of Vital Statistics or by some similarly named agency.

VNO *Verbond van Nederlandse Ondernemingen,* one of two Dutch confederations of employers' associations.

vocational guidance A transaction, usually after extensive testing, wherein an individual is counseled on a possible vocation in light of test scores, personal impressions, etc.

vocational training Training designed to give skills in a specific trade, as contrasted with the more general term, education.

Vogel Approximation Method (VAM) A method used in linear programming, using the following steps: 1) for each row and each column, the differences between the two lowest cell costs are found and posted; slack is included and considered the same as any other cost is; 2) the largest difference of a row or a column is chosen; 3) the maximum possible quantity to available lowest cost cell in the selected row or column is assigned; 4) if a row or column is satisfied, the difference is eliminated and all other unfilled cell costs in that row or column are considered no longer available by filling them in with a zero; 5) after each assignment, new differences for effective rows and columns should be calculated.

void contract An effort to enter an agreement that is contrary to law or to public policy as interpreted by the courts. Thus, no contract ever exists.

voidable contract An agreement or contract between two parties wherein one party has the right o decide whether to go on with the contract or to have it declared void.

voir dire *law* A preliminary examination to determine whether a witness or juryman has an interest in a case.

volatility *finance* See B-risk.

volenti non fit injuria Latin for "voluntary assumption of risk."

volition Will.

voluntary bankruptcy Bankruptcy proceedings that are started by the debtor who is seeking to wind up his affairs.

voluntary conveyance *law* A transfer of property without consideration.

Vorstand The board of directors of the Zurich Stock Exchange. Also refers to the management board of a German company.

VPC *La vente par correspondance,* French term for mail order.

Vuoso classification System used in Czechoslovakia to analyze and classify components and equipment and to provide statistics for optimizing tool design.

W

wage freeze A prohibition on wage increases, usually mandated by government during periods of crisis, such as a war.

wage-price spiral A term denoting that an increase in wages must ultimately result in an increase in prices, and this action will continue in an upward spiral.

wages and motivation Wages tend to motivate employees to seek the next higher wage, not to work harder or smarter.

Wages Council Act A 1959 consolidation of earlier wage legislation.

wages of management The wages or salary a manager could earn if he hired out to another employer. This measure is sometimes used to gauge whether a man in business for himself can actually earn as much as if he sold his time to someone else.

wage structure The interrelationships of wages in different types of industries and in different types of employees.

wage-work bargaining Collective bargaining in the United Kingdom that takes work performance into account.

Wagner Act Known officially as the National Labor Relations Act, this piece of legislation was passed as a result of the hard work of New York Senator Robert Ferdinand Wagner in 1935. It gave unions considerably more power than they had previously had. In fact, the unions obtained so much power and grew so rapidly during the late Depression years and the early World War II years that they were accused of hindering the war effort. The National Labor Relations Act was greatly amended by the Taft-Hartley Act of 1947, which gave greater balance to labor-management relations.

waiters Name denoting uniformed attendants at the London Stock Exchange.

waiver *law* A general legal doctrine concerning the voluntary abandonment by a person of some or all of his rights.

waiver of premium *insurance* A rider sometimes found on a live insurance policy that guarantees the continued payment of premiums if the insured becomes disabled and is unable to pay.

Wales Tourist Board Address: 7 Park Place, Cardiff CF1 3UJ.

Wall Street The main street of New York's banking and financial center.

Walrasian model A system in which all economic variables are considered endogenous and all the variables not included are noneconomic, such as technology conditions or psychological demand factors.

want *economics* A desire or need for something that is never translated into demand, often from lack of sufficient money.

warehouse receipt A document issued by a warehouse for goods stored.

warehousing loan A loan made using goods stored in a warehouse as collateral.

warranty A guarantee made by one party that certain facts are true.

warranty deed A deed in which the

grantor guarantees certain matters, for example, that the grantee will enjoy peaceful ownership and that if he does not, the grantor will bear the expense of defending the title.

WASP Acronym for Workshop Analysis and Scheduling Programming. In the United States, the acronym stands for white Anglo-Saxon Protestant.

waste *law* Damage done by people to real estate.

wasting asset A capital asset that is consumed in use.

water rights *law* The rights of owners of adjacent land and of the public to waters such as rivers and lakes.

Water Supply Industry Training Board An agency established in June 1965 in the United Kingdom under the Industrial Training Act of 1964, Address: 104A Park Street, London W1.

watered stock Stock issued by a corporation that is in excess of its true assets.

waybill (WB) A statement of goods in a shipment along with shipping instructions.

wealth Anything useful and owned by human beings. Term sometimes used to refer to the combined nonhuman assets of a nation.

wealth tax Often called a "net-wealth tax" and levied by several countries on all wealth above a specified amount.

Weather Bureau (WB) U.S. agency of the Department of Commerce responsible for assembling meteorological data and assisting private weather-reporting systems throughout the nation.

weather theory of the business cycle The theory that weather is the prime determinant of agricultural prosperity or depression, and, since agriculture is basic to a nation's economy, weather thus will influence the entire economy.

Weber's Law A theory that if a salary structure is to have uniform incentive value, the salary levels should increase in geometric proportions.

weighted average 1. A measure of the arithmetic mean in which the relative importance of each item is taken into account. Each item is multiplied by the number of items having that same value, then all items are summed, and the sum is divided by the number of items. 2. An average in which weights (specific values) are assigned to the items to be averaged.

weighted sample A term for a sample with a specific bias rather than random sampling.

Weights and Measures Act of 1963 Legislation in the United Kingdom requiring that the weights of all prepackaged and packaged goods must be revealed on the package.

welfare clause The clause in the Constitution of the United States authorizing the federal government to provide for the "general welfare" of its citizens. Until the Great Depression, the courts held that this simply referred to the guarantees made specifically in other parts of the Constitution, but now the term has been broadened to mean almost anything that society demands.

welfare economics A theoretical approach to economics that analyzes economic data in terms of maximizing human welfare for the greatest number, and not merely maximizing profits for the entrepreneur.

Wellington Stock Exchange One of five New Zealand stock exchanges. (*See* Section VII)

Wertpapiersteuer The securities tax on bonds when they are issued for the first time on the Vienna Stock Exchange.

Westman Personnel Classification Test An intelligence test that includes both analogy-type questions and mathematical computations.

w-factor *psychology* Spearman's label for a trait of persistence, goal striving, and freedom from distractions. A willingness to forgo immediate goals in order to work for a major, and often remote, end.

white-collar trade union A union composed of primarily clerical or other white-collar workers. This type of union has become more prevalent as industries have turned to fewer assembly-line workers and to more automation and "mental"-type workers.

white land A term used in the United Kingdom to describe land that is not being developed and is not in the planning stage for development.

WHO World Health Organization.

whole method Training in the United Kingdom that is not divided up into segments, but is taught as a whole course.

Wholesale Price Index Published by the Department of Trade in the United Kingdom.

Wiener Börse Vienna Stock Exchange. (*See* Section VII)

will A document by which a person at death bequeaths his property to others. The document is usually considered valid only if made by a person of sound mind, or legal age, without coercion, and signed in the presence of witnesses. Laws on wills vary somewhat among the states.

Will Temperament Test A measure of such traits as persistence, flexibility, speed of decision, and emotional control as revealed through handwriting.

Winkelbörsen Illegal groups dealing in securities in Austria.

Winnipeg Stock Exchange One of six in Canada. (*See* Section VII)

withdrawal 1. *psychology* The action of mentally removing oneself from a real and troubling situation and resorting to sleeping, daydreaming, alcohol, or illegal drugs. 2. *economics* Saving or otherwise pulling money out of the circular flow of income.

withdrawal symptoms *psychology* Such general reactions as asocial behavior, tendency to criticize others, overresponse to flattery and hypersensitivity to criticism, and avoidance of competitive situations.

withdrawing reaction *psychoanalysis* Any behavior that either consciously or unconsciously affords some protection to the ego or the superego from reality.

withholding tax Money withheld from a worker's paycheck for income-tax purposes or withheld from Social Security or from some other social program.

without prejudice a legal term indicating than an action, such as an offer to settle, is made without any admissions or waivers by the action.

WMCW World Movement of Christian Workers.

Wonderlic Personnel Test A twelve-minute screening measure of intelligence used in selecting personnel for high-level industrial positions.

Woodworth Personal Data Sheet Designed by R. S. Woodworth in 1917, it was one of the first questionnaires for self-appraisal intended to reveal the presence or the absence of neurotic symptoms. Used on soldiers in World War I.

Wool Auctions Specialist commodity exchange in the United Kingdom.

Wool, Jute and Flax Industry Training Board Established in 1964 under the 1964 Industrial Training Act in the United Kingdom. Address: 55 Well Street, Bradford BD1 5PW.

word association test An attempt to explore the thought processes by making a record of sequential free associations, one word suggesting another, etc.

work curve A graphic representation of increments and decrements in output, physical or mental, during successive units of time.

workers' control A somewhat ethereal expression which generally denotes workers' control of corporations under capitalism through the ownership. It is also related to "worker participation."

workers' directors A term referring to the practice in the United Kingdom of having representatives from the workers' groups (or unions) on the Board of Directors of the corporation. This approach has been tried in a limit way in both the United Kingdom and the United States, but it has gained little momentum.

workers' participation A broad concept for bringing the ideas of workers into the realm of management. It is seen sometimes as a motivational factor for employees, and also a part of the answer to job satisfaction. "Participation in management" is being used in nearly all industrial countries either through quality groups or some other designation. At this point in time, the concept seems to work best in industrial, assembly-line situations.

working assets The total of all types of stocks, including raw materials, work in progress, and finished goods, along with cash in hand and amounts due from debtors.

working days lost A concept usually denoting the number of days of a job that are lost because of strikes or other labor disputes. Sometimes denotes absenteeism due to illness, etc.

Working Together Campaign A non-government agency in the United Kingdom that seeks to increase communications and cooperation among academics and industrialists. Address: Room G4, Portland House, Stag Place, London SW1E 5BG.

work measurement Methods used, such as time and motion studies, to gauge the efficiency of the workplace and the worker.

work-to-rule A term denoting an action by workers in the United States who do not strike or close a plant, but slow production to a pace that pleases them.

World Bank International bank for reconstruction and development.

World Confederation of Labor (WLC) Established in 1920 as the International Foundation of Christian Trade Unions (IFCTU). Changed name in 1968. Has member trade unions in more than ninety countries. Address: 50 rue Joseph II, Brussels 1040, Belgium.

World Federation of Scientific Workers Set up in 1946 in the United Kingdom to promote interaction of scientists among all nations. Address: 40 Goodge Street, London WIP IFH.

World Federation of Trade Unions (WFTU) Organized in 1945 by trade union federations from more than fifty countries. Address: Address: WFTU, Nam, Curieovych 1, Prague 1, Czechoslovakia.

World Health Organization (WHO) A special agency of the United Nations, established in 1945. Address: Avenue Appia, 1211, Geneva, Switzerland.

World Meteorological Organization (WMO) An agency of the United Nations. Address: 41 avenue Guiseppe Motta, Geneva, Switzerland.

World Movement of Christian Workers (WMCW) Established in 1961. Address: 20 rue Belliard, Brussels 4, Belgium.

worry factor *insurance* The anxiety caused by being underinsured.

wrist-finger speed A type of psychomotor skill test, measuring the ability to make rotary and other wrist movements.

writ A written order by a court directing a court officer to perform a specific act, such as seizing property.

write-down reducing the value of an asset on the company books.

write-up The overstating of assets on the company books, or the written report on a meeting, experiment, etc.

write-off To periodically reduce the value of an asset on the company books, or to write down a debt which will likely not be paid.

writ of assistance *law* A writ of a court directing a sheriff to evict the defendant from real estate and to place the plaintiff in possession of the real estate.

writ of error *law* 1. A writ directing the judges of a court to examine the record leading to the judgment in a case. 2. A writ directing a lower court to send the record to an appellate court for review.

wrongful dismissal A term for unfair, or perhaps illegal, firing from a job.

X

X-axis The horizontal axis on a graph.

xenophobia A morbid dread of strangers or of unfamiliar customs.

Y

Y-axis The vertical axis on a graph.

yen Basic unit of Japanese currency. (*See* Appendix D)

yield to maturity The internal rate of return on a bond when held to maturity.

Yugoslav central bank *Narodna Banka Jugoslavije.* (*See* Section VII)

Yugoslav chamber of commerce Federal Chamber of Economy, Terazije 23, POB 1003, Belgrade.

Z

Zeigarnik effect The compulsion in some individuals to accomplish a task or to achieve a certain result.

zero correlation A lack of any association between two distributions of scores.

Zero Defects, as a motivating force The promotion of achieving near perfection in the production of a specific product has proven to be a motivator, especially in higher echelon people or highly skilled people.

Zollner illusion Parallel lines that appear to slant because they are crossed by short diagonal lines.

zone freight rate One freight rate applicable to shipments from any of the points in one area or zone to any of the points in another.

zoning laws Ordinances or laws passed by cities and towns restricting the use of land. The different zones are designated as residential, commercial, industrial, business, etc.

Zurich stock exchange *See* Section VII.

Appendix A:
International Business Travel

Introduction

In the past, international business travel reasons has applied to a limited number of people, and many of these people were from large, often multi-national, corporations. This will not be the case in our one-world economy, and for that reason this section is included in this volume.

My discussion will be primarily philosophical; pragmatic issues such as local tipping customs, "where to eat" information, and other tourist information will be left to other publications. I shall deal with matters that directly relate to the question of how business people can sell themselves and their firms to the people they are visiting.

Two types of business people, in the main, will be engaged in foreign traveling. There are the contract-makers—those top people who speak with authority from their firms—and those technical people who travel overseas as installers or repairers of technical equipment. In addition, of course, there will be those representatives of service industries that will proliferate in the 1990s as their international business increases.

Large companies will have in-house staff who will train others in international customs and human relations. Medium-sized companies and small companies will be breaking new foreign ground, and most of them will need help. Help is available. Most major airlines have rather complete booklets on nearly every nation, and many of these are attuned to business travel. Major travel agencies also frequently print such material. No person, therefore, need undertake a trip unprepared.

One such publication is entitled *Guide To Business Travel in Asia.* It is distributed by Northwest Airlines and was published for their use by Passport Books, a division of NTC Publishing Group in Lincolnwood, Illinois, USA 60646—1975, 1989. It is a veritable gold mine of information on Bangkok, Hong Kong, Macao, Manila, Osaka, Seoul, Shanghai, Singapore, Taipei, Tokyo.

There are at least two other sources of information in this volume that could be helpful for making the overseas business traveler more comfortable. They are the listing of embassies of the nations of the world that are located in Washington, D.C. and New York (section II) and the listing of banks of other major nations (in section VII). There is also a listing of major U.S. banks (in section VII), each of which has an International Department.

I want to discuss some areas that might make a difference to the success or failure of a trip.

Attitude

It is widely accepted that many Americans are not good advertisements for the United States when they go abroad. Just in the past few months, a recurrent ad has been appearing on television, picturing that know-it-all American who goes abroad to "teach those foreigners something about the good old U.S. know-how" only to make an utter fool of himself. This type of attitude has been so widely discussed over the past fifty years that it surely must have more than a grain of truth in it.

Several things ought to be remembered. Most of the countries of the world where a business person might be expected to go have been in existence a lot longer than the United States. The United States became rich and powerful in a relatively short time. Americans are still fledglings in international affairs, and the other countries are well aware of that. So a business person should never approach another country as if he were a "superior" condescending to visit an "inferior". In the first place, it is not true, and even if it were, one would be foolish to make such an assumption or to take such an attitude.

Any country that business people might go to will have much to teach them. Business people should always go to foreign countries as learners. The business person should be steeped in the nation's history and customs and then go to learn more. And the business person should not be afraid to let the people of foreign nations know that he is privileged to be there and that he wants to learn from them all that he can.

Business people should never pass judgment on things they see and hear. If they have strong opinions, they should keep them to themselves. Business people should always remember they are there to learn, to sell themselves, to sell their company and their product or service. Therefore, it is helpful to assume a posture of rational humility.

If business people travel with the right attitude, chances for successful trips will be increased

Subjects Not for Discussion

As with domestic business relations, appropriate sensitivity should be applied to matters of race, religion, sex, and politics. It is probably wisest to avoid discussions on these topics altogether.

When visiting a country with which the home country has been at war in the past, the business person should never let the subject come up if possible. Some U.S. business people are still making enemies of the Japanese and the Germans and the Vietnamese because of bygone events. This is foolish on its face. The business person should let the past be the past and work for today and tomorrow.

The business person should not denigrate the competition nor speak poorly of the product or service that the host country is now using, even if the business person may be visiting to displace outmoded products and services.

How to Dress on a Foreign Trip

Almost all of the booklets that I have recommended say that conservative business suits, for either men or women, are acceptable anywhere the business person travels. The type of suit or the weight of suit will be decided by the climate and season of the country visited. Even in countries where the business suit is not yet everyday wear, hosts may very well receive you in such dress, so you can be assured of always being appropriately dressed. It should be kept in mind that special evening wear may be necessary on some visits.

International Business Can Be Fun

Few things in business are as stimulating as being introduced to international trade. I got my initiation in the late 1950s and early 1960s. The man who got me started was a world traveler of many years, Rear Admiral (Ret.) F. R. L. Tuthill.

He introduced me to the inner workings of foreign business and foreign relations. He carefully taught me the somewhat stilted English that one used in correspondence in those days. It is likely that technology has changed much of that. But in those years, I assisted in hosting people from Japan, Ireland, England, France, Germany, Italy, India, and other countries. I learned a lot about business protocol in those days and continued the practice of international trade for some time after.

One thing I learned from the people I met was that they all responded to gracious hospitality and to the genteel treatment we tried to give all of them. And we won many of them as long-time friends and customers.

Not all foreign experiences are pleasurable. As there are crooks and frauds in the United States, so there are in other countries as well. Sorting them out requires the same procedures followed in the United States.

Conclusion

I was thinking the other day about my sitting in a little Greek restaurant in Illinois when the news of Pearl Harbor came over the radio. I knew, somewhat vaguely, where the Hawaiian Islands were, but I had never heard of Pearl Harbor. Now, the world is a much smaller place.

But Americans still know too little about world geography and about other languages. The manager in a one-world economy would be well advised to get a really good world globe, a first-rate world atlas, and a first-rate encyclopedia of world geography for the office. The business person should be armed at all times with a current copy of *The World Almanac and Book of Facts,* published by Scripps Howard Company, an imprint of Pharos Books, 200 Park Avenue, New York, NY 10166. This book is updated annually and costs less than ten dollars. You should never be without one. Virtually any data one might ever need, from any country in the world, can be found there.

Appendix B:
Useful Toll-Free Numbers in
the United States

NOTE: Users should understand that telephone numbers are subject to change and/or revocation. These were in use January 1, 1990.

Car Rentals

Alamo Rent-A-Car, except Florida	800-327-9633
American International Rent-A-Car	800-527-0202
Avis Rent-A-Car	800-331-1212
International	800-331-2112
Budget Rent-A-Car	800-527-0700
Dollar Rent-A-Car	800-421-6868
General Rent-A-Car	800-327-7607
Hertz Rent-A-Car, except Oklahoma	800-654-3131
Canada	800-654-3001
National Car Rental, except Minnesota	800-328-4567

Communications/News

Commodity News Service	800-255-6490
Dow Jones News Retrieval	800-257-5114
Western Union International, Telegrams/Telex/ Cablegrams/Mailgrams/General Information	800-325-6000

Courier/Messenger Services

Airport Couriers, Inc.	800-221-4495
Federal Express	800-238-5355

| Special Courier Service | 800-221-3400 |
| World Courier Service | 800-221-6600 |

Finance/Currency Information Services

| Deak International Inc. | 800-424-1186 |
| Dun and Bradstreet | 800-526-0651 |

Government

Conservation of Renewable Energy	
Inquiry Referral Service	800-523-2929
Alaska and Hawaii	800-233-3071
Energy Hotline (Insulation and Energy)	800-342-3722
Environmental Protection Agency National	
Response Center (Toxic chemicals and Oil Spills)	800-424-8802
Fair Housing and Equal Opportunity	
(Dept. Housing and Urban Development)	800-424-8590
Fraud Task Force Hotline	
(General Accounting Office)	800-424-8590
Hazardous Waste Hotline (Resources	
Conservation and Recovery Act Superfund)	800-424-9346
Senior Citizens	800-342-9871
Small Business Administration Publications	
Hotline	800-368-5855
Washington, D.C.	800-653-7561
U.S. Department of Defense	
Nuclear Energy	800-336-3068
U.S. Export-Import Bank Hotline	800-424-5201

Hotels/Motels/Inns

American Hotels, except Nebraska	800-228-3278
Amfac Hotels	800-227-4700
Best Western Hotels, except Arizona	800-528-1234
CN Hotels	800-268-9143
CP Hotels	800-828-7447
Canada	800-268-9411

Helmsley Hotels	800-221-4982
(in New York, St. Moritz)	800-221-4774
Hilton Hotels (Texas)	800-445-8667
(in other states ask Information)	
Holiday Inns, U.S. and Canada	800-465-4329
Howard Johnson Motor Lodges, except Oklahoma	800-654-2000
Hyatt Hotels	800-228-9000
Marriott Hotels	800-228-9290
Preferred Hotel Association	800-323-7500
Quality Inns USA	800-228-5151
Ramada Inns USA	800-228-2828
Sheraton Hotels USA, except Missouri	800-325-3535
Canada-East	800-268-9393
Canada-West	800-268-9330
Sonesta International Hotels USA,	
except Massachusetts	800-343-7170
Travelodge USA	800-255-3050
Trust Houses Forte USA	800-223-5672
Canada	800-268-9761
Westin Hotels USA and Canada	800-228-3000

NOTE: An AT & T toll-free 800 directory can be obtained by writing:

AT&T Toll-Free 800 Directory
Room 24C36
55 Corporate Drive
Bridgewater, NJ 08807

AT&T toll-free directory assistance can be had by calling 1-800-555-1212.

Appendix C:
Useful International Area Codes
and National Airlines

COUNTRY/CODE	CAPITAL/CODE	HRS. FROM EST	NATIONAL AIRLINE(S)
Argentina 54	Buenos Aires 1	+2	Aerolineas Argentinas
Australia 61	Canberra 62	+15	Quantas
Belgium 32	Brussels 22	+6	Sabena
Brazil 55	Brasilia 61	+2	Varig
Canada *(direct dial)*	Ottawa	EST	Air Canada
Colombia 57	Bogota 1	EST	Avianca
Egypt 20	Cairo 2	+7	EgyptAir
France 33	Paris 13, 14, 16	+6	Air France
Germany 49	Berlin	+6	Lufthansa
Hong Kong 852	Hong Kong 5	+13	Cathay Pacific Airways
India 91	Delhi 11	+10.5	Air India
Indonesia 62	Jakarta 21	+12	Garuda Indonesian Airways
Israel 972	Jerusalem 2	+7	El Al
Italy 39	Rome 6	+6	Alitalia
Japan 81	Tokyo 3	+14	Japan Air Lines
Malaysia 60	Kuala Lumpur 3	+13	MAS

COUNTRY/CODE	CAPITAL/CODE	HRS. FROM EST	NATIONAL AIRLINE(S)
Mexico 52	Mexico City 5	-1	Mexicana and Aeromexico
Netherlands 31	Amsterdam 6	+6	KLM
Nigeria 234	Lagos 1	+6	Nigeria Airways
Philippines 63	Manila 2	+13	Philippine Airways
Saudia Arabia 966	Riyadh 1	+8	Saudia
Singapore 65	Singapore	+13	Singapore Airlines
South Africa 27	Pretoria 12	+7	SAA
South Korea 82	Seoul 2	+14	Korean Airlines
Spain 34	Madrid 1	+6	Iberia International
Sweden 46	Stockholm 8	+6	SAS
Switzerland 41	Berne 31	+6	Swissair
Taiwan 886	Taipei 2	+13	CAL
United Kingdom 44	London 1	+5	British Airways
United States	Washington	EST	
Venezuela 58	Caracas 2	+1	Viasa

Appendix D:
World Currencies

COUNTRY	CURRENCY	VALUE, AS RELATED TO THE U.S. DOLLAR, 1988
Afghanistan	Afghani	50.60 = $1
Albania	Lek	6.19 = $1
Algeria	Dinar	5.29 = $1
Andorra	French franc and Spanish peseta	(Valued same.)
Angola	Kwanza	30.53 = $1
Antigua & Barbuda	East Caribbean dollar	2.70 = $1
Argentina	Austral	9.20 = $1
Australia	Dollar	1.23 = $1
Austria	Schilling	12.16 = $1
Bahamas, The	Dollar	1.00 = $1
Bahrain	Dinar	0.38 = $1
Bangladesh	Taka	31.50 = $1
Barbados	Dollar	2.01 = $1
Belgium	Franc	36.15 = $1
Belize	Belize dollar	2.00 = $1

COUNTRY	CURRENCY	VALUE, AS RELATED TO THE U.S. DOLLAR, 1988
Benin	CFA Franc	281.00 = $1
Bhutan	Ngultrum	12.00 = $1
Bolivia	Peso	2,230.00 = $1
Botswana	Pula	0.40 = $1
Brazil	Cruzeiro	163.00 = $1
Brunei Darussalam	Brunei dollar	2.10 = $1
Bulgaria	Lev	1.15 = $1
Burkina Faso	CFA Franc	281.00 = $1
Burma	Kyat	6.22 = $1
Burundi	Franc	131.00 = $1
Cambodia	Riel	4.00 = $1
Cameroon	CFA Franc	281.00 = $1
Canada	Dollar	1.23 = $1
Cape Verde	Escudo	89.27 = $1
Central African Republic	CFA Franc	281.00 = $1
Chad	CFA Franc	281.00 = $1
Chile	Peso	246.00 = $1
China	Yuan	3.72 = $1
Colombia	Peso	290.00 = $1
Comoros	CFA Franc	281.00 = $1
Congo	CFA Franc	281.00 = $1
Costa Rica	Colone	74.00 = $1
Cote d'Ivoire	CFA Franc	281.00 = $1
Cuba	Peso	1.28 = $1

COUNTRY	CURRENCY	VALUE, AS RELATED TO THE U.S. DOLLAR, 1988
Cyprus	Pound	2.17 = $1
Czechoslovakia	Koruna	5.48 = $1
Denmark	Krone	6.57 = $1
Djibouti	Franc	176.00 = $1
Dominica	East Caribbean dollar	2.70 = $1
Dominican Republic	Peso	5.25 = $1
Ecuador	Sucre	475.00 = $1
Egypt	Pound	2.28 = $1
El Salvador	Colon	5.00 = $1
Equatorial Guinea	Bipkwele	281.00 = $1
Ethiopia	Bir	2.07 = $1
Fiji	Dollar	1.31 = $1
Finland	Markaa	4.08 = $1
France	Franc	5.82 = $1
Gabon	CFA Franc	281.00 = $1
Gambia, The	Dalasi	67.00 = $1
Germany	Mark	1.72 = $1
Ghana	Cedi	20.00 = $1
Greece	Drachma	137.00 = $1
Grenada	East Caribbean dollar	2.70 = $1
Guatemala	Quetzal	2.50 = $1
Guinea	Franc	339.00 = $1
Guinea-Bissau	Peso	649.00 = $1
Guyana	Dollar	10.00 = $1
Haiti	Gourde	5.00 = $1

COUNTRY	CURRENCY	VALUE, AS RELATED TO THE U.S. DOLLAR, 1988
Honduras	Lempira	2.00 = $1
Hungary	Forint	47.00 = $1
Iceland	Kronur	38.90 = $1
India	Rupee	13.51 = $1
Indonesia	Rupiah	1,673.00 = $1
Iran	Rial	66.83 = $1
Iraq	Dinar	0.31 = $1
Ireland	Pound	0.64 = $1
Israel	Shekel	1.58 = $1
Italy	Lira	1,283.00 = $1
Jamaica	Dollar	5.48 = $1
Japan	Yen	125.00 = $1
Jordan	Dinar	0.33 = $1
Kenya	Shilling	17.02 = $1
Kiribati	Australian dollar	1.23 = $1
Korea, North	Won	0.94 = $1
Korea, South	Won	746.00 = $1
Kuwait	Dinar	0.29 = $1
Laos	New kip	35.00 = $1
Lebanon	Pound	363.00 = $1
Lesotho	Maloti	0.47 = $1
Liberia	Dollar	1.00 = $1
Libya	Dinar	0.28 = $1
Liechtenstein	Swiss franc	1.44 = $1
Luxembourg	Franc	34.2 = $1

COUNTRY	CURRENCY	VALUE, AS RELATED TO THE U.S. DOLLAR, 1988
Madagascar	Franc	166.00 = $1
Malawi	Kwacha	247 = $1
Malaysia	Ringgit	0.56 = $1
Maldives	Rufiyaa	8.50 = $1
Mali	Franc	281.00 = $1
Malta	Pound	0.31 = $1
Mauritania	Ouguiya	0.73 = $1
Mauritius	Rupee	12.78 = $1
Mexico	Peso	2,281.00 = $1
Mongolia	Tugrik	3.36 = $1
Morocco	Dirham	7.93 = $1
Mozambique	Metical	403.00 = $1
Nepal	Rupee	21.90 = $1
Netherlands	Guilder	1.93 = $1
New Zealand	Dollar	1.42 = $1
Nicaragua	Cordoba	70.00 = $1
Niger	CFA Franc	281.00 = $1
Nigeria	Naira	0.23 = $1
Norway	Kroner	6.27 = $1
Oman	Rial Omani	0.38 = $1
Pakistan	Rupee	17.22 = $1
Panama	Balboa	1.00 = $1
Papua New Guinea	Kina	0.87 = $1
Paraguay	Guarani	550.00 = $1
Peru	Sol	33.00 = $1

COUNTRY	CURRENCY	VALUE, AS RELATED TO THE U.S. DOLLAR, 1988
Philippines	Peso	21.01 = $1
Poland	Zloty	400.00 = $1
Portugal	Escudo	140.80 = $1
Qatar	Riyal	0.27 = $1
Romania	Leu	13.96 = $1
Rwanda	Franc	74.00 = $1
St. Christopher	East Caribbean dollar	2.70 = $1
Saint Lucia	East Caribbean dollar	2.70 = $1
Saint Vincent & the Grenadines	East Caribbean dollar	2.70 = $1
Sao Tome & Principe	Dobra	35.00 = $1
Saudi Arabia	Riyal	3.74 = $1
Senegal	CFA Franc	281.00 = $1
Seychelles	Rupee	5.23 = $1
Sierra Leone	Leone	0.04 = $1
Singapore	Dollar	2.02 = $1
Solomon Islands	Dollar	2.03 = $1
Somalia	Shilling	100.00 = $1
South Africa	Rand	2.24 = $1
Spain	Peseta	114.30 = $1
Sri Lanka	Rupee	30.89 = $1
Sudan	Pound	0.22 = $1
Suriname	Guilder	1.78 = $1
Swaziland	Lilangeni	0.47 = $1
Sweden	Krona	6.00 = $1

COUNTRY	CURRENCY	VALUE, AS RELATED TO THE U.S. DOLLAR, 1988
Switzerland	Franc	1.44 = $1
Syria	Pound	11.22 = $1
Taiwan	New Taiwan dollar	28.60 = $1
Tanzania	Shilling	93.73 = $1
Thailand	Baht	25.15 = $1
Togo	CFA Franc	281.00 = $1
Tonga	Pa'anga	1.40 = $1
Trinidad & Tobago	Dollar	3.60 = $1
Tunisia	Dinar	0.80 = $1
Tuvalu	Australian dollar	
Uganda	Shilling	60.00 = $1
Union of Soviet Socialist Republics (USSR)	Ruble	0.69 = $1
United Arab Emirates	Dirham	3.67 = $1
United Kingdom of Great Britain and Northern Ireland	Pound	0.55 = $1
Uruguay	New Peso	330.00 = $1
Vanuatu	Australian dollar & Vanuatu Franc	110.00 = $1
Venezuela	Bolivar	31.25 = $1
Vietnam	Dong	80.00 = $1
Western Samoa	Tala	0.48 = $1
North Yemen	Rial	9.76 = $1
South Yemen	Dinar	0.35 = $1
Yugoslavia	Dinar	1,532.00 = $1

COUNTRY	CURRENCY	VALUE, AS RELATED TO THE U.S. DOLLAR, 1988
Zaire	Zaire	161.00 = $1
Zambia	Kwacha	0.12 = $1
Zimbabwe	Dollar	0.58 = $1

Appendix E:
Weights and Measures

Common Conversions:

TO CHANGE	TO	MULTIPLY BY
Acres	Hectares	0.4047
Bushels (U.S.)	Hectoliters	0.3521
Centimeters	Inches	0.3973
Cubic feet	Cubic meters	0.0283
Cubic meters	Cubic feet	35.3145
Cubic meters	Cubic yards	1.3079
Cubic yards	Cubic meters	0.7645
Feet	Meters	0.3048
Gallons (U.S.)	Liters	3.7854
Grains	Grams	0.0648
Grams	Grains	15.4321
Grams	Ounces avoirdupois	0..0353
Hectares	Acres	2.4710
Hectoliters	Bushels (U.S.)	2.8378
Inches	Millimeters	25.4000
Inches	Centimeters	2.5400
Kilograms	Pounds apothecaries' or troy	2.6792
Kilograms	Pounds avoirdupois	2.2046
Kilometers	Miles	0.6214
Liters	Gallons (U.S.)	0.2642

TO CHANGE	TO	MULTIPLY BY
Liters	Pecks	0.1135
Liters	Pints dry	1.8162
Liters	Pints liquid	2.1133
Liters	Quarts dry	0.9081
Liters	Quarts liquid	1.0567
Meters	Feet	3.2808
Meters	Yards	1.0936
Metric tons	Tons long	0.9842
Metric tons	Tons short	1.1023
Miles	Kilometers	1.6103
Millimeters	Inches	0.0394
Ounces avoirdupois	Grams	28.3495
Pecks	Liters	8.8098
Pints dry	Liters	0.5506
Pints liquid	Liters	0.4732
Pounds apothecaries' or troy	Kilograms	0.3732
Pounds avoirdupois	Kilograms	0.4536
Quarts dry	Liters	1.1012
Quarts liquid	Liters	0.9463
Square feet	Square meters	0.0929
Square meters	Square feet	10.7639
Square meters	Square yards	1.1960
Square yards	Square meters	0.8361
Tons long	Metric tons	1.0160
Tons short	Metric tons	0.9072
Yards	Meters	0.9144

Metric Weight

10 milligrams = 1 centigram
10 centigrams = 1 decigram
10 decigrams = 1 gram

10 grams = 1 decagram
10 decagrams = 1 hectogram
10 hectograms = 1 kilogram
100 kilograms = 1 quintal
10 quintals = 1 metric ton

Liquid Measure

10 milliliters = 1 centiliter
10 centiliters = deciliter
10 deciliters = 1 liter
10 liters = 1 decaliter
10 decaliters = l hectoliter
10 hectoliters = 1 kiloliter

Linear Measure

10 millimeters = 1 centimeter
10 centimeters = 1 decimeter
10 decimeters = 1 meter
10 meters = 1 decameter
10 decameters = 1 hectometer
10 hectometers = 1 kilometer

Square Measure

100 square millimeters = 1 square centimeter
100 square centimeters = 1 square decimeter
100 square decimeters = 1 square meter
100 square meters = 1 square decameter
100 square decameters = 1 square hectometer
100 square hectometers = 1 square kilometer

Cubic Measure

1000 cubic millimeters = 1 cubic centimeter
1000 cubic centimeters = 1 cubic decimeter
1000 cubic decimeters = 1 cubic meter

Customary Metric Conversions

Linear Measure

1 inch = 25.4 millimeters
1 inch = 2.54 centimeters

1 foot = 30.48 centimeters
1 foot = 3.048 decimeters
1 foot = 0.3048 meter

1 yard = 0.9144 meter

1 mile = 1609.3 meters
1 mile = 1.6093 kilometers

0.03937 inch = 1 millimeter
0.3937 inch = 1 centimeter
3.937 inches = 1 decimeter

39.37 inches = 1 meter
3.2808 feet = 1 meter
1.0936 yards = 1 meter

3280.8 feet = 1 kilometer
1093.6 yards = 1 kilometer
0.62137 mile = 1 kilometer

Dry Measure

1 quart = 1.1012 liters
1 peck = 8.8098 liters
1 bushel = 35.239 liters

0.90808 quart = 1 liter
0.11351 peck = 1 liter
0.028378 bushel = 1 liter

Liquid Measure

1 fluid ounce = 29.573 milliliters

1 quart = 9.4635 deciliters
1 quart = 0.94635 liter

1 gallon = 3.7854 liters
0.033814 fluid ounce = 1 milliliter
3.3814 fluid ounce = 1 deciliter

33.814 fluid ounces = 1 liter
1.0567 quarts = 1 liter
0.26417 gallon = 1 liter

Weight

1 grain = 0.064799 gram
1 avoirdupois ounce = 28.350 grams
1 troy ounce = 31.103 grams
1 avoirdupois pound = 0.45359 kilogram
1 troy pound = 0.37324 kilogram

1 short ton (0.8929 long ton) = 907.18 kilograms
1 short ton = 0.90718 metric ton

1 long ton (1.1200 short tons) = 1016.0 kilograms
1 long ton = 1.0160 metric tons

15.432 grains = 1 gram
0.0035274 avoirdupois ounce = 1 gram
0.032151 troy ounce = 1 gram

2.2046 avoirdupois pounds = 1 kilogram

0.98421 long ton = 1 metric ton
1.1023 short tons = 1 metric ton

Square Measure

1 square inch = 645.16 square millimeters
1 square inch = 6.4516 square centimeters
1 square foot = 929.03 square centimeters
1 square foot = 9.2903 square decimeters
1 square foot = 0.092903 square meter
1 square yard = 0.83613 square meter
1 square mile = 2.5900 square kilometers

0.0015500 square inch = 1 square millimeter
0.15500 square inch = 1 square centimeter

15.500 square inches = 1 square decimeter
0.10764 square foot = 1 square decimeter

1.1960 square yards = 1 square meter
0.38608 square mile = 1 square kilometer

Cubic Measure

1 cubic inch = 16.387 cubic centimeters
1 cubic inch = 0.016387 liter
1 cubic foot = 0.028317 cubic meter
1 cubic yard = 0.76455 cubic meter
1 cubic mile = 4.16818 cubic kilometers

0.061023 cubic inch = 1 cubic centimeter
61.023 cubic inches = 1 cubic decimeter
35.315 cubic feet = 1 cubic decimeter
1.3079 cubic yards = 1 cubic meter
0.23990 cubic mile = 1 cubic kilometer

Appendix F:
World Times

Times are computed from 12:00 noon, Eastern Standard Time. An asterisk indicates that the time listed is on the next day.

Afghanistan: 9:30 p.m.
Albania: 6:00 p.m.
Algeria: 5:00 p.m.
Andorra: 6:00 p.m.
Angola: 6:00 p.m.
Antigua: 1:00 p.m.
Argentina: 2:00 p.m.
Australia
    Perth: 1:00 a.m.*
    Adelaide: 2:30 a.m.*
    Brisbane: 3:00 a.m.*
Austria: 6:00 p.m.
Azores: 4:00 p.m.
Bahamas: 12:00 noon
Bahrain: 9:00 p.m.
Bangladesh: 11:00 p.m.
Barbados: 1:00 p.m.
Belgium: 6:00 p.m.
Belize: 11:00 p.m.
Benin: 6:00 p.m.
Bermuda: 1:00 p.m.

Bhutan: 11:00 p.m.

Bolivia: 1:00 p.m.

Botswana: 7:00 p.m.

Brazil: 2:00 p.m.

Brunei: 1:00 a.m.

Bulgaria: 7:00 p.m.

Burkino Faso: 5:00 p.m.

Burma: 11:30 p.m.

Burundi: 8:00 p.m.

Cambodia: 12:00 midnight

Cameroon: 6:00 p.m.

Canada

    Victoria: 9:00 a.m.

    Calgary: 10:00 a.m.

    Winnipeg: 11:00 a.m.

    Toronto: 12:00 noon

    Halifax: 1:00 p.m.

Cape Verde: 3:00 p.m.

Central African Republic: 6:00 p.m.

Chad: 6:00 p.m.

Chile: 1:00 p.m.

China, Mainland: 1:00 a.m.*

China, Taiwan: 1:00 a.m.*

Colombia: 12:00 noon

Comoro Islands: 8:00 p.m.

Congo: 6:00 p.m.

Cook Islands: 7:00 a.m.

Costa Rica: 11:00 a.m.

Cuba: 1:00 p.m.

Cyprus: 7:00 p.m.

Denmark: 6:00 p.m.

Djibouti: 8:00 p.m.

Dominica: 1:00 p.m.

Dominican Republic: 12:00 noon

Ecuador: 12:00 noon

Egypt: 7:00 p.m.
El Salvador: 11:00 a.m.
England: 5:00 p.m.
Equatorial Guinea: 6:00 p.m.
Ethiopia: 8:00 p.m.
Falkland Islands: 1:00 p.m.
Faeroe Islands: 6:00 p.m.
Finland: 7:00 p.m.
France: 6:00 p.m.
French Guiana: 1:00 p.m.
Gabon: 6:00 p.m.
Gambia: 1:00 p.m.
Germany: 6:00 p.m.
Ghana: 5:00 p.m.
Gibraltar: 6:00 p.m.
Gilbert Islands: 6:00 a.m.
Greece: 7:00 p.m.
Greenland: 2:00 p.m.
Grenada: 1:00 p.m.
Guadeloupe: 1:00 p.m.
Guam: 3:00 a.m.
Guatemala: 11:00 a.m.
Guinea: 5:00 p.m.
Guinea-Bissau: 4:00 p.m.
Guyana: 1:15 p.m.
Haiti: 12:00 noon
Honduras: 11:00 a.m.
Hong Kong: 1:00 a.m.
Hungary: 6:00 p.m.
Iceland: 5:00 p.m.
India: 10:30 p.m.
Indonesia: 12:00 midnight
Iraq: 8:00 p.m.
Ireland: 5:00 p.m.
Isle of Man: 5:00 p.m.

Israel: 6:00 p.m.
Italy: 6:00 p.m.
Ivory Coast: 5:00 p.m.
Jamaica: 12:00 noon
Japan: 2:00 a.m.*
Jordan: 7:00 p.m.
Kenya: 8:00 p.m.
Korea, North: 2:00 a.m.
Korea, South: 2:00 a.m.
Kuwait: 8:00 p.m.
Laos: 12:00 midnight
Lebanon: 7:00 p.m.
Leeward Islands: 1:00 p.m.
Lesotho: 7:00 p.m.
Liberia: 6:00 p.m.
Libya: 7:00 p.m.
Liechtenstein: 6:00 p.m.
Luxembourg: 6:00 p.m.
Madagascar: 8:00 p.m.
Malawi: 7:00 p.m.
Malaysia: 1:00 a.m.
Maldives: 10:00 p.m.
Mali: 5:00 p.m.
Malta: 6:00 p.m.
Martinique: 1:00 p.m.
Mauritania: 5:00 p.m.
Mauritius: 9:00 p.m.
Mexico
    Hermosillo: 10:00 p.m.
    Mexico City: 11:00 p.m.
Monaco: 6:00 p.m.
Mongolia: 12:00 midnight*
Montserrat: 1:00 p.m.
Morocco: 5:00 p.m.
Mozambique: 7:00 p.m.
Namibia (Southwest Africa): 7:00 p.m.

Nepal: 11:00 p.m.
The Netherlands: 6:00 p.m.
Netherlands Antilles: 1:00 p.m.
New Caledonia: 4:00 a.m.
New Zealand: 5:00 a.m.
Nicaragua: 11:00 a.m.
Niger: 6:00 p.m.
Nigeria: 6:00 p.m.
Northern Ireland: 5:00 p.m.
Norway: 6:00 p.m.
Oman: 9:00 p.m.
Pakistan: 10:00 p.m.
Panama: 12:00 noon
Papua New Guinea: 3:00 a.m.*
Paraguay: 1:00 p.m.
Peru: 12:00 noon
Philippines: 1:00 a.m.*
Poland: 6:00 p.m.
Portugal
    mainland: 6:00 p.m.
    Madeira: 5:00 p.m.
Puerto Rico: 1:00 p.m.
Qatar: 9:00 p.m.
Reunion: 9:00 p.m.
Rumania: 7:00 p.m.
Russia
    Moscow: 8:00 p.m.
    Gorki: 9:00 p.m.
Rwanda: 8:00 p.m.
St. Christopher
    Nevis-Anguilla: 1:00 p.m.
St. Lucia: 1:00 p.m.
St. Vincent: 1:00 p.m.
San Marino: 6:00 p.m.
Sao Tome and Principe: 6:00 p.m.
Saudi Arabia: 8:00 p.m.

Scotland: 5:00 p.m.
Senegal: 5:00 p.m.
Seychelles: 9:00 p.m.
Sierra Leone: 5:00 p.m.
Singapore: 1:00 a.m.
Solomon Islands: 3:00 a.m.
Somalia: 8:00 p.m.
South Africa: 7:00 p.m.
Spain: 6:00 p.m.
Sri Lanka: 10:30 p.m.
Sudan: 7:00 p.m.
Suriname: 1:30 p.m.
Swaziland: 7:00 p.m.
Sweden: 6:00 p.m.
Syria: 7:00 p.m.
Tahiti: 7:00 p.m.
Tanzania: 8:00 p.m.
Tasmania: 3:00 a.m.*
Thailand: 12:00 midnight
Togo: 5:00 p.m.
Transkei: 7:00 p.m.
Trinidad and Tobago: 1:00 p.m.
Tunisia: 6:00 p.m.
Turkey: 7:00 p.m.
Turks and Caicos Islands: 12:00 noon
Uganda: 8:00 p.m.
United Arab Emirates: 9:00 p.m.
United States
    Honolulu: 7:00 a.m.
    Anchorage: 7:00 a.m.
    Los Angeles: 9:00 a.m.
    Denver: 10:00 a.m.
    Houston: 11:00 a.m.
    Washington, D.C.: 12:00 noon
Uruguay: 2:00 p.m.

Uzbekistan: 11:00 p.m.

Vatican City: 6:00 p.m.

Venezuela: 1:00 p.m.

Vietnam: 1:00 a.m.*

Virgin Islands (British): 1:00 p.m.

Virgin Islands (United States): 1:00 p.m.

Western Samoa: 6:00 a.m.

West Indies: 1:00 p.m.

Windward Islands: 1:00 p.m.

Yemen, Arab Republic: 8:00 p.m.

Yemen, People's Democratic Republic of: 8:00 p.m.

Zaire: 6:00 p.m.

Zambia: 7:00 p.m.

Zimbabwe: 7:00 p.m.

The World's Time Zones

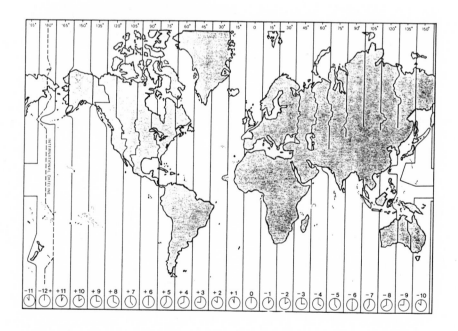

North American Time Zones

Bibliography

Aguayo, Rafael. *Dr. Deming: The American Who Taught the Japanese about Quality.* New York: A Lyle Stuart Book, Published by Carol Publishing Company, 1990.

Albert, Kenneth, editor-in-chief. *Handbook of Business Problem Solving.* New York: McGraw-Hill Book Company, 1980.

Bloom, Allan. *The Closing of the American Mind.* New York: Simon and Schuster, 1987.

Bittel, Lester R. *Management by Exception.* New York: McGraw-Hill Book Company, 1964.

Blake, Robert R, and Jane Srygley Mouton. *Productivity—The Human Side.* New York: Barron's Bilingual Business Guides, Barrons Educational Series, Inc. Japanese ed., 1988; Korean ed., 1988; French ed., 1987; German ed., 1987; Spanish ed., 1987.

Blanchard, Kenneth, and Robert Lorber. *Putting the One-Minute Manager to Work.* New York: William Morrow and Company, Inc., 1984.

Bolling, Richard and John Bowles. *America's Competitive Edge—How to Get Our Country Moving Again.* New York: McGraw-Hill Book Company, 1982.

Butterfield, Arthur S. *Practical Spanish-English, English-Spanish Dictionary.* New York: Hippocrene Books, 1983.

Congressional Directory 100th Congress. Washington, D.C.: United States Government Printing Office.

Carlisle, Elliott. *"Mac" Conversations About Management.* New York: McGraw-Hill Book Company, 1983.

Cassell Staff. *Cassell's French and English Dictionary.* New York: Collier Books, McMillan Publishing Co., 1968.

Culligan, Matthew J., G. Suzanne Deakins, and Arthur Young. *Back to Basics Management.* New York: Facts on File, 1983.

Cummings, L. S., and W. E. Scott, editors. *Readings in Organizational Behavior and Human Performance.* Homewood, Ill.: Richard D. Irwin, Inc., and the Dorsey Press, 1969.

Coulter, Dr. Arthur N., Jr. *Synergetics—An Adventure in Human Development.* Englewood Cliffs, N.J.: Prentice-Hall, Inc. 1976.

Drucker, Peter F. *Managing in Turbulent Times.* New York: Harper & Row, Publishers, 1980.

———. *Men, Ideas and Politics.* New York: Harper & Row, Publishers, 1971.

———. *The Age of Discontinuity.* New York: Harper & Row, Publishers, 1969.

———. *The Practice of Management.* New York: Harper & Row, Publishers, 1954.

———. *Technology, Management and Society.* New York: Harper & Row, Publishers, 1970.

———. *Managing For Results.* New York: Harper & Row, Publishers, 1964.

———. *Management: Responsibilities and Practices.* New York: Harper & Row, Publishers, 1974.

———. *Innovation and Entrepreneurship.* New York: Harper & Row, Publishers, 1985.

Davis, Ralph Courrier. *The Fundamentals of Top Management.* New York: Harper & Row, Publishers, 1985.

Deutsch, Mitchell F. *Doing Business With the Japanese.* New York: New American Library, 1983.

Downes, John and Elliot Goodman. *Barron's Finance and Investment Handbook.* New York: Barron's, 1987.

Ewing, David. *The Managerial Mind.* New York: The Free Press, 1964.

Erlichman, John. *The China Card.* New York: Simon & Schuster, 1986.

Fargis, Paul, and Sheree Dykoffsky. *The New York Public Library Desk Reference.* New York: A Stonesong Press Book, 1989.

Gardner, Lloyd C. *Approaching Vietnam From World War II through Dienbienphu.* New York: W. W. Norton & Co., 1988.

Garraty, John A., and Peter Gay, editors. *The Columbia History of the World.* New York: Harper & Row, Publishers, 1972.

Goble, Frank. *A Third Force: The Psychology of Abraham Maslow.* New York: Grossman Publishers, 1970.

Gordon, Dr. Thomas. *Leadership Effectiveness Training—L.E.T.* Ridgefield, Conn.: Wyden Books, 1977.

Gifis, Steven H. *Dictionary of Legal Terms.* New York: Barron's Educational Series, Inc., 1983.

Grun, Bernard. *The Time Tables of History,* Simon & Schuster, New York, 1979.

Harvard Business Review Editors. *Harvard Business Review on Human Relations.* New York: Harper & Row, Publishers, 1979.

Harvard Business Review Editors. *Harvard Business Review on Management.* New York: Harper & Row, Publishers, 1975.

Harriman, Philip L. *Handbook of Psychological Terms.* Paterson, N.J.: Littlefield, Adams and Company, 1959.

Halberstam, David. *The Reckoning.* New York: William Morrow and Company, 1986.

Heyel, Carl, editor. *The Encyclopedia of Management.* 3d ed. New York: Van Nostrand Reinhold Company, 1982.

Herzberg, Frederick. *Managerial Choice.* Homewood, Ill.: Dow-Jones Irwin, 1976.

Hoffman, Mark S., editor. *The World Almanac* 1991. New York: A Scripps Howard Company, an imprint of Pharos Books.

Johannsen, Hano and G. Terry Page. *The International Dictionary of Business.* Englewood Cliffs, N.J.: Prentice-Hall, Inc., 1981.

Johnson, Paul. *Modern Times: The World From the Twenties to the Eighties.* New York: Harper & Row, Publishers, 1983.

Langenscheidt's *German and English Dictionary.* New York: Washington Square Press, Inc., 1963.

Lederer, William J. and Eugene Burdick. *The Ugly American.* New York: Fawcett Crest, 1958.

Levy, Judith S., and Agnes Greenhall. *The Concise Columbia Encyclopedia.* New York: Columbia University Press, 1983.

Lye, Keith, general editor. *Encyclopedia of World Geography.* New York: Dorset Press, 1989.

Masatsugu, Mitsuyuki. *The Modern Samurai Society: Duty and Dependence in Contemporary Japan.* New York: AMA COM, 1982.

Maccoby, Michael. *The Leader.* New York: Simon and Schuster, 1981.

MacKenzie, R. Alec. *The Time Trap.* New York: AMA COM, 1972.

McCormick, Mona. *The New York Times Guide to Reference Materials,* rev. ed. New York: Times Books, 1970.

The New York Times Encyclopedic Almanac. New York: Times Books, 1970.

Nemmers, Erwin Esser. *Dictionary of Business and Economics.* Paterson, N.J.: Littlefield, Adams and Co., 1959.

Ouchi, William. *Theory Z—How American Business Can Meet the Japanese Challenge.* Reading, Mass: Addison-Wesley Publishing Company, 1981.

Odiorne, George S. *MBO II.* Belmont, Calif.: David S. Lake, Pubs., Inc., 1979.

Peter, Dr. Laurence J. *The Peter Pyramid: Or Will We Ever Get the Point.* New York: William Morrow and Company, Inc., 1986.

——. *The Peter Plan-A Proposal For Survival.* New York: William Morrow and Company, 1976.

Peter, Dr. Laurence J., and Raymond Hull. *The Peter Principle: Why Things Always Go Wrong.* New York: William Morrow and Company, Inc. 1969.

Parkinson, C. Northcote. *Parkinson's Law.* Boston: Houghton Mifflin Co., 1980.

Palmer, Stuart. *Role Stress—How To Handle Everyday Tension.* Englewood Cliffs, N.J.: Prentice-Hall, Inc., 1981.

Peters, Thomas J., and Robert H. Waterman, Jr. *In Search of Excellence—Lessons from America's Best Run Companies.* New York: Harper & Row, Publishers, 1982.

Reader's Digest Atlas of the World. Pleasantville, N.Y.: Reader's Digest Assn., 1987.

Reuters Glossary of International and Financial Terms New York: Coward-McCain, Inc., 1982.

Spence, Jonathan D. *The Search for Modern China.* New York: W. W. Norton and Co., 1990.

Sayles, Leonard. *Managerial Behavior.* New York: McGraw-Hill Book Company, 1964.

Strauss, George, and Leonard R. Sayles. *Personnel—The Human Problems of Management.* Englewood Cliffs, N.J.: Prentice-Hall, Inc., 1960.

Sutermeister, Robert A. *People and Productivity.* New York: McGraw-Hill Book Company, Inc., 1963.

Shave, Gordon A. *Nuts, Bolts, and Gut-Level Management.* West Nyack, N.Y.: Parker Publishing Company, 1974.

Silva, Michael, and Bertil Sjogren. *Europe 1992 and The New World Power Game.* New York: John Wiley & Sons, 1990.

U.S. Dept. of Commerce, Bureau of the Census. *Statistical Abstract of the United States.* Washington, D.C.: U.S. Printing Office, annual publication.

The Statistical History of the United States: From Colonial Times to the Present. Stamford, Conn.: Fairfield Publishers, Inc. 1969. Distributed by: Horizon Press, Inc.

Terry, George R. *Principles of Management.* 6th ed. Homewood, Ill.: Richard D. Irwin, Inc., 1972.

Terry, John V. *Dictionary for Business and Finance.* 2d ed. Fayetteville, Ark.: The University of Arkansas Press, 1990.

Waldron, Arthur. *The Great Wall of China: From History to Myth.* New York: Cambridge University Press, 1990.

Williams, Rosalind. *Practical French-English, English-French Dictionary.* New York: Hippocrene Books, 1983.

World Development Report 1987. New York: Oxford University Press.

Yankelovich, Daniel. *New Rules: Searching For Fulfillment in a World Turned Upside Down.* New York: Random House, 1981.